WINNING SCHOLA

A STUDENT'S GUIDE TO ENTRANCE AWARDS

AT WESTERN CANADIAN UNIVERSITIES AND

COLLEGES

MICHAEL J. HOWELL

Winning Scholarships

A STUDENT'S GUIDE TO ENTRANCE AWARDS AT WESTERN CANADIAN UNIVERSITIES AND COLLEGES

UNIVERSITY OF TORONTO PRESS

Toronto Buffalo London

© University of Toronto Press Incorporated 1994
Toronto Buffalo London
Printed in Canada

ISBN 0-8020-7481-2

Printed on acid-free paper

Canadian Cataloguing in Publication Data

Howell, Michael J.

Winning scholarships: a student's guide to
entrance awards at Western Canadian universities
and colleges

Includes index.
ISBN 0-8020-7481-2

1. Scholarships – Canada, Western. 2. Student aid
– Canada, Western. I. Title.

LB2339.C3H69 1994   378.3'4'09712   C94-931390-4

To my parents, Winnifred and John Howell.
They've never stopped educating their
eight children and numerous grandchildren.

Contents

Introduction

"EXPLORER DISCOVERS HIDDEN TREASURE." Every year we see head-lines like this; someone finds fame and fortune because he or she looked where no one else did. All across western Canada thou-sands of students are winning millions of dollars in scholarship money because they knew how and where to find it. Thousands of other students could have won but didn't, because they lacked a good guide.

This book is intended to help any student who is planning to attend university or college to locate and apply for some of the hidden treasure that's out there, some of which goes unclaimed for years and years. Of course, this book doesn't have all the answers and that's where your adventure begins. With this book as a start-ing-point it's almost certain you'll find scholarship money and awards for which you can apply. It won't all be easy. There will be blind alleys and wild-goose chases. Scholarships disappear and others are created. You'll have to work at it and take some chances. It's a little like Indiana Jones using his father's diary to find the Holy Grail, only you won't need a bullwhip. And there's more than just scholarship money at stake.

Many of the colleges and universities in Canada are looking at more than just the marks of their applicants, especially in the professional programs. They are more interested in the whole person.

This book will help you prepare yourself for the challenges that lie ahead. Have a look at the chapters and you will see that this process will involve your teachers and your parents. It's going to be a team effort, but you are the focus of it. You will determine whether or not you will be successful. Let's begin the adventure!

Acknowledgements

I would like to express my gratitude to all the university and college administrators who were so helpful in my research. In addition, I would like to thank the following:

- Province of British Columbia, Ministry of Education
- Canadian Merit Scholarship Foundation
- Central Okanagan Bursary and Scholarship Society
- Student Services, Gabriel Dumont Institute
- Student Services, Deparment of Education, Government of the Northwest Territories
- Alberta Students Finance Board
- Alberta Heritage Fund
- Yukon Education, Advanced Education Branch
- Saskatchewan Education, Student Development and Career Resources
- Student Assistance Centre, Assiniboine Community College
- Manitoba Education and Training

I am very deeply impressed by the extent of the generosity of human and financial capital in western Canada. It is a great place for students who are starting a scholarship quest.

MICHAEL J. HOWELL

WINNING SCHOLARSHIPS:

A STUDENT'S GUIDE TO ENTRANCE AWARDS

AT WESTERN CANADIAN UNIVERSITIES AND

COLLEGES

1 What are scholarships? What helps win them?

It's a good idea to gather a lot of information before setting out on any hunt. The word scholarship itself has many uses and misuses, so let's take a look at some of the jargon.

A scholarship is an award of money or assistance that a student receives to help cover the expense of further education. Most scholarships are based on merit. Merit usually refers to excellence in such things as academic achievement, music, or sports. The financial needs of the applicants are not usually taken into account, so that even people from wealthy families can win them. Scholarships can take the form of money or credit given to a student directly or money given to a college or university in the form of tuition or residence payments for a student. Scholarships are not a new idea. They have been around for a long time, and that is why there are so many of them and why they can be so hard to find.

You many be wondering why universities and colleges give out scholarships. It sounds a bit like a merchant paying someone to shop in his or her store. Universities and colleges award scholarships to attract the most talented students. There are eighteen universities and fifty-one major colleges in Western Canada. Because these institutions are in competition with each other for students, all of them feel the need to offer financial incentives to bring in talented students. It is important to have good students in order to get and keep good professors. If an institution has good professors then it will get more research grants from the government. So there are a lot of reasons why it is in the best interest of the college or university to offer good students money to go there. These places also hope that when you have graduated and found a good job you will donate money to your old school! Above all else, most scholarships are designed to recognize and encourage excellence.

Some scholarships are established to attract a certain type of student. Post-secondary education is not only serious work and nothing more. In fact, colleges and universities are like small towns with a very strong sense of community. There is a rich social life and more clubs and teams than in any high school. In order for this life to continue, new members must be found each year to replace the people who have graduated. As we shall see, many of the "big money" scholarships are directed at people who get good marks but also get involved in their school and community.

Before we look at such scholarships we had better clear up a few other terms that can cause confusion. The first one is "bursary." This generally refers to a grant of money awarded on the basis of financial need: usually, it's necessary to prove that you need the money. Some places also consider academic achievement and other matters before awarding a bursary. You are probably thinking: "Wouldn't that make it more like a scholarship?" And it gets more confusing: some places consider financial need when awarding scholarships. Are these bursaries too? You'll just have to be very careful when you are checking into such things. Keep asking questions until you clear up all the mysteries!

One term that is fairly easy to understand is "award." This is usually a cash prize and/or trophy of some kind given to a student for outstanding achievement. Awards (sometimes called prizes) are usually given out by private groups or foundations to support a particular interest.

One other term you may see is "fellowship." Fellowships are usually awarded to people who are completing their undergraduate studies so that they can go on for more education at the graduate level. (If you find other terms in this book that you are not clear about, check the glossary at the back.)

As you look at scholarships you may notice a few patterns. One thing that is quite obvious is the differences in the amounts. Some scholarships are worth only a few hundred dollars while others are worth a lot; the University of British Columbia National Scholarship pays out $26,000 over four years. Many of the universities now have prestigious high-value President's or Chancellor's scholarships. The catch is that they expect the winner to go to that university. You can't take the President's scholarship from the University of Regina and then go to Simon Fraser University. The people giving out the money are looking for a commitment. That's why they also give the money out over four years and the winner has to maintain a certain average while at the university. There's no free lunch, especially when it comes to scholarships. The donors want to encourage you to continue to strive for excellence.

As a rule, the greater the value of the scholarship, the more work is involved in winning it. Many of the big scholarships have lengthy application forms that we will look at in detail later on. Applicants are also required to get two or three letters of recommendation. In addition, you may be asked to write one or two essays on a given topic. There may even be an interview. It sounds like a lot of work, but you have to remember that once you have set yourself up to try for one scholarship you might as well apply for several. At present there is no central authority that limits the amount of scholarship money a student can try out for.

You may be wondering why you have to do so much. It's possible that all this paperwork is a kind of test. A student who can't sit down and fill out a few forms doesn't deserve to win a big scholarship. If applying for scholarships was easy, everyone would be doing it.

Another reason why scholarships are based on more than just marks is something known as mark inflation. Each province's and territory's high schools have their own standards. The universities are aware of this, and they weigh each high school according to how its students do in their first year of post-secondary education, when they face more uniform standards at the university.

Marks are also tricky because some people take summer school and night school in the hope that they can get higher grades there. Some students have been known to repeat courses that they passed the first time in order to raise the mark. Marks by themselves are not always the best indicator of achievement. It's just too easy to figure out ways to get high marks. Besides, no institution wants to give thousands of dollars to someone who cares only about marks. For that kind of money, they want someone who is an "all-rounder." An all-rounder is a person who gets good marks, does community service, shows athletic and/or artistic ability, and may also play a musical instrument. It sounds like a lot, but in most cases a student isn't expected to do it all at the same time. Therfore, you could do a couple of things in each year of high school and then have all your bases covered when it comes time to fill in the scholarship forms. We'll look into this aspect in detail in a later chapter.

It's worth noting that – even if no scholarship is involved – many professional programs like architecture, nursing, and medicine are now looking for more than just marks on the application forms. Nobody likes to work with a bookworm. Social skills are important for success. Besides, as the Canadian economy moves to an information and service base from a resource and industry one, the ability to work with people will become more important.

In terms of working with people, the two areas that show up on scholarship applications in one form or another involve community service and extracurricular activities.

Community service and extracurricular activities

Community service is work done on a volunteer basis in a student's neighbourhood, town, city, or church. It may involve a regular commitment of time, such as running a Sunday school or assisting with the Cub Scouts or Girl Guides. Alternatively, it may be the kind of activity that happens only once a year, such as tree planting or the Terry Fox Run. Students interested in doing community service may be amazed to discover the number of service groups that exist in even the smallest towns. Such groups as the Kinsmen, Knights of Columbus, Lions, Optimists, and Rotarians are all busy working for the good of their communities. There are also various services like distress centres and drop-in centres in most towns. Some of the larger urban centres have volunteer centres that act as "employment agencies" for people looking to do volunteer work. Hospitals and other institutions usually have some kind of volunteer coordinator to find places for volunteers.

So all that remains for you to get involved is to find an area of community service that interests you and to offer your services. You must realize that this means making a commitment to people, and that this should not be entered into lightly or just so you look good. A dilettante who flits from one activity to another for short periods of time doesn't carry as much weight as someone who makes a long-term commitment to a good cause. Nor should you expect to be paid for good works. Many organizations have ways of recognizing the work of their volunteers with banquets and awards. If you accept a paycheck, however, the work normally cannot be counted as community service. An exception to this might be the honorarium paid to counsellors at camps for handicapped children.

Extracurricular activities are those that are offered by the school but not for credit. It is much easier to find out about all the extracurricular activities if there is a student handbook. Most teaching departments feel obliged to do something for the school community in addition to teaching their subjects. The physical education department usually has year-round sports with teams for every grade competing with other schools. As well, there may be intramural sports in which teams play only in the school. The art department may have a design club that produces posters and other artwork for the school. There may well be an auto club, computer club, chess and games club, and even a radio-controlled-vehicles club. Most schools also have a students' council, yearbook, and student newspaper. Most of these activities take place before school, at lunchtime, or after school. It is up to you to investigate all the clubs and teams that are of interest and go to the meetings.

A number of scholarship forms specifically request a detailed description of any leadership experience the candidate might have. This is where the person who has stayed with certain activities and acquired a leadership role over time comes out ahead of the dilettante. It looks very good if a student develops from, say, the yearbook photographer one year to assistant editor the next year and finishes off as the editor in the third year. Such a student can be seen to be capable and worthy of promotion. In most provinces specific leadership training camps are offered, which students can attend for a few days to learn about management techniques. Aside from being a team captain or club manager there are other ways to develop leadership skills. Participating in the students' council is a great experience, especially if re-election shows that you have the approval of your peers.

To sum it all up then, community service is work done for the community for no payment and extracurricular activities are those done in and around the school for no academic credit. You should try not to put the same activity in both categories when filling out forms. Most students usually have more extracurricular activities than community-service ones, and so something like a Christmas food drive organized by the school to help feed people in the area might be considered community service as opposed to an extracurricular activity. As much as possible, and without fabrication, you should try to eliminate both repetition and blank spaces on your application forms.

Above all, pick activities that interest you. In this way you can really put your heart into it. It would also be very useful to pick volunteer work in a field that you are considering for a career. For example, if you are thinking of becoming a doctor, then volunteer work in a hospital or with the St John's Ambulance would be ideal. Most schools of medicine look for an early commitment to such work when considering an applicant.

If you are very shy about volunteering, why not go in with a friend and try to find something you can work on together? You may also consider joining an exceptionally good program that combines leadership, extracurricular activitie, and community service: the Duke of Edinburgh Award. This international program has a Gold, Silver, and Bronze award for successful participants. The DEA is usually run out of high schools. If there isn't a group in your school you may want to talk to a favourite teacher about starting one. The addresses of the offices of the Duke of Edinburgh Awards are:

National Office

The Executive Director
The Duke of Edinburgh's Award
Young Canadians Challenge
207 Queen's Quay West
P.O. Box 124
Toronto, Ontario
M5J 1A7

Regional Offices
Alberta (and North West Territories)

The Regional Director
The Duke of Edinburgh's Award
Young Canadians Challenge
Alberta and North West Territories
Suite 010, 611 – 10 Avenue S.W.
Calgary, Alberta
T2R 0B2

British Columbia (and Yukon Territory)

The Regional Director
The Duke of Edinburgh's Award
Young Canadians Challenge
British Columbia and Yukon Territory
212 – 633 Courtney Street
Victoria, British Columbia
V8W 1B8

Manitoba

The Provincial Director
The Duke of Edinburgh's Award
Young Canadians Challenge
Manitoba
Suite 2308, 7 Evergreen Place
Winnipeg, Manitoba
R3L 2T3

Saskatchewan

The Provincial Director
The Duke of Edinburgh's Award
Young Canadians Challenge
Saskatchewan
1870 Lorne Street
Regina, Saskatchewan
S4P 2L7

Don't forget: some scholarships have been around for a long time and their sponsors have seen a lot of tricks. The sponsors are wary of what they call "résumé builders." A résumé is a short document that describes an applicant's personal history and includes such things as education and work experience. There are people who make a point of padding their résumés with a wide variety of activities undertaken for a short period of time. The résumé builders will not get very good letters of recommendation because they didn't commit themselves to anything for very long. Résumé builders are trying to look good on paper. This is the wrong approach.

In the third chapter we will look at ways to build up your character and not just your résumé. Take a moment now, however, to leaf through the section at the back of the book that shows all the various scholarships. I think you'll be amazed by the variety that's out there. You will find that the high-value scholarships are looking for three things: excellent marks, community service, and extracurricular activities. They may not use those terms exactly, but that it what is generally required to win.

2 Who gets scholarships? Who doesn't?

Whenever I ask students about the kind of people who get scholarships I am always surprised by their answers. Most students seem think to that only super-brains in other schools win scholarships. The other answer I get is that only real bookworms win scholarships – really serious, dull, no-fun-at-all types. In reality, these answers say a lot about the people who give them. I strongly suspect that because they think they can't win a scholarship they believe there must be something weird about those who do.

I first became interested in scholarships while sitting through a high school graduation ceremony. As a teacher, I have to go through this exercise at least once a year. It gets a little repetitive, so one time I started to go through the program to see who was winning what. To my amazement, a small group of students seemed to be winning the bulk of all the awards. When I began to do some research on this group I discovered that they had a few things in common.

First, they were fairly confident people. I'm sure they thought of themselves as winners. They seemed to have definite goals and plans. These people had their heads up and knew what they wanted. Not surprisingly, many were going into professions like medicine, engineering, and architecture.

Secondly, these people had been involved in school activities. Most of them had joined clubs. Many had been in school teams, the band, or theatrical productions. Some had done all these things plus the yearbook and student government too.

Many of these students had also been involved in community activities of some kind. They had volunteered their time to good causes. They hadn't just watched things happen, they had made things happen.

Almost all these people had good grades, 80 per cent and up. Most had some subjects in the 90 per cent range. These were students who had earned the respect of their teachers. In fact, such marks aren't so hard to get if a regular effort is maintained.

Some of these students had shown leadership ability. They didn't lead student rebellions, however. They had worked with the school administration on various projects.

Nearly all these students were fairly conservative in their outlook and manner of dress. There weren't any with shaven heads or calculators hanging on their belts. What really surprised me was just how ordinary these winners were. They weren't geniuses and they seemed to have good social lives. In fact, many of these people were quite popular.

It was clear to me that scholarships weren't some kind of compensation for being bookworms. Instead, they seemed to be the reward for making the most out the high school experience. The really strange thing is that the winners weren't that much different from those who didn't win.

Who doesn't win scholarships?

This may sound like a silly question to be asking. A lot of people don't win. However, it's very clear to me that there are many people who should have won something and didn't. It's worth looking at some of the reasons why this happens to make sure that this doesn't happen to you.

The two big enemies of success in most things are ignorance and apathy. I once asked a poor student if he knew the difference between the two and he replied, "I don't know and I don't care!" He said more than he realized. A lot of students don't win scholarships and awards because they don't know about them, so they can't apply. I've been collecting all kinds of stories from people who missed out on big money and recognition because nobody told them that it was waiting to be had. I've also seen instances where scholarship money has sat for years just waiting for someone to apply for it!

In my first year at university I met a classmate who was filling in a very fancy-looking form. When I inquired about it, I was told it was a scholarship acceptance form. When I asked, "How did you get that?" he replied, "I was the only one to apply for it!"

A student of mine named Paul missed a deadline for a University of Western Ontario President's scholarship by about a week. I called the university to ask for a short extension and they refused. Paul sort of shrugged and made a "sour grapes" statement about not being good enough anyway. When Paul went into residence at Western he met another student who had won the scholarship and Paul discovered that he had a better record than the winner.

My best friend in high school knew about the available scholarships because I had told him that I was applying for them. At the end of my senior year I was awarded the Signode Canada scholarship and Mark didn't get anything. Now I know that his grades were a lot better than mine, but because he didn't apply, he lost out.

Not long ago, I was speaking to a parent's group about scholarships. One woman told me that her son didn't do any sports, didn't like school clubs, didn't enter contests, and didn't do any community service. She asked if he could still win any scholarships. I said that he could still win an entrance scholarship at a university or college if he had excellent marks, but his lack of involvement would keep him from getting any of the big scholarships. I had the feeling that this mother took all this a little badly. I hastened to point out that no one had a right to any scholarship. All the candidates get judged on their own merits. A student who has nothing special can't expect to stand a chance.

I bet I could write an entire book of sad stories about how ignorance and apathy have smothered success. I could fill another book with stories I've heard of people who discovered untapped scholarship and bursary money. If you ask your parents and your teachers, I'm positive they will have similar stories to tell. My hope is that you will make full use of this book to ensure that you are a success. Don't forget; from what I have seen there isn't much difference between winners and losers. It all starts with wanting to win.

3 How to make the most of your high school years

So far we have seen that there are millions of dollars in scholarships available and that there is nothing all that special about the people who win them. The winning combination seems to be the following: very good marks, extracurricular activities, and community service. It also helps that the winners learned to plan carefully and made good use of their time. The winners were able to find support at home and school and make use of this help to accomplish a lot of good things during their high school years. Teachers and parents will play an important role in your success story. However, you are the key player in all this. Let's look at the high school experience and see how you can make the most of it.

In every western province and the territories students need four years to graduate from Grade 12. You can expect to see between twenty-five to thirty-five different teachers over this time. You will enter high school as a "minor niner" and graduate as a capable, confident adult. With luck, you can use this time to acquire experiences and friendships that will last you a lifetime. You will also be faced with major choices in terms of which career path to take. There's a lot to do in your high school years and too many students don't get it right.

I think the worst mistake you can make in high school is sitting things out. Of course, it's not easy in grade nine, going from being the big kid at the elementary school to a junior in the larger environment of the high school. Your first impulse may be to hide out until you think it's safe or until you get bigger. As a result, very few Grade 9 students get involved in extracurricular activities. This is a very unfortunate state of affairs. Since no one is going to be looking very closely at your Grade 9 and 10 marks this is the best time to get involved in other things. As long as your work habits are good and you get all your credits you should consider getting involved in extracurricular activities and doing community service. Also, there are even math contests, art contests, and essay contests available starting in Grade 9. There are sports teams that start in Grade 9.

So what it comes down to is a question of confidence. Those Grade 9 students who tell me that they can't get involved in school activities because their marks will go down are really saying that they are just too shy and afraid to admit it. This is not a winning attitude. The first secret of success in planning for scholarships is to get involved and stay involved.

Another big mistake that students make is not wanting to make a commitment concerning their future. They get so good at putting it off that they get to their last year and don't know what to put down on their university and college application forms. This is much too late. It's wise to have a fairly good idea about career plans by the time you finish Grade 11. This is because many university programs require certain senior-level courses. Since most people start taking these courses in Grades 11 or 12 it would be good to know which ones you will need for university.

There are many ways to explore career options in high school. You can talk to a guidance counsellor who can give you tests to determine your interests and aptitudes. You can do co-op courses where you can earn credits while working for, say, a veterinarian. In this way you can test out a potential career to see if it is what you really want. It isn't fair to expect you to have a career all planned out by Grade 9. However, you should be considering a few possibilities.

Let's have a look at a complete plan for a high school career. We'll start in Grades 9 and 10, the years of exploration and discovery. Your marks aren't so important as getting off to a good start in high school. You should select courses that challenge your abilities. You should be trying all the different clubs and teams to find the right ones for your personal style. These grades are ideal for getting started in community service. Don't forget to watch for things like the Royal Canadian Legion Remembrance Day competitions. I had one student take a single poem and win four Legion prizes with it. She received both trophies and cash as her entry progressed from the local branch to the provincial level. Many competitions in high school have an intermediate level. Ask your teachers to let you know if they see any competitions that you could enter. If you show a little initiative I'm sure you will discover a lot of ways you can start winning early in high school.

Grade 11 is for choosing and planning. You must make a few career choices in this grade. You must plan your approach to post-secondary education. You should also be looking for scholarship opportunities. As in the earlier grades you should be trying out for teams and clubs, but by this time you should know what suits you best. There are numerous science, math, and English contests for senior-level students. The University of Waterloo, for example, sponsors the Descartes Math Contest and uses the results from this contest in its selection process. Try writing tests of this kind in every grade you can. They will help you get used to the style. Your senior years are also an ideal time for going on an exchange to, say, France or Quebec. These are also your best years for participating in student government or working on the yearbook. Don't forget to keep up your community-service activities.

It's best to consider your senior year to be the year of achievement. Marks are critical now. You must give nearly all your energies to getting the highest average you can. You must also put in a lot of time applying to post-secondary institutions and applying for scholarships. This is not the year to get involved in activities that take up a lot of your time, such as the school play. You should continue to compete in the various math and science contests, however, and you should be good at them by now. If possible, avoid taking on a part-time job in this year. It could cost you a scholarship or even a chance to get into the program you want if your marks drop. I know it isn't easy, but try to avoid complicated romantic attachments in Grade 12. You may feel that you have found true love, but quite possibly the two of you will be going into different programs at different universities. I have seen students with great potential lose it all to romantic difficulties. Your final year at high school may well determine the course of the rest of your life. It should be the crowning glory of an incredible high school career. Don't blow it!

Here's a high school planner to help you keep track of your progress. I give these to all the Grade 8 students coming to my school every year. I know that a lot of the students will never bother to look at them again. These are the people who won't win scholarships. Those students who take the time to think ahead soon discover that there are ways to develop themselves at high school and have fun doing it. Remember: there is no one right way to do well at high school. However, if you can make yourself into a creative, well-rounded individual then you have made the most of your high school years.

High school planner

Name:

School(s):

Grade 9	*Description*	*Dates*	*Teachers*
Clubs			
Teams			
Band			
Theatre			
Contests			
Community service			

Grade 10	*Description*	*Dates*	*Teachers*
Clubs			
Teams			
Band			
Theatre			
Contests			
Community service			

Grade 11	*Description*	*Dates*	*Teachers*
Clubs			
Teams			
Student government			
Exchange(s)			
Contests			
Community service			

Grade 12	*Description*	*Dates*	*Teachers*
Contests			
Clubs			
Community service			

Mentors

As you can see in the planner, there is a column for the names of
teachers who are the coaches and managers of the various activities.
During your high school years you will work with at least thirty
different teachers. If possible, you should try to stay on good terms
with all of them. This isn't always easy, I know, and I'm not advising
that you try to be a goody-two-shoes for four years straight. However,
you will need letters of recommendation from your teachers, so it
wouldn't hurt to get to know a few of them a little better by joining
the clubs and teams they run. Ideally, you should try to find one or
two teachers who can be your mentors. A mentor is an experienced
and trusted adviser. Your mentor would keep an eye open for contests
or scholarships that might interest you, and might help you when the
time comes to fill out application forms. Your guidance counsellor
could be a mentor: I'm always amazed by the number of senior
students who tell me that they have never seen their guidance
counsellor. There are no prizes for going it alone. Smart students take
full advantage of the resources available in the school. A mentor is
also a perfect candidate to write letters of recommendation for you.

It may sound a little formal right now, but you don't have to walk
up to a teacher and say, "Will you mentor me?" The relationship is
more like a friendship. You find one or two teachers you like and seek
out their advice from time to time. In return you could help them by
volunteering your time to help coach one of their teams or clubs. It's
well known in the business world that if you want to succeed you had
better find a good mentor. See the section of the book on scholarship
coaching for more information about this.

Clubs

Most schools have numerous athletic teams, so you shouldn't have
any trouble finding sports to get involved in, whether you play
competitively with other schools or simply intramurally. Intramural
mean "within the walls" and refers to those teams that play for
enjoyment inside the school.

Clubs are usually groups that are recognized and sometimes funded
by the student council. Most high schools require that every team and

club have a member of the teaching staff as a supervisor. In fact, all teachers are expected to get involved in the life of the school by coaching teams clubs or, say, directing the school play. Teachers look bad if they don't get involved in something. You may discover that you and your mentor share a strong interest in astronomy. It might be possible then to set up your own astronomy club that meets regularly to discuss the topic and arrange for guest speakers and field trips. The best thing about setting up your own clubs at school is that you get more choice and more control over the activities that take place. You also may get some valuable experience in leadership and management.

At my school I offer a number of clubs during the lunch hour. Each one meets in my room on a different day of the week. The clubs change each year and new ones are added and others fade away as students get older and graduate. I encourage the students in each club to elect leaders who are in charge of running the meetings. In this way, I am free to work with a lot of different groups at the same time. The leaders consult with me about anything they may need.

The list of activities in my enrichment program this year was as follows:

Monday: CONTEST CLUB. This group meets every week to share ideas about essay contests and scholarships. We made a point of watching for any art or essay contests coming into the school. Even though students were competing they were still supportive of one another. Some of the Grade 9 students who joined this club won in the local Royal Canadian Legion Remembrance Day poetry and poster contest. Eventually, these students got involved in science contests and national programs like Forum for Young Canadians.

Monday: SPECIAL PROJECTS GROUP. This group meets to prepare graphics for the school and community. It plans designs, and calligraphy for diplomas. We even have a button-making machine and have made money for charity by selling buttons for various school and community events.

Tuesday: CHESS TEAM. This team meets to play chess and prepare for provincial chess tournaments held in the spring.

Wednesday: MODEL UNITED NATIONS CLUB. This club combines politics, world affairs, and play-acting. The Model United Nations allows students to act as representatives of various countries in a United Nations assembly where issues like acid rain and Middle East conflict are discussed. In December of each year this club hosts a regional assembly where other schools select countries and send delegates. There are also large provincial assemblies.

Thursday: SCHOOLREACH TEAM. This activity is based on the old CBC program, "Reach for the Top." The new name is "Schoolreach" and it is played in much the same way, with two teams of four students trying to buzz in fastest with the correct answers to general-knowledge questions. It is possible to get to the national level in competitive play.

Friday: HISTORICAL SIMULATIONS AND GAMES CLUB. This group meets at least once a week to play all manner of games based on historical events like the Second World War. We have a special shelf where games in progress can be stored.

AMNESTY INTERNATIONAL CLUB. This club was started by a student who had an interest in helping political prisoners. The student found her own adviser, set up guest speakers and even assemblies, and organized various school-wide activities to draw attention to the plight of political prisoners.

It doesn't take much more than interest to set up clubs and keep them going. You and a few friends could probably set up any number of clubs at your school. Don't forget to find a teacher to act as adviser. Check with them about your school's procedures for clubs. Don't be afraid to go to the student council for money. There's usually no problem finding an empty classroom at lunchtime or after school. If you can't get one, try talking to the school librarian. You'll find that most teachers are very willing to help a student who shows some drive and vision.

You may be wondering how you will find the time to get all these things done. Don't forget that you have four or five years to do this. That should be enough if you use your time properly.

Time management

We are all time travellers. Our trips start when we are born and continue for several decades. In all that time we will spend years watching television, months on the phone, and so on. Without some kind of personal control, we could spend all our lives doing menial tasks and never find the time to do the very important things in life. The people who win scholarships accomplish this by seizing control of their own time and investing it wisely. You may be wondering how the "all-rounders" find the time for extracurricular activities and community service. The truth is that they don't *find* the time, they *make* the time. The average person wastes a lot of time. You probably lose at least two hours a day through inefficient time management. Many people dislike the concept of time management because it suggests that people are tied to a clock and have to run around like robots. But these same people usually claim that there isn't enough time in the day to get all their work done. Clearly everyone has the same time in a day, only some people make better use of it.

The funny thing is that we don't all experience time in the same way. Here's an experiment you can try with your friends or family. All you need is a pen, some paper, and a watch that shows the passage of seconds. Ask everyone to close their eyes and put their heads down. Tell them that they are to raise their hand when they think a full minute has passed after you give the "start" signal. Remind all of your participants to remain silent for the exercise. Your job is to watch the clock and the hands and write down each person's estimate of one minute. Depending on the size of the group you will find that the estimates for the minute length will stretch from thirty to ninety seconds. Time really is relative. We all experience it differently.

To understand how you use your time it is necessary to keep track of it. Here's an exercise you should try. Have a look at the circle in figure 1. Around the edge of the circle are numbers from 1 to 24. This pie diagram can be used to record your time use down to the nearest half-hour. What you must do is keep the diagram with you at all times for one full day and sketch in what you are doing at any given hour. Don't try to fill in anything in advance. Keep a record of the day as it actually happens. Use the circle as if it were a clock. If you wake up at 7:00 AM, then start your record there. If you go to bed at 11:00 PM, then this would be the 23rd hour of your day. You may wish to try keeping track of your time for a full week in order to get a better view of your situation. Then you will really know how you are spending your 24 hours every day.

This clock exercise will show you that there is at least an hour every day when you aren't doing anything. It could be that you are waiting for a bus or just goofing off during the lunch hour. Like most young people you probably watch too much television. You may also find

A.M.

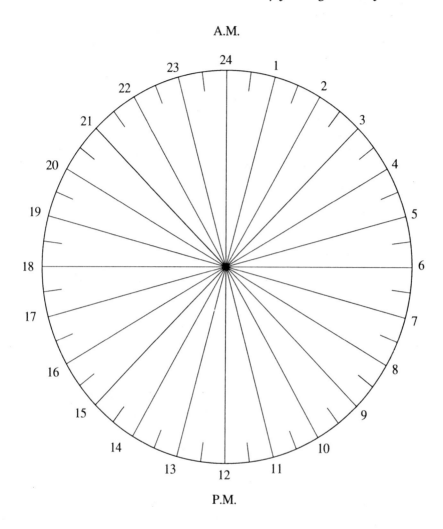

P.M.

Figure 1 Time-use diagram

Use this pie chart to record how you are using your time during an average day. Write down your activities in the space next to the hour at which they take place. This is based on a 24-hour clock: anything in the PM half is like the usual time with 12 added to it. For example, 2 PM would be 14 o'clock and 6 PM would be 18 o'clock. Don't forget to keep track of your day as it happens. Don't write it down in advance or try to remember it later. You'll be amazed when you see where your time is going.

time slots that can be recycled into two-for-one time; you could read a book while waiting for your bus instead of just standing there. By using your time more efficiently you can get more out of every day. This is how you can find the time to get better grades, join extracurricular activities, and do community service.

Long-term time planning is very important. Most schools have some kind of student calendar so that you can write down key dates. Get into the habit of using one of these. Nothing is more disturbing than missing an important date, especially if it involves a scholarship deadline. A time-planning book gives you control of the passage of your time. In one sense, when you write down under February 25 the words "Math test, chapters 1 to 19" you are making a prediction for your own future. You can see yourself writing a math test that day. Too many students walk into class and say, "A test today? I don't remember anything about a test today! This is so unfair." It is possible for some time travellers to get lost.

Another important bit of time management revolves around the course selections that you make in each year of high school. I have seen good students forced to come back for an extra term to pick up one last credit. It wouldn't be very much fun to have to do math and science courses in your final year. A smart move would be to take your math courses at an accelerated rate, perhaps one per term if possible. You will have eight or ten semesters in high school and there are several math courses you could take. Math course are hated by most students. This is unfortunate because a well-done math course can produce a very high mark to help with your average. I'd even go so far as to suggest that most people are more likely to get a mark in the 90 per cent range in math than English or history. English and history courses are graded on essays and written exams. It is very hard to write extremely good material when you are just learning a subject. In these subjects different teachers look for different things. Math, on the other hand, is largely the application of skills that can be practised and perfected. Answers are generally right or wrong. Mathematics is basically a language. Once you know the basic rules and the key terms you can improve with practice. This is a very important consideration because it is the average of your final marks that plays a critical part in the winning of entrance scholarships from the universities and colleges.

Since most university and scholarship applications are due by February or March, you would do best to have at least one free period in the first term of your last year in order to have time to fill out all the forms. It is essential that your applications go well, so give this matter top priority in your time planning. If you organize yourself properly it should be possible to apply for all the scholarships for which you are eligible.

Another time trick will help with the university application procedure. Because it takes time to process all the applications each year the universities have to use the mid-term marks for the second term. This means that if you are a slow starter you might be penalized by a low mid-term mark. You are better off working hard at the beginning of your last term to ensure a high mid-term mark. But don't think that you can slack off after those marks go in. The final mark is important for a number of reasons, including scholarships offered later in the school year.

At present, scientists cannot manufacture time. This means that we must all make the best use of the time that we have. It won't happen overnight, but you can learn to be a better time traveller.

4 Applying for awards

Once you have decided to apply for a scholarship the real work begins. Since you get only one chance to make a first impression, it is critical that you spend some time on your application. You will find the personal student record in this chapter useful for organizing all your information. Fill out the form carefully and then let your parents and your scholarship coach take a look at it to be sure that you haven't missed anything.

Nearly all the universities in Western Canada have prestigious scholarships that require special attention. These are sent out to high school principals or guidance departments each year with the instruction that only one candidate should be chosen from each school. The reason for this limitation is to ensure that only the very best students will be considered for these awards.

Most of the big scholarships have some kind of set application procedure and a deadline. If you have done some research you should know the scholarships for which you are eligible. Your next move is to work through the requirements carefully. Resist the temptation to scribble down one copy and send it off. If this is your attitude you might as well not bother wasting the postage. This is especially true if you have been asked to be the candidate for your school. If you don't really want to put in the time, then decline the honour and let someone else apply for it. I get more than a little angry when I ask a student to represent the school and then am told too late that he or she wasn't really interested and didn't complete the application. Not only does that attitude let the school down, it selfishly wastes an opportunity that could have gone to someone else.

Scholarship application forms are not easy to complete. The main reason why potential candidates don't apply is because there is too much work involved. However, there really isn't too much involved in filling out a scholarship form. A typical form is two pages long. The front side of the first page describes the scholarship and lists the selection criteria. The back side of the first page has spaces for personal information like your name, address, school, the program applied for, and the names of your references. The other sections of the application form ask for such things as

- a list of your extracurricular activities and community service;
- your employment history;
- a description of any prizes, awards, medals, or distinctions you have received while in high school;
- a recent transcript of your high school marks;
- a comparative assessment by a teacher that gives your rank in the graduating class (top 5 per cent or top 10 per cent and so on); and
- a recommendation from the principal (often a checklist of characteristics in addition to an anecdotal comment).

Some of the university scholarship applications require a short essay, usually of no longer than 600 words. The topics for these essays vary from year to year but involve the attitudes and values of the applicant in some way. These essays are judged on their form and content. This means that the essays should be well written and creative. Many scholarship sponsors are disappointed by the quality of applications they receive. They cannot believe that students with academic averages over 90 per cent write so poorly. Messy applications are also a frequent complaint. It is a good idea to spend some time on your paperwork. It represents you. The following are lists of dos and don'ts for scholarship application forms.

Dos and Don'ts

Do list

Do make sure that you are doing your rough draft on a photocopy of the form and not an original.

Do get your parents and scholarship coach to proofread your rough draft. Everyone makes mistakes. You won't get it right the first time.

Do be certain that you have read over the instructions carefully before you begin, taking careful note of the deadline date. Look at all the questions and make a note of the ones that you will want to discuss with your coach.

Do try to be creative. Unless it is stated explicitly otherwise, feel free to personalize your application with a good photograph of yourself or by enclosing an additional reference or two. Coloured paper can brighten any application but remember to be tasteful. Remember also that it's hard to read things written on dark-coloured paper.

Do apply for as many scholarships as possible. Once you have done all the preparation for one the rest are easier to complete. As a rule your odds of winning something increase as you enter more competitions. At present there is no limit to the number of scholarships that you can win.

Do be sure to type the final copy. If you must do it by hand, use blue or black ink and space your writing carefully. Your form may be photocopied later so it must be legible. It is also important to keep all your forms, letters of recommendation, transcripts, and so on neatly together, so you will want to send off your application in some kind of folder. Most stationery stores have a good selection of two-pocket folders.

Do take the time to make a photocopy of your entire application and file it away safely. It may be useful if the original goes missing or if you have to prepare a similar application. You may also find the form useful if you get called for an interview.

Do make sure that you have your own Social Insurance Number (SIN). You may need it for some applications. Apply for it before the scholarship busy season starts.

Do remember that it is best to get your completed application to the sponsor at least three or four weeks before the final deadline. Last-minute entries don't give you enough time to do a thorough job.

Do keep track of all the scholarships for which you have applied and especially of the date by which you should receive a reply. This might spare you some anxious days of waiting and wondering.

Do ask your scholarship coach for help if you get stuck while filling out the forms. This is your first time at it, but the coach will likely have more experience with the application process. If necessary, the coach can contact the sponsor for more information.

Don't list

Don't let the original copy of the application form get soiled or dog-eared. Keep it stored flat in a proper-sized envelope. Don't fold your material if you can help it since it might be photocopied later.

Don't forget to give your references at least a week to produce a letter of recommendation for you. Supply them with a copy of your personal information form, instructions concerning the scholarship you are applying for, and an addressed envelope with postage attached. In some cases the reference letters must be sent in with the application, and so you must ask your references to return the letters to you. Because letters of reference are so important, there is a special section of this chapter that describes them in detail.

Don't forget to send thank-you notes to the people who write your letters of recommendation. It's only proper courtesy. You may also need other letters from them in the future.

Don't ever lie on an application form. If you are ever found to be a fraud, it could mean that you could lose your good name as well as a scholarship.

Don't do your "good" copy the first time; do at least one rough copy. You may discover that one of your entries in one part of the application can be moved to fill a blank somewhere else without appearing to be out of place. This is why it is so important to do at least one rough copy.

Don't leave any unanswered sections on your application. Just because you've drawn a blank there's no reason to leave one. It's usually possible to come up with a truthful answer by "thinking laterally." An example of this is the student who found a section in the Shad Valley Centre for Creative Technology application that asked about his entrepreneurial experience. He told his mentor that he had never run his own business and so had nothing to put down in this space. It turned out, however, that he had repaired car stereos for a garage owner, taking numerous stereos home and fixing them there. In effect, this student was acting as a private contractor being paid on a piecework basis. After more prompting this student realized that his hobby of fixing computers and VCRs was more like a business. So by careful thought, a blank became a good solid answer.

Don't forget to check to be sure that you are sending everything that was requested. You may have to remind people about sending off the letters of recommendation. If you must meet a deadline, send in a note with the application stating that a letter of recommendation from Mrs So-and-so will be sent shortly.

Don't miss deadlines. Some scholarship deadlines are taken very seriously. If a sponsor has a large number of good applications, why should he or she wait for you?

Don't send important documents by ordinary mail. A little extra money will buy fast, secure delivery through Priority Post or a courier. Your school may be willing to cover the costs of sending off your application.

Above all, don't talk yourself out of trying. Nobody can guarantee you any prizes, but it is an absolute certainty that if you don't try then you cannot win. Let the scholarship selection committee make the final choice. If the application procedure has discouraged you then go and talk it over with your parents or scholarship coach. I have seen too many great students and potential winners talk themselves out of applying. There's no shame in losing when you are competing with the very best. Besides, if you do everything right, then you might win, and just think of how good that would feel. Scholarships mean both fame and money. Get your share.

Application etiquette

When applying for any award of scholarship it is essential that the applicant observe proper business etiquette. Letters should be typed and polite. Never pester a scholarship sponsor with phone calls. Checking every three days to see how your application is doing will not improve your chances and may have a negative effect.

In the case of many university and college scholarships there is no application deadline because candidates will be selected on the basis of admission information such as senior-year grades and program. In the case of all the scholarships listed in this book, there will be a deadline date if a separate application is required. Don't waste your time and that of the sponsor by sending letters inquiring about scholarships that don't require any application form. Always remember: some sponsors give away these awards out of a sense of generosity. They are doing you a favour. Nobody will appreciate a greedy or pushy candidate. In fact, classy recipients always send thank-you letters to show their appreciation for the recognition and the money.

Requesting letters of recommendation

Applications for scholarships and many university and college programs require letters of reference (also known as letters of recommendation). You will need at least three letters for most scholarships. These letters are usually required from such people as your teachers, principal, or employer. You may also request letters from the organizations for which you do volunteer work.

Don't be shy about asking for such letters from your teachers. It is usually an honour for a teacher to be asked to do this because it suggests the student values that teacher's opinion. Unfortunately, not all teachers understand both the honour or the importance of writing good letters of recommendation. Now and then a teacher will forget about the letter, and that can hamper your application. Such a failure is a shame, because it is very likely that someone took the time to write a letter of recommendation for that teacher sometime in the past. Here is a way to ensure that you always get the letters of recommendation that you need.

Every teacher knows that students are more likely to do homework if the assignment is written down so the students won't forget it. It stands to reason that if you want to be sure that a teacher doesn't forget your letter of recommendation you should give written instructions. Here is a typical letter from a student to a teacher concerning a letter of recommendation. This note should be given to the teacher in person so that he or she can connect your name to your face. Teachers see thousands of students during their careers, so don't feel badly if your favourite teacher needs a little reminder about who you are.

Dear Mrs Brown:

I am applying to the education program at the University of Victoria and also for the President's Scholarship there. Would you please write letters of recommendation for both of these for me?

I have attached the reference form for the concurrent education program. I have also included the description of the scholarship that was sent to me, along with a copy of my personal student record which shows all my high school activities.

The concurrent education reference form must be sent back with my application, so please return it to me when you are finished. The letter of recommendation for the scholarship must be sent separately, and so I have prepared a stamped, addressed envelope for you. Both applications are due before the end of March.

Thanks for your help. Let me know if you need any more information.

Yours truly,

David Lurie

Notice how the letter requests two reference letters at the same time. It is unlikely that the teacher will change much of the information in the two letters anyway. Here are a few other tips concerning letters of reference/recommendation:

Seek out teachers who really know you. Don't be afraid to track them down if they or you have changed schools.

Get people who have first-hand knowledge of all your good works both in and out of the classroom.

Ask teachers who teach the subject(s) related to your scholarship or university application. For example, ask your biology teacher if you are applying for a biology program.

Always ask for more letters than you need. This gives you a choice of letters or an extra one in case one person doesn't come through.

Let the teacher know what the application is looking for so that he or she can mention it specifically. If creativity is one of the criteria, ask the teacher to address your creative side in their letter.

Sample questions

You may wish to use this sample list of questions to practise your style. They are drawn from a variety of different types of scholarship forms. As much as possible, try to answer in well-written, full sentences. Point-form answers are to be avoided unless specifically requested by the scholarship sponsor.

What is your long-term goal? Please explain how your academic progress has contributed to this goal.

What is your most significant achievement?

What are your hobbies and why do you enjoy them?

What kinds of creative work have you done? (Include music, art, computers, essays, or poetry)

Write a brief paragraph about the most inspiring book you have ever read. What was special about it?

What magazines do you read regularly?

Once you get into the process of filling out application forms, you will discover that they are very similar to the Personal Student Record Form at the end of this chapter. The trick is to organize all your personal information in advance. Then you can concentrate on the more unusual questions like the ones above. It is important to give good answers to the creative essay–style questions. It is not unusual for me to ask a student to rewrite an answer three or four times. Don't expect your first try to be golden. When you are answering questions about your career goals be sure to talk about your sense of community. Too many students focus only on themselves in application forms and come across as narrow and selfish. Your goals should include concern for serving the needs of others.

You must keep a well-organized file for all your scholarship information and forms. If you are systematic it will be easier to apply for more scholarships without all the paper becoming a hopeless jumble in one of your school binders. You may wish to use the sample organizer provided here to help you track your application paper.

Name of scholarship	Deadline date	Names of references	Date of response
1.			
2.			
3.			
4.			
5.			
6.			
7.			

Interviews

Interviews are an important part of some scholarships application processes. Some bursary applications require interviews as well. It is usually a good sign to be granted an interview because it means that your application form was interesting to the scholarship sponsors and they want to have a better look at you. The bad news is that very few students in high school have ever had a proper interview. Most of the jobs that students get don't require long interviews: if you can flip a hamburger and mop a floor you're hired. As you get into the world of careers and full-time jobs you will discover that interview skills are critical to your success. Many post-secondary programs like teaching and architecture require interviews as well, as part of the admission procedures, so it is vital that you get experience in high school.

An interview is a chance for someone who is interested in you to find out if you are the right person. You in turn get a chance to see if you would like to get involved with the people who are interviewing you. It's not just a question of what you know; an interview is a social experience. A good interview should allow both you and the interviewer to say, "This is who I am." The other issue is, "Is this the right person?"

It sounds easy enough, but the circumstances surrounding an interview cause most people to get nervous. It can be a very formal situation, which is very unnatural for most of us. The worst aspect is that the interview focuses largely on you personally. Sometimes there can be two or three or more people in the room looking at you and asking you questions. When I applied to the School of Architecture at the University of Waterloo I had nine people interview me at the same time. Interviews can make you feel like some kind of zoo exhibit.

I think the best way to approach interviews of all kinds is to think of them as little stage plays without a script. You are the star actor and the interviewer is part of the supporting cast. You will feel just like a stage actor does before a show starts. Even old pros still get nervous before they go on. The trick is to keep your nervousness from affecting your performance. Actors practise their parts and go over them several times to ensure that they will not forget their lines or freeze up. You can do the same thing when preparing for an interview. First, find out when the interview is and where it will take place. Also, ask who will be interviewing you. Next, think about your costume; what you will wear to the interview. Then, start doing your research about the interview. If you are going for a scholarship interview at a university, make a point of doing a lot of reading about the place. Talk to someone who went there recently. There's probably some teacher at your high school who has attended that university. It's important to bring specific information to the interview.

Now that you have the setting and background research taken care of you can focus on the actual interview. Most interviews take between twenty and forty minutes. This means that you will have to be able to talk for at least half the time of the interview. You know that the interviewer will be looking at your background, so write down a list of your skills and abilities. You will find the Personal Student Record to be very useful. You can expect to be asked about your weaknesses. In the case of a scholarship interview you can expect to be asked why you deserve to get the scholarship. For all these questions you should have prepared answers written and practised beforehand. Just like a stage actor you must practise your interview skills. Get a friend, parent, or teacher to give you an interview. It will seem a little strange at first. You will probably want to go into the interview and just "be yourself." Unfortunately, a long interview is likely to make someone feel a little foolish if they have "been themselves" for five minutes and then spent twenty minutes in awkward silence. Resist the temptation to trust your luck. Practise, practise, practise. One of my students told me that after all the practice interviews the real thing seemed easy.

Make sure that you arrive early for your interview. It's a good idea to find out well in advance which room you are supposed to be in. Remember to relax while waiting. Interviews are often behind schedule, so don't let the delay disturb you. Think positively and avoid anyone who is having a panic attack in the waiting room; distress can be contagious. If you are troubled by sweaty palms keep a small ziplock bag of talcum powder in your pocket or purse and rub a small amount into your hands just before going to the interview. This will make your hands feel dry and smooth. Keep the powder off your clothes, though, especially a dark outfit.

Remember to smile as much as possible. If you go in all serious and quiet you won't come across very well. A smile increases your "face value." Don't be surprised if the interviewer starts to smile back. A positive attitude is essential in any interview. Eye contact is important as well. Always look directly at the person to whom you are speaking. Avoid the temptation to look away. You may want to practise maintaining eye contact in a mirror or with friends.

Videotaping a practice interview will give you a chance to see how you look. Most high schools have video cameras that you can use if you don't have one of your own.

The following is a list of questions you should know how to answer:

"Tell us a little about yourself."
"Why did you choose our university?"
"What are your long term career goals?"
"What kind of people do you like to associate with?"
"Would you describe yourself as a moral person?"
"Can you describe a moral dilemma that you experienced recently?"
"How will you be creative in your future studies?"
"Do you prefer to work with people or objects?"
"What advice would you give politicians today?"
"Give an example of something scholarly."
"What makes a good leader?"
"What clubs or teams do you plan on joining when you come here?"
"Do you plan to continue to do community service while at university?"
"If there was a colour that best described you, what would it be?"
"Why do you think you deserve this scholarship?"

Don't be upset if someone is taking notes during your interview. If there are a lot of people to interview, there will be different teams of interviewers. If they are to compare their results, they must collect written scores. No doubt you will feel very ill at ease when you say something and an interviewer starts to write. You must resist the temptation to ask, "Did I give the right answer?" or "How am I doing, anyway?" This sort of behaviour shows that you are nervous and insecure. There are usually no right answers in an interview, but there certainly is the wrong kind of behaviour. Try to avoid nervous tapping, throat clearing, looking away, and awkward, defensive postures. I have seen students wrap their arms around one knee and rock back and forth during a practice interview. Others have flapped their hands like wings; this can be very distracting. You must practice a relaxed posture and slow breathing. Pause before answering any questions. Speak slowly and clearly. Look at the person who asked the question. If you can master these qualities you will find that you will enjoy the interview more. Who knows? You may even learn to relax and to take charge of an interview when you meet an interviewer who is more nervous than you are.

Most interviewers like to make little speeches during the interview. While some of this is pompous, these speeches can contain important information. Listen carefully because you can gain some idea about the attitudes of the interviewer. You can then try to make an appropriate response to the speech. Never interrupt an interviewer. The more time that the interviewer spends talking, the more time you have to think over your responses.

The end of an interview is a difficult time for everyone. You must never look at your watch, although the interviewer might. Remember to stay relaxed during the interview or you will get up stiffly and even a little lightheaded. Most interviewers will finish by saying, "Well, I wonder if you have any questions?" Most people can't wait to get out of the room and so they say, "Uh, no, I don't think so." This is a bad answer. Surely you have heard something during the interview that you want to talk about. Ask at least one good question before you go. You may want to write up three or four final questions beforehand, but be sure that they haven't been answered during the interview or you will look silly asking them.

Finish the interview with a smile even if you feel it went miserably. Inexperience will make you think that you acted like an idiot, but you probably did well. Don't ask whether or not you will hear from them. They will get back to you when they are ready. Shake hands with everyone in the room before you go. Leave with dignity and then go get yourself a drink of water and some fresh air. Your performance is over. If you get a phone call telling you that you were unsuccessful in your quest for a scholarship, try to turn misfortune to your benefit and ask why you didn't succeed. Don't feel bad if you are not a winner. You must keep on trying.

Personal student record

Since most students apply for scholarships in their year of graduation
they find that time often runs short and the quality of their paperwork
suffers. When it comes down to a choice between doing well on a
term essay or sweating over the details of a scholarship form students
usually choose to put their time into their schoolwork and forget
about the scholarships. In order to help you prepare for all the various
forms you will likely see in your last year of high school, the following form should be completed in the first term of that year. The
reference column refers to the person(s) who can substantiate your
record. This form should *not* be sent out with your applications.
However, you could give it to people who are writing letters of
recommendation for you to give them background information.

Full name: _____   SIN number: _____

Parents names: Employers:

_____   _____

_____   _____

University/College choices:

1 _____ 2 _____ 3 _____

_____   _____   _____

Program(s): _____

_____

_____

Special characteristics (physical disabilities, allergies, identified
learning disability, giftedness): _____

_____

_____

Extenuating circumstances (events that had an effect upon recent
school performance like a death in the immediate family, prolonged

illness or injury, family bankruptcy or unemployment, frequent change of schools or travel, including exchanges): ⸺

_____

_____

_____

Awards (school awards and prizes for academic subjects and athletics and community recognition; e.g., Junior Citizen of the Year):

AwardYear   *Reference person*

_____

_____

Extracurricular activities (clubs, teams, yearbook, student government, stage, committees):

Type   Year   *Reference person*

_____

_____

Community service (any volunteer work done outside the school):

Type   Year   *Reference person*

_____

_____

Leadership experience (team captain, coach, manager):

Type   Year   *Reference person*

_____

_____

Music training (both in and out of school):

Instrument   *Year*   *Level reached*

_____

_____

Hobbies, interests and recreational sports: _____

_____

_____

_____

Personal strengths: _____

_____

_____

_____

Personal weaknesses: _____

_____

_____

_____

Career goals: _____

_____

_____

_____

Work experience (especially jobs that involve entrepreneurial skills or positions of responsibility):

Position	*Year*	*Employer*

5 Scholarships and taxes

Like most good things, scholarships are eligible for taxation by the Government of Canada. This is not a major disaster because the income of most students is usually low. Also, many of the big money scholarships are doled out year by year or term by term because continuance is dependent upon the recipient maintaining a certain grade point average. As a result, no one taxation year should have a massive amount of taxable scholarship income. The one exception might be the freshman year if a student has won a number of high school awards plus university or college entrance scholarships. In a riveting document, number IT-75R2, Revenue Canada sets down:

> Scholarships and bursaries may be defined as amounts paid or benefits given to students to enable them to pursue their education, usually at a university, college or other educational institution and to proceed towards obtaining a degree, diploma (e.g., one issued by a college to a plumber or electrician), or other certificate of graduation. Normally, a student is not expected to do specific work for the payer in exchange for such amounts. All amounts received by a taxpayer in a year as or on account of scholarship, fellowship or bursary, or a prize for achievement in a field of endeavour ordinarily carried on by the taxpayer, are included in income by virtue of paragraph 56(1)(n) of the Act to the extent that the total of these amounts received in the year exceeds $500. Such amounts are included in income in the year received.

Loosely translated, the current process is to total all scholarships, fellowships, and bursaries. If the total is $500 or less, it is not to be reported. If the total is more than $500, then a $500 tax-free exemption is subtracted and the remaining amount entered under line 130 of the tax form as "Other Income."

Many students may not have been filing tax returns during high school. This may not be such a smart idea since there are tax credits available that can be transferred to parents. Don't wait until you are away from home at university or college to try to figure out your income taxes. Start looking at the responsibilities and benefits of prompt taxation returns while you are in high school.

6 Notes for parents

Parents are an important part of every scholarship winner's team. A student spends only thirty hours in school every week. That leaves one hundred and thirty-eight hours when you are somewhere else, and most likely a lot of it is spent at home. Home is a student's base of operations and parents should be partners.

Some parents feel that the best way to get their children into the best universities with scholarships is to send them to expensive private schools. This is not necessarily true. If a student has a good plan and good support then he or she can be successful just about anywhere. It shouldn't be too hard for parents to support the school program of their children. Aside from the necessities like clothing and food, parents can provide advice, encouragement, and, when necessary, discipline. Most adolescents will admit that one of their big concerns is whether parents care or not. Rejection by the parents plays a big part in juvenile delinquency. The reverse is also true. Successful students will acknowledge the assistance of their parents. Sports stars are always saying "Hi, Mom!" on television.

The best thing that parents can do is to create a home environment that encourages good work habits and also recognizes success without being pushy. I have seen students driven into hospital because of the pressure from their parents to get high marks. As we have seen, marks have only a partial role to play and they are no predictor of success in life. It is important that parents share a more balanced view of the high school experience. This means that they should ask about the extracurricular activities and the community service of their children.

It may mean that they themselves get involved in some of these things, if only as "taxi driver" for various events.

Since marks matter most in the last couple of years of high school, parents should concentrate in the early years on identifying areas of weakness and working on them. If necessary, a tutor could be hired to help with a problem subject like math. Parents should also encourage their children to develop good work habits. Bright students often slide by in high school, using their dazzling verbal skills and charm to do well. As a result, Grade 12 comes as a surprise and university or college comes as a shock. Students have come back from their first term of post-secondary education to tell me that their marks have dropped 20 per cent and that they have been working like dogs. University is no place to try to develop good work habits.

The best place to learn how to work is in the home. Parents should be sure that the following things are in place:

1 Students should have a quiet, well-lit and well-ventilated room in which to work.

2 Students should choose a study hour and stick to it every night. Even if there is no homework, the student can review and organize notes to study. It may even be possible to do work in advance. This hour should be uninterrupted. Phone calls should be avoided. Parents should not interrupt either.

3 Every high school student should have some kind of booklet for keeping track of assignment deadlines, tests, and so on. Many high schools now have student handbooks. Parents should check to make sure such a thing is in place and in use.

4 Parents shouldn't be afraid to check up on the work habits of their children. There should be some homework every week, if not every night. If a student is coming home empty-handed and not succeeding, then a call to the teachers is in order. Don't go bothering the principal. It would be best to talk to each teacher first. Nothing bothers teachers more than to be called into the principal's office to be told of a parental complaint. This is known as a "cold prickly" in the education business. It will not help school and home relations.

5 Parents often overlook superior teaching ability. Calling a teacher to thank him or her for coaching a team or helping with an essay contest is what is known as a "warm fuzzy." Teachers can't get enough of them and neither can principals. Clearly, a large part of the parents' role lies in encouraging both the teachers and the students.

6 Every term, high schools hold parents nights. Almost always the parents of the successful students come to see the teachers. The parents of troubled students rarely come out. So there is a clear connection between parents, teachers, and student success. If they work together, success is guaranteed. The moral is that parents should make a point of attending school meetings and even join school committees. If it is not possible to find time to visit the school, then parents should be particulary attentive to any newsletters sent out by the school and call back if they have any questions.

7 Every student needs a computer to do well these days. It's one of those investments that the whole family can benefit from. A typed essay will usually do better than a handwritten one. In addition, some of the word-processing programs have excellent features for graphics and spelling checks.

8 Many students have part-time jobs. These can be valuable for students, but such work should not interfere with school. Parents should limit working hours to the weekends. If possible, no senior student should be working after school, especially those in their final year. After all, you can't buy high school credits.

9 Although pleasant, family trips in the middle of the school year can be very disruptive for students and teachers. A lot of material must be covered in a very short time in most courses. Most teachers don't think a trip to the United States in February is a valid excuse for missing class time. This sort of thing gives the impression that education is a low priority for some families. If trips must happen, students should get work from the teacher in advance to make up for the material that will be missed.

Parents should ask the high school if there is a scholarship coach. It isn't sufficient that there are lists of scholarships in the guidance office. There really should be someone to whom students can turn for help when they are applying. There should also be a scholarship selection committee at school, and parents may be welcome to join it. The role of this committee will be to make sure that the best students are applying for as many scholarships as possible. In addition, this committee will be responsible for most of the awards and bursaries given by the high school to graduating students. Since many of these awards come from community groups like the Legion or the Kinsmen, parents can help to promote the creation of scholarships by the groups they are involved in.

For scholarships, parents can be a big help in filling out and proof-reading applications forms. Also, many employers have scholarships for the children of their employees. Parents should look into this possibilty, including any offered by their previous employers. Parents should also ask their employers to establish such scholarships if none exist at present. There is a list of employer scholarships in chapter 14. Parents pay the lion's share of post-secondary education costs. They should not be shy about getting involved with the issues mentioned here. Quite apart from helping their own children, positive changes in the high school environment can have a lasting beneficial effect on hundreds of future students.

Registered Education Savings Plans

The word "scholarship" has numerous meanings, ranging from a monetary reward for academic excellence to the quality of knowledge gained through study. Scholarship is an overused word that has been misapplied in many areas.

One such case involves the registered education savings plans (RESP) that call themselves scholarships. A normal RESP involves money set aside by a parent or someone else and invested to help fund a child's education. The donor does not get any tax deduction on this money, but it gains interest that is not taxed until it is withdrawn. There are four major RESP trust funds that call themselves scholarships. These are:

– Canadian Scholarship Trust Fund
– Heritage Scholarship Trust Foundation
– University Scholarship Foundation
– Foundation Universitas (Quebec)

Although the word "scholarship" features prominently in these names, these are really savings plans that demand regular, long-term payments before any "scholarship" money is paid out to the student. Academic merit is not one of the criteria for getting money out. Students with a 60 average get the same amount as students with a 90 average provided that someone has kept up the payments in the RESP. In addition, these plans require significant enrolment fees and depository charges. Although all these RESPs are run by non-profit organizations, there are various drains on the funds in the form of administrative and advertising costs. There seems to be no end of application forms for such programs sitting in boxes in doctor's and dentist's waiting rooms. Some of these funds even offer little bibs to babies in maternity wards. Recently the Canadian Scholarship Trust Plan was offering an RESP prize in packages of diapers to help promote that trust plan.

A brief look at the prospectus documents reveals that all these so-called scholarship programs operate in much the same way. In the first year of university or college a student would receive only the principal paid into the fund over the years, which would be about $2000 per investment unit. This would vary according to the age of the child when the RESP was initiated. For up to three years following, a student would receive a "scholarship" that would come from the interest money in the fund. It is important to note that in order to be eligible for this money, the student must attend an institution recognized by the fund. The organizers of these RESPs also reserve the right to discontinue funding if a student leaves a program or takes a year off. These restrictions make these investments fairly inflexible. It's presumptuous to assume that a newborn baby will be going to go to college or university. If a child doesn't go on to post-secondary education the RESPs will refund only the principal or allow a sibling to take over the "scholarship."

I can only assume that these programs are called scholarships to entice status-seeking people to join. Proud parents can then claim, "Our Mary is at university on a scholarship!" It does sound better than "She's got an RESP." But really, these aren't scholarships as we have defined them in this book. You don't have to pay large sums to get a real scholarship. You win them for being good at something.

Undoubtedly the cost of university is a major burden and one that is bound to increase in the future. A wise family would do well to prepare in advance. However, since the world changes so quickly it is important to have more flexibility and control over any savings programs. In effect, a family could set up its own "scholarship fund" in the form of an RESP. Many financial institutions offer them along with their RRSP products. It's worth noting that there are limits to the amount of money that can be placed in an RESP – currently no more than $1500 per year.

Another method is to take out whole-life insurance policies on the child that would be cashed in later as required. This has the benefit of giving the child insurance coverage as she or he grows up. Any savings plan for children should allow for a wide range of options later in life. The money may fund a house, travel, a business, or a wedding. If parents set too narrow a focus for their children they could just be buying trouble in the future. It is important to let children know that just because money is being set aside for education there is no guarantee that they will be assured of going to college or university or that is the only goal their parents wish for them. Students should have good marks and a record of community service and extracurricular involvement. Since few scholarships have a means test to determine financial need, even a student with an RESP should plan on applying for them. There's no law that says you have to go broke while attending university.

Young families should build future education costs into their long-term financial planning. Professional advice should be sought early in the life of any child to ensure it has a bright future. Don't forget: everyone at university or college discovers that there is never enough time during exams and never enough money left near the end of the second term.

7 Scholarship coaches

As we have seen, you will need help from your parents and your high school to be able to make the most of your chances of getting scholarships. It is important to find a good mentor who knows about scholarships. Every high school should have someone in charge of helping students with their scholarship applications. This person might be called the scholarship coach. This part of the book deals with the role of these people.

A scholarship coach is a special kind of mentor. Most likely it will be someone with experience with scholarships who can help with applications. Some scholarships you can apply for yourself and others are automatic when you apply to the college or university that offers them. In all cases, you will do better if you get some knowledgeable help from someone at the school. A good scholarship coach can help you in every year of high school. You should be able to get advice on how to get better grades, which courses to take, and what activities to join. You'll benefit from the experience and training of a scholarship coach just as a runner improves with a good track coach: like the runner, you can get motivated and improve your performance over the years.

If you discover that your high school does not have a scholarship coach of some kind you may wish to have a talk with your guidance counsellor. There may not even be a scholarship selection committee at your school. You may wish to offer your help in setting one up. Perhaps your parents can assist you in this. Don't storm into guidance making demands, though. I'm sure you'll find that most schools are receptive to the idea of helping their students to excel. It wouldn't hurt for students to read over this chapter on scholarship coaching. You may gain more insight into the process by which scholarships are awarded. Don't forget: you and the scholarship coach have to work together just like a runner and a track coach. You must listen to the advice of the coach and put in a good effort. Don't expect the scholarship coach to do everything for you. After all; you're the one who is getting all the fame and money!

Who should be a scholarship coach?

If a school is serious about supporting the development of its students, it would be wise to appoint a member of the staff as a scholarship coach. In very large schools more than one may be required. Ideally, the coach should be given time in his or her work schedule to work with students. The best people for this job are staff members who have a flexible timetable with few fixed classes, such as guidance counsellors or special-education resource teachers. It seems logical that the best department to manage the scholarships is guidance. However, since many gifted students apply for scholarships, it may fall to the gifted-program coordinator. In any case the person or persons who take on the coaching role must have a good background knowledge of scholarships, courses, and institutions. Above all, the coach must have the ability to communicate with young people and know how to motivate them.

Once a scholarship coach has been found he or she can begin to make plans. It is best to think of dealing initially with every student in the school and also with the senior classes at the local elementary school. This large population will yield a more manageable number of students who are willing and able to be coached; this is much the way another kind of coach would proceed in picking a volleyball team. Unlike the athletic type; the scholarship coach must work with the school staff to help them with such things as letters of recommendation. The staff can be of great help by providing the coach with the names of promising students and of the various contests that enter the school addressed to department heads. An important part of the job of a scholarship coach is to connect the right student with the right opportunity.

The job description of the scholarship coach should run something like this:

1 Working with students in Grades 8–12 on various contests, programs, and scholarship applications. This includes motivating students to apply for scholarships and giving them moral support during the application process.
2 Assisting school staff in the preparation of letters of recommendation.
3 Making regular presentations to classes, teachers, and parent groups in regard to scholarships. This includes visits to the feeder schools to talk to the Grade 8 classes and their parents.
4 Counselling students about their school activities, education plans, and career goals.
5 Contacting colleges and universities to get information about programs and scholarships, and also contacting private organizations about scholarships.
6 Maintaining records of student applications for scholarships as well as sending out press releases as needed.
7 Organizing a staff scholarship committee for the selection of suitable candidates each year.
8 Actively seeking support from local businessess and service groups for high school scholarships and awards for graduating students going on to higher education. For example, *Reader's Digest* offers one-year subscriptions to the valedictorians of graduating classes of Canadian high schools. One student from each high school can be nominated each year. (For more information, contact the Valedictorian Subscription Program, Reader's Digest Magazines Ltd, 215 Redfern Ave., Westmount, Quebec H3Z 2V9.)
9 Teaching personal development courses like Career Planning or Human Relations.

This last item is worth examining. Teaching courses like Career Planning or Human Relations allows the scholarship coach to have first-hand experience with the students being coached. It also helps the coach write meaningful letters of recommendation. The courses could address the concept of personal development, education and career planning, and other survival skills not taught in most other courses. An important component of such a course is the strong emphasis on community service. Many students reach senior high without having worked for their community. If Canadian society is going to avoid some of the social problems rampant in the United States it is critical that the education system begin to connect students with their communities. The Human Relations course can also assist senior students with their communication skills, especially with résumés and interviews. In short, such a course is intended to help students get a sense of who they are, what they want, and how they can present themselves to get it. There would be a unit on how students can prepare themselves to apply for scholarships

When does scholarship coaching begin?

There are "flashcard parents" intent on developing the potential of their children at an early age. This process is known as "hothousing" because it is intended to force development just as a greenhouse promotes early seed germination. Children are not plants, however, and they may grow to resist parental pressure to steer them down a given path before they are ready. The concept of scholarship coaching involves a partnership between students, parents, and mentors. It is based on positive motivation and personal growth and not on the headlong rush for fame and riches. Ideally, the process of preparing for scholarships should be valuable in itself. The actual attainment of the award is an exciting by-product.

Since a vast majority of scholarship and university application forms seek information about high school activities, it makes sense to begin to think about this matter just before students enter Grade 9. For most students Grade 9 marks the transition from elementary to secondary school. Grade 8 students are thirteen or fourteen years old and mature enough, with some exceptions, to grasp the idea of beginning to shape their own futures. Physical changes have started to take place to mark the transition from childhood to adolescence. As well, Grade 8 students are required to make choices as to what courses, and at what level, they will be taking at high school. It makes sense that someone should talk to Grade 8 students about how to make the most of their high school years.

Each high school draws Grade 9 students from smaller feeder schools around it. The scholarship coach should visit these schools at about the time the Grade 8 students are making their choices for Grade 9. Many parents leave course selection in the hands of their children and the elementary school guidance counsellor. As a result, some students take general-level courses instead of advanced-level ones and vice versa. Some students pick their courses so that they can stay with friends. This is unlikely to work out, especially in the larger high schools that may have ten or more Grade 9 classes for some subjects. Some students overlook enrichment courses in Grade 9, thinking that they will play it safe in order to get high marks. This is wrongheaded because no one will be looking back to their Grade 9 marks whereas some people will be looking to see if a student has sought out challenges. If it is appropriate, a Grade 9 student should try to take enriched courses to gain more creative experiences. The scholarship coach should visit the elementary schools to discuss enrichment courses and the clubs and teams that will be available next year at the high school. The coach must meet with each Grade 8 class to give them this information and answer any questions that they may have. A large part of this effort is meant to alert the students to the potential to win and to motivate them to get started early.

Whenever I visit a Grade 8 class to talk about high school I take along what I call the "road show." I have a series of overheads that show what scholarships are and how to get them. I talk about all the wonderful teams, clubs, and other activities that are available at high school and I show slides of students having fun at these activities. I give each of them a list of the clubs and activities. I also talk about community service, and then I give each student a copy of the high school planner from chapter 3 in the hope that each student will start thinking about joining in school activities in Grade 9 instead of Grade 11, when it is too late to try some things.

It would be wishful thinking to hope that every Grade 8 student will run out and start getting involved at high school. I know that those old enemies ignorance and apathy will stop many students from doing anything. However, I do expect a number of good students will see things in a better light. I hope they will avoid the problems of some of my senior students, who have complained that no one told them what was needed for success in high school and beyond.

Selecting scholarship candidates

Many scholarships are directed at high school students. The best way for scholarship sponsors to find applicants is to notify the high schools, usually through letters sent to the principal or the head of guidance. The trouble is that these notices don't always get to the students who could act on them. I get the occasional opportunity to visit other high schools to talk about scholarships and I visit every guidance office to see the kind of systems that are in place for students to find out about scholarships. In many cases I find that there is only a dusty and neglected folder that has a few old scholarship forms. When I ask about this I am told that none of the kids is interested and that at that school has ever won anyway. That's a system, all right: one that guarantees failure every time.

The more enlightened high schools and certainly most of the private schools are much more active in the promotion of their students. These schools have something like a scholarship coach who works with students on an ongoing basis. Scholarship lists are kept up to date and are posted on a regular basis. There is a scholarship selection committee to help choose candidates from the school. There is plenty of support from the principal when it comes time to write letters of recommendation. Parents and local organizations have contributed money and awards to recognize student achievement. The local paper publishes the names and pictures of the winners. In short, such schools know the value of scholarships to everyone involved and make it a priority to encourage students to apply for them. Not surprisingly these schools have winners every year. Everyone can take pride when a number of students at a high school are recognized by prestigious institutions. In a time when education is being criticized, a winning school can assert its superiority. Scholarships recognize those things that make a high school great: academic achievement and student involvement in extracurricular activities and community service. These things can make a high school the centre of a community and a good place to be for the growing adolescent. Surely this is more important than having a champion volleyball team. Although athletics teams are important, all schools should be putting at least as much effort into coaching their students to be good scholarship candidates.

The following is a step-by-step process for getting scholarship information into the hands of students and helping them to use it.

Step 1

All scholarship forms that enter the school should be photocopied and a copy filed in a binder to which students have access. The original forms should be sent to the school's scholarship coach. The coach should look over the criteria for the scholarship and then announce them to the teachers at one of the regular staff meetings. Names of prospective candidates should be solicited from the staff.

Step 2

Once the scholarship coach has generated a list of names, a selection committee should meet to choose the most appropriate candidate(s) from the list. Most scholarships specify that only one or two people may be submitted by each school. It is in no one's best interest to send in applications from every single potential candidate. To avoid inequities, the selection committee should try to keep track of all the various attributes of the high-achieving students in the school. The following form might assist the committee in deciding who should be applying for the various scholarships. Every student in the senior year should have filled out this form. It could also be used to help decide the recipients of the awards offered by the high school.

SENIOR STUDENT INFORMATION FORM

Name: _____   Homeroom: _____

_____   _____

Grade 12 courses: _____

_____

University/College choices:

1 _____ 2 _____ 3 _____

_____   _____   _____

Proposed course of study: _____

Extracurricular activities (teams, clubs, music, etc.) and community service: _____

_____

_____

Awards: _____

_____

_____

Other information (disabilities, family situation, health problems, financial need): _____

_____

_____

Release: I acknowledge that this information will be used by the school as required.

Signature: _____

This form could also be used to help decide on such things as the valedictorian and the subject award winners for the senior year. With this information it should be easy to sort out a short list of possible candidates for scholarships, especially those linked with a certain university or college. If a student has not applied to that institution, there's no point in them applying for any scholarships there.

The scholarship coach then takes the short list of students and checks the academic standing of each potential candidate to make sure they meet the minimum requirement. The students who remain on the list are the ones who should be asked to apply for the scholarship. It is very important that all this screening take place before any students are approached. Today's high school students are under enough pressure without discovering that they were considered as scholarships candidates and found unworthy for some reason. Confidentiality must be the watchword of the scholarship coach and the selection committee.

Step 3
Once the scholarship coach has the list of acceptable candidates, it is necessary to arrange a one-to-one meeting with each of the selected students to discuss the scholarship. These meetings usually begin with a shy candidate asking "Why me?" An important part of the coach's job is to convince the student that she or he is qualified to apply for the scholarship. Once modesty has succumbed to flattery it is necessary to deal with the pros and cons of applying for the scholarship. The pro side is great: money and fame. Even so, some students have convinced themselves that they won't need the money, so why bother applying? The scholarship coach must learn to stifle derisive laughter on such occasions and must hasten to point out the long-term career benefits that come from the recognition that scholarships confer. They look great on a résumé. Some students don't want to apply for a scholarship because they are afraid it will force them to go to their second or third choice of schools. The coach must point out to such students that other factors could prevent them from attending their first choice of university. Students should optimize all their chances of attending college or university. Ideally, a well-developed student should be accepted at all of the places he or she has applied to, and be offered scholarships from each of them. This outcome might

necessitate a tough choice in June, but students generally survive such an ordeal.

There is a negative side to applying for scholarships. One of the biggest deterrents is the time involved in filling out the forms, organizing references, and so on. Even though the potential rate of pay is thousands of dollars per hour, some students still won't apply. The odds of winning a scholarship are much better than winning a lottery and those odds improve with the quality of the application. The scholarship coach should refer the applicant to the fourth chapter of this book, dealing with the application process.

Some students claim that they would rather not apply for scholarships if it means that they must compete with their friends for them. It is usually best if the scholarship coach does not tell candidates about the other applicants from the same school. It is especially important to avoid making comparisons between competing candidates, even though the students may pressure the coach to do so.

It is also very important that the scholarship coach and selection committee refrain from informing other staff and the community about candidates until something has been won. Some scholarships will send word that a student has passed the first stage of the application process. I don't like to broadcast this morsel of good news, as it puts more pressure on the students and seems to increase their fear of failure.

I think the real reason why students decline the honour of applying for scholarships is fear of failure. High school seniors are wrapped up in getting into university or college. They are concerned about finances, marks, and whether or not they will be accepted. If they fail, they will do so in plain view of a large number of friends and teachers. Applying for a scholarship involves risking even more failure and rejection. Some students think that if they don't get the scholarship the school will reject them. Quite the reverse is true. Even if they don't win first prize, universities often acknowledge worthy applicants with other scholarships or early acceptance. It could be argued that making a good application for a scholarship gives the student another foot in the door.

It's important that stressed-out senior students realize that life involves risk. If you start playing it safe at 18 you'll be comatose by age 30. Scholarship applicants have nothing to lose but time and everything to gain. There will never be another opportunity to try for so much fame and money. It is possible to achieve a resounding success that the entire community will know about. After high school classmates specialize and go in various directions. High school is the last time students can expect to see the same familiar faces year after year. What better way to leave it than by graduating as a winner?

And what about failure? The scholarship coach owes it to the unsuccessful applicant to say a few words of encouragement. I tell my students that it is an honour to represent the school. We are not ashamed of failure because the best effort was put forward in a competition with the best in the country. They must not take it as personal rejection. High schools have awards, and these can be given in recognition of a student's efforts in representing the school. In addition, the very process of learning how to present themselves is valuable to students.

One of my students used all of her scholarship application experience to win herself a coveted place in a program at York University in her second year there.

It is important to note that the school plays a critical role in the awarding of scholarships. There must be a selection committee, a scholarship coach and, above all, a determination on the part of the school administration to support the staff and students in the quest for scholarships. Time and resources must be allocated by the principal if the scholarship coaching is going to successful in the long term.

8 For teachers and others: Writing letters of recommendation

Many scholarship applications require what are called letters of reference from a teacher and/or the principal. In reality these are letters of recommendation because their purpose is to promote a candidate. Letters of reference are generally more guarded documents used to verify an employee's previous employment. These are said to be "sealed with a shrug and opened with a smile" because they tend to be vague. This is not the style needed for scholarship applications because they would appear to be "damning with faint praise." Here is an example:

To whom it may concern:

Tom Swift was a student in my Grade 9 advanced mathematics course at Clearwater High School. He is also in my Grade 12 Algebra course. He works hard on his math and had an mid-term mark of 86%

Yours truly,

Thomas Teecher

Although well-intentioned, this letter has several failings. First, it lacks direction. It is not addressed to anyone in particular, nor does it indicate that the student is a worthy candidate for a scholarship or university program. If this letter arrived on the wrong desk, it might never get to the right one.

While it is true that writing letters is very much a matter of personal style, a few points should be covered in any letter of recommendation. A teacher or other referee can expect to get the following from a student before drafting a good letter of recommendation:

- A copy of the applicant's personal student record showing all the relevant information concerning the student's background, extracurricular involvement, and so on
- Clear instructions as to whom the letter should be sent, and information about what the letter is in aid of, whether it is for a scholarship or a specific university or college program
- A stamped, addressed envelope
- A definite deadline date

With this information it is possible to write a rough draft. This should be shown to the student to ensure that it is what is wanted. Some freedom-of-information acts require that such letters must be shown to the subject of the document on request anyway. As a rule, these letters do not have to be much longer than one page. It is usually unnecessary to include "laundry lists" of the student's achievements because these are usually covered in the application form. The main role of this letter is to show how the student meets the criteria of the scholarship sponsor. If the sponsor is looking for creative people, for example, the letter of recommendation should stress creativity. Here are some examples of letters that had the right style.

Ms Katherine George
Student Alumni Association
University of Waterloo
Waterloo, Ontario
N2L 3G1

Dear Ms George:

I am pleased to recommend Charlene Knowlton for the Student Alumni Award for Outstanding Extracurricular Involvement. There aren't many activities at Sutton District High School that haven't had the benefit of Charlene's involvement. Her list of achievements defies replication in this short letter.

Charlene became involved in extracurricular activities early in her high school career and has stayed involved all the way through. I am truly impressed by her maturity and energy. Charlene has managed to achieve excellent academic performance along with phenomenal participation in many of my enrichment programs. In fact, the Model United Nations, Science Olympics, and Schoolreach teams would not have run at all were it not for Charlene.

I believe that Charlene Knowlton is a worthy candidate for your award. As a Waterloo alumnus I encourage our best students to attend there. Charlene is one of our very best and she will be a definite asset to the community life at the University of Waterloo.

Yours truly,

Michael J. Howell
Assistant Head
Special Education Dept.

This letter is short and to the point. It clearly links Charlene with the award she is trying to win. As much as possible, I tried to refer to those things I had seen first-hand, but I acknowledged her other achievements. Here is another example:

Mayor Bob Johnston and Council
Township of Georgina, Civic Centre
Sutton West, Ontario
L0E 1R0

Dear Sirs:

I am writing to you to recommend Alison Armitage as Junior Citizen of the Year. Alison is a gifted student at Sutton District High School, and the school and the community have been the recipients of her talents. She has been involved in numerous activities at the school and Alison has done a lot of volunteer work in the community including three years at a summer camp for mentally and physically challenged children. Alison has also taught Sunday school at her church for four years. Not surprisingly, she has received many awards for her good works. She is also an excellent student.

Most recently, Alison helped to organize and run a teen sexuality program at Sutton District High School called Choices and Challenges. As always, Alison displayed maturity and concern for others. She was the natural leader in my leadership class.

It is also worth noting that Alison Armitage is the supervisor of the student workers at the Georgina Public Library in Keswick.

I am sure that you will agree that our community is fortunate to have people like Alison Armitage. By recognizing citizenship in her we encourage it in others.

Yours truly,

M.J. Howell

Note that the style is positive and emphatic. It should be the objective of anyone writing letters of recommendation to convince the selection committee that this is the person they are seeking.

The following is a letter written by a teacher named Susan Milne for Jennifer Couturier. It is different from my style of writing letters, but it still gets the point across very well. If it has any faults at all, it may be that it has too much detail. As well, it is not directed at a specific person.

University of Guelph
Office of the Registrar
Re: President's Scholarship

Jennifer Couturier has asked me to write a letter of reference in support of her application for a University of Guelph President's Scholarship. It is a pleasure for me to do this as I believe Jennifer is a unique student who deserves some recognition for her abilities. She is very poised and she possesses many attributes which will make her successful in whatever task she undertakes.

I have known Jennifer for the past three years in my capacity both as a teacher and as a staff adviser for our school's yearbook.

In my first year as yearbook adviser Jennifer was one of the co- editors. She made my job very easy as she was extremely organized and very easy to work with. I always knew that her pages would be done before the deadline and that they would be well designed. Part of this job involved working in the darkroom where we developed all of the black and white pictures that were needed. Jennifer was quite confident in this area and she even taught me how to print pictures. As an editor, she had the added responsibilities of being on the executive for the student council and doing the work that they required of her. Jennifer was the "backbone" of the yearbook committee and she worked very well with the other students.

Jennifer has also been a student in both my Finite and Calculus OAC classes. Last year she was the top student in my Finite class and she earned a mark of 99% on her final exam. She is also going to be one of the top one or two students in my Calculus class this semester.

Jennifer is a diligent worker who strives for perfection at all times. She has not been as involved in school activities recently as she was in Grades 9 through 11. This was because she recognized that she would be putting a great deal of time into her OAC courses and she would not have time for extracurricular work. This may be seen as a drawback for this award, but I feel it is another example of Jennifer's ability to organize and prioritize her affairs. She always plans ahead and sets goals for herself and these are things that will make her successful.

Jennifer is a very intelligent student who is well liked and respected by her peers. I know that she would be good candidate for a President's Scholarship.

Susan Milne

Although letters of recommendation are products of individual style, it is essential that they convey a positive note of promotion for students. If they do not, they may do more harm than good.

Forms

Some universities' programs and many scholarships have developed their own reference forms instead of requesting letters of recommendation. No doubt this was done to standardize the application process. Since teachers have individual styles of writing letters it seems to make sense to tie them all down to a fill-in-the-blank system that allows for comparison between candidates.

At first glance a form seems to be easier for the person making the recommendation. For one thing, it may not require typing later. In fact, forms are trickier and usually require more time and attention than a personal letter of recommendation. Teachers must resist the temptation to simply write something in the spaces and send it off.

For example, some forms ask a question like "In your estimation is the candidate (a) one in ten, (b) one in a hundred, or (c) one in a thousand in terms of his/her ability." Alternatively, the form may request the student's rank in the class. This can pose problems if the teacher is ranking two or more students or the high school does not rank students by classes.

In general, a recommendation/reference form should be approached as if it were a test. Read the entire form over carefully and sketch out your answers in rough on a photocopy of the original. Try not to leave any blanks. If more information is needed, ask the student. Avoid repeating the same items in different sections.

Some forms stipulate that they are to be completed by the principal. Given the kind of care and attention required, it's difficult for such busy people to find the time to do a good job of it. A wise principal usually delegates the writing of such forms or letters to a teacher who knows the student or perhaps the scholarship coach. It is important that the principal read the ghostwriter's work carefully before signing it, and a copy should be kept on file. This is in case the principal gets a phone call about the student from the institution.

Many application forms require official high school transcripts. Since students cannot send their own transcripts they often request that they be sent by the person writing their letter of reference. These can be found in the student records, usually maintained by the guidance office of most high schools. To be considered official, photocopied transcripts must be signed by the principal or the head of guidance and carry the school seal. Please note, however, that every school has set procedures for use of the student records and student transcripts. Anyone seeking access to these files must know these procedures and have proper authorization.

A few final points for those writing letters of recommendation:

If you can't find the time to do a good job, decline the request to write the letter.

If you do accept, spend some time thinking and doing rough drafts.

If you need more information, contact the student or the scholarship coach.

Don't forget the deadline! Send the letter off promptly. The student is counting on you.

Don't be vague. Your main objective is to promote the student's application.

If you are unsure of your style, show a draft to the scholarship coach or the student.

It is very important to keep a copy on file of all letters that you write. This will protect you and save you a lot of effort later if the same student asks you to write another letter of recommendation.

Whenever possible, type your letters on the school or other letterhead. This makes them more official-looking and easy to identify.

9 Important odds and ends

Sports scholarships

Western Canada

Many students who are athletic want to know if there are sports scholarships in Canada. They hear about all the big money deals that are offered to college-bound athletes in the United States. The good news is that there are a number of sports scholarships in Canada. The bad news is that these awards aren't worth as much as those offered south of the border. In fact, sports scholarships are strictly regulated in most Canadian colleges and universities. The reason for this is because of the problems that have emerged under the American way of handling scholarships.

In the United States there are powerful "booster clubs" made up of alumni who want to see their old school or "Alma Mater" continue to do well in sports. Further pressure is added because of valuable television broadcasts of major college basketball and football games. These booster clubs raise millions of dollars each year to be used for athletic scholarships to attract gifted athletes to a college. In competing for athletes some colleges have been known to overlook entrance requirements so that gifted athletes who are poor students can gain admission. Because these students cannot handle the usual course load special courses must be set up. There have even been reports of powerful coaches telling professors to pass an athlete with poor grades so that he can continue to play for the college. Some students discover that once they are injured and no longer able to play they lose their scholarships. Recently, American authorities have moved to prevent these kinds of abuses of sports scholarships.

Luckily, universities and colleges in western Canada have learned from these mistakes and have made regulations to prevent post-secondary athletics from distorting the educational process at college and universities.

Most universities in Canada do not offer any purely athletic entrance scholarships. The Canadian Interuniversity Athletic Union (CIAU) regulates the following sports at Canadian universities:

- men's/women's basketball
- men's/women's cross-country running
- men's/women's soccer
- men's/women's swimming
- men's/women's track & field
- men's/women's volleyball
- men's football
- men's ice hockey
- men's wrestling
- women's field hockey

The CIAU requires of its member institutions that:

1 all awards must be for continuing students (2nd year and up);
2 all awards are approved by the board of governors;
3 awards are administered by the university awards office; and
4 booster clubs are not allowed to offer financial incentives to students.

Only Simon Fraser University in British Columbia offers American-style athletic scholarships to new students. You may have to leave Canada if you want to get paid well for playing a sport at a university.

In terms of colleges, there isn't much in the way of scholarship money, and even that seems to be shrinking owing to budget cuts. Given the physical size of western Canada, the cost of transportation for teams is a major issue, along with equipment and facilities costs.

In Alberta the Alberta Colleges Athletic Conference (ACAC) sets down rules for financial support to athletes:

Rule 1: At any member institution, the only acceptable form of aid which can be given to a student specifically to participate in athletic activities shall be financial, and shall not exceed the established tuition of the specifice institution. An athlete receiving a full ($1000) Jimmy Condon Scholarship shall not be eligible to receive any other *direct* scholarship, i.e. Jimmy Condon Scholarship *plus* tuition-fee scholarship.

Also: Housing (room and board) provided at less than local market rates is interpreted as a form of financial aid to student athletes.

Rule 2: Any scholarships that exceed tuition or a Jimmy Condon Scholarship provided to the institution by an individual, group, foundation, or agency, and administered by the college must comply with the following:

The recipient must be an ACAC eligible athlete who has successfully completed one full academic year as a full-time student at the ACAC member institution where the award is available unless an identical award is made available to all participating institutions in a given sport (i.e. AAHA Scholarship).

The award must not be contingent upon continued athletic participation by the recipient.

The award must be forwarded by the sponsor to the college attended by the recipient, and must be administered to the recipient through the College Awards Office or its equivalent.

The award must not exceed one thousand dollars ($1000.00) in Canadian funds.

An athlete may not receive more than one thousand dollars (CDN) in scholarships over and above a Jimmy Condon Scholarship, Charles S. Noble Scholarship, or a tuition scholarship in any one academic year.

The award or scholarship has received ACAC approval.

In addition to various provincial sources of finances for athletes, the federal government has extended assistance for student athletes offered through Sports Canada. This program is designed to assist Canadian athletes who have fulfilled a long-term training commitment and who have represented Canada in international sporting events. Only athletes who have been "carded" (met the appropriate national qualifications) will be eligible. The benefits include tuition fees and a monthly living allowance of $450. For further information contact

Athlete Assistance Program
Fitness and Amateur Sport
365 Laurier Avenue West
Ottawa, Ontario
K1A 0X6

American sports scholarships

If a gifted Canadian athlete wants to gain access to American sports scholarships, there is an American company that can help them do it: College Prospects of America Inc. This company has offices in Kelowna, North Vancouver, Calgary, and Winnipeg. Canadian students fill out a profile of themselves, with references from their coaches outlining their athletic abilities. These profiles are reproduced and then sent on to American colleges in the hopes that the students will receive scholarship offers from them. The cost of this service is about $650 (U.S.).

It is worth noting that, while the American colleges have the money to offer athletes, they also expect performance for their dollar. Canadian athletes planning a move to the United States should think ahead. American colleges tend to look at a cumulative grade-point average that includes all marks from Grades 9 to 12. In addition, athletes must qualify through the Scholastic Aptitude Test, which is widely used in the United States to determine the academic qualifications of college and university applicants.

Before accepting an undergraduate athletic scholarship in a foreign country it is important to remember a few key points. Many people meet their future spouses while at university. Friendships are made that will last a lifetime. It would be a shame to leave all that behind when it came time to return to Canada. You can't assume that you will be allowed to stay in that other country once you have completed your studies there. It's also worth noting that the dream of a career in professional sports remains just a dream for the vast bulk of college players. Never forget that a sports career is transitory at best, but a solid education will be valuable for the rest of your life.

For most people university and college marks the first time they have left home for a prolonged period of time. It can involve a new routine and a different workload. All of this is very stressful and many students catch what is called the "Freshman Flu." An American sports scholarship will mean moving from home to a different country where you may not know anyone on campus, and then finding that, on top of all your school work, you are expected to devote a lot of time to your sports team. After all, that's why they invited you. It would be very wise, therefore, to visit a distant campus before accepting a scholarship there. You must know what you are getting into.

If you have visited a foreign campus and satisfied yourself that it is acceptable, be very careful about all your paperwork. You may find that you can still qualify for provincial student loans. Given the history of American athletic scholarships, candidates should be sure to get all the terms and conditions of the award in writing. Be wary of any promises made by a booster club member. There should not be any secret scholarships. If there are any concerns, students should contact the student awards office at the college or university before they accept any sports scholarships. There are always rumours of special secret deals being offered to talented athletes to entice them to go to a certain university in North America. Remember that such inducements are not officially authorized by the university, and therefore there is no guarantee that anything will come of it. The ultimate test of such things is that if you can't put it on a résumé then it is probably not worth accepting.

Scholarship information services

The recent explosion of scholarship information services may be due to the tough economic times or to tuition increases. They are not a new concept, however. Since I started researching scholarships I have found four information companies that once existed and then disappeared. In theory, it doesn't hurt to get as much information as you can concerning scholarships. In practice, you must be careful not to fall into a "smash and grab" approach to your quest. As this book has attempted to show, the sponsors of most scholarships are looking for a specific type of recipient. No reputable information service will be able to change who you are or guarantee you a scholarship. Only you can do that through your own actions. All these services can really do is to sell you information.

Name of Company	*Charge*
Cash for College P.O. Box 9090 1105 Wellington Road South London, Ontario N6E 1V0	$75
College Prospects of America, Inc. P.O. Box 52027 North Vancouver, B.C. V7J 3T2 (This company offers a separate service for student athletes considering American sports scholarships)	$650 (U.S.)
Scholarship Advisory Service 1051 Cedarglen Gate, Unit 46 Mississauga, Ontario L5C 3A7	$60 to $755
Student Scholarship Services of Canada 272 St George Street Suite 303 Moncton, New Brunswick E1C 1W5	$100
Canadian High School Information Service P.O. Box 20075 Ottawa, Ontario K1N 9N5	$50

All of these services claim to have national databases that are constantly being updated. Some of them actually guarantee that you will win a scholarship or they will refund your fee. The only catch is that you must apply to every single scholarship they recommend to you and then send them proof of rejection for all of them. This is a safe bet for the scholarship infomation companies! I can't imagine too many people will want to publicly trumpet such momumental failure, even to get a refund. Also be wary of any company that claims to know of every last scholarship. It will take me three books to cover just the entrance scholarships in Canada. The information is in a constant state of flux as new scholarships appear and others disappear. I would distrust any one source of information.

Your quest for scholarships is very much your own. Don't expect that someone will do all the work for you. The bottom line is that you should not invest more money in scholarship information than you could reasonably expect to win. Also, remember that most of the information you are buying is in the public domain, which means it is probably in libraries, high school guidance offices, and, as you would expect, university and college calendars. Of course, I invite you to make complete use of the verified information I have included in the scholarship lists at the back of this book. A little time spent with the cross-reference section will locate several scholarships for which you could apply. You can't buy scholarships; you have to earn them.

An approximate first-year budget

Money – and the lack of it – is probably the greatest concern for students these days. Can you afford to go to university or college? Will there be a high-paying job to go into after graduation to make the expense worthwhile? It's a good idea to face the first of these questions head on by having a budget. Nobody really likes budgets because they seem to make life so two-dimensional. All the spontaneity goes out of things when you are constantly counting pennies. Even so, you'd better do a rough draft now, before you are far from home and out of time and money. Don't worry about your second year and the ones after that. Your first year will likely be your worst year financially, because you don't yet know all angles of how to live like a student. Once you get experienced, you will find ways to do things cheaply, often in the company of fellow students who are struggling to survive by pooling resources, splitting the rent, and generally living on the cheap.

Fill in the spaces below as best you can. If you have to make an approximation for an amount, talk to your friends and parents to ensure that it is a reasonable guess. In any case, make sure your estimates are a little on the high side.

The first step is to calculate all of your *expenses* (the universities and colleges will supply most of this information in their calendars):

Item	Amount
Tuition (2 terms)	$
Residence fees (2 terms) OR Rent and food for 9 months (Note: Residence life is more fun but also more expensive.)	
Local transportation (car, bus pass, bike)	
Long-range transportation (bus, train, airfare) for trips home: at least 3 round trips for each academic year	
Recreation (beer, pizza, social events)	
Special equipment (lab fees, sports, computer, camera)	
Clothing	
Textbooks	
Medical/dental (Check to see if you are covered by a parental health plan)	
Miscellaneous: stamps, phone bill, magazines, etc.	
Total Expenses:	$

No doubt you are terrified by the amount of money it costs to go to school. Let's have a look at the good news: your *sources of income.* Some of these will just have to involve good guesses.

Item	Amount
Savings/Registered Education Savings Plan	$
High school scholarships	
Employer scholarships	
University/college scholarships	
Government loans	
Government grants	
Bursaries	
Parent contributions	
Part-time employment income	
Other sources	
Total Income for First Year:	$

Now subtract the Total Assets from the Total Expenses to see how you are likely to do. Is there a shortfall? If there is, don't despair yet. Most budgets that people draw up deal with only financial capital. Experts have identified two other kinds of capital: human and social.

Human capital can be loosely defined as the value of the skills and education of individual people. In fact, your education is a major investment in your own human capital. While at college or university, you should find ways to apply the human capital that you already have. One former student of mine, who was studying in a music program, was desperately short of money. I suggested that she and her friends get permission to "busk," or play for donations, at a local mall. This may not lead to a recording contract, but it is one way to make money and get some practice time in. In my own case, I took a job as a teaching assistant to a professor whom I admired very much. The money wasn't great, but the experience was very valuable.

I was also in a architecture cooperative education program, which meant that I alternated between work and university studies every four months. Not only was I working to finance four months of university at a time, I was gaining valuable experience.

I left full-time employment when I went back to the University of Calgary to obtain my Bachelor of Education, and of course I missed getting a paycheck. Rather than work in a grocery store to make some extra money, I joined the Canadian Armed Forces Reserves. Although I found the discipline and training to be rather challenging, the experience was certainly more interesting than stocking shelves. I was also able to get extensive training as a medic. I took summer courses with the militia and eventually had the opportunity to teach courses for 14 Calgary Service Battalion. I found my commanding officers to be understanding about allowing me to give priority to my university studies. I realize that this experience is not for everyone, but it worked for me. If you are interested, you'll find that most major cities have a military unit. In fact, the Canadian Armed Forces offers the Regular Officer Training Program (ROTP) as one way to fund most of your post-secondary education. The catch is that you must serve with the Forces for a few years after you graduate.

Notice how all of the examples cited – busking, teacher assistant, and Reserves – combine both financial capital and human capital. This is known as getting a "twofer," or two for one.

Social capital can be defined as the value you obtain from your social network. One of the biggest problem for most students in their first year is that they have been completely cut off from the world they grew up in, and have little social contact in their new life. My advice is to get involved in clubs and teams and try to meet people. Does this sound familiar? It should, because it is the advice I give to students entering Grade 9. Your social contacts will lead to study buddies, room-mates, lab partners, carpools, book exchanges, great parties, job prospects, and lifelong friends. You may also find a mentor or two at university or college if you are very fortunate. Don't forget one little rule: every first-year student is as new to the campus as you are. Meet as many people as you can, and don't be shy about building a new social network.

At this point you may be thinking of redoubling your efforts to acquire scholarships. You may also want to think about starting a "Help Chest" where you stock up on such things as pens, pencils, paper, computer disks, binders, shampoo, and chocolate. It may not sound like much compared to expenses in the thousands of dollars, but the morale-boosting effect of such positive efforts is not to be underestimated. It will also demonstrate to your family that you are serious about continuing your education.

You can usually count on some help from your parents. I knew one fellow who used to send his dirty laundry home and get clean laundry and baked goods sent back by his mother. It was a major letdown when she refused to adopt me.

Entrance scholarships are the most important kind of academic award because they assist you in your most difficult year. After first year, you will be hitting the job market in April, not June. This gives you the possibility of four months of employment to help fund the next eight months of school. In addition, you may qualify for bursaries and scholarships available to students in second and third years. Most important of all, after your first year you should be more aware of the hidden student social network. This involves things like sharing a house with classmates instead of going into residence, checking the bulletin board for rides home, and learning a hundred other ways to save money by sharing with others in the same situation as you.

Don't be shy about getting student loans. Every provincial and territorial education ministry has a branch that deals with student loans. The best source of such information is your high school guidance office. You must be especially careful in filling out the forms for student loans in order to get the maximum amount. Again, ask for help from your guidance counsellors. Many of my students have expressed concern about taking on a lot of debt to finance their educations. It took me ten years to finally pay off all my student loans, but I have never regretted borrowing the money. The best plan is to apply for student loans and then bank the money as a reserve. Don't touch it until you have no other choice. Careful conservation of student loans might see you through a lean year.

The biggest mistake you can make is to put off your education. Costs will continue to go up. If you work for a long time, you'll definitely get used to a regular paycheck, and you may get too comfortable to enter into the frugal life of a student. In the end, remember that education is the best investment in yourself. The sooner you start, the greater the benefit you will gain from it.

The future for scholarships

As in many other areas, Canada is underdeveloped in terms of scholarships compared with the rest of the world. Most scholarships are not well promoted. This means that true competition is not occurring to determine the most meritorious candidate, which is not in the best interests of either the students or the sponsors of the awards.

Hand in hand with promotion goes accountability. It is important to let the public know who is winning the scholarships. There is a risk that scholarships could become a matter of "insider information": only those in the know will win. Again, this is detrimental to the entire concept of scholarships as a means of promoting excellence. In a multicultural society it is essential that there be no bias in the selection process, but because of the dual lack of promotion and of public accountability there is always the risk that various forms of discrimination may occur. In many countries, most notably the United States, scholarships are a major factor in the funding of post-secondary education. Billions of dollars are awarded every year to thousands of students. Much of this money comes from private sources. Instead of being a preserve for a lucky few, scholarships are a support to a very large number of students.

As post-secondary education costs rise here in Canada, it is essential that every level of government do more to increase the number of scholarships from both public and private sources. As well, these governments must also take more interest in the fair administration of scholarships, and not just at the point of taxation. Scholarships could play a valuable role in motivating and supporting students in the future. They could be especially valuable in developing weak areas of the infrastructure of this country, such as research and development of high technology or promotion of environmental awareness. At present scholarships play a very passive role in Canadian education.

Specifically, scholarships could be used to promote positive change in this country. The C.D. Howe Scholarship allows students from Quebec to study at the University of Toronto in English and students from outside Quebec to study at Laval in French. More of these types of education exchanges would do much to help break down the "two solitudes" that still threaten Canadian unity.

Demographic reports suggest that a lot of money will soon be going from thrifty older generations to younger ones in the form of inheritances. Careful thought should be given to the idea of using some of this bounty to create scholarships to help promote the beliefs and values of the donors. Most universities and colleges would be delighted to help donors set up a scholarship or bursary, and nearly all have some kind of resource development office.

Such awards could be used to encourage those students who were leaders in their high schools and communities to continue their good work. The scholarships will free such people from financial pressures and leave them with time to continue helping others and developing themselves.

Parents should be talking with employers about setting up some kind of employer scholarships. Every high school should have at least one scholarship coach and a scholarship committee. There should also be an ongoing attempt to create scholarships in the high school for high-achieving students who are going on to higher education. If parents, school, employers, and government start working on creating scholarships, a lot of the post-secondary student funding problems can be solved.

In the final analysis, scholarships are a reward for excellence. There are few areas of human endeavour that wouldn't benefit from an incentive to try harder. Scholarships are proof that it pays to excel. The combination of fame plus money is a powerful lure for young people. Many seek both in arenas far removed from the school system and even through illegal means like gangs. High schools have it within their power to get students thinking about their educations with renewed energy and interest. Far from being a perquisite of a rich élite, scholarships can and should be used to promote better people and a better country. Every high school in the country should be grooming its students to apply for scholarships, because they can be the catalyst for more cooperation among parents, students, and schools. In this way we can make better use of our greatest resource: the young people of Canada.

10 Using the scholarship lists

So far we have been looking at the concept of scholarships and how to make long-term plans to get them. The mentoring, scholarship planning, coaching, and parental involvement all come together when you sit down and go through these lists of scholarships. You will no doubt find several scholarships for which you can apply. Do not hesitate to try several.

Be systematic in your approach to mailing for information. You will find that you can use the same letters with just a simple change of address and a few other alterations. With any luck your high school guidance office may already have many of the forms you need. And don't forget that there are numerous in-course scholarships offered to students in the later years of college and university programs. Your scholarship quest isn't coming to an end here: it's just beginning.

It's worth noting that there are almost as many bursaries as scholarships offered by universities and colleges. Bursaries are funds given to students who can demonstrate financial need. You will find lists of bursaries in the college and university course calendars right after the scholarship descriptions. As a rule, the institutions don't award them in the first term, and some places do not offer them to first-year students because so much money is allocated to entrance scholarships. There will be some general information about bursaries and other sources of funds later in this chapter.

There are more than 1500 different scholarships described in the scholarship lists that follow. If you consider that there may be three or four winners for some of the scholarships listed, that means there are thousands of awards available to you. The typical scholarship is worth around $2000. Thus, there are millions of dollars to had by skilful explorers. And don't forget: a scholarship means both fame as well as money.

How you use the scholarship lists will depend on where you are in your education. If you are in Grade 9 or 10 you will probably not have decided on a program of study or even whether or not you are going to college or university. In this case, the best thing would be to look over the lists to find scholarships that may apply to you in future. In particular, look at such things as the minimum average required and the basis of the scholarship. These are the criteria that will be used in awarding the scholarship to someone. You should be looking to see if you are doing enough community service, for example, and if necessary plan to go out and get involved in something so that you will be ready when the time comes to apply for these awards.

It's important to bear in mind that scholarships are always in a state of change. Old ones disappear and new ones come along. As a result, despite rigorous research and verification, this list cannot be the ultimate last word about scholarships. It is just a guide for your personal quest. You still have an adventure ahead of you as you search for scholarships that suit you.

If you are a senior student about to enter your last year of high school you must use this scholarship list in a much more specific manner. First, you must decide what program you wish to pursue. Next, you must decide where the best place is to find that program. There are usually several possible choices of institution and you will have to decide where you want to spend the next two to four years of your life. It is a good idea to visit the various campuses before you make your final choice. In the case of universities you will pick three. If you are having trouble choosing you may wish to refer to an excellent book by Dyanne Gibson called *Gibson's Student Guide to Western Canadian Universities* published by University of Toronto Press.

College applications are organized on much the same lines by your guidance department. They will assist you in the selection of college programs.

Once you have chosen a program and a short list of possible institutions, it's time to look over the scholarship lists. There are four groups of scholarships. The first is university scholarships listed by province and in alphabetical order by name of university. The lists for each university are organized along the same lines as the official descriptions of the scholarships in the university calendars. You will find that some universities give a lot of detail and others do not. The University of Calgary offers students a very useful scholarship handbook. There are 500 different entrance scholarships at western Canadian universities, and more than 300 at the colleges. (Don't forget that some scholarships are given to two or three people each year. There are thousands of Canada Scholars, for example.) The college scholarships are organized in this book in the same way as those for the universities. In both cases the address for obtaining more information or application forms is shown under the name of the institution in the lists at the end of this chapter.

The third listing in the book is of general scholarships that are not tied to any particular institution. These are scholarships that are offered by foundations, governments, and unions and are open to the public. These scholarships are listed alphabetically by province and the address for each is included as part of the listing. To avoid repetition and confusion any awards offered at more than one institution – the Canada Scholarship for example – are listed in the general section. National scholarships and awards will be listed under the code "CA/" in the General list.

The last list of scholarships are those offered by employers for the dependents of their workers *only*. The list is not complete, but indicates the kind of help that is available. There is no point in applying to any of the employer-sponsored awards unless one of your parents or guardians works or once worked for the company in question. Dependents of retired workers often qualify for such scholarships, but verify this point when you write for an application form.

If one or both of your parents works for a large company that doesn't offer a scholarship to the children of employees, then perhaps it's time a company scholarship was established. Westinghouse Canada offers both a public scholarship and one for the families of employees.

Reading the entries

With nearly a thousand different scholarships to look over it is important that you learn how to use the scholarship list efficiently. Here is a brief description of how each entry is set up:

CODE: This is the distinct "licence plate" for each scholarship in the list. The first letters indicate the province or territory; and so the scholarships are all listed alphabetically by province and territory (AB = Alberta; BC = British Columbia; MB = Manitoba; NT = Northwest Territories; SK = Saskatchewan; YT = Yukon Territories; CA = Canada). The second letters are an abbreviation of the name of the sponsor of the scholarship. Next is the number given to the scholarship in the database. It does not imply any ranking except to indicate where the scholarship appeared in the lists provided by the sponsor. The last letter will be "u" for university, "c" for college, "e" for employer, or "g" for general public. Here's an example: SK/REG003/u means the third scholarship listed in the University of Regina calendar.

NAME: This is the official name of the scholarship.

PROGRAM: This deals with the program(s) that the scholarship may apply to. If there are numerous possibilities, the terms "Various" or "Any" have been used.

BASIS: These are the criteria by which the scholarship will be awarded. This includes such factors as academic achievement, community service, and special concerns like leadership skill or place of residence. If an application form is required it will be noted in this part of the description.

MINIMUM AVERAGE: This is the minimum academic average that the student should have to be considered for the scholarship. This is usually based on senior-year marks. Simply having the minimum average may not guarantee you a scholarship. There's always someone out there with a higher average than you. At present, the typical range of minimum averages for most institutions is about 80–85 per cent. Don't confuse the minimum average for scholarships with the minimum average for admission to programs. (In some cases the GPA value is shown).

VALUE: This is the nearest dollar value that can be found for the scholarship. It is the total amount that an award would be worth if the recipient received it for the longest possible time. For example, a

$2500 entrance scholarship renewable for up to three more years would list at $10,000. In the case of scholarships worth the value of the tuition fees an approximation has been used. Some institutions, like the University of Alberta, increase the value of their scholarships each year automatically. In a few cases, the total amount of award money is divided up differently each year for some scholarships. In such cases the word "total" will follow the amount shown.

TERMS: This is a description of how the scholarship will be paid out to the student, with the renewal criteria if such apply. Most of the small scholarships are offered to the recipients for one year only. The larger renewable scholarships often have a minimum academic average that must be maintained for the recipient to receive the scholarship in the following year.

NUMBER OF AWARDS: There may be three or four scholarships with the same name. This is the number of that particular scholarship that are offered to students each year.

DEADLINE FOR APPLICATIONS: Most scholarships are offered to students automatically upon application to a university or college. However, the high-value scholarships and those offered by outside agencies and employers usually require some kind of application form, to be submitted by a given date so that all applications can be considered at once. If such is the case, an approximate month and date will be shown in this section. Remember that it is best to send in your application well in advance of the deadline. Also, it is advisable to send your material by priority post. Bear in mind that most scholarship sponsors abide by their own deadlines so don't expect sympathy for late applications.

Please note that in some cases it was not possible to get such information as "Number of Awards" for each scholarship. When you see "N/A" this means that the information was not available. "N/R" means the information is not relevant in this case. Sometimes the value and number of awards varies because the source of funds has a variable rate of interest from year to year.

Asking for more information

Remember that the best source of information concerning a scholarship is the sponsor who offers it. Here is a sample letter that makes a short and concise request for information.

Student Awards Office
Any University
Somewhere, Manitoba

Dear Sirs:

I am a high school senior at Sutton District High School and I am applying to Any University to enter in September 1993.

I am interested in obtaining information about the Ferntree Scholarship offered by your university. Please include an application form. I have enclosed a self-addressed envelope for your convenience.

Yours truly,

Ima Student

Enclosure.

This letter will work for getting information about most scholarships from any source. There's no point in giving a lot of your life history in this letter since it will most likely be answered by a secretary anyway. Since some scholarships are run by non-profit organizations, it doesn't hurt to send a *stamped*, self-addressed envelope. It will certainly guarantee a prompt reply rather than the possibility of none at all. A Canadian stamp doesn't cost that much and the scholarship sponsor will appreciate your consideration.

At this point your confidence may be disappearing faster than snowflakes in June. Again, I can only remind you that ignorance and apathy are the two major reasons that people don't get scholarships. This book can help with the first part, but you've got to beat apathy on your own. Your chances of winning a scholarship aren't bad even when you look at the mathematical odds. Some scholarships attract only two applicants for one award. There are others that attract hundreds of applicants for three awards. These odds are still much better than any lottery going. The good news is that scholarships aren't awarded by some kind of lucky draw from a barrel of entries. The quality of your application can dramatically improve your odds of winning, as can the number of scholarships you apply for. In essence, the answer to ignorance and apathy is quality and quantity. Also, there is no limit to the number of scholarships for which you can apply, although some of the larger scholarships are "not tenable" with other awards. This means that some institutions won't permit you to receive two large awards simultaneously.

Scholarships with specific requirements

As you look through the scholarship lists you will notice that there are scholarships designed for members of special-interest groups. If you are curious about your eligibility for any particular scholarship, then you should contact the sponsor.

Some scholarships have had to change to keep up with the times. One such was the Leonard Foundation Scholarship. Established in 1916 the scholarships were awarded only to white, Anglo-Saxon Protestants until this limitation was challenged in court. In the present description of Leonard Foundation scholarships no mention of race is made and it says that "preference in the selection of students for financial assistance shall be given to the children of the following: a member of the Clergy (i.e., an official minister of any religion; School Teachers; Persons who have served in Her Majesty's military, naval or air forces; Graduates of the Royal Military College of Canada; Members of the Engineering Institute of Canada; and Members of the Mining and Metallurgical Institute of Canada."

The word "preference" is the key. It comes up time and again with special-interest scholarships. It seems to imply that while anyone may apply for the scholarship it will likely go to someone meeting the special criteria.

In addition, some scholarships are restricted to students entering specific programs. Some programs, such as engineering and music, enjoy the advantage of having numerous scholarships.

In Chapter 15, you can find lists of scholarships divided by special interests and programs. The entries are cross-referenced by code number to the main entries in the university and college lists. Remember that these are only part of the total number of awards do not have specific requirements and are open to students in any program.

Deadlines for applying

Deadlines are a critical part of applying for scholarships. In Chapter 15, you will find a list of deadlines, also cross-referenced to code numbers of individual awards. A large number of the dates are in the spring. This allows the sponsor to see your final grades and your choices of institution. Deadlines are very important, so don't miss them. Also, deadlines may change from year to year – so get your application in well before the date listed.

Bursaries and other sources of funds

It would be nice if everyone could get a scholarship to help to pay for post-secondary education. Unfortunately, this simply isn't possible. The good news is that all the skills you have acquired for your scholarship quest can help you find other sources of funds for your further education. Most students find themselves running short of money during university or college. Some students send letters home begging for more money and others try to live on a diet of macaroni and cheese. You should plan your budget well in advance so there won't be any surprises. Here are a few ideas to consider if you think money is going to be tight. You'll want these supports in place in advance of your need for them! Start your search in your high school guidance office and then talk to the university or college student awards or student services office. Many high schools and school boards have their own scholarships.

The most obvious place to start is with government assistance programs. For most students this means your provincial or territorial government's student assistance program. Be very careful when filling out these forms. And don't be afraid to appeal the decision if you think you haven't received enough support.

A bursary is money given to a student who has financial need.

There are almost as many bursaries as scholarships offered by the universities and colleges. While there is no fame involved in obtaining a bursary there is no shame either. Applicants usually have to meet a minimum academic standing and establish their financial need. Many institutions do not give out their bursaries until the second term of the academic year. All bursaries require the completion of an application form. Again, take the time to do a good job on the paperwork. And don't be surprised if you are required to go in for an interview as well.

If money is very short because, say, your scholarship cheque hasn't arrived, then ask if your institution has some kind of emergency loan program. Also a number of places have interesting work/study programs where deserving students are given jobs on the campus to help fund their educations. This isn't the same as a co-op program, but it's helpful none the less.

There are some very good programs offered to Canadian Forces personnel and their families. The following organizations will provide loans for qualified applicants:

Canadian Forces Personnel Assistance Fund
245 Cooper Street, 6th Floor
Ottawa, Ontario
K2P 0G2

Air Force, RCAF Benevolent Fund
100 Metcalfe Street
Ottawa, Ontario
K1A 0K2

The Royal Canadian Navy Benevolent Fund
P.O. Box 505
Ottawa, Ontario
K1P 5P6

In the case of military personnel it may also be worth checking with

Veterans Affairs Canada
East Memorial Building
284 Wellington Street
Ottawa, Ontario
K1A 0P4

Hopefully, some of these suggestions will work for you. If worst comes to worst you may have to ask your rich uncle for a loan (every family seems to have one). You may have to swallow your pride to get an education, but it is well worth the effort. If all else has failed and you must leave school to get work, consider taking post-secondary correspondence courses or going to school at night. Your education is the best investment, and the sooner you have it the better off you will be.

Addresses of Western Canadian universities and colleges

Most of the universities list their scholarships somewhere in their course calendars, usually near the back of the book. Some post-secondary institutions like Grande Prairie Regional College and University of British Columbia publish specific entrance scholarship booklets. In general the community colleges aren't so organized about scholarships; some of them put out leaflets, while others may put something in their student handbooks.

The best source of information concerning a specific scholarship is the institution that offers it. The addresses listed below are the best places to mail your inquiries. (The scholarship list code is not part of the mailing address; it is the "address" for each scholarship in this book).

Included in the list of universities are addresses of any colleges that offer their own scholarships but are affiliated with a particular institution. These colleges are connected with the universities and are not to be confused with the community colleges. These colleges may offer special courses and programs; the universities with which they are affiliated recognize them and grant degrees based on this work. A college that is linked to a university shares the first part of the scholarship identification number. For example, St Thomas More College at the University of Saskatchewan is listed as SK/SASTM0/u. The SK stands for Saskatchewan, the SAS for the University, and TM0 for St Thomas More College. Please note that only those colleges that have their own scholarships are listed here.

Western Canadian universities	*Scholarship list code*

ALBERTA

Student Awards Office 103 Administration Building University of Alberta 252 Athebasca Hall Edmonton, Alberta T6G 2M7	AB/ALB000/u
The Registrar Athabasca University Box 10,000 Athabasca, Alberta T0G 2R0	AB/ATH000/u

The Registrar
Athabasca University
Southern Regional Office
3rd Floor
1040 – 7 Avenue S.W.
Calgary, Alberta
T2P 3G9

The Registrar
Athabasca University
Northern Regional Office
2nd Floor, 108 Street Building
9942 – 108 Street
Edmonton, Alberta
T5K 2J5

The Registrar
Athabasca University
Fort McMurray Centre
607, Plaza II
8600 Franklin Avenue
Fort McMurray, Alberta
T9H 2J5

Financial Aid Office Augustana University College 4901 – 46 Avenue Camrose, Alberta T4V 2R3	AB/AUG000/u
Student Awards and Financial Aid Room 124 McKinnie Library Block University of Calgary 2500 University Drive, N.W. Calgary, Alberta T2N 1N4	AB/CAL000/u

Registrar
Concordia College
7128 Ada Boulevard
Edmonton, Alberta
T5B 4E4

AB/CDA000/u

Financial Aid and Awards Office
University of Lethbridge
4401 University Drive West
Lethbridge, Alberta
T1K 3M4

AB/LET000/u

BRITISH COLUMBIA

Office of Awards and Financial Aid
Brock Hall
University of British Columbia
#1036 – 1874 East Mall
Vancouver, British Columbia
V6T 1Z1

BC/BRI000/u

Student Services
University of Northern British Columbia
P.O. Bag 1950
Prince George, British Columbia
V2L 5P2

BC/UNBC00/u

The Registrar
Open Learning Agency
7671 Alderbridge Way
Richmond, British Columbia
V6X 1Z9

BC/OLA000/u

Liaison and Awards
Office of the Registrar
Simon Fraser University
Burnaby, British Columbia
V5A 1S6

BC/SFU000/u

Director, Financial Aid
Trinity Western University
7600 Glover Road
Langley, British Columbia
V3A 6H4

BC/TWU000/u

Office of the Administrative Registrar
University of Victoria
Box 3025
Victoria, British Columbia
V8W 3P2

BC/VIC000/u

MANITOBA

Scholarship/Awards Office Brandon University 270 18th Street Brandon, Manitoba R7A 6A9	MB/BRN000/u
Registrar Collège universitaire de Saint-Boniface 200, avenue de la Cathédrale Saint-Boniface, Manitoba R2H 0H7	MB/CUSB00/u
Awards Office University of Manitoba 424 University Centre Winnipeg, Manitoba R3T 2N2	MB/MAN000/u

(Affiliated with the University of Manitoba)
Registrar   MB/MANSJ0/u
St John's College,
University of Manitoba
400 Dysart Road
Winnipeg, Manitoba
R3T 2M6

Registrar   MB/MANSP0/u
St Paul's College
University of Manitoba
430 Dysart Road
Winnipeg, Manitoba
R3T 2M6

Awards Office   MB/WNG000/u
University of Winnipeg
515 Portage Avenue
Winnipeg, Manitoba
R3B 2E9

(Affiliated with the University of Winnipeg)
Secretary   MB/WNGMS0/u
Menno Simons College
University of Winnipeg,
515 Portage Avenue
Winnipeg, Manitoba
R3B 2E9

SASKATCHEWAN

Assistant Registrar, Awards   SK/REG000/u
University of Regina
Regina, Saskatchewan
S4S 0A2

(Affiliated with the University of Regina)
Awards Officer
Room 301, Campion College
University of Regina
Regina, Saskatchewan
S4S 0A2

SK/REGC00/u

Luther College Academic Office
Room 200, Luther College
University of Regina
Regina, Saskatchewan
S4S 0A2

SK/REGL00/u

SIFC Scholarship Committee
Saskatchewan Indian Federated College
Room 127, College West
University of Regina
Regina, Saskatchewan
S4S 0A2

SK/REGS00/u

Scholarships and Awards Officer
University of Saskatchewan
Saskatoon, Saskatchewan
S7N 0W0

SK/SAS000/u

(Affiliated with the University of
Saskatchewan)
Scholarship Committee
Dean's Office
St Peter's College
P.O. Box 10
Muenster, Saskatchewan
S0K 2Y0

SK/SASSP0/u

Student Services
St Thomas More College
1437 College Drive
Saskatoon, Saskatchewan
S7N 0W6

SK/SASTM0/u

Western Canadian Colleges

Scholarship list codes

ALBERTA

Assistant Registrar
Alberta College
10041 – 101 Street
Edmonton, Alberta
T5J 0S3

AB/ALT000/c

Financial Aid and Awards Officer
Alberta College of Art
1407 14th Avenue N.W.
Calgary, Alberta
T2N 4R3

AB/ACA000/c

Administrative Secretary   AB/FAIR00/c
Dean of Student Services
Fairview College
P.O. Box 3000
Fairview, Alberta
T0H 1L0

Awards and Financial Aid Officer   AB/GPRC00/c
Grande Prairie Regional College
10726 16th Avenue
Grande Prairie, Alberta
T8V 4C4

Registrar   AB/GMC000/c
Grant MacEwan Community College
P.O. Box 1796
Edmonton, Alberta
T5J 2P2

Student Awards Officer   AB/KEY000/c
Keyano College
8115 Franklin Avenue
Fort McMurray, Alberta
T9H 2H7

Financial Aid and Awards Office   AB/LAKE000/c
Bag 5100
Lakeland College
Vermilion Campus
Vermilion, Alberta
T0B 4M0

  Registrar
  Lakeland College
  Lloydminster Campus
  4420 50th Avenue
  Lloydminster, Alberta
  T9V 0W2

Student Awards   AB/LETH00/c
Lethbridge Community College
3000 College Drive South
Lethbridge, Alberta
T1K 1L6

Student Loans/Scholarships   AB/MED000/c
Medicine Hat College
299 College Drive
Medicine Hat, Alberta
T1A 3Y6

Financial Aid and Awards
Mount Royal College
A139C, Kirby Hall
4825 Richard Road S.W.
Calgary, Alberta
T3E 6K6

AB/MRC000/c

Counselling Office
Northern Alberta Institute of Technology
11762 – 106 Street
Edmonton, Alberta
T5G 2R1

AB/NAIT00/c

Registrar
Olds College
Olds, Alberta
T0M 1P0

AB/OLDS00/c

Registrar
Old Sun Community College
P.O. Box 339
Gleichen, Alberta
T0J 1N0

AB/OLSUN0/c

Financial Aid Officer
Red Deer College
56th Avenue / 31st Street
Red Deer, Alberta
T4N 5H5

AB/REDD00/c

Scholarship/Awards Officer
Southern Alberta Institute of Technology
1301 Sixteenth Avenue N.W.
Calgary, Alberta
T2M 0L4

AB/SAIT00/c

BRITISH COLUMBIA

Co-ordinator
Financial Aid Department
British Columbia Institute of Technology
3700 Willingdon Avenue
Burnaby, British Columbia
V5G 3H2

BC/BCIT00/c

Registrar
Camosun College
3100 Foul Bay Road
Victoria, British Columbia
V8P 5J2

BC/CAM000/c

Student Finance Office   BC/CUC000/c
Canadian Union College
P.O. Box 430
College Heights, Alberta
T0C 0Z0

Supervisor, Financial Aid   BC/CAP000/c
Capilano College
2055 Purcell Way
North Vancouver, British Columbia
V7J 3H5

Awards Officer   BC/CBO000/c
Cariboo College
P.O. Box 3010
Kamloops, British Columbia
V2C 5N3

Director of Student Services   BC/COL000/c
Columbia College
6037 Marlborough Avenue
Burnaby, British Columbia
V5H 3L6

Principal   BC/COQ000/c
Coquitlam College
516 Brookmere Avenue
Coquitlam, British Columbia
V3J 1W9

Student Finances and Placement Office   BC/DGS000/c
Douglas College
P.O. Box 2503
New Westminster, British Columbia
V3L 5B2

Counselling Co-ordinator   BC/EKCC00/c
East Kootenay Community College
P.O. Box 8500
Cranbrook, British Columbia
V1C 5L7

Financial Awards Office   BC/ECCAD0/c
The Emily Carr College of Art and Design
1399 Johnston Street
Granville Island
Vancouver, British Columbia
V6H 3R9

Student Loans and Awards   BC/KWA000/c
Kwantlen College
P.O. Box 9030
Surrey, British Columbia
V3T 5H8

Student Services
Malaspina College
900 Fifth Street
Nanaimo, British Columbia
V9R 5S5

BC/MAL000/c

Financial Aid Office
College of New Caledonia
3330 22nd Avenue
Prince George, British Columbia
V2N 1P8

BC/NEWC00/c

Student Awards and Financial Aid
Northern Lights College
11401 8th Street
Dawson Creek, British Columbia
V1G 4G2

BC/NOLT00/c

Registrar
North Island College
156 Manor Drive
Comox, British Columbia
V9N 6P7

BC/NIS000/c

Financial Aid Office
Northwest Community College
P.O. Box 726
Terrace, British Columbia
V8G 4C2

BC/NWC000/c

Financial Awards Assistant
Okanagan College
3333 College Way
Kelowna, British Columbia
V1Y 4X8

BC/OKA000/c

Captain Roman Piechocki
Pacific Marine Training Institute
265 West Esplanade
North Vancouver, British Columbia
V7M 1A5

BC/PMTI00/c

Financial Aid
Selkirk College
P.O. Box 1200
Castlegar, British Columbia
V1N 3J1

BC/SELK00/c

Financial Aid Office
University College of the
    Fraser Valley
45600 Airport Road
Chilliwack, British Columbia
V2P 6T4

BC/UCFV00/c

Registrar   BC/VAN000/c
Vancouver Community College
King Edward Campus
1155 East Broadway
Box 24620, Station C
Vancouver, British Columbia
V5T 4N3

Student Services Office
Vancouver Community College
Langara Campus
100 West 49th Avenue
Vancouver, British Columbia
V5Y 2Z6

MANITOBA

Co-ordinator   MB/ACC000/c
The Student Assistance Centre
Assiniboine Community College
P.O. Box 935
1430 Victoria Avenue East
Brandon, Manitoba
R7A 2A9

Counselling Area   MB/KEE000/c
Keewatin Community College
P.O. Box 3000
The Pas, Manitoba
R9A 1M7

Financial Aid Office   MB/RRC000/c
Red River Community College
Building C, 3rd Floor
2055 Notre Dame Avenue
Winnipeg, Manitoba
R3H 0J9

NORTHWEST TERRITORIES

Corporate Development Officer   NT/ARC000/c
Arctic College
P.O. Box 1769
Yellowknife, Northwest Territories
X1A 2P3

SASKATCHEWAN

Registrar   SK/CTRC00/c
Carlton Trail Regional College
P.O. Box 720
Humboldt, Saskatchewan
S0K 2A0

The Scholarship Committee
Cumberland Regional College
P.O. Box 2225
Nipawin, Saskatchewan
S0E 1E0

SK/CUMB00/c

Student Services
Cypress Hills Regional College
129 2nd Avenue, N.E.
Swift Current, Saskatchewan
S9H 2C6

SK/CYP000/c

Registrar
Northlands Career College
Air Ronge Campus
P.O. Box 1000
Air Ronge, Saskatchewan
S0J 3G0

SK/NCC000/c

Co-ordinator of Student Services
North West Regional College
1381 101st Street
North Battleford, Saskatchewan
S9A 0Z9

SK/NWR000/c

Registrar
Parkland Regional College
P.O. Box 790
Melville, Saskatchewan
S0A 2P0

SK/PAR000/c

Registrar
Prairie West Regional College
113 Third Avenue West
P.O. Box 700
Biggar, Saskatchewan
S0K 0M0

SK/PWRC00/c

Registrar
Saskatchewan Indian Institute
   of Technologies
201 Robin Crescent
Saskatoon, Saskatchewan
S7L 6M8

SK/SIIT00/c

Registrar
Saskatchewan Institute of Applied
   Science and Technology
Kelsey Campus
P.O. Box 1520
Saskatoon, Saskatchewan
S7K 3R5

SK/SIA000/c

Registrar   SK/SRC000/c
Southeast Regional College
22 Third Street N.E.
Wcyburn, Saskatchewan
S4H 0V9

YUKON TERRITORY

Registrar   YK/YKN000/c
Yukon College
Box 2799
Whitehorse, Yukon
Y1A 5K4

11 University awards

University of Alberta

CODE: AB/ALB001/u
NAME: Leadership Awards
PROGRAM: Any
BASIS: Awarded to high school graduates in the top 10% of their class academically who possess exceptional leadership qualities as demonstrated by service, school, and/or community involvement. An application is required.
MINIMUM AVERAGE: N/A
VALUE: $5000.00
TERMS: One year only. Value of these awards varies from $1000 to $5000. Some awards are reserved for students tranferring from an Alberta community college.
NUMBER OF AWARDS: 60
DEADLINE FOR APPLICATIONS: March 15

CODE: AB/ALB002/u
NAME: Max Wyman Memorial Entrance Scholarship
PROGRAM: Any
BASIS: The U of Alberta's most prestigious award is based on demonstrated exceptional leadership, service, and community involvement and superior academic achievement.
MINIMUM AVERAGE: N/A
VALUE: $5000.00
TERMS: One year only
NUMBER OF AWARDS: 9
DEADLINE FOR APPLICATIONS: March 15

CODE: AB/ALB003/u
NAME: Millar Western Entrance Scholarships
PROGRAM: Any
BASIS: Awarded on the basis of superior academic achievement, leadership, and community involvement. These scholarships are reserved for students from Alberta and Saskatchewan entering the 1st year of a degree program.
MINIMUM AVERAGE: N/A
VALUE: $2500.00
TERMS: One year only
NUMBER OF AWARDS: 18
DEADLINE FOR APPLICATIONS: March 15

CODE: AB/ALB004/u
NAME: William and Mary Hawrysh Memorial Scholarships
PROGRAM: Any
BASIS: Open to graduates of Alberta

high schools who are entering 1st year at the U of A. Awarded on the basis of superior academic achievement, leadership abilities, extracurricular activities, and community involvement.
MINIMUM AVERAGE: N/A
VALUE: $2500.00
TERMS: One year only
NUMBER OF AWARDS: 18
DEADLINE FOR APPLICATIONS: March 15

CODE: AB/ALB005/u
NAME: Copp Family Scholarships
PROGRAM: Any
BASIS: Candidates must be in the top 10% of applicants academically and must have demonstrated extracurricular and community involvement. These scholarships are available to college students transferring to the University or those entering 1st year.
MINIMUM AVERAGE: N/A
VALUE: $2500.00
TERMS: One year only
NUMBER OF AWARDS: 10
DEADLINE FOR APPLICATIONS: March 15

CODE: AB/ALB006/u
NAME: Harold and Florence Mosley Leadership Scholarships
PROGRAM: Any
BASIS: Restricted to Canadian citizens entering a degree program at the U of A. Awarded on the basis of superior academic achievement, leadership abilities, extracurricular activities, and community involvement.
MINIMUM AVERAGE: N/A
VALUE: $2500.00
TERMS: One year only
NUMBER OF AWARDS: 4
DEADLINE FOR APPLICATIONS: March 15

CODE: AB/ALB007/u
NAME: Elizabeth Imrie Memorial Leadership Award
PROGRAM: Any
BASIS: Awarded to an individual who is entering the 1st year of an undergraduate program from high school. The selection is based on superior academic achievement.
MINIMUM AVERAGE: N/A
VALUE: Varies
TERMS: One year only
NUMBER OF AWARDS: 1
DEADLINE FOR APPLICATIONS: October 15

CODE: AB/ALB008/u
NAME: Charlotte A. and J. Garner Caddel Memorial Leadership Scholarship
PROGRAM: Any
BASIS: Offered to a graduate of a high school in the County of Strathcona who best combines superior academic achievement with demonstrated community service and leadership qualities.
MINIMUM AVERAGE: 80.00
VALUE: $1000.00
TERMS: One year only
NUMBER OF AWARDS: 1
DEADLINE FOR APPLICATIONS: April 15

CODE: AB/ALB009/u
NAME: BL Montgomery Scholarship in Engineering
PROGRAM: Civil, Mechanical, Electrical, Geological, Metallurgical, Computer, Mining, Surveying, or Petrochemical Engineering
BASIS: Awarded on the basis of academic standing, extracurricular activities, work experience, community involvement, and evidence of maturity.
MINIMUM AVERAGE: 85.00
VALUE: $12000.00
TERMS: $3000 per year, renewable in the recipient's 2nd, 3rd, and 4th years
NUMBER OF AWARDS: 1
DEADLINE FOR APPLICATIONS: January 1

CODE: AB/ALB010/u
NAME: William Norman Grace Memorial Bursaries

PROGRAM: Business
BASIS: Restricted to a student who has been an Alberta resident for at least 12 months prior to application. The selection is based on superior academic achievement. Preference is given to students entering the Faculty of Business.
MINIMUM AVERAGE: 85.00
VALUE: $2500.00
TERMS: One year only
NUMBER OF AWARDS: 1
DEADLINE FOR APPLICATIONS: July 15

CODE: AB/ALB011/u
NAME: Jean Patoine Scholarship
PROGRAM: Faculté Saint-Jean
BASIS: Restricted to Albertans whose first language is French and who are entering Faculté Saint-Jean. Candidates should apply to the Faculté. The selection is based on academic standing and extracurricular involvement.
MINIMUM AVERAGE: 85.00
VALUE: $2000.00
TERMS: One year only
NUMBER OF AWARDS: 1
DEADLINE FOR APPLICATIONS: March 15

CODE: AB/ALB012/u
NAME: Robert Telger Entrance Scholarships
PROGRAM: Any
BASIS: Restricted to Canadian citizens who have completed Grades 10, 11, and 12 in Alberta. The selection is based on superior academic achievement and financial need.
MINIMUM AVERAGE: 85.00
VALUE: $1500.00
TERMS: One year only
NUMBER OF AWARDS: 3
DEADLINE FOR APPLICATIONS: July 15

CODE: AB/ALB013/u
NAME: Dr. F.P. Galbraith Entrance Scholarships
PROGRAM: Any
BASIS: Awarded on the basis of superior academic achievement and financial need to students entering 1st year.
MINIMUM AVERAGE: 85.00
VALUE: Varies
TERMS: One year only
NUMBER OF AWARDS: 12
DEADLINE FOR APPLICATIONS: July 15

CODE: AB/ALB014/u
NAME: Harvey S. Perkins Scholarship
PROGRAM: Any
BASIS: To be awarded annually to a student entering 1st year on the basis of superior academic achievement.
MINIMUM AVERAGE: 85.00
VALUE: $1500.00
TERMS: One year only
NUMBER OF AWARDS: 15
DEADLINE FOR APPLICATIONS: October 15

CODE: AB/ALB015/u
NAME: Maurice Arnold Solberg Memorial Scholarship
PROGRAM: Humanities
BASIS: Awarded for superior academic achievement and moral character to a 1st-year student from the Special Areas District of Alberta. This special area extends east of Drumheller to the Saskatchewan border and north of Suffield Military Range to Neutral Hills.
MINIMUM AVERAGE: 85.00
VALUE: $2000.00
TERMS: One year only
NUMBER OF AWARDS: 1
DEADLINE FOR APPLICATIONS: July 15

CODE: AB/ALB016/u
NAME: Edmonton Northlands Entrance Scholarship
PROGRAM: Any degree program
BASIS: Restricted to residents of Alberta on the basis of superior academic achievement. Candidates must be entering 1st year at the U of A.
MINIMUM AVERAGE: 85.00
VALUE: $1500.00

TERMS: One year only
NUMBER OF AWARDS: 1
DEADLINE FOR APPLICATIONS: July 15

CODE: AB/ALB017/u
NAME: University of Alberta Entrance Scholarships
PROGRAM: Any
BASIS: Awarded to students entering 1st year at the U of A. The selection is based on superior academic achievement.
MINIMUM AVERAGE: 85.00
VALUE: Varies
TERMS: One year only
NUMBER OF AWARDS: Varies
DEADLINE FOR APPLICATIONS: July 15

CODE: AB/ALB018/u
NAME: Clare Drake Hockey Award
PROGRAM: Any
BASIS: Offered to a student registered full-time in a degree program at the U of A. Recipients must be members of the Golden Bears Hockey Squad and nominated by the Department of Athletics.
MINIMUM AVERAGE: 75.00
VALUE: $1500.00
TERMS: One year only. Students must have a matriculation avg. of 75% from U.S. and Canadian high schools or a GPA of at least 6.5.
NUMBER OF AWARDS: Varies

CODE: AB/ALB019/u
NAME: Adam Kryczka Memorial Hockey Scholarship
PROGRAM: Any
BASIS: Offered to a student registered full-time in a degree program at the U of A. Recipients must be members of the Golden Bears Hockey Squad, and preference will be given to goaltenders. Nominated by the Department of Athletics.
MINIMUM AVERAGE: 75.00
VALUE: $1500.00
TERMS: One year only. Candidates must have a GPA of 6.5 at the university level.

NUMBER OF AWARDS: 1
DEADLINE FOR APPLICATIONS: July 15

CODE: AB/ALB020/u
NAME: Canadian Federation of University Women, Edmonton Scholarship
PROGRAM: Any
BASIS: Awarded on the basis of superior academic standing to a student entering the 1st year of a degree program at the U of A.
MINIMUM AVERAGE: 85.00
VALUE: $1400.00
TERMS: $1000 will be awarded on entering 2nd year, providing a GPA of at least 6.5 is maintained.
NUMBER OF AWARDS: 1
DEADLINE FOR APPLICATIONS: July 15

CODE: AB/ALB021/u
NAME: Gardiner Brothers Scholarships in Food Science
PROGRAM: Food Science
BASIS: Restricted to students graduating from an Alberta high school entering a B.Sc. Food Science program. Awarded on the basis of high academic standing and on performance in a personal interview (or essay). Candidates should apply to the Department of Food Science.
MINIMUM AVERAGE: 85.00
VALUE: $1000.00
TERMS: One year only
NUMBER OF AWARDS: 3
DEADLINE FOR APPLICATIONS: July 15

CODE: AB/ALB022/u
NAME: Oil Service Charitable Organization Entrance Scholarship
PROGRAM: Rehabilitation Medicine
BASIS: Restricted to students entering Rehabilitation Medicine from high school. The selection is based on superior academic standing and financial need. Preference will be given to students from Alberta or Saskatchewan.
MINIMUM AVERAGE: 85.00

VALUE: $2000.00
TERMS: One year only. Value and
number of awards may vary.
NUMBER OF AWARDS: Varies
DEADLINE FOR APPLICATIONS: July 15

CODE: AB/ALB023/u
NAME: MacEachran Memorial
Scholarship in Education
PROGRAM: Education
BASIS: Restricted to students from an
Alberta high school entering 1st
year at the Faculty of Education.
Awarded on the basis of superior
academic standing.
MINIMUM AVERAGE: 85.00
VALUE: $800.00
TERMS: One year only
NUMBER OF AWARDS: 2
DEADLINE FOR APPLICATIONS: July 15

CODE: AB/ALB024/u
NAME: Viscount Bennett Scholarships
PROGRAM: Any
BASIS: Restricted to students who
have resided for at least 5 consecu-
tive years in Calgary, or within 20
miles of that city, or in Banff Na-
tional Park. Based on academic
standing and satisfactory personal
qualities. Financial need may be
considered.
MINIMUM AVERAGE: 85.00
VALUE: $1000.00
TERMS: One year only
NUMBER OF AWARDS: 6
DEADLINE FOR APPLICATIONS: July 15

CODE: AB/ALB025/u
NAME: Rosa H. Wolters Entrance
Scholarship
PROGRAM: Any
BASIS: Restricted to students graduat-
ing from a high school in the
County of Vermillion Valley #24.
Awarded to students entering 1st
year at the U of A on the basis of
superior academic achievement.
MINIMUM AVERAGE: 85.00
VALUE: $600.00
TERMS: One year only

NUMBER OF AWARDS: 1
DEADLINE FOR APPLICATIONS: July 15
CODE: AB/ALB026/u
NAME: Harry W. Bass Memorial
Bursaries
PROGRAM: Any
BASIS: Awarded on the basis of supe-
rior academic standing and finan-
cial need to students entering 1st
year at the U of A.
MINIMUM AVERAGE: 85.00
VALUE: $1000.00
TERMS: One year only
NUMBER OF AWARDS: 6
DEADLINE FOR APPLICATIONS: July 15

CODE: AB/ALB027/u
NAME: Margaret Ann (Hardy)
Simpson Award
PROGRAM: Arts
BASIS: Awarded to a student entering
the 1st year in the Faculty of Arts.
The selection is based on superior
academic achievement.
MINIMUM AVERAGE: 85.00
VALUE: $500.00
TERMS: One year only
NUMBER OF AWARDS: 2
DEADLINE FOR APPLICATIONS: July 15

CODE: AB/ALB028/u
NAME: Canadian Foundation of
Poliomyelitis and Rehabilitation
Bursaries (Alberta)
PROGRAM: Rehabilitation Medicine
BASIS: Restricted to students entering
the 1st year of Rehabilitation Medi-
cine. The selection is based on aca-
demic standing.
MINIMUM AVERAGE: 85.00
VALUE: $800.00
TERMS: One year only. It is expected
that recipients will carry on their
profession in Alberta for a reason-
able period after graduation.
NUMBER OF AWARDS: 1
DEADLINE FOR APPLICATIONS: July 15

CODE: AB/ALB029/u
NAME: Saddle Lake Steinhauer
Entrance Scholarship

PROGRAM: Any
BASIS: Awarded on the basis of academic achievement and community service with native peoples to a student entering the 1st year at the U of A. Preference will be given to native students who will be nominated by Native Student Services.
MINIMUM AVERAGE: 85.00
VALUE: $1000.00
TERMS: One year only
NUMBER OF AWARDS: 1

CODE: AB/ALB030/u
NAME: Dr. K.A. Clark Memorial Bursary
PROGRAM: Any
BASIS: Awarded to a student from the Fort McMurray area entering 1st year at the U of A. The selection is based on superior academic standing and financial need. This award may be offered to an undergraduate student.
MINIMUM AVERAGE: 85.00
VALUE: $800.00
TERMS: One year only
NUMBER OF AWARDS: 1
DEADLINE FOR APPLICATIONS: July 15

CODE: AB/ALB031/u
NAME: TransAlta Utilities Entrance Scholarships
PROGRAM: Any
BASIS: Awarded to students entering 1st year at the U of A whose homes are in areas served by TransAlta Utilities Corporation either directly or indirectly.
MINIMUM AVERAGE: 85.00
VALUE: $750.00
TERMS: One year only
NUMBER OF AWARDS: 5
DEADLINE FOR APPLICATIONS: July 15

CODE: AB/ALB032/u
NAME: Percy Clubine Memorial Scholarship
PROGRAM: Agriculture
BASIS: Awarded on the basis of superior academic standing to students entering 1st year in the Faculty of Agriculture.
MINIMUM AVERAGE: 85.00
VALUE: $1000.00
TERMS: One year only
NUMBER OF AWARDS: 4
DEADLINE FOR APPLICATIONS: July 15

CODE: AB/ALB033/u
NAME: Mildred Rowe Weston Memorial Scholarships
PROGRAM: Any
BASIS: Awarded to students from rural Alberta. Preference will be given to students having completed courses through the Alberta Correspondence School. The selection is based on superior academic achievement and financial need.
MINIMUM AVERAGE: 85.00
VALUE: $600.00
TERMS: One year only
NUMBER OF AWARDS: 3
DEADLINE FOR APPLICATIONS: July 15

CODE: AB/ALB034/u
NAME: Alma Mater Entrance Scholarships
PROGRAM: Any
BASIS: Offered to students entering 1st year. The selection is based on superior academic achievement and financial need.
MINIMUM AVERAGE: 85.00
VALUE: $600.00
TERMS: One year only
NUMBER OF AWARDS: 3
DEADLINE FOR APPLICATIONS: July 15

CODE: AB/ALB035/u
NAME: Dymtro O. Pawluk Scholarships
PROGRAM: Any
BASIS: Awarded on the basis of superior academic standing and financial need to students entering 1st year at the U of A.
MINIMUM AVERAGE: 85.00
VALUE: $600.00
TERMS: One year only
NUMBER OF AWARDS: 2
DEADLINE FOR APPLICATIONS: July 15

CODE: AB/ALB036/u
NAME: Harry A. and Frances
Lepofsky Friedman Award
PROGRAM: Any
BASIS: Offered to a Native Indian or
Eskimo student on the basis of satisfactory academic achievement.
Candidates will be nominated by
the Office of Native Student Services.
MINIMUM AVERAGE: 70.00
VALUE: $1500.00
TERMS: One year only
NUMBER OF AWARDS: 1
DEADLINE FOR APPLICATIONS: July 15

CODE: AB/ALB037/u
NAME: Moe Lieberman Scholarship
PROGRAM: Any
BASIS: Awarded on the basis of academic standing and financial need.
Consideration will be given to
merit in football. A candidate will
be nominated by the Department of
Athletics in October of the 1st year.
Students in other years may be
considered.
MINIMUM AVERAGE: 80.00
VALUE: $600.00
TERMS: One year only
NUMBER OF AWARDS: 1

CODE: AB/ALB038/u
NAME: David Butchart Pope
Scholarships
PROGRAM: Agriculture and Forestry
BASIS: Awarded to graduates of Alberta high schools on the basis of
academic standing and financial
need. Preference will be given to
rural students who are, or have
been, members of the Boys' or
Girls' Clubs.
MINIMUM AVERAGE: 85.00
VALUE: $1000.00
TERMS: One year only
NUMBER OF AWARDS: 3
DEADLINE FOR APPLICATIONS: July 15

CODE: AB/ALB039/u
NAME: Alberta Egg Producers
Scholarships
PROGRAM: Agriculture or Home Economics
BASIS: Restricted to 1st-year students
entering Agriculture or Home Economics. Awarded on the basis of
high academic standing.
MINIMUM AVERAGE: 85.00
VALUE: $500.00
TERMS: One year only
NUMBER OF AWARDS: 2
DEADLINE FOR APPLICATIONS: July 15

CODE: AB/ALB040/u
NAME: Ralph and Isabel Steinhauer
Scholarship
PROGRAM: Any
BASIS: Awarded on the basis of superior academic achievement and financial need to a native student
entering the U of A.
MINIMUM AVERAGE: 85.00
VALUE: $500.00
TERMS: One year only
NUMBER OF AWARDS: 1
DEADLINE FOR APPLICATIONS: July 15

CODE: AB/ALB041/u
NAME: City of Edmonton Entrance
Scholarship
PROGRAM: Any
BASIS: Restricted to Edmonton residents. Awarded on the basis of
superior academic achievement
and financial need.
MINIMUM AVERAGE: 85.00
VALUE: $500.00
TERMS: One year only
NUMBER OF AWARDS: 1
DEADLINE FOR APPLICATIONS: July 15

CODE: AB/ALB042/u
NAME: Lloyd Thomas Award in
Music
PROGRAM: Music
BASIS: Awarded on the basis of academic standing and musical merit
to a student entering the Bachelor
of Music program. A candidate will
be nominated by the Music faculty
following an admission audition.
Preference will be given to a clarinet student entering 1st year.

MINIMUM AVERAGE: 85.00
VALUE: $750.00
TERMS: One year only
NUMBER OF AWARDS: 1

CODE: AB/ALB043/u
NAME: Nickle Family Foundation Prize
PROGRAM: Any
BASIS: Candidates must be Canadian citizens or landed immigrants. Awarded on the basis of performance in a scholarship examination held at local schools on the 3rd Tuesday in February. Apply through Alberta high school principals.
MINIMUM AVERAGE: 85.00
VALUE: $500.00
TERMS: One year only
NUMBER OF AWARDS: 1
DEADLINE FOR APPLICATIONS: July 15

CODE: AB/ALB044/u
NAME: Trans Mountain Pipe Line Company Ltd Scholarships
PROGRAM: Any
BASIS: Restricted to students whose homes are along the route of the Trans Mountain Pipe Line in Alberta and Edmonton west to the provincial boundary. Preference will be given to students from outside the city of Edmonton. The selection is based on superior academic achievement.
MINIMUM AVERAGE: 85.00
VALUE: $700.00
TERMS: One year only
NUMBER OF AWARDS: 2
DEADLINE FOR APPLICATIONS: July 15

CODE: AB/ALB045/u
NAME: Melcor Developments Ltd Scholarship
PROGRAM: Faculty of Business
BASIS: Restricted to students from Alberta high schools entering 1st year in the Faculty of Business. The selection is based on superior academic achievement.

MINIMUM AVERAGE: 85.00
VALUE: $350.00
TERMS: One year only
NUMBER OF AWARDS: 1
DEADLINE FOR APPLICATIONS: July 15

CODE: AB/ALB046/u
NAME: University of Alberta Entrance Scholarships
PROGRAM: Any
BASIS: Awarded to students entering 1st year at the U of A. The selection is based on superior academic achievement.
MINIMUM AVERAGE: 85.00
VALUE: Varies
TERMS: One year only
NUMBER OF AWARDS: Varies
DEADLINE FOR APPLICATIONS: July 15

CODE: AB/ALB047/u
NAME: PEO Memorial Scholarship
PROGRAM: Bachelor of Science in Nursing
BASIS: Restricted to a student entering the Bachelor of Science in Nursing program from an Alberta high school. The selection is based on superior academic achievement.
MINIMUM AVERAGE: 85.00
VALUE: $200.00
TERMS: One year only
NUMBER OF AWARDS: 1
DEADLINE FOR APPLICATIONS: July 15

CODE: AB/ALB048/u
NAME: Edmonton Musical Club Scholarship in Music
PROGRAM: Bachelor of Music
BASIS: Restricted to students graduating from an Alberta high school and entering the Bachelor of Music program. The selection is based on superior academic achievement and is made by the Department of Music following either auditions admissions or end of 1st term.
MINIMUM AVERAGE: 85.00
VALUE: $750.00
TERMS: One year only
NUMBER OF AWARDS: 1

DEADLINE FOR APPLICATIONS:
September 1
CODE: AB/ALB049/u
NAME: Peace River Pioneer Memorial
Bursaries
PROGRAM: Any
BASIS: Restricted to Alberta high
school graduates whose homes lie
north of township 68 and west of
the 5th meridian who are entering
1st year at the U of A. The selection is based on academic achievement and financial need.
MINIMUM AVERAGE: 85.00
VALUE: $7500.00 maximum
TERMS: One year only. Number and
value varies up to a total of $7500.
NUMBER OF AWARDS: Varies
DEADLINE FOR APPLICATIONS: July 15

Athabaska University

CODE: AB/ATH000/u
NAME: Athabasca University has no
entrance awards.

Augustana University College

CODE: AB/AUG001/u
NAME: Academic Scholarships
PROGRAM: Any
BASIS: Awarded on the basis of
Augustana admission average as
defined in the calendar. An application is required.
MINIMUM AVERAGE: 80.00
VALUE: Varies
TERMS: One year only. 25% of tuition
with an average between 80% and
89.9%; 50% of tuition for 90% or
over.
NUMBER OF AWARDS: Varies
DEADLINE FOR APPLICATIONS: June 1

CODE: AB/AUG002/u
NAME: Presidential Scholarships
PROGRAM: Any
BASIS: Awarded on the basis of
Augustana admission average as
defined in the calendar, and demonstrated leadership qualities. An
application is required.
MINIMUM AVERAGE: 90.00
VALUE: Equals full tuition fees.
TERMS: One year only
NUMBER OF AWARDS: 2
DEADLINE FOR APPLICATIONS: June 1

CODE: AB/AUG003/u
NAME: University Incentive
Scholarship
PROGRAM: Any
BASIS: Awarded to non-Alberta resident Canadian students entering
Augustana. The selection is based
on demonstrated leadership qualities. An application is required.
MINIMUM AVERAGE: 70.00
VALUE: $400.00
TERMS: One year only
NUMBER OF AWARDS: Varies
DEADLINE FOR APPLICATIONS: June 1

CODE: AB/AUG004/u
NAME: Athletic Performance Grants
PROGRAM: Any
BASIS: Awarded on the basis of leadership qualities and proficiency
and potential in one of: basketball,
biathlon, curling, hockey, or cross-country skiing. A list of competitions, achievements, and awards
must accompany the application.
MINIMUM AVERAGE: 60.00
VALUE: $300.00
TERMS: One year only. Value varies
from $300 to 25% of tuition. The
number of awards will not exceed
number of athletes on the teams.
NUMBER OF AWARDS: See above.
DEADLINE FOR APPLICATIONS: June 1

CODE: AB/AUG005/u
NAME: Fine Arts Performance Grants
PROGRAM: Fine Arts
BASIS: Awarded for proficiency and
potential in one of: drama, flute,
guitar, organ, piano, studio art,
and voice. For Music, candidates

should contact the Fine Arts Dept. to arrange an audition/interview. For Drama, a teacher recommendation and VHS tape of audition are required. Studio Art requires a portfolio.
MINIMUM AVERAGE: 60.00
VALUE: $300.00
TERMS: One year only. Value varies from $300 to 25% of tuition.
NUMBER OF AWARDS: Varies
DEADLINE FOR APPLICATIONS: June 30

CODE: AB/AUG006/u
NAME: Leadership Scholarships
PROGRAM: Any
BASIS: Awarded for demonstrated leadership qualities in church, school, and community. A detailed description of these activities must accompany the application. A reference letter is required.
MINIMUM AVERAGE: 60.00
VALUE: $600.00
TERMS: One year only
NUMBER OF AWARDS: 8
DEADLINE FOR APPLICATIONS: June 1

CODE: AB/AUG007/u
NAME: Lutheran Leadership Scholarships
PROGRAM: Any
BASIS: Awarded for demonstrated leadership qualities in and commitment to the Lutheran Church. A reference letter is required with the application.
MINIMUM AVERAGE: 60.00
VALUE: $600.00
TERMS: One year only
NUMBER OF AWARDS: 30
DEADLINE FOR APPLICATIONS: June 1

University of Calgary

CODE: AB/CAL001/u
NAME: Alumni Association of the University of Calgary Scholarship
PROGRAM: Any
BASIS: Awarded to a Canadian citizen or landed immigrant entering a Fall session at the U of C. Academic merit, contribution to high school and/or community life, and academic promise will be considered.
MINIMUM AVERAGE: 75.00
VALUE: $3000.00
TERMS: One year only
NUMBER OF AWARDS: 1
DEADLINE FOR APPLICATIONS: March 15

CODE: AB/CAL002/u
NAME: Chancellor's Club Scholarships
PROGRAM: Any
BASIS: Awarded to Canadian citizens or landed immigrants entering a Fall session at the U of C. Academic merit, contribution to high school and/or community life, and academic promise will be considered.
MINIMUM AVERAGE: 75.00
VALUE: $24,000.00
TERMS: $6000 per year. Renewable in the 2nd, 3rd, and 4th years provided the recipient maintains a minimum grade-point average of 3.0 for each year of study.
NUMBER OF AWARDS: 10
DEADLINE FOR APPLICATIONS: March 15

CODE: AB/CAL003/u
NAME: Copp Family Scholarships
PROGRAM: Any
BASIS: Awarded to Canadian citizens or landed immigrants entering a Fall session at the U of C. Academic merit, contribution to high school and/or community life, and academic promise will be considered.
MINIMUM AVERAGE: 75.00
VALUE: $3000.00
TERMS: One year only
NUMBER OF AWARDS: 6
DEADLINE FOR APPLICATIONS: March 15

CODE: AB/CAL004/u
NAME: Gordon Edward Wright Scholarship
PROGRAM: Any
BASIS: Awarded to Canadian citizens

or landed immigrants entering a Fall session at the U of C. Academic merit, contribution to high school and/or community life, and academic promise will be considered.

MINIMUM AVERAGE: 75.00
VALUE: $3000.00
TERMS: One year only
NUMBER OF AWARDS: 1
DEADLINE FOR APPLICATIONS: March 15

CODE: AB/CAL005/u
NAME: Joyce Margret Wright Scholarship
PROGRAM: Pre-management courses
BASIS: Awarded to a Canadian citizen or landed immigrant entering a Fall session at the U of C. Academic merit, contribution to high school or community life, and academic promise will be considered.
MINIMUM AVERAGE: 75.00
VALUE: $3000.00
TERMS: One year only
NUMBER OF AWARDS: 1
DEADLINE FOR APPLICATIONS: March 15

CODE: AB/CAL006/u
NAME: Elizabeth and James McKenzie Andrews Bursaries
PROGRAM: Bachelor of Education
BASIS: Awarded to Alberta high school graduates intending to pursue a Bachelor of Education degree at the U of C. Academic merit and financial need will be considered.
MINIMUM AVERAGE: 65.00
VALUE: $12,500.00
TERMS: $2000 in 1st year and $3500 in 2nd, 3rd, and 4th years, providing the recipient maintains a minimum grade-point average of 2.60 for each year of study.
NUMBER OF AWARDS: 4
DEADLINE FOR APPLICATIONS: July 15

CODE: AB/CAL007/u
NAME: Alex R. Cummings Bursary
PROGRAM: Faculty of Engineering
BASIS: Awarded on the basis of academic merit and financial need to a student entering 1st year in the Faculty of Engineering.
MINIMUM AVERAGE: 65.00
VALUE: $2500.00
TERMS: One year only
NUMBER OF AWARDS: 1
DEADLINE FOR APPLICATIONS: July 15

CODE: AB/CAL008/u
NAME: Calgary Flames Award
PROGRAM: Any
BASIS: Offered to students entering their 1st year at the U of C who are members of the U of C Dinosaur ice-hockey team. The names will be recommended by the Director of Athletics and the head ice-hockey coach.
MINIMUM AVERAGE: 80.00
VALUE: $3000.00
TERMS: Value varies to a maximum of $3000.
NUMBER OF AWARDS: Varies

CODE: AB/CAL009/u
NAME: Dinosaur Football's 5th Quarter Association Awards
PROGRAM: Any
BASIS: Awarded to students entering 1st year who are members of the Dinosaur football team. The selection is made by the Director of Athletics and the head football coach.
MINIMUM AVERAGE: 80.00
VALUE: $2500.00
TERMS: One year only. Amount varies.
NUMBER OF AWARDS: Varies

CODE: AB/CAL010/u
NAME: Thomas S. Dobson Scholarship
PROGRAM: Conjoint program, Faculty of Nursing
BASIS: Awarded to a student entering 1st year of the conjoint program in the Faculty of Nursing. Academic merit and extracurricular activities will be considered.
MINIMUM AVERAGE: 75.00

VALUE: $2500.00
TERMS: One year only
NUMBER OF AWARDS: 1
DEADLINE FOR APPLICATIONS: July 15
CODE: AB/CAL011/u
NAME: Dr. A. Downey Memorial Award
PROGRAM: Any
BASIS: Offered to a student with above-average academic achievement, entering 1st year. Some preference will be given to a student intending a career in dentistry. The recipient must have played minor hockey.
MINIMUM AVERAGE: N/A
VALUE: $600.00
TERMS: One year only
NUMBER OF AWARDS: 1
DEADLINE FOR APPLICATIONS: July 15

CODE: AB/CAL012/u
NAME: John and Sarra Fabbro Scholarships
PROGRAM: Any
BASIS: Offered to students entering 1st year from a separate-school system in Alberta. To be eligible, students must have successfully completed Italian 30.
MINIMUM AVERAGE: 75.00
VALUE: $1500.00
TERMS: One year only
NUMBER OF AWARDS: 2
DEADLINE FOR APPLICATIONS: July 15

CODE: AB/CAL013/u
NAME: F.L. Fenwick Scholarship in Music
PROGRAM: Music (pipe organ)
BASIS: Offered to a student enrolled in or entering the Bachelor of Music program. The award is based on the recomendation of the audition jury or the spring jury. Preference is given to an organist, but students studying harpsicord may be considered.
MINIMUM AVERAGE: N/A
VALUE: $2500.00

TERMS: One year only
NUMBER OF AWARDS: 1

CODE: AB/CAL014/u
NAME: Fortune Industries Ltd Matriculation Bursary
PROGRAM: General Studies
BASIS: Offered to a student entering the 1st year in the Faculty of General Studies who intends to pursue a Bachelor of Commerce degree. This award is based on financial need and academic merit.
MINIMUM AVERAGE: 65.00
VALUE: $100.00
TERMS: This award may be renewable provided the recipient continues to have financial need and maintains a satisfactory academic record.
NUMBER OF AWARDS: 1
DEADLINE FOR APPLICATIONS: July 15

CODE: AB/CAL015/u
NAME: Bob Grainger Matriculation Bursary
PROGRAM: Any
BASIS: Offered to a student entering the 1st year in any faculty. This award is based on academic merit, extracurricular activities, and financial need.
MINIMUM AVERAGE: 65.00
VALUE: $2000.00
TERMS: One year only
NUMBER OF AWARDS: 1
DEADLINE FOR APPLICATIONS: July 15

CODE: AB/CAL016/u
NAME: Bob Grainger Matriculation Bursary, Bow Valley Area
PROGRAM: Any
BASIS: Offered to a student entering the 1st year in any program. This award is based on academic merit, extracurricular activities, and financial need. Preference will be given to graduates of a high school in the Bow Valley area west of Calgary.
MINIMUM AVERAGE: 65.00
VALUE: $2000.00
TERMS: One year only

NUMBER OF AWARDS: 1
DEADLINE FOR APPLICATIONS: July 15

CODE: AB/CAL017/u
NAME: Home Oil Company Limited
Centennial Matriculation Bursaries
PROGRAM: Management, Engineering,
General Studies, Computer Science,
Geology, or Geophysics
BASIS: Offered to Canadian citizens or
landed immigrants entering the 1st
year. This award is based on academic merit, extracurricular activities, and financial need.
MINIMUM AVERAGE: 65.00
VALUE: $1000.00
TERMS: One year only
NUMBER OF AWARDS: 5
DEADLINE FOR APPLICATIONS: July 15

CODE: AB/CAL018/u
NAME: W.G. (Bill) Howard Memorial
Foundation Matriculation
Scholarships
PROGRAM: Engineering
BASIS: Offered to students entering
1st-year Engineering. This award is
based on academic merit and extracurricular activities. Candidates
must have demonstrated leadership
ability through involvement in the
community, clubs, and organizations in high school.
MINIMUM AVERAGE: 75.00
VALUE: $500.00
TERMS: One year only
NUMBER OF AWARDS: 2
DEADLINE FOR APPLICATIONS: July 15

CODE: AB/CAL019/u
NAME: Kappa Alpha Theta Alumnae
Club of Calgary Scholarship
PROGRAM: Any
BASIS: Offered to a female student
entering the 1st year of any faculty.
The recipient must have completed
Grade 12 at a Calgary high school.
The award will be based on academic merit.
MINIMUM AVERAGE: 75.00
VALUE: $400.00

TERMS: One year only
NUMBER OF AWARDS: 1
DEADLINE FOR APPLICATIONS: July 15

CODE: AB/CAL020/u
NAME: William Keyte Memorial
Bursaries
PROGRAM: Any
BASIS: Offered to students from the
Special Areas District (Hanna,
Youngstown, Oyen, Cereal, etc.)
entering the 1st year of any faculty.
Awarded primarily on the basis of
financial need and academic standing.
MINIMUM AVERAGE: 65.00
VALUE: $8000.00
TERMS: $2000 per year, renewable for
3 more years provided the recipient maintains a minimum gradepoint average of 2.60 for each year
of study.
NUMBER OF AWARDS: 4
DEADLINE FOR APPLICATIONS: July 15

CODE: AB/CAL021/u
NAME: Kirby Memorial Scholarship
PROGRAM: Music
BASIS: Offered to a student entering
the 1st year of the Bachelor of Music program. The selection is based
on audition or jury by the Department of Music, with preference
being given to a student who is
preparing to study voice.
MINIMUM AVERAGE: N/A
VALUE: $500.00
TERMS: One year only
NUMBER OF AWARDS: 1

CODE: AB/CAL022/u
NAME: Joyce Margaret Locke
Scholarships
PROGRAM: Music
BASIS: Offered to students in the
Bachelor of Music program studying violin, violincello, viola, or
string bass. The selection is based
on performance before either the
spring jury or the audition jury.
MINIMUM AVERAGE: N/A

VALUE: $1000.00
TERMS: One year only
NUMBER OF AWARDS: 4

CODE: AB/CAL023/u
NAME: Ross A. MacKimmie Bursary
PROGRAM: Any
BASIS: Offered to a student of Native Canadian ancestry (status Indian, non-status Indian, Métis, Inuit) entering 1st year at the U of C. The selection is based on academic merit and financial need.
MINIMUM AVERAGE: 65.00
VALUE: $1000.00
TERMS: One year only
NUMBER OF AWARDS: 1
DEADLINE FOR APPLICATIONS: July 15

CODE: AB/CAL024/u
NAME: McCaig Family Matriculation Bursary
PROGRAM: Any
BASIS: Offered to a student entering 1st year at the U of C. The selection is based on academic merit and financial need.
MINIMUM AVERAGE: 65.00
VALUE: $500.00
TERMS: One year only
NUMBER OF AWARDS: 1
DEADLINE FOR APPLICATIONS: July 15

CODE: AB/CAL025/u
NAME: Melcor Developments Ltd Bursary
PROGRAM: General Studies
BASIS: Offered to a student entering 1st-year Faculty of General Studies who has indicated the intention to pursue studies in the Faculty of Management. The award is based on academic merit and financial need.
MINIMUM AVERAGE: 65.00
VALUE: $350.00
TERMS: One year only
NUMBER OF AWARDS: 1
DEADLINE FOR APPLICATIONS: July 15

CODE: AB/CAL026/u
NAME: Gerald Robert Mortimer and

Victor Emanuel Mortimer Scholarships and Bursaries
PROGRAM: General Studies
BASIS: Offered to students who attended high school in the Judicial District of Calgary, excluding the City of Calgary, for at least 2 consecutive years. The award is based on academic merit and, in some cases, financial need.
MINIMUM AVERAGE: 65.00
VALUE: $1400.00
TERMS: One year only
NUMBER OF AWARDS: 12
DEADLINE FOR APPLICATIONS: July 15

CODE: AB/CAL027/u
NAME: Department of Music Awards
PROGRAM: Music
BASIS: Offered to students entering or enrolled in the Bachelor of Music program. Awarded on the recommendation of the audition jury or on musical ability and academic standing.
MINIMUM AVERAGE: N/A
VALUE: Varies
TERMS: One year only
NUMBER OF AWARDS: Varies

CODE: AB/CAL028/u
NAME: Department of Music Entrance Awards
PROGRAM: Music
BASIS: Offered to students entering the Bachelor of Music program. Awarded on the recommendation of the audition jury and on musical ability.
MINIMUM AVERAGE: N/A
VALUE: Up to $1000.00
TERMS: One year only
NUMBER OF AWARDS: Varies

CODE: AB/CAL029/u
NAME: Department of Music Prize
PROGRAM: Music
BASIS: Offered to a student enrolled in or entering the Bachelor of Music program. The recipient will be chosen on the basis of contribution

to the musical life of the Department in the previous academic year or the recommendation of the audition jury.

MINIMUM AVERAGE: N/A
VALUE: $2000.00
TERMS: One year only
NUMBER OF AWARDS: 1

CODE: AB/CAL030/u
NAME: Hans M. Nielsen Memorial Matriculation Bursary
PROGRAM: Engineering
BASIS: Offered to Canadian citizens who are permanent residents of Alberta entering 1st-year Engineering. The award is based on academic merit and financial need.
MINIMUM AVERAGE: 65.00
VALUE: $1000.00
TERMS: One year only
NUMBER OF AWARDS: 3
DEADLINE FOR APPLICATIONS: July 15

CODE: AB/CAL031/u
NAME: Senator the Honourable H.A. Olson Scholarship
PROGRAM: Any
BASIS: Awarded for academic performance in Grade 12 to a matriculant from Alberta entering the 1st year of any faculty. Preference will be given to those graduating from a high school within the 1968 boundaries of the federal electoral constituency of Medicine Hat.
MINIMUM AVERAGE: 75.00
VALUE: $1200.00
TERMS: One year only. Recipients must be living south of latitude 51 degrees.
NUMBER OF AWARDS: 1
DEADLINE FOR APPLICATIONS: July 15

CODE: AB/CAL032/u
NAME: Gary A.S. Owen Bursary
PROGRAM: General Studies
BASIS: Awarded to a student entering the 1st year of post-secondary studies in the Faculty of General Studies who has completed high school in a rural community. Consideration will be given to financial need and academic standing.
MINIMUM AVERAGE: 65.00
VALUE: $1000.00
TERMS: One year only
NUMBER OF AWARDS: 1
DEADLINE FOR APPLICATIONS: July 15

CODE: AB/CAL033/u
NAME: Myrtle Cochran Paget Memorial Bursary
PROGRAM: Music (Violin)
BASIS: Offered to a student in the Bachelor of Music program majoring in violin. Preference will be given to a student entering the 1st year of the program. The selection is based on audition or jury by the Department of Music. Financial need considered.
MINIMUM AVERAGE: 65.00
VALUE: $850.00
TERMS: One year only
NUMBER OF AWARDS: 1
DEADLINE FOR APPLICATIONS: June 15

CODE: AB/CAL034/u
NAME: John D. Petrie, Q.C., Memorial Matriculation Bursary
PROGRAM: Any
BASIS: Offered to a student entering 1st year at the U of C. The selection is based on academic merit and financial need. To be eligible, recipients must be Canadian citizens or landed immigrants.
MINIMUM AVERAGE: 65.00
VALUE: $1000.00
TERMS: One year only
NUMBER OF AWARDS: 1
DEADLINE FOR APPLICATIONS: July 15

CODE: AB/CAL035/u
NAME: Pinnacle Resources Ltd. Bursary
PROGRAM: Any
BASIS: Offered to a student entering 1st year at the U of C. The selection is based on academic merit, financial need, and extracurricular

activities. Candidates must have graduated from a high school in the Provost, Westlock, or Athabasca area.
MINIMUM AVERAGE: 65.00
VALUE: $3000.00
TERMS: One year only
NUMBER OF AWARDS: 1
DEADLINE FOR APPLICATIONS: July 15

CODE: AB/CAL036/u
NAME: Garrett Shawn Prentice Matriculation Award
PROGRAM: Any
BASIS: Offered to a graduate of the bilingual program at Branton Junior High who is entering the 1st year in any undergraduate faculty. The award is based on academic merit on Grade 12 University entrance requirements.
MINIMUM AVERAGE: 75.00
VALUE: $1500.00
TERMS: One year only
NUMBER OF AWARDS: 1
DEADLINE FOR APPLICATIONS: July 15

CODE: AB/CAL037/u
NAME: Richard M. Proctor Memorial Bursaries
PROGRAM: Any
BASIS: Offered to students entering 1st year who have academic merit, financial need, and have participated in the Uncles or Aunts at Large programs. Sons and daughters of current Canadian Progress Club Calgary Downtown members may be considered.
MINIMUM AVERAGE: 65.00
VALUE: $1200.00
TERMS: One year only
NUMBER OF AWARDS: 2
DEADLINE FOR APPLICATIONS: July 15

CODE: AB/CAL038/u
NAME: Punjabi Students Association Bursaries
PROGRAM: Any
BASIS: Offered to a male and a female student entering 1st year at the U

of C. The selection is based on academic merit, and financial need. Preference will be given to students who have shown active interest in the Punjabi community.
MINIMUM AVERAGE: 65.00
VALUE: $500.00
TERMS: One year only
NUMBER OF AWARDS: 2
DEADLINE FOR APPLICATIONS: July 15

CODE: AB/CAL039/u
NAME: Ringette Calgary Scholarships
PROGRAM: Any
BASIS: Offered on the basis of academic merit to students entering 1st year. To be eligible, applicants must be members in good standing in Ringette Calgary and must have been active players for the past 2 years.
MINIMUM AVERAGE: 75.00
VALUE: $700.00
TERMS: One year only
NUMBER OF AWARDS: 2
DEADLINE FOR APPLICATIONS: July 15

CODE: AB/CAL040/u
NAME: Alberta–N.W.T. Command Royal Canadian Legion Bursaries
PROGRAM: Any
BASIS: A candidate must be the son or daughter of a deceased or disabled veteran, an ex–service man or woman, or the son, grandson, daughter, or granddaughter of ex–service personnel, and a native-born or naturalized Canadian domicilied in Alberta or Northwest Territories.
MINIMUM AVERAGE: 65.00
VALUE: $500.00
TERMS: One year only
NUMBER OF AWARDS: 2
DEADLINE FOR APPLICATIONS: July 15

CODE: AB/CAL041/u
NAME: Royal Canadian Legion (Branch 288) Scholarship
PROGRAM: Any
BASIS: Offered to a student entering

1st year who is a graduate of Bert Church High School in Airdrie. The award is given on the basis of academic merit to a student with the highest matriculation average who is not receiving an Alexander Rutherford Scholarship
MINIMUM AVERAGE: 75.00
VALUE: $1000.00
TERMS: One year only
NUMBER OF AWARDS: 1
DEADLINE FOR APPLICATIONS: July 15

CODE: AB/CAL042/u
NAME: Polyna Savridi Memorial Matriculation Scholarship
PROGRAM: Bachelor of Music
BASIS: Offered to a vocal-music student entering 1st year in the Bachelor of Music program. The selection is based on musical ability and the recommendation of the audition jury.
MINIMUM AVERAGE: N/A
VALUE: $500.00
TERMS: One year only
NUMBER OF AWARDS: 1

CODE: AB/CAL043/u
NAME: Servpro Cleaning DR Ltd Bursary
PROGRAM: General Studies leading to Bachelor of Commerce degree
BASIS: Offered to a student entering 1st-year Faculty of General Studies who intends to pursue a Bachelor of Commerce degree. This award is based on financial need and satisfactory academic merit.
MINIMUM AVERAGE: 65.00
VALUE: $300.00
TERMS: Renewable in subsequent years provided the recipient continues to have financial need and maintains a satisfactory academic record.
NUMBER OF AWARDS: 1
DEADLINE FOR APPLICATIONS: July 15

CODE: AB/CAL044/u
NAME: Norman Ronald Silver Memorial Matriculation Scholarship

PROGRAM: Any
BASIS: Offered to a graduate of Henry Wise Wood High School who is entering 1st year. To be eligible for this award, applicants must have exhibited strong citizenship qualities.
MINIMUM AVERAGE: 75.00
VALUE: $800.00
TERMS: One year only
NUMBER OF AWARDS: 1
DEADLINE FOR APPLICATIONS: July 15

CODE: AB/CAL045/u
NAME: Student's Union Matriculation Bursary
PROGRAM: Any
BASIS: Offered to a student entering 1st year at the U of C. The award is based on academic merit, financial need, extracurricular activities, and demonstrated leadership ability.
MINIMUM AVERAGE: 65.00
VALUE: $500.00
TERMS: One year only
NUMBER OF AWARDS: 1
DEADLINE FOR APPLICATIONS: July 15

CODE: AB/CAL046/u
NAME: Anthony Thibaudeau Matriculation Bursary
PROGRAM: Pre-management courses
BASIS: Offered to a student entering 1st year at the U of C and intending to pursue a Bachelor of Commerce degree with a concentration in Insurance and Risk Management. The selection is based on academic merit and financial need.
MINIMUM AVERAGE: 65.00
VALUE: $2000.00
TERMS: One year only
NUMBER OF AWARDS: 1
DEADLINE FOR APPLICATIONS: July 15

CODE: AB/CAL047/u
NAME: Douglas (Yeung) Tims Memorial Bursary
PROGRAM: Any
BASIS: Offered to a student entering 1st year at the U of C. The award

is based on academic merit, financial need and extracurricular activities involving contribution to the community. Preference will be given to Calgary Chinese School students.
MINIMUM AVERAGE: 65.00
VALUE: $600.00
TERMS: One year only
NUMBER OF AWARDS: 1
DEADLINE FOR APPLICATIONS: July 15

CODE: AB/CAL048/u
NAME: TransAlta Utilities Matriculation Scholarships
PROGRAM: Any
BASIS: Offered to students entering 1st year at the U of C. The students' homes must be in an area served directly or indirectly by TransAlta Utilities Corporation. The awards are based on academic merit and consideration is given to financial need.
MINIMUM AVERAGE: 75.00
VALUE: $750.00
TERMS: One year only
NUMBER OF AWARDS: 5
DEADLINE FOR APPLICATIONS: July 15

CODE: AB/CAL049/u
NAME: John Tsafalas Memorial Bursary
PROGRAM: Any
BASIS: Offered to a student entering 1st year at the U of C. The award is based on academic merit and financial need.
MINIMUM AVERAGE: 65.00
VALUE: $500.00
TERMS: One year only
NUMBER OF AWARDS: 1
DEADLINE FOR APPLICATIONS: July 15

CODE: AB/CAL050/u
NAME: University of Calgary Academic Scholarship for Frosh Students
PROGRAM: Any
BASIS: Offered to students entering 1st year at the U of C. Four awards are based on academic merit and one

is based on academic merit and non-academic activities and achievements.
MINIMUM AVERAGE: 75.00
VALUE: $1000.00
TERMS: One year only
NUMBER OF AWARDS: 5
DEADLINE FOR APPLICATIONS: July 15

CODE: AB/CAL051/u
NAME: University of Calgary Bursaries for Frosh Students
PROGRAM: Any
BASIS: Offered to students entering 1st year at the U of C. Four awards are based on academic merit and one is based on academic merit and non-academic activities and achievements.
MINIMUM AVERAGE: 65.00
VALUE: $500.00
TERMS: One year only
NUMBER OF AWARDS: 5
DEADLINE FOR APPLICATIONS: July 15

CODE: AB/CAL052/u
NAME: University of Calgary Maths Extension Programme Prize
PROGRAM: Any
BASIS: Offered to students enrolled in the University of Calgary Maths Extension Programme at Western Canada High School. The awards will be based on proficiency in the program. The Department of Mathematics and Statistics recommends recipients.
MINIMUM AVERAGE: N/A
VALUE: $500.00
TERMS: One year only. The awards are tenable only at the U of C. A recipient must enroll as a matriculated frosh student within 2 years.
NUMBER OF AWARDS: 2

CODE: AB/CAL053/u
NAME: University of Calgary Matriculation Merit Awards
PROGRAM: Any
BASIS: Offered on the basis of aca-

demic merit to students entering 1st year at the U of C.
MINIMUM AVERAGE: N/A
VALUE: Varies
TERMS: One year only
NUMBER OF AWARDS: Varies
DEADLINE FOR APPLICATIONS: July 15

CODE: AB/CAL054/u
NAME: University of Calgary Men's Basketball Awards
PROGRAM: Any
BASIS: To be eligible, frosh students must be members of the U of C men's basketball team. The selection is made by the Director of Athletics and the men's basketball coach.
MINIMUM AVERAGE: 80.00
VALUE: Up to $3000.00
TERMS: One year only
NUMBER OF AWARDS: Varies

CODE: AB/CAL055/u
NAME: University of Calgary Men's Volleyball Awards
PROGRAM: Any
BASIS: To be eligible, a frosh student must be a member of the U of C men's volleyball team. The name of the recipient is recommended by the Director of Athletics and the men's volleyball coach.
MINIMUM AVERAGE: 80.00
VALUE: $1000.00
TERMS: One year only
NUMBER OF AWARDS: N/A
DEADLINE FOR APPLICATIONS: July 15

CODE: AB/CAL056/u
NAME: University of Calgary Scholarships for Frosh Outside of Alberta
PROGRAM: Any
BASIS: These awards are open to frosh students who obtain their matriculation outside of Alberta. Two awards are based on academic merit and one is based on academic merit with consideration to non-academic activities and achievements.

MINIMUM AVERAGE: 75.00
VALUE: $1000.00
TERMS: One year only. One or more of these awards are available to students who have completed high school outside Canada.
NUMBER OF AWARDS: 3
DEADLINE FOR APPLICATIONS: July 15

CODE: AB/CAL057/u
NAME: University of Calgary Support Staff Matriculation Bursary
PROGRAM: Any
BASIS: Available only to the dependent children of the U of C Support Staff employees who hold regular or sessional full-time positions and who have completed 3 or more years of service. The dependents of deceased employees may also apply.
MINIMUM AVERAGE: 65.00
VALUE: $1600.00
TERMS: One year only. Recipients must be Canadian citizens or landed immigrants. Academic merit and financial need will be considered.
NUMBER OF AWARDS: 1
DEADLINE FOR APPLICATIONS: July 15

CODE: AB/CAL058/u
NAME: University of Calgary Women's Basketball Awards
PROGRAM: Any
BASIS: To be eligible, frosh students must be members of the U of C women's basketball team. The selection is made by the Director of Athletics and the women's basketball coach.
MINIMUM AVERAGE: 80.00
VALUE: Up to $3000.00
TERMS: One year only
NUMBER OF AWARDS: Varies

CODE: AB/CAL059/u
NAME: Madam Valda Bursary
PROGRAM: Faculty of Fine Arts
BASIS: Offered to a student entering 1st year of any program in the

Faculty of Fine Arts. The award is based primarily on financial need with academic merit also to be considered.
MINIMUM AVERAGE: 65.00
VALUE: $1000.00
TERMS: One year only
NUMBER OF AWARDS: 1
DEADLINE FOR APPLICATIONS: July 15

CODE: AB/CAL060/u
NAME: Vernon V. Van Sant, Jr, Memorial Matriculation Bursary
PROGRAM: Any
BASIS: Offered to a student entering 1st year at the U of C. The selection is based on academic merit and financial need. To be eligible, recipients must be Canadian citizens or landed immigrants and have completed Grade 12 at an Alberta high school.
MINIMUM AVERAGE: 65.00
VALUE: $1000.00
TERMS: One year only
NUMBER OF AWARDS: 1
DEADLINE FOR APPLICATIONS: July 15

CODE: AB/CAL061/u
NAME: Viscount Bennett Matriculation Scholarships
PROGRAM: Any
BASIS: Open to students who have resided for at least 5 consecutive years in Calgary, or within 32 km of that city, or in Banff National Park. Awarded on the basis of academic attainment, good character, and satisfactory personal qualities.
MINIMUM AVERAGE: N/A
VALUE: $1000.00
TERMS: One year only
NUMBER OF AWARDS: 4
DEADLINE FOR APPLICATIONS: July 15

CODE: AB/CAL062/u
NAME: West Canadian Graphic Scholarship
PROGRAM: Any
BASIS: Offered to a student of outstanding academic merit entering 1st year at the U of C.
MINIMUM AVERAGE: 75.00
VALUE: $400.00
TERMS: One year only
NUMBER OF AWARDS: 1
DEADLINE FOR APPLICATIONS: July 15

CODE: AB/CAL063/u
NAME: Mildred Rowe Weston Memorial Scholarships
PROGRAM: Any
BASIS: Applicants must have taken at least Grade 12 in a rural Alberta high school and lived outside of any of the major cities of Alberta. Preference will be given to students who have taken correspondence courses. The selection is based on academic merit.
MINIMUM AVERAGE: 75.00
VALUE: $600.00
TERMS: One year only. If there is a tie in academic merit for selection purposes, financial need will also be considered.
NUMBER OF AWARDS: 3
DEADLINE FOR APPLICATIONS: July 15

CODE: AB/CAL064/u
NAME: Don Wright Prizes
PROGRAM: Bachelor of Music
BASIS: Offered to students enrolled in or entering the Bachelor of Music program. The recipients will be chosen on the basis of contribution to the musical life of the Department in the previous academic year or on the recommendation of the audition jury.
MINIMUM AVERAGE: N/A
VALUE: $1000.00
TERMS: One year only
NUMBER OF AWARDS: 2

CODE: AB/CAL065/u
NAME: University of Calgary Transfer Scholarships
PROGRAM: Any
BASIS: Offered on the basis of academic standing to students who

have received advanced credits for the equivalent of at least 5 full courses completed at another post-secondary institution. Students must be entering 2nd or 3rd year.
MINIMUM AVERAGE: 3.20
VALUE: Up to $1500.00
TERMS: One year only
NUMBER OF AWARDS: Varies
DEADLINE FOR APPLICATIONS: June 15

Concordia College

CODE: AB/CDA001/u
NAME: Concordia College has no entrance scholarships.

University of Lethbridge

CODE: AB/LET001/u
NAME: Chinook Scholarships
PROGRAM: Any
BASIS: Awarded on the basis of superior academic attainment and qualities of leadership. An application form, with 2 letters of reference, high school transcripts, letter of application, and essay must be received at the Students Awards Office.
MINIMUM AVERAGE: 80.00
VALUE: $5000.00
TERMS: Two payments of $2500 each.
NUMBER OF AWARDS: 3
DEADLINE FOR APPLICATIONS: April 1

CODE: AB/LET002/u
NAME: University of Lethbridge Achievement Scholarships
PROGRAM: Any
BASIS: Awarded on the basis of superior academic achievement and performance in extracurricular activities. An application form, with a letter of reference from a high school official, and high school transcripts must be received at the Students Awards Office.
MINIMUM AVERAGE: 80.00
VALUE: $1500.00

TERMS: One year only
NUMBER OF AWARDS: 20
DEADLINE FOR APPLICATIONS: April 1

CODE: AB/LET003/u
NAME: Early Entrance Scholarships
PROGRAM: Any
BASIS: Awarded on the basis of academic achievement, as evidenced by actual and predicted matriculation grades. An application form, with a letter of reference, and high school transcripts must be received at the Students Awards Office.
MINIMUM AVERAGE: 80.00
VALUE: $1000.00
TERMS: One year only
NUMBER OF AWARDS: 10
DEADLINE FOR APPLICATIONS: April 1

CODE: AB/LET004/u
NAME: University of Lethbridge Entrance Scholarships
PROGRAM: Any
BASIS: Awarded on the basis of academic proficiency (admission average). An application form and high school transcripts must be sent to the Students Awards Office.
MINIMUM AVERAGE: 80.00
VALUE: $1500.00 maximum
TERMS: One year only
NUMBER OF AWARDS: May vary
DEADLINE FOR APPLICATIONS: July 15

CODE: AB/LET005/u
NAME: Oliver Collumbell Kelly Memorial Scholarship
PROGRAM: Any
BASIS: Offered to a resident from the Town of Claresholm, Alberta, or the Claresholm district, who graduated with honours at Willow Creek Composite High School. Candidates must enter the U of L without previous post-secondary education.
MINIMUM AVERAGE: 80.00
VALUE: $1000.00
TERMS: One year only

NUMBER OF AWARDS: Varies
DEADLINE FOR APPLICATIONS: July 15

CODE: AB/LET006/u
NAME: Entrance and Continuing Scholarships
PROGRAM: Any
BASIS: Offered to students entering the U of L immediately following high school.
MINIMUM AVERAGE: 80.00
VALUE: $6000.00
TERMS: $1500 per year for a maximum of 4 years provided a grade-point average of at least 3.5 is maintained in a full course load.
NUMBER OF AWARDS: 3
DEADLINE FOR APPLICATIONS: July 15

CODE: AB/LET007/u
NAME: Frank M. and Lila Linn Thompson Scholarship
PROGRAM: Any
BASIS: Available to students entering the U of L directly from high schools within the City of Lethbridge, in the year immediately following graduation from high school. Awarded on the basis of high Grade 12 grades.
MINIMUM AVERAGE: 80.00
VALUE: $2000.00
TERMS: One year only. Two payments of $1000 each.
NUMBER OF AWARDS: 3
DEADLINE FOR APPLICATIONS: July 15

CODE: AB/LET008/u
NAME: Lethbridge Science Fair Scholarship
PROGRAM: Any
BASIS: Awarded for academic proficiency and placing first, second, or third with an exhibit at the Lethbridge Science Fair at the senior high school level.
MINIMUM AVERAGE: 80.00
VALUE: $600.00
TERMS: One year only. Two payments of $300 each.
NUMBER OF AWARDS: 3
DEADLINE FOR APPLICATIONS: July 15

CODE: AB/LET009/u
NAME: Archdeacon Cecil Swanson Scholarship
PROGRAM: English or History
BASIS: Awarded for academic proficiency and financial need. Preference is given to a student majoring in English or History.
MINIMUM AVERAGE: 80.00
VALUE: $500.00
TERMS: One year only. Two payments of $250 each.
NUMBER OF AWARDS: 1
DEADLINE FOR APPLICATIONS: July 15

CODE: AB/LET010/u
NAME: Bigelow Fowler Clinic Scholarship
PROGRAM: Pre-Medicine
BASIS: For a student enrolled in the pre-Medicine program
MINIMUM AVERAGE: 80.00
VALUE: $500.00
TERMS: One year only. Two payments of $250 each.
NUMBER OF AWARDS: 1
DEADLINE FOR APPLICATIONS: July 15

CODE: AB/LET011/u
NAME: Entrance Scholarship in Fine Arts
PROGRAM: B.F.A.(Art), B.F.A.(Drama), B.Mus.
BASIS: Awarded on the basis of academic proficiency and demonstrated interest in Fine Arts to students entering the U of L for the 1st time.
MINIMUM AVERAGE: 80.00
VALUE: $1000.00
TERMS: One year only. Amount of award varies from $500 to $1000. Two equal payments.
NUMBER OF AWARDS: 3
DEADLINE FOR APPLICATIONS: July 15

CODE: AB/LET012/u
NAME: Czechoslovak Canadian Cultural Society Scholarship
PROGRAM: Any
BASIS: Preference will be given to students who have demonstrated

interest in Czechoslovak culture and history.
MINIMUM AVERAGE: 80.00
VALUE: $500.00
TERMS: One year only. Two equal payments of $250.
NUMBER OF AWARDS: 1
DEADLINE FOR APPLICATIONS: July 15

CODE: AB/LET013/u
NAME: Ellison Enterprises Ltd Scholarship
PROGRAM: Any
BASIS: For a graduate from Raymond High School
MINIMUM AVERAGE: 80.00
VALUE: $650.00
TERMS: One year only. Two equal payments of $325.
NUMBER OF AWARDS: 1
DEADLINE FOR APPLICATIONS: July 15

CODE: AB/LET014/u
NAME: Home Oil Company Limited Scholarship
PROGRAM: Management or Engineering
BASIS: Awarded on the basis of demonstrated academic proficiency, good citizenship, and sportsmanship to students enrolling in Management or Engineering.
MINIMUM AVERAGE: 80.00
VALUE: $500.00
TERMS: One year only. Two equal payments of $250.
NUMBER OF AWARDS: 4
DEADLINE FOR APPLICATIONS: July 15

CODE: AB/LET015/u
NAME: Palliser Distillers Scholarships
PROGRAM: Any
BASIS: The selection is based on academic achievement.
MINIMUM AVERAGE: 80.00
VALUE: $500.00
TERMS: One year only. Two equal payments of $250.
NUMBER OF AWARDS: 4
DEADLINE FOR APPLICATIONS: July 15

CODE: AB/LET016/u
NAME: Robert H. Parsons Scholarship
PROGRAM: Any
BASIS: Awarded for demonstrated academic proficiency and potential for group leadership. An application and transcripts must be submitted to the Financial Aid and Student Awards Office.
MINIMUM AVERAGE: 80.00
VALUE: $700.00
TERMS: One year only. Two equal payments of $350.
NUMBER OF AWARDS: 1
DEADLINE FOR APPLICATIONS: July 15

CODE: AB/LET017/u
NAME: Mary Agnes Crow Scholarships
PROGRAM: Any
BASIS: Offered to a student entering the U of L for the 1st time. Preference for one scholarship should be given to a graduate living in the Barons School district, provided that such candidate is of sound moral character and meets entrance requirements.
MINIMUM AVERAGE: 80.00
VALUE: $1100.00
TERMS: One year only. Two equal payments of $550.
NUMBER OF AWARDS: 1
DEADLINE FOR APPLICATIONS: July 15

CODE: AB/LET018/u
NAME: Mildred Rowe Weston Scholarship
PROGRAM: Any
BASIS: Awarded for demonstrated academic proficiency and financial need to a student from rural Alberta. Preference will be given to students having completed courses through the Alberta Correspondence School.
MINIMUM AVERAGE: 80.00
VALUE: $600.00
TERMS: One year only. Two equal payments of $300.
NUMBER OF AWARDS: 1
DEADLINE FOR APPLICATIONS: July 15

CODE: AB/LET019/u
NAME: Canada Winter Games Scholarship
PROGRAM: Any
BASIS: Awarded to a resident of southern Alberta for high achievement in athletics at the high school level, contribution to the community, and demonstrated academic proficiency.
MINIMUM AVERAGE: 80.00
VALUE: $300.00
TERMS: One year only
NUMBER OF AWARDS: 1
DEADLINE FOR APPLICATIONS: July 15

CODE: AB/LET020/u
NAME: Royal Canadian Legion Alberta–N.W.T. Command Bursaries
PROGRAM: Any
BASIS: Awarded for academic proficiency and financial need to students domiciled in Alberta or N.W.T., entering the U of L who are: sons/grandsons or daughters/granddaughters of a deceased or disabled war veteran or ex–service person.
MINIMUM AVERAGE: 80.00
VALUE: $500.00
TERMS: One year only. Two equal payments of $250.
NUMBER OF AWARDS: 2
DEADLINE FOR APPLICATIONS: July 15

CODE: AB/LET021/u
NAME: TransAlta Utilities Scholarship
PROGRAM: Engineering Transfer Program
BASIS: Offered to a graduate of an Alberta high school. Candidates must be from an area served either directly or indirectly by TransAlta Utilities. Awarded on the basis of academic proficiency and financial need.
MINIMUM AVERAGE: 80.00
VALUE: $500.00
TERMS: One year only
NUMBER OF AWARDS: 1
DEADLINE FOR APPLICATIONS: July 15

CODE: AB/LET022/u
NAME: Neil D. Holmes Bursary
PROGRAM: Biology
BASIS: Offered to new 1st-year students commencing a degree program at the U of L. Awarded on the basis of academic proficiency, potential for biological research, and financial need. No application is required.
MINIMUM AVERAGE: 80.00
VALUE: $300.00
TERMS: One year only
NUMBER OF AWARDS: 1

CODE: AB/LET023/u
NAME: IODE Awards in Music
PROGRAM: At least one Music course
BASIS: Awarded to full-time students who have demonstrated outstanding promise as performing musicians, upon the initial studio audition.
MINIMUM AVERAGE: 80.00
VALUE: $250.00
TERMS: One year only
NUMBER OF AWARDS: 2
DEADLINE FOR APPLICATIONS: July 15

CODE: AB/LET024/u
NAME: William Asbury Buchanan Bursary
PROGRAM: Any
BASIS: Awarded on the basis of academic proficiency and financial need to a student whose residence is either in the Lethbridge Public School District, the Lethbridge Separate School District, or the County of Lethbridge.
MINIMUM AVERAGE: 80.00
VALUE: $150.00
TERMS: One year only
NUMBER OF AWARDS: 1
DEADLINE FOR APPLICATIONS: July 15

CODE: AB/LET025/u
NAME: College Transfer Scholarships
PROGRAM: Any
BASIS: Offered to students entering the U of L from Medicine Hat

College, Red Deer C, Grande Prairie C, Mount Royal C, and East Kootenay C on the basis of one scholarship for each college.
MINIMUM AVERAGE: N/A
VALUE: $2000.00
TERMS: One year only. Two payments of $1000.
NUMBER OF AWARDS: 5
DEADLINE FOR APPLICATIONS: July 15

CODE: AB/LET026/u
NAME: Transfer Student Scholarships
PROGRAM: Any
BASIS: Offered to students entering the U of L for the 1st time with a minimum of 8 transfer courses taken during the last academic year. Application and documentation must be sent to the Awards Office.
MINIMUM AVERAGE: N/A
VALUE: $1000.00
TERMS: One year only. Two payments of $500.
NUMBER OF AWARDS: 2
DEADLINE FOR APPLICATIONS: July 15

CODE: AB/LET027/u
NAME: Lethbridge Community College Transfer Scholarships
PROGRAM: Any
BASIS: Offered to students from Lethbridge CC entering full-time studies towards a U of L degree. Candidates must have completed at least one year of full-time studies at the College in the academic year prior to application.
MINIMUM AVERAGE: N/A
VALUE: $500.00
TERMS: One year only
NUMBER OF AWARDS: 2
DEADLINE FOR APPLICATIONS: July 15

CODE: AB/LET028/u
NAME: School of Nursing Entrance Scholarship
PROGRAM: Bachelor of Nursing
BASIS: Offered to students entering the Bachelor of Nursing program.

Awarded on the basis of academic proficiency from the Diploma School of Nursing.
MINIMUM AVERAGE: N/A
VALUE: $500.00
TERMS: One year only
NUMBER OF AWARDS: 3
DEADLINE FOR APPLICATIONS: July 15

CODE: AB/LET029/u
NAME: William S. Kizema Memorial Scholarships
PROGRAM: Any
BASIS: For students entering for the 1st time as freshman or transfer students continuing a degree program at the U of L. Transfer students must have successfully completed the equivalent of at least 8 semester courses in the year prior to application.
MINIMUM AVERAGE: N/A
VALUE: $2000.00
TERMS: One year only. Two payments of $1000 each.
NUMBER OF AWARDS: 6
DEADLINE FOR APPLICATIONS: July 15

CODE: AB/LET030/u
NAME: Gerald Trechka Memorial Scholarship
PROGRAM: Any
BASIS: For a student entering the U of L for the 1st time or a student continuing a program of study at this institution. Preference will be given to a student with a physical disability.
MINIMUM AVERAGE: N/A
VALUE: $1000.00
TERMS: One year only. Two payments of $500 each.
NUMBER OF AWARDS: 1
DEADLINE FOR APPLICATIONS: July 15

CODE: AB/LET031/u
NAME: Fine Arts Entrance Scholarship (Art)
PROGRAM: Bachelor of Fine Arts (Art)
BASIS: Offered to students commencing a program of study leading to

the B.F.A. (Art) degree. Open to either new 1st year students or new transfer students. Awarded for artistic excellence and academic proficiency. An interview and/or portfolio review is required.
MINIMUM AVERAGE: 70.00
VALUE: $1000.00
TERMS: One year only. Two payments of $500 each.
NUMBER OF AWARDS: 1
DEADLINE FOR APPLICATIONS: July 15

CODE: AB/LET032/u
NAME: Fine Arts Entrance Scholarship Dramatic Arts
PROGRAM: Bachelor of Fine Arts (Dramatic Arts)
BASIS: Offered to students commencing a program of study leading to the B.F.A. (Dramatic Arts) degree. Open to new 1st-year students or new transfer students. Awarded for artistic excellence and academic proficiency. An audition and/or portfolio review is required.
MINIMUM AVERAGE: 70.00
VALUE: $1000.00
TERMS: One year only. Two payments of $500 each.
NUMBER OF AWARDS: 1
DEADLINE FOR APPLICATIONS: July 15

CODE: AB/LET033/u
NAME: Fine Arts Entrance Scholarship (Music)
PROGRAM: Bachelor of Music
BASIS: Offered to students commencing a program of study leading to the B.Mus. degree program. Open to new 1st-year students or new transfer students. Awarded for artistic excellence and academic proficiency. An audition and interview will be required.
MINIMUM AVERAGE: 70.00
VALUE: $1000.00
TERMS: One year only. Two payments of $500 each.
NUMBER OF AWARDS: 1
DEADLINE FOR APPLICATIONS: July 15

CODE: AB/LET034/u
NAME: Louise Needham Scholarship
PROGRAM: Music
BASIS: Offered to students commencing a degree program of study at the U of L with a major in Music. Awarded for academic proficiency and demonstrated artistic excellence. An audition and interview will be required. Apply to the Awards Office and Department of Music.
MINIMUM AVERAGE: 70.00
VALUE: $1000.00
TERMS: One year only. Two payments of $500 each.
NUMBER OF AWARDS: 1
DEADLINE FOR APPLICATIONS: July 15

CODE: AB/LET035/u
NAME: Joseph Dorner Memorial Bursary
PROGRAM: Any
BASIS: For a student entering the U of L for the 1st time or a student continuing a program of study. Preference will be given to students who have a permanent address in, or whose parents reside in Granum, Alberta, or its Municipal District.
MINIMUM AVERAGE: 70.00
VALUE: $600.00
TERMS: One year only
NUMBER OF AWARDS: 10
DEADLINE FOR APPLICATIONS: July 15

CODE: AB/LET036/u
NAME: Scholarship for the Physically Disabled
PROGRAM: Any
BASIS: For a physically disabled student entering or continuing a program of study at the U of L. A physician's statement and indication of the nature and degree of impairment are required with the application.
MINIMUM AVERAGE: 70.00
VALUE: $500.00
TERMS: One year only

NUMBER OF AWARDS: 1
DEADLINE FOR APPLICATIONS: July 15
CODE: AB/LET037/u
NAME: Ryan Imbach Memorial
Bursary for the Hearing Impaired
PROGRAM: Any
BASIS: For a hearing-impaired student
entering or continuing a program
of study at the U of L. Academic

proficiency and financial need are
considered. A physician's state-
ment and indication of the nature
and degree of impairment are re-
quired with the application.
MINIMUM AVERAGE: 70.00
VALUE: $300.00
TERMS: One year only
NUMBER OF AWARDS: 1
DEADLINE FOR APPLICATIONS: July 15

BRITISH COLUMBIA

University of British Columbia

CODE: BC/BRI001/u
NAME: National Scholarships
PROGRAM: Any
BASIS: Awarded to outstanding stu-
dents entering UBC from secon-
dary schools in Canada. Applica-
tions are available at the UBC
Awards Office. A recent transcript
is required.
MINIMUM AVERAGE: 80.00
VALUE: $26,000.00
TERMS: $6500 per year. Renewable
provided the recipient retains a
satisfactory academic standing.
NUMBER OF AWARDS: 10
DEADLINE FOR APPLICATIONS: April 15

CODE: BC/BRI002/u
NAME: Mount Pleasant Branch #177 –
Royal Canadian Legion Scholarship
PROGRAM: Any
BASIS: Awarded to a student entering
UBC from a Canadian secondary
school. The applicant must be a
Canadian citizen. Academic
achievement, community service,
and extracurricular activites will be
considered. Applications are
available at the UBC Awards
Office.

MINIMUM AVERAGE: 80.00
VALUE: $20,000.00
TERMS: $5000 per year. Renewable
provided the recipient retains a
satisfactory academic standing.
NUMBER OF AWARDS: 1
DEADLINE FOR APPLICATIONS: April 15

CODE: BC/BRI003/u
NAME: Bert Henry Memorial
Scholarships
PROGRAM: Any
BASIS: Awarded on the basis of
scholarly achievement to a student
entering UBC from a senior secon-
dary school. Applications are
available at the UBC Awards
Office.
MINIMUM AVERAGE: 80.00
VALUE: $18,000.00
TERMS: $4500 per year. Renewable
provided the recipient retains a
satisfactory academic standing.
NUMBER OF AWARDS: 1
DEADLINE FOR APPLICATIONS: April 15

CODE: BC/BRI004/u
NAME: Chancellor's Entrance Scholarships (from Secondary School)
PROGRAM: Any
BASIS: Awarded on the basis of scholarly achievement to students entering UBC from senior secondary
schools. Applications are available

at the UBC Awards Office. A recent transcript is required.
MINIMUM AVERAGE: 80.00
VALUE: $14,000.00
TERMS: $3500 per year. Renewable provided the recipient retains a satisfactory academic standing.
NUMBER OF AWARDS: 20
DEADLINE FOR APPLICATIONS: April 15

CODE: BC/BRI005/u
NAME: Chancellor's Entrance Scholarships (from Regional Colleges)
PROGRAM: Any
BASIS: Awarded on the basis of scholarly achievement to students entering UBC from regional colleges. Applications are available at the UBC Awards Office. A recent transcript is required.
MINIMUM AVERAGE: 80.00
VALUE: $14,000.00
TERMS: $3500 per year. Renewable provided the recipient retains a satisfactory academic standing.
NUMBER OF AWARDS: 5
DEADLINE FOR APPLICATIONS: May 15

CODE: BC/BRI006/u
NAME: President's Entrance Scholarships
PROGRAM: Any
BASIS: Awarded to outstanding students entering undergraduate programs at UBC from senior secondary schools. Applications are available at the UBC Awards Office. A recent transcript is required.
MINIMUM AVERAGE: N/A
VALUE: $8400.00
TERMS: $3000 in the 1st year and a minimum of $1800 per annum for a further 3 years provided a 1st-class academic average (80%) is maintained.
NUMBER OF AWARDS: 25
DEADLINE FOR APPLICATIONS: April 15

CODE: BC/BRI007/u
NAME: UBC Royal Institution Entrance Scholarships

PROGRAM: Any
BASIS: Awarded on the basis of scholarly achievement to outstanding students entering undergraduate programs at UBC from senior secondary schools. Applications are available at the UBC Awards Office. A recent transcript is required.
MINIMUM AVERAGE: N/A
VALUE: $8400.00
TERMS: $3000 in the 1st year and a minimum of $1800 per annum for a further 3 years provided a 1st-class average (80%) or better is maintained.
NUMBER OF AWARDS: 5
DEADLINE FOR APPLICATIONS: April 15

CODE: BC/BRI008/u
NAME: Charles A. and Jane C.A. Banks Foundation Entrance Scholarships (I)
PROGRAM: Faculties of Science, Applied Science (Engineering), Forestry, or Agricultural Science
BASIS: Awarded on the basis of scholarly achievement to students entering specified undergraduate programs at UBC from senior secondary schools. Applications are available at the UBC Awards Office. A transcript, 2 references, and an essay are required.
MINIMUM AVERAGE: N/A
VALUE: $7900.00
TERMS: $2500 in the 1st year and $1800 per annum for up to 3 more years of study provided a 1st-class academic average (80% minimum) is maintained.
NUMBER OF AWARDS: 5
DEADLINE FOR APPLICATIONS: April 15

CODE: BC/BRI009/u
NAME: Charles A. and Jane C.A. Banks Foundation Entrance Scholarships (II)
PROGRAM: Faculties of Science, Applied Science (Engineering), Forestry, or Agricultural Science
BASIS: Awarded on the basis of schol-

arly achievement to students entering specified undergraduate programs at UBC from a regional college or another university. Applications are available at the UBC Awards Office. A transcript, 2 references, and an essay are required.
MINIMUM AVERAGE: N/A
VALUE: $7900.00
TERMS: $2500 in the 1st year and $1800 per annum for up to 3 more years of study provided a 1st-class academic average (80% minimum) is maintained.
NUMBER OF AWARDS: 4
DEADLINE FOR APPLICATIONS: April 15

CODE: BC/BRI010/u
NAME: University of BC Agricultural Sciences Alumni Entrance Scholarship
PROGRAM: Agricultural Science
BASIS: Awarded to a student entering full-time studies at UBC. Applications are available at the UBC Awards Office. A transcript is required.
MINIMUM AVERAGE: 80.00
VALUE: $7400.00
TERMS: $2000 in the 1st year and at least $1800 per annum for up to 3 more years of study provided a 1st-class academic average (80% minimum) is maintained.
NUMBER OF AWARDS: 1
DEADLINE FOR APPLICATIONS: April 15

CODE: BC/BRI011/u
NAME: Expo 86 Scholarship
PROGRAM: Engineering
BASIS: Awarded to students entering full-time studies at UBC. Applications are available at the UBC Awards Office. A transcript is required.
MINIMUM AVERAGE: N/A
VALUE: $10,000.00
TERMS: $2500 per year through completion of the 1st degree provided the recipient retains a 1st-class academic average (80% minimum).

NUMBER OF AWARDS: 2
DEADLINE FOR APPLICATIONS: April 15

CODE: BC/BRI012/u
NAME: C.K. Choi Scholarship in Engineering
PROGRAM: Engineering
BASIS: Awarded to a student entering full-time studies in Engineering at UBC. Applications are available at the UBC Awards Office. A transcript is required.
MINIMUM AVERAGE: 80.00
VALUE: $10,000.00
TERMS: $2500 per year through completion of the 1st degree provided the recipient retains a 1st-class academic average (80% minimum).
NUMBER OF AWARDS: 1
DEADLINE FOR APPLICATIONS: April 15

CODE: BC/BRI013/u
NAME: University of BC Forestry Alumni Division Scholarship
PROGRAM: Faculty of Forestry
BASIS: Awarded to a student entering full-time studies at UBC. Applications are available at the UBC Awards Office. A transcript is required.
MINIMUM AVERAGE: 80.00
VALUE: $7400.00
TERMS: $2000 in the 1st year and at least $1800 per annum for up to 3 more years of study provided a 1st-class academic average (80% minimum) is maintained.
NUMBER OF AWARDS: 1
DEADLINE FOR APPLICATIONS: April 15

CODE: BC/BRI014/u
NAME: School of Music 25th Anniversary Entrance Scholarships
PROGRAM: Music
BASIS: Awarded to students entering studies at the School of Music. The awards are made to students who obtain high scores on auditions, interviews, and theory tests conducted in May. Prospective students are automatically considered.

MINIMUM AVERAGE: 80.00
VALUE: $2000.00
TERMS: One year only
NUMBER OF AWARDS: 2
DEADLINE FOR APPLICATIONS: April 15

CODE: BC/BRI015/u
NAME: Harry and Frances Adaskin
Scholarship
PROGRAM: Music
BASIS: Awarded to students entering
or continuing studies at the School
of Music. Preference will be given
to gifted string instrumentalists.
Financial need will be considered.
Awarded by faculty recommenda-
tion.
MINIMUM AVERAGE: N/A
VALUE: $1600.00
TERMS: One year only
NUMBER OF AWARDS: 2
DEADLINE FOR APPLICATIONS: April 15

CODE: BC/BRI016/u
NAME: Adelphian Scholarship
PROGRAM: Various fields: Agriculture,
Forestry, Medicine, Dentistry,
Nursing, and Teaching
BASIS: Awarded to students from
other countries beginning or con-
tinuing graduate or undergraduate
studies at UBC. The selection is
based on academic standing, prom-
ise of success in the proposed pro-
gram, and financial need. An appli-
cation is required.
MINIMUM AVERAGE: 75.00
VALUE: $3200.00
TERMS: One year only
NUMBER OF AWARDS: Varies
DEADLINE FOR APPLICATIONS: May 15

CODE: BC/BRI017/u
NAME: Allied Officers Auxiliary
Bursary
PROGRAM: Any
BASIS: Awarded to a student in any
year or faculty on the basis of
scholastic ability and financial
need. Applicants must be a veteran
of World War Two or the son or

daughter of a veteran. Applications
are required.
MINIMUM AVERAGE: N/A
VALUE: $400.00
TERMS: One year only
NUMBER OF AWARDS: 1
DEADLINE FOR APPLICATIONS: June 30

CODE: BC/BRI018/u
NAME: E.A. Alm Bursary
PROGRAM: Any
BASIS: Awarded to a student in any
year or faculty on the basis of
scholastic ability and financial
need. Applicants must be of Swe-
dish descent through either the
father or the mother and a resident
of BC for at least 12 months prior
to application.
MINIMUM AVERAGE: N/A
VALUE: $250.00
TERMS: One year only
NUMBER OF AWARDS: 1
DEADLINE FOR APPLICATIONS: June 30

CODE: BC/BRI019/u
NAME: Architectural Institute of
British Columbia Scholarship
PROGRAM: Architecture
BASIS: Awarded to a student entering
1st-year Architecture and having
the highest academic standing
among applicants possessing a
degree from a university in BC
seeking admission to the School.
Awarded by faculty recommenda-
tion.
MINIMUM AVERAGE: 75.00
VALUE: $1000.00
TERMS: One year only
NUMBER OF AWARDS: 1

CODE: BC/BRI020/u
NAME: Association of Administrative
and Professional Staff of UBC
Scholarship
PROGRAM: Any
BASIS: Awarded to a student entering
or continuing full-time studies.
Applicants will be considered in
the following order: children or

spouses of AAPS, or members enrolled at UBC, or a UBC student who has earned high scholastic standing.
MINIMUM AVERAGE: 75.00
VALUE: $2200.00
TERMS: One year only
NUMBER OF AWARDS: 1
DEADLINE FOR APPLICATIONS: May 15

CODE: BC/BRI021/u
NAME: Chan Fong Gan Au Memorial Bursary
PROGRAM: Faculty of Arts and Faculty of Science
BASIS: One award is made to a student of Chinese ancestry entering the Faculty of Arts from Grade 12 and the other is made to a student of Chinese ancestry entering the Faculty of Science from Grade 12.
MINIMUM AVERAGE: N/A
VALUE: $900.00
TERMS: One year only
NUMBER OF AWARDS: 2
DEADLINE FOR APPLICATIONS: June 30

CODE: BC/BRI022/u
NAME: Bacon, Donaldson and Associates Scholarship in Metallurgy
PROGRAM: Metallurgical Engineering
BASIS: Awarded to a student entering any year of the metallurgical engineering program. The selection is based on academic ability and financial need. Awarded by faculty recommendation.
MINIMUM AVERAGE: 75.00
VALUE: $500.00
TERMS: One year only
NUMBER OF AWARDS: 1

CODE: BC/BRI023/u
NAME: Sutro Bancroft Bursary
PROGRAM: Any
BASIS: Awarded to a student entering UBC who was either born in Greece or born in Canada to Greek parents. An application is required.
MINIMUM AVERAGE: N/A
VALUE: $750.00

TERMS: One year only
NUMBER OF AWARDS: 1
DEADLINE FOR APPLICATIONS: June 30

CODE: BC/BRI024/u
NAME: Birks Family Foundation Bursary
PROGRAM: Any
BASIS: Awarded to students in any year or program who are experiencing financial need. An application is required.
MINIMUM AVERAGE: N/A
VALUE: Varies
TERMS: May be renewable.
NUMBER OF AWARDS: Varies
DEADLINE FOR APPLICATIONS: October 1

CODE: BC/BRI025/u
NAME: Dr. and Mrs. A.M. Bomstead Scholarship in Piano
PROGRAM: Music
BASIS: Awarded to gifted and accomplished students beginning or continuing studies in the School of Music. Students majoring in violin performance receive first consideration, but some awards go to those majoring in piano performance.
MINIMUM AVERAGE: N/A
VALUE: $9000.00
TERMS: Several scholarships will be awarded, totalling $9000. Recipients may re-apply each year.
NUMBER OF AWARDS: Varies

CODE: BC/BRI026/u
NAME: Karen Bomstead Memorial Scholarship in Piano
PROGRAM: Music
BASIS: Awarded to promising pianists beginning or continuing studies in the School of Music. Both piano majors and concentrators are eligible. The selection is based on a recommendation by the School of Music.
MINIMUM AVERAGE: N/A
VALUE: $1500.00
TERMS: One or more scholarships will

be awarded, totalling $1500. Recipients may re-apply each year.
NUMBER OF AWARDS: Varies

CODE: BC/BRI027/u
NAME: Borden Packaging and Industrial Products – Canada Scholarship
PROGRAM: Chemistry, Chemical Engineering, Forestry, Education
BASIS: Awarded to a student entering 1st year at UBC who is planning a career in the fields of chemistry, chemical engineering, forest products or wood utilization, or teaching. Need, academic ability, and community and school involvement will be considered.
MINIMUM AVERAGE: 75.00
VALUE: $500.00
TERMS: One year only
NUMBER OF AWARDS: 1
DEADLINE FOR APPLICATIONS: May 15

CODE: BC/BRI028/u
NAME: British Columbia Forestry Association Bursary
PROGRAM: Faculty of Forestry
BASIS: Awarded to a student beginning or continuing studies in the Faculty of Forestry who has been active in the Junior Forest Warden program
MINIMUM AVERAGE: N/A
VALUE: $200.00
TERMS: One year only
NUMBER OF AWARDS: 1
DEADLINE FOR APPLICATIONS: June 30

CODE: BC/BRI029/u
NAME: British Columbia Institute of Agrologists Scholarship
PROGRAM: Faculty of Agricultural Sciences
BASIS: Awarded to a student entering the degree course in Agricultural Sciences for the first time. Scholastic standing, farm background, and participation in community activities will be considered. Awarded on the recommendation of the Dean of the Faculty of Agricultural Sciences.
MINIMUM AVERAGE: 75.00
VALUE: $300.00
TERMS: One year only
NUMBER OF AWARDS: 1

CODE: BC/BRI030/u
NAME: BC Teachers Credit Union Bursary
PROGRAM: Faculty of Education
BASIS: Awarded to members of the BC Teachers Credit Union or to sons and daughters of members in good standing. Academic achievement and financial need will be considered.
MINIMUM AVERAGE: N/A
VALUE: $400.00
TERMS: One year only
NUMBER OF AWARDS: 1
DEADLINE FOR APPLICATIONS: June 30

CODE: BC/BRI031/u
NAME: BC Telephone NITEP Bursary
PROGRAM: Faculty of Education
BASIS: Awarded to Status and Non-status Indian students in the NITEP program on the recommendation of the Faculty of Education.
MINIMUM AVERAGE: N/A
VALUE: $3250.00
TERMS: Renewable
NUMBER OF AWARDS: Varies
DEADLINE FOR APPLICATIONS: October 1

CODE: BC/BRI032/u
NAME: Ruth S. Bryson Soroptimist Scholarship in Family and Nutritional Sciences
PROGRAM: School of Family and Nutritional Sciences
BASIS: Awarded to a student entering 1st year in the School of Family and Nutritional Sciences on the recommendation of the School.
MINIMUM AVERAGE: 75.00
VALUE: $675.00
TERMS: One year only
NUMBER OF AWARDS: 1

CODE: BC/BRI033/u
NAME: Burnaby Writers Society
Scholarship
PROGRAM: Creative Writing
BASIS: Awarded to a student entering,
or continuing in, a program leading
to a degree in Creative Writing.
Awarded on the recommendation
of the Department of Creative
Writing. Preference will be given to
a student from the Burnaby area.
MINIMUM AVERAGE: N/A
VALUE: $200.00
TERMS: One year only
NUMBER OF AWARDS: 1

CODE: BC/BRI034/u
NAME: Burrard Charitable Foundation
Bursary for the Visually Impaired
PROGRAM: Any
BASIS: This award is made to a visual-
ly impaired student by application
to the Committee on Awards for
Students with Disabilities.
MINIMUM AVERAGE: N/A
VALUE: $500.00
TERMS: One year only
NUMBER OF AWARDS: 1
DEADLINE FOR APPLICATIONS: October
15

CODE: BC/BRI035/u
NAME: Dr. Gordon C. Butler
Memorial Bursary
PROGRAM: Health or Social Sciences
BASIS: Awarded to Status or Non-
status Indians or Inuit enrolled or
currently majoring in health or so-
cial sciences at UBC.
MINIMUM AVERAGE: N/A
VALUE: $500.00
TERMS: One year only
NUMBER OF AWARDS: 3
DEADLINE FOR APPLICATIONS: June 30

CODE: BC/BRI036/u
NAME: Harriet Sarah Byrne
Scholarship
PROGRAM: Health Sciences
BASIS: Awarded to encourage a dis-
abled student or a student demon-
strating an interest and ability in
the problems of the disabled. Pref-
erence will be given to a woman
undertaking studies in the health
sciences. Awarded by faculty
recommendation.
MINIMUM AVERAGE: 75.00
VALUE: $1000.00
TERMS: One year only
NUMBER OF AWARDS: 1

CODE: BC/BRI037/u
NAME: Ian T. Cameron Memorial
Bursary
PROGRAM: Faculty of Forestry
BASIS: Awarded to a needy student
who is beginning or continuing
studies in the Faculty of Forestry.
Preference will be given to stu-
dents who have been active in the
Junior Forest Warden program.
MINIMUM AVERAGE: N/A
VALUE: $1000.00
TERMS: One year only
NUMBER OF AWARDS: 1
DEADLINE FOR APPLICATIONS: June 30

CODE: BC/BRI038/u
NAME: Canadian Armed Forces
University Training Scholarship
PROGRAM: Any
BASIS: Awarded on the basis of aca-
demic proficiency and military
leadership and management skills
to candidates who are currently
serving with the Canadian Armed
Forces (Reserve) and proceeding
with their uiversity studies. Can-
didates should apply to their com-
manding officer.
MINIMUM AVERAGE: 75.00
VALUE: $1000.00
TERMS: One year only
NUMBER OF AWARDS: 3
DEADLINE FOR APPLICATIONS:
November 1

CODE: BC/BRI039/u
NAME: Canadian Army Remembrance
Scholarship
PROGRAM: Any

BASIS: Awarded to the descendents of those who have served in the armed forces of Canada. Preference will be given to undergraduate students.
MINIMUM AVERAGE: 75.00
VALUE: $1000.00
TERMS: One year only
NUMBER OF AWARDS: 5
DEADLINE FOR APPLICATIONS: May 15

CODE: BC/BRI040/u
NAME: CBC Prize in Playwriting
PROGRAM: Any
BASIS: Any winter or summer students at UBC may submit an original play of at least a half-hour in length to the Chairman of the Creative Writing Department.
MINIMUM AVERAGE: N/A
VALUE: $300.00
TERMS: If the winning entry is broadcast by the CBC, additional fees will be paid to the prize recipient.
NUMBER OF AWARDS: 5
DEADLINE FOR APPLICATIONS: April 1

CODE: BC/BRI041/u
NAME: C.K. Choi Scholarship in Secondary Education
PROGRAM: Bachelor of Education (Secondary)
BASIS: Awarded on the recommendation of the Faculty of Education to an outstanding student entering the Bachelor of Education (Secondary) program.
MINIMUM AVERAGE: 80.00
VALUE: $5000.00
TERMS: This award is intended to cover the costs of one year of study and will be disbursed in 3 equal payments.
NUMBER OF AWARDS: 1

CODE: BC/BRI042/u
NAME: Margaret McDavid Fordyce Clark Memorial Scholarship
PROGRAM: Any full-time program at UBC
BASIS: Awarded to a woman student who, being eligible to compete for Government of BC scholarships, obtains the highest standing among women students in the province in the Grade 12 exams conducted by the Ministry of Education.
MINIMUM AVERAGE: 80.00
VALUE: $1000.00
TERMS: One year only
NUMBER OF AWARDS: 1
DEADLINE FOR APPLICATIONS: April 15

CODE: BC/BRI043/u
NAME: Zella Collins Scholarship
PROGRAM: Social Work
BASIS: Awarded to a student or students entering or continuing in the School of Social Work. The School will recommend students who are worthy and deserving.
MINIMUM AVERAGE: 75.00
VALUE: $325.00
TERMS: One year only
NUMBER OF AWARDS: 1

CODE: BC/BRI044/u
NAME: Columbia College A.J. Mouncey Memorial Scholarship
PROGRAM: Any full-time program
BASIS: Awarded to a student of Columbia College who is proceeding in the Fall to full program of study at UBC. The award is made to a student selected on the basis of high academic standing.
MINIMUM AVERAGE: 75.00
VALUE: $850.00
TERMS: One year only
NUMBER OF AWARDS: 1
DEADLINE FOR APPLICATIONS: May 15

CODE: BC/BRI045/u
NAME: Marion Copp Bursary
PROGRAM: Any
BASIS: Awarded to students from rural areas and preference is given to visually impaired or physically handicapped students. Candidates for this award are selected from applicants for affiliation awards for visually impaired and/or physically disabled students.

MINIMUM AVERAGE: N/A
VALUE: $500.00
TERMS: One year only
NUMBER OF AWARDS: Varies
DEADLINE FOR APPLICATIONS: June 30

CODE: BC/BRI046/u
NAME: Council of Forest Industries Bursary
PROGRAM: Faculty of Forestry
BASIS: Awarded to a student who has been a resident of BC for the previous 2 years and have been engaged for at least one summer session, or the equivalent thereof, in employment in the coastal sector of the BC forest industry.
MINIMUM AVERAGE: N/A
VALUE: $1000.00
TERMS: One year only
NUMBER OF AWARDS: 1
DEADLINE FOR APPLICATIONS: June 30

CODE: BC/BRI047/u
NAME: Margaret Ruth Crawford Scholarship
PROGRAM: Faculty of Arts
BASIS: Awarded to a student from Britannia Secondary School (Vancouver) who is entering the Faculty of Arts at UBC from Grade 12. Preference is given to a student with high standing in English 12.
MINIMUM AVERAGE: 75.00
VALUE: $450.00
TERMS: One year only
NUMBER OF AWARDS: 1
DEADLINE FOR APPLICATIONS: May 15

CODE: BC/BRI048/u
NAME: Elizabeth M. Crichton-Carver Memorial Scholarship
PROGRAM: Faculty of Arts
BASIS: Awarded to a student who is entering the Faculty of Arts at UBC. Preference is given to disabled students. Financial need may be considered.
MINIMUM AVERAGE: 75.00
VALUE: $200.00
TERMS: One year only

NUMBER OF AWARDS: 1
DEADLINE FOR APPLICATIONS: October 15

CODE: BC/BRI049/u
NAME: Lewis Cuming Scholarship
PROGRAM: Any
BASIS: Awarded to a deserving graduate of the seondary school(s) of Chase, BC, who is beginning or continuing studies at UBC. Consideration is given to candidates recommended by the Board of School Trustees of School District No. 24, Kamloops, BC.
MINIMUM AVERAGE: 75.00
VALUE: $1000.00
TERMS: One year only
NUMBER OF AWARDS: 1
DEADLINE FOR APPLICATIONS: May 15

CODE: BC/BRI050/u
NAME: Roy Daniells Scholarship in Creative Writing
PROGRAM: Any
BASIS: Open to students in Grade 12 in BC secondary schools beginning studies in any faculty at UBC. Candidates must submit to the Dept. of Creative Writing: 12–20 pages of creative writing and a brief personal statement.
MINIMUM AVERAGE: N/A
VALUE: $250.00
TERMS: One year only
NUMBER OF AWARDS: 1
DEADLINE FOR APPLICATIONS: August 1

CODE: BC/BRI051/u
NAME: Delta Gamma Bursary for the Blind
PROGRAM: Any
BASIS: Awarded to a blind student requiring financial assistance to enable him or her to enter or proceed to further studies at UBC.
MINIMUM AVERAGE: N/A
VALUE: $250.00
TERMS: One year only
NUMBER OF AWARDS: 1
DEADLINE FOR APPLICATIONS: October 15

CODE: BC/BRI052/u
NAME: Delta Gamma Society, Alpha Province Bursary
PROGRAM: Any
BASIS: Awarded to a visually impaired student. Preference will be given to a student from British Columbia.
MINIMUM AVERAGE: N/A
VALUE: $950.00
TERMS: One year only
NUMBER OF AWARDS: 1
DEADLINE FOR APPLICATIONS: October 15

CODE: BC/BRI053u
NAME: Delta Gamma Society Bursary in Education
PROGRAM: Faculty of Education
BASIS: Awarded to a single mother who is entering or enrolled in a teacher education program in the Faculty of Education.
MINIMUM AVERAGE: N/A
VALUE: $500.00
TERMS: One year only
NUMBER OF AWARDS: 1
DEADLINE FOR APPLICATIONS: October 1

CODE: BC/BRI054/u
NAME: Diachem Industries Scholarship
PROGRAM: Any
BASIS: Awarded on the basis of academic proficiency, leadership, and soccer ability to talented soccer players entering UBC. Recommendation for these scholarships will be made by the Director of Athletic and Sport Services.
MINIMUM AVERAGE: 75.00
VALUE: $500.00
TERMS: One year only
NUMBER OF AWARDS: 5

CODE: BC/BRI055/u
NAME: Alex Drdul Memorial Bursary
PROGRAM: Any
BASIS: One is awarded to a student entering UBC from Cariboo College and another to a student entering UBC from a high school in School District 24 (Kamloops). Candidates must have at least a 2nd-class average.
MINIMUM AVERAGE: N/A
VALUE: $1000.00
TERMS: One year only
NUMBER OF AWARDS: 2
DEADLINE FOR APPLICATIONS: June 3

CODE: BC/BRI056/u
NAME: Kathleen Elliott Memorial Scholarship
PROGRAM: Bachelor of Education (Elementary)
BASIS: Awarded on the recommendation of the Faculty of Education to a student entering or continuing in the Bachelor of Education (Elementary) program who has demonstrated abilities in art and is specializing in Art Education at the elementary level.
MINIMUM AVERAGE: 75.00
VALUE: $1500.00
TERMS: One year only
NUMBER OF AWARDS: 1

CODE: BC/BRI057/u
NAME: Engineering Physics Scholarship
PROGRAM: Engineering Physics
BASIS: Awarded on the recommendation of the Director of Engineering Physics to students beginning or continuing studies in Engineering Physics. The selection is based upon academic standing and extracurricular activities.
MINIMUM AVERAGE: 75.00
VALUE: $500.00
TERMS: One year only
NUMBER OF AWARDS: Varies

CODE: BC/BRI058/u
NAME: EXPO 86 Scholarship
PROGRAM: Engineering
BASIS: Awarded on the recommendation of the Dean of Applied Sciences to students beginning or continuing studies in Engineering.

MINIMUM AVERAGE: 75.00
VALUE: $2500.00
TERMS: One year only
NUMBER OF AWARDS: 3

CODE: BC/BRI059/u
NAME: Faculty Women's Club Jubilee Bursary
PROGRAM: Any
BASIS: Awarded to mature women beginning or continuing studies at UBC.
MINIMUM AVERAGE: N/A
VALUE: $1200.00
TERMS: One year only
NUMBER OF AWARDS: Varies
DEADLINE FOR APPLICATIONS: October 1

CODE: BC/BRI060/u
NAME: Faculty Women's Club Magaret MacKenzie Scholarship
PROGRAM: Any
BASIS: Awarded to a woman entering UBC for the 1st time and registering in an undergraduate program. Preference is given to a student with a demonstrated interest in hiking and cross-country skiing. Financial need will be considered.
MINIMUM AVERAGE: 75.00
VALUE: $1250.00
TERMS: One year only
NUMBER OF AWARDS: 1
DEADLINE FOR APPLICATIONS: May 15

CODE: BC/BRI061/u
NAME: Ferguson Scholarship
PROGRAM: Any
BASIS: Awarded to a graduate of a secondary school in School District No. 7 with 1st preference given to a student from L.V. Rogers Secondary School. Financial need will be considered.
MINIMUM AVERAGE: 75.00
VALUE: $350.00
TERMS: One year only
NUMBER OF AWARDS: 1
DEADLINE FOR APPLICATIONS: May 15

CODE: BC/BRI062/u
NAME: Harry Franklin Memorial Award

PROGRAM: Any
BASIS: Awarded to an entering or continuing student who exhibits high standards of leadership and basketball ability. The award is made on the recommendation of the Director of Athletic and Sports Services.
MINIMUM AVERAGE: N/A
VALUE: $1500.00 maximum
TERMS: One year only
NUMBER OF AWARDS: Varies

CODE: BC/BRI063/u
NAME: Mary and Jane Fyfe-Smith Memorial Bursary
PROGRAM: Various
BASIS: Awarded to native Indian students entering or in attendance in the Schools of Social Work, Nursing, Education, or Law.
MINIMUM AVERAGE: N/A
VALUE: $1500.00
TERMS: One year only
NUMBER OF AWARDS: 3
DEADLINE FOR APPLICATIONS: June 30

CODE: BC/BRI064/u
NAME: Walter H. Gage Bursary
PROGRAM: Any, including part-time studies
BASIS: Awarded to BC secondary school graduates or long-time residents of the province beginning or continuing attendance at UBC. Candidates must have a sound academic standing. Financial need will be considered.
MINIMUM AVERAGE: N/A
VALUE: Varies
TERMS: One year only. A total of $27,000. will be distributed.
NUMBER OF AWARDS: Varies
DEADLINE FOR APPLICATIONS: October 1

CODE: BC/BRI065/u
NAME: Sylvia and Sarah Garvie Scholarship
PROGRAM: Electrical Engineering and Mechanical Engineering
BASIS: Awarded to BC high school students entering electrical or

mechanical engineering. Selection will be made on the recommendation of the Faculty of Applied Science. Financial need will be considered.

MINIMUM AVERAGE: 75.00
VALUE: $2250.00
TERMS: One year only
NUMBER OF AWARDS: 2

CODE: BC/BRI066/u
NAME: Gay and Lesbians of UBC Bursary
PROGRAM: Any
BASIS: Any gay or lesbian UBC students may submit an application for UBC affiliation bursaries to the Awards and Financial Aid Office.
MINIMUM AVERAGE: N/A
VALUE: $300.00
TERMS: One year only
NUMBER OF AWARDS: 1
DEADLINE FOR APPLICATIONS: June 30

CODE: BC/BRI067/u
NAME: Robert C. Gibson Bursary
PROGRAM: Any
BASIS: These awards are made to disabled students at UBC.
MINIMUM AVERAGE: N/A
VALUE: $1600.00
TERMS: One year only. There may be one or more awards from this fund.
NUMBER OF AWARDS: 1 or more
DEADLINE FOR APPLICATIONS: October 15

CODE: BC/BRI068/u
NAME: Eileen R. Gilley Soroptimist Scholarship in Music
PROGRAM: Music
BASIS: Awarded to a student entering Music for the 1st time and majoring in Piano. The scholarship is awarded on the recommendation of the School of Music.
MINIMUM AVERAGE: N/A
VALUE: $700.00
TERMS: One year only
NUMBER OF AWARDS: 1

CODE: BC/BRI069/u
NAME: Girl Guides of Canada Vancouver Area Council Elizabeth Rogers Trust Scholarship
PROGRAM: Any
BASIS: Awarded to active members of the Girl Guide Movement in Vancouver, West Vancouver, North Vancouver (City or District), Richmond, or Burnaby. Applicants' interest in Girl Guide activities will be considered.
MINIMUM AVERAGE: N/A
VALUE: $300.00
TERMS: One year only. Recipients assume a moral obligation to maintain association with the Girl Guides Movement.
NUMBER OF AWARDS: 2
DEADLINE FOR APPLICATIONS: May 15

CODE: BC/BRI070/u
NAME: Frank Gnup Memorial Award
PROGRAM: Any
BASIS: Applicants must possess high academic standing, display strong leadership qualities, be active in athletics, and intend to pursue the latter interest at UBC, primarily in football. A special application for this award may be made at the Awards Office.
MINIMUM AVERAGE: N/A
VALUE: $1500.00
TERMS: One year only
NUMBER OF AWARDS: 1
DEADLINE FOR APPLICATIONS: May 15

CODE: BC/BRI071/u
NAME: Duncan Hamilton Bursary
PROGRAM: Any
BASIS: Awarded to selected students who would otherwise be unable to begin or continue their studies at UBC. Character, ability, and promise will be considered.
MINIMUM AVERAGE: N/A
VALUE: $5000.00
TERMS: One year only. The donors hope that when circumstances permit, recipients of the bursaries will,

in turn, provide funds to assist deserving students.
NUMBER OF AWARDS: Varies
DEADLINE FOR APPLICATIONS: October 1

CODE: BC/BRI072/u
NAME: Imlah Bursary
PROGRAM: Any
BASIS: Awarded to students who have graduated from a secondary school in School District 40 (New Westminster).
MINIMUM AVERAGE: N/A
VALUE: $2400.00
TERMS: One year only
NUMBER OF AWARDS: Varies
DEADLINE FOR APPLICATIONS: June 30

CODE: BC/BRI073/u
NAME: IODE Coronation Chapter (1902–1960) Memorial Bursary
PROGRAM: Any
BASIS: Awarded to a worthy and deserving woman beginning or continuing studies at UBC. Consideration will be given to financial need, academic standing, and promise of service to the Commonwealth and Empire, with special preference for desecendents of veterans.
MINIMUM AVERAGE: N/A
VALUE: $400.00
TERMS: One year only
NUMBER OF AWARDS: 1
DEADLINE FOR APPLICATIONS: October 1

CODE: BC/BRI074/u
NAME: Annie B. Jamieson Scholarship
PROGRAM: Any
BASIS: Awarded to students entering UBC from Grade 12 of a Vancouver secondary school who have high scholastic standing and show evidence of those qualities of character that make for leadership in community affairs and interest in world events.
MINIMUM AVERAGE: N/A
VALUE: $4500.00
TERMS: One year only
NUMBER OF AWARDS: Varies
DEADLINE FOR APPLICATIONS: April 15

CODE: BC/BRI075/u
NAME: Japanese-Canadian Citizens' Association BC Centennial Scholarship
PROGRAM: Any
BASIS: Awarded to a Canadian student of Japanese ancestry residing in BC and proceeding from Grade 12 to a full course of study at UBC. Scholastic ability, character, promise of achievement, and extracurricular activites will be considered.
MINIMUM AVERAGE: 75.00
VALUE: $1000.00
TERMS: One year only
NUMBER OF AWARDS: 1
DEADLINE FOR APPLICATIONS: May 15

CODE: BC/BRI076/u
NAME: A. Johnson Bursary
PROGRAM: Any
BASIS: Awarded to a male student who received his secondary education in Britain, preferably at Cheltenham School. Applications should be sent to The A. Johnson Bursary Committee, Office of the Agent General, BC House, 1 Regent St., London, SW1Y 4NS, England.
MINIMUM AVERAGE: 75.00
VALUE: $6000.00
TERMS: Renewable for an additional 3 years. Tuition fees will also be covered by this bursary. There will be $1500 given in the 1st year to cover relocation costs.
NUMBER OF AWARDS: 1
DEADLINE FOR APPLICATIONS: March 31

CODE: BC/BRI077/u
NAME: Thomas Holmes Johnson Bursary
PROGRAM: Any
BASIS: Awarded to students who have attended high school in Prince Rupert, BC. Applications must include letters of recommendation from the applicant's principal and 3 Prince Rupert residents who hold university degrees.

MINIMUM AVERAGE: N/A
VALUE: $2200.00
TERMS: One year only. One of the awards will normally go to a son or daughter of member of good standing of Tyee Lodge No. 66, A.F.A.M.
NUMBER OF AWARDS: 3
DEADLINE FOR APPLICATIONS: June 30

CODE: BC/BRI078/u
NAME: Douglas T. Kenny Bursary for Disabled Students
PROGRAM: Any
BASIS: Awarded to physically disabled students who need wheelchairs or other artificial aids to carry out their studies at UBC.
MINIMUM AVERAGE: N/A
VALUE: $1100.00
TERMS: One year only. This amount may be divided into more than one award.
NUMBER OF AWARDS: 1 or more
DEADLINE FOR APPLICATIONS: October 15

CODE: BC/BRI079/u
NAME: Janet Ketcham Bursary
PROGRAM: Any
BASIS: Awarded to First Nations students. Preference is given to students who have demonstrated an interest in serving their Native community.
MINIMUM AVERAGE: N/A
VALUE: $1000.00
TERMS: One year only
NUMBER OF AWARDS: Varies
DEADLINE FOR APPLICATIONS: June 30

CODE: BC/BRI080/u
NAME: Khaki University and YMCA Memorial Fund Bursary
PROGRAM: Any
BASIS: Awarded to undergraduates, preferably the sons, daughters, and grandchildren of veterans of World War One.
MINIMUM AVERAGE: N/A
VALUE: $100.00

TERMS: One year only
NUMBER OF AWARDS: 22
DEADLINE FOR APPLICATIONS: June 30

CODE: BC/BRI081/u
NAME: Anne Evelyn Kirkby Bursary
PROGRAM: Any
BASIS: Awarded to mature students and Native Indian students (both Status and Non-status).
MINIMUM AVERAGE: N/A
VALUE: $4500.00
TERMS: One year only
NUMBER OF AWARDS: Varies
DEADLINE FOR APPLICATIONS: October 1

CODE: BC/BRI082/u
NAME: Labatt Breweries of British Columbia Scholarships
PROGRAM: Any
BASIS: Awarded to students who are resident in British Columbia and who are proceeding directly from Grade 12 to a full course of study at UBC. The selection is based upon scholastic standing, character, and interest in school and community affairs.
MINIMUM AVERAGE: N/A
VALUE: $1000.00
TERMS: One year only
NUMBER OF AWARDS: 2
DEADLINE FOR APPLICATIONS: April 15

CODE: BC/BRI083/u
NAME: T.E. and M.E. Ladner Memorial Scholarship
PROGRAM: Any
BASIS: Awarded to a resident of Delta Municipality on the basis of scholastic standing, character, and financial need. Application must include: names and addresses of parents, length of their residence in the Delta area, and details of financial circumstances.
MINIMUM AVERAGE: 75.00
VALUE: $1900.00
TERMS: One year only
NUMBER OF AWARDS: 1
DEADLINE FOR APPLICATIONS: May 15

CODE: BC/BRI084/u
NAME: Harold Lauer B'nai B'rith Foundation Bursary
PROGRAM: Any
BASIS: These awards are made to students who would be unable to attend university without financial assistance.
MINIMUM AVERAGE: N/A
VALUE: $750.00
TERMS: One year only
NUMBER OF AWARDS: 2
DEADLINE FOR APPLICATIONS: October 1

CODE: BC/BRI085/u
NAME: Legallais-Mackie Memorial Bursary
PROGRAM: Any
BASIS: Awarded to a worthy and deserving student who completed high school in Vernon, BC.
MINIMUM AVERAGE: N/A
VALUE: $300.00
TERMS: One year only
NUMBER OF AWARDS: 1
DEADLINE FOR APPLICATIONS: October 1

CODE: BC/BRI086/u
NAME: John B. Macdonald Alumni Bursary
PROGRAM: Any
BASIS: Awarded to students entering UBC in the Fall from regional colleges in BC. The selection of winners is based on academic ability and financial need.
MINIMUM AVERAGE: N/A
VALUE: $12,500.00
TERMS: One year only
NUMBER OF AWARDS: Varies
DEADLINE FOR APPLICATIONS: June 30

CODE: BC/BRI087/u
NAME: Patricia Ann Macdonald Memorial Scholarship
PROGRAM: Any
BASIS: Awarded to a blind or physically disabled student attending UBC. The recipient must be in a program leading to a degree with definite vocational goals and a high grade average. Applications are available from the UBC Awards Office.
MINIMUM AVERAGE: 75.00
VALUE: $2400.00
TERMS: One year only
NUMBER OF AWARDS: More than 1 award may be offered.
DEADLINE FOR APPLICATIONS: October 15

CODE: BC/BRI088/u
NAME: W.H. MacInnes Entrance Scholarship in English
PROGRAM: Any
BASIS: Awarded to the 3 students entering UBC with the highest standing in English Literature 12. To be eligible a candidate must write the scholarship examinations conducted in January or June by the Ministry of Education, Victoria, BC.
MINIMUM AVERAGE: 80.00
VALUE: $1250.00 for first place
TERMS: One year only. The other two scholarships are worth $1000 and $750.
NUMBER OF AWARDS: 3
DEADLINE FOR APPLICATIONS: April 15

CODE: BC/BRI089/u
NAME: W.H. MacInnes Entrance Scholarship in Latin
PROGRAM: Any
BASIS: Awarded to the 3 students entering UBC with the highest standing in Latin 12. To be eligible a candidate must write the scholarship examinations conducted in January or June by the Ministry of Education, Victoria, BC.
MINIMUM AVERAGE: 80.00
VALUE: $1250.00 for first place
TERMS: One year only. The other two scholarships are worth $1000 and $750.
NUMBER OF AWARDS: 3
DEADLINE FOR APPLICATIONS: April 15

CODE: BC/BRI090/u
NAME: W.H. MacInnes Entrance
Scholarship in Mathematics
PROGRAM: Any
BASIS: Awarded to the 3 students entering UBC with the highest standing in Mathematics 12. To be eligible a candidate must write the scholarship examinations conducted in January or June by the Ministry of Education, Victoria, BC.
MINIMUM AVERAGE: 80.00
VALUE: $1250.00 for first place
TERMS: One year only. The other two scholarships are worth $1000 and $750.
NUMBER OF AWARDS: 3
DEADLINE FOR APPLICATIONS: April 15

CODE: BC/BRI091/u
NAME: Cheryl McKay Bursary for the Visually Impaired
PROGRAM: Any
BASIS: These awards are made to assist visually impaired students.
MINIMUM AVERAGE: N/A
VALUE: $1500.00
TERMS: Total value of all awards is $1500.
NUMBER OF AWARDS: Varies
DEADLINE FOR APPLICATIONS: October 15

CODE: BC/BRI092/u
NAME: Norman Mackenzie Alumni Entrance Scholarship
PROGRAM: Any
BASIS: For BC Grade 12 graduates entering UBC. The selection is based on: scholastic achievement, community service, and extracurricular activities. Contact: Norman Mackenzie Alumni Screening Committee, UBC Alumni Association, 6251 Cecil Green Park Rd., Vancouver, BC, V6T 1W5.
MINIMUM AVERAGE: 80.00
VALUE: $2400.00
TERMS: One year only. Not tenable with other major UBC entrance scholarships.
NUMBER OF AWARDS: 27
DEADLINE FOR APPLICATIONS: April 1

CODE: BC/BRI093/u
NAME: Norman A. Mackenzie College Scholarships
PROGRAM: Any
BASIS: For students proceeding from a BC community college to UBC. A 200-word personal statement is required as part of the application. Contact: Norman Mackenzie Alumni Screening Committee, UBC Alumni Association, 6251 Cecil Green Park Rd., Vancouver, BC, V6T 1W5.
MINIMUM AVERAGE: 80.00
VALUE: $1250.00
TERMS: One year only
NUMBER OF AWARDS: 6
DEADLINE FOR APPLICATIONS: April 1

CODE: BC/BRI094/u
NAME: Louise Elliot McLuckie Bursary
PROGRAM: Any
BASIS: Awarded to worthy and deserving students entering UBC from Grade 12. In selecting candidates, recommendations from high school principals will be given favourable consideration.
MINIMUM AVERAGE: N/A
VALUE: $22,000.00 (total)
TERMS: One year only
NUMBER OF AWARDS: Varies
DEADLINE FOR APPLICATIONS: April 15

CODE: BC/BRI095/u
NAME: Elizabeth and Diana McManus Memorial Bursary
PROGRAM: Any
BASIS: Awarded to the sons, daughters, or legal dependents of members of Branch No. 48, Royal Canadian Legion, or, failing suitable candidates, to a student or students in any year and faculty. Academic standing and financial need will be considered.
MINIMUM AVERAGE: N/A

VALUE: $1850.00
TERMS: One year only
NUMBER OF AWARDS: Varies
DEADLINE FOR APPLICATIONS: June 30

CODE: BC/BRI096/u
NAME: Mrs. H.R. MacMillan Bursary
PROGRAM: Any
BASIS: Awarded to women students with good academic standing to begin or continue attendance at UBC. Special preference will be shown to those whose circumstances make it necessary to be self-supporting.
MINIMUM AVERAGE: N/A
VALUE: $8000.00 (total)
TERMS: One year only
NUMBER OF AWARDS: Varies
DEADLINE FOR APPLICATIONS: October 1

CODE: BC/BRI097/u
NAME: Joy Messaros Memorial Bursary
PROGRAM: Any, including part-time
BASIS: Awarded to a student with a physical disability who demonstrates financial need and determination to overcome obstacles caused by the physical disability. (This does not include those with sensory loss of sight or hearing or learning disablities alone.)
MINIMUM AVERAGE: N/A
VALUE: $750.00
TERMS: One year only
NUMBER OF AWARDS: 1
DEADLINE FOR APPLICATIONS: October 15

CODE: BC/BRI098/u
NAME: Margaret Morrow Scholarship, Nelson, BC
PROGRAM: Any
BASIS: Awarded to a student who has graduated from a high school in School District 7 (Nelson, BC) with 1st preference to a student from L.V. Rogers Secondary School. Financial need will be considered.
MINIMUM AVERAGE: 75.00

VALUE: $1000.00
TERMS: One year only. When possible, this award will go to a male or female in alternating years.
NUMBER OF AWARDS: 1
DEADLINE FOR APPLICATIONS: May 15

CODE: BC/BRI099/u
NAME: School of Music, Keyboard Division Scholarship
PROGRAM: School of Music
BASIS: Awarded to an outstanding keyboard performance major entering the School of Music. The award is made on the recommendation of the School.
MINIMUM AVERAGE: 75.00
VALUE: $200.00
TERMS: One year only
NUMBER OF AWARDS: 1

CODE: BC/BRI100/u
NAME: School of Music, Twenty-fifth Anniversary Scholarship
PROGRAM: School of Music
BASIS: Awarded to students entering the School of Music. These awards are made on the recommendation of the School.
MINIMUM AVERAGE: 75.00
VALUE: $6000.00 (total). The value of these scholarships varies from $750 to $2000 per student.
TERMS: One year only
NUMBER OF AWARDS: Varies
DEADLINE FOR APPLICATIONS: April 15

CODE: BC/BRI101/u
NAME: Alan W. Neill Memorial Scholarship
PROGRAM: Any
BASIS: Awarded to a student resident in the Comox-Alberni Electoral District who is proceeding from Grade 12 to studies at UBC. The selection is based on personal qualities, character, and achievement.
MINIMUM AVERAGE: 75.00
VALUE: $900.00
TERMS: One year only

NUMBER OF AWARDS: 1
DEADLINE FOR APPLICATIONS: May 15

CODE: BC/BRI102/u
NAME: Percy W. Nelms Memorial
    Scholarship
PROGRAM: Any
BASIS: Awarded to a student resident
    in British Columbia, north of the
    Peace River, who is entering UBC
    for the 1st time. The selection is
    based on academic ability, promise,
    and personal qualities.
MINIMUM AVERAGE: 75.00
VALUE: $300.00
TERMS: One year only
NUMBER OF AWARDS: 1
DEADLINE FOR APPLICATIONS: April 15

CODE: BC/BRI103/u
NAME: PEO Sisterhood Chapter B
    Bursary
PROGRAM: Any degree program
BASIS: Awarded to a woman from the
    New Westminster area who is be-
    ginning or continuing her studies
    at UBC in a full course load lead-
    ing to a degree. This award is
    made to a student who has good
    standing, shows promise, and has
    financial need.
MINIMUM AVERAGE: N/A
VALUE: $500.00
TERMS: One year only
NUMBER OF AWARDS: 1
DEADLINE FOR APPLICATIONS: October 1

CODE: BC/BRI104/u
NAME: PEO Sisterhood Chapter BD –
    Evah Chase Butler Memorial
    Bursary
PROGRAM: Any
BASIS: Awarded to female students
    who have graduated from secon-
    dary schools in School Districts 37
    (Delta) and 38 (Richmond).
MINIMUM AVERAGE: N/A
VALUE: $250.00
TERMS: One year only
NUMBER OF AWARDS: 2
DEADLINE FOR APPLICATIONS: October 1

CODE: BC/BRI105/u
NAME: PEO Sisterhood Chapter B
    Bursary for the Blind
PROGRAM: Any degree program
BASIS: Awarded to a blind woman
    who is beginning or continuing her
    studies at UBC in a full course load
    leading to a degree. Awarded on
    the recommendation of the Crane
    Library. Academic standing and
    financial need will be considered.
MINIMUM AVERAGE: N/A
VALUE: $500.00
TERMS: One year only
NUMBER OF AWARDS: 1
DEADLINE FOR APPLICATIONS: October
    15

CODE: BC/BRI106/u
NAME: Percy W. Perris Salmon Arm
    Scholarship
PROGRAM: Any ·
BASIS: Awarded to a student entering
    or continuing studies at UBC
    whose home is in School District
    No. 89 (Shuswap). The selection is
    made on the basis of academic
    standing, personal qualities, and
    financial need.
MINIMUM AVERAGE: 75.00
VALUE: $1350.00
TERMS: One year only
NUMBER OF AWARDS: 1
DEADLINE FOR APPLICATIONS: May 15

CODE: BC/BRI107/u
NAME: Elwood Peskett Memorial
    Bursary
PROGRAM: Any
BASIS: Awarded to a student whose
    home is in School District No. 15
    (Penticton, Kaleden, Naramata)
    and who has satisfactory academic
    standing, participates actively in
    athletics, and needs financial assist-
    ance.
MINIMUM AVERAGE: N/A
VALUE: $400.00
TERMS: One year only
NUMBER OF AWARDS: 1
DEADLINE FOR APPLICATIONS: June 30

CODE: BC/BRI108/u
NAME: Sperry Phillips Memorial Bursary
PROGRAM: Faculty of Agricultural Sciences or the School of Family and Nutritional Sciences
BASIS: Awarded to a student on the basis of academic ability, 4-H membership, and financial need. The application submitted should contain full details regarding partcipation in 4-H Club activites and school and community affairs.
MINIMUM AVERAGE: N/A
VALUE: $700.00
TERMS: One year only
NUMBER OF AWARDS: 1
DEADLINE FOR APPLICATIONS: June 30

CODE: BC/BRI109/u
NAME: John Oliver Piercy Memorial Scholarship
PROGRAM: Any
BASIS: Awarded to a student from northern or central Vancouver Island (School Districts 69-72, 84, and 85) with preference given to a student entering UBC directly from Grade 12.
MINIMUM AVERAGE: 75.00
VALUE: $1500.00
TERMS: One year only
NUMBER OF AWARDS: 1
DEADLINE FOR APPLICATIONS: April 15

CODE: BC/BRI110/u
NAME: Marion Ricker Memorial Scholarship in Nursing
PROGRAM: Bachelor of Science in Nursing
BASIS: Awarded on the recommendation of the Director of the School of Nursing to a registered nurse who is entering or continuing a program leading to the degree of B.S.N. Preference is given to a mature student.
MINIMUM AVERAGE: 75.00
VALUE: $500.00
TERMS: One year only
NUMBER OF AWARDS: 1

CODE: BC/BRI111/u
NAME: Joseph P. Ruffel Scholarship in Science
PROGRAM: Faculty of Science
BASIS: Awarded to a male student beginning or continuing undergraduate or graduate studies in the Faculty of Science. It is awarded to the student who has an outstanding academic record and who shows promise of success in his chosen field.
MINIMUM AVERAGE: N/A
VALUE: $1850.00
TERMS: One year only
NUMBER OF AWARDS: 1
DEADLINE FOR APPLICATIONS: June 30

CODE: BC/BRI112/u
NAME: RCAF Veterans' Bursary
PROGRAM: Any
BASIS: These bursaries are available for RCAF Veterans of the War 1939–45 and for their dependents. Awards are made on the basis of scholastic standing and financial need.
MINIMUM AVERAGE: 75.00
VALUE: $1750.00 (total)
TERMS: One year only
NUMBER OF AWARDS: Several bursaries will be awarded.

CODE: BC/BRI113/u
NAME: Nancy Ryckman Scholarship
PROGRAM: Any
BASIS: Awarded to students who have completed at least one year at a college or university and who attended high school in the East Kootenays. Awarded on the basis of character and intellectual promise.
MINIMUM AVERAGE: 75.00
VALUE: $1500.00
TERMS: One year only
NUMBER OF AWARDS: Varies
DEADLINE FOR APPLICATIONS: May 15

CODE: BC/BRI114/u
NAME: St Philip's Anglican Church Bursary

PROGRAM: Any
BASIS: Awarded to Native Indian students. Preference is given to Nonstatus Indians.
MINIMUM AVERAGE: N/A
VALUE: $2300.00
TERMS: One year only
NUMBER OF AWARDS: Varies
DEADLINE FOR APPLICATIONS: June 30

CODE: BC/BRI115/u
NAME: Sikh Students' Association Scholarship
PROGRAM: Any
BASIS: Awarded to an undergraduate student in financial need.
MINIMUM AVERAGE: 75.00
VALUE: $400.00
TERMS: One year only
NUMBER OF AWARDS: 1
DEADLINE FOR APPLICATIONS: May 15

CODE: BC/BRI116/u
NAME: Terminal City Club Memorial Scholarship
PROGRAM: Any
BASIS: Awarded to sons or daughters of members or employees of the Club who are beginning or continuing their studies at UBC.
MINIMUM AVERAGE: 75.00
VALUE: $500.00
TERMS: One year only
NUMBER OF AWARDS: 1
DEADLINE FOR APPLICATIONS: May 15

CODE: BC/BRI117/u
NAME: David Thom Scholarship
PROGRAM: Faculty of Agriculture
BASIS: There is one award for the student who has passed Grade 12 with the highest standing and who is registered for the 1st time in the Faculty of Agriculture. Awarded on the recommendation of the Faculty.
MINIMUM AVERAGE: 75.00
VALUE: $450.00
TERMS: One year only. There are other scholarships in the later years of undergraduate study.
NUMBER OF AWARDS: 1

CODE: BC/BRI118/u
NAME: Truck Loggers Association Scholarship
PROGRAM: Forestry
BASIS: These scholarships are awarded to students entering 1st-year Forestry with high standing who are worthy and deserving of encouragement and assistance. Awarded on the recommendation of the Faculty.
MINIMUM AVERAGE: 75.00
VALUE: $1000.00
TERMS: One year only
NUMBER OF AWARDS: 3

CODE: BC/BRI119/u
NAME: Chitose Uchida Memorial Prize
PROGRAM: Bachelor of Education Program
BASIS: Awarded on the recommendation of the Faculty of Education to a student entering the Bachelor of Education program with high standing in Arts courses.
MINIMUM AVERAGE: N/A
VALUE: $250.00
TERMS: One year only
NUMBER OF AWARDS: 1

CODE: BC/BRI120/u
NAME: U.S.A. Alumni Scholarship
PROGRAM: Any
BASIS: Awarded on the basis of academic standing and personal qualities to permanent residents of the United States. The special application form is available from: The President, Friends of UBC Inc., 1739 – 172 Place N.E., Bellevue, Washington, 98008, USA.
MINIMUM AVERAGE: 75.00
VALUE: $2500.00
TERMS: One year only
NUMBER OF AWARDS: 3
DEADLINE FOR APPLICATIONS: April 1

CODE: BC/BRI121/u
NAME: University of BC Alumni Southern California Scholarship
PROGRAM: Any

BASIS: Offered, with preference in the following order, to a student (a) whose home is in Southern California; (b) whose home is in the United States; (c) at the discretion of the University. Awarded on the basis of academic standing, personal qualities, and need.
MINIMUM AVERAGE: 75.00
VALUE: $500.00
TERMS: One year only
NUMBER OF AWARDS: 1
DEADLINE FOR APPLICATIONS: May 15

CODE: BC/BRI122/u
NAME: Vancouver Estonian Society Scholarship
PROGRAM: Any
BASIS: Awarded to a student beginning or continuing a course of study at UBC. Eligible candidates must be a member, or the son or daughter of a member, of the Vancouver Estonian Society. Academic standing, personal qualities, and need are considered.
MINIMUM AVERAGE: 75.00
VALUE: $200.00
TERMS: One year only
NUMBER OF AWARDS: 1
DEADLINE FOR APPLICATIONS: May 15

CODE: BC/BRI123/u
NAME: Vancouver Fire Fighters' Union Local No. 18 Bursary
PROGRAM: Any
BASIS: Awarded to a student beginning or continuing studies at UBC. The award is made to a physically disabled student who needs financial assistance.
MINIMUM AVERAGE: N/A
VALUE: $650.00
TERMS: One year only
NUMBER OF AWARDS: 1
DEADLINE FOR APPLICATIONS: October 15

CODE: BC/BRI124/u
NAME: Harold Anderson White Scholarship

PROGRAM: Any
BASIS: Awarded to a student of the Protestant faith beginning or continuing studies at UBC from Grade 12, from a secondary school in School District No. 1 (Fernie).
MINIMUM AVERAGE: 75.00
VALUE: $5000.00
TERMS: Renewable for a further 3 years of study at UBC subject to continued satisfactory academic performance.
NUMBER OF AWARDS: 1
DEADLINE FOR APPLICATIONS: May 15

CODE: BC/BRI125/u
NAME: Edmond T. Wong Bursaries
PROGRAM: Any
BASIS: Awarded to needy students with good academic averages who are proceeding from Grade 12 to a full course of study at UBC. These awards are offerd to graduates of Britannia Secondary School, Vancouver Technical Secondary School, and Templeton Secondary School.
MINIMUM AVERAGE: N/A
VALUE: $500.00
TERMS: One year only
NUMBER OF AWARDS: 4
DEADLINE FOR APPLICATIONS: June 15

CODE: BC/BRI126/u
NAME: Amy Woodland Scholarship
PROGRAM: Any
BASIS: Awarded to academically worthy and deserving students who have, for at least 2 years, attended the Amy Woodland Elementary School, Pinewood Elementary School, or Steeples Elementary School at Cranbrook. Candidates should contact the School Trustees for applications.
MINIMUM AVERAGE: N/A
VALUE: $600.00
TERMS: One year only
NUMBER OF AWARDS: 2
DEADLINE FOR APPLICATIONS: April 15

CODE: BC/BRI127/u
NAME: World University Service of Canada Bursary
PROGRAM: Any
BASIS: Awarded to a student refugee on the recommendation of the World University Service of Canada, UBC Local Committee.
MINIMUM AVERAGE: N/A
VALUE: $4000.00
TERMS: One year only. Awarded to defray the costs of books and tuition.
NUMBER OF AWARDS: 1

CODE: BC/BRI128/u
NAME: Yates Memorial Scholarship Fund
PROGRAM: Any
BASIS: Awarded to promising and deserving candidates beginning or continuing studies at UBC who have high academic standing or financial need. First preference is given to veterans of World War Two, then to their sons, daughters, and grandchildren.
MINIMUM AVERAGE: 75.00
VALUE: $2500.00
TERMS: One year only
NUMBER OF AWARDS: Varies
DEADLINE FOR APPLICATIONS: May 15

CODE: BC/BRI129/u
NAME: Katherine Ann Young Memorial Bursary
PROGRAM: Any
BASIS: Awarded to a student entering UBC from Grade 12. The award is intended to assist a promising student residing outside of the metropolitan areas of Vancouver or Victoria, who, without such assistance, would be unable to attend university.
MINIMUM AVERAGE: 75.00
VALUE: $600.00
TERMS: One year only
NUMBER OF AWARDS: 1
DEADLINE FOR APPLICATIONS: April 15

CODE: BC/BRI130/u
NAME: Zonta Club of Vancouver Bursary
PROGRAM: Any undergraduate or professional program
BASIS: Awarded to a student enrolled full-time in any undergraduate or professional program. The award is made to Canadian citizens or permanent residents who graduated from a BC high school.
MINIMUM AVERAGE: N/A
VALUE: $400.00
TERMS: One year only
NUMBER OF AWARDS: 1
DEADLINE FOR APPLICATIONS: October 15

CODE: BC/BRI131/u
NAME: Father David Bauer Scholarship (not administered by UBC)
PROGRAM: Any
BASIS: Awarded on the basis of academic ability, leadership qualities, and hockey ability to a BC resident entering UBC. Candidates should apply to the Father David Bauer Scholarship Committee, P.O. Box 10424, Pacific Centre, Suite 1300 – 777 Dunsmuir Street, Vancouver, BC V7Y 1K2.
MINIMUM AVERAGE: N/A
VALUE: $1000.00
TERMS: One year only. In the event there is no suitable candidate, the scholarship may be withheld.
NUMBER OF AWARDS: 1
DEADLINE FOR APPLICATIONS: July 1

CODE: BC/BRI132/u
NAME: Hongkong Bank Foundation Scholarship (not administered by UBC)
PROGRAM: Economics, Philosophy, or Political Science
BASIS: Awarded to a Hong Kong resident entering UBC to major in economics, philosophy, or political science. Applications are distributed in high schools in Hong Kong by the Foundation.

MINIMUM AVERAGE: 75.00
VALUE: Varies
TERMS: This is a 4-year scholarship that covers annual tuition costs, room, board, health insurance, round-trip excursion flight, and other expenses.
NUMBER OF AWARDS: 1

CODE: BC/BRI133/u
NAME: Worthington Memorial, IODE Bursary (not administered by UBC)
PROGRAM: Any
BASIS: Awarded to a member of the BC Regiment or the Cadet Corp of the BC Regiment who is beginning or continuing his or her studies at UBC. Financial need and service record will be considered. Candidates should apply to the Commanding Officer, BC Regiment.
MINIMUM AVERAGE: N/A
VALUE: $300.00
TERMS: One year only
NUMBER OF AWARDS: 1

Open Learning Agency

CODE: BC/OLA000/u
NAME: Open Learning Agency has no entrance awards.

Simon Fraser University

CODE: BC/SFU001/u
NAME: Simon Fraser Entrance Scholarships
PROGRAM: Any
BASIS: Awarded on the basis of excellent academic performance and potential to BC students entering full-time studies at SFU. The application must include a résumé, a 1000-word essay, 2 letters of recommendation, and a transcript of grades.
MINIMUM AVERAGE: 80.00
VALUE: $30,000.00
TERMS: The award is disbursed over 8 semesters, provided the recipient meets the renewal criteria.

NUMBER OF AWARDS: Varies
DEADLINE FOR APPLICATIONS: April 1

CODE: BC/SFU002/u
NAME: Simon Fraser Alumni Leadership Scholarship
PROGRAM: Any
BASIS: Awarded to students from BC entering SFU. The selection is based on extraordinary leadership, community service, citizenship, and high academic standing. An application is required.
MINIMUM AVERAGE: 80.00
VALUE: $25,000.00
TERMS: The award is disbursed over 8 semesters, provided the recipient meets the renewal criteria.
NUMBER OF AWARDS: Varies
DEADLINE FOR APPLICATIONS: April 1

CODE: BC/SFU003/u
NAME: Gordon M. Shrum Entrance Scholarships
PROGRAM: Any
BASIS: Awarded to BC students entering full-time studies at SFU. The selection is based on academic performance, commitment to school and community service, leadership, volunteer activity, music, the arts, or athletics. An application is required.
MINIMUM AVERAGE: 80.00
VALUE: $20,000.00
TERMS: The award is disbursed over 8 semesters, provided the recipient meets the renewal criteria.
NUMBER OF AWARDS: Varies
DEADLINE FOR APPLICATIONS: April 1

CODE: BC/SFU004/u
NAME: BC Regional Summit Scholarships
PROGRAM: Any
BASIS: Awarded on the basis of academic excellence to outstanding BC students entering SFU from each BC college region. An application is required.
MINIMUM AVERAGE: 80.00

VALUE: $3000.00
TERMS: The award is disbursed over 2 semesters, provided the recipient meets the renewal criteria.
NUMBER OF AWARDS: Varies
DEADLINE FOR APPLICATIONS: April 1

CODE: BC/SFU005/u
NAME: Summit Scholarships
PROGRAM: Any
BASIS: Awarded to outstanding BC applicants in recognition of academic excellence. An application is required.
MINIMUM AVERAGE: 80.00
VALUE: $3000.00
TERMS: Prizes are disbursed over 2 semesters.
NUMBER OF AWARDS: Varies
DEADLINE FOR APPLICATIONS: April 14

CODE: BC/SFU006/u
NAME: Jack Diamond Scholarships
PROGRAM: Any
BASIS: Awarded on the basis of academic and athletic excellence to BC students entering SFU. An application is required. Potential candidates are identified by SFU and nominated by the Director of Athletics.
MINIMUM AVERAGE: 80.00
VALUE: $3000.00
TERMS: The award is disbursed over 2 semesters, provided the recipient meets the renewal criteria.
NUMBER OF AWARDS: Varies
DEADLINE FOR APPLICATIONS: April 1

CODE: BC/SFU007/u
NAME: Dean's Scholarships in Communication
PROGRAM: Applied Science
BASIS: Applicants must submit a personal statement about his/her technical, creative, or management experience in communication. The statement should include school and/or extra-school experience related to communication.

MINIMUM AVERAGE: 80.00
VALUE: $6000.00
TERMS: The award is disbursed over 4 semesters, provided the recipient meets the renewal criteria.
NUMBER OF AWARDS: Varies
DEADLINE FOR APPLICATIONS: April 1

CODE: BC/SFU008/u
NAME: Dean's Scholarship in Computer Sciences
PROGRAM: Faculty of Applied Sciences – Computing Sciences
BASIS: Awarded to academically promising BC secondary school graduates entering the Faculty of Arts at SFU. The application must include principal's nomination, 2 letters of reference, an autobiographical essay, and a 1000–1500-word essay.
MINIMUM AVERAGE: 80.00
VALUE: $6000.00
TERMS: The award is disbursed over 4 semesters, provided the recipient meets the renewal criteria. Winners may also be considered for a Canada Scholarship.
NUMBER OF AWARDS: Varies
DEADLINE FOR APPLICATIONS: April 1

CODE: BC/SFU009/u
NAME: Paul Cote Scholarship in Engineering Science
PROGRAM: Faculty of Engineering Sciences
BASIS: The application for this scholarship must include a transcript of marks, 2 letter of recommendation, and a 1500-word personal statement.
MINIMUM AVERAGE: 80.00
VALUE: $6000.00
TERMS: The award is disbursed over 4 semesters, provided the recipient meets the renewal criteria. Winners of this scholarship may be considered for a Canada Scholarship.
NUMBER OF AWARDS: Varies
DEADLINE FOR APPLICATIONS: April 1

CODE: BC/SFU010/u
NAME: Dean's Scholarship in Kinesiology
PROGRAM: Faculty of Applied Sciences – Kinesiology
BASIS: Awarded to academically promising BC secondary school graduates entering the Faculty of Arts at SFU. The application must include principal's nomination, 2 letters of reference, an autobiographical essay, and a 300-word essay.
MINIMUM AVERAGE: 80.00
VALUE: $6000.00
TERMS: The award is disbursed over 4 semesters, provided the recipient meets the renewal criteria.
NUMBER OF AWARDS: Varies
DEADLINE FOR APPLICATIONS: April 1

CODE: BC/SFU011/u
NAME: Dean's Scholarship in Archaeology
PROGRAM: Faculty of Arts – Archaeology
BASIS: Awarded to academically promising BC secondary school graduates entering the Faculty of Arts at SFU. The application must include principal's nomination, 2 letters of reference, an autobiographical essay, and a 1500-word subject essay.
MINIMUM AVERAGE: 80.00
VALUE: $6000.00
TERMS: The award is disbursed over 4 semesters, provided the recipient meets the renewal criteria.
NUMBER OF AWARDS: Varies
DEADLINE FOR APPLICATIONS: April 1

CODE: BC/SFU012/u
NAME: Dean's Promising Artist Scholarships in Fine and Performing Arts
PROGRAM: Faculty of Arts: Dance, Film, Music, Theatre, Visual Arts, or Interdisciplinary study
BASIS: Awarded to academically promising BC secondary school graduates entering SFU. The application must include principal's nomination, 2 letters of reference, an autobiographical essay, and a 1000–1500-word essay. Evidence of creative/critical ability is required.
MINIMUM AVERAGE: 80.00
VALUE: $6000.00
TERMS: The award is disbursed over 4 semesters, provided the recipient meets the renewal criteria.
NUMBER OF AWARDS: Varies
DEADLINE FOR APPLICATIONS: April 1

CODE: BC/SFU013/u
NAME: Dean's Ezzat A. Fattah Scholarship in Criminology
PROGRAM: Faculty of Arts – Criminology
BASIS: Awarded to academically promising BC secondary school graduates entering the Faculty of Arts at SFU. The application must include principal's nomination, 2 letters of reference, an autobiographical essay, and a 1000-word subject essay.
MINIMUM AVERAGE: 80.00
VALUE: $6000.00
TERMS: The award is disbursed over 4 semesters, provided the recipient meets the renewal criteria.
NUMBER OF AWARDS: Varies
DEADLINE FOR APPLICATIONS: April 1

CODE: BC/SFU014/u
NAME: Dean's Scholarship in Economics
PROGRAM: Faculty of Arts – Economics
BASIS: Awarded to academically promising BC secondary school graduates entering the Faculty of Arts at SFU. The application must include principal's nomination, 2 letters of reference, an autobiographical essay, and a 1500-word subject essay.
MINIMUM AVERAGE: 80.00
VALUE: $6000.00

TERMS: The award is disbursed over 4 semesters, provided the recipient meets the renewal criteria.
NUMBER OF AWARDS: Varies
DEADLINE FOR APPLICATIONS: April 1

CODE: BC/SFU015/u
NAME: Dean's Scholarship in English
PROGRAM: Faculty of Arts English
BASIS: Awarded to academically promising BC secondary school graduates entering the Faculty of Arts at SFU. The application must include principal's nomination, 2 letters of reference, an autobiographical essay, and a 1500-word subject essay.
MINIMUM AVERAGE: 80.00
VALUE: $6000.00
TERMS: The award is disbursed over 4 semesters, provided the recipient meets the renewal criteria.
NUMBER OF AWARDS: Varies
DEADLINE FOR APPLICATIONS: April 1

CODE: BC/SFU016/u
NAME: Dean's Genevieve Bird Scholarship in French
PROGRAM: Faculty of Arts – French
BASIS: Awarded to academically promising BC students. The application must include principal's nomination, 2 letters of reference, an autobiographical essay, a cassette tape of the applicant reading a French prose passage, an exam, and 2 essays.
MINIMUM AVERAGE: 3.50
VALUE: $6000.00
TERMS: The award is disbursed over 4 semesters, provided the recipient meets the renewal criteria.
NUMBER OF AWARDS: Varies
DEADLINE FOR APPLICATIONS: April 1

CODE: BC/SFU017/u
NAME: Dean's Archie MacPherson Scholarship in Geography
PROGRAM: Faculty of Arts – Geography
BASIS: Awarded to academically promising BC secondary school graduates entering the Faculty of Arts at SFU. The application must include principal's nomination, 2 letters of reference, an autobiographical essay, and a 1500-word subject essay.
MINIMUM AVERAGE: 80.00
VALUE: $6000.00
TERMS: The award is disbursed over 4 semesters, provided the recipient meets the renewal criteria.
NUMBER OF AWARDS: Varies
DEADLINE FOR APPLICATIONS: April 1

CODE: BC/SFU018/u
NAME: Dean's Amelia Douglas Scholarship in History
PROGRAM: Faculty of Arts – History
BASIS: Awarded to academically promising BC secondary school graduates entering the Faculty of Arts at SFU. The application must include principal's nomination, 2 letters of reference, an autobiographical essay, and a 1500-word subject essay.
MINIMUM AVERAGE: 80.00
VALUE: $6000.00
TERMS: The award is disbursed over 4 semesters, provided the recipient meets the renewal criteria.
NUMBER OF AWARDS: Varies
DEADLINE FOR APPLICATIONS: April 1

CODE: BC/SFU019/u
NAME: Dean's Franz Boas Scholarship in Linguistics
PROGRAM: Faculty of Arts – Linguistics
BASIS: Awarded to academically promising BC secondary school graduates entering the Faculty of Arts at SFU. The application must include principal's nomination, 2 letters of reference, an autobiographical essay, and a 1500-word subject essay.
MINIMUM AVERAGE: 80.00
VALUE: $6000.00
TERMS: The award is disbursed over 4 semesters, provided the recipient meets the renewal criteria.

NUMBER OF AWARDS: Varies
DEADLINE FOR APPLICATIONS: April 1

CODE: BC/SFU020/u
NAME: Dean's Scholarship in Philosophy
PROGRAM: Faculty of Arts – Philosophy
BASIS: Awarded to academically promising BC secondary school graduates entering the Faculty of Arts at SFU. The application must include principal's nomination, 2 letters of reference, an autobiographical essay, and a 1500-word subject essay.
MINIMUM AVERAGE: 80.00
VALUE: $6000.00
TERMS: The award is disbursed over 4 semesters, provided the recipient meets the renewal criteria. Not tenable with other SFU scholarships.
NUMBER OF AWARDS: Varies
DEADLINE FOR APPLICATIONS: April 1

CODE: BC/SFU021/u
NAME: Dean's Scholarship in Political Science
PROGRAM: Faculty of Arts – Political Science
BASIS: Awarded to academically promising BC secondary school graduates entering the Faculty of Arts at SFU. The application must include principal's nomination, 2 letters of reference, an autobiographical essay, and a 1500-word subject essay.
MINIMUM AVERAGE: 80.00
VALUE: $6000.00
TERMS: The award is disbursed over 8 semesters, provided the recipient meets the renewal criteria.
NUMBER OF AWARDS: Varies
DEADLINE FOR APPLICATIONS: April 1

CODE: BC/SFU022/u
NAME: Dean's Scholarship in Sociology and Anthropology
PROGRAM: Faculty of Arts – Sociology and Anthropology
BASIS: Awarded to academically promising BC secondary school graduates entering the Faculty of Arts at SFU. The application must include principal's nomination, 2 letters of reference, an autobiographical essay, and a 1500-word subject essay.
MINIMUM AVERAGE: 80.00
VALUE: $6000.00
TERMS: The award is disbursed over 4 semesters, provided the recipient meets the renewal criteria.
NUMBER OF AWARDS: Varies
DEADLINE FOR APPLICATIONS: April 1

CODE: BC/SFU023/u
NAME: Dean's Captain Quadra Scholarship in Spanish
PROGRAM: Faculty of Arts – Spanish
BASIS: Awarded to academically promising BC secondary school graduates entering the Faculty of Arts at SFU. The application must include principal's nomination, 2 letters of reference, an autobiographical essay, and a 1500-word essay in English, French, or Spanish.
MINIMUM AVERAGE: 80.00
VALUE: $6000.00
TERMS: The award is disbursed over 4 semesters, provided the recipient meets the renewal criteria.
NUMBER OF AWARDS: Varies
DEADLINE FOR APPLICATIONS: April 1

CODE: BC/SFU024/u
NAME: Dean's Helena Gutteridge Scholarship in Women's Studies
PROGRAM: Faculty of Arts – Women's Studies
BASIS: Awarded to academically promising BC secondary school graduates entering the Faculty of Arts at SFU. The application must include principal's nomination, 2 letters of reference, an autobiographical essay, and a 1500-word essay.
MINIMUM AVERAGE: 80.00
VALUE: $6000.00
TERMS: The award is disbursed over 4

semesters, provided the recipient meets the renewal criteria.
NUMBER OF AWARDS: Varies
DEADLINE FOR APPLICATIONS: April 1

CODE: BC/SFU025/u
NAME: Dean's Entrance Scholarships in the Faculty of Business Administration
PROGRAM: Business Administration
BASIS: Awarded to academically promising BC students who excel in Business Administration. A 500-word essay is required with the application.
MINIMUM AVERAGE: 80.00
VALUE: $6000.00
TERMS: The award is disbursed over 4 semesters, provided the recepient meets the renewal criteria.
NUMBER OF AWARDS: Varies
DEADLINE FOR APPLICATIONS: April 14

CODE: BC/SFU026/u
NAME: P.D. McTaggart-Cowan Scholarships in Biology
PROGRAM: Biology
BASIS: Awarded on the basis of applicant's 300-word essay that indicates his/her interest in Biology, personal goals, and objectives. Selected candidates will be interviewed.
MINIMUM AVERAGE: 80.00
VALUE: $6000.00
TERMS: The award is disbursed over 4 semesters, provided the recipient meets the renewal criteria.
NUMBER OF AWARDS: Varies
DEADLINE FOR APPLICATIONS: April 1

CODE: BC/SFU027/u
NAME: P.D. McTaggart-Cowan Scholarships in Chemistry
PROGRAM: Chemistry
BASIS: Awarded on the basis of a 300-word essay that describes the applicant's interest in Chemistry and the results of the SFU Prize Examination in Chemistry.
MINIMUM AVERAGE: 80.00
VALUE: $6000.00

TERMS: The award will be disbursed over 4 semesters.
NUMBER OF AWARDS: Varies
DEADLINE FOR APPLICATIONS: April 1

CODE: BC/SFU028/u
NAME: P.D. McTaggart-Cowan Scholarships in Mathematics
PROGRAM: Mathematics
BASIS: Awarded on the basis of a 300-word essay describing the applicant's interest in Mathematics, personal goals, and career objectives. In addition, the results of the American High School Mathematics Examination (AHSME) will be considered.
MINIMUM AVERAGE: 80.00
VALUE: $6000.00
TERMS: The award is disbursed over 4 semesters, provided the recipient meets the renewal criteria.
NUMBER OF AWARDS: Varies
DEADLINE FOR APPLICATIONS: April 1

CODE: BC/SFU029/u
NAME: P.D. McTaggart-Cowan Scholarships in Physics
PROGRAM: Physics
BASIS: Awarded on the basis of a 300-word essay outlining interest in Physics and personal goals. The results of the Canadian Association of Physicists (CAP) Examination will also be considered.
MINIMUM AVERAGE: 80.00
VALUE: $6000.00
TERMS: These scholarships will be disbursed over 4 semesters, provided the recipient meets the renewal criteria.
NUMBER OF AWARDS: Varies
DEADLINE FOR APPLICATIONS: April 1

CODE: BC/SFU030/u
NAME: Dean's Scholarship in Management and Systems Science
PROGRAM: Faculty of Science – Management and Systems Science
BASIS: The candidates should have an A grade on the Algebra 12 exam or

Geometry, Calculus, Statistics, or Computing Science subjects, or high performance on the AHSME or Euclid exam. A 500-word essay and letters of recommendation are required.
MINIMUM AVERAGE: 80.00
VALUE: $6000.00
TERMS: The award is disbursed over 4 semesters, provided the recipient meets the renewal criteria. Winners may also be considered for a Canada Scholarship.
NUMBER OF AWARDS: Varies
DEADLINE FOR APPLICATIONS: April 1

CODE: BC/SFU031/u
NAME: Gordon M. Shrum National Scholarships
PROGRAM: Any
BASIS: Awarded to Canadian citizens or permanent residents who are entering SFU from outside BC. The application must include transcripts, referees reports, an autobiographical essay, and a résumé. Academic performance, community service, and ability in music, art, and athletics are considered.
MINIMUM AVERAGE: 80.00
VALUE: $20,000.00
TERMS: The awards will be disbursed over 8 semesters, provided the recipients meet the renewal criteria. BC residents are not eligible for this award.
NUMBER OF AWARDS: Varies
DEADLINE FOR APPLICATIONS: April 1

CODE: BC/SFU032/u
NAME: Kenneth Strand National Scholarship
PROGRAM: Any
BASIS: Awarded to Canadian citizens or permanent residents who are entering SFU from outside BC. The application must include transcripts, referees reports, an autobiographical essay, and a résumé. The selection is based on academic excellence.

MINIMUM AVERAGE: 80.00
VALUE: $3000.00
TERMS: The awards will be disbursed over 2 semesters, provided the recipients meet the renewal criteria. BC residents are not eligible for this award.
NUMBER OF AWARDS: Varies
DEADLINE FOR APPLICATIONS: April 1

CODE: BC/SFU033/u
NAME: Jack Diamond National Entrance Scholarships
PROGRAM: Any
BASIS: Awarded to Canadian citizens or permanent residents who are entering SFU from outside BC. The selection is based on academic and athletic excellence. Potential candidates for this award are identified by SFU and nominated by the Director of Athletics.
MINIMUM AVERAGE: 80.00
VALUE: $3000.00
TERMS: The awards will be disbursed over 2 semesters, provided the recipients meet the renewal criteria.
NUMBER OF AWARDS: Varies
DEADLINE FOR APPLICATIONS: April 1

CODE: BC/SFU034/u
NAME: Honourable William M. Hamilton Scholarship
PROGRAM: Any
BASIS: Awarded to Canadian citizens or permanent residents who are transfering to SFU from a College or Institute. The application must include transcripts, referees reports, an autobiographical essay, and a résumé. Leadership and academic potential will be considered.
MINIMUM AVERAGE: 80.00
VALUE: $10,000.00
TERMS: The awards will be disbursed over 4 semesters, provided the recipients meet the renewal criteria.
NUMBER OF AWARDS: 4
DEADLINE FOR APPLICATIONS: April 1

CODE: BC/SFU035/u
NAME: Ken Caple Scholarships
PROGRAM: Any
BASIS: Awarded to Canadian citizens or permanent residents who are transfering to SFU from a College or Institute. The application must include transcripts, referees reports, an autobiographical essay, and a résumé. Academic perfomance will be considered.
MINIMUM AVERAGE: 80.00
VALUE: $3000.00
TERMS: The awards will be disbursed over 2 semesters, provided the recipients meet the renewal criteria.
NUMBER OF AWARDS: Varies
DEADLINE FOR APPLICATIONS: April 1

Trinity Western University

CODE: BC/TWU001/u
NAME: President's Scholarships
PROGRAM: Any
BASIS: Awarded to entering students on the basis of academic achievement in the best 6 subjects, 4 of which must be Grade 12 academic courses. The President's Awards application form is available from the TWU Financial Aid Office.
MINIMUM AVERAGE: 80.00
VALUE: $8000.00
TERMS: Renewable for 3 more years at $2000 per year.
NUMBER OF AWARDS: 20
DEADLINE FOR APPLICATIONS: April 15

CODE: BC/TWU002/u
NAME: President's Leadership Award
PROGRAM: Any
BASIS: Awarded on the basis of academic achievement in the best 6 subjects, 4 of which must be Grade 12 academic courses. Applicants must have leadership potential and/or experience. The President's Awards application form is available from the TWU Financial Aid Office.
MINIMUM AVERAGE: 75.00
VALUE: $2000.00
TERMS: One year only. The award is half tuition and half residence.
NUMBER OF AWARDS: 20
DEADLINE FOR APPLICATIONS: April 15

CODE: BC/TWU003/u
NAME: Trinity Western Entrance Scholarship
PROGRAM: Any
BASIS: Awarded to entering students on the basis of academic achievement. Application forms are available from the TWU Financial Aid Office. A transcript of grades is required.
MINIMUM AVERAGE: 75.00
VALUE: $500.00 maximum
TERMS: One year only
NUMBER OF AWARDS: Depends on the funds available.
DEADLINE FOR APPLICATIONS: April 1

CODE: BC/TWU004/u
NAME: Trinity Western Academic Scholarship
PROGRAM: Any
BASIS: Awarded to entering students on the basis of academic achievement. Application forms are available from the TWU Financial Aid Office.
MINIMUM AVERAGE: 75.00
VALUE: $500.00 maximum
TERMS: One year only
NUMBER OF AWARDS: Depends on the funds available.
DEADLINE FOR APPLICATIONS: March 1

CODE: BC/TWU005/u
NAME: Christian Ministries Bursary
PROGRAM: Any
BASIS: Awarded to applicants who are involved in full-time Christian work or have parents who are. Application forms are available from the Financial Aid Office.
MINIMUM AVERAGE: 75.00
VALUE: $500.00
TERMS: One year only

NUMBER OF AWARDS: Depends on the funds available.

DEADLINE FOR APPLICATIONS: April 1

CODE: BC/TWU006/u
NAME: Trinity Western Bursary
PROGRAM: Any
BASIS: Awarded to applicants on the basis of financial need. Application forms are available from the Financial Aid Office.
MINIMUM AVERAGE: 60.00
VALUE: $1200.00
TERMS: One year only. Amount may vary.
NUMBER OF AWARDS: Depends on the funds available.
DEADLINE FOR APPLICATIONS: April 1

University of Northern British Columbia

CODE: BC/UNBC01/u
NAME: Entrance Awards
PROGRAM: Various
BASIS: The University of Northern British Columbia is the first new university in Canada in 25 years. It is expected to offer scholarships and bursaries.
MINIMUM AVERAGE: N/A
VALUE: N/A
TERMS: UNBC is currently developing an entrance scholarship program.
NUMBER OF AWARDS: N/A

University of Victoria

CODE: BC/VIC001/u
NAME: President's Entrance Scholarships
PROGRAM: Any.
BASIS: Awarded to British Columbia secondary school graduates who are entering U Vic. Recipients will have achieved a total score of 2000 or higher on their best 3 Provincial Scholarship examinations.
MINIMUM AVERAGE: 80.00
VALUE: $2500.00

TERMS: One year only
NUMBER OF AWARDS: 20
DEADLINE FOR APPLICATIONS: April 15

CODE: BC/VIC002/u
NAME: President's Regional Entrance Scholarships
PROGRAM: Any
BASIS: Four scholarships are awarded within each college region of BC to students with high academic standing and broad interests who are entering U Vic. directly from BC secondary schools or regional colleges. An application is required. Applicants from a regional college must include transcripts of interim and final marks.
MINIMUM AVERAGE: 80.00
VALUE: $2000.00
TERMS: One year only
NUMBER OF AWARDS: 60
DEADLINE FOR APPLICATIONS: April 15

CODE: BC/VIC003/u
NAME: David Brousson Entrance Scholarship
PROGRAM: Any
BASIS: Awarded to a student entering U Vic. directly from a BC secondary school or regional college. The selection is based on academic achievement.
MINIMUM AVERAGE: 80.00
VALUE: $2000.00
TERMS: One year only
NUMBER OF AWARDS: 1
DEADLINE FOR APPLICATIONS: April 15

CODE: BC/VIC004/u
NAME: Ralph Barbour Burry Memorial Scholarship in Music
PROGRAM: Music
BASIS: Awarded to Music students on the basis of excellence in music. In the case of two equally gifted candidates, need will be the determining factor. The selection is made by the Senate Committee on Awards upon the recommendation of the School of Music.

MINIMUM AVERAGE: N/A
VALUE: $800.00
TERMS: One year only. Amount of awards may vary.
NUMBER OF AWARDS: 3
DEADLINE FOR APPLICATIONS: April 15

CODE: BC/VIC005/u
NAME: L. and G. Butler Scholarship for the Disabled
PROGRAM: Any
BASIS: Awarded on the basis of academic performance to a disabled student entering or continuing studies at U Vic. Application forms may be obtained from the Office of the Administrative Registrar.
MINIMUM AVERAGE: 80.00
VALUE: $650.00
TERMS: One year only
NUMBER OF AWARDS: 1
DEADLINE FOR APPLICATIONS: April 15

CODE: BC/VIC006/u
NAME: Canadian Union of Public Employees Scholarships
PROGRAM: Any
BASIS: Open to the sons and daughters of members of contributing locals of CUPE of the Greater Victoria area entering 1st year at U Vic. The selection is based on academic standing. An application is required.
MINIMUM AVERAGE: 80.00
VALUE: $300.00
TERMS: One year only
NUMBER OF AWARDS: 1
DEADLINE FOR APPLICATIONS: August 31

CODE: BC/VIC007/u
NAME: C.H. Dowling Memorial Award
PROGRAM: Humanities or Social Sciences
BASIS: Awarded to a Native Indian student who is a resident of BC and is entering U Vic. directly from Grade 12 or a regional college. The

selection is made on the basis of scholastic achievement.
MINIMUM AVERAGE: 80.00
VALUE: $500.00
TERMS: One year only
NUMBER OF AWARDS: 1
DEADLINE FOR APPLICATIONS: April 15

CODE: BC/VIC008/u
NAME: Gertrude Huntly Durand Memorial Scholarship
PROGRAM: Music
BASIS: Awarded to a piano student in any year of the Bachelor of Music program who has demonstrated potential in the areas of accompanying or teaching. The selection is made by the Senate Committee on Awards upon the recommendation of the School of Music.
MINIMUM AVERAGE: N/A
VALUE: $800.00
TERMS: One year only
NUMBER OF AWARDS: 1
DEADLINE FOR APPLICATIONS: April 15

CODE: BC/VIC009/u
NAME: Faculty of Engineering – Dean's Entrance Scholarships
PROGRAM: Faculty of Engineering
BASIS: Awarded to students of high academic standing who are entering the Faculty of Engineering at U Vic. directly from BC secondary schools or regional colleges.
MINIMUM AVERAGE: 80.00
VALUE: $2000.00
TERMS: One year only
NUMBER OF AWARDS: 1
DEADLINE FOR APPLICATIONS: April 15

CODE: BC/VIC010/u
NAME: Walter J. Fletcher Piano Scholarship
PROGRAM: Music
BASIS: Awarded to an outstanding student in any year of the Bachelor of Music program whose principal instrument is the piano. The selection is made by the Senate Committee on Awards upon the recom-

mendation of the School of Music. An audition is required.
MINIMUM AVERAGE: N/A
VALUE: $550.00
TERMS: One year only
NUMBER OF AWARDS: 1
DEADLINE FOR APPLICATIONS: April 15

CODE: BC/VIC011/u
NAME: Alyden Hamber IODE Entrance Scholarship
PROGRAM: Any
BASIS: Awarded to a deserving female student entering the 1st year at U Vic. Applicants must write the BC Scholarship examinations.
MINIMUM AVERAGE: 80.00
VALUE: $600.00
TERMS: One year only
NUMBER OF AWARDS: 1
DEADLINE FOR APPLICATIONS: April 15

CODE: BC/VIC012/u
NAME: Harbord Insurance Ltd Scholarship
PROGRAM: Music
BASIS: Awarded to the most promising scholar leaving School District No. 6 who intends to specialize in music. The selection is made by the Senate Committee on Awards upon the recommendation of the School of Music. An audition is required.
MINIMUM AVERAGE: N/A
VALUE: $1000.00
TERMS: One year only
NUMBER OF AWARDS: 1
DEADLINE FOR APPLICATIONS: April 15

CODE: BC/VIC013/u
NAME: Willard E. Ireland Entrance Scholarship
PROGRAM: Music
BASIS: Awarded to an outstanding student entering the School of Music at U Vic. The selection is made by the Senate Committee on Awards upon the recommendation of the School of Music after the auditions.
MINIMUM AVERAGE: N/A

VALUE: $1600.00
TERMS: One year only. Value may vary.
NUMBER OF AWARDS: 3
DEADLINE FOR APPLICATIONS: April 15

CODE: BC/VIC014/u
NAME: J.J. Johannesen Scholarship in Music Performance
PROGRAM: Music
BASIS: Awarded to music students from any part of the world demonstrating excellence and/or potential in performance, as soloists, in the areas of strings, piano, and flute. The selection is made upon the recommendation of the School of Music after the auditions.
MINIMUM AVERAGE: N/A
VALUE: $1500.00
TERMS: One year only. One or 2 awards of equal amounts up to a total of $1500 will be awarded annually.
NUMBER OF AWARDS: 3
DEADLINE FOR APPLICATIONS: April 15

CODE: BC/VIC015/u
NAME: Betty and Gilbert Kennedy Entrance Scholarship in Engineering
PROGRAM: Faculty of Engineering
BASIS: Awarded to an outstanding student entering the Faculty of Engineering from a BC secondary school or regional college.
MINIMUM AVERAGE: 80.00
VALUE: $2000.00
TERMS: One year only
NUMBER OF AWARDS: 1
DEADLINE FOR APPLICATIONS: April 15

CODE: BC/VIC016/u
NAME: Labatt Breweries of British Columbia Ltd Scholarship
PROGRAM: Any
BASIS: Awarded to a BC resident entering full-time studies at U Vic. directly from Grade 12. The selection is based upon scholastic standing, character, extracurricular activ-

ities, community service, and government scholarship examination results.
MINIMUM AVERAGE: 80.00
VALUE: $1000.00
TERMS: One year only
NUMBER OF AWARDS: 1
DEADLINE FOR APPLICATIONS: April 15

CODE: BC/VIC017/u
NAME: Alexander and Mary Mackenzie Entrance Scholarship
PROGRAM: Any
BASIS: Awarded to a student entering U Vic. who was involved in a secondary school or community anti-drug and alcohol program. A letter of recommendation from the program director must accompany the application.
MINIMUM AVERAGE: N/A
VALUE: $250.00
TERMS: One year only
NUMBER OF AWARDS: 1
DEADLINE FOR APPLICATIONS: April 15

CODE: BC/VIC018/u
NAME: Evelyn Marchant MacLaurin Memorial Scholarships in Music
PROGRAM: Music
BASIS: Awarded to outstanding students pursuing a degree in music. Preference will be given to newly admitted students entering the School of Music. The selection of recipients is made by the Senate Committee upon the recommendation of the School of Music.
MINIMUM AVERAGE: N/A
VALUE: $800.00
TERMS: One year only. Value of awards may vary.
NUMBER OF AWARDS: Varies
DEADLINE FOR APPLICATIONS: April 15

CODE: BC/VIC019/u
NAME: John Locke Malkin Entrance Scholarships
PROGRAM: Any
BASIS: Awarded to students of exceptional academic promise entering U Vic. from a secondary school or college. Candidates must apply in writing to the U Vic. Senate Committee on Awards or be nominated by their high schools.
MINIMUM AVERAGE: 80.00
VALUE: $22,500.00
TERMS: $4,500 per year for 5 years provided the recipient maintains a GPA of at least 7.0. Some scholarships may be worth $3000 per year.
NUMBER OF AWARDS: 6
DEADLINE FOR APPLICATIONS: March 15

CODE: BC/VIC020/u
NAME: T.S. McPherson Entrance Scholarships
PROGRAM: Any
BASIS: Awarded to students of exceptional promise entering U Vic. on the basis of BC Provincial Scholarship examinations, academic standing, breadth of interest, and leadership qualities. Candidates should apply directly to the Senate Committee on Awards.
MINIMUM AVERAGE: 80.00
VALUE: $12,000.00
TERMS: Renewable for $3000 per year provided a minimum GPA of 7.5 is maintained in a full program. Two of the scholarships will have a value of $4500.
NUMBER OF AWARDS: 10
DEADLINE FOR APPLICATIONS: March 15

CODE: BC/VIC021/u
NAME: George Nelms Memorial Scholarship
PROGRAM: Science
BASIS: Awarded to a student with high academic standing who is entering U Vic. directly from a secondary school or college in Northern British Columbia or the Peace River district of Alberta. The selection is based on academic achievement.
MINIMUM AVERAGE: N/A
VALUE: N/A
TERMS: One year only

NUMBER OF AWARDS: 1
DEADLINE FOR APPLICATIONS: April 15

CODE: BC/VIC022/u
NAME: 25th Olympiad Scholarship
PROGRAM: Any
BASIS: Awarded to a student entering U Vic. who has demonstrated a record of outstanding athletic achievements while maintaining a high academic standing. The application must include a letter of recommendation from the athlete's coach.
MINIMUM AVERAGE: 80.00
VALUE: $2000.00
TERMS: One year only
NUMBER OF AWARDS: 1
DEADLINE FOR APPLICATIONS: April 15

CODE: BC/VIC023/u
NAME: Performance Scholarship in Music
PROGRAM: Music
BASIS: Awarded to students for outstanding achievement in performance. The selection is made by the Senate Committee on Awards upon the recommendation of the School of Music. The selection is based on auditions.
MINIMUM AVERAGE: N/A
VALUE: N/A
TERMS: One year only
NUMBER OF AWARDS: Varies
DEADLINE FOR APPLICATIONS: April 15

CODE: BC/VIC024/u
NAME: Douglas Ross Memorial Scholarship
PROGRAM: Music
BASIS: Awarded to a new or returning student for outstanding achievement in piano performance. The selection is made by the Senate Committee on Awards upon the recommendation of the School of Music. The selection is based on an audition.
MINIMUM AVERAGE: N/A
VALUE: $425.00

TERMS: One year only
NUMBER OF AWARDS: 1
DEADLINE FOR APPLICATIONS: April 15

CODE: BC/VIC025/u
NAME: Herbert and Eva Schaefer String Scholarship
PROGRAM: Music
BASIS: Awarded to outstanding student(s) of violin, viola, cello, or double bass entering or continuing in the Music program at either the graduate or undergraduate level.
MINIMUM AVERAGE: N/A
VALUE: Value is equal to tuition.
NUMBER OF AWARDS: Number of awards may vary.
DEADLINE FOR APPLICATIONS: April 15

CODE: BC/VIC026/u
NAME: School of Physical Education Entrance Scholarship
PROGRAM: School of Physical Education
BASIS: Open to a student transferring into the School of Physical Education from a college or university. The selection of the recipient is made by the Senate Committee on Awards upon the recommendation of the Faculty of Education.
MINIMUM AVERAGE: 80.00
VALUE: $375.00
TERMS: One year only
NUMBER OF AWARDS: 1
DEADLINE FOR APPLICATIONS: April 15

CODE: BC/VIC027/u
NAME: Daisie Thirlwall Scholarships in Violin
PROGRAM: Music
BASIS: Awarded to gifted violinists who demonstrate excellence or potential in performance. In the case of two equally qualified candidates, need will be the determining factor. The selection is made by the Senate Committe on Awards after the auditions.
MINIMUM AVERAGE: N/A
VALUE: Varies

TERMS: One year only. Amounts of awards may vary. Other string instrumentalists may be considered if there are no qualified violinist candidates.
NUMBER OF AWARDS: 3
DEADLINE FOR APPLICATIONS: April 15

CODE: BC/VIC028/u
NAME: University of Victoria Entrance Scholarships
PROGRAM: Any
BASIS: Awarded to students with high academic standing who are entering U Vic. directly from BC secondary schools or regional colleges.
MINIMUM AVERAGE: 80.00
VALUE: $2000.00
TERMS: One year only
NUMBER OF AWARDS: 1
DEADLINE FOR APPLICATIONS: April 15

CODE: BC/VIC029/u
NAME: West Kootenay Power Scholarship
PROGRAM: Any
BASIS: Awarded to a student who is graduating from a secondary school in the West Kootenay Power service region. A candidate must demonstrate a record of extracurricular activities, community service, leadership, and sports. An application is required.
MINIMUM AVERAGE: 70.00
VALUE: $1500.00
TERMS: One year only
NUMBER OF AWARDS: 1
DEADLINE FOR APPLICATIONS: April 15

CODE: BC/VIC030/u
NAME: University of Victoria Science Fair Award
PROGRAM: Any
BASIS: The president of the University will award $500 to the student who presents the exhibit judged to be the best of those presented by senior students at the Vancouver Island Regional Science Fair.
MINIMUM AVERAGE: N/A

VALUE: $500.00
TERMS: One year only. The award is only tenable when and if the winner registers in a full-time program of studies at U Vic.
NUMBER OF AWARDS: 1

CODE: BC/VIC031/u
NAME: Brian Williams Memorial Scholarship
PROGRAM: Any
BASIS: Awarded to students entering U Vic. who intend to be involved in the University rugby program. Application forms may be obtained from the Office of the Administrative Registrar. A letter of reference from the rugby coach is required.
MINIMUM AVERAGE: 70.00
VALUE: $500.00
TERMS: One year only
NUMBER OF AWARDS: 3
DEADLINE FOR APPLICATIONS: April 15

CODE: BC/VIC032/u
NAME: Victoria Musical Arts Society Scholarship
PROGRAM: School of Music
BASIS: Awarded to an outstanding student, entering or continuing in the School of Music and intending to pursue a career in music. The student must have been a resident of the Greater Victoria area for at least 2 years.
MINIMUM AVERAGE: N/A
VALUE: $1500.00
TERMS: One year only. Previous recipients of this award are not permitted to reapply in subsequent years.
NUMBER OF AWARDS: 1
DEADLINE FOR APPLICATIONS: April 15

MANITOBA

Brandon University

CODE: MB/BRN001/u
NAME: R.D. Bell String Scholarships
PROGRAM: Music (full-time studies)
BASIS: Awarded to outstanding orchestral string students entering any year of the Music program.
MINIMUM AVERAGE: 80.00
VALUE: Varies
TERMS: Scholarships include part of the cost of tuition and for some students, the travel expenses to Brandon University.
NUMBER OF AWARDS: Varies
DEADLINE FOR APPLICATIONS: May 1

CODE: MB/BRN002/u
NAME: Beta Sigma Phi Entrance Scholarship
PROGRAM: Any
BASIS: Awarded to a female student who has achieved excellent high school standing in the year immediately prior to admission to full-time studies at Brandon U. Application forms are available from the Awards Office.
MINIMUM AVERAGE: N/A
VALUE: $1000.00
TERMS: This scholarship will not be given to a student who has received any other entrance award.
NUMBER OF AWARDS: 1
DEADLINE FOR APPLICATIONS: May 1

CODE: MB/BRN003/u
NAME: Procop and Dora Bilous Memorial Scholarship
PROGRAM: Political Science
BASIS: Awarded to a student entering Brandon U for the 1st time and enrolling in a 1st-year Political Science course or its equivalent. The selection is based on academic merit and financial need.
MINIMUM AVERAGE: 75.00
VALUE: $100.00
TERMS: One year only
NUMBER OF AWARDS: 1
DEADLINE FOR APPLICATIONS: May 1

CODE: MB/BRN004/u
NAME: Brandon University Board of Governors Entrance Scholarship
PROGRAM: Any
BASIS: Awarded to a student entering Brandon U in a 1st-year program. Applicants must submit to the Awards Office an application for admission, a scholarship application form, and an official transcript of marks for the last 2 years of high school.
MINIMUM AVERAGE: 80.00
VALUE: Varies
TERMS: One year only
NUMBER OF AWARDS: Varies
DEADLINE FOR APPLICATIONS: May 1

CODE: MB/BRN005/u
NAME: Brandon University Entrance Scholarship to the Music Program
PROGRAM: Music program
BASIS: Awarded to a student entering the University Music program who demonstrates special ability in an audition at the School of Music. Scholarship auditions will be held in May. Application forms are available from the School of Music Secretary.
MINIMUM AVERAGE: 80.00
VALUE: $200.00
TERMS: One year only
NUMBER OF AWARDS: 1
DEADLINE FOR APPLICATIONS: April 1

CODE: MB/BRN006/u
NAME: Elizabeth Ann Bremner Award
PROGRAM: Geography
BASIS: Awarded to a graduate of Neepawa Area Collegiate who has

completed at least 2 Geography high school credits and is registering in Geography courses at Brandon U. The selection is made on the basis of academic merit and citizenship.

MINIMUM AVERAGE: 75.00
VALUE: $200.00
TERMS: One year only
NUMBER OF AWARDS: 1
DEADLINE FOR APPLICATIONS: April 1

CODE: MB/BRN007/u
NAME: James Christie Memorial Scholarship
PROGRAM: Any
BASIS: Awarded to a graduate of the Souris Collegiate who attends Brandon U in his/her graduating year. If no suitable candidate is available from Souris, the scholarship may be awarded to a southwestern Manitoba graduate.
MINIMUM AVERAGE: 75.00
VALUE: $1000.00
TERMS: Renewable in the 2nd year.
NUMBER OF AWARDS: 1
DEADLINE FOR APPLICATIONS: May 1

CODE: MB/BRN008/u
NAME: Sarah Harriet Hall Memorial Academic Scholarships
PROGRAM: B.A., B.Sc., B.Ed., B.Mus., and B.G.S.
BASIS: Awarded to the best student entering the 1st year of each of the following programs: B.A., B.Sc., B.Ed., B.Mus., and B.G.S., on the basis of academic excellence and proficiency in extracurricular activities. Letters of recommendation are required.
MINIMUM AVERAGE: 80.00
VALUE: Varies
TERMS: Renewable provided a full course load and a 3.50 GPA is maintained.
NUMBER OF AWARDS: 5
DEADLINE FOR APPLICATIONS: May 1

CODE: MB/BRN009/u
NAME: G.F. MacDowell Entrance Scholarships
PROGRAM: Any
BASIS: Awarded to students entering full-time 1st-year studies at Brandon U immediately following graduation from an accredited Canadian high school.
MINIMUM AVERAGE: 80.00
VALUE: $800.00
TERMS: One year only. Value varies.
NUMBER OF AWARDS: Varies
DEADLINE FOR APPLICATIONS: May 1

CODE: MB/BRN010/u
NAME: Professor G. MacNeill Memorial Scholarship
PROGRAM: Arts
BASIS: Awarded to a Province of Manitoba student entering the Arts program at Brandon U with the highest proficiency in a language or languages other than English in his/her Grade 12 studies.
MINIMUM AVERAGE: 80.00
VALUE: $800.00
TERMS: One year only
NUMBER OF AWARDS: 1
DEADLINE FOR APPLICATIONS: May 1

CODE: MB/BRN011/u
NAME: Masonic Past Masters' Association of Manitoba Entrance Scholarship
PROGRAM: Arts or Science
BASIS: Awarded to 2 students applying for admission to either the Faculty of Arts or the Faculty of Science who have high academic standing in high school and who have financial need.
MINIMUM AVERAGE: 80.00
VALUE: $200.00
TERMS: One year only
NUMBER OF AWARDS: 2
DEADLINE FOR APPLICATIONS: May 1

CODE: MB/BRN012/u
NAME: Orchard Memorial Entrance Scholarship

PROGRAM: Music
BASIS: Awarded to a student of outstanding promise entering one of the School of Music degree programs.
MINIMUM AVERAGE: 80.00
VALUE: $650.00
TERMS: One year only
NUMBER OF AWARDS: 1
DEADLINE FOR APPLICATIONS: May 1

CODE: MB/BRN013/u
NAME: Terry Penton Memorial Entrance Scholarship
PROGRAM: Any
BASIS: Awarded to a Grade 12 southwestern Manitoba high school graduate entering Brandon U. A letter of recommendation from the high school principal is required, testifying to the applicant's exemplary community service and proven ability.
MINIMUM AVERAGE: 75.00
VALUE: $1000.00
TERMS: One year only
NUMBER OF AWARDS: 1
DEADLINE FOR APPLICATIONS: May 1

CODE: MB/BRN014/u
NAME: Robbins Entrance Scholarships
PROGRAM: Any
BASIS: Awarded to students entering Brandon U on the basis of academic excellence, extracurricular activities and community service. Application forms are available from the Awards Office.
MINIMUM AVERAGE: 80.00
VALUE: $1000.00
TERMS: One year only
NUMBER OF AWARDS: 1
DEADLINE FOR APPLICATIONS: May 1

CODE: MB/BRN015/u
NAME: Carl and Lyle Sanders Scholarships in Music
PROGRAM: Music
BASIS: Awarded to students entering the music program. Scholarship auditions will take place in May.

Application forms are available from the Secretary, School of Music.
MINIMUM AVERAGE: N/A
VALUE: $400.00
TERMS: One year only
NUMBER OF AWARDS: 2
DEADLINE FOR APPLICATIONS: May 1

CODE: MB/BRN016/u
NAME: Simplot Canada Limited Entrance Scholarship
PROGRAM: Any
BASIS: Awarded to a student who has lived on a farm and/or has been actively involved in a farm operation in Manitoba or eastern Saskatchewan east of Highway #6. Two letters of reference must accompany the application form.
MINIMUM AVERAGE: 80.00
VALUE: $1000.00
TERMS: One year only
NUMBER OF AWARDS: 1
DEADLINE FOR APPLICATIONS: May 1

CODE: MB/BRN017/u
NAME: Simplot Canada Limited Scholarship
PROGRAM: Any
BASIS: Applicants must be children of Simplot Canada Ltd employees. The company's Scholarship Application form is available from the Awards Office and requires information re: educational aims, chosen career, and plans for accomplishment.
MINIMUM AVERAGE: 80.00
VALUE: $500.00
TERMS: One year only
NUMBER OF AWARDS: 1
DEADLINE FOR APPLICATIONS: September 3

CODE: MB/BRN018/u
NAME: Mary Smart Scholarships
PROGRAM: School of Music degree program
BASIS: Awarded on the basis of performance to students entering any

year of the School of Music degree program. The School of Music Scholarship Committee for that year may designate a preferred instrument or voice in each year.
MINIMUM AVERAGE: N/A
VALUE: Varies
TERMS: One year only
NUMBER OF AWARDS: Varies
DEADLINE FOR APPLICATIONS: May 1

CODE: MB/BRN019/u
NAME: James Harvey Tolton Memorial Scholarship
PROGRAM: Agriculture
BASIS: Awarded to a Grade 12 southwestern Manitoba high school graduate who is entering 1st year Agriculture at Brandon U.
MINIMUM AVERAGE: 80.00
VALUE: $450.00
TERMS: One year only
NUMBER OF AWARDS: 1
DEADLINE FOR APPLICATIONS: May 1

CODE: MB/BRN020/u
NAME: Westman Dental Group Scholarship
PROGRAM: Pre-Dental
BASIS: Awarded to a student who registers at Brandon U in subjects which lead to a career in dentistry or dental hygiene. Application forms are available from the Awards Office.
MINIMUM AVERAGE: 80.00
VALUE: $450.00
TERMS: One year only
NUMBER OF AWARDS: 1
DEADLINE FOR APPLICATIONS: May 1

Collège universitaire de Saint-Boniface

CODE: MB/CUSB01/u
NAME: Bourses de l'Oeuvre
PROGRAM: Des programmes d'études à plein temps au CUSB
BASIS: Offertes à des étudiantes et des étudiants de la 12e année des écoles franco-manitobaines et d'im-

mersion française du Manitoba. Personne ne peut faire de demande pour l'une des bourses. Elles sont décemée par le personnel de chaque école secondaire.
MINIMUM AVERAGE: N/A
VALUE: $500.00
TERMS: Pour la première année
NUMBER OF AWARDS: 20

CODE: MB/CUSB02/u
NAME: Bourses pour les sports
PROGRAM: Des programmes d'études à plein temps au CUSB
BASIS: Des bourses sont décernées à des étudiantes et des étudiants de la 12e année (pour leur excellence dans un activité sportive particulière) qui ont maintainu une moyenne de C+, qui sont engagés dan une équipe intercollégiale du CUSB.
MINIMUM AVERAGE: N/A
VALUE: $400.00
TERMS: Pour la première année
NUMBER OF AWARDS: N/A

University of Manitoba

CODE: MB/MAN001/u
NAME: Leader of Tomorrow Scholarships
PROGRAM: Any "direct entry" faculty or school
BASIS: Applicants must have demonstrated evidence of leadership qualities and future potential, a high level of communication skills, community involvement, and special abilities like athletics, literary accomplishments, or languages. An interview may be required.
MINIMUM AVERAGE: 90.00
VALUE: $3000.00
TERMS: One year only. Open to Manitoba residents only.
NUMBER OF AWARDS: 5
DEADLINE FOR APPLICATIONS: June 25

CODE: MB/MAN002/u
NAME: Isabel Auld Entrance Scholarship

PROGRAM: Agricultural and Food Sciences, Arts, Education, Fine Arts, Human Ecology, Music, Nursing, Physical Education, or Science
BASIS: Awarded to a Manitoba or northwestern Ontario high school graduate entering the University. The selection is based on academic achievement. The application for admission must be made by February 1.
MINIMUM AVERAGE: 90.00
VALUE: $6000.00
TERMS: $1500 per year, renewable for up to 4 years. Not tenable with other entrance scholarships.
NUMBER OF AWARDS: 1
DEADLINE FOR APPLICATIONS: February 1

CODE: MB/MAN003/u
NAME: Queen Elizabeth II Entrance Scholarships
PROGRAM: Agricultural and Food Sciences, Arts, Education, Fine Arts, Human Ecology, Music, Nursing, Physical Education, or Science
BASIS: Awarded to Manitoba or northwestern Ontario high school graduates entering the University. The selection is based on academic achievement. The application for admission must be made by February 1.
MINIMUM AVERAGE: 90.00
VALUE: $1000.00
TERMS: One year only. Not tenable with other entrance scholarships.
NUMBER OF AWARDS: 5
DEADLINE FOR APPLICATIONS: February 1

CODE: MB/MAN004/u
NAME: Guertin Centennial Scholarships
PROGRAM: Agricultural and Food Sciences, Arts, Education, Fine Arts, Human Ecology, Music, Nursing, Physical Education, or Science
BASIS: Awarded to Manitoba or northwestern Ontario high school grad-

uates entering the University. The selection is based on academic achievement. The application for admission must be made before February 1.
MINIMUM AVERAGE: 90.00
VALUE: $1000.00
TERMS: One year only. Not tenable with other entrance scholarships.
NUMBER OF AWARDS: 5

CODE: MB/MAN005/u
NAME: Hogg Centennial Scholarships
PROGRAM: Agricultural and Food Sciences, Arts, Education, Fine Arts, Human Ecology, Music, Nursing, Physical Education, or Science
BASIS: Awarded to Manitoba or northwestern Ontario high school graduates entering the University. The selection is based on academic achievement. The application must be made before February 1.
MINIMUM AVERAGE: 90.00
VALUE: $1000.00
TERMS: One year only. Not tenable with other entrance scholarships.
NUMBER OF AWARDS: 5

CODE: MB/MAN006/u
NAME: University of Manitoba Entrance Scholarships
PROGRAM: Any
BASIS: Awarded to Manitoba or northwestern high school graduates who have applied for "early consideration" for admission to the University by February 1. The selection is based on academic achievement. An application is not required.
MINIMUM AVERAGE: 80.00
VALUE: $500.00
TERMS: One year only. Not tenable with other entrance scholarships.
NUMBER OF AWARDS: 150

CODE: MB/MAN007/u
NAME: Chown Centennial Scholarships
PROGRAM: Any
BASIS: One scholarship is allotted to

each high school in Manitoba and northwest Ontario that prepares students to enter any degree pro gram at the University. Each school may nominate an outstanding high school graduate each June.
MINIMUM AVERAGE: 80.00
VALUE: $500.00
TERMS: One year only. Not tenable with other entrance scholarships.
NUMBER OF AWARDS: N/A

CODE: MB/MANSJ1/u
NAME: St John's College Entrance Scholarships
PROGRAM: Various
BASIS: Selection is based on academic standing.
MINIMUM AVERAGE: N/A
VALUE: $3200.00 total
TERMS: St John's College has 2 scholarships of $1000 and 1 of $1200.
NUMBER OF AWARDS: 3

CODE: MB/MANSP1/u
NAME: St Paul's College Entrance Scholarships
PROGRAM: Various
BASIS: Selection is based on academic achievement.
MINIMUM AVERAGE: N/A
VALUE: Varies
TERMS: St. Paul's College offers 6 entrance scholarships ranging in value from $330 to $1200.
NUMBER OF AWARDS: 6

University of Winnipeg

CODE: MB/WNG001/u
NAME: Alumni Entrance Awards
PROGRAM: Any
BASIS: Awarded to students completing high school in Manitoba. Application is by high school principal's nomination only, with one student from each school chosen on the basis of academic achievement, extracurricular activities, community service, and leadership.
MINIMUM AVERAGE: 80.00

VALUE: $2500.00
TERMS: One year only. Not to be held in conjunction with any other entrance scholarships offered by the University.
NUMBER OF AWARDS: 10
DEADLINE FOR APPLICATIONS: April 1

CODE: MB/WNG002/u
NAME: Francis Winston Armstrong Entrance Scholarship
PROGRAM: Any
BASIS: Awarded to a student with financial need and with good academic standing who is entering the University for the 1st time.
MINIMUM AVERAGE: 80.00
VALUE: $225.00
TERMS: One year only
NUMBER OF AWARDS: 1
DEADLINE FOR APPLICATIONS: March 2

CODE: MB/WNG003/u
NAME: Elinor F.E. Black Entrance Scholarship
PROGRAM: Any
BASIS: Awarded to a student with good academic standing who is entering the University for the 1st time.
MINIMUM AVERAGE: 80.00
VALUE: $100.00
TERMS: One year only
NUMBER OF AWARDS: 1
DEADLINE FOR APPLICATIONS: March 2

CODE: MB/WNG004/u
NAME: James H. Cameron Memorial Scholarship
PROGRAM: Any
BASIS: Awarded to a Manitoba high school graduate who has high academic standing. Preference will be given to a candidate who has graduated from a high school from the West Central Core in Winnipeg and whose family members served in the military.
MINIMUM AVERAGE: 80.00
VALUE: $400.00
TERMS: One year only

NUMBER OF AWARDS: 1
DEADLINE FOR APPLICATIONS: March 2

CODE: MB/WNG005/u
NAME: C.A. DeFehr Memorial
Entrance Scholarship in Mennonite
Studies
PROGRAM: At least 1 course of Mennonite studies
BASIS: Awarded to a student entering
the University on the basis of his/
her matriculation standing and on
the condition that he/she register
in at least one course in Mennonite
studies. A special application is
required.
MINIMUM AVERAGE: 80.00
VALUE: $150.00
TERMS: One year only
NUMBER OF AWARDS: 1
DEADLINE FOR APPLICATIONS: March 2

CODE: MB/WNG006/u
NAME: Henry Edmison Duckworth
Entrance Scholarships
PROGRAM: Any
BASIS: Awarded to entering students
of exceptional promise.
MINIMUM AVERAGE: 80.00
VALUE: $500.00
TERMS: One year only
NUMBER OF AWARDS: 5
DEADLINE FOR APPLICATIONS: March 2

CODE: MB/WNG007/u
NAME: Carl N. Halstead Memorial
Scholarship in History
PROGRAM: Any
BASIS: Awarded to a full-course
student in The Collegiate obtaining
the highest mark in History 300
who is continuing studies at the
University in a program consisting
of at least 4 full courses.
MINIMUM AVERAGE: 80.00
VALUE: $100.00
TERMS: One year only
NUMBER OF AWARDS: 5
DEADLINE FOR APPLICATIONS: March 2

CODE: MB/WNG008/u
NAME: International Baccalaureate
Entrance Scholarships
PROGRAM: Any
BASIS: Awarded to students who are
entering the University for the 1st
time on the basis of the International Baccalaureate Diploma. Applicants must have a grade total of at
least 30, including the extended
essay and the Theory of Knowledge course.
MINIMUM AVERAGE: 70.00
VALUE: $1200.00
TERMS: One year only
NUMBER OF AWARDS: Varies
DEADLINE FOR APPLICATIONS: March 2

CODE: MB/WNG009/u
NAME: Leonard Krueger Scholarship
PROGRAM: Any
BASIS: Awarded to both a male and a
female graduate in Grade 12 at The
Collegiate who receive the highest
academic standing in that year and
who continue their studies at the U
of Winnipeg.
MINIMUM AVERAGE: 80.00
VALUE: $65.00
TERMS: One year only
NUMBER OF AWARDS: 2
DEADLINE FOR APPLICATIONS: March 2

CODE: MB/WNG010/u
NAME: Alfred Duncan Longman
Scholarship
PROGRAM: Any
BASIS: Awarded to a full-course student in The Collegiate who
acheives the highest mark in English 300 who is entering a program
at the U of Winnipeg of at least 4
courses.
MINIMUM AVERAGE: 80.00
VALUE: $450.00
TERMS: One year only
NUMBER OF AWARDS: 1
DEADLINE FOR APPLICATIONS: March 2

CODE: MB/WNG011/u
NAME: Manitoba Blue Cross Entrance Award
PROGRAM: Any
BASIS: Awarded on the basis of financial need and high overall academic standing in Grade 12 to a student entering any full-time program. A special application is required.
MINIMUM AVERAGE: 80.00
VALUE: $500.00
TERMS: One year only
NUMBER OF AWARDS: 1
DEADLINE FOR APPLICATIONS: March 2

CODE: MB/WNG012/u
NAME: Manitoba United Church Women's Scholarship
PROGRAM: Any
BASIS: Awarded to any United Church student of the Conference of Manitoba on the basis of scholarship, character, and other considerations. A special application is required.
MINIMUM AVERAGE: 80.00
VALUE: $450.00
TERMS: One year only
NUMBER OF AWARDS: 1
DEADLINE FOR APPLICATIONS: March 2

CODE: MB/WNG013/u
NAME: Masonic Past Masters' Association of Manitoba Entrance Scholarship
PROGRAM: Any
BASIS: Awarded to a student who has high academic standing and financial need. A special application is required.
MINIMUM AVERAGE: 80.00
VALUE: $250.00
TERMS: One year only
NUMBER OF AWARDS: 1
DEADLINE FOR APPLICATIONS: March 2

CODE: MB/WNG014/u
NAME: Dr. Annie Mae Moore Memorial Entrance Scholarships
PROGRAM: Any
BASIS: Awarded to deserving students with good academic standing. Awards are to be divided between rural and urban Manitoba residents. A special application is required.
MINIMUM AVERAGE: 80.00
VALUE: $300.00
TERMS: One year only
NUMBER OF AWARDS: 4
DEADLINE FOR APPLICATIONS: March 2

CODE: MB/WNG015/u
NAME: Natanis Agnes Phillips Memorial Entrance Scholarships
PROGRAM: Any
BASIS: Awarded to 3 outstanding high school graduates entering the University.
MINIMUM AVERAGE: 80.00
VALUE: $500.00
TERMS: One year only
NUMBER OF AWARDS: 3
DEADLINE FOR APPLICATIONS: March 2

CODE: MB/WNG016/u
NAME: Cecil Essadelle Rombrough Memorial Entrance Scholarship
PROGRAM: Any
BASIS: Awarded to an outstanding graduate of a Winnipeg high school who is entering the University.
MINIMUM AVERAGE: 80.00
VALUE: $550.00
TERMS: One year only
NUMBER OF AWARDS: 1
DEADLINE FOR APPLICATIONS: March 2

CODE: MB/WNG017/u
NAME: Special Entrance Scholarships
PROGRAM: Any
BASIS: Awarded to all graduates of Manitoba high schools with at least five 300 credits. A maximum of one approved 305 credit may be included. (Note: these scholarships are funded by the James T. Watson Scholarship Fund and MacBean Foundation.)
MINIMUM AVERAGE: 90.00
VALUE: $1200.00

TERMS: One year only. Students with
an average of less than 90% may
receive an $800 scholarship.
NUMBER OF AWARDS: 120
DEADLINE FOR APPLICATIONS: March 2

CODE: MB/WNG018/u
NAME: H. Emerson Snyder Entrance
Scholarship
PROGRAM: Any
BASIS: Awarded on the basis of out-
standing scholarship, character,
and citizenship to a high school
graduate entering the University. A
special application is required.
MINIMUM AVERAGE: 80.00
VALUE: $375.00
TERMS: One year only
NUMBER OF AWARDS: 1
DEADLINE FOR APPLICATIONS: March 2

CODE: MB/WNG019/u
NAME: Luella Sprung Memorial
Entrance Scholarship
PROGRAM: Any
BASIS: Awarded to an outstanding
high school graduate entering the
University.
MINIMUM AVERAGE: 80.00
VALUE: $275.00
TERMS: One year only
NUMBER OF AWARDS: 1
DEADLINE FOR APPLICATIONS: March 2

CODE: MB/WNG020/u
NAME: Gladys K. Thompson
Memorial Entrance Scholarship
PROGRAM: Any
BASIS: Awarded to a student of St
James Collegiate, Silver Heights
Collegiate, or Sturgeon Creek Re-
gional Secondary School who is
entering the University with high
academic standing and has shown
excellence in English. A special ap-
plication is required.
MINIMUM AVERAGE: 80.00
VALUE: $125.00
TERMS: One year only
NUMBER OF AWARDS: 1
DEADLINE FOR APPLICATIONS: March 2

CODE: MB/WNG021/u
NAME: Chancellor P.H.T. Thorlakson
Entrance Scholarships
PROGRAM: Any
BASIS: Awarded to 2 outstanding high
school graduates entering the U of
Winnipeg.
MINIMUM AVERAGE: 80.00
VALUE: $750.00
TERMS: One year only
NUMBER OF AWARDS: 2
DEADLINE FOR APPLICATIONS: March 2

CODE: MB/WNG022/u
NAME: War Amputations (Manitoba
Branch) Entrance Scholarships
PROGRAM: Any
BASIS: Awarded to Manitoba residents
with financial need who are enter-
ing the University and who are
either handicapped or the children
of handicapped persons. A special
application is required.
MINIMUM AVERAGE: 80.00
VALUE: $350.00
TERMS: One year only
NUMBER OF AWARDS: 4
DEADLINE FOR APPLICATIONS: March 2

CODE: MB/WNG023/u
NAME: Manitoba Blue Cross Bursary
for a Student with Special Needs
PROGRAM: Any
BASIS: Awarded to a student who is
entering full-time studies at the
University and who must incur ad-
ditional expenses owing to a physi-
cal or other handicap.
MINIMUM AVERAGE: 80.00
VALUE: $500.00
TERMS: One year only
NUMBER OF AWARDS: 1
DEADLINE FOR APPLICATIONS: March 2

CODE: MB/WNG024/u
NAME: Manitoba Blue Cross
Travellers Bursary
PROGRAM: Any
BASIS: Awarded on the basis of finan-
cial need and high overall aca-
demic standing in Grade 12 to a

student from rural Manitoba who must travel more than 100 km to enter a full-time program of studies at the U of Winnipeg.
MINIMUM AVERAGE: 80.00
VALUE: $500.00
TERMS: One year only
NUMBER OF AWARDS: 1
DEADLINE FOR APPLICATIONS: March 2

CODE: MB/WNGMS1/u
NAME: Menno Simons College Entrance Scholarships
PROGRAM: Various
BASIS: The selection is based on academic achievement.
MINIMUM AVERAGE: N/A
VALUE: Varies
NUMBER OF AWARDS: 4

SASKATCHEWAN

University of Regina

CODE: SK/REG001/u
NAME: Elmer Shaw Entrance Scholarship
PROGRAM: Any
BASIS: Awarded to students from Saskatchewan entering the University with the highest standing, based on the average of specified Grade 11 and 12 academic subjects. An application is required.
MINIMUM AVERAGE: 90.00
VALUE: $4500.00
TERMS: One year only. Paid in 2 instalments.
NUMBER OF AWARDS: 1
DEADLINE FOR APPLICATIONS: April 30

CODE: SK/REG002/u
NAME: Entrance Scholarships
PROGRAM: Any
BASIS: Awarded to students from Saskatchewan entering the University with the highest standing in specified Grade 11 and 12 academic subjects. An application is required.
MINIMUM AVERAGE: 90.00
VALUE: $4300.00
TERMS: One year only. Paid in 2 instalments.
NUMBER OF AWARDS: 5
DEADLINE FOR APPLICATIONS: April 30

CODE: SK/REG003/u
NAME: Entrance Scholarships
PROGRAM: Any
BASIS: Awarded to students from Saskatchewan entering the University with the highest standing based on the average of specified Grade 11 and 12 academic subjects. An application is required.
MINIMUM AVERAGE: 90.00
VALUE: $2900.00
TERMS: One year only. Paid in 2 instalments.
NUMBER OF AWARDS: 3
DEADLINE FOR APPLICATIONS: April 30

CODE: SK/REG004/u
NAME: Entrance Scholarships
PROGRAM: Any
BASIS: Awarded to students from Saskatchewan entering the University with the highest standing, based on the average in specified Grade 11 and 12 academic subjects. An application is required.
MINIMUM AVERAGE: 90.00
VALUE: $1300.00
TERMS: One semester only. Paid in 2 instalments.
NUMBER OF AWARDS: 6
DEADLINE FOR APPLICATIONS: April 30

CODE: SK/REG005/u
NAME: Allan Blakeney Entrance Scholarship

PROGRAM: Any
BASIS: Awarded to a student from Saskatchewan entering the University. The selection is based on academic achievement and participation in activities like model United Nations, student government, youth parliaments, etc. A letter of reference is required with the application.
MINIMUM AVERAGE: 75.00
VALUE: $1000.00
TERMS: One year only
NUMBER OF AWARDS: 1
DEADLINE FOR APPLICATIONS: April 30

CODE: SK/REG006/u
NAME: Elmer Shaw Special Talent Entrance Scholarship
PROGRAM: Any
BASIS: Awarded to a student from Saskatchewan entering the University directly from high school. The award will be made on the basis of academic achievement and for outstanding talent and/or leadership. Applications are available from high school principals.
MINIMUM AVERAGE: 70.00
VALUE: $1500.00
TERMS: One semester only
NUMBER OF AWARDS: 1
DEADLINE FOR APPLICATIONS: September 1

CODE: SK/REG007/u
NAME: Elmer Shaw Entrance Bursaries
PROGRAM: Any
BASIS: Awarded to students from Saskatchewan entering the University directly from high school. The award will be made on the basis of leadership, community service, and financial need. Applications are available from high school principals.
MINIMUM AVERAGE: 70.00
VALUE: $1500.00
TERMS: One semester only
NUMBER OF AWARDS: 2

DEADLINE FOR APPLICATIONS: September 1

CODE: SK/REG008/u
NAME: Faculty of Science 10th Anniversary Scholarship
PROGRAM: Science
BASIS: Awarded to a student graduating from a Saskatchewan high school who intends to pursue a degree program in science at the University. The application to the Dean of Science must include career plans and transcripts. The average for Grades 10, 11, and 12 is considered.
MINIMUM AVERAGE: 85.00
VALUE: $4600.00
TERMS: One year only. Paid out in 3 instalments.
NUMBER OF AWARDS: 1
DEADLINE FOR APPLICATIONS: March 1

CODE: SK/REG009/u
NAME: Fine Arts Entrance Scholarships
PROGRAM: Scholarships per program: 2 for Music, 1 for Theatre Program, 1 for Film and Video Program, 1 for Visual Arts Program, and 1 undesignated.
BASIS: Awarded on the basis of academic qualifications and artistic talents. A letter of application and transcript are required to the appropriate department. An audition, or portfolio, or video submission is required, depending upon program.
MINIMUM AVERAGE: 75.00
VALUE: $1300.00
TERMS: One semester only
NUMBER OF AWARDS: 6
DEADLINE FOR APPLICATIONS: April 15

CODE: SK/REG010/u
NAME: Dr. George and Helen Ferguson Entrance Scholarship
PROGRAM: Any
BASIS: Awarded to a student who attended the Dr. George Ferguson

School in Regina and who completed Saskatchewan Grade 12. Based on academic standing, extracurricular activites, sports, and community service. Candidates should apply to the U of R Alumni Association.
MINIMUM AVERAGE: 70.00
VALUE: $1000.00
TERMS: One semester only
NUMBER OF AWARDS: 1
DEADLINE FOR APPLICATIONS: May 15

CODE: SK/REG011/u
NAME: IPSCO Inc. Scholarships
PROGRAM: Any
BASIS: Awarded to Saskatchewan students entering the University from Grade 12. The selection is based on academic standing, leadership skills, need, and an interest in working in the steel industry.
MINIMUM AVERAGE: 80.00
VALUE: $6000.00
TERMS: $1500 per year. Recipients who maintain a high academic record will receive the scholarship in each of the 4 years of their program.
NUMBER OF AWARDS: Varies
DEADLINE FOR APPLICATIONS: August 15

CODE: SK/REG012/u
NAME: SSEA Groome Memorial Scholarship
PROGRAM: Faculty of Education, Art Education
BASIS: Awarded to student from a Saskatchewan high school who are planning to major in Art Education. A letter of application and statement of high school standing must be sent to the Co-ordinator of Student Program Counselling, Faculty of Education.
MINIMUM AVERAGE: 75.00
VALUE: $250.00
TERMS: One semester only
NUMBER OF AWARDS: 1
DEADLINE FOR APPLICATIONS: August 15

CODE: SK/REG013/u
NAME: 13 CJME Santa's Anonymous Bursary
PROGRAM: Any
BASIS: Awarded on the basis of financial need to a Regina resident entering the U of Regina immediately following high school. An application is available from the Awards Office.
MINIMUM AVERAGE: 70.00
VALUE: $1500.00
TERMS: One semester only
NUMBER OF AWARDS: 1
DEADLINE FOR APPLICATIONS: September 1

CODE: SK/REG014/u
NAME: J.A. Toupin Memorial Scholarship
PROGRAM: Any
BASIS: Awarded to a 1st-year student residing in Saskatchewan who is an immediate member of the family of a current or former employee of the Saskatchewan Wheat Pool. Applicants must demonstrate a commitment to community service.
MINIMUM AVERAGE: 75.00
VALUE: $750.00
TERMS: One semester only
NUMBER OF AWARDS: 1
DEADLINE FOR APPLICATIONS: September 1

CODE: SK/REG015/u
NAME: University of Regina Alumni Senate District Scholarship
PROGRAM: Any
BASIS: Awarded to a student entering the U of Regina in the Fall semester with the highest high school admission average in each of the 12 Senate districts. No application is required.
MINIMUM AVERAGE: N/A
VALUE: $1000.00
TERMS: One semester only. Not tenable with any other major scholarships.
NUMBER OF AWARDS: 12

CODE: SK/REG016/u
NAME: IODE James Henderson LL.D. Chapter Bursary
PROGRAM: Any
BASIS: Applicants must be entering the University from a Regina high school. Academic standing, extracurricular activities, and need will be considered. Candidates should apply to Bursary Committee Convenor, 114 Michener Dr., Regina, Saskatchewan S4V 0G8. A reference letter is required.
MINIMUM AVERAGE: 70.00
VALUE: $1000.00
TERMS: One year only. Payable in 2 instalments, subject to the recipient maintaining satisfactory academic standing.
NUMBER OF AWARDS: 1
DEADLINE FOR APPLICATIONS: June 1

CODE: SK/REG017/u
NAME: Garth Edward Usick Memorial Bursary
PROGRAM: Preference given to applicants entering or continuing in Computer Science, Economics, or Administration
BASIS: Awarded to a student who uses a wheelchair as the result of a spinal-cord injury.
MINIMUM AVERAGE: 70.00
VALUE: $500.00
TERMS: One semester only
NUMBER OF AWARDS: 1
DEADLINE FOR APPLICATIONS: September 1

CODE: SK/REG018/u
NAME: Bert Fox/Ferguson University of Regina Alumni Entrance Scholarship
PROGRAM: Any
BASIS: Awarded to a student who has completed Grade 12 at Bert Fox Composite School in Fort Qu'Appelle and is entering the University. The selection is based on academic standing, student and community activities, and sports involvement. An application is required.
MINIMUM AVERAGE: 70.00
VALUE: $750.00
TERMS: One semester only
NUMBER OF AWARDS: 1
DEADLINE FOR APPLICATIONS: June 30

CODE: SK/REG019/u
NAME: Red Carpet Food Services Faculty of Physical Activities Studies Entrance Scholarship
PROGRAM: Bachelor of Physical Activities Studies degree
BASIS: Awarded to the student with the highest weighted percentage average entering the Faculty of Physical Activites Studies directly from high school. No application is required.
MINIMUM AVERAGE: 75.00
VALUE: $1000.00
TERMS: One semester only
NUMBER OF AWARDS: 1

CODE: SK/REG020/u
NAME: Anne Rigney Entrance Scholarship
PROGRAM: Faculty of Arts
BASIS: Awarded to the most outstanding Canadian student entering the Faculty of Arts directly from high school. A letter of reference must accompany the application.
MINIMUM AVERAGE: 75.00
VALUE: $3000.00
TERMS: One year only. Paid in 2 instalments of $1500 each. An average of 75% must be maintained in the 1st semester to receive the 2nd instalment.
NUMBER OF AWARDS: 1
DEADLINE FOR APPLICATIONS: April 30

CODE: SK/REG021/u
NAME: University of Regina Special Entrance Scholarships
PROGRAM: Any
BASIS: Awarded to recognize students who may not qualify for a regular entrance scholarship. Applicants

should have a special area of expertise: artistic, musical, athletic, or community involvement. A letter of reference must accompany the application.
MINIMUM AVERAGE: 80.00
VALUE: $1300.00
TERMS: One semester only
NUMBER OF AWARDS: 4
DEADLINE FOR APPLICATIONS: April 30

CODE: SK/REG022/u
NAME: Professor Peter Ventre Entrance Scholarship
PROGRAM: Preference is given to applicants entering the Faculty of Physical Activities Studies.
BASIS: Awarded to students who are graduating from high school and entering the University. Students will be evaluated on their involvement in and contribution to the sport of rugby.
MINIMUM AVERAGE: 75.00
VALUE: $500.00
TERMS: One semester only
NUMBER OF AWARDS: 1
DEADLINE FOR APPLICATIONS: September 1

CODE: SK/REG023/u
NAME: Frederick W. and Bertha A. Wenzel Entrance Bursary
PROGRAM: Pre-medicine
BASIS: Awarded to a Canadian citizen or landed immigrant graduating from a Saskatchewan high school. Financial need will be considered. An application is required.
MINIMUM AVERAGE: 80.00
VALUE: Value equal to tuition fees for 2 semesters and a partial allowance for books.
TERMS: Renewable
NUMBER OF AWARDS: 1
DEADLINE FOR APPLICATIONS: April 30

CODE: SK/REG024/u
NAME: Groome Memorial Scholarship
PROGRAM: Art Education, Faculty of Education

BASIS: Awarded to a high school graduate entering the Faculty of Education. An application and transcript must be sent to the Dean, Faculty of Education, the University of Regina.
MINIMUM AVERAGE: N/A
VALUE: $150.00
TERMS: One year only
NUMBER OF AWARDS: 1
DEADLINE FOR APPLICATIONS: August 1

CODE: SK/REGC01/u
NAME: Kramer Limited Scholarship (Campion College)
PROGRAM: Any
BASIS: Awarded to a 1st-year Campion student entering with the highest academic averages. Preference is given to a student from rural Saskatchewan. No application is required.
MINIMUM AVERAGE: 75.00
VALUE: $1000.00
TERMS: One year only
NUMBER OF AWARDS: 1

CODE: SK/REGC02/u
NAME: Reverend Isidore Gorski Scholarships (Campion College)
PROGRAM: Any
BASIS: Awarded to 1st-year Campion students entering with the highest academic averages. No application is required.
MINIMUM AVERAGE: 75.00
VALUE: $400.00
TERMS: One year only
NUMBER OF AWARDS: 5

CODE: SK/REGC03/u
NAME: Archbishop O'Neill Memorial Scholarship (Campion College)
PROGRAM: Any
BASIS: Awarded to a 1st-year Campion student entering with the highest academic averages. No application is required.
MINIMUM AVERAGE: 75.00
VALUE: $300.00
TERMS: One year only
NUMBER OF AWARDS: 1

CODE: SK/REGC04/u
NAME: Emmet A. McCusker Memorial Scholarship (Campion College)
PROGRAM: Any
BASIS: Awarded to a 1st-year Campion student entering with the highest academic averages. No application is required.
MINIMUM AVERAGE: 75.00
VALUE: $300.00
TERMS: One year only
NUMBER OF AWARDS: 1

CODE: SK/REGC05/u
NAME: Arthur Braun Memorial Scholarship (Campion College)
PROGRAM: Any
BASIS: Awarded to a 1st-year Campion student entering with the highest academic averages. No application is required.
MINIMUM AVERAGE: 75.00
VALUE: $300.00
TERMS: One year only
NUMBER OF AWARDS: 1

CODE: SK/REGC06/u
NAME: Reverend Daniel Hannin, S.J., Memorial Scholarship (Campion College)
PROGRAM: Any
BASIS: Awarded to a 1st-year Campion student entering with the highest academic averages. No application is required.
MINIMUM AVERAGE: 75.00
VALUE: $300.00
TERMS: One year only
NUMBER OF AWARDS: 1

CODE: SK/REGC07/u
NAME: Reverend William J. Kearns, S.J., Memorial Scholarship (Campion College)
PROGRAM: Any
BASIS: Awarded to a 1st-year Campion student entering with the highest academic averages. No application is required.
MINIMUM AVERAGE: 75.00
VALUE: $300.00

TERMS: One year only
NUMBER OF AWARDS: 1

CODE: SK/REGC08/u
NAME: Joseph Duffy Memorial Scholarship (Campion College)
PROGRAM: Any
BASIS: Awarded to a 1st-year Campion student entering with the highest academic averages. No application is required.
MINIMUM AVERAGE: 75.00
VALUE: $300.00
TERMS: One year only
NUMBER OF AWARDS: 1

CODE: SK/REGC09/u
NAME: Dorothy Boyle Scholarship (Campion College)
PROGRAM: Any
BASIS: Awarded to a 1st-year Campion student entering with the highest academic averages. No application is required.
MINIMUM AVERAGE: 75.00
VALUE: $300.00
TERMS: One year only
NUMBER OF AWARDS: 1

CODE: SK/REGC10/u
NAME: Patricia MacNeill Memorial Scholarship (Campion College)
PROGRAM: Any
BASIS: Awarded to a 1st-year Campion student entering with the highest academic averages. No application is required.
MINIMUM AVERAGE: 75.00
VALUE: $300.00
TERMS: One year only
NUMBER OF AWARDS: 1

CODE: SK/REGC11/u
NAME: Catholic Women's League Scholarships (Campion College)
PROGRAM: Any
BASIS: Awarded to 1st-year Campion students whose mothers are members of the Catholic Women's League. Applications may be obtained from any parish council.
MINIMUM AVERAGE: 75.00

VALUE: $300.00
TERMS: One year only
NUMBER OF AWARDS: 2
DEADLINE FOR APPLICATIONS: August 15

CODE: SK/REGC12/u
NAME: Jesuit Fathers Entrance Bursaries (Campion College)
PROGRAM: Any
BASIS: Awarded to 1st-year Campion students on the basis of financial need, academic achievement, and extracurricular activities. Applications are available from high schools or the Campion College Registrar's Office.
MINIMUM AVERAGE: 75.00
VALUE: $500.00
TERMS: One year only
NUMBER OF AWARDS: 2
DEADLINE FOR APPLICATIONS: August 15

CODE: SK/REGC13/u
NAME: Knights of Columbus, Conseil Langevin Scholarship (Campion College)
PROGRAM: Preference will be given to those intending to major in French.
BASIS: Awarded to a 1st-year Campion student receiving the highest mark (at least 75%) in Grade 12 French. The recipient must be registered in a French class. Application forms are available from high schools or the Campion College Registrar's Office.
MINIMUM AVERAGE: 75.00
VALUE: $250.00
TERMS: One year only
NUMBER OF AWARDS: 1
DEADLINE FOR APPLICATIONS: August 15

CODE: SK/REGC14/u
NAME: Saskatchewan Irish Club, Mary Reid Memorial Scholarship (Campion College)
PROGRAM: Any
BASIS: Awarded to a 1st-year Campion student. Preference is given to a student of Irish descent who graduated from a Saskatchewan high school. Application forms are available from high schools or the Campion College Registrar's Office.
MINIMUM AVERAGE: 75.00
VALUE: $300.00
TERMS: One year only
NUMBER OF AWARDS: 1
DEADLINE FOR APPLICATIONS: August 15

CODE: SK/REGC15/u
NAME: Reverend John Toth Scholarship (Campion College)
PROGRAM: Any
BASIS: Awarded to a 1st-year Campion student who is a Miller High School graduate with the highest mark in Grade 12 English. No application is required.
MINIMUM AVERAGE: 75.00
VALUE: $500.00
TERMS: One year only
NUMBER OF AWARDS: 1

CODE: SK/REGL01/u
NAME: Philip Assman Memorial Scholarships (Luther College)
PROGRAM: Any
BASIS: Awarded to Luther College High School graduates considering a church vocation and attending Luther College, University of Regina. A Luther College Application Form must be submitted.
MINIMUM AVERAGE: 80.00
VALUE: $250.00
TERMS: One year only
NUMBER OF AWARDS: 4
DEADLINE FOR APPLICATIONS: September 12

CODE: SK/REGL02/u
NAME: Harold A. Dietrich University Bursaries (Luther College)
PROGRAM: Any
BASIS: Awarded to Luther students who are Canadian citizens, Lutheran, and demonstrate academic

achievement. Financial need will also be considered. A Luther College Application Form must be submitted.
MINIMUM AVERAGE: 85.00
VALUE: $4000.00
TERMS: $1000 per year. Renewable for up to 4 years upon reapplication.
NUMBER OF AWARDS: 4
DEADLINE FOR APPLICATIONS: September 12

CODE: SK/REGL03/u
NAME: Entrance Scholarships for Excellence and Achievement (Luther College)
PROGRAM: Any
BASIS: Awarded to students entering Luther College with the highest Grade 12 averages. A Luther College Application Form must be submitted.
MINIMUM AVERAGE: 80.00
VALUE: $500.00
TERMS: One year only. Value varies with number and quality of applicants.
NUMBER OF AWARDS: Varies
DEADLINE FOR APPLICATIONS: September 12

CODE: SK/REGL04/u
NAME: Liefeld Music Scholarship (Luther College)
PROGRAM: Music
BASIS: Awarded to a student entering or continuing studies at Luther College who demonstrates academic excellence. A Luther College Application Form must be submitted.
MINIMUM AVERAGE: 80.00
VALUE: $500.00
TERMS: One year only
NUMBER OF AWARDS: 1
DEADLINE FOR APPLICATIONS: September 12

CODE: SK/REGL05/u
NAME: Liefeld – Taube Science Scholarship (Luther College)
PROGRAM: Luther Faculty of Science

BASIS: Awarded to a student entering or continuing studies at Luther College who demonstrates academic excellence. A Luther College Application Form must be submitted.
MINIMUM AVERAGE: 85.00
VALUE: $800.00
TERMS: One year only
NUMBER OF AWARDS: 1
DEADLINE FOR APPLICATIONS: September 12

CODE: SK/REGL06/u
NAME: Laurence M. Maxwell Memorial Scholarship (Luther College)
PROGRAM: Any
BASIS: Awarded to a student from rural Saskatchewan entering or continuing studies at Luther College who has demonstrated good character and industry, high academic potential, and financial need. A Luther College Application Form must be submitted.
MINIMUM AVERAGE: 80.00
VALUE: $500.00
TERMS: One year only
NUMBER OF AWARDS: 1
DEADLINE FOR APPLICATIONS: September 12

CODE: SK/REGL07/u
NAME: Caroline Niebergall Scholarship (Luther College)
PROGRAM: Any
BASIS: Awarded to a student entering or continuing studies at Luther College who is preparing for Christian service. Financial need and academic performance will be considered. A Luther College Application Form must be submitted.
MINIMUM AVERAGE: 80.00
VALUE: $100.00
TERMS: One year only
NUMBER OF AWARDS: 1
DEADLINE FOR APPLICATIONS: September 12

CODE: SK/REGL08/u
NAME: St Mark's Lutheran Church

Anniversary Scholarship (Luther College)
PROGRAM: Any
BASIS: Awarded to a student entering or continuing studies at Luther College. Financial need is considered. Preference is given to a member of the Lutheran Church (ELCIC) preparing for the ministry or church-related work. A Luther College Application Form must be submitted.
MINIMUM AVERAGE: 80.00
VALUE: $250.00
TERMS: One year only
NUMBER OF AWARDS: 1
DEADLINE FOR APPLICATIONS: September 12

CODE: SK/REGL09/u
NAME: Robert and Gertrude Wagner Music Scholarship (Luther College)
PROGRAM: Music
BASIS: Awarded to a student entering or continuing studies at Luther College who demonstrates proficiency in Music and attains high academic achievement. A Luther College Application Form must be submitted.
MINIMUM AVERAGE: 80.00
VALUE: $500.00
TERMS: One year only
NUMBER OF AWARDS: 1
DEADLINE FOR APPLICATIONS: September 12

CODE: SK/REGS01/u
NAME: Eastview Rotary Indian/ Native Entrance Scholarship (SIFC)
PROGRAM: Any
BASIS: Awarded to a 1st-year Indian/ Native SIFC student at the U of Regina. Applicants must have demonstrated good citizenship and leadership. Application forms are available from the SIFC Student Services Office.
MINIMUM AVERAGE: N/A
VALUE: $500.00
TERMS: One year only

NUMBER OF AWARDS: 1
DEADLINE FOR APPLICATIONS: February 28

CODE: SK/REGS02/u
NAME: Information Systems Management Scholarship (SIFC)
PROGRAM: General Arts and Science Program
BASIS: Awarded to the highest qualifying SIFC student of Native ancestry who meets the University entrance requirements. The recipient must indicate an intention to enter the SIFC Administration Program after 1st year of the general Arts and Science program.
MINIMUM AVERAGE: N/A
VALUE: $2000.00
TERMS: $500 per year for 4 years. Renewable each fiscal year provided a satisfactory academic average is maintained and the Computer Science core is completed.
NUMBER OF AWARDS: 1
DEADLINE FOR APPLICATIONS: February 28

CODE: SK/REGS03/u
NAME: SIFC Entrance Scholarship
PROGRAM: General Arts and Science Program
BASIS: Awarded to a Saskatchewan Treaty Indian, Non-status Indian, or Métis who is graduating from high school and has been accepted by SIFC. Application forms are available from the SIFC Student Services Office.
MINIMUM AVERAGE: 70.00
VALUE: $1000.00
TERMS: One year only
NUMBER OF AWARDS: 1
DEADLINE FOR APPLICATIONS: October 31

University of Saskatchewan

CODE: SK/SAS001/u
NAME: Sarah Jane Abrey Bursaries

PROGRAM: College of Education
BASIS: Offered to entering or undergraduate Saskatchewan resident male students on the basis of academic achievement, community service, character, leadership, and financial need. Applications are available from the Dean's Office, College of Education.
MINIMUM AVERAGE: N/A
VALUE: $1800.00
TERMS: Renewable
NUMBER OF AWARDS: Varies
DEADLINE FOR APPLICATIONS: September 30

CODE: SK/SAS002/u
NAME: Charles Edward Bell Scholarship
PROGRAM: Bachelor of Education
BASIS: Awarded to a student entering or enrolled in the B.E. degree program. The selection is based on academic achievement. No application is required.
MINIMUM AVERAGE: N/A
VALUE: $700.00
TERMS: One year only
NUMBER OF AWARDS: Varies

CODE: SK/SAS003/u
NAME: Chase Memorial Scholarships
PROGRAM: Any
BASIS: Awarded to students of North American Indian descent with demonstrated financial need. Candidates should submit an application to the Registrar's Office along with proof of Indian descent and a Preliminary Statement of High School Marks.
MINIMUM AVERAGE: N/A
VALUE: $1500.00
TERMS: Renewable upon re-application
NUMBER OF AWARDS: 8
DEADLINE FOR APPLICATIONS: April 15

CODE: SK/SAS004/u
NAME: C95 Bursary

PROGRAM: Music
BASIS: Awarded to a graduating Saskatoon high school student entering the 1st year in the Bachelor of Music or Bachelor of Music in Music Education program. Applications are available from the Department of Music.
MINIMUM AVERAGE: N/A
VALUE: $1000.00
TERMS: One year only
NUMBER OF AWARDS: 1
DEADLINE FOR APPLICATIONS: July 1

CODE: SK/SAS005/u
NAME: R.E. DuWors Scholarship
PROGRAM: Any
BASIS: Offered to a student entering any college. The selection is based on demonstrated ability in middle-distance running and/or cross-country running, combined with academic achievement. A summary of track accomplishments must accompany the General Application.
MINIMUM AVERAGE: N/A
VALUE: $500.00
TERMS: One year only
NUMBER OF AWARDS: 1
DEADLINE FOR APPLICATIONS: April 15

CODE: SK/SAS006/u
NAME: Entrance Scholarships in Music
PROGRAM: Music
BASIS: Awarded to students entering the Department of Music. The selection is based on the entrance audition and high school average. No application is required.
MINIMUM AVERAGE: N/A
VALUE: Varies
TERMS: One year only
NUMBER OF AWARDS: Varies

CODE: SK/SAS007/u
NAME: Farm Credit Corporation Canada Scholarships
PROGRAM: College of Agriculture
BASIS: Awarded on the basis of academic achievement and com-

munity service to 4-H members entering their 1st year. Applications are available from: 4-H Office, Rural Service Centre, 3735 Thatcher Ave., Saskatoon, Saskatchewan S7K 2H6.
MINIMUM AVERAGE: N/A
VALUE: $500.00
TERMS: One year only
NUMBER OF AWARDS: 4
DEADLINE FOR APPLICATIONS: July 31

CODE: SK/SAS008/u
NAME: Pearl Finley Scholarships
PROGRAM: Any
BASIS: Awarded to students from the Kerrobert School Unit. Selection will be based on financial need and academic achievement. Candidates should apply on the General Application for Undergraduate Awards and submit a Preliminary Statement of High School Marks.
MINIMUM AVERAGE: N/A
VALUE: $500.00
TERMS: One year only
NUMBER OF AWARDS: 4
DEADLINE FOR APPLICATIONS: April 15

CODE: SK/SAS009/u
NAME: Maureen Hayes Memorial Scholarship
PROGRAM: College of Education
BASIS: Awarded to 1st-year students in the College of Education who are members of the Newman Center and are enrolled in at least one course offered by St Thomas More College. No application is required.
MINIMUM AVERAGE: N/A
VALUE: $150.00
TERMS: One year only
NUMBER OF AWARDS: 3
DEADLINE FOR APPLICATIONS: April 15

CODE: SK/SAS010/u
NAME: Howard Henderson Memorial Bursary (Agriculture)
PROGRAM: Any
BASIS: Awarded to an active member of a 4-H or similar club who is a resident of the area included in Agricultural Representative Districts 25, 26, 27, or 31. The selection is based on need, participation, and interest in livestock. Candidates should apply to the Dean's Office, Agriculture.
MINIMUM AVERAGE: N/A
VALUE: $500.00
TERMS: One year only
NUMBER OF AWARDS: 1
DEADLINE FOR APPLICATIONS: October 15

CODE: SK/SAS011/u
NAME: Hoechst Bursary
PROGRAM: School or College of Agriculture
BASIS: Awarded to a member of a 4-H club entering 1st year. The selection is based on financial need, 4-H involvement, and academic ability. Applications are available from: 4-H Office, Rural Service Centre, 3735 Thatcher Ave, Saskatoon, Saskatchewan S7K 2H6.
MINIMUM AVERAGE: N/A
VALUE: $500.00
TERMS: One year only
NUMBER OF AWARDS: 1
DEADLINE FOR APPLICATIONS: July 15

CODE: SK/SAS012/u
NAME: Harry R. Hunking Scholarship
PROGRAM: Any
BASIS: Awarded to a student graduating from one of the collegiate institutes of Saskatoon. The selection is based on outstanding athletic ability combined with academic proficiency. Candidates should apply on the General Application for Entrance Awards, including high school marks.
MINIMUM AVERAGE: N/A
VALUE: $900.00
TERMS: One year only
NUMBER OF AWARDS: 1
DEADLINE FOR APPLICATIONS: April 15

CODE: SK/SAS013/u
NAME: India Canada Cultural Association Bursary
PROGRAM: Any
BASIS: Awarded to a student entering 1st year who has either a parent or parents from India who are of Indo-Canadian ancestry. The selection is based on academic achievement and community service. Candidates should apply on the General Application for Entrance Awards.
MINIMUM AVERAGE: N/A
VALUE: $250.00
TERMS: One year only
NUMBER OF AWARDS: 1
DEADLINE FOR APPLICATIONS: April 15

CODE: SK/SAS014/u
NAME: Richard Glenn Johnston Bursaries
PROGRAM: Any
BASIS: Offered to students from the postal districts of Radisson, Borden, and Maymont, Saskatchewan. The selection is based on academic achievement and financial need. Preference will be given to students who have completed at least one year of study.
MINIMUM AVERAGE: N/A
VALUE: $700.00
TERMS: One year only
NUMBER OF AWARDS: 2
DEADLINE FOR APPLICATIONS: June 1

CODE: SK/SAS015/u
NAME: Constable Brian King Memorial Bursaries
PROGRAM: Any
BASIS: Awarded to Saskatchewan high school graduates on the basis of financial need, demonstrated involvement in school and community activities, sports involvement, and academic potential. The application must include letters of recommendation and a transcript.
MINIMUM AVERAGE: N/A
VALUE: $1300.00

TERMS: One year only
NUMBER OF AWARDS: 5
DEADLINE FOR APPLICATIONS: April 15

CODE: SK/SAS016/u
NAME: Knights of Columbus Bursaries
PROGRAM: Any at St Thomas More College
BASIS: Awarded to full-time students entering their 1st year at St Thomas More College. The selection is based on academic achievement and financial need. Applications are available from Room 216, St Thomas More College.
MINIMUM AVERAGE: N/A
VALUE: $500.00
TERMS: One year only. Not tenable with any other scholarships, bursaries, or awards totalling over $1000.
NUMBER OF AWARDS: 3
DEADLINE FOR APPLICATIONS: October 1

CODE: SK/SAS017/u
NAME: Moore Memorial Award
PROGRAM: Preference is given to students entering the College of Engineering.
BASIS: Awarded to a student whose residence, or that of his or her immediate family at the time of application, is within the postal districts of the town of Francis or the village of Abernethy. The selection is based on academic achievement. Candidates should apply through the Registrar.
MINIMUM AVERAGE: N/A
VALUE: $1400.00
TERMS: One year only
NUMBER OF AWARDS: 1
DEADLINE FOR APPLICATIONS: April 15

CODE: SK/SAS018/u
NAME: Evan and Elsie Morgan Scholarship
PROGRAM: Music
BASIS: Awarded to a string student entering the Bachelor of Music or

the Bachelor of Music in Music Education degree progam. The selection is based on performance and academic ability. An audition is required.

MINIMUM AVERAGE: N/A
VALUE: Varies
TERMS: One year only
NUMBER OF AWARDS: 1
DEADLINE FOR APPLICATIONS: July 1

CODE: SK/SAS019/u *
NAME: Beatrice Murray Agriculture Entrance Scholarship
PROGRAM: Bachelor of Science in Agriculture
BASIS: Awarded to a female student entering the B.S.A. degree program with the highest admission average. No application is required.
MINIMUM AVERAGE: N/A
VALUE: $1500.00 (approx.)
TERMS: One year only
NUMBER OF AWARDS: 1

CODE: SK/SAS020/u
NAME: Frances Elizabeth Murray Scholarship
PROGRAM: Bachelor of Science in Agriculture
BASIS: Awarded to a student entering any college at the U of Saskatchewan. This scholarship will be awarded to a student applicant for the University Entrance Scholarships who is not chosen in that competition.
MINIMUM AVERAGE: N/A
VALUE: $1000.00
TERMS: One year only
NUMBER OF AWARDS: 1
DEADLINE FOR APPLICATIONS: April 15

CODE: SK/SAS021/u
NAME: Evelyn Norgord Scholarship in Education
PROGRAM: Education
BASIS: Offered to a student who attended Grade 3 or 4 in Biggar or resides within 25 km of the town. Preference is given to applicants

who wish to teach in an elementary school in rural Saskatchewan. Candidates should apply to the Assistant Dean of the College of Education.
MINIMUM AVERAGE: N/A
VALUE: To be determined.
TERMS: One year only
NUMBER OF AWARDS: 1
DEADLINE FOR APPLICATIONS: September 30

CODE: SK/SAS022/u
NAME: Halvor and Betty Norgord Scholarship in Education
PROGRAM: Education
BASIS: Offered to a student who attended elementary school in the Town of Watrous or who resides within 25 km of the town. Preference is given to applicants who wish to teach in an elementary school in rural Saskatchewan. Candidates should apply to the Assistant Dean of Education.
MINIMUM AVERAGE: N/A
VALUE: To be determined.
TERMS: One year only
NUMBER OF AWARDS: 1
DEADLINE FOR APPLICATIONS: September 30

CODE: SK/SAS023/u
NAME: Phi Delta Kappa Scholarship in Education
PROGRAM: Education
BASIS: Eligible applicants must have graduated from selected school boards in Saskatchewan. The application is available from the Assistant Dean, College of Education. Community service, leadership, and research potential are considered. A reference is required.
MINIMUM AVERAGE: 80.00
VALUE: $250.00
TERMS: One year only
NUMBER OF AWARDS: 1
DEADLINE FOR APPLICATIONS: September 30

CODE: SK/SAS024/u
NAME: Potash Corporation of Saskatchewan Scholarship
PROGRAM: Any college at the U of Saskatchewan
BASIS: Offered to a 4-H member entering 1st year. The selection is based on academic ability, community involvement, and demonstrated 4-H leadership skills. Applications are available from the 4-H Office, Rural Service Centre, 3735 Thatcher St., Saskatoon, Saskatchewan, S7K 2H6.
MINIMUM AVERAGE: N/A
VALUE: $500.00
TERMS: One year only
NUMBER OF AWARDS: 1
DEADLINE FOR APPLICATIONS: July 31

CODE: SK/SAS025/u
NAME: Louis Riel Scholarship
PROGRAM: Any
BASIS: Awarded to a Métis student from Saskatchewan. Proof of Métis descent is required with the General Application.
MINIMUM AVERAGE: N/A
VALUE: $6000.00
TERMS: $1500 per year, renewable for up to 4 or more years of undergraduate study.
NUMBER OF AWARDS: 1
DEADLINE FOR APPLICATIONS: April 15

CODE: SK/SAS026/u
NAME: St Thomas More College Entrance Scholarships
PROGRAM: Any at St Thomas More College
BASIS: Offered to a student entering St Thomas More College. The application is available from Room 216 at the College.
MINIMUM AVERAGE: N/A
VALUE: $150.00
TERMS: One year only
NUMBER OF AWARDS: 1
DEADLINE FOR APPLICATIONS: October 1

CODE: SK/SAS027/u
NAME: Salikin Diabetes Scholarships
PROGRAM: Any college at the U of Saskatchewan
BASIS: Awarded to students with diabetes entering 1st year. Eligible candidates must have graduated from a high school in the Saskatoon and District boundaries of the local diabetes association. Medical documentation must accompany the General Application for Awards.
MINIMUM AVERAGE: N/A
VALUE: $500.00
TERMS: One year only
NUMBER OF AWARDS: 3
DEADLINE FOR APPLICATIONS: April 15

CODE: SK/SAS028/u
NAME: SASKEXPO '86 Bursary
PROGRAM: Any
BASIS: Awarded to a student entering the University. The selection is based on school and community activities, leadership potential, academic abilities, and financial need. References and a list of activities must acccompany the General Application for Awards.
MINIMUM AVERAGE: N/A
VALUE: $1500.00
TERMS: One year only. The award will alternate between the U of Saskatchewan and Simon Fraser U (BC).
NUMBER OF AWARDS: 1
DEADLINE FOR APPLICATIONS: April 15

CODE: SK/SAS029/u
NAME: SaskTel Scholarships
PROGRAM: Preference is given to applicants registered in Commerce, Computational Sciences, and Engineering.
BASIS: Offered to students in degree programs directly related to telecommunications. The selection is based on academic achievement, career interest, financial need, and community service. Preference is

given to designated minority-group members.
MINIMUM AVERAGE: N/A
VALUE: $2000.00
TERMS: One year only
NUMBER OF AWARDS: 1
DEADLINE FOR APPLICATIONS: July 1

CODE: SK/SAS030/u
NAME: Clare and Margaret Sherrard Memorial Scholarship
PROGRAM: Any program
BASIS: Offered to graduates of a Saskatchewan high school.
MINIMUM AVERAGE: N/A
VALUE: $1500.00
TERMS: One year only. Students holding a Clare and Margaret Sherrard Scholarship from Balfour Collegiate are not eligible.
NUMBER OF AWARDS: 2
DEADLINE FOR APPLICATIONS: April 15

CODE: SK/SAS031/u
NAME: Bill Story Memorial Bursary in Agriculture
PROGRAM: College of Agriculture
BASIS: Awarded to a rural Saskatchewan student entering the College of Agriculture. The selection is based on demonstrated financial need and satisfactory academic performance. Candidates should apply to the Dean's Office, Agriculture.
MINIMUM AVERAGE: N/A
VALUE: $500.00
TERMS: One year only
NUMBER OF AWARDS: 1
DEADLINE FOR APPLICATIONS: October 15

CODE: SK/SAS032/u
NAME: Toupin Family Memorial Bursary
PROGRAM: Any
BASIS: Awarded to a student graduating from a secondary school of St Paul's Roman Catholic Separate School Division No. 20 in Saskatoon. The selection is based on academic achievement, financial need, and leadership qualities.
MINIMUM AVERAGE: N/A
VALUE: $1000.00
TERMS: One year only. The bursary will be awarded in 2 equal parts, provided the conditions of the bursary continue to be met.
NUMBER OF AWARDS: 1
DEADLINE FOR APPLICATIONS: April 15

CODE: SK/SAS033/u
NAME: University Entrance Scholarships
PROGRAM: Any
BASIS: Awarded to students entering a full program of studies. The selection is based on academic achievement in Grades 10, 11, and 12. Candidates should submit the General Application for Entrance Scholarships to the Registrar's Office.
MINIMUM AVERAGE: 90.00
VALUE: $4200.00
TERMS: One year only
NUMBER OF AWARDS: 9
DEADLINE FOR APPLICATIONS: April 15

CODE: SK/SAS034/u
NAME: University of Saskatchewan Alumni Association Scholarships
PROGRAM: Any
BASIS: Awarded to students entering a full program of studies. The selection is based on academic achievement in high school. Candidates should submit the General Application for Entrance Scholarships to the Registrar's Office.
MINIMUM AVERAGE: N/A
VALUE: $1000.00
TERMS: One year only. Recipients must commence studies in the year the scholarship is awarded.
NUMBER OF AWARDS: 42
DEADLINE FOR APPLICATIONS: April 15

CODE: SK/SAS035/u
NAME: Allen Memorial Scholarship of the Turtleford School District

PROGRAM: Any program
BASIS: Awarded to a student from Turtleford High School. The selection is based on academic achievemment in Grades 11 and 12 and contributions to the welfare of the school. No application is required.
MINIMUM AVERAGE: N/A
VALUE: $800.00
TERMS: One year only. To be eligible, candidates must have completed Grades 11 and 12 at the high school.
NUMBER OF AWARDS: 1

CODE: SK/SAS036/u
NAME: Clark Scholarship in Memory of Gertrude Evelyn Clark (Newmann)
PROGRAM: Any program
BASIS: Awarded to a student from St Walburg School. The selection is based on academic achievemment in Grades 10, 11, and 12 and contributions to the welfare of the school. Applications are available from the Principal, St Walburg School.
MINIMUM AVERAGE: N/A
VALUE: $950.00
TERMS: One year only. To be eligible, candidates must have completed Grades 11 and 12 at the high school.
NUMBER OF AWARDS: 1

CODE: SK/SAS037/u
NAME: C.F.M. Misselbrook Scholarship Fund
PROGRAM: Any program
BASIS: Awarded to a student who graduated from a school within the corporate limits of the Town of Nipawin in 1978 or in a subsequent year. The selection is based on one's academic record and financial need. Applications are available from the Nipawin School Divisional Office.
MINIMUM AVERAGE: N/A
VALUE: Varies

TERMS: One year only
NUMBER OF AWARDS: 1
DEADLINE FOR APPLICATIONS: June 1

CODE: SK/SAS038/u
NAME: VanBlaricom Scholarship for Tisdale School Division No. 53
PROGRAM: Any program
BASIS: Awarded to students graduating from any of the high schools in the Tisdale School Division. Applications are available from the Secretary-Treasurer of the Tisdale School Division, No. 53, Box 400, Tisdale, Saskatchewan S0E 1T0.
MINIMUM AVERAGE: N/A
VALUE: $300.00
TERMS: One year only
NUMBER OF AWARDS: 8

CODE: SK/SASSP1/u
NAME: Frank and Elizabeth Weber Scholarship (St Peter's College)
PROGRAM: Arts and Science
BASIS: Awarded to students entering full-time studies at St Peter's College. The selection is based on high school academic achievement. One copy of the final Grade 12 marks must be submitted to the Dean's Office by August 15.
MINIMUM AVERAGE: N/A
VALUE: Varies with the number of scholarships given.
TERMS: One year only
NUMBER OF AWARDS: Varies with entrance marks of applicants.
DEADLINE FOR APPLICATIONS: September 30

CODE: SK/SASSP2/u
NAME: Thomas and Marie Clandinin Scholarship (St Peter's College)
PROGRAM: Arts and Science
BASIS: Awarded to students entering full-time studies at St Peter's College. The selection is based on high school academic achievement. One copy of final Grade 12 marks must be submitted to the Dean's Office by August 15.

MINIMUM AVERAGE: N/A
VALUE: $400.00
TERMS: One year only. The amount is determined by interest rates.
NUMBER OF AWARDS: Varies
DEADLINE FOR APPLICATIONS: September 30

CODE: SK/SASSP3/u
NAME: Co-operative Work Scholarship (St Peter's College)
PROGRAM: Any
BASIS: Awarded to 1st- or 2nd-year students on the basis of a written proposal. Financial need will be considered.
MINIMUM AVERAGE: N/A
VALUE: $500.00
TERMS: One year only. The students receive tuition in exchange for a project or other work.
NUMBER OF AWARDS: Varies
DEADLINE FOR APPLICATIONS: September 30

CODE: SK/SASSP4/u
NAME: St Peter's College Entrance Scholarships
PROGRAM: Arts and Sciences
BASIS: Awarded to full-time students entering St Peter's College. The selection is based on Grade 12 average.
MINIMUM AVERAGE: N/A
VALUE: $700.00
TERMS: One year only. Value varies between $300 and $700.
NUMBER OF AWARDS: Varies
DEADLINE FOR APPLICATIONS: September 30

CODE: SK/SASTM1/u
NAME: St Thomas More College First-Year Scholarships
PROGRAM: Any
BASIS: Awarded to students entering STM College.
MINIMUM AVERAGE: N/A
VALUE: $150.00
TERMS: One year only. STM students who have received the U of Sas-

katchewan Entrance Scholarship or many other scholarships are not eligible. (Note: St Thomas More Applicants should also see SK/SAS016/u and SK/SAS026/u.)
NUMBER OF AWARDS: 20
DEADLINE FOR APPLICATIONS: September 30

CODE: SK/SASTM2/u
NAME: St Thomas More Knights of Columbus First-Year Scholarships
PROGRAM: Various
BASIS: Awarded to students entering 1st year at STM College in English, Economics, French, History, Philosophy, Political Studies, Pyschology, Religious Studies, and Sociology. An additional scholarship will be offered to the top applicants in the 4 programs.
MINIMUM AVERAGE: N/A
VALUE: $500.00
TERMS: One year only. STM students who have received the U of Saskatchewan Entrance Scholarship or many other scholarships are not eligible.
NUMBER OF AWARDS: 13
DEADLINE FOR APPLICATIONS: September 30

CODE: SK/SASTM3/u
NAME: Rose Voytilla Scholarship
PROGRAM: An undergraduate program leading to the Catholic priesthood.
BASIS: Awarded to an STM student who is pursuing an undergraduate program in preparation for the Catholic priesthood. Students applying for this scholarship are to provide a letter describing their intention of commitment to pursuing such studies.
MINIMUM AVERAGE: N/A
VALUE: $500.00
TERMS: One year only
NUMBER OF AWARDS: 1
DEADLINE FOR APPLICATIONS: September 30

CODE: SK/SASTM4/u
NAME: Knights of Columbus Bursaries
PROGRAM: Any
BASIS: Awarded to full-time students entering 1st year at STM College. Awarded on the basis of academic achievement and need. Normally, 2 of these are given to dependents of Saskatoon Chapter Knights of Columbus Councils, while the 3rd is open to other students.
MINIMUM AVERAGE: N/A
VALUE: $500.00
TERMS: One year only. Not tenable with any other scholarships and/or bursaries totalling over $1000.
NUMBER OF AWARDS: 3
DEADLINE FOR APPLICATIONS: September 30

CODE: SK/SASTM5/u
NAME: Maureen Haynes Memorial Scholarship
PROGRAM: Education
BASIS: Awarded to 1st-year students in the College of Education who are members of the Newman Centre and are enrolled in at least one course offered by St Thomas More College. No application is required.
MINIMUM AVERAGE: N/A
VALUE: $150.00
TERMS: One year only
NUMBER OF AWARDS: 3
DEADLINE FOR APPLICATIONS: September 30

ALBERTA

Alberta College of Art

CODE: AB/ACA001/c
NAME: ACA Alumni Association Award
PROGRAM: Foundation Program
BASIS: Applicants must be applying for full-time studies in the ACA Foundation Program and submit: a portfolio, a statement of purpose, transcripts, and a scholarship application. The selection is based on the merit of the entrance portfolio submitted.
MINIMUM AVERAGE: N/A
VALUE: $300.00
TERMS: One year only
NUMBER OF AWARDS: Varies
DEADLINE FOR APPLICATIONS: May 10

CODE: AB/ACA002/c
NAME: Continuing Arts Association Foundation Scholarship
PROGRAM: Foundation Program
BASIS: Applicants must be graduates of a separate or public Calgary high school entering full-time studies in the ACA Foundation Program and must submit: a portfolio, a statement of purpose, transcripts, and a scholarship application.
MINIMUM AVERAGE: N/A
VALUE: $300.00
TERMS: One year only
NUMBER OF AWARDS: 1
DEADLINE FOR APPLICATIONS: May 10

CODE: AB/ACA003/c
NAME: Eaton Scholarship
PROGRAM: Foundation Program
BASIS: Applicants must be applying for full-time studies in the Foundation Program and submit: a portfolio, a statement of purpose, transcripts, and a 750-word statement of intent giving reasons why the applicant should be considered for the Eaton Scholarship.
MINIMUM AVERAGE: N/A
VALUE: $4000.00
TERMS: $2000 will be awarded upon entering the ACA Foundation program and $2000 in the 2nd year, provided the returning recipient holds a GPA of 3.0 or more.
NUMBER OF AWARDS: 1
DEADLINE FOR APPLICATIONS: May 10

Alberta College

CODE: AB/ALT000/c
NAME: Alberta College does not offer any entrance scholarhips.

Fairview College

CODE: AB/FAIR01/c
NAME: Fairview College Tuition Scholarships
PROGRAM: Any career program of studies at Fairview College
BASIS: Awarded to students from various school boards in British Columbia and Alberta. One student will be chosen by the School District Superintendents. Applicants should apply directly to their school district's superintendent.
MINIMUM AVERAGE: N/A
VALUE: Awards equal to the value of 1st-year tuition fees.
TERMS: One year only. Recipients must enter programs directly from high school or Adult Upgrading programs.
NUMBER OF AWARDS: 41
DEADLINE FOR APPLICATIONS: June 30

Grande Prairie Regional College

CODE: AB/GPRC01/c
NAME: A.C.T. Auxiliary Bursary
PROGRAM: Any
BASIS: Awarded to full-time Peace area students who are entering or continuing studies at GPRC. Applicants must have been out of full-time studies for 3 years. The selection is based on financial need and satisfactory academic achievement.
MINIMUM AVERAGE: 5.00
VALUE: $500.00
TERMS: One year only
NUMBER OF AWARDS: 2
DEADLINE FOR APPLICATIONS: September 15

CODE: AB/GPRC02/c
NAME: Academic Staff Association Bursary
PROGRAM: Any
BASIS: Awarded to a full-time student who is entering GPRC. The selection is based on financial need, academic achievement, and college/community involvement.
MINIMUM AVERAGE: 5.00
VALUE: Equals tuition fees.
TERMS: One year only
NUMBER OF AWARDS: 1
DEADLINE FOR APPLICATIONS: September 15

CODE: AB/GPRC03/c
NAME: Alberta Power Limited Bursary
PROGRAM: Any
BASIS: Awarded to a full-time student who is entering GPRC. The selection is based on financial need, academic achievement, and college/community involvement.
MINIMUM AVERAGE: 5.00
VALUE: Equals tuition fees.
TERMS: One year only
NUMBER OF AWARDS: 1
DEADLINE FOR APPLICATIONS: September 15

CODE: AB/GPRC04/c
NAME: Alberta Union of Provincial Employees Bursary
PROGRAM: Any
BASIS: Awarded to members in good standing of the AUPE, or the son, daughter, legal ward, or spouse of a member. The selection is based on financial need and satisfactory academic achievement.
MINIMUM AVERAGE: 5.00
VALUE: Equals tuition fees.
TERMS: One year only
NUMBER OF AWARDS: 1
DEADLINE FOR APPLICATIONS: September 15

CODE: AB/GPRC05/c
NAME: Margaret Andersen Bursary

PROGRAM: Any
BASIS: Awarded to a full-time student who is entering GPRC. The selection is based on financial need, academic achievement, and college/community involvement.
MINIMUM AVERAGE: 5.00
VALUE: Equals tuition fees.
TERMS: One year only
NUMBER OF AWARDS: 1
DEADLINE FOR APPLICATIONS: September 15

CODE: AB/GPRC06/c
NAME: Henry N. Anderson Scholarship
PROGRAM: Bachelor of Education
BASIS: Awarded to a student with the highest academic standing entering the 1st year of the Bachelor of Education program at GPRC.
MINIMUM AVERAGE: 7.50
VALUE: Equals tuition fees.
TERMS: One year only
NUMBER OF AWARDS: 1
DEADLINE FOR APPLICATIONS: September 15

CODE: AB/GPRC07/c
NAME: Army, Navy and Air Force Veterans in Canada Award
PROGRAM: Various
BASIS: One Academic Development Bursary will be awarded to an entering or continuing full-time student registered in Academic Development. Another bursary will be awarded to a disabled full-time student. The selection for both is based on financial need.
MINIMUM AVERAGE: 7.50
VALUE: $500.00
TERMS: One year only
NUMBER OF AWARDS: 2
DEADLINE FOR APPLICATIONS: September 15

CODE: AB/GPRC08/c
NAME: BLHS Reunion '86 Bursary
PROGRAM: Any except university transfer programs

BASIS: Awarded to a Grade 12 student from Beaverlodge High School in any program excluding university transfer programs. The selection is based on financial need.
MINIMUM AVERAGE: 5.00
VALUE: $800.00
TERMS: One year only
NUMBER OF AWARDS: 1
DEADLINE FOR APPLICATIONS: September 15

CODE: AB/GPRC09/c
NAME: Beta Sigma Phi Bursary
PROGRAM: Any
BASIS: Applicants must be mature, full-time students who are Canadian citizens and in need of financial assistance. Priority will go to a female student.
MINIMUM AVERAGE: 5.00
VALUE: $300.00
TERMS: One year only
NUMBER OF AWARDS: 1
DEADLINE FOR APPLICATIONS: September 15

CODE: AB/GPRC10/c
NAME: Bowes Family Mature Student Bursary
PROGRAM: Any
BASIS: Awarded to a part-time or full-time student who is entering or continuing studies at GPRC. Applicants must have been out of full-time studies for 5 years. The selection is based on financial need and satisfactory academic achievement.
MINIMUM AVERAGE: 5.00
VALUE: Varies
TERMS: One year only
NUMBER OF AWARDS: Varies
DEADLINE FOR APPLICATIONS: September 15

CODE: AB/GPRC11/c
NAME: Elizabeth Jean Butler Scholarships
PROGRAM: Any
BASIS: Awarded to any current Grade 12 graduates from the entire Peace

region. Priority will go to applicants who have been a resident of the Bear Canyon–Cherry Point District and have completed grades 7, 8, and 9 at Bear Canyon Central School.
MINIMUM AVERAGE: 5.00
VALUE: Varies
TERMS: One year only
NUMBER OF AWARDS: Varies
DEADLINE FOR APPLICATIONS:
September 15

CODE: AB/GPRC12/c
NAME: Canadian Forest Products Bursary
PROGRAM: Any
BASIS: Awarded to full-time entering or continuing students who reside in the Peace region. The selection is based on financial need and satisfactory academic standing.
MINIMUM AVERAGE: 5.00
VALUE: $1000.00
TERMS: One year only
NUMBER OF AWARDS: 2
DEADLINE FOR APPLICATIONS:
September 15

CODE: AB/GPRC13/c
NAME: CFGP Performing Arts Scholarship
PROGRAM: Performing Arts
BASIS: Awarded to any entering or continuing student from a Peace Country high school who demonstrates ability and a clearly defined career path in the performing arts and has made a contribution to the performing-arts community. Financial need is considered.
MINIMUM AVERAGE: 7.50
VALUE: Varies
TERMS: One year only
NUMBER OF AWARDS: Varies
DEADLINE FOR APPLICATIONS:
September 15

CODE: AB/GPRC14/c
NAME: Chicken Village Office Administration Bursary
PROGRAM: Office Administration
BASIS: Awarded to a part-time Office Administration student. The selection is based on financial need and academic achievement.
MINIMUM AVERAGE: 7.50
VALUE: $300.00
TERMS: One year only
NUMBER OF AWARDS: 1
DEADLINE FOR APPLICATIONS:
September 15

CODE: AB/GPRC15/c
NAME: Daily Herald-Tribune Bursary
PROGRAM: Any
BASIS: Awarded to a full-time student who is entering GPRC. The selection is based on financial need, academic achievement, and college/community involvement.
MINIMUM AVERAGE: 5.00
VALUE: $300.00
TERMS: One year only
NUMBER OF AWARDS: 1
DEADLINE FOR APPLICATIONS:
September 15

CODE: AB/GPRC16/c
NAME: Edmonton Northlands Mature Student Bursary
PROGRAM: Any
BASIS: Awarded to part-time or full-time students who are entering GPRC. Applicants must have been out of full-time studies for 5 years. The application must include a 500-word statement of educational/career plans. Preference is given to a rural student.
MINIMUM AVERAGE: 5.00
VALUE: $1000.00
TERMS: One year only
NUMBER OF AWARDS: 2
DEADLINE FOR APPLICATIONS:
September 15

CODE: AB/GPRC17/c
NAME: Edmonton Northlands Pre-Employment Trades Bursaries
PROGRAM: Pre-Employment Trades
BASIS: Awarded to entering students

in any one of the Pre-Employment trades. The selection is based on financial need, attendance, and work habits. No application is necessary.
MINIMUM AVERAGE: 5.00
VALUE: $300.00 approx.
TERMS: One year only. Value equals tuition fees.
NUMBER OF AWARDS: Varies
DEADLINE FOR APPLICATIONS:
September 15

CODE: AB/GPRC18/c
NAME: Fairview Health Complex District #59 Nursing Bursary
PROGRAM: Nursing
BASIS: Awarded to a 1st-year nursing student from the Fairview Health Complex District #59 on the basis of academic standing, community involvement, and financial need.
MINIMUM AVERAGE: 5.00
VALUE: $500.00
TERMS: One year only
NUMBER OF AWARDS: 1
DEADLINE FOR APPLICATIONS:
September 15

CODE: AB/GPRC19/c
NAME: Elsworth Foy Memorial Bursary
PROGRAM: Agriculture, Education, Forestry, or Nursing
BASIS: Awarded to residents of the Peace River region who come from a rural background. Preference will be given to students entering Agriculture. The selection is based on academic achievement and financial need.
MINIMUM AVERAGE: 5.00
VALUE: $600.00
TERMS: One year only
NUMBER OF AWARDS: 2
DEADLINE FOR APPLICATIONS:
September 15

CODE: AB/GPRC20/c
NAME: Angel Fraser Memorial Scholarship
PROGRAM: Any

BASIS: Awarded to a full-time student entering GPRC. The selection is based on financial need and a brief statement of career goals.
MINIMUM AVERAGE: 7.50
VALUE: Varies
TERMS: One year only
NUMBER OF AWARDS: Varies
DEADLINE FOR APPLICATIONS:
September 15

CODE: AB/GPRC21/c
NAME: Grande Prairie Amateur Games Society Award
PROGRAM: Visual and Performing Arts or Physical Education and Athletics
BASIS: Awarded to full-time entering or continuing students who are residents of the city of Grande Prairie or the immediate surrounding area. The selection is based on academic standing and financial need.
MINIMUM AVERAGE: 7.50
VALUE: Varies
TERMS: One year only. Number of awards varies.
NUMBER OF AWARDS: 2 minimum
DEADLINE FOR APPLICATIONS:
September 15

CODE: AB/GPRC22/c
NAME: Grande Prairie Business and Professional Women's Club Bursary
PROGRAM: Any
BASIS: Awarded to a mature student who is a Canadian citizen, resides in the Peace River area, is in need of financial assistance, and displays academic competence. The application must include 2 letters of reference. Preference is given to female applicants.
MINIMUM AVERAGE: 5.00
VALUE: $1000.00
TERMS: One year only
NUMBER OF AWARDS: 1
DEADLINE FOR APPLICATIONS:
September 15

CODE: AB/GPRC23/c
NAME: Grande Prairie Petroleum Association Bursary
PROGRAM: Any
BASIS: Awarded to a female and a male dependent of Grande Prairie Petroleum Association members. The selection is based on financial need and academic standing. A special application form is available from the awards office.
MINIMUM AVERAGE: 5.00
VALUE: $1000.00
TERMS: One year only. Dependents of the Northern Alberta Petroleum Association may be considered if suitable Grande Prairie candidates are not found.
NUMBER OF AWARDS: 2
DEADLINE FOR APPLICATIONS: September 15

CODE: AB/GPRC24/c
NAME: Grande Prairie Regional College Music Faculty Scholarships
PROGRAM: Music
BASIS: Awarded to selected students on the basis of a vocal audition or an audition on their major instrument. Eligible candidates must be enrolled in a minimum of 3 courses in music. One of these must involve a major music ensemble.
MINIMUM AVERAGE: 7.50
VALUE: Varies
TERMS: One year only
NUMBER OF AWARDS: Varies
DEADLINE FOR APPLICATIONS: September 15

CODE: AB/GPRC25/c
NAME: GPRC Wolf Pac Booster Club Athletic Bursaries
PROGRAM: Any
BASIS: Awarded to students with athletic ability on any of the following ACAC teams: Badminton, Basketball, Hockey, Volleyball, or Curling. Candidates should apply to: GPRC Wolf Pac Booster Club, c/o the Co-ordinator of Athletics,

GPRC, 10726 106th Ave., Grande Prairie, Alberta T8V 4C4
MINIMUM AVERAGE: 5.00
VALUE: Equals tuition fees.
TERMS: To be divided equally per semester. Not tenable with the Jimmie Condon Scholarship.
NUMBER OF AWARDS: Varies
DEADLINE FOR APPLICATIONS: September 15

CODE: AB/GPRC26/c
NAME: Archie Harvey Memorial Bursary
PROGRAM: Any
BASIS: Awarded to an entering or continuing student on the basis of financial need and satisfactory academic standing.
MINIMUM AVERAGE: 5.00
VALUE: $300.00
TERMS: One year only
NUMBER OF AWARDS: 1
DEADLINE FOR APPLICATIONS: September 15

CODE: AB/GPRC27/c
NAME: IOF Bachelor of Physical Education Bursary
PROGRAM: Bachelor of Physical Education
BASIS: Awarded to a 1st- or 2nd-year student. The selection is based on scholastic ability and financial need. The application must include a transcript of marks and a letter describing hobbies, interests, and extracurricular activities.
MINIMUM AVERAGE: 5.00
VALUE: $500.00
TERMS: One year only
NUMBER OF AWARDS: 1
DEADLINE FOR APPLICATIONS: September 15

CODE: AB/GPRC28/c
NAME: IOF Computer Systems Technology Bursary
PROGRAM: Computer Systems Technology
BASIS: Awarded to a student who is a

graduate of a Grande Prairie high school. The selection is based on scholastic ability and financial need. The application must include a transcript of marks and a letter describing hobbies, interests, and extracurricular activities.
MINIMUM AVERAGE: 5.00
VALUE: $500.00
TERMS: One year only
NUMBER OF AWARDS: 1
DEADLINE FOR APPLICATIONS: September 15

CODE: AB/GPRC29/c
NAME: IOF Early Childhood Development Bursary
PROGRAM: Early Childhood Development
BASIS: Awarded to a 1st- or 2nd-year student. The selection is based on scholastic ability and financial need. The application must include a transcript of marks and a letter describing hobbies, interests, and extracurricular activities.
MINIMUM AVERAGE: 5.00
VALUE: $500.00
TERMS: One year only
NUMBER OF AWARDS: 1
DEADLINE FOR APPLICATIONS: September 15

CODE: AB/GPRC30/c
NAME: Jazz North Scholarships
PROGRAM: Diploma or Bachelor of Music
BASIS: Awarded to outstanding musicians participating in the Jazz North Festival. The selection will be made by the adjudicators at the festival. No application is necessary, but candidates must be enrolled in a stage band at Jazz North.
MINIMUM AVERAGE: 7.50
VALUE: Varies
TERMS: One year only
NUMBER OF AWARDS: Varies
DEADLINE FOR APPLICATIONS: March 31

CODE: AB/GPRC31/c
NAME: Edgar Jebb Memorial Nursing Bursary
PROGRAM: Nursing
BASIS: Awarded to a 1st-year nursing student who plans to continue into 2nd year. Preference will be given to the son, daughter, or grandchild of a veteran.
MINIMUM AVERAGE: 5.00
VALUE: Varies
TERMS: One year only
NUMBER OF AWARDS: 1
DEADLINE FOR APPLICATIONS: September 15

CODE: AB/GPRC32/c
NAME: Dorothy Kovak Memorial Scholarship
PROGRAM: Nursing
BASIS: Awarded to full-time students who are entering or continuing in the Nursing program at GPRC. The selection is based on financial need and academic achievement.
MINIMUM AVERAGE: 7.50
VALUE: Varies
TERMS: One year only
NUMBER OF AWARDS: Varies
DEADLINE FOR APPLICATIONS: September 15

CODE: AB/GPRC33/c
NAME: B.J. Laninga Memorial Bursary
PROGRAM: Bachelor of Education
BASIS: Awarded to a full-time student who is entering or continuing in the Bachelor of Education program at GPRC. The selection is based on financial need and satisfactory academic achievement. Preference is given to a Canadian citizen.
MINIMUM AVERAGE: 5.00
VALUE: Varies
TERMS: One year only
NUMBER OF AWARDS: 1
DEADLINE FOR APPLICATIONS: September 15

CODE: AB/GPRC34/c
NAME: Honoré Maisonneuve Bursary

PROGRAM: Any
BASIS: Awarded to a full-time student who is entering or continuing a program of study at GPRC. The selection is based on financial need and overall academic achievement.
MINIMUM AVERAGE: 5.00
VALUE: $325.00
TERMS: One year only
NUMBER OF AWARDS: 1
DEADLINE FOR APPLICATIONS: September 15

CODE: AB/GPRC35/c
NAME: Nordic Development David Willis Memorial Bursary
PROGRAM: Any
BASIS: Awarded to a full-time student who is entering GPRC. The selection is based on financial need, academic achievement, and college/community involvement.
MINIMUM AVERAGE: 5.00
VALUE: $350.00
TERMS: One year only
NUMBER OF AWARDS: 1
DEADLINE FOR APPLICATIONS: September 15

CODE: AB/GPRC36/c
NAME: Peace River District Graduate Association Scholarship
PROGRAM: Any
BASIS: Awarded to a student in the city or county of Grande Prairie. The selection is based on the final marks for high school matriculation.
MINIMUM AVERAGE: 7.50
VALUE: $700.00
TERMS: One year only. Also tenable at other institutions.
NUMBER OF AWARDS: 1
DEADLINE FOR APPLICATIONS: September 15

CODE: AB/GPRC37/c
NAME: Northwestern Utilities Bursary
PROGRAM: Any
BASIS: Awarded to a full-time student who is entering GPRC. The selec-

tion is based on financial need, academic achievement, and college/community involvement.
MINIMUM AVERAGE: 5.00
VALUE: Equals tuition fees.
TERMS: One year only
NUMBER OF AWARDS: 1
DEADLINE FOR APPLICATIONS: September 15

CODE: AB/GPRC38/c
NAME: Peace River Livestock Association Bursary
PROGRAM: Various livestock-related programs (e.g., Pre-Veterinary)
BASIS: Awarded to a Peace Country student enrolled in a livestock-oriented program. The selection is based on financial need and academic achievement.
MINIMUM AVERAGE: 5.00
VALUE: $400.00
TERMS: One year only
NUMBER OF AWARDS: 1
DEADLINE FOR APPLICATIONS: September 15

CODE: AB/GPRC39/c
NAME: Performing Arts Awards
PROGRAM: Drama
BASIS: Awarded to a student from the Regional High School Drama Festival who is interested in pursuing a career in drama. Another award will go to an applicant to the drama program on the basis of an interview.
MINIMUM AVERAGE: 7.50
VALUE: Equals tuition fees.
TERMS: One year only
NUMBER OF AWARDS: 1
DEADLINE FOR APPLICATIONS: September 15

CODE: AB/GPRC40/c
NAME: President's Ball Bursaries
PROGRAM: Any
BASIS: Awarded to a full-time entering or continuing student at GPRC. The selection is based on financial need, satisfactory academic

achievement, and/or college/community involvement.
MINIMUM AVERAGE: 5.00
VALUE: Varies
TERMS: One year only
NUMBER OF AWARDS: Varies
DEADLINE FOR APPLICATIONS:
September 15

CODE: AB/GPRC41/c
NAME: Reed Stenhouse Limited Bursary
PROGRAM: Business Administration
BASIS: Awarded to a student enrolled in Business Administration program. The selection is based on financial need and academic achievment
MINIMUM AVERAGE: 5.00
VALUE: Equals tuition fees.
TERMS: One year only
NUMBER OF AWARDS: 1
DEADLINE FOR APPLICATIONS:
September 15

CODE: AB/GPRC42/c
NAME: Rehabilitation Practitioner Bursary
PROGRAM: Rehabilitation Practitioner
BASIS: Awarded to a full-time student entering or continuing in the Rehabilitation Practitioner program. The selection is based on financial need and academic performance.
MINIMUM AVERAGE: 5.00
VALUE: Varies
TERMS: One year only
NUMBER OF AWARDS: Varies
DEADLINE FOR APPLICATIONS:
September 15

CODE: AB/GPRC43/c
NAME: Royal Canadian Legion, Alberta–N.W.T.
PROGRAM: Any
BASIS: Applicants must be native or naturalized Canadians and the sons, daughters, grandsons, or granddaughters of ex–service personnel or veterans, living or deceased. The selection is based on

financial need and satisfactory scholastic record.
MINIMUM AVERAGE: 7.50
VALUE: $500.00
TERMS: One year only
NUMBER OF AWARDS: 2
DEADLINE FOR APPLICATIONS:
September 15

CODE: AB/GPRC44/c
NAME: Royal Canadian Legion Branch #54 Bursary
PROGRAM: Any
BASIS: Awarded to students from the Peace River region, with preference given to the sons, daughters, grandsons, or granddaughters of ex–service personnel or veterans, living or deceased. The selection is based on financial need and previous academic work.
MINIMUM AVERAGE: 5.00
VALUE: $500.00
TERMS: One year only
NUMBER OF AWARDS: Varies
DEADLINE FOR APPLICATIONS:
September 15

CODE: AB/GPRC45/c
NAME: Florrie E. Shumard Bursary
PROGRAM: Any
BASIS: Awarded to a Berwyn area student entering or continuing studies at GPRC. If necessary, students from a wider rural area between Fairview and Peace River may be considered. Awarded on the basis of financial need and academic achievement.
MINIMUM AVERAGE: 5.00
VALUE: Varies
TERMS: One year only
NUMBER OF AWARDS: Varies
DEADLINE FOR APPLICATIONS:
September 15

CODE: AB/GPRC46/c
NAME: Henrick Solheim and Andy Haugen Bursary
PROGRAM: Bachelor of Commerce or Pre-Law

BASIS: Awarded to an entering student on the basis of financial need, academic achievement, and college/community involvement.
MINIMUM AVERAGE: 5.00
VALUE: $300.00
TERMS: One year only
NUMBER OF AWARDS: Varies
DEADLINE FOR APPLICATIONS: September 15

CODE: AB/GPRC47/c
NAME: Willis Repka Pre-Law Scholarship
PROGRAM: Pre-law
BASIS: Awarded to an entering student or continuing student on the basis of financial need, academic standing, and participation in student government, community affairs, or athletics.
MINIMUM AVERAGE: 7.50
VALUE: Varies
TERMS: One year only
NUMBER OF AWARDS: 1
DEADLINE FOR APPLICATIONS: September 15

CODE: AB/GPRC48/c
NAME: Henry Wise Wood Memorial Bursary
PROGRAM: Any program related to Agriculture
BASIS: Awarded to a full-time student from the Alberta and BC Peace River Block whose parents derive the major portion of their income from farming. The selection is based on academic achievement and financial need.
MINIMUM AVERAGE: 5.00
VALUE: $500.00
TERMS: One year only
NUMBER OF AWARDS: 1
DEADLINE FOR APPLICATIONS: September 15

Grant MacEwan Community College

CODE: AB/GRMC000/c
NAME: Grant MacEwan Community College does not offer entrance scholarships.

Keyano College

CODE: AB/KEY001/c
NAME: Keith Agnew Memorial Bursary
PROGRAM: Any
BASIS: Awarded to a life or ordinary member, or the son/daughter or ordinary member of Branch #165 of the Legion. Proof of Legion membership must be provided. The selection is based on financial need.
MINIMUM AVERAGE: 60.00
VALUE: $500.00
TERMS: Renewable only during the applicant's current registration period.
NUMBER OF AWARDS: 1
DEADLINE FOR APPLICATIONS: September 25

CODE: AB/KEY002/c
NAME: Alberta Union of Public Employees (AUPE) Bursary
PROGRAM: Any
BASIS: Awarded to members in good standing of the Alberta Union of Public Employees or sons, daughters, legal wards, or spouses of members. Dependents of retired or deceased members are eligible. The selection is based on financial need and academic achievement.
MINIMUM AVERAGE: 60.00
VALUE: $300.00
TERMS: One year only
NUMBER OF AWARDS: 2
DEADLINE FOR APPLICATIONS: September 25

CODE: AB/KEY003/c
NAME: Business and Professional Women's Club of Fort McMurray Bursary
PROGRAM: Any
BASIS: Awarded to a mature female student who is re-entering the education system and can demonstrate financial need.
MINIMUM AVERAGE: 60.00
VALUE: $500.00
TERMS: One year only
NUMBER OF AWARDS: 1
DEADLINE FOR APPLICATIONS: September 25

CODE: AB/KEY004/c
NAME: Canadian Union of Public Employees (CUPE) Local 2157 Bursary
PROGRAM: Any
BASIS: Awarded to a full-time Keyano student who is enrolled in a program of at least 8 weeks' duration. The selection is based on financial need and academic achievement. Preference is given to a CUPE member, or the spouse, child, or grandchild of same.
MINIMUM AVERAGE: 60.00
VALUE: $500.00
TERMS: One year only
NUMBER OF AWARDS: 1
DEADLINE FOR APPLICATIONS: September 25

CODE: AB/KEY005/c
NAME: City of Fort McMurray Bursary
PROGRAM: Any
BASIS: Awarded to a student who previously attended a Fort McMurray high school for at least 2 years and is enrolled in a certificate or diploma program at Keyano.
MINIMUM AVERAGE: 60.00
VALUE: $250.00
TERMS: One year only
NUMBER OF AWARDS: 1
DEADLINE FOR APPLICATIONS: September 25

CODE: AB/KEY006/c
NAME: Edmonton Northlands Single Parent Bursary
PROGRAM: Any
BASIS: Awarded to full-time students who are single parents and are enrolled in a certificate or diploma program.
MINIMUM AVERAGE: 60.00
VALUE: $1000.00
TERMS: One year only
NUMBER OF AWARDS: 3
DEADLINE FOR APPLICATIONS: September 25

CODE: AB/KEY007/c
NAME: Keyano College Alumni Bursary
PROGRAM: Career or University Transfer
BASIS: Awarded to any registered member of the Alumni Association, his/her spouse, or dependent who is attending as a full-time student. Awarded on the basis of financial need, past academic performance, and alumni involvement. Proof of membership is required.
MINIMUM AVERAGE: 60.00
VALUE: $250.00
TERMS: One year only
NUMBER OF AWARDS: 1
DEADLINE FOR APPLICATIONS: September 25

CODE: AB/KEY008/c
NAME: Royal Canadian Legion Branch No. 165 Bursary
PROGRAM: Any
BASIS: Awarded to life or ordinary members or the sons/daughters of members of McMurray Branch #165 of the Legion. Recipients must be full-time students. Proof of Legion membership must be provided.
MINIMUM AVERAGE: 60.00
VALUE: $300.00
TERMS: Renewable. Recipients must reapply prior to their next registration period.

NUMBER OF AWARDS: 1
DEADLINE FOR APPLICATIONS:
September 25

CODE: AB/KEY009/c
NAME: Ted Walter Bursary
PROGRAM: Any
BASIS: Awarded to a Native (Treaty, Bill C31, or Métis) student enrolled full-time in a certficate or diploma program. Based on financial need and satisfactory academic achievement.
MINIMUM AVERAGE: 60.00
VALUE: $500.00
TERMS: One year only
NUMBER OF AWARDS: 1
DEADLINE FOR APPLICATIONS:
September 25

CODE: AB/KEY010/c
NAME: C.D. MacRae Business Education Bursary
PROGRAM: Business Education
BASIS: Awarded to a former student of Fort McMurray Composite High School. The selection is based on financial need and academic achievement.
MINIMUM AVERAGE: 60.00
VALUE: $500.00
TERMS: One year only
NUMBER OF AWARDS: 1
DEADLINE FOR APPLICATIONS:
September 25

CODE: AB/KEY011/c
NAME: Westbridge C.B.S. Entrance Award
PROGRAM: Computer Business Systems
BASIS: Awarded to a local high school graduate enrolled in the C.B.S. program. The recipient will have a Grade 12 average of 65% and will have shown community involvement.
MINIMUM AVERAGE: 60.00
VALUE: $500.00
TERMS: One year only
NUMBER OF AWARDS: 1

DEADLINE FOR APPLICATIONS:
September 25

CODE: AB/KEY012/c
NAME: Donna Cyprien Award
PROGRAM: Early Childhood Development
BASIS: Awarded to a student entering the Early Childhood Development program who has obtained the prerequisites for ECD in the Fort Chipewyan community by attending either the local high school or the Fort Chipewyan Keyano Campus.
MINIMUM AVERAGE: 60.00
VALUE: $150.00
TERMS: One year only
NUMBER OF AWARDS: 1
DEADLINE FOR APPLICATIONS:
September 25

CODE: AB/KEY013/c
NAME: Chris Ryan Memorial Bursary
PROGRAM: Nursing
BASIS: Awarded to a student who has graduated from Grade 12 or completes College Preparation. Awarded on the basis of financial need and community involvement.
MINIMUM AVERAGE: 60.00
VALUE: $300.00
TERMS: One year only
NUMBER OF AWARDS: 1
DEADLINE FOR APPLICATIONS:
September 25

CODE: AB/KEY014/c
NAME: Ron Wolff Bursary
PROGRAM: Nursing
BASIS: Awarded to a Grade 12 graduate enrolled in the 1st year of the Nursing program. Awarded on the basis of academic achievement and financial need.
MINIMUM AVERAGE: 60.00
VALUE: $500.00
TERMS: One year only
NUMBER OF AWARDS: 1
DEADLINE FOR APPLICATIONS:
September 25

CODE: AB/KEY015/c
NAME: Dr. Nicholson Bachelor of Arts
Entrance Award
PROGRAM: Bachelor of Arts
BASIS: Awarded to a local high school
graduate who enrolls in the Bachelor of Arts program. Awarded on
the basis of financial need.
MINIMUM AVERAGE: 60.00
VALUE: $550.00
TERMS: One year only
NUMBER OF AWARDS: 1
DEADLINE FOR APPLICATIONS:
September 25

CODE: AB/KEY016/c
NAME: Delta Catalytic Corporation
Engineering Award
PROGRAM: University Transfer –
Engineering
BASIS: Awarded to a student entering
the University Transfer – Engineering program. Awarded on the basis
academic achievement and financial need.
MINIMUM AVERAGE: 60.00
VALUE: $500.00
TERMS: One year only
NUMBER OF AWARDS: 1
DEADLINE FOR APPLICATIONS:
September 25

Lakeland College

CODE: AB/LAKE01/c
NAME: Earle Associate Consulting
Scholarship
PROGRAM: Business Administration,
Lloydminster Campus
BASIS: Available to a 1st-year full-time
Lakeland student. The award is
based on high school academic
achievement and contributions to
school and/or community life.
MINIMUM AVERAGE: N/A
VALUE: $300.00
TERMS: One year only
NUMBER OF AWARDS: 1
DEADLINE FOR APPLICATIONS: August 1

CODE: AB/LAKE02/c
NAME: Ed Jenson and Family
Scholarship
PROGRAM: University Transfer
BASIS: Awarded to a student entering
full-time credit program in University Transfer. The selection is based
on satisfactory academics, leadership in school and community activities, and positive attitude.
Musical interest and talent may be
considered.
MINIMUM AVERAGE: N/A
VALUE: $400.00
TERMS: One year only
NUMBER OF AWARDS: 1
DEADLINE FOR APPLICATIONS: August 1

CODE: AB/LAKE03/c
NAME: Herman Huber Award
PROGRAM: Any at the Vermillion
Campus
BASIS: Awarded to an Alberta resident entering a full-time program.
The selection is based on commitment to academic achievement in
high school and a short autobiographical essay describing contributions made to school and/or
community life.
MINIMUM AVERAGE: N/A
VALUE: $200.00
TERMS: One year only
NUMBER OF AWARDS: 1
DEADLINE FOR APPLICATIONS: August 1

CODE: AB/LAKE04/c
NAME: Husky Oil Entrance
Scholarships
PROGRAM: Heavy Oil Technician (full-time), Lloydminster Campus
BASIS: Awarded to students entering
full-time studies. The selection is
based on commitment to academic
achievement in high school and a
short autobiographical essay describing contributions made to
school and/or community life.
MINIMUM AVERAGE: N/A
VALUE: $300.00
TERMS: One year only

NUMBER OF AWARDS: 2
DEADLINE FOR APPLICATIONS: August 1

CODE: AB/LAKE05/c
NAME: ISPAS Wildlife Refuge Scholarship
PROGRAM: Environmental Sciences, Vermillion Campus
BASIS: Available to a 1st-year full-time Lakeland student. The award is based on high school academic achievement and contributions to school and/or community life. Recipients must be Canadian citizens, with 1st preference given to Alberta students.
MINIMUM AVERAGE: N/A
VALUE: $500.00
TERMS: One year only
NUMBER OF AWARDS: 2
DEADLINE FOR APPLICATIONS: August 1

CODE: AB/LAKE06/c
NAME: John Dahmer Community Involvement Scholarship
PROGRAM: Any, at any Lakeland campus
BASIS: Awarded to an Alberta resident entering a full-time program. The selection is based on commitment to academic achievement in high school and a short autobiographical essay describing contributions made to school and/or community life.
MINIMUM AVERAGE: N/A
VALUE: $300.00
TERMS: One year only
NUMBER OF AWARDS: 1
DEADLINE FOR APPLICATIONS: August 1

CODE: AB/LAKE07/c
NAME: Lakeland College Scholarship for Excellence
PROGRAM: Any, at any Lakeland campus
BASIS: Available to matriculated students entering full-time studies. These awards are based on academic merit throughout the applicant's high school career, contribu-

tions to school and/or community life, and an indication of academic promise.
MINIMUM AVERAGE: N/A
VALUE: $1000.00
TERMS: One year only
NUMBER OF AWARDS: 1
DEADLINE FOR APPLICATIONS: August 1

CODE: AB/LAKE08/c
NAME: Matt and Mary McDonald Memorial Award
PROGRAM: Any, at any Lakeland campus
BASIS: Awarded to a student entering full-time studies at Lakeland. The selection is based on a commitment to academic achievement in high school and community and/or school involvement, with preference given for 4-H involvement.
MINIMUM AVERAGE: N/A
VALUE: $400.00
TERMS: One year only
NUMBER OF AWARDS: 1
DEADLINE FOR APPLICATIONS: August 1

CODE: AB/LAKE09/c
NAME: Colchester and District Agricultural Society Scholarship
PROGRAM: Agriculture-related
BASIS: Awarded on the basis of academic achievement and a short autobiographical essay describing the applicant's contribution to school and/or community life. Preference will be given to Alberta residents of Strathcona County.
MINIMUM AVERAGE: N/A
VALUE: Varies
TERMS: One year only
NUMBER OF AWARDS: 1
DEADLINE FOR APPLICATIONS: August 1

CODE: AB/LAKE10/c
NAME: Peter J. Gulak Entrance Scholarship
PROGRAM: Business Administration, Lloydminster Campus
BASIS: Awarded to a student entering full-time studies. The selection is

based on academic merit, contributions to school and/or community life, and indications of academic promise.

MINIMUM AVERAGE: N/A
VALUE: $500.00
TERMS: One year only
NUMBER OF AWARDS: 1
DEADLINE FOR APPLICATIONS: August 1

Lethbridge Community College

CODE: AB/LETH01/c
NAME: Alberta Treasury Branches Bursary
PROGRAM: Agricultural Technology
BASIS: Awarded to an Alberta resident whose parents are currently engaged in agricultural production in Alberta. Candidates must have an interest in the field of Agriculture/Business. The selection is based on academic achievement, leadership, and school activities.
MINIMUM AVERAGE: N/A
VALUE: $500.00
TERMS: One year only
NUMBER OF AWARDS: 1
DEADLINE FOR APPLICATIONS: September 1

CODE: AB/LETH02/c
NAME: Andy Anderson Student Leadership Award
PROGRAM: Any career program
BASIS: Awarded to a graduate of a City of Lethbridge High School, entering a 2-year career program at Lethbridge CC. Leadership qualities in high school will be considered.
MINIMUM AVERAGE: N/A
VALUE: $350.00
TERMS: One year only
NUMBER OF AWARDS: 1
DEADLINE FOR APPLICATIONS: September 1

CODE: AB/LETH03/c
NAME: Canada Winter Games Scholarship
PROGRAM: Any career program
BASIS: Awarded to residents of Southern Alberta who are active in athletics at the high school level, have contributed to the community, and have demonstrated academic proficiency.
MINIMUM AVERAGE: N/A
VALUE: $1000.00
TERMS: One year only. Value of awards varies.
NUMBER OF AWARDS: Varies
DEADLINE FOR APPLICATIONS: September 1

CODE: AB/LETH04/c
NAME: Dr. Frank Christie Award
PROGRAM: Prepatory Upgrading
BASIS: Awarded to mature students (19 years of age and over, out of high school at least one year) and with dependents. Financial need will be considered.
MINIMUM AVERAGE: N/A
VALUE: $175.00
TERMS: One year only. Awarded in 2 instalments.
NUMBER OF AWARDS: 2
DEADLINE FOR APPLICATIONS: September 1

CODE: AB/LETH05/c
NAME: Canbra Food Educational Award
PROGRAM: Any full-time program
BASIS: Open to dependents of Canbra Foods employees. In the absence of an eligible dependent, graduates of City of Lethbridge high schools will be considered. The selection is based on high school average and financial need.
MINIMUM AVERAGE: N/A
VALUE: $500.00
TERMS: One year only. Not tenable with any other award of greater value.

NUMBER OF AWARDS: 1
DEADLINE FOR APPLICATIONS: July 15
CODE: AB/LETH06/c
NAME: Frank M. and Lila Linn
Thompson Scholarship (I)
PROGRAM: Any
BASIS: Awarded to students who obtain the highest average in Grade 12 marks of all high school students in the City of Lethbridge. The selection is also based on the same criteria as the Alexander Rutherford Scholarships (see AB/ALHER1/g, p. 274).
MINIMUM AVERAGE: N/A
VALUE: $500.00
TERMS: One year only
NUMBER OF AWARDS: Approx. 4
DEADLINE FOR APPLICATIONS:
September 1

CODE: AB/LETH07/c
NAME: Frank M. and Lila Linn
Thompson Scholarship (II)
PROGRAM: Nursing
BASIS: Awarded to students on the basis of the highest academic average of the five 30 Level courses required to enter the Nursing program. The applicants must also have achieved satisfactory pre-admission test scores prior to acceptance into the Nursing program.
MINIMUM AVERAGE: N/A
VALUE: $600.00
TERMS: One year only
NUMBER OF AWARDS: 3
DEADLINE FOR APPLICATIONS:
September 1

CODE: AB/LETH08/c
NAME: Frank M. and Lila Linn
Thompson Scholarship (III)
PROGRAM: Nursing
BASIS: Awarded to mature students based on the highest academic average of the three 30 Level courses required to enter the Nursing program. The applicants must also have achieved satisfactory pre-admission test scores prior to acceptance into the Nursing program.
MINIMUM AVERAGE: N/A
VALUE: $600.00
TERMS: One year only
NUMBER OF AWARDS: 2
DEADLINE FOR APPLICATIONS:
September 1

CODE: AB/LETH09/c
NAME: Lethbridge Community
College Entrance Scholarship
PROGRAM: Any credit certificate/
diploma program
BASIS: For full-time students entering Lethbridge CC. The selection is based on academic achievement in high school or upgrading courses taken at the post-secondary level. Financial need will also be considered.
MINIMUM AVERAGE: N/A
VALUE: $500.00
TERMS: One year only. Not tenable with other awards.
NUMBER OF AWARDS: Varies
DEADLINE FOR APPLICATIONS:
September 1

CODE: AB/LETH10/c
NAME: Siguard E. Hansen Scholarship
PROGRAM: Nursing
BASIS: For students entering the Nursing program at Lethbridge CC. The selection is based on high school academic achievement or academic achievement in the LCC Upgrading Program.
MINIMUM AVERAGE: N/A
VALUE: $500.00
TERMS: One year only. Not tenable with other awards.
NUMBER OF AWARDS: Approx. 3
DEADLINE FOR APPLICATIONS:
September 1

CODE: AB/LETH11/c
NAME: Vencl Hrncirik Memorial
Scholarship
PROGRAM: Agricultural Technology

BASIS: Awarded to a graduate from the County of Lethbridge entering the Agricultural Technology program.
MINIMUM AVERAGE: N/A
VALUE: $100.00
TERMS: One year only
NUMBER OF AWARDS: 1
DEADLINE FOR APPLICATIONS: September 1

CODE: AB/LETH12/c
NAME: William Asbury Buchanan Bursary
PROGRAM: Any
BASIS: Awarded to an outstanding student in the Lethbridge, Lethbridge Separate, or County of Lethbridge school districts. The selection is based on academic standing, financial need, and extracurricular activities.
MINIMUM AVERAGE: N/A
VALUE: $250.00
TERMS: One year only
NUMBER OF AWARDS: 1
DEADLINE FOR APPLICATIONS: September 1

Medicine Hat College

CODE: AB/MED001/c
NAME: Major Academic Excellence Scholarships
PROGRAM: Any
BASIS: Awarded to entering students on the basis of the average of their 6 best high school subjects, including English 30, Math 30, Math 31, Social 30, Biology 30, Physics 30, French 30, German 30, or equivalents.
MINIMUM AVERAGE: 86.00
VALUE: $1000.00
TERMS: One year only. Awarded in 2 equal payments.
NUMBER OF AWARDS: Up to 10
DEADLINE FOR APPLICATIONS: September 4

CODE: AB/MED002/c
NAME: First Year Academic Scholarships
PROGRAM: Any
BASIS: Awarded to entering students on the basis of the average of their 4 best high school subjects, including English 30, Math 30, Math 31, Social 30, Biology 30, Physics 30, French 30, German 30, or equivalents.
MINIMUM AVERAGE: 75.00
VALUE: $200.00
TERMS: One year only
NUMBER OF AWARDS: Varies
DEADLINE FOR APPLICATIONS: September 4

CODE: AB/MED003/c
NAME: Medicine Hat College Tuition Waiver
PROGRAM: Any 5 full-credit courses in a University Transfer, Certificate, or Diploma program.
BASIS: Awarded to an entering student from each of the designated high schools in southeastern Alberta.
MINIMUM AVERAGE: N/A
VALUE: Equals 1st-semester tuition fees.
TERMS: One year only
NUMBER OF AWARDS: Varies
DEADLINE FOR APPLICATIONS: September 4

CODE: AB/MED004/c
NAME: Service Recognition Scholarships
PROGRAM: Any
BASIS: Awarded to students with a record of community, school, and College service. Recipients will be expected to assist with various campus functions; e.g., peer tutors and athletic team managers.
MINIMUM AVERAGE: N/A
VALUE: Varies. These scholarships are dependent on the availability of funds.
TERMS: One year only

NUMBER OF AWARDS: Varies
DEADLINE FOR APPLICATIONS:
September 4

CODE: AB/MED005/c
NAME: Technician/Technology
Scholarships
PROGRAM: Computer Aided Drafting
Technology Certificate, Computer
Systems Technology Diploma, or
Power Engineering Technology
Diploma
BASIS: Awarded to students entering
technology courses. The selection is
based on the average of their best 4
high school academic subjects.
MINIMUM AVERAGE: 75.00
VALUE: $500.00
TERMS: One year only
NUMBER OF AWARDS: 4
DEADLINE FOR APPLICATIONS:
September 4

CODE: AB/MED006/c
NAME: Alberta Energy Company
Scholarships
PROGRAM: Business Administration,
Commerce, Computer Science,
Engineering, or Computer Systems
Technology
BASIS: Awarded to students with out-
standing academic potential. Finan-
cial need will also be considered.
Candidates must be graduates of a
high school in Alberta.
MINIMUM AVERAGE: 75.00
VALUE: $750.00
TERMS: One year only
NUMBER OF AWARDS: 4
DEADLINE FOR APPLICATIONS:
September 4

CODE: AB/MED007/c
NAME: Angus Gordon Scholarship
PROGRAM: Bachelor of Science or
Commerce, with an emphasis on
accounting
BASIS: Awarded to a student entering
Medicine Hat College
MINIMUM AVERAGE: 75.00
VALUE: Varies

TERMS: One year only
NUMBER OF AWARDS: 1
DEADLINE FOR APPLICATIONS:
September 4

CODE: AB/MED008/c
NAME: Medicine Hat and District
Chamber of Commerce
PROGRAM: Computer Systems Tech-
nology, Office Technology, Busi-
ness Administration, or Travel
Consultant
BASIS: Awarded to a student entering
Medicine Hat C. The selection is
based on academic performance
and financial need.
MINIMUM AVERAGE: 75.00
VALUE: $300.00
TERMS: One year only
NUMBER OF AWARDS: 1
DEADLINE FOR APPLICATIONS:
September 4

CODE: AB/MED009/c
NAME: Eileen Sissons Memorial
Scholarships
PROGRAM: Education, with a music
major
BASIS: Awarded to students in 1st and
2nd year. Early Childhood Devel-
opment students may be con-
sidered.
MINIMUM AVERAGE: N/A
VALUE: $500.00
TERMS: One year only
NUMBER OF AWARDS: 2
DEADLINE FOR APPLICATIONS:
September 4

CODE: AB/MED010/c
NAME: Estelle and Malcolm McArthur
Scholarships
PROGRAM: Library Science or Educa-
tion
BASIS: Awarded to students enrolling
in Medicine Hat C from Cypress
School Division #4; i.e., Irvine,
Schuler, Walsh, or Seven Persons
area.
MINIMUM AVERAGE: N/A
VALUE: Varies

TERMS: One year only
NUMBER OF AWARDS: 4
DEADLINE FOR APPLICATIONS:
September 4

CODE: AB/MED011/c
NAME: I.X.L. Industries Scholarships
PROGRAM: University Transfer Engineering
BASIS: Awarded to a student achieving exceptional academic achievement in high school who is registered in the University Transfer Engineering program. Where possible, the student should have a career interest in Ceramic or Industrial Engineering.
MINIMUM AVERAGE: N/A
VALUE: $400.00
TERMS: One year only. I.X.L. Industries may be able to consider continued support in the form of summer employment.
NUMBER OF AWARDS: 1
DEADLINE FOR APPLICATIONS:
September 4

CODE: AB/MED012/c
NAME: TransAlta Utilities Corporation Engineering Scholarship
PROGRAM: Engineering
BASIS: Awarded to students who reside in an area served directly or indirectly by TransAlta Utilities. The selection is based on matriculation academic excellence.
MINIMUM AVERAGE: N/A
VALUE: Varies
TERMS: One year only
NUMBER OF AWARDS: 1
DEADLINE FOR APPLICATIONS:
September 4

CODE: AB/MED013/c
NAME: Alberta Wheat Pool "Henry Wise Wood Bursary"
PROGRAM: Any
BASIS: Awarded to a rural student. The selection is based on academic achievement and financial need. The recipient's parents must reside in Alberta or in the Peace River block of BC, and derive the major portion of their income from farming.
MINIMUM AVERAGE: N/A
VALUE: $500.00
TERMS: One year only
NUMBER OF AWARDS: 1
DEADLINE FOR APPLICATIONS:
September 4

CODE: AB/MED014/c
NAME: Bar Association of Medicine Hat Scholarship
PROGRAM: Any
BASIS: Awarded to students entering Medicine Hat C. Financial need will also be considered.
MINIMUM AVERAGE: 80.00
VALUE: $150.00
TERMS: One year only
NUMBER OF AWARDS: 2
DEADLINE FOR APPLICATIONS:
September 4

CODE: AB/MED015/c
NAME: Big M Lincoln Mercury Sales (1988) Ltd Award
PROGRAM: Any
BASIS: Awarded to a graduating rural high school student entering Medicine Hat C. A high academic average and financial need will be considered.
MINIMUM AVERAGE: N/A
VALUE: $250.00
TERMS: One year only
NUMBER OF AWARDS: 1
DEADLINE FOR APPLICATIONS:
September 4

CODE: AB/MED016/c
NAME: Harry Hutchings Memorial Bursary
PROGRAM: Any
BASIS: Awarded to a high school student entering Medicine Hat C. The selection is based on the average of 5 matriculation subjects.
MINIMUM AVERAGE: 70.00
VALUE: Varies

TERMS: One year only
NUMBER OF AWARDS: 1
DEADLINE FOR APPLICATIONS:
September 4

CODE: AB/MED017/c
NAME: Independent Order of Odd
Fellows Centennial Scholarship
PROGRAM: University Transfer Science
program, with preference given to
those applicants interested in pur-
suing a career in optometry.
BASIS: Awarded to a graduate of the
school districts in Medicine Hat
and the municipal district of Cy-
press. Financial need will be con-
sidered.
MINIMUM AVERAGE: 75.00
VALUE: Varies
TERMS: One year only
NUMBER OF AWARDS: 1
DEADLINE FOR APPLICATIONS:
September 4

CODE: AB/MED018/c
NAME: Medicine Hat Masonic Lodge
#2 A.F. & A.M.
PROGRAM: University Transfer Science
program
BASIS: Awarded to either a 1st-year or
2nd-year student. Financial need
will be considered.
MINIMUM AVERAGE: 75.00
VALUE: Varies
TERMS: One year only
NUMBER OF AWARDS: 1
DEADLINE FOR APPLICATIONS:
September 4

CODE: AB/MED019/c
NAME: Medicine Hat Exhibition and
Stampede Scholarships
PROGRAM: Various
BASIS: Awarded to students enrolled
in an approved course of study at
Medicine Hat College who are
chosen as the Queen or Princess of
the Medicine Hat Exhibition and
Stampede. Recipients must display
community leadership and interest
in Western issues.

MINIMUM AVERAGE: N/A
VALUE: $3000.00
TERMS: One year only
NUMBER OF AWARDS: 3
DEADLINE FOR APPLICATIONS:
September 4

CODE: AB/MED020/c
NAME: Métis Nations Local #8
Scholarships
PROGRAM: Early Childhood Develop-
ment, Computer Systems Technol-
ogy, Computer Aided Drafting,
Industrial Generalist, or Office
Technology
BASIS: Awarded to student(s) who are
of Métis or Native Indian back-
ground in recognition of those who
contribute their time and effort to
create awareness of the Métis Na-
tion Local #8.
MINIMUM AVERAGE: N/A
VALUE: Varies
TERMS: One year only
NUMBER OF AWARDS: Varies
DEADLINE FOR APPLICATIONS:
September 4

CODE: AB/MED021/c
NAME: Métis Nations Reuben Lee
Local #8
PROGRAM: Any full-time program
BASIS: Awarded to a Métis student.
Preference will be give to relatives
or members of Local #8, or those
who are eligible for full member-
ship in the Métis Nations of Alber-
ta. Financial need and potential for
academic successs will be con-
sidered.
MINIMUM AVERAGE: N/A
VALUE: Varies
TERMS: One year only. Under certain
circumstances, non-Métis appli-
cants may be considered.
NUMBER OF AWARDS: 1
DEADLINE FOR APPLICATIONS:
September 4

CODE: AB/MED022/c
NAME: Ottrey Memorial Scholarship

PROGRAM: Any
BASIS: In awarding this scholarship, preference will be given to students with a physical handicap and/or those who have demonstrated courage in continuing their education.
MINIMUM AVERAGE: N/A
VALUE: Varies
TERMS: One year only
NUMBER OF AWARDS: 1
DEADLINE FOR APPLICATIONS: September 4

CODE: AB/MED023/c
NAME: Troy McLaughlin Memorial Scholarship
PROGRAM: Any
BASIS: Awarded to Crescent Heights High School graduates enrolling in full-time studies at Medicine Hat C. Academic achievement and extracurricular involvement will be considered. Preference will be given to participants in the high school band program.
MINIMUM AVERAGE: N/A
VALUE: Varies
TERMS: One year only
NUMBER OF AWARDS: 1
DEADLINE FOR APPLICATIONS: September 4

CODE: AB/MED024/c
NAME: A & B Steel & Aluminum (1979) Ltd Scholarship
PROGRAM: Trades
BASIS: Awarded to a student entering a Trades program at Medicine Hat C. This award is based on potential for success and financial need.
MINIMUM AVERAGE: N/A
VALUE: $350.00
TERMS: One year only
NUMBER OF AWARDS: 1
DEADLINE FOR APPLICATIONS: September 4

CODE: AB/MED025/c
NAME: Brooks Bulletin Scholarship (Brooks Campus)
PROGRAM: Education
BASIS: Awarded to Brooks and County High School students who are enrolled in an Education program.
MINIMUM AVERAGE: N/A
VALUE: $350.00
TERMS: One year only. Value of awards vary.
NUMBER OF AWARDS: Varies
DEADLINE FOR APPLICATIONS: September 4

CODE: AB/MED026/c
NAME: Irvine Chinook Club Scholarship
PROGRAM: Any
BASIS: Awarded to a student who is currently enrolled at Irvine High School who achieves an average of at least 65% on any five Grade 12 matriculation subjects. Candidates should apply to the Secretary, Irvine Chinook Club, Irvine AB, or contact the Irvine High School principal.
MINIMUM AVERAGE: 65.00
VALUE: $250.00
TERMS: One year only. Tenable at Medicine Hat C only.
NUMBER OF AWARDS: 1
DEADLINE FOR APPLICATIONS: August 15

Mount Royal College

CODE: AB/MRC001/c
NAME: Board of Governors Entrance Scholarship
PROGRAM: Any
BASIS: For a Grade 12 high school graduate entering Mount Royal C. Awarded on the basis of academic excellence in Grade 12. A copy of an official high school transcript must accompany the scholarship application.
MINIMUM AVERAGE: 75.00
VALUE: $1500.00
TERMS: One year only

NUMBER OF AWARDS: 1
DEADLINE FOR APPLICATIONS: October 31

CODE: AB/MRC002/c
NAME: City of Calgary Scholarships
PROGRAM: Any
BASIS: Awarded to graduates of Calgary high schools. An official high school transcript must accompany the application.
MINIMUM AVERAGE: 75.00
VALUE: $700.00
TERMS: One year only
NUMBER OF AWARDS: 3
DEADLINE FOR APPLICATIONS: October 31

CODE: AB/MRC003/c
NAME: Dr. George W. Kerby Memorial Scholarship
PROGRAM: Any
BASIS: For a Grade 12 high school graduate entering Mount Royal C. Awarded on the basis of academic proficiency in Grade 12 matriculation courses. A copy of an official high school transcript must accompany the scholarship application.
MINIMUM AVERAGE: 75.00
VALUE: $600.00
TERMS: One year only
NUMBER OF AWARDS: 1
DEADLINE FOR APPLICATIONS: October 31

CODE: AB/MRC004/c
NAME: Mount Royal College Entrance Scholarships
PROGRAM: Any
BASIS: For 1st-year students enrolled full-time in any program at Mount Royal C. Awarded on the basis of academic proficiency in Grade 12 matriculation courses. A copy of an official high school transcript must accompany the scholarship application.
MINIMUM AVERAGE: 75.00
VALUE: $600.00
TERMS: One year only

NUMBER OF AWARDS: 1
DEADLINE FOR APPLICATIONS: October 31

CODE: AB/MRC005/c
NAME: Native Calgarian Society Scholarship
PROGRAM: Any
BASIS: Awarded to a full-time student who was born in Calgary and who has demonstrated academic proficiency in Grade 12. An official high school transcript must accompany the application.
MINIMUM AVERAGE: 75.00
VALUE: $100.00
TERMS: One year only
NUMBER OF AWARDS: 1
DEADLINE FOR APPLICATIONS: October 31

CODE: AB/MRC006/c
NAME: Nickle Family Foundation Scholarship – Business Administration
PROGRAM: Business Administration
BASIS: Awarded to a full-time student enrolled in the 1st year of Business Adminstration who is a graduate of a southern Alberta high school. Academic proficiency in Grade 12 will be considered. An official high school transcript must accompany the application.
MINIMUM AVERAGE: N/A
VALUE: Varies
TERMS: One year only
NUMBER OF AWARDS: 1
DEADLINE FOR APPLICATIONS: October 31

CODE: AB/MRC007/c
NAME: Nickle Family Foundation Scholarship – Engineering
PROGRAM: Engineering
BASIS: Awarded to a full-time student enrolled in the 1st year of Engineering who is a graduate of a southern Alberta high school. Academic proficiency in Grade 12 will be considered. An official high

school transcript must accompany the application.
MINIMUM AVERAGE: 75.00
VALUE: Varies
TERMS: One year only
NUMBER OF AWARDS: 1
DEADLINE FOR APPLICATIONS: October 31

CODE: AB/MRC008/c
NAME: Jim Sinclair Insurance Bursary
PROGRAM: General Insurance and Business Administration
BASIS: Awarded to a full-time student enrolled in the 1st year of the General Insurance and Business Adminstration program. Academic proficiency and financial need will be considered. An official high school transcript must accompany the application.
MINIMUM AVERAGE: N/A
VALUE: Varies
TERMS: One year only
NUMBER OF AWARDS: 1
DEADLINE FOR APPLICATIONS: October 31

CODE: AB/MRC009/c
NAME: TransAlta Utilities Engineering Scholarship
PROGRAM: Engineering
BASIS: Awarded to a full-time student enrolled in the 1st year of Engineering who is a graduate of an Alberta high school in an area served by TransAlta Utilities Corporation. Academic proficiency and financial need will be considered. An application is required.
MINIMUM AVERAGE: 75.00
VALUE: $500.00
TERMS: One year only
NUMBER OF AWARDS: 1
DEADLINE FOR APPLICATIONS: October 31

CODE: AB/MRC010/c
NAME: Athletic Grants in Aid for MRC

PROGRAM: Any
BASIS: Awarded to students who participate in the Athletic Program at Mount Royal C on the basis of financial need and athletic abaility. Applications should be requested from the Mount Royal Athletics Department.
MINIMUM AVERAGE: 2.00
VALUE: Grants cover tuition fees.
TERMS: Renewable
NUMBER OF AWARDS: Varies
DEADLINE FOR APPLICATIONS: October 30

CODE: AB/MRC011/c
NAME: Jimmie Condon Athletic Scholarships
PROGRAM: Any
BASIS: Awarded to students enrolled full-time at Mount Royal C who have earned a position on an intercollegiate team. Academic standing will be considered. Applications should be requested from the Mount Royal Athletics Department.
MINIMUM AVERAGE: N/A
VALUE: $1000.00
TERMS: Recipients may reapply for subsequents years, provided they remain on an athletic team.
NUMBER OF AWARDS: Varies
DEADLINE FOR APPLICATIONS: October 30

Northern Alberta Institute of Technology

CODE: AB/NAIT00/c
NAME: NAIT does not offer any entrance scholarships.

Olds College

CODE: AB/OLDS00/c
NAME: Olds College does not offer any entrance scholarships.

Old Sun Community College

CODE: AB/OLSUN0/c
NAME: Old Sun Community College offers no entrance scholarships.

Red Deer College

CODE: AB/REDD01/c
NAME: Alberta/NWT Command of the Royal Canadian Legion Award
PROGRAM: Any
BASIS: Available to sons and daughters of ex-service people. Open to Alberta residents who enter Red Deer C in a full-time program. The selection is based on academic standing, financial need, and participation in school and community affairs.
MINIMUM AVERAGE: 62.00
VALUE: $500.00
TERMS: One year only
NUMBER OF AWARDS: 2
DEADLINE FOR APPLICATIONS: September 15

CODE: AB/REDD02/c
NAME: Canwest Publishers Adult Re-Entry Award
PROGRAM: College Preparatory or General Developmental Studies
BASIS: Available to students 23 years of age or older who have had their education/training interrupted and are returning to school. Awarded on the basis of financial need, academic ability, and career goals.
MINIMUM AVERAGE: 62.00
VALUE: $350.00
TERMS: One year only
NUMBER OF AWARDS: 2
DEADLINE FOR APPLICATIONS: September 15

CODE: AB/REDD03/c
NAME: Canwest Publishers Adult Status Award
PROGRAM: Any
BASIS: Awarded to a student beginning full-time studies at Red Deer C who has been admitted as an adult-status student. The selection is based on financial need, academic ability, and career goals.
MINIMUM AVERAGE: 62.00
VALUE: $200.00
TERMS: One year only
NUMBER OF AWARDS: 1
DEADLINE FOR APPLICATIONS: September 15

CODE: AB/REDD04/c
NAME: Canwest Publishers College Prepratory Entry Awards
PROGRAM: High School Level Study
BASIS: Awarded to students who have completed the Red Deer C Adult Basic Education program and are proceeding to high school-level study. The selection is based on financial need, career goals, and a commitment to finish the College Prepatory Program.
MINIMUM AVERAGE: 2.30
VALUE: $250.00
TERMS: One year only
NUMBER OF AWARDS: 2

CODE: AB/REDD05/c
NAME: Canwest Publishers General and Developmental Studies
PROGRAM: General and Developmental Studies
BASIS: Awarded to students who are entering the General and Developmental Studies program with an intent to move to a major in literature, English, or journalism. The selection is based on standing in high school English and financial need.
MINIMUM AVERAGE: 62.00
VALUE: $500.00
TERMS: One year only
NUMBER OF AWARDS: 3
DEADLINE FOR APPLICATIONS: September 15

CODE: AB/REDD06/c
NAME: Canwest Publishers Masters Re-Entry to Education Award
PROGRAM: Any
BASIS: Awarded to a student who is 40 years of age or older and beginning full-time studies at Red Deer C. The selection is based on established goals, commitment to life-long learning, financial need, and previous academic standing.
MINIMUM AVERAGE: 62.00
VALUE: $250.00
TERMS: One year only
NUMBER OF AWARDS: 1
DEADLINE FOR APPLICATIONS: September 15

CODE: AB/REDD07/c
NAME: Central Alberta Teachers' Convention Association Educational Award
PROGRAM: Bachelor of Education
BASIS: Awarded to a student who has one or both parents employed in a certified position with various Alberta Teachers' Association locals in Central Alberta. The selection is based on academic standing and participation in school and community affairs.
MINIMUM AVERAGE: 62.00
VALUE: $500.00
TERMS: One year only
NUMBER OF AWARDS: 1
DEADLINE FOR APPLICATIONS: September 15

CODE: AB/REDD08/c
NAME: Charles Henry Snell City of Red Deer Engineering Scholarship
PROGRAM: Engineering
BASIS: Awarded to a student entering 1st year at Red Deer C. Preference is given to students indicating an intention of specializing in surveying engineering. Applicant must be a Canadian citizen or landed immigrant. The selection is based on academic standing.
MINIMUM AVERAGE: 62.00

VALUE: $500.00
TERMS: One year only
NUMBER OF AWARDS: 1
DEADLINE FOR APPLICATIONS: September 15

CODE: AB/REDD09/c
NAME: County of Red Deer #23 Tuition Award
PROGRAM: Any
BASIS: Awarded to a student who is a resident of the County of Red Deer (City of Red Deer not included) entering 1st year at Red Deer C. The selection is based on academic standing, financial need, and participation in school and community activities.
MINIMUM AVERAGE: 62.00
VALUE: $300.00
TERMS: One year only. Award includes a plaque.
NUMBER OF AWARDS: 1
DEADLINE FOR APPLICATIONS: September 15

CODE: AB/REDD10/c
NAME: Edmonton Northlands Biology Technology Award
PROGRAM: Biology Technology
BASIS: Awarded to a student entering 1st year at Red Deer C. The selection is based on academic performance and financial need.
MINIMUM AVERAGE: 62.00
VALUE: $250.00
TERMS: One year only.
NUMBER OF AWARDS: 1
DEADLINE FOR APPLICATIONS: September 15

CODE: AB/REDD11/c
NAME: Edmonton Northlands College Preparatory Award
PROGRAM: College Preparatory
BASIS: Awarded to a student entering 1st year of full-time studies at Red Deer C. The selection is based on financial need and career goal-setting.
MINIMUM AVERAGE: N/A

VALUE: $250.00
TERMS: One year only. Award includes a plaque.
NUMBER OF AWARDS: 1
DEADLINE FOR APPLICATIONS:
September 15

CODE: AB/REDD12/c
NAME: Edmonton Northlands Computer Systems Technology Award
PROGRAM: Computer Systems Technology
BASIS: Awarded to a student entering 1st year of full-time studies at Red Deer C. The selection is based on academic performance and financial need.
MINIMUM AVERAGE: 62.00
VALUE: $250.00
TERMS: One year only
NUMBER OF AWARDS: 1
DEADLINE FOR APPLICATIONS:
September 15

CODE: AB/REDD13/c
NAME: Edmonton Northlands Education – Elementary Award
PROGRAM: Bachelor of Education (Elementary)
BASIS: Awarded to a student entering 1st year of full-time studies at Red Deer C. The selection is based on academic performance and financial need.
MINIMUM AVERAGE: 62.00
VALUE: $250.00
TERMS: One year only
NUMBER OF AWARDS: 1
DEADLINE FOR APPLICATIONS:
September 15

CODE: AB/REDD14/c
NAME: Edmonton Northlands Education – Secondary Award
PROGRAM: Bachelor of Education (Secondary)
BASIS: Awarded to a student entering 1st year of full-time studies at Red Deer C. The selection is based on academic performance and financial need.

MINIMUM AVERAGE: 62.00
VALUE: $250.00
TERMS: One year only
NUMBER OF AWARDS: 1
DEADLINE FOR APPLICATIONS:
September 15

CODE: AB/REDD15/c
NAME: Edmonton Northlands Rehabilitation Services Award
PROGRAM: Rehabilitation Services
BASIS: Awarded to a student entering 1st year of full-time studies at Red Deer C. The selection is based on academic performance and financial need.
MINIMUM AVERAGE: 62.00
VALUE: $250.00
TERMS: One year only
NUMBER OF AWARDS: 1
DEADLINE FOR APPLICATIONS:
September 15

CODE: AB/REDD16/c
NAME: Georgia Belknap Endowment Early Childhood Education Entrance Award
PROGRAM: Early Childhood Development
BASIS: Awarded to a student entering 1st year of full-time studies at Red Deer C. The selection is based on academic performance and financial need.
MINIMUM AVERAGE: 62.00
VALUE: $500.00
TERMS: One year only
NUMBER OF AWARDS: 1
DEADLINE FOR APPLICATIONS:
September 15

CODE: AB/REDD17/c
NAME: Georgia Belknap Endowment Teacher Assistant Entrance Award
PROGRAM: Teacher Assistant
BASIS: Awarded to a student entering 1st year of full-time studies at Red Deer C. The selection is based on academic performance and financial need.
MINIMUM AVERAGE: 62.00

VALUE: $500.00
TERMS: One year only
NUMBER OF AWARDS: 1
DEADLINE FOR APPLICATIONS:
September 15

CODE: AB/REDD18/c
NAME: Helen Anderson Smith
Pharmacy Technician Bursary
PROGRAM: Pharmacy Technician
BASIS: Awarded to a student entering
1st year of full-time studies at Red
Deer C. The selection is based on
financial need.
MINIMUM AVERAGE: 62.00
VALUE: $500.00
TERMS: One year only
NUMBER OF AWARDS: 1
DEADLINE FOR APPLICATIONS:
September 15

CODE: AB/REDD19/c
NAME: Henry Wise Wood Memorial
Award
PROGRAM: Preference is given to ap-
plicants studying an agriculture-
related program.
BASIS: Awarded to a student from
Alberta or Northern British Colum-
bia whose parents, spouse, or him/
herself derive the major portion of
their income from agriculture. The
selection is based on academic
standing and financial need.
MINIMUM AVERAGE: 62.00
VALUE: $500.00
TERMS: One year only
NUMBER OF AWARDS: 1
DEADLINE FOR APPLICATIONS:
September 15

CODE: AB/REDD20/c
NAME: Ian Cannon Memorial Bursary
PROGRAM: College Preparatory
BASIS: Awarded to a student who is
entering the College Preparatory
Program at Red Deer C as a
mature-status applicant. The selection is based on financial need and
evidence of an effort towards self-
improvement.

MINIMUM AVERAGE: N/A
VALUE: $400.00
TERMS: One year only
NUMBER OF AWARDS: 1
DEADLINE FOR APPLICATIONS:
September 15

CODE: AB/REDD21/c
NAME: Imperial Oil Limited
Scholarship
PROGRAM: Computer Systems Tech-
nology or the Business Administra-
tion
BASIS: Awarded to a student entering
the Computer Systems Technology
progam and to one entering the
Business Administration program.
The selection is based on academic
achievement.
MINIMUM AVERAGE: 66.00
VALUE: $500.00
TERMS: One year only
NUMBER OF AWARDS: 2
DEADLINE FOR APPLICATIONS:
September 15

CODE: AB/REDD22/c
NAME: Red Deer College Students'
Association Bachelor of Arts
Entrance Award
PROGRAM: Bachelor of Arts
BASIS: Awarded to a student entering
full-time studies in the Bachelor of
Arts program at Red Deer C. The
selection is based on outstanding
academic achievement.
MINIMUM AVERAGE: 66.00
VALUE: $250.00
TERMS: One year only
NUMBER OF AWARDS: 1
DEADLINE FOR APPLICATIONS:
September 15

CODE: AB/REDD23/c
NAME: Red Deer College Students'
Association General Studies
Entrance Award
PROGRAM: General Studies
BASIS: Awarded to a student entering
full-time studies in the General
Studies program at Red Deer C.

The selection is based on academic performance and financial need.
MINIMUM AVERAGE: 62.00
VALUE: $250.00
TERMS: One year only
NUMBER OF AWARDS: 1
DEADLINE FOR APPLICATIONS: September 15

CODE: AB/REDD24/c
NAME: Shauna O'Sullivan Memorial Award in Theatre
PROGRAM: Theatre Studies
BASIS: Awarded to a successful applicant to the performance major of the Theatre Studies program at Red Deer C. Candidates should apply to the Chairperson of Theatre Studies, stating interest in Theatre Studies, and past experience in school or community theatre.
MINIMUM AVERAGE: N/A
VALUE: $150.00
TERMS: One year only
NUMBER OF AWARDS: 1
DEADLINE FOR APPLICATIONS: September 15

CODE: AB/REDD25/c
NAME: TransAlta Utilities Engineering Award
PROGRAM: Bachelor of Science in Engineering
BASIS: Awarded to a student entering the 1st year of full-time studies at Red Deer C. The recipient must have graduated from an Alberta high school in an area served by TransAlta Utilities Corporation. The selection is based on academic proficiency and financial need.
MINIMUM AVERAGE: 62.00
VALUE: $100.00
TERMS: One year only
NUMBER OF AWARDS: 1
DEADLINE FOR APPLICATIONS: September 15

Southern Alberta Institute of Technology

CODE: AB/SAIT01/c
NAME: Alberta "75" Scholarship (Gliding)
PROGRAM: Award rotates between AXT, AMT, and AET, 2 programs per year
BASIS: Awarded to students enrolled in career training programs in the aviation or aerospace industries.
MINIMUM AVERAGE: 2.00
VALUE: $300.00
TERMS: One year only. Award to be applied toward introductory flight training with Cu-Nim Gliding Club.
NUMBER OF AWARDS: 2
DEADLINE FOR APPLICATIONS: April 30

CODE: AB/SAIT02/c
NAME: Ben S. Plumer Bursary (Alberta Wheat Pool)
PROGRAM: Any
BASIS: Awarded to rural applicants from Alberta and the BC/Peace River block whose parents derive their principal income from farming. The selection is based on financial need and academic achievement.
MINIMUM AVERAGE: N/A
VALUE: $500.00
TERMS: One year only
NUMBER OF AWARDS: 1
DEADLINE FOR APPLICATIONS: July 15

CODE: AB/SAIT03/c
NAME: Calgary Filipino Lions Club
PROGRAM: Any
BASIS: Awarded to a 1st- or 2nd-year student who is a resident of Alberta and meets minimum academic requirements. Preference will be given to applicants of Filipino descent.
MINIMUM AVERAGE: 1.00
VALUE: $300.00
TERMS: One year only

NUMBER OF AWARDS: Varies
DEADLINE FOR APPLICATIONS: July 15

CODE: AB/SAIT04/c
NAME: Leonie Richard Endowment
PROGRAM: Preference is given to programs related to the food-service industry (e.g., Hotel and Restaurant Administration, Professional Cooking, Commercial Baking)
BASIS: Awarded to a female student who is a single parent and entering or returning to SAIT to further her education.
MINIMUM AVERAGE: N/A
VALUE: Varies
TERMS: One year only. Not tenable with other awards.
NUMBER OF AWARDS: 1
DEADLINE FOR APPLICATIONS: July 15

CODE: AB/SAIT05/c
NAME: Don Moore Award
PROGRAM: Recreation Facility Operations and Maintenance
BASIS: Awarded to a 1st-year student who is a resident of Alberta. The selection is based on academic achievement and personal qualities, indicative of success in the field.
MINIMUM AVERAGE: 3.00
VALUE: $500.00
TERMS: One year only
NUMBER OF AWARDS: 1
DEADLINE FOR APPLICATIONS: March 31

CODE: AB/SAIT06/c
NAME: North Canadian Forest Industry
PROGRAM: Any at SAIT
BASIS: Awarded to a 1st-year student who has resided north of Township 68 and west of the 5th meridian in Alberta for one year or longer. Candidates should apply to the Student Awards Officer, Grande Prairie Regional, Grande Prairie, Alberta T8V 4C4.

MINIMUM AVERAGE: 3.00
VALUE: $500.00
TERMS: One year only. Recipients must agree to return to the specified area of Alberta upon the completion of their education.
NUMBER OF AWARDS: 2
DEADLINE FOR APPLICATIONS: March 31

CODE: AB/SAIT07/c
NAME: George W. Kerby IODE
PROGRAM: Any at SAIT
BASIS: Awarded to a student who has completed his or her academic upgrading at AVC and will be attending SAIT as a full-time student in the Fall.
MINIMUM AVERAGE: N/A
VALUE: N/A
TERMS: One year only
NUMBER OF AWARDS: 1

CODE: AB/SAIT08/c
NAME: H.A. Woodroofe Memorial Award
PROGRAM: Industrial Electronics Technology
BASIS: For a student entering the IXT program.
MINIMUM AVERAGE: 65.00 in Math 30
VALUE: $500.00
TERMS: One year only
NUMBER OF AWARDS: 1

CODE: AB/SAIT09/c
NAME: SAIT Caretaking and Custodial Staff Bursary
PROGRAM: Any at SAIT
BASIS: Awarded to a student who is being supported by a single parent while attending SAIT. Applicants must be Canadian citizens.
MINIMUM AVERAGE: 1.00
VALUE: Varies
TERMS: One year only
NUMBER OF AWARDS: N/A
DEADLINE FOR APPLICATIONS: July 15

BRITISH COLUMBIA

British Columbia Institute of Technology

CODE: BC/BCIT01/c
NAME: BCIT Alumni Association Entrance Award
PROGRAM: Any full-time Technology or Trades program at BCIT
BASIS: Candidates must be Canadian citizens or permanent residents entering BCIT at least one year after high school. Academic standing, extracurricular activites and/or community service will be considered. An application and letters of reference are required.
MINIMUM AVERAGE: N/A
VALUE: Equal to one year's tuition.
TERMS: One year only
NUMBER OF AWARDS: Up to 12 awards will be given.
DEADLINE FOR APPLICATIONS: August 2

CODE: BC/BCIT02/c
NAME: President's Entrance Award Program
PROGRAM: Any full-time Technology or Trades program at BCIT
BASIS: Candidates must have combined high achievement with active participation in school/community activites. An application and 2 letters of reference are required. A nomination form is required from the candidate's secondary school.
MINIMUM AVERAGE: N/A
VALUE: Equal to tuition
TERMS: One year only
NUMBER OF AWARDS: 60
DEADLINE FOR APPLICATIONS: April 15

CODE: BC/BCIT03/c
NAME: Pacific Foundation of Applied Technology, Otto A. Kloss Awards
PROGRAM: Various Trades programs at BCIT

BASIS: Applicants must have participated in extracurricular activities and/or community service and be well motivated in the pursuit of their chosen career. An application is required.
MINIMUM AVERAGE: C+
VALUE: $1500.00
TERMS: One year only
NUMBER OF AWARDS: 4
DEADLINE FOR APPLICATIONS: August 2

CODE: BC/BCIT04/c
NAME: Sea Island Entrance Bursaries
PROGRAM: Aircraft Maintenance, Aircraft Structures, Gas Turbine Technician, and Avionic
BASIS: Applicants must submit a BCIT Trades Bursary application form, available from the Financial Aid and Awards Office. The selection is based on financial need.
MINIMUM AVERAGE: N/A
VALUE: Varies
TERMS: One year only. The combined value of all Sea Island bursaries will be $2000.
NUMBER OF AWARDS: Varies
DEADLINE FOR APPLICATIONS: September 30

CODE: BC/BCIT05/c
NAME: Simons Foundation Entrance Awards for Women
PROGRAM: Any full-time Trades program and various Technology courses
BASIS: Female students wishing to apply must complete a BCIT Entrance Awards application, available from the Financial Aid and Awards Office.
MINIMUM AVERAGE: N/A
VALUE: $500.00
TERMS: One year only. There is one scholarship for a female student

entering a Trades program and one for a female student entering a Technology program.

NUMBER OF AWARDS: 2
DEADLINE FOR APPLICATIONS: August 2

CODE: BC/BCIT06/c
NAME: Teck Corporation Entrance Award
PROGRAM: Mining
BASIS: Awarded on the basis of financial need to employees (or their dependents) of Teck or Teck-affiliated companies, students whose permanent residence is near a Teck mine, or students entering the Mining program.
MINIMUM AVERAGE: N/A
VALUE: $1200.00
TERMS: One year only
NUMBER OF AWARDS: 1
DEADLINE FOR APPLICATIONS: August 2

CODE: BC/BCIT07/c
NAME: Workers' Compensation Board Entrance Scholarships
PROGRAM: Occupational Health and Safety
BASIS: Awarded to students entering the BCIT Occupational Health and Safety program. Students accepted to this program will be notified of the application procedures.
MINIMUM AVERAGE: N/A
VALUE: These scholarships are worth 50% of the 1st-year tuition fees.
TERMS: One year only
NUMBER OF AWARDS: 6

CODE: BC/BCIT08/c
NAME: BC Dairy Foundation Entrance Awards
PROGRAM: Food Technology
BASIS: Awarded on the basis of academic standing in high school to students entering the Food Technology program. Preference will be shown to students who are sons/daughters of individuals working in the dairy industry. An application is required.

MINIMUM AVERAGE: N/A
VALUE: $1000.00
TERMS: One year only
NUMBER OF AWARDS: 2
DEADLINE FOR APPLICATIONS: August 2

CODE: BC/BCIT09/c
NAME: David Lloyd Entrance Awards
PROGRAM: Any full-time Technology or Trades program
BASIS: Applicants must be residents of the Sunshine Coast School District with preference given to those from Pender Harbour. The selection is based on marks and participation in school and/or community activities.
MINIMUM AVERAGE: N/A
VALUE: $1500.00
TERMS: One year only
NUMBER OF AWARDS: 6
DEADLINE FOR APPLICATIONS: August 2

CODE: BC/BCIT10/c
NAME: BCIT High Tech High Promise Entrance Award
PROGRAM: Any full-time Trades program
BASIS: Applicants must submit a BCIT Entrance Award application, available from the Financial Aid and Awards Office.
MINIMUM AVERAGE: N/A
VALUE: $750.00
TERMS: One year only
NUMBER OF AWARDS: 1
DEADLINE FOR APPLICATIONS: August 2

CODE: BC/BCIT11/c
NAME: CFOX Broadcast Entrance Awards for Women and First Nations Students
PROGRAM: Broadcast Communications
BASIS: Applicants must submit a BCIT Entrance Award application, available from the Financial Aid and Awards Office.
MINIMUM AVERAGE: N/A
VALUE: $4000.00
TERMS: One year only. One award is

available for a female student and one for a First Nations student.

NUMBER OF AWARDS: 2
DEADLINE FOR APPLICATIONS: August 2

CODE: BC/BCIT12/c
NAME: Elsie Boone/North Shore Lions Club Entrance Award
PROGRAM: Any full-time Technology or Trades program
BASIS: Applicants must be entering BCIT directly from Grade 12, have a physical disability, and be a resident of North or West Vancouver.
MINIMUM AVERAGE: N/A
VALUE: Equal to one year's tuition.
TERMS: One year only
NUMBER OF AWARDS: 1
DEADLINE FOR APPLICATIONS: August 2

CODE: BC/BCIT13/c
NAME: BCIT December 6 Memorial Award for Women in Engineering
PROGRAM: Electronics Technology or any 2-year program in the School of Engineering Technology
BASIS: The selection is based on standing in high school and any post-secondary courses taken, plus participation in school/community activities.
MINIMUM AVERAGE: N/A
VALUE: Equal to one year's tuition.
TERMS: One year only
NUMBER OF AWARDS: 1
DEADLINE FOR APPLICATIONS: August 2

CODE: BC/BCIT14/c
NAME: Cy and Emerald Keyes Entrance Award
PROGRAM: Mining
BASIS: Awarded on the basis of financial need.
MINIMUM AVERAGE: N/A
VALUE: $1000.00
TERMS: One year only
NUMBER OF AWARDS: 1
DEADLINE FOR APPLICATIONS: August 2

Camosun College

CODE: BC/CAM000/c
NAME: Camosun College does not offer any entrance scholarships.

Canadian Union College

CODE: BC/CUC001/c
NAME: Valedictorian of the Class Scholarship
PROGRAM: Any
BASIS: Awarded to any high school valedictorian entering Canadian Union C.
MINIMUM AVERAGE: N/A
VALUE: $750.00
TERMS: One year only
NUMBER OF AWARDS: Varies

CODE: BC/CUC002/c
NAME: Salutorian of the Class Scholarship
PROGRAM: Any
BASIS: Awarded to any high school salutorian entering Canadian Union C.
MINIMUM AVERAGE: N/A
VALUE: $500.00
TERMS: One year only
NUMBER OF AWARDS: Varies

CODE: BC/CUC003/c
NAME: Other Academic Scholarships
PROGRAM: Any
BASIS: Awarded to any high school students entering Canadian Union C. Awarded on the basis of academic merit.
MINIMUM AVERAGE: N/A
VALUE: $300.00
TERMS: One year only
NUMBER OF AWARDS: Varies

Capilano College

CODE: BC/CAP001/c
NAME: Capilano College Board Entrance Scholarships
PROGRAM: Any

BASIS: Awarded to students entering Capilano C on the basis of academic merit. There will be one scholarship for each high school in the College region.
MINIMUM AVERAGE: 3.50
VALUE: The scholarships consist of a tuition waiver for 2 consecutive academic terms.
TERMS: One year only
NUMBER OF AWARDS: N/A
DEADLINE FOR APPLICATIONS: August 30

CODE: BC/CAP002/c
NAME: Capilano College English Scholarship
PROGRAM: Academic Studies
BASIS: Awarded to students entering Capilano C on the basis of an essay contest which is open to all Grade 12 students who are graduating in the current year. Contact the English Department for more information.
MINIMUM AVERAGE: N/A
VALUE: The scholarships consist of a tuition waiver. Book prizes will also be awarded.
TERMS: One year only
NUMBER OF AWARDS: Varies
DEADLINE FOR APPLICATIONS: April 15

CODE: BC/CAP003/c
NAME: Science Faculty and Staff Scholarships
PROGRAM: Pure and Applied Sciences
BASIS: Awarded to students currently taking a full Grade 12 course load and expecting to graduate with high marks. Information is available from the Pure and Applied Sciences program at the College.
MINIMUM AVERAGE: N/A
VALUE: $500.00
TERMS: One year only
NUMBER OF AWARDS: 2
DEADLINE FOR APPLICATIONS: May 15

CODE: BC/CAP004/c
NAME: Science Tuition Scholarships
PROGRAM: Full-time Pure and Applied Sciences
BASIS: Awarded to students obtaining a GPA of at least 3.5 in a specified set of four Grade 12 courses. Information is available from the Pure and Applied Sciences Program at the College.
MINIMUM AVERAGE: 3.50
VALUE: The awards consist of a tuition waiver for the Fall term.
TERMS: One year only
NUMBER OF AWARDS: Varies
DEADLINE FOR APPLICATIONS: May 15

CODE: BC/CAP005/c
NAME: Science Textbook Publishers' Awards
PROGRAM: Full-time Pure and Applied Sciences
BASIS: Awarded to students with a high GPA entering a Science program. Information is available from the Science Division office (Rm 471, 4th Floor, H Bldg.) at the College.
MINIMUM AVERAGE: 3.50
VALUE: The awards consist of 1st-year science textbooks.
TERMS: One year only
NUMBER OF AWARDS: Varies

Cariboo College

CODE: BC/CBO001/c
NAME: CUPE Local 3500 Bursary
PROGRAM: Any
BASIS: Awarded to a son, daughter, or other legal dependent of a CUPE Local #3500 member (or deceased member) who has held membership for at least 2 years. Academic achievement and financial need will be considered.
MINIMUM AVERAGE: 60.00
VALUE: $1000.00
TERMS: One year only. Awarded in 2 instalments of $500 each in November and January.
NUMBER OF AWARDS: 1
DEADLINE FOR APPLICATIONS: September 15

CODE: BC/CBO002/c
NAME: Drdul, Alex Memorial
Bursaries
PROGRAM: Academic
BASIS: Awarded to a student from School District 24 who is entering an academic program at University College of the Cariboo (UCC).
MINIMUM AVERAGE: 70.00
VALUE: $1000.00
TERMS: One year only
NUMBER OF AWARDS: 1
DEADLINE FOR APPLICATIONS: September 15

CODE: BC/CBO003/c
NAME: Macmillan, H.R. Indian Training Fund
PROGRAM: Any
BASIS: Available to status Indians registered in the Williams Lake District taking courses of not less than 3 weeks' duration. Application forms are available at Williams Lake campus or the Kamloops campus Financial Aid Office.
MINIMUM AVERAGE: N/A
VALUE: Varies
TERMS: One year only
NUMBER OF AWARDS: Varies
DEADLINE FOR APPLICATIONS: There are various application deadlines: March 15, May 31, November 15.

CODE: BC/CBO004/c
NAME: UCC Entrance Scholarships
PROGRAM: Any
BASIS: Awarded to a Grade 12 student entering UCC from each of the provinically accredited secondary schools in the CC region. Awarded on the basis of academic achievement and leadership qualities. Candidates should apply through the high school counselling office.
MINIMUM AVERAGE: N/A
VALUE: $800.00
TERMS: One year only
NUMBER OF AWARDS: 16
DEADLINE FOR APPLICATIONS: September 15

CODE: BC/CBO005/c
NAME: UCC Sports Task Force Entrance Scholarships
PROGRAM: Any
BASIS: Awarded to top-ranking high school graduates entering full-time studies at UCC and participating in the UCC Athletics program. Applications are available from high school counsellors or the Financial Aid and Awards Office.
MINIMUM AVERAGE: N/A
VALUE: $800.00
TERMS: One year only
NUMBER OF AWARDS: 10
DEADLINE FOR APPLICATIONS: March 13

CODE: BC/CBO006/c
NAME: UCC Student Financial Aid Fund
PROGRAM: Any
BASIS: This fund may provide scholarships and bursaries to students who qualify for the UCC Scholarship Program or who complete a bursary application.
MINIMUM AVERAGE: N/A
VALUE: Varies
TERMS: Candidates may reapply.
NUMBER OF AWARDS: Varies
DEADLINE FOR APPLICATIONS: September 15

CODE: BC/CBO007/c
NAME: Underwriters Insurance Agencies Award
PROGRAM: Any in the Visual and Performing Arts Department
BASIS: Awarded to a needy student who is registered in a program in the Visual and Performing Arts Dept.
MINIMUM AVERAGE: N/A
VALUE: $200.00
TERMS: One year only
NUMBER OF AWARDS: 1
DEADLINE FOR APPLICATIONS: September 15

CODE: BC/CBO008/c
NAME: John Thomas Gramiak Prize

PROGRAM: Engineering, Nursing or Business Administration preferred
BASIS: Awarded to a student graduating from Kamloops Secondary School who demonstrates good work habits and community involvement, and who enrolls at UCC. Applications are available from high school counselling offices. Proof of admission to UCC is required.
MINIMUM AVERAGE: N/A
VALUE: Varies
TERMS: One year only
NUMBER OF AWARDS: 1
DEADLINE FOR APPLICATIONS: May 30

CODE: BC/CBO009/c
NAME: Sharon Anne Kask Memorial Bursary
PROGRAM: Education-oriented programs
BASIS: Awarded to a female student graduating from Norkam Secondary School and enrolling at UCC with the intent of pursuing a career in Elementary Education. Commitment to teaching and extracurricular activities will be considered. An application is required.
MINIMUM AVERAGE: N/A
VALUE: $600.00
TERMS: One year only
NUMBER OF AWARDS: 1
DEADLINE FOR APPLICATIONS: May 30

CODE: BC/CBO010/c
NAME: Charles Marshall Endowment
PROGRAM: Education or Nursing
BASIS: Two scholarships will be awarded to graduates of Chase Secondary School who are enrolling in Nursing or Education at UCC. One scholarship will be awarded to a student from Barriere Secondary School. Applications are available from high school counsellors.
MINIMUM AVERAGE: N/A
VALUE: $1000.00
TERMS: One year only

NUMBER OF AWARDS: 3
DEADLINE FOR APPLICATIONS: May 30

CODE: BC/CBO011/c
NAME: Rose Hill Farmers' Institute Bursaries
PROGRAM: Any
BASIS: Awarded to students from the Knutsford area. The selection will be based on financial need and academic standing. Applicants must have completed Grade 10 or higher. Applications are available from the Financial Aid and Awards Office.
MINIMUM AVERAGE: N/A
VALUE: $200.00
TERMS: One year only
NUMBER OF AWARDS: 2
DEADLINE FOR APPLICATIONS: May 1

CODE: BC/CBO012/c
NAME: Rose Hill Farmers' Institute – Heritage Bursary
PROGRAM: Any
BASIS: The selection will be based on financial need and academic standing. Applicants must have completed Grade 10 or higher. Applications are available from the Financial Aid and Awards Office.
MINIMUM AVERAGE: N/A
VALUE: $500.00
TERMS: One year only
NUMBER OF AWARDS: 1
DEADLINE FOR APPLICATIONS: May 15

CODE: BC/CBO013/c
NAME: Soroptomist International of the Americas Awards, Kamloops Branch
PROGRAM: Vocational or Technical training
BASIS: Awarded to promote upward mobility in mature women, assisting them in their efforts toward training and entry into the labour market. Applications are available from the Financial Aid and Awards Office.
MINIMUM AVERAGE: N/A

VALUE: $1500.00
TERMS: One year only
NUMBER OF AWARDS: 1
DEADLINE FOR APPLICATIONS: December 15

College of New Caledonia

CODE: BC/NEWC01/c
NAME: College of New Caledonia Entrance Scholarships
PROGRAM: Any at New Caledonia College
BASIS: Entrance scholarships will be distributed to students graduating from high schools in the New Caledonia region, including School Districts #28, 55, 56, and 57. A letter of application, recommendation letter, and transcipt must be submitted.
MINIMUM AVERAGE: 70.00
VALUE: $1000.00
TERMS: $500 will be disbursed in September, another $500 in January.
NUMBER OF AWARDS: 5
DEADLINE FOR APPLICATIONS: December 31

CODE: BC/NEWC02/c
NAME: College of New Caledonia Entrance Bursaries
PROGRAM: Any full-time program at New Caledonia College
BASIS: Awarded to graduates of high schools in the College region who can demonstrate financial need. Applicants must complete the Application for CNC Admission Bursary and submit a letter of recommendation and transcript to the Financial Aid Officer.
MINIMUM AVERAGE: 60.00
VALUE: $900.00
TERMS: One year only. Paid in 2 instalments of $450 in September and January.
NUMBER OF AWARDS:
DEADLINE FOR APPLICATIONS: May 31

CODE: BC/NEWC03/c
NAME: Canadian National Scholarships for Women
PROGRAM: Entry Level Training, Power Engineering, Welding, Electronics Technology, Engineering Graphics and Design Technology, or Co-operative Apprecticeship
BASIS: Awarded to a female student entering one of a selected number of vocational/technical programs at the C of New Caledonia. The selection is based on demonstrated interest in the chosen field of study.
MINIMUM AVERAGE: 60.00
VALUE: $500.00
TERMS: One year only
NUMBER OF AWARDS: 1
DEADLINE FOR APPLICATIONS: July 29

CODE: BC/NEWC04/c
NAME: Dr. Hu Stephen Memorial Bursary
PROGRAM: Any full-time program at New Caledonia College
BASIS: Awarded to Nechako Valley Secondary School students whose achievement has been noteworthy because of hard work and devotion to learning. Financial need will be considered. The selection of recipients is made by the Principal.
MINIMUM AVERAGE: N/A
VALUE: $1000.00
TERMS: One year only
NUMBER OF AWARDS: 2
DEADLINE FOR APPLICATIONS: July 29

CODE: BC/NEWC05/c
NAME: Rotary Club of Vanderhoof
PROGRAM: Office Administration
BASIS: Awarded to full-time students entering the Office Administration program at the Nachako campus. Applicants must complete the Standard College bursary form and a Rotary Club of Vanderhoof Application form. Financial need will be considered.
MINIMUM AVERAGE: N/A

VALUE: $500.00
TERMS: One year only. Failure to complete the program may result in a request to repay the bursary.
NUMBER OF AWARDS: 2
DEADLINE FOR APPLICATIONS: August 15

Columbia College

CODE: BC/COL001/c
NAME: Columbia College Entrance Scholarships
PROGRAM: Any
BASIS: Awarded to outstanding academic students who are completing at least their 2nd semester of full-time studies and are planning to register for a subsequent semester. Scholarships are awarded on the basis of overall GPA and faculty recommendation.
MINIMUM AVERAGE: 75.00
VALUE: $750.00
TERMS: One year only. Applications may also be made in February and October.
NUMBER OF AWARDS: 12
DEADLINE FOR APPLICATIONS: June 15

Coquitlam College

CODE: BC/COQ000/c
NAME: Coquitlam College offers no entrance scholarships.

Douglas College

CODE: BC/DGS001/c
NAME: CJP Architects Scholarship
PROGRAM: Any
BASIS: Available to a graduate of Thomas Haney Centre Secondary School entering Douglas College.
MINIMUM AVERAGE: 80.00
VALUE: $500.00
TERMS: One year only
NUMBER OF AWARDS: 4
DEADLINE FOR APPLICATIONS: April 1

CODE: BC/DGS002/c
NAME: Coquitlam 1991 BC Summer Games Award
PROGRAM: Any
BASIS: Available to graduates of Coquitlam High School entering Douglas C. The selection is based on extracurricular activities and community service. Financial need will be considered. A letter of recommendation and transcript are required.
MINIMUM AVERAGE: 3.00
VALUE: $500.00
TERMS: One year only
NUMBER OF AWARDS: 4
DEADLINE FOR APPLICATIONS: April 1

CODE: BC/DGS003/c
NAME: Douglas College Entrance Scholarships
PROGRAM: Any full-time program
BASIS: Available to graduates of a senior secondary school in the Douglas C area. The selection is based on major involvement in extracurricular activities and community service. The principal's nomination and reference are required.
MINIMUM AVERAGE: 81.50
VALUE: Equals the tuition fees for 1st year.
TERMS: Renewable for a 2nd year.
NUMBER OF AWARDS: 8
DEADLINE FOR APPLICATIONS: April 1

CODE: BC/DGS004/c
NAME: Douglas College Music Scholarships
PROGRAM: Full-time University Transfer – Music program at Douglas College
BASIS: Awarded on the basis of audition performances with accepted theory entrance standings. The selection is made by the Music Department after May auditions.
MINIMUM AVERAGE: N/A
VALUE: $500.00
TERMS: One year only

NUMBER OF AWARDS: 2
DEADLINE FOR APPLICATIONS: May 1
CODE: BC/DGS005/c
NAME: Royal Visit 1983 Scholarship
PROGRAM: Any full-time program
BASIS: Applicant must be a graduate
of a senior secondary school in the
Douglas C region. The selection is
based on participation in extracur-
ricular activites and community
service.
MINIMUM AVERAGE: 3.00
VALUE: $600.00
TERMS: One year only
NUMBER OF AWARDS: 1
DEADLINE FOR APPLICATIONS: April 1

CODE: BC/DGS006/c
NAME: United Association of
Plumbers and Pipefitters, Local 170
Entrance Scholarships
PROGRAM: Any
BASIS: Applicants must be sons,
daughters, or legal dependents of a
member of the United Association
of Plumbers and Pipefitters, Local
170. Academic achievement will be
considered.
MINIMUM AVERAGE: N/A
VALUE: $300.00
TERMS: One year only
NUMBER OF AWARDS: 2
DEADLINE FOR APPLICATIONS: April 1

East Kootenay Community College

CODE: BC/EKCC01/c
NAME: Crestbrook Forest Industries
Ltd, Rotary Club of Cranbrook
Scholarship
PROGRAM: Forestry-related program
BASIS: Awarded to a meritorious stu-
dent from the district of Cranbrook
entering a full-time program at
EKCC. Applicants must be Cana-
dian citizens or landed immigrants.
MINIMUM AVERAGE: 70.00
VALUE: $1000.00

TERMS: One year only
NUMBER OF AWARDS: 1
DEADLINE FOR APPLICATIONS: April 15

CODE: BC/EKCC02/c
NAME: East Kootenay Community
College Entrance Scholarships
PROGRAM: Any
BASIS: Awarded to senior high school
graduates entering a full-time pro-
gram at EKCC. Applicants must be
Canadian citizens or landed immi-
grants.
MINIMUM AVERAGE: 70.00
VALUE: $1000.00
TERMS: One year only
NUMBER OF AWARDS: 15
DEADLINE FOR APPLICATIONS: April 15

CODE: BC/EKCC03/c
NAME: Paul Sims Memorial
Scholarship
PROGRAM: Any
BASIS: Awarded to students entering
or continuing a full-time program
at EKCC. Applicants must be
Canadian citizens or landed immi-
grants.
MINIMUM AVERAGE: 70.00
VALUE: $500.00
TERMS: One year only
NUMBER OF AWARDS: 1
DEADLINE FOR APPLICATIONS: April 15

Emily Carr College of Art and Design

CODE: BC/ECCAD0/c
NAME: Emily Carr College of Art and
Design has no entrance scholar-
ships.

Kwantlen College

CODE: BC/KWA001/c
NAME: Phyllis Addinall Bauer
Memorial Scholarship
PROGRAM: Business-related program
BASIS: Awarded to a mature female
student who is a single parent

enrolled in a Kwantlen C program having a business orientation. Previous scholastic and business attainment will be considered.
MINIMUM AVERAGE: N/A
VALUE: $150.00
TERMS: One year only
NUMBER OF AWARDS: 1
DEADLINE FOR APPLICATIONS: October 15

CODE: BC/KWA002/c
NAME: Dorothy Calvert Memorial Award
PROGRAM: Any recognized 13-week-long course that will lead to opportunities for employment.
BASIS: The candidate must be a female resident of Langley, Surrey, North Delta, or White Rock returning to school after at least 10 years' absence from high school.
MINIMUM AVERAGE: N/A
VALUE: $500.00
TERMS: One year only
NUMBER OF AWARDS: 1
DEADLINE FOR APPLICATIONS: September 30

CODE: BC/KWA003/c
NAME: Cloverdale Paint Scholarship
PROGRAM: Any
BASIS: Awarded to a full-time student at Kwantlen C who is a Canadian citizen and a resident of BC or Alberta. The selection is based on community service and career and/or entrepreneurial objectives. Preference is shown to relations of Cloverdale Paint employees.
MINIMUM AVERAGE: N/A
VALUE: $750.00
TERMS: One year only
NUMBER OF AWARDS: 1
DEADLINE FOR APPLICATIONS: September 30

CODE: BC/KWA004/c
NAME: Elizabeth Foundation Bursary
PROGRAM: Any
BASIS: Awarded to students who are

residents of the White Rock area south of the Nicomekl River and King George Highway or who have attended Earl Marriott, Semiahmoo, or White Rock Secondary Schools. The recipient must display ability in art, music, drama, etc.
MINIMUM AVERAGE: N/A
VALUE: $400.00
TERMS: One year only. The recipient must be enrolled in at least 2 cultural courses in a calendar year.
NUMBER OF AWARDS: 2
DEADLINE FOR APPLICATIONS: September 30

CODE: BC/KWA005/c
NAME: Gingell Scholarship
PROGRAM: Any
BASIS: Applicants must be enrolled in a minimum of 12 credits or equivalent. Scholastic or business achievement and participation in community activities will be considered. Applications are available from the Financial Awards Office.
MINIMUM AVERAGE: N/A
VALUE: $150.00
TERMS: One year only. The award is provided in the Fall semester. In the event that a suitable candidate is not found, the award may be made in the Spring.
NUMBER OF AWARDS: 1
DEADLINE FOR APPLICATIONS: September 30

CODE: BC/KWA006/c
NAME: Ann Hass Memorial Bursary
PROGRAM: Any
BASIS: Awarded to a female Richmond student who requires financial assistance to complete her education. Applications are available at the Financial Aid Office.
MINIMUM AVERAGE: N/A
VALUE: $150.00
TERMS: One year only
NUMBER OF AWARDS: 1
DEADLINE FOR APPLICATIONS: November 30

CODE: BC/KWA007/c
NAME: Kwantlen College Entrance Awards
PROGRAM: Any
BASIS: Work experience, volunteer activities, and previous educational achievements will be considered. Two letters of recommendation from employers or community leaders should accompany the application. Applications are available from the Financial Awards Office.
MINIMUM AVERAGE: N/A
VALUE: $1000.00
TERMS: One year only. The award will be applied toward tuition fees for a student entering a full-time program commencing on the next enrolment date.
NUMBER OF AWARDS: 12
DEADLINE FOR APPLICATIONS: September 30

CODE: BC/KWA008/c
NAME: Kwantlen College Entrance Scholarships
PROGRAM: Any
BASIS: An applicant must have graduated as one of the most qualified students from his or her secondary school in an academic or vocational field, and must intend to be a direct-entry student at Kwantlen C. Applications are available at all high schools.
MINIMUM AVERAGE: N/A
VALUE: $1000.00
TERMS: One year only. The award will be applied toward tuition fees and college bookstore charges.
NUMBER OF AWARDS: 24
DEADLINE FOR APPLICATIONS: March 31

CODE: BC/KWA009/c
NAME: Jason R. MacPhail Memorial Award
PROGRAM: Business, Accounting, or Marketing
BASIS: Awarded to a male and a female student from Richmond Senior Secondary School, Matthew McNair Secondary School, or Stevenson Secondary School. The selection is based on academic achievement, letters of recommendation, and high school transcripts.
MINIMUM AVERAGE: N/A
VALUE: $1200.00
TERMS: One year only
NUMBER OF AWARDS: 2
DEADLINE FOR APPLICATIONS: September 30

CODE: BC/KWA010/c
NAME: Student Association Award
PROGRAM: Any
BASIS: Awarded to a male and a female student enrolled at Kwantlen C. Financial need, potential in area of study, and community or college volunteer activities will be considered
MINIMUM AVERAGE: N/A
VALUE: $500.00
TERMS: One year only
NUMBER OF AWARDS: 2
DEADLINE FOR APPLICATIONS: September 30

CODE: BC/KWA011/c
NAME: Surrey Chapter of IODE Bursary
PROGRAM: Health Sciences
BASIS: Applicants must be Canadian citizens with good scholastic ability. Financial need will be considered. Preference will be shown to Surrey residents.
MINIMUM AVERAGE: 3.00
VALUE: $400.00
TERMS: Consideration will be given to a previous recipient making application for a 2nd-year term.
NUMBER OF AWARDS: 1
DEADLINE FOR APPLICATIONS: September 30

CODE: BC/KWA012/c
NAME: Ernest Westerman Memorial Bursary
PROGRAM: Any
BASIS: Awarded to a male and a fe-

male student from a Surrey secondary school who demonstrate financial need and academic achievement.

MINIMUM AVERAGE: N/A
VALUE: $1000.00
TERMS: One year only
NUMBER OF AWARDS: 2
DEADLINE FOR APPLICATIONS: September 30

CODE: BC/KWA013/c
NAME: Women's Equity Bursary
PROGRAM: Women's Studies or related course work in non-traditional fields, leading to a degree, certificate, or diploma
BASIS: Awarded to a female student enrolled in either full-time or part-time studies of not less than one year. Financial need will be considered.
MINIMUM AVERAGE: N/A
VALUE: $500.00
TERMS: One year only
NUMBER OF AWARDS: 1
DEADLINE FOR APPLICATIONS: September 30

Malaspina College

CODE: BC/MAL001/c
NAME: Nicholas Plecas Endowment Entrance Scholarships in Science
PROGRAM: Science
BASIS: Awarded to students entering Malaspina C. The selection is based on academic achievement.
MINIMUM AVERAGE: 70.00
VALUE: Equals full tuition.
TERMS: One year only
NUMBER OF AWARDS: 4
DEADLINE FOR APPLICATIONS: April 30

CODE: BC/MAL002/c
NAME: Malaspina College Forestry Technology Entrance Award
PROGRAM: Forestry Technology
BASIS: Awarded to mature students entering Malaspina C. The selection

is based on academic achievement and financial need.
MINIMUM AVERAGE: 70.00
VALUE: $500.00
TERMS: One year only
NUMBER OF AWARDS: 2
DEADLINE FOR APPLICATIONS: June 30

CODE: BC/MAL003/c
NAME: Bill Rowntree Memorial Award
PROGRAM: Any
BASIS: Awarded to a mature student entering full-time studies at Malaspina C. The selection is based on achievement in part-time studies or upgrading courses.
MINIMUM AVERAGE: 70.00
VALUE: $500.00
TERMS: One year only
NUMBER OF AWARDS: 1
DEADLINE FOR APPLICATIONS: June 30

CODE: BC/MAL004/c
NAME: University Womens Club of Nanaimo
PROGRAM: Any
BASIS: Awarded to a mature female student entering full-time studies at Malaspina C. The selection is based on academic achievement in part-time studies or upgrading courses, community service, and financial need.
MINIMUM AVERAGE: 70.00
VALUE: $500.00
TERMS: One year only
NUMBER OF AWARDS: 1
DEADLINE FOR APPLICATIONS: June 30

New Caledonia College. *See* College of New Caledonia

North Island College

CODE: BC/NIS000/c
NAME: North Island College does not offer any entrance scholarships.

Northern Lights College

CODE: BC/NOLT01/c
NAME: Northern Lights College
Award of Excellence
PROGRAM: Any
BASIS: Awarded to a high school
graduate on the basis of a qualify-
ing project such as an essay, scien-
tific experiment, shop technique,
business procedure, or a nutrition
or textile project. Projects must be
submitted to a Campus Principal.
MINIMUM AVERAGE: N/A
VALUE: Equals tuition credits.
TERMS: One year only
NUMBER OF AWARDS: 1
DEADLINE FOR APPLICATIONS: April 30

CODE: BC/NOLT02/c
NAME: International Student Tai Chi
Chuan Scholarship
PROGRAM: Any
BASIS: This scholarship assists a can-
didate who is adept at Yang Style
Tai Chi Chuan and who meets the
College admission requirements to
study at Northern Lights C. Can-
didates should apply to the Inter-
national Education Coordinator at
the Fort St. John campus.
MINIMUM AVERAGE: N/A
VALUE: $2000.00
TERMS: One year only. The purpose is
to attract expert instruction in Tai
Chi Chuan to the Peace River Re-
gion.
NUMBER OF AWARDS: 1

CODE: BC/NOLT03/c
NAME: Northern Mixedwood
Scholarship
PROGRAM: Any
BASIS: Preference for this award is
given to a pre–Forestry University
Transfer student enrolled at the
College. A high school student en-
tering the College in any program
who has a career interest in the
forestry industry is also eligible.
An application is required.

MINIMUM AVERAGE: N/A
VALUE: $500.00
TERMS: One year only
NUMBER OF AWARDS: 1

Northwest Community College

CODE: BC/NWC001/c
NAME: Northwest Community
College Entrance Scholarships
PROGRAM: Any
BASIS: Applicants must be graduates
from BC School Districts 50, 52, 54,
80, 88, and 92 and be enrolled in
full-time programs at Northwest
CC.
MINIMUM AVERAGE: 75.00
VALUE: Varies with program.
TERMS: Scholarship is a tuition reduc-
tion based on high school grades:
A average, 100%; B+ Average, 75%;
B Average, 50%.
NUMBER OF AWARDS: Varies
DEADLINE FOR APPLICATIONS:
September 30

Okanagan University College

CODE: BC/OKA001/c
NAME: Berge & Company Entrance
Award
PROGRAM: Arts/Science
BASIS: Awarded on the basis of aca-
demic achievement and financial
need.
MINIMUM AVERAGE: 75.00
VALUE: $500.00
TERMS: One year only
NUMBER OF AWARDS: Varies
DEADLINE FOR APPLICATIONS: July 15

CODE: BC/OKA002/c
NAME: Coca Cola Bottling Entrance
Scholarship
PROGRAM: Career or Technology
BASIS: Awarded on the basis of aca-
demic achievement. An application

and transcript of final grades are required.
MINIMUM AVERAGE: 75.00
VALUE: $500.00
TERMS: One year only
NUMBER OF AWARDS: Varies
DEADLINE FOR APPLICATIONS: July 15

CODE: BC/OKA003/c
NAME: Michael Doyle Memorial Award
PROGRAM: Any
BASIS: Awarded to a handicapped student attending the Kelowna Centre of Okanagan UC for the first time on the basis of academic achievement. Recipients must be permanent residents of BC. Financial need will be considered.
MINIMUM AVERAGE: N/A
VALUE: $500.00
TERMS: One year only
NUMBER OF AWARDS: Varies
DEADLINE FOR APPLICATIONS: May 31

CODE: BC/OKA004/c
NAME: Okanagan Mainline Real Estate Board Awards
PROGRAM: Any
BASIS: Recipients must be residents of the region withing the boundaries of the Okanagan Mainline Real Estate Board. The selection is based on academic achievement and financial need. Applicants interested in real estate careers may receive preference.
MINIMUM AVERAGE: 75.00
VALUE: $500.00, but may vary.
TERMS: One year only
NUMBER OF AWARDS: 4
DEADLINE FOR APPLICATIONS: July 15

CODE: BC/OKA005/c
NAME: Okanagan University College International Access Award
PROGRAM: Any
BASIS: Awarded to students from developing countries studying at Okanagan UC. Application forms are available from the International Education Office, Kelowna Centre.
MINIMUM AVERAGE: N/A
VALUE: Varies
TERMS: Includes tuition fees, books and supplies, accommodation, transportation, and miscellaneous expenditures.
NUMBER OF AWARDS: Varies
DEADLINE FOR APPLICATIONS: June 30

CODE: BC/OKA006/c
NAME: Okanagan University College President's Entrance Scholarships
PROGRAM: Any
BASIS: Awarded to graduates of secondary schools in the Okanagan UC region on the basis of scholastic achievement, leadership qualities, and extracurricular participation. An application is required.
MINIMUM AVERAGE: 80.00
VALUE: $2310.00
TERMS: Award is worth tuition and approximately $1000 cash. A full course load must be taken. Not tenable with any other entrance scholarships.
NUMBER OF AWARDS: 18
DEADLINE FOR APPLICATIONS: March 31

CODE: BC/OKA007/c
NAME: Penticton Auto Dealers Association Automotive Studies Bursary.
PROGRAM: Automotive Technology Co-op or Entry Level Automotive
BASIS: Awarded to a resident of Penticton and District Community. Academic achievement and financial need will be considered.
MINIMUM AVERAGE: 60.00
VALUE: $250.00
TERMS: One year only
NUMBER OF AWARDS: 2
DEADLINE FOR APPLICATIONS: April 30

CODE: BC/OKA008/c
NAME: Penticton Centre Award Fund
PROGRAM: Any at Penticton Centre

BASIS: Awarded to a resident of Penticton and District Community. Academic achievement will be considered.
MINIMUM AVERAGE: 75.00
VALUE: Varies
TERMS: One year only
NUMBER OF AWARDS: 2
DEADLINE FOR APPLICATIONS: September 15

CODE: BC/OKA009/c
NAME: Penticton Chamber of Commerce Business Scholarship
PROGRAM: Any business and/or tourism program at Penticton Centre
BASIS: Awarded on the basis of academic achievement and financial need.
MINIMUM AVERAGE: 75.00
VALUE: $500.00
TERMS: One year only
NUMBER OF AWARDS: 2
DEADLINE FOR APPLICATIONS: September 15

CODE: BC/OKA010/c
NAME: Penticton Kinette Entrance Bursary
PROGRAM: Any
BASIS: Awarded on the basis of academic achievement and financial need. Preference will be shown to members of Kinsmen/Kinette families.
MINIMUM AVERAGE: 75.00
VALUE: $500.00
TERMS: One year only
NUMBER OF AWARDS: 1
DEADLINE FOR APPLICATIONS: May 31

CODE: BC/OKA011/c
NAME: Penticton Plaza Bursary
PROGRAM: Any
BASIS: Awarded to permanent residents of the Penticton community on the basis of academic achievement and financial need. Preference will be given to students who are single parents.

MINIMUM AVERAGE: 75.00
VALUE: $500.00
TERMS: One year only
NUMBER OF AWARDS: 2
DEADLINE FOR APPLICATIONS: May 31

CODE: BC/OKA012/c
NAME: Penticton University Women's Club Bursary
PROGRAM: Any
BASIS: Awarded to permanent residents of the area from Summerland to Osoyoos and west to Princeton attending at Penticton Centre. Preference will be given to mature females returning to studies and in financial need. An application is required.
MINIMUM AVERAGE: 75.00
VALUE: $300.00
TERMS: One year only
NUMBER OF AWARDS: 2
DEADLINE FOR APPLICATIONS: September 15

CODE: BC/OKA013/c
NAME: Real Estate Foundation Fund Awards
PROGRAM: Any related to real estate
BASIS: Awarded to students pursing studies and careers related to real estate. Preference may be given to applicants who are licensed real estate agents or immediate family members of real estate agents. Academic achievement and financial need will be considerd
MINIMUM AVERAGE: 75.00
VALUE: Varies
TERMS: One year only
NUMBER OF AWARDS: 4
DEADLINE FOR APPLICATIONS: July 15

CODE: BC/OKA014/c
NAME: Robert Allison Bursary for Non-Status Indians
PROGRAM: Any
BASIS: Awarded to students who are the descendents of Native Indians and whose circumstances make it necessary to be self-supporting.

MINIMUM AVERAGE: 75.00
VALUE: Varies
TERMS: The award funds may be given to one or more recipients.
NUMBER OF AWARDS: Varies
DEADLINE FOR APPLICATIONS: May 31

CODE: BC/OKA015/c
NAME: Rotary Club of Salmon Arm Award
PROGRAM: Any
BASIS: Awarded to deserving Salmon Arms Centre students
MINIMUM AVERAGE: 75.00
VALUE: $825.00
TERMS: One year only
NUMBER OF AWARDS: 2
DEADLINE FOR APPLICATIONS: May 31

CODE: BC/OKA016/c
NAME: Sun-Rype Products Ltd, $500 Entrance Scholarships
PROGRAM: Any
BASIS: Awarded to graduates of senior secondary schools in the Okanagan UC region on the basis of academic achievement, community service, and extracurricular activities. Applications are available from the high school guidance offices after February 1.
MINIMUM AVERAGE: 75.00
VALUE: $500.00
TERMS: One year only
NUMBER OF AWARDS: 3
DEADLINE FOR APPLICATIONS: July 15

CODE: BC/OKA017/c
NAME: Vernon Film Society Entrance Scholarship
PROGRAM: Humanities
BASIS: Open to graduates of a Vernon high school planning a degree with a major in one of the Humanities at the Kalamalka Centre. Academic achievement and financial need will be considered. Applications are available at the high school.
MINIMUM AVERAGE: 75.00
VALUE: $500.00
TERMS: One year only

NUMBER OF AWARDS: N/A
DEADLINE FOR APPLICATIONS: August 31

CODE: BC/OKA018/c
NAME: Walrod Memorial Scholarship Fund
PROGRAM: Any
BASIS: Awarded to high-ranking secondary students of the Central Okanagan School District #23 entering their 1st year of full-time study at Okanagan UC. Application forms are available from the high schools.
MINIMUM AVERAGE: 75.00
VALUE: Varies
TERMS: One year only
NUMBER OF AWARDS: 1
DEADLINE FOR APPLICATIONS: July 15

Pacific Marine Training Institute

CODE: BC/PMTI01/c
NAME: B.C. Supercargoes Association Bursary
PROGRAM: Shipping and Marine Operations
BASIS: Applicants should contact the Shipping and Marine Operations Dept. directly for the selection criteria and application information.
MINIMUM AVERAGE: N/A
VALUE: $600.00
TERMS: One year only
NUMBER OF AWARDS: 1

CODE: BC/PMTI02/c
NAME: ILWU Local 514 – Ship and Deck Foremen
PROGRAM: Shipping and Marine Operations
BASIS: Applicants should contact the Department directly for the selection criteria and application information.
MINIMUM AVERAGE: N/A
VALUE: $500.00
TERMS: One year only
NUMBER OF AWARDS: 1

CODE: BC/PMTI03/c
NAME: National Transportation Club
Bursary
PROGRAM: Shipping and Marine
Operations
BASIS: Applicants should contact the
Department directly for the selec-
tion criteria and application infor-
mation.
MINIMUM AVERAGE: N/A
VALUE: $1500.00
TERMS: One year only
NUMBER OF AWARDS: 1

CODE: BC/PMTI04/c
NAME: Vancouver Port Corporation
Bursary
PROGRAM: Shipping and Marine
Operations
BASIS: Applicants should contact the
Department directly for the selec-
tion criteria and application infor-
mation.
MINIMUM AVERAGE: N/A
VALUE: $1000.00
TERMS: One year only
NUMBER OF AWARDS: 1

CODE: BC/PMTI05/c
NAME: Chamber of Shipping of BC
"Peter N. Russell" Award
PROGRAM: Shipping and Marine
Operations
BASIS: Applicants should contact the
Department directly for the selec-
tion criteria and application infor-
mation.
MINIMUM AVERAGE: N/A
VALUE: $500.00
TERMS: One year only
NUMBER OF AWARDS: 1

Selkirk College

CODE: BC/SELK01/c
NAME: Selkirk College Entrance
Scholarships
PROGRAM: Any program at Selkirk
College
BASIS: One award is offered to a grad-
uating student from each of the 12
high schools in the Selkirk C

region. The selection is made on
the basis of academic achievement
and leadership by the guidance
counsellors at each high school.
MINIMUM AVERAGE: N/A
VALUE: $500.00
TERMS: One year only
NUMBER OF AWARDS: 12

University College of the Fraser Valley

CODE: BC/UCFV01/c
NAME: Aldergrove Agricultural
Association Bursary
PROGRAM: Agricultural Technology at
UCFV
BASIS: Awarded to a student enrolling
in a full-time program (20 credits
per semester). Applications are
available from the Aldergrove
Agricultural Association, Box 1053,
Aldergrove, BC V0X 1A0 or the
UCFV Financial Aid Office.
MINIMUM AVERAGE: N/A
VALUE: $500.00
TERMS: One year only
NUMBER OF AWARDS: 1
DEADLINE FOR APPLICATIONS: July 31

CODE: BC/UCFV02/c
NAME: Chilliwack Horticultural
Society Scholarships
PROGRAM: Agricultural
BASIS: Awarded to students who
intend to make a career in horti-
culture. Preference will be given a
Chilliwack area student. Appli-
cations are available from Chilli-
wack Horticultural Society, c/o
46511 Mayfair Ave., Chilliwack, BC
V2P 3J3 or UCFV Financial Aid
Office.
MINIMUM AVERAGE: N/A
VALUE: $300 for a 1st-year student
and $300 for a 2nd-year student.
TERMS: Renewable
NUMBER OF AWARDS: Varies
DEADLINE FOR APPLICATIONS:
September 1

CODE: BC/UCFV03/c
NAME: Lobb Memorial Scholarship
PROGRAM: Aviation
BASIS: Awarded to students entering or continuing their enrolment in the UCFV Aviation program. Preference will be given to Mission students. Applications are available from Mission Foundation, c/o Keith Cameron, School District No. 75, 33046 4th Ave., Mission, BC V2V 1S5.
MINIMUM AVERAGE: N/A
VALUE: $1000.00
TERMS: One year only
NUMBER OF AWARDS: Varies

CODE: BC/UCFV04/c
NAME: Michelene Catherine Allard Memorial Fine Arts Bursary
PROGRAM: Fine Arts
BASIS: Awarded to Canadian citizens who live or have lived in the Chilliwack area. An applicant must demonstrate financial need and satisfactory academic progress. Applications are available from the UCFV Financial Aid Office.
MINIMUM AVERAGE: N/A
VALUE: $1000.00
TERMS: Amount may vary. This bursary is to be used for tuition, books, and supplies.
NUMBER OF AWARDS: 1
DEADLINE FOR APPLICATIONS: October 31

CODE: BC/UCFV05/c
NAME: University College of the Fraser Valley Athletic Scholarship
PROGRAM: Any full-time program
BASIS: Awarded to full-time UCFV students who are participating in a recognized college team sport. Candidates must meet the athletic eligibility requirements. New students qualify on the basis of 1st-term grades, not high school grades.
MINIMUM AVERAGE: 2.50

VALUE: Equals a tuition waiver worth 9 credits (maximum) per semester.
TERMS: Renewable
NUMBER OF AWARDS: 1

CODE: BC/UCFV06/c
NAME: University College of the Fraser Valley Athletic Tuition Waiver
PROGRAM: Any full-time program
BASIS: Awarded to full-time UCFV students who are participating in a recognized college team sport. Candidates must be excellent athletes who meet the athletic eligibility requirements as determined by the coaching staff and the BCCAA.
MINIMUM AVERAGE: 2.80
VALUE: $1000.00
TERMS: Not tenable with any other UCFV entrance scholarships.
NUMBER OF AWARDS: 2

CODE: BC/UCFV07/c
NAME: UCFV Basic Education and Development Tuition Scholarships
PROGRAM: Any full-time program
BASIS: Awarded to part-time students who have completed any basic education and development program in the past year and who intend to continue into full-time studies at UCFV. Applications are available from Student Services, Abbotsford Campus.
MINIMUM AVERAGE: N/A
VALUE: Equals a tuition waiver.
TERMS: One year only
NUMBER OF AWARDS: 2
DEADLINE FOR APPLICATIONS: May 15

CODE: BC/UCFV08/c
NAME: University College of the Fraser Valley Bursaries
PROGRAM: Any
BASIS: For full-time students who have identified vocational or academic objectives and who require and merit financial assistance. Also eligible are mature

students, single parents, and those in upgrading and short-duration courses. A financial aid form is required.
MINIMUM AVERAGE: N/A
VALUE: $1200.00
TERMS: Renewable
NUMBER OF AWARDS: 2

CODE: BC/UCFV09/c
NAME: University College of the Fraser Valley Student Society Bursary
PROGRAM: Any
BASIS: Awarded to entering full-time students who have been involved in the high school community on a volunteer basis. A letter of application and 2 personal recommendations must be sent to the UCFV Student Society Awards Selection Committee.
MINIMUM AVERAGE: 3.00
VALUE: Varies
TERMS: One year only
NUMBER OF AWARDS: 2
DEADLINE FOR APPLICATIONS: May 15

CODE: BC/UCFV10/c
NAME: UCFV Tuition Waiver Scholarships for High School Students
PROGRAM: Any
BASIS: Awarded to entering full-time students who have participated actively in the school community. Leadership, determination, effort, and academic standing will be considered. Candidates should apply to the University College Awards Selection Committee.
MINIMUM AVERAGE: 3.00
VALUE: Varies
TERMS: One year only
NUMBER OF AWARDS: 15
DEADLINE FOR APPLICATIONS: May 15

Vancouver Community College

CODE: BC/VAN001/c

NAME: Bernard G. Robinson Scholarship (Langara Campus)
PROGRAM: Criminal Justice
BASIS: Candidates must be students pursuing studies in programs to enhance their careers in criminal justice. Financial need, a record of previous formal education, and demonstrated commitment to advancing the cause of criminal justice are necessary. An application is required.
MINIMUM AVERAGE: N/A
VALUE: $500.00
TERMS: One year only
NUMBER OF AWARDS: 1

CODE: BC/VAN002/c
NAME: British Columbia Forest Products Entrance Scholarship (Langara Campus)
PROGRAM: Any full-time program
BASIS: Awarded to a student entering full-time studies at Langara who has been the legal dependent of an employee of the Company for at least one year. Scholastic achievement in the final 2 years of high school will be considered. An application is required.
MINIMUM AVERAGE: 70.00
VALUE: $250.00
TERMS: One year only
NUMBER OF AWARDS: 1
DEADLINE FOR APPLICATIONS: July 1

CODE: BC/VAN003/c
NAME: Duncan McCallum Athletic Scholarship (Langara Campus)
PROGRAM: Any
BASIS: Awarded to a student entering at least 12 credit hour of studies at Langara who is a starting member of a VCC athletic team.
MINIMUM AVERAGE: 3.50
VALUE: $500.00
TERMS: One year only
NUMBER OF AWARDS: 1

MANITOBA

Assiniboine Community College

CODE: MB/ACC000/c
NAME: Assiniboine Community College offers no entrance scholarships.

Keewatin Community College

CODE: MB/KEE000/c
NAME: Keewatin Community College offers no entrance scholarships.

Red River Community College

CODE: MB/RRC001/c
NAME: Tom O'Brien Memorial Entrance Scholarship
PROGRAM: Any full-time certificate or diploma program
BASIS: Awarded to a male and a female student who are Manitoba residents entering Red River CC. Academic merit, school or community involvement, and financial need will be considered. An application, transcripts, and letters of reference are required.
MINIMUM AVERAGE: N/A
VALUE: Equals the cost of tuition and student fees for one year.
TERMS: One year only
NUMBER OF AWARDS: 2
DEADLINE FOR APPLICATIONS: July 31

NORTHWEST TERRITORIES

Arctic College

CODE: NT/ARC001/c
NAME: A Western Arctic Scholarship
PROGRAM: Commerce, Forestry, Engineering, or Recreation
BASIS: Applicants must be residents of the western regions of the NWT planning to attend Arctic C or a technical school or university in Alberta. Awarded on the basis of academic ability and participation in extracurricular activities. An application is required.
MINIMUM AVERAGE: N/A
VALUE: $800.00
TERMS: One year only. Applicants must be grade 12 graduates.
NUMBER OF AWARDS: 3
DEADLINE FOR APPLICATIONS: July 15

CODE: NT/ARC002/c
NAME: Canadian National Scholarship for Women
PROGRAM: Environmental Technology or Renewable Resources
BASIS: Awarded to a female applicant accepted for a program starting in the Fall semester. The award is based on the applicant's description of interest in a blue-collar career.

MINIMUM AVERAGE: N/A
VALUE: $500.00
TERMS: One year only
NUMBER OF AWARDS: 1
DEADLINE FOR APPLICATIONS: August 15

CODE: NT/ARC003/c
NAME: Canada Scholars for Technology
PROGRAM: Environmental Technology or Renewable Resources

BASIS: Awarded to 2 students from the Nunatta Campus and 2 from the Thebacha Campus. At least 50% of the recipients will be female. An application is required.
MINIMUM AVERAGE: 80.00
VALUE: $6000.00
TERMS: $2000 per year, renewable provided an 80% average is maintained in a full course load.
NUMBER OF AWARDS: 4
DEADLINE FOR APPLICATIONS: June 1

SASKATCHEWAN

Carleton Trail Regional College

CODE: SK/CTRC00/c
NAME: Carlton Trail Regional College offers no entrance scholarships.

Cumberland Regional College

CODE: SK/CUMB01/c
NAME: Carson & Company Scholarship
PROGRAM: Any
BASIS: Awarded to a full-time student enrolled at the Cumberland Regional C University Centre in Melfort. A letter of application stating financial need, community involvement, and eligibility and a recent transcript of marks are required.
MINIMUM AVERAGE: N/A
VALUE: $300.00
TERMS: One year only
NUMBER OF AWARDS: 1
DEADLINE FOR APPLICATIONS: January 7

CODE: SK/CUMB02/c
NAME: City of Melfort Scholarship
PROGRAM: Any

BASIS: Awarded to a full-time student enrolled at the Cumberland Regional C University Centre in Melfort. A letter of application stating financial need, community involvement, and eligibility and a recent transcript of marks are required.
MINIMUM AVERAGE: N/A
VALUE: $500.00
TERMS: One year only
NUMBER OF AWARDS: 1
DEADLINE FOR APPLICATIONS: January 7

CODE: SK/CUMB03/c
NAME: Melfort Journal Scholarship
PROGRAM: Any
BASIS: Awarded to a full-time student enrolled at the Cumberland Regional C University Centre in Melfort. A letter of application stating financial need, community involvement, and eligibility and a recent transcript of marks are required.
MINIMUM AVERAGE: N/A
VALUE: $500.00
TERMS: One year only
NUMBER OF AWARDS: 1
DEADLINE FOR APPLICATIONS: January 7

CODE: SK/CUMB04/c
NAME: Melfort Knights of Columbus Scholarship

PROGRAM: Any
BASIS: Awarded to full-time students enrolled at the Cumberland Regional C University Centre in Melfort. The recipients must be from the City of Melfort and area. One scholarship will go to a rural student and another to an urban one. An application is required. Candidates should contact the Grand Knight, Melfort Knights of Columbus, Council #5788, Box 433, Melfort, Saskatchewan S0E 1A0.
MINIMUM AVERAGE: N/A
VALUE: $300.00
TERMS: One year only
NUMBER OF AWARDS: 2
DEADLINE FOR APPLICATIONS: January 7

CODE: SK/CUMB05/c
NAME: MUCC Post-Graduation Committee Scholarship
PROGRAM: Technical program or university classes
BASIS: Awarded to full-time students enrolled at Cumberland Regional C. A letter of application stating career plans, financial need, community involvement, and eligibility and a recent transcript of marks are required.
MINIMUM AVERAGE: N/A
VALUE: $300.00
TERMS: One year only
NUMBER OF AWARDS: 2
DEADLINE FOR APPLICATIONS: January 7

CODE: SK/CUMB06/c
NAME: Melfort Rotary Club Scholarships
PROGRAM: Any
BASIS: Awarded to full-time students from the Melfort area enrolled at the Cumberland Regional C University Centre in Melfort. A letter of application stating financial need, community involvement, and eligibility and a recent transcript of marks are required.
MINIMUM AVERAGE: N/A
VALUE: $300.00

TERMS: One year only. Not tenable with any other scholarships or bursaries.
NUMBER OF AWARDS: 2
DEADLINE FOR APPLICATIONS: January 7

CODE: SK/CUMB07/c
NAME: Melfort School Division Scholarship
PROGRAM: Any
BASIS: Awarded to an MUCC graduate enrolled at the University Program Centre in Melfort. A letter of application stating financial need, community involvement, and eligibility and a recent transcript of marks are required.
MINIMUM AVERAGE: N/A
VALUE: $500.00
TERMS: One year only
NUMBER OF AWARDS: 1
DEADLINE FOR APPLICATIONS: January 7

CODE: SK/CUMB08/c
NAME: Porcupine Plain Board of Trade Scholarship (Porcupine Plains)
PROGRAM: Any
BASIS: Awarded to a graduate of the Hudson Bay School Division or Bjorkdale High School who is a enrolled as a full-time university student at the Cumberland Regional C site in Porcupine Plain. An application is required.
MINIMUM AVERAGE: N/A
VALUE: $500.00
TERMS: One year only
NUMBER OF AWARDS: 1
DEADLINE FOR APPLICATIONS: January 7

CODE: SK/CUMB09/c
NAME: Tiger Lily School Division Scholarship
PROGRAM: Any
BASIS: Awarded to a student enrolled in full-time studies at the University Centre in Melfort who is a recent graduate of the Tiger Lily School Division. Academic ability, community service, leadership, and

financial need will be considered. An application is required. Contact the Director of Education, Tiger Lily School Division #54, Melfort, Saskatchewan S0E 1A0
MINIMUM AVERAGE: N/A
VALUE: $500.00
TERMS: One year only.
NUMBER OF AWARDS: 1
DEADLINE FOR APPLICATIONS: September 11

CODE: SK/CUMB10/c
NAME: Nipawan Royal Canadian Legion Bursary
PROGRAM: Any
BASIS: Awarded to a full-time student at Cumberland Regional C in Nipawin. Applicants will be assessed on their academic record and financial need.
MINIMUM AVERAGE: N/A
VALUE: $500.00
TERMS: One year only
NUMBER OF AWARDS: 1
DEADLINE FOR APPLICATIONS: September 11

CODE: SK/CUMB11/c
NAME: Tisdale Recorder Scholarship (Tisdale Campus)
PROGRAM: Technical program
BASIS: Awarded to a Tisdale resident enrolled in full-time studies at the College. Preference will be given to applicants who require financial assistance in order to achieve their educational goals. An application is required. Community leadership will be considered.
MINIMUM AVERAGE: N/A
VALUE: $250.00
TERMS: One year only
NUMBER OF AWARDS: 1
DEADLINE FOR APPLICATIONS: January 7

CODE: SK/CUMB12/c
NAME: Town of Tisdale Scholarship (Tisdale Campus)
PROGRAM: Technical program
BASIS: Awarded to a Tisdale resident

enrolled in full-time studies at the Tisdale campus. Leadership, community involvement, and financial need will be considered. An application is required, including a letter outlining educational plans and a letter of reference.
MINIMUM AVERAGE: N/A
VALUE: $500.00
TERMS: One year only
NUMBER OF AWARDS: 1
DEADLINE FOR APPLICATIONS: September 11

CODE: SK/CUMB13/c
NAME: Dataport Computer Centre Scholarship
PROGRAM: Businesss Certificate I or Office Education
BASIS: Awarded to a full-time student enrolled in either the Business Certificate I or Office Education program. An application is required.
MINIMUM AVERAGE: N/A
VALUE: $200.00
TERMS: One year only
NUMBER OF AWARDS: 1
DEADLINE FOR APPLICATIONS: January 7

Cypress Hills Regional College

CODE: SK/CYP001/c
NAME: Cypress Hills Regional College Entrance Award
PROGRAM: University – 1st year full-time
BASIS: Awarded to a student entering full-time studies at Cypress Hills Regional C. A combination of academic standing and financial need will be considered.
MINIMUM AVERAGE: N/A
VALUE: $1000.00
TERMS: One year only
NUMBER OF AWARDS: 1
DEADLINE FOR APPLICATIONS: October 15

CODE: SK/CYP002/c
NAME: South Saskatchewan Pipelines Scholarship
PROGRAM: Post-secondary program
BASIS: Awarded to a College-region resident entering full-time studies at Cypress Hills Regional C with high academic standing.
MINIMUM AVERAGE: N/A
VALUE: $1000.00
TERMS: One year only
NUMBER OF AWARDS: 1
DEADLINE FOR APPLICATIONS: October 15

CODE: SK/CYP003/c
NAME: Sask Oil Scholarship
PROGRAM: Any full-time SIAST program
BASIS: Awarded on the basis of academic standing and financial need to an adult returning to school full time after an absence of one year.
MINIMUM AVERAGE: N/A
VALUE: $200.00
TERMS: One year only
NUMBER OF AWARDS: 1
DEADLINE FOR APPLICATIONS: October 15

CODE: SK/CYP004/c
NAME: Swift Current Kiwanis Club Scholarship
PROGRAM: Any
BASIS: Awarded to a student graduating from Grade 12 at Swift Current Comprehensive High School and enrolling in a full-time program at Cypress Hills Regional C in the Fall. Applications are available from SCCHS Student Services.
MINIMUM AVERAGE: N/A
VALUE: $200.00
TERMS: One year only
NUMBER OF AWARDS: 1
DEADLINE FOR APPLICATIONS: October 15

Northlands Career College

CODE: SK/NCC000/c
NAME: Northlands Career College offers no entrance scholarships.

North West Regional College

CODE: SK/NWR001/c
NAME: Canadian Tire Scholarship
PROGRAM: North West Regional College university program
BASIS: Awarded to graduates of John Paul II Collegiate or the North Battleford Comprehensive High School. The selection is based on marks, community activities, education and career goals, and letters of recommendation. An application and transcript are required.
MINIMUM AVERAGE: 80.00
VALUE: $250.00
TERMS: One year only
NUMBER OF AWARDS: 1
DEADLINE FOR APPLICATIONS: September 30

CODE: SK/NWR002/c
NAME: Adult Basic Education Scholarship
PROGRAM: A full-time post-secondary credit program (Institute or University)
BASIS: Awarded to a graduate of a Grade 10, 11, or 12 Adult Basic Education (ABE) program at North West Regional C. Applicants must submit an application form, an official transcript of ABE marks, and a letter of recommendation from an instructor.
MINIMUM AVERAGE: 80.00
VALUE: $500.00
TERMS: One year only
NUMBER OF AWARDS: 1
DEADLINE FOR APPLICATIONS: September 30

CODE: SK/NWR003/c
NAME: RE/MAX Scholarship
PROGRAM: Full-time Saskatchewan Institute of Applied Technology program or North West Regional C university program
BASIS: Awarded to students entering NWRC on the basis of marks, community activities, education and career goals, and letters of recommendation. An application and transcript are required.
MINIMUM AVERAGE: 80.00
VALUE: $250.00
TERMS: One year only
NUMBER OF AWARDS: 1
DEADLINE FOR APPLICATIONS: September 30

CODE: SK/NWR004/c
NAME: Technical Training Scholarship
PROGRAM: Full-time Saskatchewan Institute of Applied Technology program
BASIS: Awarded to students entering NWRC on the basis of marks, community activities, education and career goals, and letters of recommendation. An application and transcript are required.
MINIMUM AVERAGE: 80.00
VALUE: $500.00
TERMS: One year only
NUMBER OF AWARDS: 1
DEADLINE FOR APPLICATIONS: September 30

Parkland Regional College

CODE: SK/PAR000/c
NAME: Parkland Regional College offers no entrance awards.

Prairie West Regional College

CODE: SK/PWRC00/c
NAME: Prairie West Regional College offers no entrance scholarships.

Saskatchewan Institute of Applied Science and Technology

CODE: SK/SIA001/c
NAME: Constable Brian King Memorial Scholarship (Kelsey)
PROGRAM: Any full-time program
BASIS: Awarded to Saskatchewan high school graduates entering Kelsey Institute. The selection is based on financial need, demonstrated involvement in school and other community activities, sports involvement, and academic potential.
MINIMUM AVERAGE: N/A
VALUE: $1000.00
TERMS: One year only
NUMBER OF AWARDS: 5
DEADLINE FOR APPLICATIONS: February 28

CODE: SK/SIA002/c
NAME: E.A. Davies Scholarship Award (Kelsey)
PROGRAM: Any full-time program
BASIS: Awarded to a Saskatchewan resident who is entering Kelsey and is a Mason, a member of the Order of Demolay, or the Order of Jobs Daughters International, or the child, stepchild, or grandchild of same. Financial need and leadership are considered.
MINIMUM AVERAGE: N/A
VALUE: $500.00
TERMS: One year only
NUMBER OF AWARDS: 1
DEADLINE FOR APPLICATIONS: September 30

CODE: SK/SIA003/c
NAME: Native Service Division Achievement Scholarship (Kelsey)
PROGRAM: One each to Adult Basic Education, Industrial Engineering Division, Health Science and Community Division
BASIS: Awarded to students of Native ancestry enrolled at Kelsey

Institute. The selection is based on academic achievement, involvement in student life activities, and community involvement.
MINIMUM AVERAGE: N/A
VALUE: $350.00
TERMS: One year only
NUMBER OF AWARDS: 1
DEADLINE FOR APPLICATIONS: February 28 and May 31

CODE: SK/SIA004/c
NAME: Health Care Educational Bursary Program (Kelsey)
PROGRAM: Diploma Nursing, Special Care Aide, Medical Laboratory Technology, Medical Radiation Technology, and Certified Combined Technician
BASIS: Applicants must be residents of the community served by St Joseph's and St Martin's Hospitals. Applications are available from the Catholic Health Council of Saskatchewan, 1705 Argyle Ave., Saskatoon, Saskatchewan S7H 2W6.
MINIMUM AVERAGE: N/A
VALUE: $450.00
TERMS: Renewable. Value of award increases in subsequent years.
NUMBER OF AWARDS: Varies

CODE: SK/SIA005/c
NAME: A.E. Smith Memorial Bursary (Kelsey)
PROGRAM: Recreation and Leisure Diploma Program or Physical Education.
BASIS: Awarded to a student who has Masonic connections or who is sponsored by a Mason. The candidate must have demonstrated leadership in athletics, especially in track, and participated in school and community activites.
MINIMUM AVERAGE: 75.00
VALUE: $300.00
TERMS: One year only
NUMBER OF AWARDS: 1
DEADLINE FOR APPLICATIONS: September 30

CODE: SK/SIA006/c
NAME: Association of Canadian Community Colleges Bursary
PROGRAM: Any full-time program
BASIS: Awarded to students enrolled in any full-time SIAST program, 32 weeks or more in duration. The application letter must include one's educational background, educational objectives, and difficulties encountered in undertaking an educational program.
MINIMUM AVERAGE: N/A
VALUE: $200.00
TERMS: One year only
NUMBER OF AWARDS: 1
DEADLINE FOR APPLICATIONS: October 30

CODE: SK/SIA007/c
NAME: Sheila Cressman Memorial Fund (Wascana Institute)
PROGRAM: ESL program – Wascana Institute
BASIS: Awarded to students enrolled in the ESL program. Financial need will be considered. Requests should be directed to Arthur Gudowski, ESL Centre.
MINIMUM AVERAGE: N/A
VALUE: N/A
TERMS: One year only
NUMBER OF AWARDS: N/A

CODE: SK/SIA008/c
NAME: McPhail Memorial Bursaries
PROGRAM: Any 2-year programs at one of the 4 SIAST campuses.
BASIS: Awarded to the sons, daughters, or wards of members of Saskatchewan Wheat Pool. The selection is based on demonstrated need, with consideration for community and school activity and academic performance.
MINIMUM AVERAGE: N/A
VALUE: $700.00
TERMS: One year only
NUMBER OF AWARDS: 3
DEADLINE FOR APPLICATIONS: July 15

Saskatchewan Indian Institute of Technologies

CODE: SK/SIIT00/c
NAME: Saskatchewan Indian Institute of Technologies does not offer any entrance awards.

Southeast Regional College

CODE: SK/SRC000/c
NAME: Southeast Regional College, does not offer any entrance scholarships.

YUKON TERRITORIES

Yukon College

CODE: YK/YKN000/c
NAME: Yukon College does not offer any entrance scholarships.

13 General awards

CANADA-WIDE

CODE: CA/AAH001/g
NAME: A.A. Heaps Scholarship
SPONSOR: Canadian Labour Congress
ADDRESS: 2841 Riverside Drive, Ottawa, Ontario K1V 8X7
PROGRAM: Any Canadian college or university program
BASIS: Candidates must be Canadian citizens or landed immigrants undertaking full-time undergraduate studies and have an interest in social reform as practised by A.A. Heaps. An essay, 2 letters of reference, and financial need will be considered.
MINIMUM AVERAGE: N/A
VALUE: $3000.00
TERMS: One year only
NUMBER OF AWARDS: Varies
DEADLINE FOR APPLICATIONS: May 7

CODE: CA/AHG001/g
NAME: Adam H. Griffith Environmental Design Award
SPONSOR: c/o R. Griffith
ADDRESS: 104 Bridlewood Boulevard, Agincourt, Ontario M1T 1R1
PROGRAM: Any
BASIS: Awarded to the student who designs the best solution to the environmental-design problem set each year. Applicants should write for an entry form that will provide detailed information. The solution may include models and drawings.
MINIMUM AVERAGE: N/A
VALUE: $500.00
TERMS: Students may re-enter the competition each year.
NUMBER OF AWARDS: 1
DEADLINE FOR APPLICATIONS: August 2

CODE: CA/AAP01/g
NAME: Athlete Assistance Program
SPONSOR: Athlete Assistance Program Manager, Fitness and Amateur Sport
ADDRESS: Journal Tower South, 365 Laurier Avenue W., Ottawa, Ontario K1A 0X6
PROGRAM: Any Canadian post-secondary program
BASIS: Applicants must be Canadian citizens or permanent residents. Athletes must be recommended by national sports governing bodies that meet the selection criteria of Sport Canada.
MINIMUM AVERAGE: N/A
VALUE: Varies

TERMS: Awards include tuition fees and a living and training allowance (to cover basic accommodation and food). Special needs may be met by request.
NUMBER OF AWARDS: Varies

CODE: CA/ACUNS1/g
NAME: Special Awards for Northern Residents
SPONSOR: Association of Canadian Universities for Northern Studies
ADDRESS: 130 Albert Street, Suite 201, Ottawa, Ontario K1P 5G4
PROGRAM: Any Canadian university program
BASIS: Open to students who live in areas of Canada north of the discontinuous permafrost line. Applicants must show commitment to the North and be able to act as resource persons in the university they are visiting. A program outline is required with the application.
MINIMUM AVERAGE: N/A
VALUE: $5000.00
TERMS: One year only. Each recipient must have a sponsor in the university who will take responsibility for developing and directing the study program.
NUMBER OF AWARDS: 2
DEADLINE FOR APPLICATIONS: January 31

CODE: CA/AFP01/g
NAME: Educational Cost Allowances for Dependants of Armed Forces Person
SPONSOR: Education Officer, Personnel Office
ADDRESS: Canadian Forces Base, Chilliwack, BC
PROGRAM: Any
BASIS: Awarded to dependents of current Armed Forces personnel who are BC residents
MINIMUM AVERAGE: N/A
VALUE: Varies
TERMS: Reimbursement for 1st year.
NUMBER OF AWARDS: Varies

CODE: CA/AIAC01/g
NAME: Automotive Industries Association of Canada Scholarship
SPONSOR: Automotive Industries Association of Canada
ADDRESS: 1272 Wellington, Ottawa, Ontario K1Y 3A7
PROGRAM: Automotive-aftermarket-industry related course
BASIS: An applicant must submit a letter detailing personal goals, school and work experience, and activities that involve community service and leadership. A letter of recommendation from a teacher is also required.
MINIMUM AVERAGE: N/A
VALUE: $700.00
TERMS: One year only
NUMBER OF AWARDS: Varies
DEADLINE FOR APPLICATIONS: October 30

CODE: CA/BAUS01/g
NAME: Bausch and Lomb Photogrammetric and Remote Sensing Scholarship
SPONSOR: Executive Manager, Canadian Institute of Surveying
ADDRESS: Box 5378, Station F, Ottawa, Ontario K2C 3J1
PROGRAM: Related to photogrammetry or remote sensing
BASIS: Applicants must submit a paper up to 4000 words in length that describes a new use of photogrammetry or remote sensing or related equipment, or an adaptation or improvement in the use of this equipment.
MINIMUM AVERAGE: N/A
VALUE: $500.00
TERMS: Award includes a 3-year membership in the Canadian Institute of Surveying.
NUMBER OF AWARDS: Varies
DEADLINE FOR APPLICATIONS: December 1

CODE: CA/BBM001/g
NAME: Bobby Bauer Memorial Award

SPONSOR: Bobby Bauer Memorial Foundation Inc.
ADDRESS: c/o The Rumpel Felt Co. Ltd, 60 Victoria Street N., P.O. Box 1283, Kitchener, Ontario N2G 4G8
PROGRAM: Any university or college program
BASIS: Awarded for scholastic achievement, sports, extracurricular activities, community service, and financial need.
MINIMUM AVERAGE: N/A
VALUE: $100.00
TERMS: One year only
NUMBER OF AWARDS: 6
DEADLINE FOR APPLICATIONS: October 30

CODE: CA/BMM001/g
NAME: Bill Mason Memorial Scholarship Fund
SPONSOR: Canadian Recreational Canoeing Association
ADDRESS: 1029 Hyde Park Road, Suite 5, Hyde Park, Ontario N0M 1Z0
PROGRAM: Outdoor Education or Environmental Studies
BASIS: Awarded on the basis of academic excellence and interest in the environment. An application is required along with a 600-word personal statement about the outdoors and the beliefs of Bill Mason, a well-known author, artist, and canoeist.
MINIMUM AVERAGE: 75.00
VALUE: $1000.00
TERMS: Awarded in 2 instalments: $700 in November and $300 in May after receipt of the year-end academic reports. Recipients may re-apply each year.
NUMBER OF AWARDS: 1
DEADLINE FOR APPLICATIONS: October 1

CODE: CA/CAP001/g
NAME: Canadian Association of Principals Student Leadership Award
SPONSOR: C.A.P. and Herff Jones Canada

ADDRESS: 331 Somerset Street West, Ottawa, Ontario K2P 0J8
PROGRAM: Any
BASIS: For graduating high school students in the top 20% of their class. An extensive application form is required, along with transcript and principal's recommendation. Leadership, community service, extracurricular activities, and special achievement are considered.
MINIMUM AVERAGE: N/A
VALUE: $1000.00
TERMS: One year only
NUMBER OF AWARDS: 20
DEADLINE FOR APPLICATIONS: December 16

CODE: CA/CASH01/g
NAME: Canada Scholarships
SPONSOR: Industry, Science and Technology Canada
ADDRESS: c/o Awards Division, AUCC, 350 Albert Street, Suite 600, Ottawa, Ontario K1R 1B1
PROGRAM: Eligible Canadian post-secondary institutions
BASIS: Candidates must apply for this scholarship at each of their selected universities or colleges. Candidates must be entering full-time study in programs with no less than 60% science and engineering courses. Half of these scholarships will be awarded to women.
MINIMUM AVERAGE: 80.00
VALUE: $10,000.00
TERMS: $2500 per year, and renewable for a further 3 years provided a 1st-class standing is maintained.
NUMBER OF AWARDS: 3300
DEADLINE FOR APPLICATIONS: June 20

CODE: CA/CCAA01/g
NAME: Canada Council Aid to Artists
SPONSOR: Lise Rochon, Communications Service, The Canada Council
ADDRESS: 99 Metcalfe Street, P.O. Box 1047, Ottawa, Ontario K1P 5V8

PROGRAM: Any artistic discipline
BASIS: Grants are available to individual accomplished artists in all disciplines and specialities to help improve skills and to allow free time for creative activity.
MINIMUM AVERAGE: N/A
VALUE: Varies
TERMS: Renewable
NUMBER OF AWARDS: Varies

CODE: CA/CCLOW1/g
NAME: Mairi St. John Macdonald Scholarship
SPONSOR: Canadian Congress for Learning Opportunities for Women
ADDRESS: 47 Main Street, Toronto, Ontario M4E 2V6
PROGRAM: High school equivalency program
BASIS: Awarded to a Canadian woman who is returning to school to complete her high school education after an absence of at least 3 years.
MINIMUM AVERAGE: N/A
VALUE: $500.00
TERMS: One year only
NUMBER OF AWARDS: 1
DEADLINE FOR APPLICATIONS: August 31

CODE: CA/CCPA01/g
NAME: Canadian Cerebral Palsy Association Scholarships
SPONSOR: Canadian Cerebral Palsy Association
ADDRESS: 825 Sherbrook Street, Winnipeg, Manitoba R3A 1M5
PROGRAM: Any post-secondary program
BASIS: Candidates must have cerebral palsy. Community service and career aspirations will be considered. Letters of recommendation and an application form are required. Preference will be shown to university-bound candidates.
MINIMUM AVERAGE: N/A
VALUE: $500.00
TERMS: Recipients may reapply each year.
NUMBER OF AWARDS: 4
DEADLINE FOR APPLICATIONS: April 1

CODE: CA/CCPEP1/g
NAME: Canadian Forces – Community College Pilot Entry Plan
SPONSOR: Canadian Forces Recruiting Centre
ADDRESS: 757 West Hastings Street, Suite R125, Sinclair Centre, Vancouver, BC V6C 1A1
PROGRAM: Aviation Technology
BASIS: Available to Canadian men and women enrolled as full-time students in an aviation-technology program who have the unique qualities required to succeed in the demanding world of military aviation.
MINIMUM AVERAGE: N/A
VALUE: Varies
TERMS: Tuition for up to 3 semesters. Recipients will be expected to enrol in the Canadian Armed Forces for 3 to 5 years.
NUMBER OF AWARDS: Varies

CODE: CA/CDH001/g
NAME: C.D. Howe Memorial Foundation Scholarships
SPONSOR: Office of Student Awards, University of Toronto
ADDRESS: 214 College Street, Toronto, Ontario M5T 2Z9
PROGRAM: Any full-time program at Laval University
BASIS: Awarded on the basis of academic achievement, extracurricular activities, leadership and the extent to which the applicant's intended program of study and future plans meet the Foundation objectives. An application and references are required.
MINIMUM AVERAGE: N/A
VALUE: Varies
TERMS: Tuition and other fees, travel costs, language tutorial assistance, and room and board. Renewable

for 4 years provided a "B" standing is maintained.
NUMBER OF AWARDS: 2
DEADLINE FOR APPLICATIONS: March 1

CODE: CA/CFSA01/g
NAME: Canadian Figure Skating Association Athlete Trust Scholarship
SPONSOR: High Performance Director, Canadian Figure Skating Association
ADDRESS: 1600 James Naismith Drive, Ottawa, Ontario K1B 5N4
PROGRAM: Any full-time college or university program
BASIS: Awarded to an inactive amateur gold-medallist test skater in any discipline or a sectional competitor in a Canadian Champion qualifying event who is prepared to undertake volunteer administrative functions for the CFSA. An application is required.
MINIMUM AVERAGE: N/A
VALUE: $8000.00
TERMS: Up to $2000 per year for tuition fees. Recipients are limited to a maximum of 4 annual grants. Applications for renewal are required annually.
NUMBER OF AWARDS: 7
DEADLINE FOR APPLICATIONS: April 1

CODE: CA/CGF001/g
NAME: Canadian Golf Foundation Scholarship Awards
SPONSOR: Shore Foundation for Charitable Purposes
ADDRESS: Golf House, 1333 Dorval Drive, Oakville, Ontario L6J 4Z3
PROGRAM: Any full-time college or university program
BASIS: Candidates must have experience in competitive golf at the regional, provincial, or national level prior to application. Candidates must also indicate involvement in extracurricular activities and community service. An application is required.

MINIMUM AVERAGE: 80.00
VALUE: $16,000.00
TERMS: $4000 per year, renewable for a total of 4 years provided the academic criteria are met.
NUMBER OF AWARDS: 24
DEADLINE FOR APPLICATIONS: June 7

CODE: CA/CHF001/g
NAME: Canadian Hospitality Foundation Scholarships
SPONSOR: Canadian Hospitality Foundation
ADDRESS: 80 Bloor Street West, Suite 1201, Toronto, Ontario M5S 2V1
PROGRAM: Various at Guelph, Ryerson, and Mount St Vincent
BASIS: Awarded to students entering a degree program in Food and Beverage Management, Lodging and Institutional Management, Hotel and Food Administration, Institutional Foodservice Management or Hospitality and Tourism Management. An application and references are required.
MINIMUM AVERAGE: N/A
VALUE: $12,500.00 total
TERMS: One year only. Three of $2000, 1 of $1500, and 5 of $1000.
NUMBER OF AWARDS: 9
DEADLINE FOR APPLICATIONS: May 31

CODE: CA/CIME01/g
NAME: Denis Cressey Marine Engineering Scholarship Trust
SPONSOR: Chairman, Board of Trustees
ADDRESS: Canadian Institute of Marine Engineering, #10 – 1934 Barclay Street, Vancouver, BC V6G 1L3
PROGRAM: Marine Engineering or related field
BASIS: Applicants must submit a letter of application giving details of educational courses or projects and stating for which purposes the grant would be used if awarded. A brief curriculum vitae should also be included.

MINIMUM AVERAGE: N/A
VALUE: $1500.00
TERMS: One year only. Amount of
award may vary.
NUMBER OF AWARDS: 1
DEADLINE FOR APPLICATIONS: May 15

CODE: CA/CMSF01/g
NAME: Canadian Merit Scholarship
Foundation Awards
SPONSOR: Canadian Merit Scholarship
Foundation
ADDRESS: R.R. #1, Wellington, Ontario
K0K 3L0
PROGRAM: Any full-time program at
specified universities
BASIS: Candidates must demonstrate
character, leadership, and commu-
nity service. Transcripts, nomina-
tion forms, and 2 short essays are
required. Interviews may follow.
Applicants must be planning to
attend the following universities:
Alberta, British Columbia, Calgary,
Dalhousie, Laval, Manitoba,
McGill, McMaster, Memorial, New
Brunswick, Queen's, Saskatchewan,
Toronto, Waterloo, Western
Ontario, York.
MINIMUM AVERAGE: 80.00
VALUE: $12,000.00
TERMS: $3000 per year plus tuition
fees. Renewable for 3 more years
provided academic (B+ or better)
and service criteria are met. In
addition to the national awards
there are 20 Regional Awards of
$1000, 25 Provincial Awards of
$500, and 45 Honour Citations
(plaques are given).
NUMBER OF AWARDS: 12
DEADLINE FOR APPLICATIONS: October
28

CODE: CA/CNA001/g
NAME: Educational Scholarship
Program
SPONSOR: Canadian Native Arts
Foundation
ADDRESS: 77 Mowat Avenue, Suite
508, Toronto, Ontario M6K 3E3

PROGRAM: Visual, performing, and
communications arts
BASIS: Awarded to students of Native ancestry entering all levels of
arts education. Artistic performance, scholastic ability, and letters
of reference will be considered.
MINIMUM AVERAGE: N/A
VALUE: Varies with applicant's requirements.
TERMS: Recipients may reapply each
year.
NUMBER OF AWARDS: Varies
DEADLINE FOR APPLICATIONS: April 15

CODE: CA/CNA002/g
NAME: Professional Development
Grants
SPONSOR: Canadian Native Arts
Foundation
ADDRESS: 77 Mowat Avenue, Suite
508, Toronto, Ontario M6K 3E3
PROGRAM: Any arts apprenticeship at
college or university
BASIS: Applicants must be of Native
ancestry entering an apprentice-
ship, college, or university pro-
gram in any kind of arts subject.
MINIMUM AVERAGE: N/A
VALUE: $1000.00
TERMS: Awards may vary in amount.
Renewable on the basis of instruc-
tors' or employers' reports.
NUMBER OF AWARDS: Varies
DEADLINE FOR APPLICATIONS: April 15

CODE: CA/CNN001/g
NAME: CN Native Educational
Awards Program
SPONSOR: Employment Equity
ADDRESS: P.O. Box 8100, Montreal,
Quebec H3C 3N4
PROGRAM: Various, leading to a career
in transportation
BASIS: Applicants must be Native
students (Inuit, Status Indians,
Non-status Indians, and Métis)
preparing for a career in the trans-
portation industry who have proof
of acceptance into one of the

eligible educational institutions. An application is required.
MINIMUM AVERAGE: N/A
VALUE: $8000.00
TERMS: $2000 per year, renewable for 3 more years. CN will also attempt to find summer employment for recipients.
NUMBER OF AWARDS: 5
DEADLINE FOR APPLICATIONS: October 31

CODE: CA/CNW001/g
NAME: CN Scholarships for Women
SPONSOR: Canadian National
ADDRESS: 935 Lagauchetière West, Montreal, Quebec H3B 2M9
PROGRAM: A technical and/or skilled trade program
BASIS: Any women entering a nontraditional career training program at selected colleges or universities may apply. Each applicant must complete the appropriate application form at the school or college and demonstrate her desire to enter a blue-collar field.
MINIMUM AVERAGE: N/A
VALUE: $500.00
TERMS: One year only. Awarded regardless of any other financial assistance and may be used by recipients to ease financial requirements during their studies.
NUMBER OF AWARDS: 66
DEADLINE FOR APPLICATIONS: August 9

CODE: CA/COPP01/g
NAME: Paul Moreland/Copp Clark Longman Award
SPONSOR: Product Development Manager, Business Studies
ADDRESS: Copp Clark Longman Ltd, 2775 Matheson Boulevard E., Mississauga, Ontario L4W 4P7
PROGRAM: Any
BASIS: Awarded to a Grade 12 student on the basis of the following: academic achievement, extracurricular and community activities,

and a 500-word essay. Candidates are usually nominated by their Business Studies teachers.
MINIMUM AVERAGE: N/A
VALUE: $1000.00
TERMS: One year only. The recipient receives an engraved plaque, as does his or her high school.
NUMBER OF AWARDS: 1
DEADLINE FOR APPLICATIONS: April 22

CODE: CA/CPA001/g
NAME: Morton Copnick Scholarship
SPONSOR: Canadian Paraplegic Association
ADDRESS: 1500 Don Mills Road, Suite 201, Don Mills, Ontario M3B 3K4
PROGRAM: Any college or university program
BASIS: Awarded to a paraplegic student engaged in studies related to physical disabilities. An application form and letters of recommendation are required.
MINIMUM AVERAGE: N/A
VALUE: $500.00
TERMS: Recipients may reapply in subsequent years.
NUMBER OF AWARDS: 1
DEADLINE FOR APPLICATIONS: August 31

CODE: CA/CPI001/g
NAME: Canadian Printing Industries Scholarship
SPONSOR: Canadian Printing Industries Association
ADDRESS: 75 Albert Street, Suite 906, Ottawa, Ontario K1P 5E7
PROGRAM: Full-time graphic arts at a Canadian school
BASIS: Scholarships are awarded on the basis of academic results and interviews with industry executives. An application is required.
MINIMUM AVERAGE: 70.00
VALUE: $800.00
TERMS: Renewable. Recipients must reapply each year.
NUMBER OF AWARDS: 46

CODE: CA/CSEA01/g
NAME: CSEA Berol Prismacolour
National Art Scholarship
SPONSOR: CSEA Berol Scholarship
Director, Commission scolaire Les
Ecores
ADDRESS: 3100, boulevard de la
Concorde Est, Bureau 210, Laval,
Quebec H7E 2B9
PROGRAM: Any art-related program
BASIS: Awarded to high school grad-
uates about to enter a recognized
post-secondary art program. Exten-
sive portfolio submission criteria
are available in the application
package.
MINIMUM AVERAGE: N/A
VALUE: $1000.00
TERMS: One year only
NUMBER OF AWARDS: 5
DEADLINE FOR APPLICATIONS: May 15

CODE: CA/CSEG01/g
NAME: Canadian Society of
Exploration Geophysicists Trust
Fund
SPONSOR: Canadian Society of Ex-
ploration Geophysicists
ADDRESS: 206 7th Avenue S.W., Room
206, Calgary, Alberta T2P 0W7
PROGRAM: Geophysics at college or
university level
BASIS: Awarded on the basis of
financial need, academic achieve-
ment, community service, and
extracurricular activities. An appli-
cation form is required.
MINIMUM AVERAGE: N/A
VALUE: $1750.00
TERMS: Candidates may reapply each
year.
NUMBER OF AWARDS: 24
DEADLINE FOR APPLICATIONS: June 30

CODE: CA/CSFS01/g
NAME: Canadian-Scandinavian
Foundation Scholarship
SPONSOR: Secretary of the Canadian-
Scandinavian Foundation
ADDRESS: c/o Department of Geog-
raphy, McGill University, 805

Sherbrooke Street W., Montreal,
Quebec H3A 2K6
PROGRAM: Fine Arts and others
BASIS: Awarded to students who wish
to study in Sweden or Finland. No
particular form is required. Study
plans, transcripts of completed
studies, and a $10 application fee
are required.
MINIMUM AVERAGE: N/A
VALUE: Varies
TERMS: A variety of scholarships are
available for Canadian students
who wish to study in a Scandinavian country . Travel costs may
be included.
NUMBER OF AWARDS: Varies
DEADLINE FOR APPLICATIONS: January
31

CODE: CA/CWF001/g
NAME: Orville Erickson Memorial
Scholarship Fund
SPONSOR: c/o Secretary, Canadian
Wildlife Foundation
ADDRESS: 2740 Queensview Drive,
Ottawa, Ontario K2B 1A2
PROGRAM: Conservation programs
BASIS: Awarded to university or
community-college students study-
ing conservation-related fields. An
application form is required along
with transcript(s) and 3 letters of
reference. Applicants must be
Canadian citizens or landed immi-
grants.
MINIMUM AVERAGE: N/A
VALUE: $1000.00
TERMS: Recipients may reapply each
year.
NUMBER OF AWARDS: 1
DEADLINE FOR APPLICATIONS: June 1

CODE: CA/CWSA01/g
NAME: Ada MacKenzie Memorial
Foundation Award to Student
Wheelchair Athletes
SPONSOR: Canadian Wheelchair Sports
Association
ADDRESS: 1600 James Naismith Drive,
Ottawa, Ontario K1B 5N4

PROGRAM: Any
BASIS: Awarded to wheelchair athletes attending post-secondary programs.
MINIMUM AVERAGE: N/A
VALUE: Varies
TERMS: Renewable
NUMBER OF AWARDS: Varies

CODE: CA/DAV001/g
NAME: Da Vinci Bursary
SPONSOR: Da Vinci Scholarship Foundation
ADDRESS: 2 Roker Crescent, Agincourt, Ontario M1S 1P4
PROGRAM: Any college or university
BASIS: These awards are for students of Italian descent who demonstrate financial need. Candidates must be of good character and not related to a director or any other officer of the Foundation. An application is required.
MINIMUM AVERAGE: 65.00
VALUE: $250.00
TERMS: Renewable provided a "B+" average is maintained.
NUMBER OF AWARDS: Varies

CODE: CA/DOE01/g
NAME: Duke of Edinburgh's Award Program Award(s)
SPONSOR: Duke of Edinburgh's Awards, BC and Yukon Division
ADDRESS: #212 – 633 Courtney Street, Victoria, BC V8W 1B8
PROGRAM: Any full-time program
BASIS: Applicants must be (or have been) active participants in the Duke of Edinburgh's Award Program. Personal achievement, and participation in school, group, and community activities will be considered. An application is required.
MINIMUM AVERAGE: N/A
VALUE: $500.00
TERMS: One year only
NUMBER OF AWARDS: 2
DEADLINE FOR APPLICATIONS: April 15

CODE: CA/DOE02/g
NAME: Duke of Edinburgh United World College Scholarship
SPONSOR: Selection Co-ordinator, United World Colleges
ADDRESS: Lester B. Pearson College of the Pacific, R.R. #1, Pearson College Drive, Victoria, BC V8X 3W9
PROGRAM: United World College programs
BASIS: Applicants must be residents of BC currently enrolled in Grades 11 or 12. Preference is given to candidates of good academic standing who have reached 17 1/2 years of age on entry to the college. One scholarship is reserved for a Status Indian living in BC.
MINIMUM AVERAGE: N/A
VALUE: Varies
TERMS: Scholarship includes 2 years at a coeducational boarding school.
NUMBER OF AWARDS: Varies
DEADLINE FOR APPLICATIONS: March 1

CODE: CA/EAN001/g
NAME: Education Awards for Native Students
SPONSOR: Petro Canada Inc.
ADDRESS: P.O. Box 2844, Calgary, Alberta T2P 3E3
PROGRAM: Canadian colleges and universities
BASIS: Awarded to students of Canadian Indian or Inuit ancestry on the basis of financial need, academic performance and potential, the appropriateness of the discipline of studies to industry, and future aspirations. An application is required.
MINIMUM AVERAGE: N/A
VALUE: $5000.00
TERMS: Renewable to a total of 4 years provided passing marks and full-time attendance is maintained. Summer employment may be provided by Petro Canada.

NUMBER OF AWARDS: 5
DEADLINE FOR APPLICATIONS: June 15

CODE: CA/EGF001/g
NAME: Elizabeth Greenshields Foundation Awards
SPONSOR: Elizabeth Greenshields Foundation
ADDRESS: 1814 Sherbrooke Street West, Suite 1, Montreal, Quebec H3H 1E4
PROGRAM: Any fine arts program
BASIS: Candidates must be artists engaged in one or all or the following: painting, drawing, printmaking, and sculpture. An application form is required.
MINIMUM AVERAGE: N/A
VALUE: $10,000.00
TERMS: Recipients may reapply in subsequent years.
NUMBER OF AWARDS: 45

CODE: CA/EIPR01/g
NAME: East Indian Professional Residents of Canada Scholarships
SPONSOR: East Indian Professional Residents of Canada
ADDRESS: 35 Northgate Crescent, Richmond Hill, Ontario L4B 2K8
PROGRAM: Any college or university program
BASIS: Awarded to students of East Indian origin who have completed at least 6 OSSD or equivalent credits by June. Application forms are available from EIPROC. An official transcript and a nomination letter from the high school principal or head of guidance is required.
MINIMUM AVERAGE: 90.00
VALUE: $1000.00
TERMS: One year only
NUMBER OF AWARDS: 3
DEADLINE FOR APPLICATIONS: June 30

CODE: CA/ESP001/g
NAME: Educational Scholarship Program
SPONSOR: Canadian Native Arts Foundation
ADDRESS: 77 Mowat Avenue, Suite 508, Toronto, Ontario M6K 3E3
PROGRAM: Visual arts, performing, and communication arts
BASIS: Awarded to students of Native ancestry entering all levels of arts education based on artistic performance, scholastic ability, and references from people familiar with the applicant's artistic ability.
MINIMUM AVERAGE: N/A
VALUE: Varies with need.
TERMS: Recipients seeking renewal must go through the entire application process each year.
NUMBER OF AWARDS: Varies
DEADLINE FOR APPLICATIONS: April 15

CODE: CA/ESSO01/g
NAME: Native Educational Awards Program
SPONSOR: Educational Awards Program, Human Resources Department
ADDRESS: Esso Resources Canada Ltd, 237 Fourth Avenue S.W., Calgary, Alberta T2P 0H6
PROGRAM: Various, related to the petroleum industry
BASIS: Applicants must be of Native ancestry and have maintained residence in BC, Alberta, Saskatchewan, Northwest Territories, or the Yukon for at least one year prior to application. Financial need, academic performance, and potential will be considered.
MINIMUM AVERAGE: N/A
VALUE: $3500.00
TERMS: One year only
NUMBER OF AWARDS: 4
DEADLINE FOR APPLICATIONS: June 15

CODE: CA/FELPR1/g
NAME: Fel-Pro Automotive Technicians Scholarship Program Awards
SPONSOR: Citizens' Scholarship Foundation of America Inc.
ADDRESS: Box 297, St Peter, Minnesota, USA 56082

PROGRAM: Various automotive programs
BASIS: Applicants must be entering Automotive Mechanic, Automotive Service Technician, Diesel Engine Mechanic, Motorcycle Mechanic, or Commercial Transport programs. Academic achievement, work experience, and community service will be considered.
MINIMUM AVERAGE: N/A
VALUE: $500.00
TERMS: Renewable. Applicants must be enrolled in a program at least 26 weeks in length that will not terminate before December 1.
NUMBER OF AWARDS: 20
DEADLINE FOR APPLICATIONS: May 1

CODE: CA/GGC01/g
NAME: Girl Guides of Canada – Guides du Canada Scholarship
SPONSOR: Girl Guides of Canada – Guides du Canada
ADDRESS: 50 Merton Street, Toronto, Ontario M4S 1A3
PROGRAM: Any recognized post-secondary program
BASIS: Applicant must be a member of the Girl Guides of Canada – Guides du Canada and under the age of 25. The selection is based on service/volunteer involvement, applicant's statement, 2 references, marks, and interests and activities.
MINIMUM AVERAGE: N/A
VALUE: Varies
TERMS: One year only. Amount varies between $500 and $1000 depending on funds available. Unsuccessful applicants may reapply the following year.
NUMBER OF AWARDS: 1
DEADLINE FOR APPLICATIONS: May 1

CODE: CA/HOL01/g
NAME: Holstein Canada Scholarship
SPONSOR: Scholarship Committee, Jane Whaley
ADDRESS: P.O. Box 610, Brantford, Ontario N3T 5R4

PROGRAM: Any
BASIS: Awarded to Regular or Junior members of Holstein Canada, or a son or daughter of a member, enrolling in a university or college. Applicants must submit a résumé of 4-H activities.
MINIMUM AVERAGE: 70.00
VALUE: $1000.00
TERMS: One year only
NUMBER OF AWARDS: 2
DEADLINE FOR APPLICATIONS: June 12

CODE: CA/HUSK01/g
NAME: Husky Oil Education Awards for Native People
SPONSOR: Staffing, Husky Oil
ADDRESS: P.O. Box 6525, Station D, Calgary, Alberta T2P 3G7
PROGRAM: Related to the Oil and Gas Industry
BASIS: Awarded to Native people (Inuit, Métis, Status Indians, Nonstatus Indians) who have been resident in BC, Alberta, or Saskatchewan for at least one year prior to applying. A demonstrated financial need and interest in the oil and gas industry are considered.
MINIMUM AVERAGE: N/A
VALUE: $3000.00
TERMS: One year only
NUMBER OF AWARDS: 4
DEADLINE FOR APPLICATIONS: June 15

CODE: CA/IFJ001/g
NAME: International Fellowships in Jewish Studies
SPONSOR: Memorial Foundation for Jewish Culture
ADDRESS: 15 East 26th Street, New York, New York 10010
PROGRAM: A field of Jewish specialization
BASIS: Any qualified scholar, researcher, or artist who posseses the knowledge and experience to formulate and implement a project in a field of Jewish specialization can apply for support.
MINIMUM AVERAGE: N/A

VALUE: $4000.00
TERMS: The value will depend on the living costs of the country in which the recipient is undertaking their studies. Renewable for one additional year.
NUMBER OF AWARDS: Varies
DEADLINE FOR APPLICATIONS: October 31

CODE: CA/IMA001/g
NAME: Imasco Scholarship
SPONSOR: Association of Colleges and Universities of Canada
ADDRESS: 350 Albert Street, Suite 600, Ottawa, Ontario K1R 1B1
PROGRAM: Any university undergraduate program
BASIS: Only for disabled students. Candidates must submit an application form, a letter from their doctor describing the type and extent of the disability, 2 letters of reference, and official academic transcripts covering the last 2 years.
MINIMUM AVERAGE: N/A
VALUE: $2000.00
TERMS: Renewable provided the recipient submits a new application and all pertinent documents.
NUMBER OF AWARDS: 5
DEADLINE FOR APPLICATIONS: June 1

CODE: CA/INAC01/g
NAME: Post-Secondary Student Assistance Program
SPONSOR: Indian and Northern Affairs, Native Education Centre
ADDRESS: 285 East 5th Avenue, Vancouver, BC V5T 1H2
PROGRAM: Any program longer than one academic year
BASIS: Applicants must be Inuit or registered as Indian and must have been residents of Canada for 12 consecutive months before the date of appplication for the Student Assistance program.
MINIMUM AVERAGE: N/A
VALUE: $1000.00

TERMS: Scholarships and bursaries are available for tuition, books, supplies, and travel and living expenses.
NUMBER OF AWARDS: Varies

CODE: CA/KMT001/g
NAME: K-Mart Scholarship Program
SPONSOR: Advertising Department, K-Mart Canada Ltd
ADDRESS: 8925 Torbram Road, Brampton, Ontario L6T 4G1
PROGRAM: Any post-secondary program
BASIS: Awarded on the basis of a lucky draw. Any scholarships won will be held in trust at National Trust until needed for post-secondary education by the winner.
MINIMUM AVERAGE: N/A
VALUE: $7500.00
TERMS: One year only. In addition to the 2 grand-prize scholarships of $7500 there will be 120 $1000 scholarships awarded, one for each store.
NUMBER OF AWARDS: 122
DEADLINE FOR APPLICATIONS: October 5

CODE: CA/KofC01/g
NAME: Knights of Columbus Canadian Scholarship Program
SPONSOR: Canadian Scholarship Committee, Knights of Columbus
ADDRESS: P.O. Drawer 1670, New Haven, Connecticut, USA 06507
PROGRAM: Any full-time undergraduate university program
BASIS: Awarded on the basis of academic excellence to the sons/ daughters of members in good standing with the Order of the Knights of Columbus.
MINIMUM AVERAGE: N/A
VALUE: $1000.00
TERMS: Renewable for up to 3 more years upon evidence of satisfactory academic performance and subject to the discretion of the Committee on Scholarships.

NUMBER OF AWARDS: 8
DEADLINE FOR APPLICATIONS: May 1

CODE: CA/LDAC01/g
NAME: Carol Thompson Memorial Scholarship
SPONSOR: Learning Disabilities Association of Canada
ADDRESS: Suite 200, 323 Chapel Street, Ottawa, Ontario K1N 7Z2
PROGRAM: Any Canadian full-time or part-time program
BASIS: Awarded to a student with learning disabilities. The application must include letters of recommendation, proof of post-secondary registration, a description of the disability and personal coping strategies, and a statement of goals.
MINIMUM AVERAGE: N/A
VALUE: $700.00
TERMS: One year only
NUMBER OF AWARDS: 1
DEADLINE FOR APPLICATIONS: May 15

CODE: CA/LEM001/g
NAME: Lemaire Co-operative Studies Awards
SPONSOR: Canadian Co-operative Association
ADDRESS: 275 Bank Street, Suite 400, Ottawa, Ontario K2P 2L6
PROGRAM: Relating to co-operative studies
BASIS: Bursaries will be provided to support students who have been involved in co-operatives, preferably in leadership positions as volunteers or employees. The applicant's course of study must involve co-operative studies. An application form is required.
MINIMUM AVERAGE: N/A
VALUE: $3000.00
TERMS: These bursaries will range from $1000 to $3000, proportional to the amount of co-operative studies undertaken. Renewable.
NUMBER OF AWARDS: 4
DEADLINE FOR APPLICATIONS: July 31

CODE: CA/LEO001/g
NAME: Leonard Foundation Financial Assistance Program
SPONSOR: Leonard Foundation
ADDRESS: c/o Canada Trust Company, 20 Eglinton Avenue E., Toronto, Ontario M4R 2E2
PROGRAM: Any Canadian college or university program
BASIS: Preference will be given to the sons and daughters of clergy, teachers, military personnel, graduates of Royal Military College, and members of the Engineering Institute of Canada and the Mining and Metallurgical Institute of Canada. An application is required.
MINIMUM AVERAGE: N/A
VALUE: $1250.00
TERMS: The amount may vary depending on the applicant's financial situation. Recipients may reapply each year until the 1st degree is completed.
NUMBER OF AWARDS: 140
DEADLINE FOR APPLICATIONS: March 15

CODE: CA/LUTH01/g
NAME: Lutheran Life University Scholarship
SPONSOR: Fraternal Department, Lutheran Life Insurance Society of Canada
ADDRESS: 470 Weber Street N., Waterloo, Ontario N2J 4G4
PROGRAM: Any full-time university degree program
BASIS: Applicant must be an individual insured by Lutheran Life and must be enrolled in, or about to enter, a full-time university degree program. Involvement in church, school, and community activities, leadership, and citizenship will all be considered.
MINIMUM AVERAGE: N/A
VALUE: $4800.00
TERMS: $1200 per year for up to 4 years, provided renewal criteria

are met. $600 is paid directly to the university each semester.
NUMBER OF AWARDS: 8
DEADLINE FOR APPLICATIONS: December 31

CODE: CA/MAS01/g
NAME: Royal Arch Masons – Ontario – Bursary Fund
SPONSOR: Royal Arch Masons of Canada in the Province of Ontario
ADDRESS: Suite 500, 3500 Dufferin Street, Toronto, Ontario M3K 1N2
PROGRAM: Any Canadian post-secondary program
BASIS: Awarded to Royal Arch Masons or members of their families
MINIMUM AVERAGE: N/A
VALUE: Varies
TERMS: May be renewed each subsequent year.
NUMBER OF AWARDS: Varies

CODE: CA/MEF01/g
NAME: Mattinson Endowment Fund Scholarship for Disabled Students
SPONSOR: Awards Division, Association of University and Colleges of Canada
ADDRESS: 350 Albert Street, Suite 600, Ottawa, Ontario K1R 1B1
PROGRAM: Most Canadian degree-granting institutions
BASIS: Restricted to disabled persons. Candidates must be Canadian citizens or permanent residents who have lived in Canada for at least 2 years as permanent residents.
MINIMUM AVERAGE: N/A
VALUE: $2000.00
TERMS: One year only – may be renewed upon reapplication. Holders of an undergraduate degree are not eligible to apply.
NUMBER OF AWARDS: Varies
DEADLINE FOR APPLICATIONS: June 1

CODE: CA/MENS01/g
NAME: Mensa Canada Scholarship Program

SPONSOR: Mensa Canada
ADDRESS: Box 1025, Station O, Toronto, Ontario M4A 2V4
PROGRAM: Any post-secondary program
BASIS: Awarded on the basis of an essay-writing competition. Topics will be selected each year. Applicants need not be Mensa members.
MINIMUM AVERAGE: N/A
VALUE: $1000.00
TERMS: Recipients may reapply each year.
NUMBER OF AWARDS: 3
DEADLINE FOR APPLICATIONS: February 28

CODE: CA/MONA01/g
NAME: Eugene A. Forsey Essay Prize
SPONSOR: Monarchy Canada, Dept. of Political Science, UBC
ADDRESS: University of British Columbia, 204 – 2075 Westbrook Mall, Vancouver, BC V6T 1Z2
PROGRAM: N/A
BASIS: This prize is offered for the best essay concerning the Monarchy in the Dominion of Canada.
MINIMUM AVERAGE: N/A
VALUE: $500.00
TERMS: There are other prizes of $200.
NUMBER OF AWARDS: Varies
DEADLINE FOR APPLICATIONS: April 1

CODE: CA/NLC01/g
NAME: Navy League of Canada Community College Entrance Scholarships
SPONSOR: Navy League of Canada, National Council
ADDRESS: 2323 Riverside Drive, 8th Floor, Ottawa, Ontario K1H 8L5
PROGRAM: Any community college program
BASIS: Awarded to Royal Canadian Sea Cadets, former Cadets, Navy League Wrenettes, or former Wrenettes who are entering a community college program of one or more years leading to a diploma.
MINIMUM AVERAGE: N/A

VALUE: $150.00
TERMS: One year only. Not available to students enrolled in the Canadian Forces on any basis whereby the government provides free tuition or grants.
NUMBER OF AWARDS: Varies
DEADLINE FOR APPLICATIONS: August 11

CODE: CA/NLC02/g
NAME: National and Saskatchewan Division Scholarship
SPONSOR: Navy League of Canada
ADDRESS: 1860 Lorne Street, Regina, Saskatchewan S4P 2L7
PROGRAM: Any
BASIS: Awarded to serving or former cadets. A letter from the unit commanding officer is required with the application.
MINIMUM AVERAGE: N/A
VALUE: $500.00
TERMS: One year only. The Saskatchewan award is worth $300.
NUMBER OF AWARDS: 2
DEADLINE FOR APPLICATIONS: July 15

CODE: CA/NLS001/g
NAME: Navy League Scholarship Award
SPONSOR: Navy League of Canada
ADDRESS: 1107 Avenue Road, Room 314, Toronto, Ontario M5N 2E4
PROGRAM: Any Canadian college or university
BASIS: For former Naval Cadets entering post-secondary education. Candidates are required to send an application, transcript, and letters of recommendation from the candidate's commanding officer and from the President of the local sponsoring committee.
MINIMUM AVERAGE: N/A
VALUE: $475.00
TERMS: One year only. College-bound applicants will receive $350. An award certifcate will also be presented.
NUMBER OF AWARDS: 5

DEADLINE FOR APPLICATIONS: August 15

CODE: CA/NLS002/g
NAME: Navy League of Canada Scholarships
SPONSOR: Navy League of Canada, National Council
ADDRESS: Suite 910, 85 Range Road, Ottawa, Ontario K1N 8J6
PROGRAM: Any at a Canadian community college
BASIS: Awarded to Royal Canadian Sea Cadets, former Sea Cadets, Navy League Wrenettes, or former Wrenettes with at least 12 months' service entering the 1st year of community college.
MINIMUM AVERAGE: N/A
VALUE: $100.00
TERMS: One year only
NUMBER OF AWARDS: Varies
DEADLINE FOR APPLICATIONS: August 11

CODE: CA/ONW001/g
NAME: Corbiere-Lavall and Two-Axe Early Awards
SPONSOR: Ontario Native Women's Association
ADDRESS: 117 North May Street, Thunder Bay, Ontario P7C 3N8
PROGRAM: Any Canadian university or community college program
BASIS: Candidates must be women of Native ancestry who show a demonstrated commitment to improving the condition of Aboriginal women politically, socially, or otherwise. An application form is required, with transcript(s) and letters of reference.
MINIMUM AVERAGE: N/A
VALUE: $1000.00
TERMS: One year only
NUMBER OF AWARDS: 2

CODE: CA/PAGE01/g
NAME: Page Program
SPONSOR: Education and Visitors Service, Applications, Public Information Office

ADDRESS: P.O. Box 1111, House of Commons, Ottawa, Ontario K1A 0A6
PROGRAM: Any full-time program at Ottawa or Carleton
BASIS: Applicants must be high school graduates who are bilingual Canadian citizens. Candidates must apply to and accept admission at either the U of Ottawa or Carleton U.
MINIMUM AVERAGE: 80.00
VALUE: $9250.00
TERMS: One year only. Transportation costs are included. Students will be required to work 15 hours per week.
NUMBER OF AWARDS: 42
DEADLINE FOR APPLICATIONS: January 15

CODE: CA/PCO001/g
NAME: Petro-Canada Olympic Torch Fund
SPONSOR: Canadian Olympic Association and Petro-Canada
ADDRESS: 1600 James Naismith Drive, Ottawa, Ontario K1B 5N4
PROGRAM: Any full-time college or university program
BASIS: Candidates must be enrolled full-time at a university or college and be a member of an athletic team there; a current or former member of a national team; or a member of a provincial or national training program. An application form and references are required.
MINIMUM AVERAGE: N/A
VALUE: $2000.00
TERMS: $2000 is awarded for university applicants and $1000 per year for college applicants. The awards are renewable for another year.
NUMBER OF AWARDS: 100
DEADLINE FOR APPLICATIONS: June 15

CODE: CA/PDG002/g
NAME: Professional Development Grants

SPONSOR: Canadian Native Arts Foundation
ADDRESS: 77 Mowat Avenue, Suite 508, Toronto, Ontario M6K 3E3
PROGRAM: Any arts apprenticeship or college/university program
BASIS: Applicants must be of Native ancestry entering an apprenticeship or college or university program in any kind of arts subject.
MINIMUM AVERAGE: N/A
VALUE: $1000.00
TERMS: Awards may vary in amount. Renewable on the basis of instructors' or employers' reports.
NUMBER OF AWARDS: Varies
DEADLINE FOR APPLICATIONS: April 15

CODE: CA/PDK001/g
NAME: Phi Delta Kappa Scholarship Grants
SPONSOR: Phi Delta Kappa Educational Foundation
ADDRESS: P.O. Box 789, Bloomington, Indiana, USA 47402
PROGRAM: Any leading to a career in teaching
BASIS: Awarded on the basis of academic achievement, letters of recommendation, written expression, interest in teaching, community service, and extracurricular activities. An application is required.
MINIMUM AVERAGE: N/A
VALUE: $1000.00
TERMS: One year only. There will be one scholarship of $2000 to the very best candidate.
NUMBER OF AWARDS: 39
DEADLINE FOR APPLICATIONS: January 31

CODE: CA/PHS001/g
NAME: Pat Humphreys Scholarship
SPONSOR: Flowers Canada – National Office
ADDRESS: 155 Suffolk Street W., Ottawa, Ontario N1H 2J7
PROGRAM: Any leading to Flowers Canada Certification
BASIS: Awarded on the basis of over-

all academic and artistic achievement and of written recommendations from florists and/or teachers and prior involvement in the florist industry. Financial need may be considered.
MINIMUM AVERAGE: N/A
VALUE: $500.00
TERMS: One year only. Scholarship funds awarded must be used for tuition only.
NUMBER OF AWARDS: 1
DEADLINE FOR APPLICATIONS: March 31

CODE: CA/PNWA01/g
NAME: Professional Native Women's Association Scholarship
SPONSOR: Professional Native Women's Association
ADDRESS: #1 – 245 East Broadway, Vancouver, BC V5T 1W4
PROGRAM: Any
BASIS: The successful applicant must be of Aboriginal ancestry and registered as a full-time student at a post-secondary institution. A copy of an academic transcript, a professional reference, and a personal reference should be included in the application.
MINIMUM AVERAGE: N/A
VALUE: Varies
TERMS: One scholarship is awarded in the Fall and another in the Spring.
NUMBER OF AWARDS: 2

CODE: CA/RCNBF1/g
NAME: Royal Canadian Naval Benevolent Fund Awards
SPONSOR: The Secretary, Western Committee, RCN Benevolent Fund
ADDRESS: CFB Esquimalt, FMO Victoria, BC V0S 1B0
PROGRAM: Any post-secondary program
BASIS: Applicants must be former members of the Naval Forces of Canada or their dependents. Financial need and educational potential will be considered. An application is required.

MINIMUM AVERAGE: N/A
VALUE: Varies
TERMS: Renewable. Recipients must supply an annual review of their progress.
NUMBER OF AWARDS: Varies

CODE: CA/RCS001/g
NAME: Raymond Crepault Scholarship
SPONSOR: c/o Canadian Association of Broadcasters
ADDRESS: P.O. Box 627 , Station B, Ottawa, Ontario K1P 5S2
PROGRAM: Communications (university level)
BASIS: For French Canadians with broadcasting experience who wish to begin or complete a program of studies in communication at the university level. An application and references are required.
MINIMUM AVERAGE: N/A
VALUE: $5000.00
TERMS: Renewable. Recipients must reapply each year. Proof of acceptance and enrolment is required.
NUMBER OF AWARDS: Varies
DEADLINE FOR APPLICATIONS: June 30

CODE: CA/ROW01/g
NAME: Pearce-Guest Awards
SPONSOR: Rowing Canada
ADDRESS: 1600 James Naismith Drive, Suite 716, Ottawa, Ontario K1B 5N4
PROGRAM: Any
BASIS: Awarded to the best male and female rowers on the basis of performance at various provincial and national regattas. No application is necessary.
MINIMUM AVERAGE: N/A
VALUE: $500.00
TERMS: Recipients may requalify through competition.
NUMBER OF AWARDS: 2

CODE: CA/ROYAL1/g
NAME: Royal Bank Native Student Awards

SPONSOR: Co-ordinator, Human Resources, Head Office, Royal Bank
ADDRESS: P.O. Box 6001, Montreal, Quebec H3G 3A9
PROGRAM: Any related to the banking industry
BASIS: Open to any Status Indian, Non-status Indian, Inuit, or Métis who is a permanent resident of Canada. The selection is based on personal and academic achievement. Financial need will be considered.
MINIMUM AVERAGE: N/A
VALUE: $16,000.00
TERMS: $4000 per year, renewable for a total of 4 years. College students will receive $4000 per year for up to 2 years.
NUMBER OF AWARDS: 5

CODE: CA/RRS001/g
NAME: Rixon Rafter Scholarship
SPONSOR: Judge Brian Stevenson Fund, c/o Mr David Neil
ADDRESS: W. Ross Macdonald School, Brantford, Ontario M3T 3J9
PROGRAM: Any
BASIS: Only for blind and visually impaired youths entering postsecondary programs.
MINIMUM AVERAGE: N/A
VALUE: $500.00
TERMS: One year only. The scholarship may vary in value from $300 to $500 depending on the number of awards in a given year.
NUMBER OF AWARDS: 2 minimum
DEADLINE FOR APPLICATIONS: September 30

CODE: CA/RWRAS1/g
NAME: Royal Westminister Regiment Association Scholarships
SPONSOR: Scholarship Committee, Royal Westminister Regiment Association
ADDRESS: Box 854, New Westminister, BC
PROGRAM: Any
BASIS: Applicants must be direct descendents, male or female, of a member of the Royal Westminister Regiment Association or the Royal Westminister Regiment CA (M). Awarded on the basis of academic standing and financial need. An application is required.
MINIMUM AVERAGE: N/A
VALUE: $250.00
TERMS: One year only
NUMBER OF AWARDS: 2
DEADLINE FOR APPLICATIONS: July 15

CODE: CA/SFAC07/g
NAME: Queen's University (Kingston, Ont.) National Bursary
SPONSOR: Students' Financial Assistance Committee, Department of Education
ADDRESS: Box 2703, Whitehorse, Yukon Y1A 2C6
PROGRAM: Any
BASIS: Awarded to applicants to Queen's University from the Provinces and Territories other than Ontario and Quebec. The selection is based on academic achievement.
MINIMUM AVERAGE: N/A
VALUE: $1985.00
TERMS: One year only
NUMBER OF AWARDS: 15
DEADLINE FOR APPLICATIONS: April 30

CODE: CA/SLBP01/g
NAME: Summer Language Bursary Program
SPONSOR: Council of Ministers of Education, Government of Canada
ADDRESS: Contact the provincial or territorial government for more information.
PROGRAM: English or French language
BASIS: This national program allows students to study English or French as a second language in various institutions across the country. These immersion programs are 6 weeks in duration and are held during the spring and summer.

MINIMUM AVERAGE: N/A
VALUE: Varies
TERMS: This program covers tuition and residence fees, but does not cover travel costs.
NUMBER OF AWARDS: Varies
DEADLINE FOR APPLICATIONS: February 18

CODE: CA/SONF01/g
NAME: Sons of Norway Foundation Scholarships
SPONSOR: Sons of Norway Foundation in Canada
ADDRESS: 311 – 6635 McKay Avenue, Burnaby, BC V5H 2X3
PROGRAM: Any community college or university program
BASIS: Awarded to students who have shown interest in Norwegian culture, history, or language. Applicants must show evidence of sound academic performance and financial need. An application is required.
MINIMUM AVERAGE: N/A
VALUE: $600.00
TERMS: One year only. There will also be 3 bursaries of $400 each.
NUMBER OF AWARDS: 6
DEADLINE FOR APPLICATIONS: June 30

CODE: CA/SORO01/g
NAME: Western Canada Regional Fellowship
SPONSOR: Soroptimist International of the Americas, Fellowship Committee
ADDRESS: 32076 Astoria Crescent, Clearbrook, BC V2T 4P5
PROGRAM: Any university program.
BASIS: Awarded to a female resident of the Western Canada region on the basis of financial need, academic goals, and potential benefit to the community. An application form is required.
MINIMUM AVERAGE: N/A
VALUE: $3000.00
TERMS: The recipient is encouraged to spend at least one year in Canada after completing her studies.
NUMBER OF AWARDS: 1

CODE: CA/STJA01/g
NAME: St John Ambulance Bursary Award Program
SPONSOR: St John Ambulance, Ontario Council
ADDRESS: 46 Wellesley Street, Toronto, Ontario M5Y 1G1
PROGRAM: Any Canadian nursing program
BASIS: Candidates must be entering a full-time nursing program at a Canadian college or university and have been involved in community service and St John Ambulance. An application form and letters of recommendation are required. Financial need will be considered.
MINIMUM AVERAGE: N/A
VALUE: Varies
TERMS: Recipients may reapply in subsequent years.
NUMBER OF AWARDS: N/A
DEADLINE FOR APPLICATIONS: March 15

CODE: CA/TFOX01/g
NAME: Terry Fox Humanitarian Award
SPONSOR: Terry Fox Humanitarian Award Program
ADDRESS: 711 – 151 Sparks Street, Ottawa, Ontario K1P 5E3
PROGRAM: Any full-time college or university program
BASIS: Candidates must be under 25 years of age and Canadian citizens or landed immigrants entering full-time studies at a Canadian college or university. Candidates must have been involved in community service and sports. An application is required.
MINIMUM AVERAGE: N/A
VALUE: $16,000.00
TERMS: $4000 per year, renewable for a further 3 years. A renewal application form is required each year.

NUMBER OF AWARDS: 40
DEADLINE FOR APPLICATIONS: February 1

CODE: CA/UCOL01/g
NAME: Norma Epstein Award for Creative Writing
SPONSOR: Registrar, University College
ADDRESS: University of Toronto, Toronto, Ontario M5S 1A1
PROGRAM: Any university program
BASIS: This contest is open to any student enrolled in undergraduate or graduate studies at a Canadian university who has written a substantial work in fiction, drama, or verse. An application form is available from the sponsor.
MINIMUM AVERAGE: N/A
VALUE: $1000.00
TERMS: This amount is awarded every 2 years.
NUMBER OF AWARDS: 1
DEADLINE FOR APPLICATIONS: May 15

CODE: CA/UCPC01/g
NAME: Ukranian Canadian Professional and Business Club Scholarships
SPONSOR: Ukranian Canadian Professional and Business Club
ADDRESS: 890 Orcrest, Kamloops, BC
PROGRAM: Any
BASIS: Awarded to a student on the basis of scholastic standing, ultimate objective, and community involvement.
MINIMUM AVERAGE: N/A
VALUE: $250.00
TERMS: One year only
NUMBER OF AWARDS: 1
DEADLINE FOR APPLICATIONS: June 30

CODE: CA/VHRT01/g
NAME: Vocational Horticulture Scholarship
SPONSOR: Professional Plant Growers Scholarship Foundation
ADDRESS: P.O. Box 27517, Lansing, Michigan, USA 48909
PROGRAM: Vocational, technical horticulture programs
BASIS: An applicant must have a major interest in horticulture with intentions of becoming a floriculture plant producer and/or operations manager upon completion of studies. Applications are accepted from Canadian students.
MINIMUM AVERAGE: 3.00
VALUE: $1000.00
TERMS: One year only. Awards range in value from $500 to $1000.
NUMBER OF AWARDS: N/A
DEADLINE FOR APPLICATIONS: August 15

CODE: CA/VIEW01/g
NAME: Views – Litton Employees Scholarships
SPONSOR: Views for the Visually Impaired
ADDRESS: 3033 Palston Road, Suite 205, Mississauga, Ontario L4Y 2Z7
PROGRAM: Any
BASIS: Blind or visually impaired candidates must submit a letter stating career goals and a description of their extracurricular activities. Proof of acceptance to a post-secondary institution is required, along with CNIB registration number.
MINIMUM AVERAGE: N/A
VALUE: $300.00
TERMS: Candidates may reapply each year.
NUMBER OF AWARDS: 2
DEADLINE FOR APPLICATIONS: December 31

CODE: CA/VIEW02/g
NAME: O.E. Bowie Award
SPONSOR: Views for the Visually Impaired
ADDRESS: 3033 Palston Road, Mississauga, Ontario L4Y 2Z7
PROGRAM: Any
BASIS: Blind or visually impaired candidates should submit a letter outlining career goals and extra-

curricular activities. Proof of acceptance at a post-secondary institution and CNIB registration number are required.
MINIMUM AVERAGE: N/A
VALUE: $300.00
TERMS: Candidates may reapply each year.
NUMBER OF AWARDS: 1
DEADLINE FOR APPLICATIONS: December 30

CODE: CA/WAMC01/g
NAME: Sophia Wood Education Award
SPONSOR: Women's Association of the Mining Industry of Canada
ADDRESS: P.O. Box 207, Postal Station A, Toronto, Ontario M5W 1B2

PROGRAM: Post-secondary mining courses
BASIS: Awarded to students who wish to enter Mining programs at Canadian post-secondary institutions. Applications are available from the Association.
MINIMUM AVERAGE: N/A
VALUE: Varies
TERMS: The amount of bursary/scholarship will vary according to the information supplied by the applicant.
NUMBER OF AWARDS: Varies
DEADLINE FOR APPLICATIONS: October 31

ALBERTA

CODE: AB/4-H001/g
NAME: Her Majesty Queen Elizabeth "the Queen Mother" Scholarships
SPONSOR: 4-H Branch, Alberta Agriculture
ADDRESS: Room 200, J.G. O'Donoghue Bldg., 7000 – 113 Street, Edmonton, Alberta T6H 5T6
PROGRAM: Agriculture, Home Economics, or Veterinary Medicine
BASIS: Awarded to students in any year at a Canadian university. The selection is based on leadership, academic achievement, and contributions to the community.
MINIMUM AVERAGE: N/A
VALUE: $1500.00
TERMS: One year only
NUMBER OF AWARDS: 3
DEADLINE FOR APPLICATIONS: July 15

CODE: AB/4-H002/g
NAME: 4-H Foundation of Alberta Scholarship

SPONSOR: 4-H Branch, Alberta Agriculture
ADDRESS: Room 200, J.G. O'Donoghue Bldg., 7000 – 113 Street, Edmonton, Alberta T6H 5T6
PROGRAM: Any
BASIS: Awarded on the basis of 4-H achievement and academic excellence to encourage the pursuit of post-secondary education.
MINIMUM AVERAGE: N/A
VALUE: $425.00
TERMS: One year only
NUMBER OF AWARDS: 1
DEADLINE FOR APPLICATIONS: July 15

CODE: AB/4-H003/g
NAME: A & E Capelle LN Herfords Scholarship
SPONSOR: 4-H Branch, Alberta Agriculture
ADDRESS: Room 200, J.G. O'Donoghue Bldg., 7000 – 113 Street, Edmonton, Alberta T6H 5T6

PROGRAM: Preference for Agriculture, Veterinary Sciences, Home Economics
BASIS: Preference is given to students from the counties of Lac St Anne and Barrhead.
MINIMUM AVERAGE: N/A
VALUE: $300.00
TERMS: One year only
NUMBER OF AWARDS: 1
DEADLINE FOR APPLICATIONS: July 15

CODE: AB/4-H004/g
NAME: Alberta Farm and Ranch Writer's Award
SPONSOR: 4-H Branch, Alberta Agriculture
ADDRESS: Room 200, J.G. O'Donoghue Bldg., 7000 – 113 Street, Edmonton, Alberta T6H 5T6
PROGRAM: Any
BASIS: Applicants must submit a 1000-word feature essay illustrating some aspect of family life. The selection is based on a combination of communication skills, community involvement, and academic standing.
MINIMUM AVERAGE: N/A
VALUE: $500.00
TERMS: One year only
NUMBER OF AWARDS: 1
DEADLINE FOR APPLICATIONS: July 15

CODE: AB/4-H005/g
NAME: Alberta Treasury Branch Scholarships
SPONSOR: 4-H Branch, Alberta Agriculture
ADDRESS: Room 200, J.G. O'Donoghue Bldg., 7000 – 113 Street, Edmonton, Alberta T6H 5T6
PROGRAM: Any Alberta university or college program
BASIS: Candidates must have been members of 4-H for at least 2 years. The awards are made on the basis of 4-H achievement, positive community involvement, and academic standing.
MINIMUM AVERAGE: N/A

VALUE: $1000.00
TERMS: One year only. One award per region.
NUMBER OF AWARDS: 7
DEADLINE FOR APPLICATIONS: July 15

CODE: AB/4-H006/g
NAME: Alberta Wheat Pool Scholarships
SPONSOR: 4-H Branch, Alberta Agriculture
ADDRESS: Room 200, J.G. O'Donoghue Bldg., 7000 – 113 Street, Edmonton, Alberta T6H 5T6
PROGRAM: Preference for Home Economics or Agriculture
BASIS: Applicants' parents must derive a major portion of their income from farming.
MINIMUM AVERAGE: N/A
VALUE: $500.00
TERMS: One year only
NUMBER OF AWARDS: 2
DEADLINE FOR APPLICATIONS: July 15

CODE: AB/4-H007/g
NAME: Alberta Ford and Mercury Dealer Scholarships
SPONSOR: 4-H Branch, Alberta Agriculture
ADDRESS: Room 200, J.G. O'Donoghue Bldg., 7000 – 113 Street, Edmonton, Alberta T6H 5T6
PROGRAM: Various
BASIS: Awarded to past or present 4-H members in good standing for 2 years who wish to pursue a certificate or diploma program that would be of value in the car dealership industry.
MINIMUM AVERAGE: N/A
VALUE: $1000.00
TERMS: One year only. One per region.
NUMBER OF AWARDS: 2
DEADLINE FOR APPLICATIONS: July 15

CODE: AB/4-H008/g
NAME: Alberta Salers Association Scholarship

SPONSOR: 4-H Branch, Alberta
Agriculture
ADDRESS: Room 200, J.G. O'Donoghue
Bldg., 7000 – 113 Street, Edmonton,
Alberta T6H 5T6
PROGRAM: Agriculture
BASIS: Awarded to past or present
4-H members. Consideration is
given to past 4-H achievements.
Preference is given to applicants
who have used Saler cattle and are
pursuing a career in Agriculture.
Applicants must submit a 200-word
essay on their future goals.
MINIMUM AVERAGE: N/A
VALUE: $500.00
TERMS: One year only
NUMBER OF AWARDS: 1
DEADLINE FOR APPLICATIONS: July 15

CODE: AB/4-H009/g
NAME: Alpha Milk Company
Scholarships
SPONSOR: 4-H Branch, Alberta
Agriculture
ADDRESS: Room 200, J.G. O'Donoghue
Bldg., 7000 – 113 Street, Edmonton,
Alberta T6H 5T6
PROGRAM: Agriculture
BASIS: Awarded on the basis of 4-H
achievements and financial need.
Preference is given to students with
a 4-H dairy background.
MINIMUM AVERAGE: N/A
VALUE: $500.00
TERMS: One year only
NUMBER OF AWARDS: 1
DEADLINE FOR APPLICATIONS: July 15

CODE: AB/4-H010/g
NAME: Bale Bandits Scholarship
SPONSOR: 4-H Branch, Alberta
Agriculture
ADDRESS: Room 200, J.G. O'Donoghue
Bldg., 7000 – 113 Street, Edmonton,
Alberta T6H 5T6
PROGRAM: Any
BASIS: Awarded on the basis of good
4-H standing and scholastic record.
MINIMUM AVERAGE: N/A

VALUE: $1000.00
TERMS: One year only
NUMBER OF AWARDS: 1
DEADLINE FOR APPLICATIONS: July 15

CODE: AB/4-H011/g
NAME: Blue Klein Memorial
Scholarship
SPONSOR: 4-H Branch, Alberta
Agriculture
ADDRESS: Room 200, J.G. O'Donoghue
Bldg., 7000 – 113 Street, Edmonton,
Alberta T6H 5T6
PROGRAM: Any
BASIS: This non-academic scholarship
is awarded to a past or present 4-H
member, in good standing for a
minimum of 4 years, who lives in
the West Central Region of Alberta
and has been a resident for at least
5 years.
MINIMUM AVERAGE: N/A
VALUE: $250.00
TERMS: One year only
NUMBER OF AWARDS: 1
DEADLINE FOR APPLICATIONS: July 15

CODE: AB/4-H012/g
NAME: Ceres International Women's
Fraternity Scholarship
SPONSOR: 4-H Branch, Alberta
Agriculture
ADDRESS: Room 200, J.G. O'Donoghue
Bldg., 7000 – 113 Street, Edmonton,
Alberta T6H 5T6
PROGRAM: Any at University of
Alberta related to agriculture
BASIS: Candidates for this scholarship
must be female students enrolled
at the U of Alberta and interested
in agriculture or rural life. Awards
are made on the basis of well-
developed communication, leader-
ship, and scholastic skills.
MINIMUM AVERAGE: N/A
VALUE: $100.00
TERMS: One year only
NUMBER OF AWARDS: 1
DEADLINE FOR APPLICATIONS: July 15

CODE: AB/4-H013/g
NAME: Dixon Shield Memorial
Scholarship
SPONSOR: 4-H Branch, Alberta
Agriculture
ADDRESS: Room 200, J.G. O'Donoghue
Bldg., 7000 – 113 Street, Edmonton,
Alberta T6H 5T6
PROGRAM: Any
BASIS: Preference is given to applicants from the County of Barrhead with a 4-H background. Otherwise, an applicant may be chosen from the Northwest 4-H Region of Alberta. The selection is based on financial need, academic achievement, and community service.
MINIMUM AVERAGE: N/A
VALUE: $425.00
TERMS: One year only
NUMBER OF AWARDS: 1
DEADLINE FOR APPLICATIONS: July 15

CODE: AB/4-H014/g
NAME: Don Matthews Scholarship
SPONSOR: 4-H Branch, Alberta
Agriculture
ADDRESS: Room 200, J.G. O'Donoghue
Bldg., 7000 – 113 Street, Edmonton,
Alberta T6H 5T6
PROGRAM: Any
BASIS: Awarded to past or present 4-H members displaying leadership abilities, community responsibility, and communication skills.
MINIMUM AVERAGE: N/A
VALUE: $200.00
TERMS: One year only. Amount may vary.
NUMBER OF AWARDS: 1
DEADLINE FOR APPLICATIONS: July 15

CODE: AB/4-H015/g
NAME: Edith Taylor Memorial
Scholarship
SPONSOR: 4-H Branch, Alberta
Agriculture
ADDRESS: Room 200, J.G. O'Donoghue
Bldg., 7000 – 113 Street, Edmonton,
Alberta T6H 5T6
PROGRAM: Any
BASIS: Awarded to 4-H members on the basis of 4-H achievement, community involvement, and financial need. Candidates must be from the Peace River region and have a minimum 2-year involvement with the 4-H program.
MINIMUM AVERAGE: N/A
VALUE: $400.00
TERMS: One year only. Amount may vary.
NUMBER OF AWARDS: 1
DEADLINE FOR APPLICATIONS: July 15

CODE: AB/4-H016/g
NAME: Farm Credit Corporation
SPONSOR: 4-H Branch, Alberta
Agriculture
ADDRESS: Room 200, J.G. O'Donoghue
Bldg., 7000 – 113 Street, Edmonton,
Alberta T6H 5T6
PROGRAM: Any
BASIS: Awarded to students entering the 1st or 2nd semester of a post-secondary program. The selection is based on community involvement and a minimum 2-year involvement with the 4-H program.
MINIMUM AVERAGE: N/A
VALUE: $300.00
TERMS: One year only. One award for each region.
NUMBER OF AWARDS: 7
DEADLINE FOR APPLICATIONS: July 15

CODE: AB/4-H017/g
NAME: Farmhouse International
Fraternity Scholarship
SPONSOR: 4-H Branch, Alberta
Agriculture
ADDRESS: Room 200, J.G. O'Donoghue
Bldg., 7000 – 113 Street, Edmonton,
Alberta T6H 5T6
PROGRAM: Any
BASIS: Awarded to a 1st- or 2nd-year male student attending the U of Alberta. Candidates must have strong communication, leadership, and scholastic skills as well as an interest in agriculture.
MINIMUM AVERAGE: N/A

VALUE: $100.00
TERMS: One year only
NUMBER OF AWARDS: 1
DEADLINE FOR APPLICATIONS: July 15

CODE: AB/4-H018/g
NAME: George Pimm Memorial
Scholarship
SPONSOR: 4-H Branch, Alberta
Agriculture
ADDRESS: Room 200, J.G. O'Donoghue
Bldg., 7000 – 113 Street, Edmonton,
Alberta T6H 5T6
PROGRAM: Any
BASIS: Awarded on the basis of 4-H
achievements and leadership skills.
Applicants must have at least 3
years of 4-H membership. Prefer-
ence is given to candidates from
the Peace River 4-H District.
MINIMUM AVERAGE: N/A
VALUE: $300.00
TERMS: One year only
NUMBER OF AWARDS: 1
DEADLINE FOR APPLICATIONS: July 15

CODE: AB/4-H019/g
NAME: Glenn Blodell Memorial
Scholarship
SPONSOR: 4-H Branch, Alberta
Agriculture
ADDRESS: Room 200, J.G. O'Donoghue
Bldg., 7000 – 113 Street, Edmonton,
Alberta T6H 5T6
PROGRAM: Any
BASIS: Awarded with preference to a
suitable 4-H candidate from the
County of Strathcona. If none is
available, then it is awarded to an
applicant from the Northwest 4-H
Region of Alberta. The selection is
based on 4-H achievement and aca-
demic excellence.
MINIMUM AVERAGE: N/A
VALUE: $100.00
TERMS: One year only
NUMBER OF AWARDS: 1
DEADLINE FOR APPLICATIONS: July 15

CODE: AB/4-H020/g
NAME: Hoechst Canada Bursary

SPONSOR: 4-H Branch, Alberta
Agriculture
ADDRESS: Room 200, J.G. O'Donoghue
Bldg., 7000 – 113 Street, Edmonton,
Alberta T6H 5T6
PROGRAM: Agriculture at an Alberta
college or university
BASIS: This is a 1st-year award given
to a current 4-H member under-
taking a degree or diploma in
Agriculture. Recipients are selected
on the basis of 4-H achievement,
academic standing, and leadership
abilities.
MINIMUM AVERAGE: N/A
VALUE: $500.00
TERMS: One year only
NUMBER OF AWARDS: 1
DEADLINE FOR APPLICATIONS: July 15

CODE: AB/4-H021/g
NAME: Inga Marr Memorial
Scholarship
SPONSOR: 4-H Branch, Alberta
Agriculture
ADDRESS: Room 200, J.G. O'Donoghue
Bldg., 7000 – 113 Street, Edmonton,
Alberta T6H 5T6
PROGRAM: Any
BASIS: Awarded to a 1st-year post-
secondary student with a back-
ground in farming.
MINIMUM AVERAGE: N/A
VALUE: $300.00
TERMS: One year only
NUMBER OF AWARDS: 1
DEADLINE FOR APPLICATIONS: July 15

CODE: AB/4-H022/g
NAME: Ken Edgerton Memorial
Scholarship
SPONSOR: 4-H Branch, Alberta
Agriculture
ADDRESS: Room 200, J.G. O'Donoghue
Bldg., 7000 – 113 Street, Edmonton,
Alberta T6H 5T6
PROGRAM: Any
BASIS: Awarded to a past or present
member of a 4-H club in the Peace
River region of Alberta who has 2
years of 4-H membership. The

selection is based on 4-H involvement, community involvement, leadership skills, and financial need.
MINIMUM AVERAGE: N/A
VALUE: $400.00
TERMS: One year only. Value may vary.
NUMBER OF AWARDS: 1
DEADLINE FOR APPLICATIONS: July 15

CODE: AB/4-H023/g
NAME: Marilyn Sue Lloyd Memorial Scholarship
SPONSOR: 4-H Branch, Alberta Agriculture
ADDRESS: Room 200, J.G. O'Donoghue Bldg., 7000 – 113 Street, Edmonton, Alberta T6H 5T6
PROGRAM: Related to Equine studies
BASIS: Awarded to past or present 4-H members, with equal consideration given to 4-H achievement and academic marks. Preference is given to students taking equine studies.
MINIMUM AVERAGE: N/A
VALUE: $150.00
TERMS: One year only
NUMBER OF AWARDS: N/A
DEADLINE FOR APPLICATIONS: July 15

CODE: AB/4-H024/g
NAME: Minburn Wild Rose Scholarship
SPONSOR: 4-H Branch, Alberta Agriculture
ADDRESS: Room 200, J.G. O'Donoghue Bldg., 7000 – 113 Street, Edmonton, Alberta T6H 5T6
PROGRAM: Any
BASIS: Applicant must have been a member of the Minburn 4-H District for a minimum of 5 years. Preference is given to students in the 1st year of a post-secondary program. The selection is based on leadership and on 4-H and community involvement.
MINIMUM AVERAGE: N/A
VALUE: $200.00
TERMS: One year only

NUMBER OF AWARDS: 1
DEADLINE FOR APPLICATIONS: July 15

CODE: AB/4-H025/g
NAME: Norma Jean Grey Scholarships
SPONSOR: 4-H Branch, Alberta Agriculture
ADDRESS: Room 200, J.G. O'Donoghue Bldg., 7000 – 113 Street, Edmonton, Alberta T6H 5T6
PROGRAM: Any
BASIS: These non-academic scholarships are awarded on the basis of 4-H club leadership, community responsibility, and communication skills, particularly in the area of public speaking.
MINIMUM AVERAGE: N/A
VALUE: $1000.00
TERMS: One year only
NUMBER OF AWARDS: 5
DEADLINE FOR APPLICATIONS: July 15

CODE: AB/4-H026/g
NAME: Pennington Memorial Scholarship
SPONSOR: 4-H Branch, Alberta Agriculture
ADDRESS: Room 200, J.G. O'Donoghue Bldg., 7000 – 113 Street, Edmonton, Alberta T6H 5T6
PROGRAM: Agriculture or related field
BASIS: Awarded on the basis of 4-H achievement, academic standing, moral character, and financial need. Preference is given to applicants from the Barrhead and Mayerthorpe district agricultural areas.
MINIMUM AVERAGE: N/A
VALUE: $1000.00
TERMS: One year only
NUMBER OF AWARDS: 2
DEADLINE FOR APPLICATIONS: July 15

CODE: AB/4-H027/g
NAME: Petro-Canada 4-H Youth Leadership Awards
SPONSOR: 4-H Branch, Alberta Agriculture
ADDRESS: Room 200, J.G. O'Donoghue

Bldg., 7000 – 113 Street, Edmonton, Alberta T6H 5T6

PROGRAM: Any

BASIS: Candidates must have been registered in 4-H for at least 2 years. The selection is based on a submitted essay outlining past achievements, involvement in local community projects, educational goals, and future plans.

MINIMUM AVERAGE: N/A

VALUE: $1000.00

TERMS: One year only

NUMBER OF AWARDS: 4

DEADLINE FOR APPLICATIONS: July 15

CODE: AB/4-H028/g

NAME: Stanley Shulan Memorial Scholarship

SPONSOR: 4-H Branch, Alberta Agriculture

ADDRESS: Room 200, J.G. O'Donoghue Bldg., 7000 – 113 Street, Edmonton, Alberta T6H 5T6

PROGRAM: Any

BASIS: This is a non-academic award given to a past or present 4-H member on the basis of leadership skills, including participation in community projects. Preference is given to applicants from the Lac Ste Anne or Barrhead districts.

MINIMUM AVERAGE: N/A

VALUE: $200.00

TERMS: One year only

NUMBER OF AWARDS: 1

DEADLINE FOR APPLICATIONS: July 15

CODE: AB/4-H029/g

NAME: Thomas Caryk Memorial Scholarship

SPONSOR: 4-H Branch, Alberta Agriculture

ADDRESS: Room 200, J.G. O'Donoghue Bldg., 7000 – 113 Street, Edmonton, Alberta T6H 5T6

PROGRAM: Agriculture preferred

BASIS: Candidates must have a minimum of 3 years of 4-H experience in the Peace River region. The

selection is made on the basis of 4-H achievement, academic performance, and financial need.

MINIMUM AVERAGE: N/A

VALUE: $500.00

TERMS: One year only

NUMBER OF AWARDS: 1

DEADLINE FOR APPLICATIONS: July 15

CODE: AB/4-H030/g

NAME: TX Bar Scholarship 1

SPONSOR: 4-H Branch, Alberta Agriculture

ADDRESS: Room 200, J.G. O'Donoghue Bldg., 7000 – 113 Street, Edmonton, Alberta T6H 5T6

PROGRAM: Veterinary Sciences

BASIS: Candidates must show a dedication to animal husbandry, and preference will be given to students from the Taber, 40 Mile (Foremost), Medicine Hat, and Brooks 4-H District Council areas.

MINIMUM AVERAGE: N/A

VALUE: $1000.00

TERMS: One year only

NUMBER OF AWARDS: 1

DEADLINE FOR APPLICATIONS: July 15

CODE: AB/4-H031/g

NAME: TX Bar Scholarship 2

SPONSOR: 4-H Branch, Alberta Agriculture

ADDRESS: Room 200, J.G. O'Donoghue Bldg., 7000 – 113 Street, Edmonton, Alberta T6H 5T6

PROGRAM: Western Canadian university Agriculture program

BASIS: Recipients of this award are individuals with excellent public speaking and leadership skills. Preference is given to students from the Taber, 40 Mile, Medicine Hat, and Brooks 4-H District Council areas.

MINIMUM AVERAGE: N/A

VALUE: $500.00

TERMS: One year only

NUMBER OF AWARDS: 1

DEADLINE FOR APPLICATIONS: July 15

CODE: AB/4-H032/g
NAME: TX Bar Scholarship 3
SPONSOR: 4-H Branch, Alberta Agriculture
ADDRESS: Room 200, J.G. O'Donoghue Bldg., 7000 – 113 Street, Edmonton, Alberta T6H 5T6
PROGRAM: Agriculture or a related field
BASIS: Candidates must have a farming background. The selection is based on outstanding achievement in 4-H. Preference is given to students from the Taber, 40 Mile, Medicine Hat, and Brooks 4-H District Council areas.
MINIMUM AVERAGE: N/A
VALUE: $400.00
TERMS: One year only
NUMBER OF AWARDS: 1
DEADLINE FOR APPLICATIONS: July 15

CODE: AB/4-H033/g
NAME: Vermillion River 4-H District Scholarship
SPONSOR: 4-H Branch, Alberta Agriculture
ADDRESS: Room 200, J.G. O'Donoghue Bldg., 7000 – 113 Street, Edmonton, Alberta T6H 5T6
PROGRAM: Any
BASIS: Candidate must have been a Vermillion River 4-H Club member for at least 3 years and active beyond the club level.
MINIMUM AVERAGE: N/A
VALUE: $200.00
TERMS: One year only
NUMBER OF AWARDS: 1
DEADLINE FOR APPLICATIONS: July 15

CODE: AB/4-H034/g
NAME: Westaskiwin District 4-H Scholarships
SPONSOR: 4-H Branch, Alberta Agriculture
ADDRESS: Room 200, J.G. O'Donoghue Bldg., 7000 – 113 Street, Edmonton, Alberta T6H 5T6
PROGRAM: Any
BASIS: Applicants must have been active members in the Wetaskiwin 4-H for a minimum of 3 years.
MINIMUM AVERAGE: N/A
VALUE: $700.00
TERMS: One year only
NUMBER OF AWARDS: 3
DEADLINE FOR APPLICATIONS: July 15

CODE: AB/4-H035/g
NAME: Wheat Board Surplus Monies Trust Scholarships
SPONSOR: 4-H Branch, Alberta Agriculture
ADDRESS: Room 200, J.G. O'Donoghue Bldg., 7000 – 113 Street, Edmonton, Alberta T6H 5T6
PROGRAM: Any
BASIS: Awarded on the basis of community involvement and outstanding achievement in 4-H.
MINIMUM AVERAGE: N/A
VALUE: $600.00
TERMS: One year only. One for each region.
NUMBER OF AWARDS: 7
DEADLINE FOR APPLICATIONS: July 15

CODE: AB/40MIL1/g
NAME: County of Forty Mile Agricultural Committee Bursaries
SPONSOR: Agricultural Field Manager
ADDRESS: County of Forty Mile #8, P.O. Box 160, Foremost, Alberta T0K 0X0
PROGRAM: Agriculture or Home Economics
BASIS: Awarded to area residents who plan to return to the County of Forty Mile upon completion of their studies.
MINIMUM AVERAGE: N/A
VALUE: $200.00
TERMS: One year only
NUMBER OF AWARDS: Varies
DEADLINE FOR APPLICATIONS: January 1

CODE: AB/AELR01/g
NAME: Alberta Environmental Laboratory and Research Centre Award
SPONSOR: Director, Alberta Environment Centre

ADDRESS: P.O. Bag 400, Vegreville, Alberta T0B 4L0
PROGRAM: Chemical Technology
BASIS: Awarded to 1st- or 2nd-year students from the Vegreville, Alberta, area.
MINIMUM AVERAGE: N/A
VALUE: Varies
NUMBER OF AWARDS: Varies

CODE: AB/AFA01/g
NAME: Visual Arts Project Grant
SPONSOR: Program Consultant, Alberta Community Development, Arts Branch
ADDRESS: 3rd Floor, 10158 – 103 Street, Edmonton, Alberta T5J 0X6
PROGRAM: Visual arts
BASIS: Awarded to Alberta residents active in visual arts to enable them to conduct projects and/or research related to the visual arts in Alberta. The application must include a résumé, slide portfolio of completed work, a budget, and a completed grant form.
MINIMUM AVERAGE: N/A
VALUE: $5000.00
TERMS: Grant amounts vary. Financial assistance will be given to cover up to 50% of the costs of the project.
NUMBER OF AWARDS: Varies
DEADLINE FOR APPLICATIONS: September 10

CODE: AB/AFA02/g
NAME: Visual Arts Study Grant
SPONSOR: Program Consultant, Alberta Community Development, Arts Branch
ADDRESS: 3rd Floor, 10 158 – 103 Street, Edmonton, Alberta T5J 0X6
PROGRAM: Visual arts
BASIS: Awarded to Alberta residents enrolling in undergraduate/diploma studies to improve their qualifications in the visual arts. Applicants must submit a résumé, a detailed budget, a slide portfolio of current work, and a description of intended program.

MINIMUM AVERAGE: N/A
VALUE: $2000.00
TERMS: Renewable. Grant amounts vary. Grant will cover up to 25% of the education costs: tuition, accommodation, travel, and materials.
NUMBER OF AWARDS: Varies
DEADLINE FOR APPLICATIONS: March 31

CODE: AB/AIIC01/g
NAME: Senator James Gladstone Memorial Scholarship
SPONSOR: Alberta Indian Investment Corporation
ADDRESS: 350 – 100 Avenue, Edmonton, Alberta T5J 0B3
PROGRAM: Business Administration
BASIS: Awarded to Treaty indians enrolled full-time in a business administration program. The selection is based upon academic proficiency and an expressed commitment to business and economic development in the Indian community. An application is required.
MINIMUM AVERAGE: N/A
VALUE: $750.00
TERMS: One year only
NUMBER OF AWARDS: 2
DEADLINE FOR APPLICATIONS: November 23

CODE: AB/ALHER1/g
NAME: Alberta Heritage Scholarships (Alexander Rutherford)
SPONSOR: Director, Heritage Scholarship Fund, Students Finance Board
ADDRESS: 10th Floor, Baker Centre, 10025 106th Street, Edmonton, Alberta T5J 1G7
PROGRAM: Any
BASIS: Awarded to Alberta residents who have demonstrated outstanding academic ability in high school. Recipients must be enrolled in a full-time post-secondary program.
MINIMUM AVERAGE: 80.00
VALUE: $1500.00
TERMS: One year only
NUMBER OF AWARDS: Varies
DEADLINE FOR APPLICATIONS: June 30

CODE: AB/ALHER2/g
NAME: Michael Luchkovich Scholarships for Career Development
SPONSOR: Alberta Heritage Scholarship Fund Office, Student Finances Board
ADDRESS: 9th Floor, Baker Centre, 10025 106th Street, Edmonton, Alberta T5J 1G7
PROGRAM: Any
BASIS: Awarded to persons who have demonstrated outstanding ability in their work and are pursuing short-term full-time study of less than 6 months, or part-time study, such as evening or home-study courses.
MINIMUM AVERAGE: N/A
VALUE: Varies
TERMS: Scholarship includes tuition fees; cost of books and related expenses may be considered.
NUMBER OF AWARDS: Varies
DEADLINE FOR APPLICATIONS: April 1

CODE: AB/ALHER3/g
NAME: Jimmie Condon Athletic Scholarships
SPONSOR: Alberta Heritage Scholarship Fund Office, Student Finances Board
ADDRESS: 9th Floor, Baker Centre, 10025 106th Street, Edmonton, Alberta T5J 1G7
PROGRAM: Any
BASIS: Qualifying athletes must be nominated by their educational facilities or sports association in Alberta.
MINIMUM AVERAGE: N/A
VALUE: $1000.00
TERMS: One year only
NUMBER OF AWARDS: Varies
DEADLINE FOR APPLICATIONS: October 15

CODE: AB/ALHER4/g
NAME: Charles S. Noble Scholarships for Study at Harvard
SPONSOR: Alberta Heritage Scholarship Fund Office, Student Finances Board
ADDRESS: 9th Floor, Baker Centre, 10025 106th Street, Edmonton, Alberta T5J 1G7
PROGRAM: Any at Harvard
BASIS: These scholarships provide the opportunity for outstanding Alberta students to pursue undergraduate study at Harvard.
MINIMUM AVERAGE: N/A
VALUE: $10,000.00
TERMS: One year only
NUMBER OF AWARDS: Varies
DEADLINE FOR APPLICATIONS: May 15

CODE: AB/ALHER5/g
NAME: Charles S. Noble Scholarships for Junior "A" Hockey
SPONSOR: Alberta Heritage Scholarship Fund Office, Student Finances Board
ADDRESS: 9th Floor, Baker Centre, 10025 106th Street, Edmonton, Alberta T5J 1G7
PROGRAM: Any post-secondary program
BASIS: These scholarships provide the incentive and means for Junior "A" hockey players to continue their post-secondary education. Qualifying athletes must be nominated by their teams.
MINIMUM AVERAGE: N/A
VALUE: $650.00
TERMS: One year only
NUMBER OF AWARDS: 5

CODE: AB/ALHER6/g
NAME: J. Percy Page Recreation Awards
SPONSOR: Alberta Heritage Scholarship Fund Office, Student Finances Board
ADDRESS: 9th Floor, Baker Centre, 10025 106th Street, Edmonton, Alberta T5J 1G7
PROGRAM: Any post-secondary program
BASIS: These scholarships foster recreational leadership in Alberta's communities by assisting dedicated

volunteers, coaches, and officials to further their training.
MINIMUM AVERAGE: N/A
VALUE: $3000.00
TERMS: Value varies to a maximum of $3000.
NUMBER OF AWARDS: Varies
DEADLINE FOR APPLICATIONS: January 1

CODE: AB/ALHER7/g
NAME: Charles S. Noble Scholarships: Junior Football
SPONSOR: Alberta Heritage Scholarship Fund Office, Student Finances Board
ADDRESS: 9th Floor, Baker Centre, 10025 106th Street, Edmonton, Alberta T5J 1G7
PROGRAM: Any post-secondary program
BASIS: These scholarships provide the incentive and means for Junior Football players to continue their post-secondary education. Qualifying athletes must be nominated by their teams.
MINIMUM AVERAGE: N/A
VALUE: $1000.00
TERMS: One year only
NUMBER OF AWARDS: 30

CODE: AB/APEGG1/g
NAME: A.P.E.G.G.A. High School Awards for Engineering, Geology and Geophysics
SPONSOR: Honours and Awards Committee, Association of Professional Engineers, Geologists and Geophysicists of Alberta
ADDRESS: 1010 One Thornton Ct, Edmonton, Alberta T5J 2E7
PROGRAM: Engineering or Geophysics
BASIS: Awarded to deserving students entering the Faculty of Engineering, Department of Geology, or Geophysics at the U of Alberta or the U of Calgary. Students in a university transfer program are also eligible.
MINIMUM AVERAGE: N/A
VALUE: Varies

TERMS: Value is equal to the tuition fees for the first year of study. One year only.
NUMBER OF AWARDS: 12
DEADLINE FOR APPLICATIONS: July 15

CODE: AB/ARC01/g
NAME: A Western Arctic Scholarship
SPONSOR: Awards Advisory Committee, c/o Director, Policy and Programs
ADDRESS: Arctic College, #1 – 5102 50th Avenue, Yellowknife, NWT X1A 3S8
PROGRAM: Commerce, Forestry, Engineering, or Recreation
BASIS: Applicants must be residents of Western NWT who are planning to attend Arctic College or a technical institute, college, or university in Alberta. Awarded on the basis of academic abilty and extracurriular activities. An application is required.
MINIMUM AVERAGE: N/A
VALUE: $800.00
TERMS: One year only
NUMBER OF AWARDS: 3
DEADLINE FOR APPLICATIONS: July 15

CODE: AB/ARPA01/g
NAME: Halladay Memorial Student Award
SPONSOR: Awards Committee, ARPA, Percy Page Centre
ADDRESS: 13 Mission Avenue, St Alberta, Alberta T8N 1H6
PROGRAM: Parks and Recreation
BASIS: Awarded to a full-time student enrolled in a program related to parks and recreation. The selection is based upon academic standing, demonstrated contribution to recreation or parks in Alberta, and work experience. An application is required.
MINIMUM AVERAGE: N/A
VALUE: Equals tuition costs.
NUMBER OF AWARDS: 1
DEADLINE FOR APPLICATIONS: May 31

CODE: AB/ARTS01/g
NAME: Ben Sauve Artstrek Bursary
SPONSOR: Director, Student Assessment
ADDRESS: Edmonton Public Schools, One Kingsway, Edmonton, Alberta T5H 4G9
PROGRAM: Any
BASIS: Awarded to an Edmonton public school student enrolled at the Artstrek Summer Drama School. Candidates must demonstrate excellent achievement in theatre and a sincere dedication to the dramatic arts. Financial need will be considered.
MINIMUM AVERAGE: N/A
VALUE: $400.00
TERMS: One year only. Value varies to a maximum of $400.
NUMBER OF AWARDS: 1

CODE: AB/ATA01/g
NAME: Education Scholarship
SPONSOR: President, Grande Prairie City Local #13
ADDRESS: Alberta Teachers' Association, Grande Prairie, Alberta
PROGRAM: Education
BASIS: Awarded to a graduate from a public or separate high school located within the city of Grande Prairie entering a Faculty of Education. The selection is based on academic achievement. The application must include a transcript of marks and a letter from the Registrar.
MINIMUM AVERAGE: N/A
VALUE: $1000.00
TERMS: One year only
NUMBER OF AWARDS: 1
DEADLINE FOR APPLICATIONS: September 30

CODE: AB/AWNA01/g
NAME: C.A. Maclean Journalism Bursary
SPONSOR: AWNA Central Office
ADDRESS: Suite 360, Terrace Plaza, 4445 Calgary Trail S., Edmonton, Alberta T6H 5R7

PROGRAM: Journalism
BASIS: Applicants must be Albertans who are either graduating high school students intending to pursue journalism studies, current journalism students, or members of AWNA who wish to return to school for refresher courses.
MINIMUM AVERAGE: N/A
VALUE: $2000.00
TERMS: One year only
NUMBER OF AWARDS: Varies
DEADLINE FOR APPLICATIONS: June 29

CODE: AB/AWP01/g
NAME: Stan Davies Agricultural Memorial Bursary
SPONSOR: Alberta Wheat Pool, Corporate Affairs Department
ADDRESS: 505 2nd Street S.W., Calgary, Alberta T2P 2P5
PROGRAM: Agriculture-related program
BASIS: Awarded to students enrolled in post-secondary agriculture program who intend to return to farming upon completing their education.
MINIMUM AVERAGE: N/A
VALUE: $800.00
TERMS: One year only
NUMBER OF AWARDS: 2
DEADLINE FOR APPLICATIONS: November 30

CODE: AB/AWP02/g
NAME: Alberta Wheat Pool Bursaries for Rural Students
SPONSOR: Extension Manager, Alberta Wheat Pool
ADDRESS: Box 2700, 505 2nd Street S.W., Calgary, Alberta T2P 2P5
PROGRAM: Preference for Agriculture or Home Economics
BASIS: Awarded to students from rural Alberta whose parents are actively engaged in farming. The selection is based on matriculation standing and financial need.
MINIMUM AVERAGE: N/A
VALUE: $3000.00
TERMS: $600 per year, renewable

provided the academic standard is maintained.
NUMBER OF AWARDS: Varies
DEADLINE FOR APPLICATIONS: August 15

CODE: AB/AWW01/g
NAME: Alberta Water and Wastewater Operator's Association Bursary
SPONSOR: Alberta Water and Wastewater Operater's Association
ADDRESS: P.O. Box 3533, Station D, Edmonton, Alberta T5L 4J6
PROGRAM: Water and Wastewater Technician
BASIS: Awarded to a student entering a Water and Wastewater Management Technician program. The selection is based on academic achievement.
MINIMUM AVERAGE: N/A
VALUE: $2000.00
TERMS: One year only
NUMBER OF AWARDS: 1
DEADLINE FOR APPLICATIONS: November 1

CODE: AB/CAB01/g
NAME: Charlie Floyd Memorial Scholarship
SPONSOR: Court Deputy, Court Aurora Borealis No. 1407
ADDRESS: P.O. Box 203, Grande Prairie, Alberta T8V 3A4
PROGRAM: Any
BASIS: This scholarship is intended for members of Court Aurora Borealis No. 1407 or their children.
MINIMUM AVERAGE: N/A
VALUE: $500.00
TERMS: One year only
NUMBER OF AWARDS: 1
DEADLINE FOR APPLICATIONS: October 31

CODE: AB/CACL01/g
NAME: Bursaries in the Field of Mental Handicap
SPONSOR: Canadian Association for Community Living
ADDRESS: 11728 Kingsway Avenue, Edmonton, Alberta T5G 0X5

PROGRAM: Any
BASIS: Awarded to students interested in the field of Mental Handicap and planning to involve themselves as volunteers or professionals and who are in need of financial assistance.
MINIMUM AVERAGE: N/A
VALUE: $1000.00
TERMS: One year only
NUMBER OF AWARDS: Varies
DEADLINE FOR APPLICATIONS: July 15

CODE: AB/CALCO1/g
NAME: Calgary Co-op Scholarship
SPONSOR: Calgary Co-op Head Office
ADDRESS: P.O. Box 8160, Calgary, Alberta T2J 2V3
PROGRAM: Any
BASIS: Awarded to a student who is a member or the dependent of a member of Calgary Co-op or other co-operatives. The selection is based on academic achievement and financial need.
MINIMUM AVERAGE: N/A
VALUE: $750.00
TERMS: One year only
NUMBER OF AWARDS: 1
DEADLINE FOR APPLICATIONS: May 30

CODE: AB/CAMH01/g
NAME: Calgary Association for the Mentally Handicapped "Teal Bursary"
SPONSOR: Calgary Association for the Mentally Handicapped
ADDRESS: 4631 Richardson Way S.W., Calgary, Alberta T3E 7B7
PROGRAM: Related to Mental Handicap
BASIS: Awarded to a resident in A.M.R. Region 4 enrolled in a full- or part-time program that will benefit mentally handicapped citizens. The selection is based on academic proficiency and comprehension of developmental handicaps. An application is required.
MINIMUM AVERAGE: N/A
VALUE: $500.00
TERMS: One year only

NUMBER OF AWARDS: 1
DEADLINE FOR APPLICATIONS: July 31

CODE: AB/CCRB01/g
NAME: Building and Construction Research Scholarship
SPONSOR: Canadian Construction Research Board, Calgary Chapter
ADDRESS: 2725 – 12 Street N.E., Calgary, Alberta T2E 7J2
PROGRAM: Any post-secondary school in Southern Alberta
BASIS: Awarded to an undergraduate student who has lived in Alberta for 3 years prior to enrolment. Applicants must intend to investigate means to improve the performance of buildings products, construction management, safety, and design.
MINIMUM AVERAGE: N/A
VALUE: Varies
TERMS: Renewable
NUMBER OF AWARDS: 2
DEADLINE FOR APPLICATIONS: February 15

CODE: AB/CFGP01/g
NAME: Roxanne Ashmead Memorial Scholarship
SPONSOR: Roxanne Ashmead Scholarship Awards, CFGP Radio
ADDRESS: 200 Windsor Court, 9835 – 101 Avenue, Grande Prairie, Alberta T8V 0X6
PROGRAM: Journalism, Radio/Television
BASIS: Awarded to students from the city of Grande Prairie, county of Grande Prairie, Spirit River School Division, or Valleyview Hillside High School who intend to follow a career path in journalism leading to radio/television reporting.
MINIMUM AVERAGE: N/A
VALUE: $375.00
TERMS: One year only
NUMBER OF AWARDS: 2
DEADLINE FOR APPLICATIONS: May 4

CODE: AB/CFGP02/g
NAME: CFGP Scholarship
SPONSOR: Scholarship Awards, CFGP Radio
ADDRESS: 200 Windsor Court, 9835 – 101 Avenue, Grande Prairie, Alberta T8V 0X6
PROGRAM: Performing arts
BASIS: Awarded to students in attendance at any school including Grand Prairie Regional College, in the city or county of Grande Prairie. Awarded for demonstrated excellence. Funds can be used for courses, seminars, or workshops.
MINIMUM AVERAGE: N/A
VALUE: $2500.00
TERMS: One year only. Funds to be divided among recipients in music, drama, and dance.
NUMBER OF AWARDS: 2
DEADLINE FOR APPLICATIONS: April 30

CODE: AB/CPA01/g
NAME: Cerebral Palsy Association in Alberta Bursary
SPONSOR: Cerebral Palsy Association in Alberta
ADDRESS: 103 St Gregory School, 5430 – 26 Avenue, Calgary, Alberta T3E 0R6
PROGRAM: Any post-secondary program
BASIS: Awarded to a student entering or enrolled in a post-secondary institution who is diagnosed as having cerebral palsy. The award is based on financial need.
MINIMUM AVERAGE: N/A
VALUE: $1000.00
TERMS: One year only. Recipients must have been an Alberta resident for a minimum of one year.
NUMBER OF AWARDS: 1
DEADLINE FOR APPLICATIONS: June 30

CODE: AB/DROC01/g
NAME: Dr. Ed O'Connor Scholarships
SPONSOR: Dr. Ed O'Connor Scholarship Committee

ADDRESS: 4552 Stanley Drive S.W.,
Calgary, Alberta T2S 2R9
PROGRAM: Any at St Francis Xavier
University, Nova Scotia
BASIS: Awarded to Alberta students
who have met the entrance re-
quirements and are enrolled at St
Francis Xavier University in Nova
Scotia. The selection is made on the
basis of financial need, academic
achievement, citizenship, and
athletic accomplishments.
MINIMUM AVERAGE: N/A
VALUE: $2000.00
TERMS: One year only
NUMBER OF AWARDS: 2
DEADLINE FOR APPLICATIONS: March 21

CODE: AB/ENM01/g
NAME: Ernest Newman Memorial
Bursary
SPONSOR: Director, Local Government
Studies, Ring House
ADDRESS: University of Alberta,
Edmonton, Alberta T6G 2E2
PROGRAM: Related to municipal
government
BASIS: Awarded to a student who is
committed to pursuing a career in
municipal administration. Finan-
cial need will be considered.
MINIMUM AVERAGE: N/A
VALUE: $1000.00
TERMS: One year only
NUMBER OF AWARDS: 1
DEADLINE FOR APPLICATIONS: June 29

CODE: AB/GPMH01/g
NAME: Iris Pollock Memorial
Scholarship
SPONSOR: Grande Prairie District
Association for the Mentally
Handicapped
ADDRESS: 8702 – 113 Street, Grande
Prairie, Alberta T8V 6K5
PROGRAM: Rehabilitation or related
field
BASIS: Applicants must be residents of
Northern Alberta and must attend
any post-secondary institution.
Awarded on the basis of academic

achievement, citizenship, and a
genuine interest in the field of
mental handicap.
MINIMUM AVERAGE: N/A
VALUE: $500.00
TERMS: One year only
NUMBER OF AWARDS: 1
DEADLINE FOR APPLICATIONS: July 31

CODE: AB/ICAA01/g
NAME: Institute of Chartered
Accountants of Alberta High
School Awards
SPONSOR: Institute of Chartered
Accountants of Alberta
ADDRESS: Suite 901, Toronto Domin-
ion Tower, Edmonton Centre,
Edmonton, Alberta T5J 2Z1
PROGRAM: Post-secondary studies in
Business
BASIS: Awarded to students who are
currently enrolled in Grade 12 and
who plan to pursue studies in
business. The selection is based on
academic standing, involvement in
school and community activites,
leadership, letters of reference, and
a 250–300-word essay.
MINIMUM AVERAGE: N/A
VALUE: $400.00 (see below)
TERMS: One year only. One recipient
will receive full tuition and there
will be 15 runner-up awards of
$400.
NUMBER OF AWARDS: 16
DEADLINE FOR APPLICATIONS: April 15

CODE: AB/IODE01/g
NAME: IODE Coronation
Matriculation Bursaries
SPONSOR: Education Secretary,
Provincial Chapter of Alberta
IODE
ADDRESS: P.O. Box 5881, Station L,
Edmonton, Alberta T6C 4G5
PROGRAM: Any Alberta university
degree program
BASIS: These awards are tenable in a
degree program at a university in
Alberta or at an affiliated college.
All candidates must have resided

in the province of Alberta for at least 3 years prior to application.
MINIMUM AVERAGE: N/A
VALUE: $800.00
TERMS: One year only
NUMBER OF AWARDS: 3
DEADLINE FOR APPLICATIONS: July 15

CODE: AB/IOF01/g
NAME: Independent Order of Foresters Scholarship
SPONSOR: Court Deputy, Court Aurora Borealis No. 1407
ADDRESS: Box 203, Grande Prairie, Alberta T8V 3A4
PROGRAM: Any
BASIS: Applicants must be a member or a child of a member of Court Aurora Borealis #1407. The selection is based on academic proficiency.
MINIMUM AVERAGE: N/A
VALUE: $150.00
TERMS: One year only. Scholarship will be awarded after proof of full-time enrolment in the Fall.
NUMBER OF AWARDS: 1

CODE: AB/KGF01/g
NAME: Keith Gilmore Foundation Scholarship
SPONSOR: Keith Gilmore Foundation
ADDRESS: 5160 Skyline Way N.E., Calgary, Alberta T2E 6V1
PROGRAM: Any agriculture program
BASIS: Awarded to students enrolled in a diploma agriculture program.
MINIMUM AVERAGE: N/A
VALUE: $500.00
TERMS: One year only
NUMBER OF AWARDS: 2
DEADLINE FOR APPLICATIONS: July 1

CODE: AB/LSTS01/g
NAME: Lord Strathcona Trust Scholarship
SPONSOR: Secretary, Lord Strathcona Trust Fund, Alberta Provincial
ADDRESS: Committee, Prairie Region Cadet Detachment Edmonton, Box 10500, Edmonton, Alberta T5J 4J5

PROGRAM: Education, Physical Education, or Recreation Management
BASIS: Awarded to students who have been serving with the cadets for at least 3 years. The application must include a letter outlining career goals, need for the scholarship, and community service. A transcript of school marks and letters of recommendation are also required.
MINIMUM AVERAGE: N/A
VALUE: $750.00
TERMS: One year only
NUMBER OF AWARDS: Varies
DEADLINE FOR APPLICATIONS: May 15

CODE: AB/MASON1/g
NAME: Masonic Bursaries
SPONSOR: Grand Secretary, Grand Lodge of Alberta, A.F. and A.M.
ADDRESS: 330 12th Avenue S.W., Calgary, Alberta T2R 0H2
PROGRAM: Various
BASIS: Awarded to applicants from Alberta high schools on the basis of financial need. Tenable at any university in Alberta or affiliated college, or any other university if the program is not available in Alberta.
MINIMUM AVERAGE: N/A
VALUE: $1000.00
TERMS: Renewable subject to financial need.
NUMBER OF AWARDS: Varies
DEADLINE FOR APPLICATIONS: April 30

CODE: AB/MHN01/g
NAME: Medicine Hat News Scholarship
SPONSOR: Medicine Hat News
ADDRESS: 3257 Dunmore Road S.E., Medicine Hat, Alberta T1A 7E6
PROGRAM: Any
BASIS: Awarded to students who are carriers or former carriers of the News.
MINIMUM AVERAGE: N/A
VALUE: $400.00
TERMS: One year only

NUMBER OF AWARDS: 2
DEADLINE FOR APPLICATIONS: August 15

CODE: AB/NACCF1/g
NAME: Dr. G.R.A. Rice Bursary
SPONSOR: Executive Director, Northern Alberta Crippled Children's Fund
ADDRESS: 111404 – 142 Street, Edmonton, Alberta T5M 1V1
PROGRAM: Any
BASIS: Awarded on the basis of financial need to a disabled student from Northern Alberta enrolled in the 1st year of a post-secondary program.
MINIMUM AVERAGE: N/A
VALUE: $5000.00
TERMS: One year only. Amount of award may vary.
NUMBER OF AWARDS: 1
DEADLINE FOR APPLICATIONS: October 1

CODE: AB/NCF01/g
NAME: North Canadian Forest Industries Bursaries
SPONSOR: Student Awards Officer
ADDRESS: Grande Prairie Regional College, Grande Prairie, Alberta T8V 4C4
PROGRAM: Any
BASIS: Available to high school graduates who have resided north of Township 68 and west of the 5th meridian in the Province of Alberta for one year or longer. Awarded on the basis of financial need and satisfactory academic standing. An application is required.
MINIMUM AVERAGE: N/A
VALUE: $500.00
TERMS: One year only
NUMBER OF AWARDS: 2

CODE: AB/NCW01/g
NAME: Métis and Non-Status Indian Professional Training Bursary
SPONSOR: Staff Development, Alberta Family and Social Services
ADDRESS: 10th Floor, Centre West, 10035 108th Street, Edmonton, Alberta T5J 3E1
PROGRAM: Social Services or Native Child Welfare
BASIS: Applicants must be either Métis or Non-status Indians and have been residents of Alberta for a minimum of 3 years. They must demonstrate a commitment to the Native community.
MINIMUM AVERAGE: N/A
VALUE: $7000.00
TERMS: This bursary has a value of $9000 if the recipient has dependents.
NUMBER OF AWARDS: Varies

CODE: AB/NEWF01/g
NAME: Althea Shears Memorial Bursary
SPONSOR: McMurray Newfoundlanders Club
ADDRESS: P.O. Box 5208, Fort McMurray, Alberta T9H 3G3
PROGRAM: Social Work and other programs
BASIS: Awarded to a student entering the Social Work program who is a member or whose parent is a member of the McMurray Newfoundlanders Club. Consideration will be given to applicants who are entering programs other than Social Work.
MINIMUM AVERAGE: N/A
VALUE: $500.00
TERMS: One year only
NUMBER OF AWARDS: 1
DEADLINE FOR APPLICATIONS: June 15

CODE: AB/NOAC01/g
NAME: Robert Hampton Gray Memorial Bursary
SPONSOR: President, Naval Officer Association of Canada (Calgary Branch)
ADDRESS: P.O. Box 6291, Station D, Calgary, Alberta T2P 2C9
PROGRAM: Any university program
BASIS: Awarded to a student who has resided in Alberta for at least 3

years. An applicant must be the direct descendant of an individual who served with the naval forces or be a past or present member of a naval corps.
MINIMUM AVERAGE: N/A
VALUE: $600.00
TERMS: One year only
NUMBER OF AWARDS: 1
DEADLINE FOR APPLICATIONS: October 15

CODE: AB/NOVA01/g
NAME: Nova Educational Awards for Natives
SPONSOR: NOVA Corporation of Alberta
ADDRESS: P.O. Box 2535, Postal Station M, Calgary, Alberta T2P 2N6
PROGRAM: Various
BASIS: Awarded to Native students (Status and Non-status Indians, Métis and Inuit) enrolled full time in Business Administration, Secretarial Arts, Office Administration, Computer Technology, or Environmental Science. An application is required.
MINIMUM AVERAGE: N/A
VALUE: $3500.00
TERMS: Renewable. Award may also include an offer of summer employment.
NUMBER OF AWARDS: 7
DEADLINE FOR APPLICATIONS: June 15

CODE: AB/P&G01/g
NAME: Proctor & Gamble Cellulose Scholarships for Peace River Area Students
SPONSOR: Scholarship Fund, Proctor and Gamble Cellulose
ADDRESS: Postal Bag 1020, Grande Prairie, Alberta T8V 3A9
PROGRAM: Commerce, Forestry, or Engineering
BASIS: Awarded to residents of Peace River. The selection is based on academic achievement and extracurricular activities.
MINIMUM AVERAGE: N/A

VALUE: $750.00
TERMS: One year only
NUMBER OF AWARDS: 7
DEADLINE FOR APPLICATIONS: July 15

CODE: AB/PACL01/g
NAME: G. Allan Roeher Institute Bursaries
SPONSOR: Alberta Association for Community Living
ADDRESS: 11728 Kingsway Avenue, Edmonton, Alberta T5G 0X5
PROGRAM: Human Service, Special Education, and MRC programs
BASIS: Applicants must submit an outline of their intended program of study, letters of reference, transcripts of academic records, a summary of past involvement in the field of mental retardation, and a personal résumé.
MINIMUM AVERAGE: N/A
VALUE: $1000.00
TERMS: One year only
NUMBER OF AWARDS: Varies
DEADLINE FOR APPLICATIONS: July 1

CODE: AB/PRPM01/g
NAME: Peace River Pioneer Memorial Bursaries
SPONSOR: Office of Student Awards, University of Alberta
ADDRESS: 252 Athabasca Hall, Edmonton, Alberta T6G 2E8
PROGRAM: University of Alberta or affiliated institutions
BASIS: Awarded to high school graduates whose homes lie north of township 68 and west of the 5th meridian in Alberta. The selection is based on superior academic achievement and financial need.
MINIMUM AVERAGE: N/A
VALUE: Varies
TERMS: One year only
NUMBER OF AWARDS: Varies
DEADLINE FOR APPLICATIONS: July 15

CODE: AB/RCL001/g
NAME: Royal Canadian Legion District #1 Bursaries

SPONSOR: District Commander, W.H.
Hakes
ADDRESS: Box 904, Spirit River,
Alberta T0H 3G0
PROGRAM: Any
BASIS: Offered to a male and a female
Grade 12 graduate who reside
within the boundaries of Royal
Canadian Legion District #1. To be
eligible, applicants must have a
parent or grandparent who served
or is serving within the armed
forces or was an Associate of the
Legion.
MINIMUM AVERAGE: N/A
VALUE: $400.00
TERMS: One year only
NUMBER OF AWARDS: 2
DEADLINE FOR APPLICATIONS: August
20

CODE: AB/RCL002/g
NAME: Royal Canadian Legion
Ladies Auxiliary Alberta–N.W.T.
Command Award
SPONSOR: Ladies Auxiliary Alberta–
N.W.T. Command
ADDRESS: Royal Canadian Legion, Box
3067, Station B, Calgary, Alberta
T2A 3E7
PROGRAM: Any post-secondary
program
BASIS: Available to 1st-year students
who are children or grandchildren
of ex–service personnel. Children
of personnel currently serving in
the forces are also eligible. Candi-
dates must be Grade 12 graduates
from a high school in Alberta or
NWT.
MINIMUM AVERAGE: N/A
VALUE: $500.00
TERMS: One year only
NUMBER OF AWARDS: Varies
DEADLINE FOR APPLICATIONS: August
29

CODE: AB/RCL003/g
NAME: Royal Canadian Legion
Camrose Branch #57 Bursaries

SPONSOR: Royal Canadian Legion
Camrose Branch #57
ADDRESS: 5703 – 48 Avenue, Camrose,
Alberta T4V 0J9
PROGRAM: Any post-secondary
program
BASIS: Six bursaries will be awarded
to children or grandchildren of
Legion members and members of
the Legion Ladies Auxiliary. Four
bursaries are available to any
member of the community who
has completed high school and
plans to pursue post-secondary
education.
MINIMUM AVERAGE: N/A
VALUE: $600.00
TERMS: One year only
NUMBER OF AWARDS: 10
DEADLINE FOR APPLICATIONS: August
15

CODE: AB/RCL004/g
NAME: Royal Canadian Legion Ladies
Auxiliary Camrose Branch #57
Bursary
SPONSOR: Scholarship Chairman,
Royal Canadian Legion Camrose
Branch #57
ADDRESS: 5703 – 48 Avenue, Camrose,
Alberta T4V 0J9
PROGRAM: Any post-secondary
program
BASIS: This bursary is awarded to
children of ex–service personnel,
veterans, and Auxiliary members
from the city or the county of
Camrose.
MINIMUM AVERAGE: N/A
VALUE: $300.00
TERMS: One year only
NUMBER OF AWARDS: 1
DEADLINE FOR APPLICATIONS:
September 15

CODE: AB/RSF01/g
NAME: Robert Spence Foundation
Awards
SPONSOR: Administrator, Robert
Spence Foundation

ADDRESS: 2523 – 19A Street S.W.,
Calgary, Alberta T2T 4Z1
PROGRAM: Any post-secondary
program (minimum 2 years)
BASIS: Awarded to needy students of
whatever race or creed. Preference
will be given to residents of the St
Famille Roman Catholic Parish in
Calgary, Alberta, or other residents
of Calgary. An application is
required.
MINIMUM AVERAGE: 70.00
VALUE: Varies
TERMS: Amount not specified.
Renewable
NUMBER OF AWARDS: Varies

CODE: AB/RVB01/g
NAME: Rocky View Bursary
SPONSOR: Assistant Superintendent,
Rocky View School Division No. 41
ADDRESS: 2616 – 18 Street N.E.,
Calgary, Alberta T2E 7R1
PROGRAM: Any
BASIS: Awarded to an adult returning
to school who resides in Rocky
View School Division. An appli-
cation is required.
MINIMUM AVERAGE: N/A
VALUE: $500.00
TERMS: One year only
NUMBER OF AWARDS: 1

CODE: AB/SFB001/g
NAME: Alberta Women's Secretariat
"Persons Case" Scholarship
SPONSOR: Director, Alberta Heritage
Scholarship Fund
ADDRESS: Student Finance Board, 9th
Floor, Baker Centre, 10025 106th
Street, Edmonton, Alberta T5J 1G7
PROGRAM: Any post-secondary pro-
gram in Alberta
BASIS: Awarded to an undergraduate
student who has lived in Alberta
for 3 years immediately prior to
enrolment. Academic achievement
and financial need will be con-
sidered.
MINIMUM AVERAGE: N/A

VALUE: $5000.00
TERMS: One year only
NUMBER OF AWARDS: Varies
DEADLINE FOR APPLICATIONS:
September 30

CODE: AB/SFB002/g
NAME: Grants for Disabled Persons
SPONSOR: Director, Alberta Heritage
Scholarship Fund
ADDRESS: Student Finances Board, 9th
Floor, Baker Centre, 10025 106th
Street, Edmonton, Alberta T5J 1G7
PROGRAM: Any post-secondary
program
BASIS: Awarded on the basis of need
to students who require special
assistance owing to physical or
mental disabilities.
MINIMUM AVERAGE: N/A
VALUE: $1000.00
TERMS: Value varies to a maximum of
$1000.
NUMBER OF AWARDS: Varies

CODE: AB/SFB003/g
NAME: Anna and John Kolesar
Memorial Scholarship
SPONSOR: Director, Alberta Heritage
Scholarship Fund
ADDRESS: Students Finance Board,
10th Floor, 10025 106th Street,
Edmonton, Alberta T5J 1G7
PROGRAM: A Faculty of Education in
Alberta
BASIS: Awarded to a student entering
a Faculty of Education who best
exemplifies academic excellence.
Applicants must be Alberta resi-
dents and be from a family where
neither parent obtained a univer-
sity degree.
MINIMUM AVERAGE: N/A
VALUE: $1200.00
TERMS: One year only
NUMBER OF AWARDS: 1
DEADLINE FOR APPLICATIONS: July 1

CODE: AB/SFB004/g
NAME: Rollie Miles Scholarship

SPONSOR: Director, Alberta Heritage Scholarship Fund
ADDRESS: Student Finances Board, 9th Floor, Baker Centre, 10025 106th Street, Edmonton, Alberta T5J 1G7
PROGRAM: Physical Education
BASIS: Awarded to a high school graduate who best exemplifies academic and athletic excellence and plans to pursue study in Physical Education. Applications are available from Edmonton high school counsellors.
MINIMUM AVERAGE: N/A
VALUE: $1000.00
TERMS: One year only
NUMBER OF AWARDS: 1
DEADLINE FOR APPLICATIONS: June 1

CODE: AB/SFB005/g
NAME: Pope John Paul II Commemorative Scholarships
SPONSOR: Director, Alberta Heritage Scholarship Fund
ADDRESS: 9th Floor, Baker Centre, 10025 106th Street, Edmonton, Alberta T5J 4P9
PROGRAM: Native Studies or International Studies
BASIS: Awarded to full-time students in Alberta. These scholarships are intended to facilitate and promote studies for the well-being of mankind through the advancement of knowledge and its effective application to contemporary problems.
MINIMUM AVERAGE: N/A
VALUE: $5000.00
TERMS: One year only
NUMBER OF AWARDS: Varies
DEADLINE FOR APPLICATIONS: July 1

CODE: AB/SFB006/g
NAME: Wayne Gretzky Scholarship
SPONSOR: Director, Alberta Heritage Scholarship Fund
ADDRESS: Student Finances Board, 9th Floor, Baker Centre, 10025 106th Street, Edmonton, Alberta T5J 1G7
PROGRAM: Any post-secondary program

BASIS: Awarded to legally blind students. The selection is based on academic achievement.
MINIMUM AVERAGE: N/A
VALUE: $1500.00
TERMS: One year only
NUMBER OF AWARDS: 1
DEADLINE FOR APPLICATIONS: October 30

CODE: AB/SOR01/g
NAME: Soroptimist Training Awards
SPONSOR: Mary Hickley
ADDRESS: R.R. #1 Airdrie, Alberta T4B 2A3
PROGRAM: Vocational or technical training
BASIS: Awarded to women entering vocational or technical training. The selection is based upon outstanding citizenship traits and contribution to school and community by various activities.
MINIMUM AVERAGE: N/A
VALUE: $1500.00
TERMS: Amount of awards varies.
NUMBER OF AWARDS: Varies
DEADLINE FOR APPLICATIONS: January 15

CODE: AB/SOR02/g
NAME: Soroptimist Foundation Scholarship
SPONSOR: Soroptimist International of Edmonton
ADDRESS: J-3 Garden Grove Village, Edmonton, Alberta T6J 2L3
PROGRAM: Various
BASIS: Awarded to mature women to assist them in their efforts toward training and entry, or re-entry, into the labour market.
MINIMUM AVERAGE: N/A
VALUE: $1500.00
TERMS: One year only
NUMBER OF AWARDS: Varies
DEADLINE FOR APPLICATIONS: December 15

CODE: AB/SPA01/g
NAME: Spina Bifida Association of Northern Alberta Scholarship

SPONSOR: Spina Bifida Association of Northern Alberta Scholarship Committee
ADDRESS: P.O. Box 9501, Postal Station S.E., Edmonton, Alberta T6E 5X2
PROGRAM: Any Canadian post-secondary institution
BASIS: Awarded to a Canadian citizen or landed immigrant disabled with Spina Bifida. Candidates must have resided in Alberta, north of Red Deer, for at least 2 years. The selection is based on motivation, maturity, and academic background.
MINIMUM AVERAGE: N/A
VALUE: $500.00
TERMS: One year only
NUMBER OF AWARDS: 1
DEADLINE FOR APPLICATIONS: August 31

CODE: AB/SYNC01/g
NAME: Syncrude Special Educational Awards
SPONSOR: Syncrude Special Education Awards Program
ADDRESS: Syncrude Canada Ltd, P.O. Bag 4023, Fort McMurray, Alberta T9H 3H5
PROGRAM: Any program relevant to the oil-sands industry
BASIS: Awarded to women who are attending a post-secondary program leading toward a non-traditional occupation (e.g., engineering, geology). Applicants must be or have been long-term residents of Northern Alberta (at least one year).
MINIMUM AVERAGE: N/A
VALUE: $2000.00
TERMS: One year only
NUMBER OF AWARDS: 2
DEADLINE FOR APPLICATIONS: June 1

CODE: AB/SYNC02/g
NAME: Syncrude Special Educational Awards for People of Native Ancestry

SPONSOR: Syncrude Special Education Awards Program
ADDRESS: Syncrude Canada Ltd, P.O. Bag 4023, Fort McMurray, Alberta T9H 3H5
PROGRAM: Any program relevant to the oil-sands industry
BASIS: Awarded to Natives (Status, Non-status or Métis) who are current or former residents of the Fort McMurrary area and are enrolled in a post-secondary program related to the oil-sands industry: engineering, commerce, computer science, secretarial arts, etc.
MINIMUM AVERAGE: N/A
VALUE: $2000.00
TERMS: One year only
NUMBER OF AWARDS: 2
DEADLINE FOR APPLICATIONS: June 1

CODE: AB/VET01/g
NAME: Children of War Dead Act (Educational Assistance)
SPONSOR: Area Counsellor, Veterans Affairs Canada
ADDRESS: 940 Canada Place, 9700 Jasper Avenue, Edmonton, Alberta T5J 4C3
PROGRAM: Any approved Canadian institution
BASIS: Awarded to certain children of deceased members of the armed forces and individuals awarded disability pensions of 48% or more through the Canadian Pension Commission.
MINIMUM AVERAGE: N/A
VALUE: Varies
TERMS: Recipients may apply the fund to post-secondary study at an approved Canadian institution.
NUMBER OF AWARDS: Varies

BRITISH COLUMBIA

CODE: BC/4-H001/g
NAME: Bill Alendal Scholarship
SPONSOR: Provincial 4-H Office, 4-H Supervisor, Rural Organization Branch
ADDRESS: BC Ministry of Agriculture and Fisheries, 101 – 3547 Skaha Lake Road, Penticton, BC V2A 7K2
PROGRAM: Any university or technical or vocational school
BASIS: Awarded to 4-H members who have completed 2 years in the 4-H program and who intend to pursue their education beyond Grade 12.
MINIMUM AVERAGE: N/A
VALUE: $225.00
TERMS: One year only
NUMBER OF AWARDS: 2
DEADLINE FOR APPLICATIONS: April 1

CODE: BC/4-H002/g
NAME: Zoe Forstbauer 4-H Scholarship
SPONSOR: BC Ministry of Agriculture
ADDRESS: #200, 42 8th Street S., Cranbrook, BC V1C 2K3
PROGRAM: Any
BASIS: Awarded to a past or present 4-H member from the Cranbrook or Creston 4-H district.
MINIMUM AVERAGE: N/A
VALUE: $600.00
TERMS: One year only
NUMBER OF AWARDS: 1
DEADLINE FOR APPLICATIONS: April 1

CODE: BC/4-H003/g
NAME: Elizabeth Haddow Memorial Scholarship
SPONSOR: Ministry of Agriculture and Fisheries
ADDRESS: 1201 103rd Avenue, 4th Floor, Dawson Creek, BC V1G 4J2
PROGRAM: Any (minimum 10 months in duration)
BASIS: Awarded to a student who is a high school graduate and a resident of the Peace River 4-H region, with a minimum of one year achieved in 4-H. An application is required.
MINIMUM AVERAGE: N/A
VALUE: Varies
TERMS: One year only
NUMBER OF AWARDS: 1
DEADLINE FOR APPLICATIONS: May 1

CODE: BC/4-H004/g
NAME: Interior Reforestation Scholarship
SPONSOR: BC Ministry of Agriculture and Fisheries
ADDRESS: #200, 42 8th Street S., Cranbrook, BC V1C 2K3
PROGRAM: Any post-secondary program
BASIS: Awarded to a student who has been a member of achievement of the Cranbrook or Creston 4-H district for the last 4 years.
MINIMUM AVERAGE: N/A
VALUE: $300.00
TERMS: One year only
NUMBER OF AWARDS: 1
DEADLINE FOR APPLICATIONS: April 1

CODE: BC/4-H005/g
NAME: Ralph Barichello Scholarship
SPONSOR: Provincial 4-H Office, 4-H Supervisor, Rural Organization Branch
ADDRESS: BC Ministry of Agriculture and Fisheries, 101 – 3547 Skaha Lake Road, Penticton, BC V2A 7K2
PROGRAM: Any university or technical or vocational school
BASIS: Awarded to 4-H members who have completed 2 years in the 4-H program and who intend to pursue their education beyond Grade 12.

MINIMUM AVERAGE: N/A
VALUE: $200.00
TERMS: One year only
NUMBER OF AWARDS: 1
DEADLINE FOR APPLICATIONS: April 1

CODE: BC/4-H006/g
NAME: 4-H Scholarships
SPONSOR: 4-H Program, Rural Organizations and Services Branch
ADDRESS: BC Ministry of Agriculture and Fisheries, 101 – 3547 Shaka Lake Road, Penticton, BC V2A 7K2
PROGRAM: Any
BASIS: Applicants must be 4-H members.
MINIMUM AVERAGE: N/A
VALUE: N/A
TERMS: Renewable
NUMBER OF AWARDS: Varies
DEADLINE FOR APPLICATIONS: March 15

CODE: BC/4-H007/g
NAME: Norgan Foundation Scholarships
SPONSOR: Provincial 4-H Office, 4-H Supervisor, Rural Organization Branch
ADDRESS: BC Ministry of Agriculture and Fisheries, 101 – 3547 Skaha Lake Road, Penticton, BC V2A 7K2
PROGRAM: University study course or equivalent
BASIS: Awarded to 4-H members who have completed 2 years in the 4-H program and who intend to pursue their education beyond Grade 12.
MINIMUM AVERAGE: N/A
VALUE: $500.00
TERMS: One year only. There is a 2nd scholarship with a value of $250.
NUMBER OF AWARDS: 2
DEADLINE FOR APPLICATIONS: April 1

CODE: BC/4-H008/g
NAME: BC Fairs Scholarships
SPONSOR: Provincial 4-H Office, 4-H Supervisor, Rural Organization Branch
ADDRESS: BC Ministry of Agriculture and Fisheries, 101 – 3547 Skaha Lake Road, Penticton, BC V2A 7K2

PROGRAM: University – Agriculture or Home Economics
BASIS: Awarded to 4-H members who have completed 2 years in the 4-H program and who intend to pursue their education beyond Grade 12.
MINIMUM AVERAGE: N/A
VALUE: $500.00
TERMS: One year only. There is a 2nd scholarship with a value of $250.
NUMBER OF AWARDS: 2
DEADLINE FOR APPLICATIONS: April 1

CODE: BC/4-H009/g
NAME: Farm Credit Corporation Scholarships
SPONSOR: Provincial 4-H Office, 4-H Supervisor, Rural Organization Branch
ADDRESS: BC Ministry of Agriculture and Fisheries, 101 – 3547 Skaha Lake Road, Penticton, BC V2A 7K2
PROGRAM: Any
BASIS: Awarded to 4-H members who have completed 2 years in the 4-H program and who intend to pursue their education beyond Grade 12.
MINIMUM AVERAGE: N/A
VALUE: $300.00
TERMS: One year only
NUMBER OF AWARDS: 4
DEADLINE FOR APPLICATIONS: April 1

CODE: BC/4-H010/g
NAME: 4-H Ranchers' Award
SPONSOR: 4-H Scholarship Committee, c/o BC Ministry of Agriculture
ADDRESS: 166 Oriole Road, Kamloops, BC V2C 4N7
PROGRAM: Any full-time program
BASIS: Awarded to a 1st-year student enrolled in any full-time program. Applicant must be a past 4-H member who has achieved within the Kamloops District.
MINIMUM AVERAGE: N/A
VALUE: $250.00
TERMS: One year only
NUMBER OF AWARDS: 1
DEADLINE FOR APPLICATIONS: November 28

CODE: BC/4-H011/g
NAME: Kamloops and District Light Horse Club
SPONSOR: 4-H Scholarship Committee, c/o BC Ministry of Agriculture
ADDRESS: 166 Oriole Road, Kamloops, BC V2C 4N7
PROGRAM: Any full-time program
BASIS: Awarded to a 1st-year student enrolling in any full-time program. Applicant must be a past or present 4-H member.
MINIMUM AVERAGE: N/A
VALUE: $500.00
TERMS: One year only
NUMBER OF AWARDS: 1
DEADLINE FOR APPLICATIONS: November 30

CODE: BC/ABCDE1/g
NAME: British Columbia Drama Scholarship
SPONSOR: President, Association of BC Drama Educators (ABCDE)
ADDRESS: 1934 Dean Park Road, Sidney, BC V8L 3V5
PROGRAM: Any
BASIS: Awarded on the basis of participation in school plays, community service, and academic standing, especially in drama/theatre courses. The application must include 2 video presentations.
MINIMUM AVERAGE: 70.00
VALUE: $1000.00
TERMS: One year only
NUMBER OF AWARDS: 1
DEADLINE FOR APPLICATIONS: May 15

CODE: BC/ACL01/g
NAME: G. Allen Roeher Institute Bursaries for College Students
SPONSOR: Education Chairman, BC Association for Community Living
ADDRESS: #300 – 30 East Sixth, Vancouver, BC V5T 4P4
PROGRAM: Various
BASIS: Applicants must submit an outline of their intended programs of study, transcripts, and letters of recommendation. A summary of past involvement in the field of mental handicap and a personal résumé are also required.
MINIMUM AVERAGE: N/A
VALUE: $1000.00
TERMS: One year only
NUMBER OF AWARDS: N/A
DEADLINE FOR APPLICATIONS: July 1

CODE: BC/AMAC01/g
NAME: Abbotsford – Matsqui Arts Council Scholarships
SPONSOR: Abbotsford – Matsqui Arts Council
ADDRESS: P.O. Box 336, Abbotsford, BC V2S 4N9
PROGRAM: Visual, performing, or literary arts
BASIS: Applicants must be Canadian citizens or landed immigrants and normally reside in Matsqui or Abbotsford. Awards will be based upon financial need and suitability of the proposed course of study. An application is required.
MINIMUM AVERAGE: N/A
VALUE: $500.00
TERMS: One year only
NUMBER OF AWARDS: 2
DEADLINE FOR APPLICATIONS: May 31

CODE: BC/APSD01/g
NAME: Province of BC Assistance Program for Students with Severe Disabilities
SPONSOR: Financial Aid and Awards Office, Ministry of Advanced Education
ADDRESS: 2nd Floor, 1106 Cook Street, Victoria, BC
PROGRAM: Any in Brititsh Columbia
BASIS: For student with severe disabilities
MINIMUM AVERAGE: N/A
VALUE: $10,000.00
TERMS: The level of assistance provided recognizes a student's extraordinary costs of goods and/or services related to a disability.
NUMBER OF AWARDS: Varies

CODE: BC/B&G001/g
NAME: Boys and Girls Club of Canada Scholarships
SPONSOR: Boys and Girls Club of British Columbia
ADDRESS: 7595 Victoria Drive, Vancouver, BC V5P 3Z6
PROGRAM: Any
BASIS: Awarded to students who have been involved in, or have a proven interest in, the Boys and Girls Club. An application is required.
MINIMUM AVERAGE: N/A
VALUE: $250.00
TERMS: One year only
NUMBER OF AWARDS: Varies
DEADLINE FOR APPLICATIONS: June 30

CODE: BC/BAC01/g
NAME: Shari Meakin Bursary
SPONSOR: Burnaby Arts Council
ADDRESS: 6450 Gilpin Street, Burnaby, BC V5G 2J3
PROGRAM: Broadcast Journalism
BASIS: Applicants must have been writing freelance fiction or non-fiction for a minimum of 5 months. Financial need will be considered. An application is required.
MINIMUM AVERAGE: N/A
VALUE: $500.00
TERMS: One year only
NUMBER OF AWARDS: 1
DEADLINE FOR APPLICATIONS: November 30

CODE: BC/BCAA01/g
NAME: BC Athletic Awards
SPONSOR: BC Administrative Centre for Sport, Recreation and Fitness
ADDRESS: 1367 West Broadway, Vancouver, BC V6H 4A9
PROGRAM: Any post-secondary program
BASIS: Awarded to athletes who haved lived in BC for the past year, are immediately below the national-team level in an Olypmic, Commonwealth Games, or Pan-American Games sport, and who are recommended by the approp-riate provincial sport-governing body.
MINIMUM AVERAGE: N/A
VALUE: $1500.00
TERMS: Renewable
NUMBER OF AWARDS: 200

CODE: BC/BCAHA1/g
NAME: BC Amateur Hockey Association Scholarship
SPONSOR: BC Amateur Hockey Association
ADDRESS: 1551 Broadmead Avenue, Victoria, BC V8P 2V1
PROGRAM: Any post-secondary program
BASIS: Candidates must be BCAHA registered members who are graduating from high school. Awarded on the basis of good sportsmanship, hockey ability, and performance or quality of contribution, as well as good school and community participation.
MINIMUM AVERAGE: N/A
VALUE: $500.00
TERMS: One year only
NUMBER OF AWARDS: 5
DEADLINE FOR APPLICATIONS: April 30

CODE: BC/BCCA01/g
NAME: BC Cattlemen's Association – Martin Riedmann Bursaries
SPONSOR: BC Cattlemen
ADDRESS: Agri-Centre, RR #2, Kamloops, BC V2C 2S3
PROGRAM: Any post-secondary program
BASIS: Awarded to graduating high school students who come from a rural area where cattle are raised. Applicants must be sponsored by a local member association of BCCA.
MINIMUM AVERAGE: N/A
VALUE: $500.00
TERMS: One year only
NUMBER OF AWARDS: 4
DEADLINE FOR APPLICATIONS: April 15

CODE: BC/BCCA02/g
NAME: Lee Christianson Scholarship

SPONSOR: BC Cattlemen's Association
ADDRESS: Agri-Centre, RR #2,
Kamloops, BC V2C 2V3
PROGRAM: Agriculture or related
studies
BASIS: Awarded to a student brought
up on a ranch of cattle-raising
enterprises, to further his/her
further education. Applicants must
be sponsored by a local member
association of the BCCA.
MINIMUM AVERAGE: N/A
VALUE: $1000.00
TERMS: One year only
NUMBER OF AWARDS: 1
DEADLINE FOR APPLICATIONS: July 30

CODE: BC/BCLA01/g
NAME: British Columbia Lung
Association Bursaries
SPONSOR: British Columbia Lung
Association
ADDRESS: 906 West Broadway,
Vancouver, BC V5Z 1K7
PROGRAM: Any post-secondary
program
BASIS: Awarded to students who have
had tuberculosis. Applicants must
write, indicating how they qualify,
their intended program of study,
and financial need.
MINIMUM AVERAGE: N/A
VALUE: Varies
TERMS: Renewable
NUMBER OF AWARDS: Varies
DEADLINE FOR APPLICATIONS:
September 1

CODE: BC/BCMEA1/g
NAME: BC Music Educators'
Association Scholarship
SPONSOR: BCMEA
ADDRESS: P.O. Box 513, Garibaldi
Highland, BC V0N 1J0
PROGRAM: Any related to public-
school music education
BASIS: Awarded to students actively
involved in the activities of the
music department. The application
must include a cassette recording
of 2 compositions.

MINIMUM AVERAGE: N/A
VALUE: $500.00
TERMS: One year only
NUMBER OF AWARDS: 2
DEADLINE FOR APPLICATIONS: May 1

CODE: BC/BCPF01/g
NAME: International Year of the
Disabled Bursaries
SPONSOR: Scholarship and Bursary
Awards Committee
ADDRESS: BC Paraplegic Foundation,
780 S.W. Marine Drive, Vancouver,
BC V6P 5Y7
PROGRAM: Any post-secondary
program
BASIS: Awarded to disabled students
who are residents of BC and Cana-
dian citizens or landed immigrants.
Merit and financial need will be
considered. An application is
required.
MINIMUM AVERAGE: N/A
VALUE: Varies
TERMS: One year only
NUMBER OF AWARDS: Varies
DEADLINE FOR APPLICATIONS: August
15

CODE: BC/BCPF02/g
NAME: John MacNeal Scholarships
SPONSOR: Scholarship and Bursary
Awards Committee
ADDRESS: BC Paraplegic Foundation,
780 S.W. Marine Drive, Vancouver,
BC V6P 5Y7
PROGRAM: Any post-secondary
program
BASIS: Applicants must be disabled
students who are residents of BC
and Canadian citizens or landed
immigrants. Awarded in recogni-
tion of academic endeavours and/
or to financially assist students. An
application is required.
MINIMUM AVERAGE: N/A
VALUE: Varies
TERMS: N/A
NUMBER OF AWARDS: Varies
DEADLINE FOR APPLICATIONS: August
15

CODE: BC/BCPF03/g
NAME: Don Vaux Scholarship
SPONSOR: Scholarship and Bursary Awards Committee
ADDRESS: BC Paraplegic Foundation, 780 S.W. Marine Drive, Vancouver, BC V6P 5Y7
PROGRAM: Any post-secondary program
BASIS: Applicants must be disabled students who are residents of BC and Canadian citizens or landed immigrants. An application is required.
MINIMUM AVERAGE: N/A
VALUE: Varies
TERMS: This scholarship is to be used specifically for tuition, tools, equipment, or books.
NUMBER OF AWARDS: Varies
DEADLINE FOR APPLICATIONS: August 15

CODE: BC/BCPF04/g
NAME: Barbara E. Adams Scholarship
SPONSOR: Scholarship and Bursary Awards Committee
ADDRESS: BC Paraplegic Foundation, 780 S.W. Marine Drive, Vancouver, BC V6P 5Y7
PROGRAM: Any post-secondary program
BASIS: Applicants must be mobility-impaired students who are residents of BC and Canadian citizens or landed immigrants. An application is required.
MINIMUM AVERAGE: N/A
VALUE: Varies
TERMS: This scholarship is to be used for tuition, books and supplies, necessary help for study purposes, or transportation costs.
NUMBER OF AWARDS: Varies
DEADLINE FOR APPLICATIONS: August 15

CODE: BC/BCPF05/g
NAME: C.W. Deans Memorial Scholarship
SPONSOR: Canadian Paraplegic Association
ADDRESS: 780 S.W. Marine Drive, Vancouver, BC V6P 5Y7
PROGRAM: Engineering preferred, but other programs considered
BASIS: Awarded to a spinal-cord-injured student entering or continuing studies at university in BC. Preference will be shown to a student in engineering. Academic record will be considered. An application is required.
MINIMUM AVERAGE: N/A
VALUE: $250.00
TERMS: One year only
NUMBER OF AWARDS: 1
DEADLINE FOR APPLICATIONS: August 15

CODE: BC/BCPF06/g
NAME: IODE Bursary for Physically Diabled Persons
SPONSOR: BC Paraplegic Foundation
ADDRESS: 780 S.W. Marine Drive, Vancouver, BC V6P 5Y7
PROGRAM: Any
BASIS: To be eligible, candidates must be disabled students who are residents of BC and Canadian citizens or landed immigrants.
MINIMUM AVERAGE: N/A
VALUE: Varies
TERMS: One year only. Monies are to be used to assist with expenses for tuition, text books, transportation, or teaching assistance.
NUMBER OF AWARDS: Varies
DEADLINE FOR APPLICATIONS: August 15

CODE: BC/BCPF07/g
NAME: Joseph David Hall Memorial Scholarship
SPONSOR: Canadian Paraplegic Association
ADDRESS: 780 S.W. Marine Drive, Vancouver, BC V6P 5Y7
PROGRAM: Any
BASIS: First preference for this scholarship will be given to physi-

cally disabled students nominated by the Canadian Paraplegic Association, BC division. Able-bodied students with outstanding academic and/or athletic records may also be considered.

MINIMUM AVERAGE: N/A
VALUE: $1650.00
TERMS: One year only
NUMBER OF AWARDS: 1
DEADLINE FOR APPLICATIONS: August 15

CODE: BC/BCWI01/g
NAME: Maple Women's Institute Scholarship
SPONSOR: BC Women's Institute
ADDRESS: #8 – 33780 Laurel Street, Abbotsford, BC V2S 1X4
PROGRAM: Any post-secondary program
BASIS: Awarded to the child of any member who has been in good standing in the BC Women's Institute for at least 3 years. Applications and letters of recommendation must be sent by the sponsoring Women's Institute.
MINIMUM AVERAGE: N/A
VALUE: $250.00
TERMS: One year only
NUMBER OF AWARDS: 1
DEADLINE FOR APPLICATIONS: August 31

CODE: BC/BCWI02/g
NAME: BC Women's Institute – Centennial Vocational Bursary
SPONSOR: BC Women's Institute
ADDRESS: 20510 Fraser Highway, Langley, BC V3A 4G2
PROGRAM: Any vocational or training school
BASIS: Awarded to a Women's Institute member or child of a member attending any vocational or training school, including arts and crafts, or correspondence course.
MINIMUM AVERAGE: N/A
VALUE: $300.00
TERMS: One year only

NUMBER OF AWARDS: 1
DEADLINE FOR APPLICATIONS: August 31

CODE: BC/BCWI03/g
NAME: BC Women's Institute Memorial Scholarship
SPONSOR: BC Women's Institute
ADDRESS: #8 – 33780 Laurel Street, Abbotsford, BC V2S 1X4
PROGRAM: Any post-secondary program
BASIS: Awarded to the child of any member who has been in good standing in the BC Women's Institute for at least 3 years. Applications and letters of recommendation must be sent by the sponsoring Women's Institute.
MINIMUM AVERAGE: N/A
VALUE: $450.00
TERMS: One year only
NUMBER OF AWARDS: 3
DEADLINE FOR APPLICATIONS: August 31

CODE: BC/BCYSA1/g
NAME: BC Youth Soccer Association Scholarship
SPONSOR: Provincial Secretary, BC Juvenile Soccer Association
ADDRESS: 1126 Douglas Road, Burnaby, BC V5C 4Z6
PROGRAM: Any
BASIS: Applicants must have been a registered player with the BCYSA for at least 3 years and actively involved in playing or coaching, or involved in administrative work in soccer. Leadership, character, and citizenship are also considered.
MINIMUM AVERAGE: 65.00
VALUE: $500.00
TERMS: One year only. Some awards are worth $300.
NUMBER OF AWARDS: 13
DEADLINE FOR APPLICATIONS: April 30

CODE: BC/BEMM01/g
NAME: Bill and Elsie More Memorial Award

SPONSOR: c/o Dr. Arthur J. More,
UBC Faculty of Education
ADDRESS: 2125 Main Mall, Vancouver,
BC V6T 1Z5
PROGRAM: Social-service professions
BASIS: Applicants must be Status or
Non-status Indian students in BC
enrolled in "helping professions"
like education, social sciences,
nursing/medicine, law, and theol-
ogy. Financial need will be consid-
ered. A letter of application is
required. Candidates can apply
anytime.
MINIMUM AVERAGE: N/A
VALUE: $1000.00
TERMS: A number of bursaries totally
$1000 will be awarded annually.
NUMBER OF AWARDS: Varies

CODE: BC/BSSC01/g
NAME: Patrick F. Graham Bursary
SPONSOR: British Sailors' Society
Canada
ADDRESS: 1412 – 675 West Hastings
Street, Vancouver, BC V6B 1N2
PROGRAM: Maritime studies
BASIS: Awarded to students training
for careers at sea. An application is
required.
MINIMUM AVERAGE: N/A
VALUE: $250.00
TERMS: One year only
NUMBER OF AWARDS: 2

CODE: BC/BVCA01/g
NAME: Bulkley Valley Cattlemen's
Association Bursary
SPONSOR: Bulkley Valley Cattlemen's
Association
ADDRESS: Box 415, Smithers, BC V0J
2X0
PROGRAM: Any
BASIS: Awarded on the basis of
academic achievement to students
who have a permanent residence in
the area between Rose Lake
Canyon and Cedarvale, BC and
have graduated from a high school
in the Bulkley Valley.
MINIMUM AVERAGE: N/A

VALUE: $250.00
TERMS: One year only
NUMBER OF AWARDS: 1
DEADLINE FOR APPLICATIONS: July 31

CODE: BC/CACC01/g
NAME: Community Arts Council of
Chilliwack Fine Arts Award
SPONSOR: Community Arts Council of
Chilliwack Awards Committee
ADDRESS: 45899 Henderson Avenue,
Chilliwack, BC V2P 2X6
PROGRAM: Fine Arts or Theatre Arts
BASIS: Awarded to past or present
residents of the Chilliwack
Regional District, to further talent
and achievement in any of the Fine
Arts or Theatre Arts. No age limit.
An application is required.
MINIMUM AVERAGE: N/A
VALUE: $200.00
TERMS: One year only
NUMBER OF AWARDS: 1
DEADLINE FOR APPLICATIONS: May 15

CODE: BC/CACC02/g
NAME: Community Arts Council of
Chilliwack Awards
SPONSOR: Community Arts Council of
Chilliwack
ADDRESS: c/o Chilliwack Arts Centre,
45899 Henderson Avenue,
Chilliwack, BC V2P 2X6
PROGRAM: Any
BASIS: Applicants must be past or
present residents of Chilliwack,
BC.
MINIMUM AVERAGE: N/A
VALUE: $200.00
TERMS: The award must be applied to
tuition.
NUMBER OF AWARDS: 3
DEADLINE FOR APPLICATIONS: May 15

CODE: BC/CACC03/g
NAME: Jenny Child Memorial Award
SPONSOR: Community Arts Council of
Chilliwack Awards Committee
ADDRESS: 45899 Henderson Avenue,
Chilliwack, BC V2P 2X6
PROGRAM: Fine Arts or Theatre Arts

BASIS: Awarded to past or present residents of the Chilliwack Regional District, to further talent and achievement in any of the Fine Arts or Theatre Arts. No age limit. An application is required.
MINIMUM AVERAGE: N/A
VALUE: $200.00
TERMS: One year only
NUMBER OF AWARDS: 1
DEADLINE FOR APPLICATIONS: May 15

CODE: BC/CACC04/g
NAME: Mary Elizabeth Allan Memorial Award
SPONSOR: Community Arts Council of Chilliwack Awards Committee
ADDRESS: 45899 Henderson Avenue, Chilliwack, BC V2P 2X6
PROGRAM: Fine Arts or Theatre Arts
BASIS: Awarded to past or present residents of the Chilliwack Regional District, to further talent and achievement in any of the Fine Arts or Theatre Arts. No age limit. An application is required.
MINIMUM AVERAGE: N/A
VALUE: $200.00
TERMS: One year only
NUMBER OF AWARDS: 1
DEADLINE FOR APPLICATIONS: May 15

CODE: BC/CACGV1/g
NAME: Community Arts Council of Greater Victoria Bursaries
SPONSOR: Community Arts Council of Greater Victoria
ADDRESS: #511 – 620 View Street, Victoria, BC V8W 1J3
PROGRAM: Various
BASIS: Awarded to students who are residents of Victoria, BC who are studying theatre, dance, music, visual arts and crafts, and creative writing. An application is required.
MINIMUM AVERAGE: N/A
VALUE: Varies
TERMS: These are tuition scholarships.
NUMBER OF AWARDS: Varies
DEADLINE FOR APPLICATIONS: March 1

CODE: BC/CACR01/g
NAME: Community Arts Council of Richmond Scholarships
SPONSOR: Community Arts Council of Richmond
ADDRESS: 5951 No. 3 Road, Richmond, BC V6X 2E3
PROGRAM: Various fine arts programs
BASIS: Awarded to students who have been residents of Richmond for at least one year prior to the time of application. Applicants must be studying performing arts, visual arts, or creative writing.
MINIMUM AVERAGE: N/A
VALUE: Varies
TERMS: These are tuition scholarships.
NUMBER OF AWARDS: Varies

CODE: BC/CAFA01/g
NAME: Coquitlam Area Fine Arts Council Grants
SPONSOR: Arts Council Office
ADDRESS: Port Moody Station Museum, 2734 Murray Street, Port Moody, BC V3H 1X2
PROGRAM: Any program in the arts
BASIS: Applicants must reside in School District #43 (Coquitlam, Port Coquitlam, Port Moody, and Belcarra). Financial need and past achievement in the chosen field of endeavour will be considered.
MINIMUM AVERAGE: N/A
VALUE: $200.00
TERMS: Grants vary in value from $50–$200.
NUMBER OF AWARDS: Varies
DEADLINE FOR APPLICATIONS: May 15

CODE: BC/CDS01/g
NAME: Canadian Daughters' Scholarship (Assembly No. 3, Kamloops)
SPONSOR: Mrs. Anne Arksey
ADDRESS: 1134 Selkirk Street, Kamloops, BC V2B 1V6
PROGRAM: Any program
BASIS: Awarded on the basis of academic excellence to a new or returning student. Applications

should include transcripts. Preference will be given to relatives of members of the Canadian Daughters.
MINIMUM AVERAGE: N/A
VALUE: $300.00
TERMS: One year only. $150 per semester.
NUMBER OF AWARDS: Varies
DEADLINE FOR APPLICATIONS: April 15

CODE: BC/CFS01/g
NAME: Barbara Hough Memorial Scholarship
SPONSOR: Catholic Family Services
ADDRESS: 150 Robson Street, Vancouver, BC V6B 2A7
PROGRAM: Any post-secondary program
BASIS: Awarded to those who have been children in care (e.g., wards of the Superintendent of Child Welfare) who are now pursuing post-secondary education. An application is required.
MINIMUM AVERAGE: N/A
VALUE: $1000.00
TERMS: Scholarships vary from $100 to $1000.
NUMBER OF AWARDS: Varies
DEADLINE FOR APPLICATIONS: April 30

CODE: BC/CFUW01/g
NAME: Canadian Federation of University Women Sunshine Coast Bursary
SPONSOR: Canadian Federation of University Women
ADDRESS: c/o Sunshine Coast Community Futures Association, P.O. Box 1591, Sechelt, BC V0N 3A0
PROGRAM: Any degree-granting institution
BASIS: Awarded to a female Sunshine Coast resident who is entering at least half-time post-secondary studies. Applicants must not be related to a member of the bursary society. An application and 2 letters of recommendation are required.

MINIMUM AVERAGE: N/A
VALUE: $500.00
TERMS: One year only
NUMBER OF AWARDS: 1
DEADLINE FOR APPLICATIONS: May 10

CODE: BC/CGAA01/g
NAME: Certified General Accountants' Association of BC Scholarship
SPONSOR: Registrar, Certified General Accountants' Association of BC
ADDRESS: 1555 West 8th Avenue, Vancouver, BC V5J 1T5
PROGRAM: Any accounting related program in BC
BASIS: The selection is based on scholastic achievement in Grades 11 and 12. An application is required.
MINIMUM AVERAGE: 70.00
VALUE: $500.00
TERMS: One year only
NUMBER OF AWARDS: 20
DEADLINE FOR APPLICATIONS: April 13

CODE: BC/CIMM01/g
NAME: South Central Interior Branch Bursary
SPONSOR: Branch Chairman, Canadian Institute of Mining and Metallurgy
ADDRESS: South Central Interior Branch, Box 3275, Kamloops, BC V2C 6B8
PROGRAM: Mining-related programs at BCIT and UBC
BASIS: Awarded to a student from the South Central Interior of BC who intends to make a career in mining and is in need of financial assistance. Applicants must send a letter indicating the criteria by which they qualify for the bursary.
MINIMUM AVERAGE: N/A
VALUE: $1000.00
TERMS: One year only
NUMBER OF AWARDS: 1
DEADLINE FOR APPLICATIONS: December 31

CODE: BC/CLRK01/g
NAME: Dr. David Clarke Bursary
SPONSOR: Chairman, South

Okanagan–Similkameen Union Board of Health

ADDRESS: 1340 Ellis Street, Kelowna, BC V1Y 1Z8

PROGRAM: Any

BASIS: Applicants must be Canadian citizens who have been residents of the South Okanagan Health Unit for at least one year. The selection is based on good character and potential for the chosen field of study.

MINIMUM AVERAGE: N/A

VALUE: $500.00

TERMS: One year only

NUMBER OF AWARDS: 1

DEADLINE FOR APPLICATIONS: April 1

CODE: BC/CNIB01/g

NAME: William and Dorothy Ferrell Scholarship

SPONSOR: Student Awards Committee, CNIB, BC–Yukon Division

ADDRESS: 100 – 5055 Joyce Street, Vancouver, BC V5R 6B2

PROGRAM: Related to services to the blind

BASIS: Awarded to visually impaired students who are pursuing studies for a career in the field of services to other blind individuals. An application is required.

MINIMUM AVERAGE: N/A

VALUE: Varies

NUMBER OF AWARDS: Varies

DEADLINE FOR APPLICATIONS: April 15

CODE: BC/CNIB02/g

NAME: June Gilmore English Memorial Fund

SPONSOR: Assistant Director, Special Education Program

ADDRESS: 844 Courtney Street, Victoria, BC V8V 2M4

PROGRAM: Any

BASIS: Awarded to visually impaired BC high school graduates who are pursuing post-secondary studies. The application must include a letter detailing extracurricular activities, medical verification of visual impairment, and a letter of recommendation.

MINIMUM AVERAGE: N/A

VALUE: $400.00

TERMS: There will be one scholarship and one bursary.

NUMBER OF AWARDS: 2

DEADLINE FOR APPLICATIONS: April 30

CODE: BC/CNIB03/g

NAME: James L. Wood Scholarship

SPONSOR: Student Awards Committee, CNIB

ADDRESS: #100 – 5055 Joyce Street, Vancouver, BC V5R 6B2

PROGRAM: Any

BASIS: Awarded to visually impaired students who are pursuing post-secondary studies. The application must include transcripts. Extra-curricular activities, community service, and financial need will be considered.

MINIMUM AVERAGE: N/A

VALUE: $500.00

TERMS: Renewable

NUMBER OF AWARDS: 2

DEADLINE FOR APPLICATIONS: June 30

CODE: BC/CNIB04/g

NAME: Robinson and Buckland Memorial Bursary (Reader Grant)

SPONSOR: Student Awards Committee, CNIB

ADDRESS: 350 East 36th Avenue, Vancouver, BC V5W 1C6

PROGRAM: Any

BASIS: Awarded to visually impaired students who are pursuing full-time post-secondary studies. An application is required.

MINIMUM AVERAGE: N/A

VALUE: $200.00

TERMS: Renewable. Paid in 2 instalments.

NUMBER OF AWARDS: Varies

DEADLINE FOR APPLICATIONS: August 15

CODE: BC/CNIB05/g

NAME: John and Dorris Corrigan Fund

SPONSOR: Mr. Fred Poon, PRCVI
ADDRESS: #106 – 1750 West 75th Avenue, Vancouver, BC V6R 4J5
PROGRAM: Any
BASIS: Awarded to visually impaired students in BC who are under 30 years and are pursuing full-time post-secondary studies. An application is required.
MINIMUM AVERAGE: N/A
VALUE: $500.00
TERMS: Amount varies to a maximum of $500. Funds are for items not covered by other funding sources.
NUMBER OF AWARDS: Varies

CODE: BC/CNIB06/g
NAME: Martha Guest Memorial Bursary
SPONSOR: Student Awards Committee, CNIB
ADDRESS: 100 – 5055 Joyce Street, Vancouver, BC V5R 6B2
PROGRAM: Any
BASIS: Awarded to blind or visually impaired students who are pursuing full-time post-secondary studies. An application is required.
MINIMUM AVERAGE: N/A
VALUE: $500.00
TERMS: One year only
NUMBER OF AWARDS: Varies
DEADLINE FOR APPLICATIONS: October 30

CODE: BC/CNIB07/g
NAME: Lorne Hassan Memorial Fund
SPONSOR: Student Awards Committee, CNIB
ADDRESS: 100 – 5055 Joyce Street, Vancouver, BC V5R 6B2
PROGRAM: Any
BASIS: Awarded to visually impaired students who are pursuing full-time post-secondary studies. An application is required.
MINIMUM AVERAGE: N/A
VALUE: $1000.00
TERMS: One year only
NUMBER OF AWARDS: Varies
DEADLINE FOR APPLICATIONS: July 30

CODE: BC/CNIB08/g
NAME: Military Police Fund
SPONSOR: Assistant Director, Special Education Programs
ADDRESS: 844 Courtenay Street, Victoria, BC V8V 2M4
PROGRAM: Any
BASIS: Awarded to visually impaired students who are pursuing full-time post-secondary studies. An application is required.
MINIMUM AVERAGE: N/A
VALUE: Varies
TERMS: This fund is for unforseen needs that cannot be met by other services and sources.
NUMBER OF AWARDS: Varies

CODE: BC/CNIB09/g
NAME: Carl G. Frink Scholarship
SPONSOR: Student Awards Committee, CNIB
ADDRESS: #100 – 5055 Joyce Street, Vancouver, BC V5R 6B2
PROGRAM: Any in BC
BASIS: Applicant must be blind, visually impaired, or deaf-blind and planning on or already attending post-secondary training in BC.
MINIMUM AVERAGE: N/A
VALUE: $1000.00
TERMS: One year only
NUMBER OF AWARDS: 1
DEADLINE FOR APPLICATIONS: May 31

CODE: BC/CNIB10/g
NAME: F.J.L. Woodcock Scholarship
SPONSOR: Student Awards Committee, CNIB
ADDRESS: #100 – 5055 Joyce Street, Vancouver, BC V5R 6B2
PROGRAM: Any in BC
BASIS: Applicants must be blind, or visually impaired, and continuing their educations. A letter of recommendation is required.
MINIMUM AVERAGE: N/A
VALUE: $400.00
TERMS: One year only. There are 2 awards for Vancouver Island

residents and 2 awards for mainland BC residents.

NUMBER OF AWARDS: 4
DEADLINE FOR APPLICATIONS: May 31

CODE: BC/CNIB11/g
NAME: Telesensory Scholarship
SPONSOR: Student Awards Committee, CNIB
ADDRESS: #100 – 5055 Joyce Street, Vancouver, BC V5R 6B2
PROGRAM: Any
BASIS: Awarded to current AER members with educational pursuits in the field of service to blind and visually impaired people.
MINIMUM AVERAGE: N/A
VALUE: $1000.00
TERMS: One year only. Value varies to a maximum of $1000.
NUMBER OF AWARDS: Varies
DEADLINE FOR APPLICATIONS: April 15

CODE: BC/CSB001/g
NAME: Arts Awards Program
SPONSOR: Coordinator, Arts Awards Program, Cultural Services Branch
ADDRESS: 5th Floor, 800 Johnson Street, Victoria, BC V8V 1X4
PROGRAM: Arts
BASIS: Award to British Columbians who are enrolled in the following disciplines: theatre, dance, music, visual arts and crafts, film and video, creative writing, arts administration, and museological and conservation studies. An application is required.
MINIMUM AVERAGE: N/A
VALUE: $1500.00
TERMS: Renewable for up to 4 years.
NUMBER OF AWARDS: Varies
DEADLINE FOR APPLICATIONS: May 31

CODE: BC/CUF01/g
NAME: Credit Union Foundation of BC Grants
SPONSOR: The Trustees, Credit Union Foundation of BC
ADDRESS: 1441 Creekside Drive, Vancouver, BC V6J 4S7

PROGRAM: Any post-secondary program in BC
BASIS: Awarded to BC resident students in financial need. Applications are available at any credit union in BC.
MINIMUM AVERAGE: N/A
VALUE: Varies
TERMS: One year only
NUMBER OF AWARDS: Varies
DEADLINE FOR APPLICATIONS: September 30

CODE: BC/CVFI01/g
NAME: Comox Valley Farmers' Institute Award
SPONSOR: Comox Valley Farmers' Institute
ADDRESS: P.O. Box 3493, Courtnay, BC V9N 6Z8
PROGRAM: Agriculture-related program
BASIS: Applicants must be between the ages of 17 and 25 and have attended school in School District #71 (Comox). Applicants must be planning to enter an agriculture-related career area.
MINIMUM AVERAGE: N/A
VALUE: $400.00
TERMS: One year only
NUMBER OF AWARDS: 1
DEADLINE FOR APPLICATIONS: May 1

CODE: BC/DAW01/g
NAME: Thomas Dawson Estate Memorial Scholarship
SPONSOR: Advisory Committee, Male Nurses Fund, Thomas Dawson Estate
ADDRESS: Royal Jubilee Hospital, 1900 Fort Street, Victoria, BC V8R 1J8
PROGRAM: Nursing
BASIS: Awarded to a male student enrolled in a School of Nursing program. An application is required.
MINIMUM AVERAGE: N/A
VALUE: $300.00
TERMS: Awarded at $300 per month for a six-month maximum.
NUMBER OF AWARDS: 1

CODE: BC/DCDH01/g
NAME: Dawson Creek and District Hospital Bursaries
SPONSOR: Personnel Department, Dawson Creek and District Hospital
ADDRESS: 11100 13th Street, Dawson Creek, BC V1G 3W8
PROGRAM: Diploma Nursing program
BASIS: This bursary is designed to provide an incentive to attract registered nurses into employment at the Dawson Creek and District Hospital. An application is required.
MINIMUM AVERAGE: N/A
VALUE: $2500.00
TERMS: Recipients of this bursary are expected to accept employment at the Dawson Creek and District Hospital for one year following graduation.
NUMBER OF AWARDS: Varies
DEADLINE FOR APPLICATIONS: February 28

CODE: BC/DHA01/g
NAME: Delta Hospital Auxiliary Award(s)
SPONSOR: Immediate Past President, Bursary Committee
ADDRESS: Delta Hospital Auxiliary, 5800 Mountain Veiw Boulevard, Delta, BC V4K 3V6
PROGRAM: Health Sciences
BASIS: Applicants must have been Delta, BC, residents for a period of not less than 2 years. Financial need will be considered.
MINIMUM AVERAGE: N/A
VALUE: $1000.00
TERMS: One year only
NUMBER OF AWARDS: 2
DEADLINE FOR APPLICATIONS: August 15

CODE: BC/DIAC01/g
NAME: Diachem Industries Limited Soccer Scholarships
SPONSOR: Diachem Industries Limited
ADDRESS: 3rd Floor, 1285 West Broadway, Vancouver, BC V6H 3Z9
PROGRAM: Any post-secondary program
BASIS: Awarded to Grade 12 graduates on the basis of proficiency in soccer, good citizenship, character, and leadership.
MINIMUM AVERAGE: 65.00
VALUE: $500.00
TERMS: One year only
NUMBER OF AWARDS: 5
DEADLINE FOR APPLICATIONS: May 15

CODE: BC/DSS01/g
NAME: Jo Heunemann Annual Memorial Bursary
SPONSOR: Irene McRae, Executive Director, Beltassist Society
ADDRESS: 11425 84th Avenue, Delta, BC V4C 2L9
PROGRAM: Social Service
BASIS: Applicants must be studying in the field of community service.
MINIMUM AVERAGE: N/A
VALUE: $100.00
TERMS: One year only
NUMBER OF AWARDS: 1

CODE: BC/ESSAY1/g
NAME: University of British Columbia Essay Competition.
SPONSOR: Office of the Dean of Arts
ADDRESS: University of British Columbia, Vancouver, BC V6T 1Z1
PROGRAM: N/A
BASIS: The competition is open to Grade 12 students in BC or the Yukon who will write an essay in their respective schools at a set time under supervised conditions. Information outlining other details will be sent to each high school.
MINIMUM AVERAGE: N/A
VALUE: $1500.00
TERMS: One time only. There are also prizes of $1000 and $500, book prizes, and certificates of merit.
NUMBER OF AWARDS: Varies

CODE: BC/FCC02/g
NAME: Fletcher Challenge Canada Awards
SPONSOR: Fletcher Challenge Canada Scholarship Program
ADDRESS: c/o National Trust Company, #900 – 666 Burrard Street, Vancouver, BC V6C 2Z9
PROGRAM: Any full-time college or university program
BASIS: Applicants must be graduating from high schools in an area of BC in which Fletcher Canada is a major employer. Applicants must be planning to attend post-secondary studies immediately after high school. Academic achievement will be considered.
MINIMUM AVERAGE: 75.00
VALUE: $1500.00
TERMS: One year only. Students entering a college program will receive $750. See entry FCC01/e for Fletcher Challenge Canada employee scholarships.
NUMBER OF AWARDS: 10
DEADLINE FOR APPLICATIONS: May 15

CODE: BC/FPLP01/g
NAME: Federal-Provincial Language Programs
SPONSOR: French Programs Co-ordinator, Modern Languages Services Branch
ADDRESS: Ministry of Education, Parliament Buildings, Victoria, BC V8V 2M4
PROGRAM: See below.
BASIS: Students who are planning to take courses in the second official language may be eligible for assist-ance. Programs available: Second-Language Monitor Program, Second-Language Study Fellow-ship, and Summer-Language Bursary program.
MINIMUM AVERAGE: N/A
VALUE: $2500.00
TERMS: One year only
NUMBER OF AWARDS: Varies

CODE: BC/GDV01/g
NAME: Geraldo Donato Vertone Scholarship
SPONSOR: Executive Director, Italian Cultural Centre Society
ADDRESS: 3075 Slocan Street, Vancouver, BC V5M 3E4
PROGRAM: Any program at a college or university
BASIS: Awarded to students of Italian origin on the basis of character strength, community services ren-dered, and community interest. A letter of application explaining the reason for applying and one letter of reference are required.
MINIMUM AVERAGE: N/A
VALUE: Varies
TERMS: Awards will not exceed the cost of half of the tuition fee needed for a full course load and funds will be paid directly to the institution.
NUMBER OF AWARDS: Varies
DEADLINE FOR APPLICATIONS: August 1

CODE: BC/GLM01/g
NAME: Grand Lodge Masonic Bursaries
SPONSOR: Grand Lodge of British Columbia
ADDRESS: Freemasons' Hall, 1495 West 8th Avenue, Vancouver, BC
PROGRAM: Any post-secondary institution in BC
BASIS: Awarded to deserving students entering post-secondary programs in British Columbia. Preference will be shown to the sons, daugh-ters, and legal wards of active members of Masonic Lodges in BC. An application is required.
MINIMUM AVERAGE: N/A
VALUE: $500.00
TERMS: Award amounts may vary.
NUMBER OF AWARDS: Varies
DEADLINE FOR APPLICATIONS: July 1

CODE: BC/HAWC01/g
NAME: Indian and Inuit Health Careers Program

SPONSOR: Regional Advisor, Indian and Inuit Health Careers Program
ADDRESS: Health and Welfare Canada, #540 – 757 Hastings Street, Vancouver, BC V6C 3E6
PROGRAM: Health sciences
BASIS: Applicants must be Canadian citizens of Indian/Inuit ancestry who have resided in Canada for at least 12 months.
MINIMUM AVERAGE: N/A
VALUE: $1000.00
TERMS: Renewable. Not tenable with any other government program awarded for the same purpose.
NUMBER OF AWARDS: Varies
DEADLINE FOR APPLICATIONS: May 15

CODE: BC/HJSO02/g
NAME: Harry Jerome Scholarship
SPONSOR: Harry Jerome Scholarship Committee
ADDRESS: c/o BC Athletics / Track & Field Association, 1200 Hornby Street, Vancouver, BC V6Z 2E2
PROGRAM: Any full-time postsecondary program
BASIS: Applicants must be Grade 12 graduates from BC who have demonstrated proficiency in track and field and qualities of character and leadership. Financial need will be considered.
MINIMUM AVERAGE: N/A
VALUE: Varies
TERMS: One year only
NUMBER OF AWARDS: 1
DEADLINE FOR APPLICATIONS: May 15

CODE: BC/HSBA01/g
NAME: BC High School Boys' Basketball Association Scholarship
SPONSOR: Mr. Ken Winslade, c/o BCHSBA
ADDRESS: 600 8th Street, New Westminster, BC V3M 3S2
PROGRAM: Any approved postsecondary program in BC
BASIS: Applicants must have demonstrated proficiency in basketball and have good qualities of character and leadership. Financial need will be considered. Three letters of recommendation are required.
MINIMUM AVERAGE: 60.00
VALUE: Varies
TERMS: One year only
NUMBER OF AWARDS: N/A
DEADLINE FOR APPLICATIONS: June 1

CODE: BC/IAS01/g
NAME: BC Indian Arts Society Memorial Bursary
SPONSOR: Honorary Secretary, BC Indian Arts Society
ADDRESS: 212 – 701 Esquimalt Road, Victoria, BC V9A 3L5
PROGRAM: Any
BASIS: Native Indian applicants must be residents of BC who are planning to enter one of the established universities or colleges in the province.
MINIMUM AVERAGE: N/A
VALUE: $150.00
TERMS: One year only
NUMBER OF AWARDS: 2

CODE: BC/ICA001/g
NAME: Institute of Chartered Accountants of BC Scholarships
SPONSOR: Institute of Chartered Accountants of BC
ADDRESS: 1133 Melville Street, Vancouver, BC V6E 4E5
PROGRAM: Accounting and Commerce preferred
BASIS: Candidates must write examinations in Math 12, Math 112, or Math 113 and one other subject chosen from a list approved by the Ministry of Education. All examinations must be written in the June examination sessions.
MINIMUM AVERAGE: N/A
VALUE: $1000.00
TERMS: One year only
NUMBER OF AWARDS: 2
DEADLINE FOR APPLICATIONS: July 1

CODE: BC/ICC01/g
NAME: Icelandic Canadian Club Scholarships

SPONSOR: Secretary of Education Committee, Icelandic Canadian Club of BC
ADDRESS: Apt. 903 – 999 Gilford, Vancouver, BC V6G 2N8
PROGRAM: Any post-secondary program in BC
BASIS: Awarded to students of Icelandic origin on the basis of academic excellence.
MINIMUM AVERAGE: N/A
VALUE: $200.00
TERMS: Renewable
NUMBER OF AWARDS: 4
DEADLINE FOR APPLICATIONS: August 15

CODE: BC/ILAF01/g
NAME: Interior Logging Association Forestry Scholarship
SPONSOR: Chairman, ILA Scholarship Committee
ADDRESS: #3 – 111 Oriole Road, Kamloops, BC V2C 4N6
PROGRAM: Forestry-related program
BASIS: Awarded to any graduating student in the ILA operating area enrolling in full-time studies in a forestry-related discipline at a Canadian college or university.
MINIMUM AVERAGE: N/A
VALUE: $1000.00
TERMS: One year only
NUMBER OF AWARDS: 1
DEADLINE FOR APPLICATIONS: July 31

CODE: BC/IOF01/g
NAME: Independent Order of Foresters Bursaries.
SPONSOR: High Secretary, High Court of British Columbia and Alaska
ADDRESS: 1902 London Street, New Westminster, BC V3M 3E5
PROGRAM: Any
BASIS: Awarded to IOF members in good standing for not less than 2 years or their dependents.
MINIMUM AVERAGE: N/A
VALUE: $500.00
TERMS: Renewable

NUMBER OF AWARDS: Varies
DEADLINE FOR APPLICATIONS: August 31

CODE: BC/JGM01/g
NAME: Joseph Golland Memorial Scholarship Award
SPONSOR: Board of Directors, Joseph Golland Memorial Scholarship Fund
ADDRESS: #911 – 525 Seymour Street, Vancouver, BC V6B 3H7
PROGRAM: Broadcast Communications
BASIS: Applicants must be BC residents who are committed to expanding their professional potential as performers, writers, directors, or those involved in related professions. An application is required.
MINIMUM AVERAGE: N/A
VALUE: $1000.00
TERMS: One year only
NUMBER OF AWARDS: 1
DEADLINE FOR APPLICATIONS: March 31

CODE: BC/JKR01/g
NAME: James Kinnaird Research Scholarships
SPONSOR: Professor Leslie Nay, BC Industrial Relations Association
ADDRESS: Faculty of Commerce and Business Administration, UBC, 2053 Main Mall, Vancouver, BC V6T 1Y8
PROGRAM: Any post-secondary program in BC
BASIS: Applicants must be capable of doing research on the following: collective bargaining, trade unionism, labour law, or dispute resolution. A curriculum vitae and research proposal must be submitted.
MINIMUM AVERAGE: N/A
VALUE: $1000.00
TERMS: Scholarships are awarded to help defray research or project costs, but may be allocated to defray tuition costs.
NUMBER OF AWARDS: N/A

CODE: BC/KFS001/g
NAME: Kermode Friendship Society
Bursary
SPONSOR: Kermode Friendship Society
ADDRESS: 3313 Kalum Street, Terrace,
BC V8G 2N7
PROGRAM: Any
BASIS: Applicants must be members of
the Kermode Friendship Society
who are continuing their post-
secondary educations. Proof of
registration and a recent transcript
are required with the application.
MINIMUM AVERAGE: N/A
VALUE: Varies
TERMS: Renewable. Amount of
bursary varies from $100 to $1000.
NUMBER OF AWARDS: Varies

CODE: BC/KHISS1/g
NAME: Robert Roshard Memorial
Trust Fund Bursary
SPONSOR: Kamloops Hearing
Impaired Support Services
Association
ADDRESS: 821 Seymour Street,
Kamloops, BC V2C 2H6
PROGRAM: Any
BASIS: Awarded to a hearing-impaired
student who has specific plans for
post-secondary education, or to a
hearing student interested in con-
tinuing education or training in
fields related to hearing impair-
ment. An application is required.
MINIMUM AVERAGE: N/A
VALUE: Varies
TERMS: Renewable
NUMBER OF AWARDS: 1
DEADLINE FOR APPLICATIONS: May 31

CODE: BC/KSCL01/g
NAME: Mary Marchi Memorial
Bursary
SPONSOR: Kootenay Society for Com-
munity Living, Regional Office
ADDRESS: 577 Baker Street, Nelson, BC
V1L 4J1
PROGRAM: Any related to the mentally
handicapped
BASIS: Awarded to a student whose

home residence is in the Kootenay
area of BC and who is pursuing
studies related to the mentally
handicapped.
MINIMUM AVERAGE: N/A
VALUE: $350.00
TERMS: One year only
NUMBER OF AWARDS: 1
DEADLINE FOR APPLICATIONS:
September 30

CODE: BC/KSCL02/g
NAME: Crystal Henson Memorial
Bursary
SPONSOR: Kootenay Society for
Community Living, Regional Office
ADDRESS: 577 Baker Street, Nelson, BC
V1L 4J1
PROGRAM: Any related to the
mentally handicapped
BASIS: Awarded to a student whose
home residence is in the Kootenay
area of BC and who is pursuing
studies related to the mentally
handicapped.
MINIMUM AVERAGE: N/A
VALUE: $350.00
TERMS: One year only
NUMBER OF AWARDS: 1
DEADLINE FOR APPLICATIONS:
September 30

CODE: BC/LAC01/g
NAME: Langley Arts Council Fine
Arts Scholarship
SPONSOR: Langley Arts Council
ADDRESS: Box 3101, Langley, BC V3A
4R3
PROGRAM: Post-secondary programs,
workshops, and conferences
BASIS: Any person who is a Langley
resident or from a family living in
the Langley area can apply for cash
scholarships in the categories of
Music/Voice, Visual Arts, Drama/
Dance, Fibre Arts, Pottery/
Sculpture, and Creative Writing.
An application is required.
MINIMUM AVERAGE: N/A
VALUE: Varies
TERMS: Each scholarship must be for

a specific course, training program, workshop or conference.
NUMBER OF AWARDS: Varies
DEADLINE FOR APPLICATIONS: March 31

CODE: BC/LFAP01/g
NAME: La Foundation André Piolat Bourses
SPONSOR: Nicole Legault, Présidente, La Foundation André Piolat
ADDRESS: 1575 Fieme Ouest, Vancouver, BC V6J 1S1
PROGRAM: Any
BASIS: Applicants must be Canadian citizens graduating with French 12 or Français-Langue 12. The selection is based on competence and interest in French, and participation in and contribution to the French community.
MINIMUM AVERAGE: N/A
VALUE: $500.00
TERMS: One year only
NUMBER OF AWARDS: Varies
DEADLINE FOR APPLICATIONS: September 1

CODE: BC/LMGS01/g
NAME: Dr. L.M. Greene Scholarship
SPONSOR: Administrator, Prince Rupert Regional Hospital
ADDRESS: 1305 Summit Avenue, Prince Rupert, BC V8J 2A6
PROGRAM: Health-care programs
BASIS: Awarded to a former Prince Rupert Senior Secondary School student who is interested in pursuing a vocation in any of the health-care fields. An application is required.
MINIMUM AVERAGE: N/A
VALUE: $500.00
TERMS: One year only
NUMBER OF AWARDS: 1

CODE: BC/LTKF01/g
NAME: Leon and Thea Koerner Foundation Grants
SPONSOR: Secretary, UBC Grants-in-Aid Fund
ADDRESS: Leon and Thea Koerner Foundation, 735 Eyremount Drive, West Vancouver, BC V7S 2A3
PROGRAM: Various
BASIS: Awards are available for BC students at the pre-professional level pursuing non-academic programs and aiming at a professional career in the arts. Talent and financial need will be considered.
MINIMUM AVERAGE: N/A
VALUE: $600.00
TERMS: Grant amounts may vary from $200 to $600. Only for students studying outside of BC.
NUMBER OF AWARDS: Varies
DEADLINE FOR APPLICATIONS: September 15

CODE: BC/MDA01/g
NAME: Derek Saltzberg Memorial Bursary
SPONSOR: Muscular Dystrophy Association of Canada
ADDRESS: #123 – 1600 West 6th Ave, Vancouver, BC V6J 1R3
PROGRAM: Any
BASIS: Applicants must be residents of BC with muscular dystrophy and entering any full-time program. An application is required.
MINIMUM AVERAGE: N/A
VALUE: $500.00
TERMS: One year only
NUMBER OF AWARDS: 1
DEADLINE FOR APPLICATIONS: August 1

CODE: BC/MDA02/g
NAME: Kit Davison Bursary
SPONSOR: Muscular Dystrophy Association of Canada
ADDRESS: #123 – 1600 West 6th Avenue. Vancouver, BC V6J 1R3
PROGRAM: Any
BASIS: Applicants must be residents of BC with muscular dystrophy entering any full-time program. An application is required.
MINIMUM AVERAGE: N/A
VALUE: $600.00
TERMS: One year only
NUMBER OF AWARDS: 1
DEADLINE FOR APPLICATIONS: August 1

CODE: BC/MINED1/g
NAME: Provincial Scholarships
SPONSOR: Examinations Branch,
Ministry of Education
ADDRESS: Parliament Buildings,
Victoria, BC V8V 2M4
PROGRAM: Any
BASIS: Open to BC Grade 12 graduates
who write Scholarship
Examinations in at least 3 courses
and achieve a score of at least 475
on the best 3 exams. Candidates
must also receive a minimum of
70% on the English examiniation.
Not tenable with a District Schol-
arship.
MINIMUM AVERAGE: N/A
VALUE: $2000.00
TERMS: There will be 10 awards of
$2000. Other qualifying students
will receive $1000 each. Academic
medals of excellence will be given
to the top 3 students.
NUMBER OF AWARDS: Varies

CODE: BC/MINED2/g
NAME: District Scholarships
SPONSOR: Examinations Branch,
Ministry of Education
ADDRESS: Parliament Buildings,
Victoria, BC V8V 2M4
PROGRAM: Any
BASIS: Awarded to graduating Grade
12 BC students who have excelled
in fields other than academics. The
requirements will be decided by
the District Scholarship Committee.
MINIMUM AVERAGE: N/A
VALUE: $500.00
TERMS: One year only. Not tenable
with the Provinical Scholarships.
Recipients receive an additional
$500 if enrolling in a recognized
post-secondary institution.
NUMBER OF AWARDS: Varies

CODE: BC/MINED3/g
NAME: Passport to Education
SPONSOR: Examinations Branch,
Ministry of Education

ADDRESS: Parliament Buildings,
Victoria, BC V8V 2M4
PROGRAM: Any approved program
BASIS: Awarded for academic
achievement to the top 30% of
students in BC high schools.
Students may redeem these credits
at a bona-fide post-secondary
institution approved by the
Ministry of Advanced Education,
Training, and Technology.
MINIMUM AVERAGE: N/A
VALUE: $500.00
TERMS: Students may earn the
following tuition credits Grade 9,
$125; Grade 10, $175; Grade 11,
$225; Grade 12, $275.
NUMBER OF AWARDS: Varies

CODE: BC/MINED4/g
NAME: Provincial Examination
Scholarship Awards Scholarship
Supplement
SPONSOR: Examinations Branch,
Ministry of Education
ADDRESS: Parliament Buildings,
Victoria, BC V8V 2M4
PROGRAM: Any approved program
BASIS: For Grade 12 Provincial
Scholarship winners who must
relocate more than 50 km from
their permanent residence to attend
BC universities, colleges, or
institutes.
MINIMUM AVERAGE: N/A
VALUE: $1500.00
TERMS: One year only
NUMBER OF AWARDS: Varies

CODE: BC/MINED5/g
NAME: Grade 12 Performance
Recognition Award
SPONSOR: Examinations Branch,
Ministry of Education
ADDRESS: Parliament Buildings,
Victoria, BC V8V 2M4
PROGRAM: Any approved program
BASIS: For Grade 12 students who
write Provinical Scholarship exams
and achieve a level just below the

scholarship level, and who must relocate more than 50 km from their permanent residence to attend BC universities, colleges, or institutes.
MINIMUM AVERAGE: N/A
VALUE: $500.00
TERMS: One year only
NUMBER OF AWARDS: Varies

CODE: BC/MMMA01/g
NAME: Mungo Martin Memorial Award Society
SPONSOR: c/o Mrs V. Rossiter
ADDRESS: 1340 Ryan Street, Victoria, BC V8T 5A7
PROGRAM: Various
BASIS: Candidates for awards must be of Indian racial background and must live in BC at the time of application. These awards are open to those who seek to do creative work to further the artistic heritage of the Indian peoples.
MINIMUM AVERAGE: N/A
VALUE: $500.00
TERMS: Awards will range from $250–$500 at the discretion of the directors.
NUMBER OF AWARDS: Varies

CODE: BC/MNA01/g
NAME: First Citizens' Fund
SPONSOR: BC Ministry of Native Affairs, Program Officer
ADDRESS: Parliament Buildings, Victoria, BC V8V 1X4
PROGRAM: Any full-time programs of at least 2 years' length
BASIS: Applicants must be Status, Non-status or Métis who were born in BC and have resided in the province for at least 6 months prior to applying. Applicants must be recommended by a Band Council or bona-fide Native organization.
MINIMUM AVERAGE: 65.00
VALUE: $2000.00
TERMS: Renewable. Bursaries of up to $2000 per academic year are available for Non-status Indian

students and $700 per academic year for Status Indians.
NUMBER OF AWARDS: Varies
DEADLINE FOR APPLICATIONS: May 31

CODE: BC/MOH001/g
NAME: Native Health Bursary
SPONSOR: Financial Aid Office, Ministry of Health
ADDRESS: 3 – 1515 Blanchard Street, Victoria, BC V8W 3C8
PROGRAM: Health sciences-related programs
BASIS: Awarded to Native Indians residing in BC who are enrolled in health-care programs in recognized post-secondary educational facilities. A recommendation must be obtained from a Band Council, Friendship Centre, or other recognized native organization.
MINIMUM AVERAGE: N/A
VALUE: Varies
TERMS: Renewable
NUMBER OF AWARDS: Varies

CODE: BC/MTCC01/g
NAME: MTC College of Business Scholarship
SPONSOR: MTC Scholarship Competition, MTC College Head Office
ADDRESS: #202, 60 8th Street, New Westminister, BC V3M 3P1
PROGRAM: Any
BASIS: An application is required.
MINIMUM AVERAGE: 3.00
VALUE: $5000.00
TERMS: Amount of award may vary. The scholarships cover any full-time diploma program of the recipient's choice.
NUMBER OF AWARDS: 3
DEADLINE FOR APPLICATIONS: April 1

CODE: BC/NGR001/g
NAME: Nancy Greene Scholarships
SPONSOR: Athlete Assistance Coordinator, Recreation and Sport Branch
ADDRESS: Ministry of Provincial

Secretary, 1200 Hornby Street, Vancouver, BC V6Z 2E2
PROGRAM: Any
BASIS: Awarded to students who combine athletic and academic achievement, leadership, and participation in school and community affairs. Applicants must be graduates of a BC senior secondary school. An application is required.
MINIMUM AVERAGE: N/A
VALUE: $1000.00
TERMS: One year only
NUMBER OF AWARDS: 26
DEADLINE FOR APPLICATIONS: May 1

CODE: BC/OFA01/g
NAME: Fairbridge Society Bursaries
SPONSOR: Secretary/Treasurer, Old Fairbridgians' Association
ADDRESS: 166 East Pender Street, Vancouver, BC
PROGRAM: Any
BASIS: Awarded to children of former members of the Prince of Wales Fairbridge School, Duncan BC.
MINIMUM AVERAGE: N/A
VALUE: $500.00
TERMS: One year only
NUMBER OF AWARDS: Varies

CODE: BC/PAA01/g
NAME: Premier's Athletic Awards
SPONSOR: Minister of Tourism, Recreation and Culture
ADDRESS: 1200 Hornby Street, Vancouver, BC V6Z 2E2
PROGRAM: Any post-secondary program in BC
BASIS: Awarded to BC athletes who train and compete in BC and who are ranked in the top 8 in the world in an Olympic event or who are members of a Canadian team ranked in the top 4 in an Olympic sport. An application is required.
MINIMUM AVERAGE: N/A
VALUE: $2500.00
TERMS: Renewable
NUMBER OF AWARDS: Varies
DEADLINE FOR APPLICATIONS: March 1

CODE: BC/PACE01/g
NAME: Pacific Association for Continuing Education Bursary
SPONSOR: c/o Dr Lawrence Fast, Vancouver Community College
ADDRESS: 1155 East Broadway, P.O. Box 24785, Station C, Vancouver, BC V5T 4N5
PROGRAM: Part-time programs
BASIS: Awarded to part-time or short-term students who are residents of BC and can demonstrate financial need.
MINIMUM AVERAGE: N/A
VALUE: $100.00
TERMS: One year only. Value of awards may vary.
NUMBER OF AWARDS: Varies

CODE: BC/PC4-H1/g
NAME: Petro-Canada 4-H Youth Leadership Award
SPONSOR: 4-H Supervisor, Rural Organizations Branch
ADDRESS: BC Ministry of Agriculture and Fisheries, 101 – 3547 Skaha Lake Road, Penticton, BC V2A 7K2
PROGRAM: Any post-secondary program
BASIS: Awarded to students who have been in 4-H for at least 2 years and are current members. Community service and leadership will be considered. A 500-word biographical essay that documents community leadership is required.
MINIMUM AVERAGE: N/A
VALUE: $1000.00
TERMS: Awards are to be used for tuition, books, and lodging.
NUMBER OF AWARDS: 2
DEADLINE FOR APPLICATIONS: April 30

CODE: BC/PCN01/g
NAME: Plateau Chapter of Nurses Award
SPONSOR: Chairman, Bursary Committee, RNABC Plateau Chapter
ADDRESS: Box 1404, Comox, BC V9N 7Z9

PROGRAM: Nursing
BASIS: Applicants must be Grade 12 graduates from the Comox Valley.
MINIMUM AVERAGE: N/A
VALUE: $250.00
TERMS: One year only
NUMBER OF AWARDS: 1
DEADLINE FOR APPLICATIONS: May 1

CODE: BC/PPCU01/g
NAME: Pacific Press Credit Union Memorial Scholarship
SPONSOR: Trustee, Pacific Press Credit Union Memorial Scholarship
ADDRESS: 2250 Granville Street, Vancouver, BC V6H 3G2
PROGRAM: Any post-secondary program
BASIS: Any student entering the 1st year of a post-secondary program whose parents and/or legal guardians are members of the Pacific Press Credit Union may apply.
MINIMUM AVERAGE: N/A
VALUE: $
TERMS: One year only
NUMBER OF AWARDS: 1

CODE: BC/PRRH01/g
NAME: Dr. R.G. Large Scholarship
SPONSOR: Office of the Administrator, Prince Rupert Regional Hospital
ADDRESS: 1305 Summit Avenue, Prince Rupert, BC V8J 2A6
PROGRAM: Nursing or Health Care
BASIS: Applicants must be graduates of Prince Rupert Senior Secondary School who are entering nursing or a health-care program.
MINIMUM AVERAGE: N/A
VALUE: $500.00
TERMS: One year only
NUMBER OF AWARDS: 2
DEADLINE FOR APPLICATIONS: June 30

CODE: BC/PTE01/g
NAME: Public Trustee Educational Assistance Fund
SPONSOR: Office of the Public Trustee, Educational Assistance Fund

ADDRESS: #600 – 808 West Hastings, Vancouver, BC V6C 9Z9
PROGRAM: Any post-secondary program
BASIS: Awarded to former permanent wards of the Superintendent of Family and Child Service of BC. Applicants must be enrolled in a post-secondary institution in BC and must provide a financial statement, recent transcript, and an outline of goals.
MINIMUM AVERAGE: N/A
VALUE: $2500.00
TERMS: Renewable. Awards are intended to help cover tuition fees, books, and transportation costs.
NUMBER OF AWARDS: Varies
DEADLINE FOR APPLICATIONS: April 1

CODE: BC/PVPA01/g
NAME: BC Principals' and Vice-Principals' Association Scholarships
SPONSOR: Scholarships, c/o BCPVPA
ADDRESS: Suite 1550 – 1185 West Georgia, Vancouver, BC V6E 4E6
PROGRAM: Any
BASIS: Awarded to students graduating in June from the BC public-education system and proceeding to post-secondary studies. Awarded on the basis of academic ability and leadership potential. Two awards are reserved for the sons and daughters of BCPVPA members.
MINIMUM AVERAGE: N/A
VALUE: $500.00
TERMS: One year only
NUMBER OF AWARDS: 12
DEADLINE FOR APPLICATIONS: September 15

CODE: BC/RAM01/g
NAME: Royal Arch Masons of British Columbia Award(s)
SPONSOR: Office of the Grand Chapter of Royal Arch Masons of BC and Yukon

ADDRESS: #104 – 1495 West 8th Avenue, Vancouver, BC V6H 1C9
PROGRAM: Any full-time program in BC
BASIS: Applicants must be children of members in good standing or deceased members of Chapters of the Order in BC or the Yukon. Financial need and academic achievement will be considered.
MINIMUM AVERAGE: N/A
VALUE: $500.00
TERMS: Renewable
NUMBER OF AWARDS: Varies
DEADLINE FOR APPLICATIONS: July 15

CODE: BC/RBM01/g
NAME: Robert Borsos Memorial Award
SPONSOR: Mary Borsos, c/o The Robert Borsos Memorial Fund
ADDRESS: R.R. # 1, Mayne Island, BC V0N 2J0
PROGRAM: Art
BASIS: Awarded to a graduate of the Gulf Island School District (includes graduates from 1987 onward) who has been accepted to an art school or college. Applications are to be one or more handwritten pages in length, detailing educational goals and financial need.
MINIMUM AVERAGE: N/A
VALUE: $500.00
TERMS: One year only
NUMBER OF AWARDS: 1
DEADLINE FOR APPLICATIONS: June 25

CODE: BC/RCL001/g
NAME: Royal Canadian Legion Branch #4 (Chilliwack) Bursaries
SPONSOR: Bursary Chairman, Royal Canadian Legion Branch #4 Office
ADDRESS: 9359 Mary Street, Chilliwack, BC V2P 4H1
PROGRAM: Any post-secondary program
BASIS: Awarded to sons or daughters of veterans killed in action, or deceased, disabled, or other veterans who are enrolling in a post-secondary institution. The award is based on achievement, need, and merit. An application is required.
MINIMUM AVERAGE: N/A
VALUE: $500.00
TERMS: One year only
NUMBER OF AWARDS: 3
DEADLINE FOR APPLICATIONS: May 15

CODE: BC/RCL002/g
NAME: Royal Canadian Legion Branch #4 (Chilliwack) Ladies Auxiliary Bursaries
SPONSOR: Bursary Chairman, Royal Canadian Legion Branch #4 Office
ADDRESS: 9359 Mary Street, Chilliwack, BC V2P 4H1
PROGRAM: Any post-secondary program
BASIS: Awarded to sons or daughters of veterans killed in action, or deceased, disabled, or other veterans who are enrolling in a post-secondary institution. The award is based on achievement, need, and merit. An application is required.
MINIMUM AVERAGE: N/A
VALUE: $500.00
TERMS: One year only
NUMBER OF AWARDS: 3
DEADLINE FOR APPLICATIONS: May 15

CODE: BC/RCL003/g
NAME: Royal Canadian Legion, Ladies Auxiliary, Branch 160, Bursary
SPONSOR: Secretary, Ladies Auxiliary, Royal Canadian Legion Branch 160
ADDRESS: 1825 Comox Avenue, Comox, BC V9N 4A3
PROGRAM: Any post-secondary program
BASIS: Available to students who attended high school in, or are residents of, the Comox Valley.
MINIMUM AVERAGE: N/A
VALUE: $500.00
TERMS: One year only
NUMBER OF AWARDS: 1
DEADLINE FOR APPLICATIONS: May 1

CODE: BC/RCL004/g
NAME: Frank Morris / Royal Canadian Legion Branch #13
SPONSOR: Branch #13, Royal Canadian Legion
ADDRESS: 4425 Legion Avenue, Terrace, BC V8G 1N7
PROGRAM: Any
BASIS: Awarded on the basis of scholastic ability and character to students from Terrace, BC entering any post-secondary program. Candidates must be related to Canadian Armed Forces veterans.
MINIMUM AVERAGE: N/A
VALUE: Varies
TERMS: One year only
NUMBER OF AWARDS: Varies
DEADLINE FOR APPLICATIONS: June 15

CODE: BC/RCLPC1/g
NAME: Royal Canadian Legion (Pacific Command) Awards
SPONSOR: Pacific Command, Royal Canadian Legion
ADDRESS: 3026 Arbutus Street, Vancouver, BC V6J 4P7
PROGRAM: Any post-secondary program
BASIS: Awarded to students in any year of a post-secondary program. Although others will be considered, preference is given to descendant children and the grandchildren of deceased, disabled, or other veterans.
MINIMUM AVERAGE: N/A
VALUE: Varies from $700 to $1300.
TERMS: Renewable
NUMBER OF AWARDS: Varies
DEADLINE FOR APPLICATIONS: May 31

CODE: BC/RCMP01/g
NAME: RCMP Veterans' Auxiliary Bursary
SPONSOR: Secretary, Women's Auxiliary
ADDRESS: 414 Valiant Drive, R.R. #3, S.13, C.8, Penticton, BC V2A 7K8

PROGRAM: Any post-secondary program
BASIS: Applicants must reside within the boundaries of the Okanagan Division of the RCMP Veteran's Association and have a parent, grandparent, or guardian who is a serving member of the RCMP or RCMP veteran. Financial need will be considered.
MINIMUM AVERAGE: N/A
VALUE: $300.00
TERMS: May be renewed.
NUMBER OF AWARDS: 2
DEADLINE FOR APPLICATIONS: July 15

CODE: BC/RIHF01/g
NAME: Royal Inland Hospital Foundation Award(s)
SPONSOR: Royal Inland Hospital Foundation
ADDRESS: 311 Columbus Street, Kamloops, BC V2C 2T1
PROGRAM: Health Sciences
BASIS: Applicants must have completed Grade 12 while residing in the Thompson Nicola District. Preference will be given to students planning to return to the Royal Inland Hospital area to practice. Scholastic achievement and community service will be considered.
MINIMUM AVERAGE: N/A
VALUE: $1000.00
TERMS: One year only
NUMBER OF AWARDS: 1
DEADLINE FOR APPLICATIONS: April 15

CODE: BC/RNF01/g
NAME: Registered Nurses Foundation of BC Bursaries
SPONSOR: Registered Nurses Foundation of BC
ADDRESS: 2855 Arbutus Street, Vancouver, BC V6J 3Y8
PROGRAM: Nursing programs
BASIS: Awarded to students who are accepted into or enrolled in various nursing programs.
MINIMUM AVERAGE: N/A
VALUE: $1000.00

TERMS: Bursaries vary in value from $300 to $1000.
NUMBER OF AWARDS: 25
DEADLINE FOR APPLICATIONS: September 15

CODE: BC/SCB01/g
NAME: Sunshine Coast Bursary
SPONSOR: Sunshine Coast Bursary and Loan Society, c/o Miss June Wilson
ADDRESS: R.R. #1, Sechelt, BC V0N 3A0
PROGRAM: Any
BASIS: Awarded to a student from the Sunshine Coast School District.
MINIMUM AVERAGE: N/A
VALUE: $500.00
TERMS: One year only
NUMBER OF AWARDS: 1

CODE: BC/SITP01/g
NAME: Soroptimist International Training Awards Program
SPONSOR: Soroptomist International of the Americas
ADDRESS: c/o Judith Hunt, 2511 West 21st Avenue, Vancouver, BC V6L 1K2
PROGRAM: Minimum of 60% of a full course load
BASIS: Applicants must be mature female stuents from Burnaby or Vancouver who are heads of households and are pursuing education to enter or return to the job market or upgrade their employment status. Financial need and goals will be considered.
MINIMUM AVERAGE: N/A
VALUE: $1500.00
TERMS: The total money available for all awards is $1500.
NUMBER OF AWARDS: Varies
DEADLINE FOR APPLICATIONS: December 15

CODE: BC/SLIPY1/g
NAME: Cardinal Josyf Slipyj Ukrainian Scholarship
SPONSOR: President, The Cardinal Josyf Slipyj Ukrainian Studies

ADDRESS: Scholarship Society, 3277 Douglas Street, Victoria, BC V8Z 3K9
PROGRAM: Ukrainian Studies
BASIS: Candidates must be enrolling in at least one course of Ukrainian Studies. The selection is based on scholastic record and financial need. Preference will be shown to BC residents. An application is required.
MINIMUM AVERAGE: N/A
VALUE: $500.00
TERMS: One year only
NUMBER OF AWARDS: Varies
DEADLINE FOR APPLICATIONS: May 30

CODE: BC/SLS001/g
NAME: Neil Libby Bursaries
SPONSOR: St Leonard's Society of Canada, c/o Excecutive Director
ADDRESS: St Leonard's North Shore, 312 Bewick Avenue, North Vancouver, BC V7M 3B7
PROGRAM: Various
BASIS: Awarded to ex-offenders who plan to take post-secondary training or job or trades training.
MINIMUM AVERAGE: N/A
VALUE: $500.00
TERMS: One year only
NUMBER OF AWARDS: 2

CODE: BC/SOR01/g
NAME: Soroptimist Youth Citizenship Awards
SPONSOR: Soroptimist Club
ADDRESS: Box 513, Abbotsford, BC V2S 5Z5
PROGRAM: Any
BASIS: Awarded to a Grade 12 graduate not over the age of 21 in recognition of service, dependability, leadership, and a clear sense of purpose.
MINIMUM AVERAGE: N/A
VALUE: $500.00
TERMS: One year only
NUMBER OF AWARDS: 1
DEADLINE FOR APPLICATIONS: December 15

CODE: BC/SPACS1/g
NAME: C.C. Thomas Scholarship
SPONSOR: Scholarship Chairman, Saanich Peninsula Arts and Crafts Society
ADDRESS: Box 2542, Sidney, BC V8L 4B9
PROGRAM: Visual arts at any BC college or university
BASIS: Awarded to students studying visual arts in a post-secondary institution. A representitive sample of work must be made available for consideration by a jury of SPAC members.
MINIMUM AVERAGE: N/A
VALUE: $500.00
TERMS: One year only
NUMBER OF AWARDS: Varies
DEADLINE FOR APPLICATIONS: January 1

CODE: BC/SPARK1/g
NAME: S.P.A.R.K.S. Scholarship
SPONSOR: City of Kamloops, Recreation and Culture Division
ADDRESS: 611A Lansdowne Street, Kamloops, BC V2C 1Y6
PROGRAM: Any post-secondary program
BASIS: Awarded to a City of Kamloops high school graduate who has participated actively in the community. Proof of registration is required with the application.
MINIMUM AVERAGE: N/A
VALUE: $250.00
TERMS: One year only
NUMBER OF AWARDS: 1
DEADLINE FOR APPLICATIONS: June 15

CODE: BC/SPEN01/g
NAME: Chris Spencer Foundation Scholarship
SPONSOR: Chris Spencer Foundation
ADDRESS: 808 – 1550 Alberni Street, Vancouver, BC V6G 1A5
PROGRAM: Any at UBC, U of Vic. or Simon Fraser U
BASIS: Applicants must be Canadian citizens who have lived in BC for

at least 9 months prior to applying. The selection is based on a demonstrated concern for others and participation in school and/or community affairs.
MINIMUM AVERAGE: 80.00
VALUE: $8000.00
TERMS: Renewable
NUMBER OF AWARDS: 2
DEADLINE FOR APPLICATIONS: May 31

CODE: BC/SSA01/g
NAME: Pam Koczapska Memorial Award
SPONSOR: Sto:lo Sitel Advisory Committee
ADDRESS: Coqualeetza Centre, Box 370, Sardis, BC V2R 1A7
PROGRAM: Any professional field
BASIS: Eligible students are those who are planning a career in education or any professional career that may benefit the Sto:lo people. Academic achievement, leadership qualities, and community service will be considered. A transcript is also required.
MINIMUM AVERAGE: N/A
VALUE: $1000.00
TERMS: One year only
NUMBER OF AWARDS: Varies

CODE: BC/SSD01/g
NAME: Assistance Program for Students with Severe Disabilities
SPONSOR: Student Services Branch, Ministry of Advanced Education
ADDRESS: Training and Technology, 2nd Floor, 16606 Cook Street, Victoria, BC V8V 3Z9
PROGRAM: Any post-secondary program
BASIS: This program may provide financial assistance to severely disabled students to cover the costs of goods and/or services needed to allow access to further education.
MINIMUM AVERAGE: N/A
VALUE: $10,000.00
TERMS: One year only

NUMBER OF AWARDS: Varies
DEADLINE FOR APPLICATIONS: August 1

CODE: BC/SSGBA1/g
NAME: BC Secondary School Girls'
Basketball Association Scholarship
SPONSOR: Steve Pettifer
ADDRESS: Centennial School, 570
Poirier Street, Coquitlam, BC V3J
6A8
PROGRAM: Any recognized post-
secondary program in BC
BASIS: Awarded on the basis of good
citizenship, character, leadership,
and basketball ability.
MINIMUM AVERAGE: 65.00
VALUE: Varies
TERMS: One year only
NUMBER OF AWARDS: Varies

CODE: BC/SSTF01/g
NAME: BCSSTFCCA Scholarship
SPONSOR: Mr Bill McNulty
ADDRESS: 1975 West 49th Avenue,
Vancouver, BC V6M 2T1
PROGRAM: Any post-secondary
program
BASIS: Applicants must be a member
of a team affiliated with the BC
Secondary School Track and Field
and Cross Country Association.
Proficiency in track and field or
cross country, good citizenship,
character, and leadership will be
considered.
MINIMUM AVERAGE: 65.00
VALUE: $250.00
TERMS: One year only
NUMBER OF AWARDS: 1

CODE: BC/STF01/g
NAME: Post-secondary Education
Assistance to Status First Nations
People
SPONSOR: Theresa Neel, Post-
secondary Indian Education
Counsellor
ADDRESS: Chilliwack Area Indian
Council, Box 73, Sardis, BC V2R
1A5

PROGRAM: Any post-secondary
program
BASIS: Awarded to Inuit or registered
Native Indian students enrolled or
accepted for enrolment in a full
program of studies at a post-
secondary institution. Applicants
must submit document proof of
status and acceptance into a post-
secondary program.
MINIMUM AVERAGE: N/A
VALUE: Varies
TERMS: Renewable
NUMBER OF AWARDS: Varies
DEADLINE FOR APPLICATIONS: June 15

CODE: BC/STJA01/g
NAME: St John Ambulance Bursaries
SPONSOR: Secretary, Bursary
Committee, St John Ambulance
ADDRESS: 6111 Cambie Street,
Vancouver, BC V5Z 3B2
PROGRAM: Nursing
BASIS: Awarded to student nurse ap-
plicants entering full-time diploma
programs. An application is re-
quired.
MINIMUM AVERAGE: N/A
VALUE: Varies
TERMS: Recipients may re-apply each
year.
NUMBER OF AWARDS: Varies
DEADLINE FOR APPLICATIONS: March 15

CODE: BC/TCDV01/g
NAME: Tubers and Chlerotic
Descendants Award
SPONSOR: Project Director
ADDRESS: 5 – 5740 Garrison Rd.,
Richmond, BC V7C 5E7
PROGRAM: Any
BASIS: Children and grandchildren of
people with tubers
MINIMUM AVERAGE: 90%
VALUE: N/A
TERMS: One year only
NUMBER OF AWARDS: 1

CODE: BC/VANF01/g
NAME: Vancouver Foundation –
Advanced Arts Study Awards
SPONSOR: Registrar, Vancouver
Academy of Music
ADDRESS: 1270 Chestnut Street,
Vancouver, BC V6J 4R9
PROGRAM: Music, Dance, or Theatre
BASIS: Awarded to students entering
an advanced-level program to
study music, dance, or theatre.
Applicants must be BC residents
and Canadian citizens or landed
immigrants.
MINIMUM AVERAGE: N/A
VALUE: $5000.00
TERMS: Amounts may vary. Recipients
may reapply.
NUMBER OF AWARDS: 15
DEADLINE FOR APPLICATIONS: May 31

CODE: BC/VSUN01/g
NAME: Vancouver Sun Scholarship for
Sun Carriers
SPONSOR: Office of Awards and
Financial Aid
ADDRESS: Brock Hall, University of
British Columbia, #1036 – 1874
East Mall, Vancouver, BC V6T
1Z1
PROGRAM: Any
BASIS: Awarded to students pro-
ceeding from Grade 12 to 1st year
at various universities in British
Columbia. To be eligible, applicants
must have been carriers of the
Vancouver Sun for at least 2 con-
secutive years. A service certificate
and application are required.
MINIMUM AVERAGE: 75.00
VALUE: $500.00
TERMS: Renewable for up to a total of
5 payments in all provided recip-
ients maintain an average of 75%
or rank in the top 10% of their year
and faculty.
NUMBER OF AWARDS: 2

CODE: BC/VSUN02/g
NAME: Vancouver Sun Special
Scholarship for Sun Carriers

SPONSOR: Officer of Awards and
Financial Aid, Brock Hall
ADDRESS: University of British
Columiba, #1036 – 1874 East Mall,
Vancouver, BC V6T 1Z1
PROGRAM: Any
BASIS: Awarded to a student proceed-
ing from Grade 12 to 1st year at
various universities in British
Columbia on the basis of extra-
curricular activities, community
service, academic achievement, and
service as a Vancouver Sun carrier.
An application is required.
MINIMUM AVERAGE: 75.00
VALUE: $500.00
TERMS: Renewable for up to a total of
5 payments in all provided
recipients maintain an average of
75% or rank in the top 10% of their
year and faculty.
NUMBER OF AWARDS: 1

CODE: BC/WAOC01/g
NAME: War Amputations of Canada,
Vancouver Branch, Bursaries
SPONSOR: Manager, War Amputations
Association of Canada
ADDRESS: 1431 West Broadway,
Vancouver, BC
PROGRAM: Any full-time program
BASIS: Awarded to the children of
active members of the Branch who
are taking a full-time course of
study beyond the Grade 12 level at
a recognized institution of learning.
Recent transcripts must be
included with the application.
MINIMUM AVERAGE: N/A
VALUE: $250.00
TERMS: One year only
NUMBER OF AWARDS: 20

CODE: BC/YBS001g
NAME: Youth Bowling Congress
Scholarship
SPONSOR: Zone Representative, Youth
Bowling Congress, c/o Principal
ADDRESS: Kitsilano Secondary School,
2550 West 10th Avenue,
Vancouver, BC V6K 2J6

PROGRAM: Any post-secondary program
BASIS: Applicants must be a regular member of a Youth Bowling Council Bowling with a recognized average based on a minimum of 21 games. The application must include 3 letters of reference. Academic achievement, leadership, and proficiency in bowling are considered.
MINIMUM AVERAGE: N/A
VALUE: Varies
TERMS: One year only
NUMBER OF AWARDS: Varies
DEADLINE FOR APPLICATIONS: April 30

CODE: BC/YMCA01/g
NAME: Adele Peet YMCA Memorial Bursary Award
SPONSOR: Chairman, Adele Peet YMCA Memorial Bursary Committee
ADDRESS: South Slope Family YMCA, 282 West 49th Avenue, Vancouver, BC V5Y 2Z5
PROGRAM: Nursing
BASIS: Applicants must be residents of the lower mainland of BC. Financial need and academic achievement will be considered.
MINIMUM AVERAGE: N/A
VALUE: $450.00
TERMS: One year only
NUMBER OF AWARDS: 1
DEADLINE FOR APPLICATIONS: October 31

CODE: BC/YMCA02/g
NAME: Hugh Christie Memorial Bursary
SPONSOR: Chairman, Hugh Christie Memorial Bursary, South Slope Family YMCA
ADDRESS: 282 West 49th Avenue, Vancouver, BC V5Y 2Z5
PROGRAM: Various
BASIS: Applicants must be planning to pursue a career in corrections, international development, social work, criminology, or YM-YWCA.

A written application and letters of reference are required.
MINIMUM AVERAGE: N/A
VALUE: $500.00
TERMS: One year only
NUMBER OF AWARDS: 1

CODE: BC/YMCA03/g
NAME: Ellen Bell Memorial Scholarship
SPONSOR: Ellen Bell YMCA Memorial Scholarship Committee
ADDRESS: YMCA of Greater Vancouver, 955 Burrard Street, Vancouver, BC V6Z 1Y2
PROGRAM: Any
BASIS: Awarded to a student who demonstrates exemplary community service. Applications must include letter(s) of reference and a short letter explaining the reason for applying.
MINIMUM AVERAGE: N/A
VALUE: $300.00
TERMS: One year only
NUMBER OF AWARDS: 1
DEADLINE FOR APPLICATIONS: March 1

CODE: BC/YT/SVI1/g
NAME: Society of Vocational Instructors of BC/Yukon Bursary
SPONSOR: Society of Vocational Instructors, c/o Bud Hallock
ADDRESS: Northwest Community College, 5331 McConnell Ave., Terrace, BC V8G 4C2
PROGRAM: Vocational programs
BASIS: Awarded to a full-time student in a vocational program at each institute that is an institutional member of the society. Recipients will be selected on the the the basis of demonstrated financial need and academic performance.
MINIMUM AVERAGE: N/A
VALUE: $100.00
TERMS: One year only
NUMBER OF AWARDS: 1

MANITOBA

CODE: MB/AGR01/g
NAME: Manitoba Agriculture Youth
Section Scholarships
SPONSOR: Manitoba Agriculture Youth
Section
ADDRESS: 810 – 401 York Avenue,
Winnipeg, Manitoba R3C 0P8
PROGRAM: Any
BASIS: N/A
MINIMUM AVERAGE: N/A
VALUE: $1000.00
TERMS: One year only
NUMBER OF AWARDS: 2

CODE: MB/CPP01/g
NAME: Canada Pension Plan
SPONSOR: CPP
ADDRESS: 153 11th Street, Brandon,
Manitoba R7A 4J5
PROGRAM: Any full-time university or
college program
BASIS: Available to the son/daughter
of parent/parents who are de-
ceased or disabled. Recipients must
be between 18 and 25.
MINIMUM AVERAGE: N/A
VALUE: $113.14 (awarded monthly)
TERMS: Renewable
NUMBER OF AWARDS: N/A

CODE: MB/DCS01/g
NAME: Vocational Rehabilitation
Program
SPONSOR: Department of Community
Services
ADDRESS: Provincial Building, The
Pas, Manitoba R9A 1M4
PROGRAM: Various
BASIS: Students who have certain
physical disabilities or other
handicaps may qualify for special
training consideration.
MINIMUM AVERAGE: N/A
VALUE: Varies
TERMS: Renewable
NUMBER OF AWARDS: Varies

CODE: MB/DVA01/g
NAME: Children of the War Dead
(Education Assistance) Act
SPONSOR: Department of Veteran
Affairs
ADDRESS: 169 Pioneer Avenue,
Winnipeg, Manitoba R3C 0H3
PROGRAM: Any post-secondary
program
BASIS: Awarded to children of
veterans whose deaths are attrib-
utable to military service.
MINIMUM AVERAGE: N/A
VALUE: Varies
TERMS: Tuiton fees and a monthly
allowance.
NUMBER OF AWARDS: Varies

CODE: MB/HYDR01/g
NAME: Employment Equity Bursaries
SPONSOR: Manitoba Hydro
ADDRESS: P.O. Box 815, Winnipeg,
Manitoba R3C 4Z4
PROGRAM: Technology or Engineer-
ing
BASIS: Eligible applicants must be
women, persons of Aboriginal
ancestry, persons from visible
minorities, or persons with a
physical or mental disability. Eli-
gible institutions include the U of
Manitoba and the Red River and
Assiniboine Community Colleges.
MINIMUM AVERAGE: N/A
VALUE: $600.00
TERMS: One year only. Awards to be
applied to tuition and books.
Recipients also get first option on a
summer job.
NUMBER OF AWARDS: Varies
DEADLINE FOR APPLICATIONS: June 30

CODE: MB/HYDR02/g
NAME: Marie Stanson Memorial
Scholarship

SPONSOR: Manitoba Hydro
ADDRESS: P.O. Box 815, Winnipeg,
Manitoba R3C 4Z4
PROGRAM: Engineering
BASIS: Awarded to a female student
entering an engineering program.
MINIMUM AVERAGE: N/A
VALUE: $600.00
TERMS: One year only. Award may include the offer of summer employment.
NUMBER OF AWARDS: 1
DEADLINE FOR APPLICATIONS: June 30

CODE: MB/HYDR03/g
NAME: Engineering Entrance
Scholarships
SPONSOR: Manitoba Hydro
ADDRESS: P.O. Box 815, Winnipeg,
Manitoba R3C 4Z4
PROGRAM: Engineering
BASIS: Awarded to a student entering
an engineering program. The $2300
award goes to a student from
Northern Manitoba, the $2100 to a
rural Manitoba student, and $1800
to a student from Winnipeg.
MINIMUM AVERAGE: N/A
VALUE: $2300.00
TERMS: One year only. Award may
include the offer of summer
employment. See "BASIS" above.
NUMBER OF AWARDS: 1
DEADLINE FOR APPLICATIONS: June 30

CODE: MB/MACLD1/g
NAME: Manitoba Association for
Children with Learning Disabilities
Annual Award
SPONSOR: Manitoba Association for
Children with Learning Disabilities
ADDRESS: 5 – 1070 Clifton Street,
Winnipeg, Manitoba R3E 2T7
PROGRAM: Learning-disability field
BASIS: Awarded to students pursuing
studies in the learning-disability
field. An application is required.
MINIMUM AVERAGE: N/A
VALUE: Varies
TERMS: Renewable
NUMBER OF AWARDS: Varies

CODE: MB/MARN01/g
NAME: Manitoba Association of
Registered Nurses Scholarships
SPONSOR: Manitoba Association of
Nurses
ADDRESS: 647 Broadway, Winnipeg,
Manitoba R3C 0X2
PROGRAM: Nursing
BASIS: Awarded to Manitoba residents
entering a recognized nursing program.
MINIMUM AVERAGE: N/A
VALUE: $500.00
TERMS: One year only
NUMBER OF AWARDS: 1

CODE: MB/MBC01/g
NAME: Manitoba Blue Cross Entrance
Scholarship
SPONSOR: Manitoba Blue Cross
ADDRESS: 1430 Victoria Avenue E.,
Brandon, Manitoba R2A 2A5
PROGRAM: Any post-secondary
program
BASIS: Awarded to Grade 12 students
coming directly into college or
university. The selection is based
on need and academic ability. Candidates should apply directly to
the post-secondary institution.
MINIMUM AVERAGE: N/A
VALUE: $500.00
TERMS: One year only
NUMBER OF AWARDS: Varies
DEADLINE FOR APPLICATIONS: June 1

CODE: MB/MBC02/g
NAME: Manitoba Blue Cross
Traveller's Award
SPONSOR: Manitoba Blue Cross
ADDRESS: 1430 Victoria Avenue E.,
Brandon, Manitoba R2A 2A5
PROGRAM: Any college or university
program
BASIS: Students graduating from
Grade 12, entering college or
university, and coming from
communities more than 100 km
away. The selection is based on
financial need and academic
ability. Apply directly to the post-secondary institution.

MINIMUM AVERAGE: N/A
VALUE: $500.00
TERMS: One year only
NUMBER OF AWARDS: Varies
DEADLINE FOR APPLICATIONS: June 1

CODE: MB/MBC03/g
NAME: Bursary for Students with Special Needs
SPONSOR: Manitoba Blue Cross
ADDRESS: 1430 Victoria Avenue E., Brandon, Manitoba R2A 2A5
PROGRAM: Any post-secondary program
BASIS: Awarded to students who have additional educational costs owing to their handicap. Candidates should apply directly to the post-secondary institutions. The selection is based on academic ability and financial need.
MINIMUM AVERAGE: N/A
VALUE: $500.00
TERMS: One year only
NUMBER OF AWARDS: Varies
DEADLINE FOR APPLICATIONS: June 1

CODE: MB/MFA01/g
NAME: Dr. Alan B. Beaven Scholarship
SPONSOR: Manitoba Forestry Association
ADDRESS: 900 Corydon Avenue, Winnipeg, Manitoba R3M 0Y4
PROGRAM: Forestry, Environmental Studies, or related program
BASIS: Applicants must have been born or raised in Manitoba. The application must include a letter of recommendation from the principal and an essay. Awarded on the basis of high school marks and/or financial need.
MINIMUM AVERAGE: N/A
VALUE: $500.00
TERMS: One year only
NUMBER OF AWARDS: Varies
DEADLINE FOR APPLICATIONS: July 31

CODE: MB/MHA01/g
NAME: Manitoba Hotel Association Scholarships
SPONSOR: Executive Assistant, Manitoba Hotel Association
ADDRESS: 1505 – 155 Carlton, Winnipeg, Manitoba R3C 3I I8
PROGRAM: Related to the hotel/ hospitality industry
BASIS: Applicants must be planning on a career in the hotel/hospitality industry.
MINIMUM AVERAGE: N/A
VALUE: $1000.00
TERMS: One year only
NUMBER OF AWARDS: 1

CODE: MB/MHSAA1/g
NAME: Manitoba High School Athletic Association Scholarships
SPONSOR: Manitoba High Schools Athletic Association
ADDRESS: 200 Main Street, Winnipeg, Manitoba R3C 4M2
PROGRAM: Any
BASIS: Applicants must be high school athletes in Manitoba.
MINIMUM AVERAGE: N/A
VALUE: $400.00
TERMS: One year only
NUMBER OF AWARDS: 4

CODE: MB/MTS001/g
NAME: Manitoba Teachers' Society Scholarships
SPONSOR: Manitoba Teachers' Society
ADDRESS: 191 Harcourt Street, Winnipeg, Manitoba R3J 3H2
PROGRAM: Education
BASIS: Awarded to full-time students in any recognized teacher-training institution in Manitoba leading to certification. An application is required.
MINIMUM AVERAGE: N/A
VALUE: $800.00
TERMS: One year only
NUMBER OF AWARDS: 5
DEADLINE FOR APPLICATIONS: May 1

CODE: MB/POW01/g
NAME: Prince of Wales / Princess Anne Bursaries

SPONSOR: Information Officer, Student Financial Assistance Branch
ADDRESS: Department of Education, 693 Taylor Avenue, Winnipeg, Manitoba R3M 3T9
PROGRAM: Any post-secondary program in Manitoba
BASIS: These bursaries are available to students of Native and Métis ancestry who are attending a post-secondary institution in Manitoba. Regular loan and bursary assistance may also be granted to these students.
MINIMUM AVERAGE: N/A
VALUE: $200.00
TERMS: One year only
NUMBER OF AWARDS: Varies

CODE: MB/PPMI01/g
NAME: Agents' Association Bursary
SPONSOR: Portage la Prairie Mutual Insurance Company
ADDRESS: c/o Awards Office, University of Winnipeg, 515 Portage Avenue, Winnipeg, Manitoba R3B 2E9
PROGRAM: Any at a university in Manitoba
BASIS: Awarded to students outside Greater Winnipeg entering a university in Manitoba.
MINIMUM AVERAGE: N/A
VALUE: $500.00
TERMS: The other bursary is worth $400.
NUMBER OF AWARDS: 2

CODE: MB/PRESS1/g
NAME: Press Radio Award
SPONSOR: Assiniboine Community College
ADDRESS: Student Assistance Centre, 1430 Victoria Avenue, Brandon, Manitoba R7A 2A9
PROGRAM: Any
BASIS: Awarded to students in 1- or 2-year programs or upgrading courses. Applicants must establish their financial need. The application deadline is the 1st Friday of every month.
MINIMUM AVERAGE: N/A
VALUE: $400.00
TERMS: Amounts vary according to need.
NUMBER OF AWARDS: Varies

CODE: MB/RCL01/g
NAME: Royal Canadian Legion Awards
SPONSOR: Brandon Office
ADDRESS: 560 13th Street E., Brandon, Manitoba R7A 5Z8
PROGRAM: Any post-secondary institutions
BASIS: Awarded to the children and grandchildren of veterans on the basis of academic standing and financial need.
MINIMUM AVERAGE: N/A
VALUE: Varies
TERMS: One year only
NUMBER OF AWARDS: Varies

CODE: MB/SOR01/g
NAME: Soroptimist Training Awards Program
SPONSOR: Peggy McKeen
ADDRESS: 12 Sykes Boulevard, Brandon, Manitoba R7B 0W6
PROGRAM: Any
BASIS: Awarded to mature women training to enter or re-enter the work force. Preference is given to applicants who are over 30 years of age.
MINIMUM AVERAGE: N/A
VALUE: $1500.00
TERMS: One year only
NUMBER OF AWARDS: Varies
DEADLINE FOR APPLICATIONS: March 26

CODE: MB/UAS01/g
NAME: Province of Manitoba University Athletic Awards
SPONSOR: University Director of Recreation and Athletic Services
ADDRESS: Each university in Manitoba manages this award.

PROGRAM: Any
BASIS: Full-time students who are graduates of high schools in Manitoba may be eligible for athletic awards funded by the Province of Manitoba if they participate in a national championship sport program sanctioned by the CIAU and the Great Plains Athletic Conference.
MINIMUM AVERAGE: N/A
VALUE: $1500.00
TERMS: Renewable
NUMBER OF AWARDS: N/A

NORTHWEST TERRITORIES

CODE: NT/ACNS01/g
NAME: Beverly and Oaminirjuao Caribou Management Scholarship Fund
SPONSOR: Association of Canadian Universities for Northern Studies
ADDRESS: 130 Albert Street, Suite 201, Ottawa, Ontario K1P 5G4
PROGRAM: Community college or university
BASIS: Awarded to Canadian citizens or permanent residents pursuing studies that will contribute to the understanding of the Barren Ground Caribou (and their habitat) in Canada. Preference is given to students who reside in a caribou-using community.
MINIMUM AVERAGE: N/A
VALUE: $1500.00
TERMS: Renewable
NUMBER OF AWARDS: 2
DEADLINE FOR APPLICATIONS: January 31

CODE: NT/DENT01/g
NAME: Dr. Don Tesar Memorial Dental Scholarship
SPONSOR: Ms. Erica Tesar
ADDRESS: Yellowknife Dental Clinic, Box 1140, Yellowknife, NT X1A 2N8
PROGRAM: Dentistry-related program
BASIS: Awarded to a NT resident who is accepted into or enrolled in any field of dentistry at a recognized college or university.
MINIMUM AVERAGE: N/A
VALUE: $1000.00
TERMS: Renewable
NUMBER OF AWARDS: 1

CODE: NT/DOH001/g
NAME: Health Bursary Program
SPONSOR: Human Resources Management, Department of Health
ADDRESS: 6th Floor, Centre Square Tower, 5022 49th Street, Box 1320, Yellowknife, NT X1A 2L9
PROGRAM: Various. The selection is based on proposed program.
BASIS: The selection is based on length of residence in NT, work history and references, length of program, and financial need. The need for trained people in the studies applied for will also be part of the selection process.
MINIMUM AVERAGE: N/A
VALUE: Varies
TERMS: This program pays for tuition and/or expenses for studies, depending on the student's financial need.
NUMBER OF AWARDS: Varies
DEADLINE FOR APPLICATIONS: May 1

CODE: NT/GNWT01/g
NAME: Igal Roth Memorial Scholarship
SPONSOR: Community Planning Division, Dept. of Municipal and Community Affairs

ADDRESS: Government of the Northwest Territories, Yellowknife, NT X1A 2L9
PROGRAM: University or college planning program
BASIS: Applicants must have been residents in the NT for at least 2 years and must submit proof of acceptance to an approved planning program as a full-time student.
MINIMUM AVERAGE: N/A
VALUE: $1000.00
TERMS: Renewable
NUMBER OF AWARDS: 3
DEADLINE FOR APPLICATIONS: August 1

CODE: NT/GNWT02/g
NAME: Grade 12 Scholarships
SPONSOR: Student Services, Department of Education
ADDRESS: Box 1320, Yellowknife, NT X1A 2L9
PROGRAM: Any approved full-time college or university program
BASIS: Recipients must have an 80% average in four Grade 12 five-credit courses (one of which must be Grade 12 English) taken at an NT high school.
MINIMUM AVERAGE: 80.00
VALUE: $500.00
TERMS: One year only
NUMBER OF AWARDS: Varies
DEADLINE FOR APPLICATIONS: June 1

CODE: NT/ICA01/g
NAME: Institute of Chartered Accountants of the NWT Scholarship
SPONSOR: Institute of Chartered Accountants
ADDRESS: P.O. Box 2433, Yellowknife, NT X1A 2P8
PROGRAM: University Commerce or Business Administration
BASIS: Awarded to an NT high school graduate entering university Commerce or Business Administration programs who are interested in entering the Chartered Accountancy profession.

MINIMUM AVERAGE: N/A
VALUE: $1000.00
TERMS: One year only
NUMBER OF AWARDS: 1
DEADLINE FOR APPLICATIONS: October 1

CODE: NT/NAPEG1/g
NAME: NAPEGG Scholarship
SPONSOR: Association of Professional Engineers, Geologists and Geophysists of the Northwest Territories
ADDRESS: Box 1962, Yellowknife, NT X1A 2P5
PROGRAM: Engineering, Geology, or Geophysics
BASIS: Awarded to a NT high school graduate entering or attending a full-time program at a Canadian university. Preference is given to highly motivated individuals with a strong academic background and demonstrated citizenship and leadership abilities.
MINIMUM AVERAGE: N/A
VALUE: $1000.00
TERMS: Renewable
NUMBER OF AWARDS: 1
DEADLINE FOR APPLICATIONS: September 30

CODE: NT/NML01/g
NAME: Nanisivik Mines Ltd Scholarships
SPONSOR: c/o Administration Superintendent
ADDRESS: Nanisivik, NT X0A 0X0
PROGRAM: Any
BASIS: Available to students who have lived in the Eastern Arctic (Baffin and Keewatin Regions). The selection is based on academic achievement, community service, leadership abilities, and length of residence in the NT.
MINIMUM AVERAGE: N/A
VALUE: $1000.00
TERMS: Renewable
NUMBER OF AWARDS: 2
DEADLINE FOR APPLICATIONS: June 30

CODE: NT/NTPC01/g
NAME: Northwest Territories Power Corporation Award
SPONSOR: Corporate Development
ADDRESS: NT Power Corporation, #402 – 5201 50th Avenue, Yellowknife, NT X1A 3S9
PROGRAM: Various
BASIS: Awarded to a NT high school graduate entering a post-secondary program that would provide the applicant with qualifications of some benefit to the Corporation.
MINIMUM AVERAGE: N/A
VALUE: $1000.00
TERMS: One year only
NUMBER OF AWARDS: 1
DEADLINE FOR APPLICATIONS: August 15

CODE: NT/NWA01/g
NAME: Native Women's Association of the NT Scholarship
SPONSOR: Native Women's Association of the NT
ADDRESS: P.O. Box 2321, Yellowknife, NT X1A 2P7
PROGRAM: Post-secondary studies
BASIS: Awarded to one First Nations woman and one Métis woman. Applicants should show a commitment to improving the situation of Aboriginal women either politically, culturally, economically, or otherwise.
MINIMUM AVERAGE: N/A
VALUE: $1500.00
TERMS: Renewable
NUMBER OF AWARDS: 2
DEADLINE FOR APPLICATIONS: July 31

CODE: NT/NWS01/g
NAME: NorthwesTel Scholarship
SPONSOR: Education Officer, Department of Education
ADDRESS: Government of the Northwest Territories, Yellowknife, NT X1A 2L9
PROGRAM: Any
BASIS: Applicants must have graduated from a NT high school within NorthwesTel's operating area. The selection is based on scholastic achievement.
MINIMUM AVERAGE: 70.00
VALUE: $500.00
TERMS: One year only
NUMBER OF AWARDS: 1

CODE: NT/NWTW01/g
NAME: NT Wildlife Federation's Louis Lemieux Scholarship
SPONSOR: Northwest Territories Wildlife Federation
ADDRESS: #3 – 4807 49th Street, Yellowknife, NT X1A 3T5
PROGRAM: Related to wildlife, environment, or conservation
BASIS: Awarded to a long-term resident of the NT currently residing in the NT. The selection is based on academic history and educational residency.
MINIMUM AVERAGE: N/A
VALUE: $1000.00
TERMS: Renewable
NUMBER OF AWARDS: 1
DEADLINE FOR APPLICATIONS: June 15

CODE: NT/SNFS01/g
NAME: Sport North Federation Scholarship
SPONSOR: Sport North Federation
ADDRESS: Box 336, Yellowknife, NT X1A 2N3
PROGRAM: Community college or university sports related
BASIS: Applicants must have completed at least one year of schooling in the NT and graduated from an NT secondary school. Candidates must be accepted into a program of phsyical education, sports administration, recreation, or sports sciences.
MINIMUM AVERAGE: N/A
VALUE: $1000.00
TERMS: One year only
NUMBER OF AWARDS: 5
DEADLINE FOR APPLICATIONS: September 30

CODE: NT/TTMF01/g
NAME: Ted Tindell Memorial
Scholarship
SPONSOR: Chairman, Ted Tindell
Memorial Scholarship Fund
ADDRESS: c/o P.O. Box 1375,
Yellowknife, NT X1A 2P1
PROGRAM: Any
BASIS: Awarded to Métis and Non-
status persons from the Northwest
Territories on the basis of academic
proficiency and financial need. An
application is required.
MINIMUM AVERAGE: N/A
VALUE: $1000.00
TERMS: One year only
NUMBER OF AWARDS: 5
DEADLINE FOR APPLICATIONS: March 8

CODE: NT/YACL01/g
NAME: Roeher Institute Bursaries
SPONSOR: Yellowknife Association for
Community Living
ADDRESS: P.O. Box 981, Yellowknife,
NT X1A 2N7
PROGRAM: Any full-time college
program
BASIS: Candidates must be recom-
mended by the Territorial Asso-
ciation of the Canadian Association
for Community Living.
MINIMUM AVERAGE: N/A
VALUE: $1000.00
TERMS: One year only
NUMBER OF AWARDS: Varies
DEADLINE FOR APPLICATIONS: July 1

CODE: NT/YDCC01/g
NAME: Yellowknife Direct Charge
Co-op Scholarship Awards
SPONSOR: Manager, Yellowknife
Direct Co-op
ADDRESS: 321 Old Airport Road,
Yellowknife, NT X1A 3T3
PROGRAM: Any
BASIS: Awarded on the basis of
demonstrated academic per-
formance, school and community
participation, and leadership
ability. Personal and school
references are required with the
application.
MINIMUM AVERAGE: N/A
VALUE: $1000.00
TERMS: One year only
NUMBER OF AWARDS: 4
DEADLINE FOR APPLICATIONS: July 15

CODE: NT/YT/BX1/g
NAME: Baxter Corporation Jean
Goodwill Scholarships
SPONSOR: Executive Director
ADDRESS: 55 Murray Street, 4th Floor,
Ottawa, Ontario K1N 5M3
PROGRAM: Nursing
BASIS: Available to Indian and Inuit
nursing students wishing to work
in the Northwest and Yukon Ter-
ritories after graduation.
MINIMUM AVERAGE: N/A
VALUE: $5000.00
TERMS: One year only
NUMBER OF AWARDS: 2
DEADLINE FOR APPLICATIONS: July 1

SASKATCHEWAN

CODE: SK/4-H01/g
NAME: Sidney Green Entrance
Scholarships
SPONSOR: 4-H Office, Rural Service
Centre
ADDRESS: 3735 Thatcher Avenue,
Saskatoon, Saskatchewan S7K 2H6

PROGRAM: Any university program
BASIS: Awarded to members of a 4-H
club in the province. The selection
is based on academic achievement,
letters of recommendation, and the
candidates' activities as 4-H
members.

MINIMUM AVERAGE: N/A
VALUE: $400.00
TERMS: One year only
NUMBER OF AWARDS: 2
DEADLINE FOR APPLICATIONS: July 15

CODE: SK/4-H02/g
NAME: Saskatchewan Grand
Proficiency Award
SPONSOR: Saskatoon Prairieland
Exhibition Corporation
ADDRESS: Exhibition Grounds,
Saskatoon, Saskatchewan S7K 4E4
PROGRAM: Any
BASIS: Awarded to a 4-H member
who participated in a very com-
petitive series of classes at the
Saskatoon Fair.
MINIMUM AVERAGE: N/A
VALUE: $1500.00
TERMS: One year only
NUMBER OF AWARDS: 1

CODE: SK/AECA01/g
NAME: Arcola East Community
Association (AECA)
SPONSOR: Dale Flichel, Vice-President,
Arcola East Community Associa-
tion
ADDRESS: 279 Michener Drive, Regina,
Saskatchewan S4V 0J1
PROGRAM: Any
BASIS: Awarded to a graduating high
school student from the area
served by the AECA whose family
is a member. The selection is based
on active volunteer involvement in
AECA community programs. Sec-
ondary criteria are school and
church involvement, in that order.
MINIMUM AVERAGE: 65.00
VALUE: $750.00
TERMS: One year only
NUMBER OF AWARDS: 1
DEADLINE FOR APPLICATIONS:
September 30

CODE: SK/AMOK01/g
NAME: AMOK Scholarship
SPONSOR: Human Resource Manager,
AMOK Ltd

ADDRESS: 825 45th Street W.,
Saskatoon, Saskatchewan S7K 3X5
PROGRAM: Any university or institute
in Saskatchewan
BASIS: Candidates must have resided
in the northern administration district for 10 years or half of their
life (whichever is less) and must be
willing to sign an agreement outlining the conditions of the
scholarship. Program of study
must be of benefit to the North.
MINIMUM AVERAGE: N/A
VALUE: $14,000.00
TERMS: Awarded in 8 instalments
over 4 years. There are 3 institute
scholarships worth $9000, paid out
in 6 instalments over 3 years.
NUMBER OF AWARDS: 9
DEADLINE FOR APPLICATIONS: June 30

CODE: SK/ASBOS1/g
NAME: Association of School Business
Officials Saskatchewan Bursary
SPONSOR: c/o Executive Secretary
ADDRESS: 3132 Mountbatten Street,
Saskatoon, Saskatchewan S7M 3T1
PROGRAM: Administration, Com-
merce, and Accounting
BASIS: Awarded to Saskatchewan high
school graduates. The selection is
based on extracurricular activities
and financial need.
MINIMUM AVERAGE: N/A
VALUE: $200.00
TERMS: One year only
NUMBER OF AWARDS: 7
DEADLINE FOR APPLICATIONS: April 19

CODE: SK/ASHE01/g
NAME: Association of Saskatchewan
Home Economists Regina Branch
Scholarship
SPONSOR: Scholarship Committee,
ASHE, Regina Branch
ADDRESS: Box 3862, Regina,
Saskatchewan S4P 3R8
PROGRAM: Home Economics,
Education, Nutrition, or Pharmacy
BASIS: Offered to a full-time student
enrolled in a Canadian College of

Home Economics or related faculty offering a degree program. The selection is based on academic achievement, extracurricular activities, and community service. An application is required.
MINIMUM AVERAGE: N/A
VALUE: $1000.00
TERMS: One year only
NUMBER OF AWARDS: 1
DEADLINE FOR APPLICATIONS: August 30

CODE: SK/BUJEA1/g
NAME: Dr. Eleanor Bujea Scholarship
SPONSOR: Scholarship Committee of Martin Collegiate
ADDRESS: Martin Collegiate, Regina, Saskatchewan
PROGRAM: Business Teacher Education Program
BASIS: Awarded to a graduate of Martin Collegiate, Regina. The recipient must have at least two business education classes, including computer studies, preferably Computer Science 30. A letter of recommendation must be sent to Martin Collegiate.
MINIMUM AVERAGE: 70.00
VALUE: $200.00
TERMS: One year only
NUMBER OF AWARDS: 1
DEADLINE FOR APPLICATIONS: May 30

CODE: SK/CAME01/g
NAME: CAMECO Entrance Scholarships
SPONSOR: Corporate Affairs, CAMECO
ADDRESS: 122 3rd Avenue N., Saskatoon, Saskatchewan S7K 2H6
PROGRAM: Any university or technical institution
BASIS: Applicants must be residents of Saskatchewan who are not currently enrolled in a post-secondary program and are planning to enter a program related to the mineral industry. The selection is based on

academic standing, community involvement, and financial need.
MINIMUM AVERAGE: N/A
VALUE: $1500.00
TERMS: Recipients must agree not to accept any financial award other than student loans.
NUMBER OF AWARDS: 5
DEADLINE FOR APPLICATIONS: June 30

CODE: SK/CHIEF1/g
NAME: Touchwood–File Hills Qu'Appelle District Chiefs Scholarships
SPONSOR: District Chiefs Branch Office
ADDRESS: Box 1549, Fort Qu'Appelle, Saskatchewan S0G 1S0
PROGRAM: Any
BASIS: Applicants must be Treaty Indians from Touchwood–File Hills Qu'Appelle area. The selection is based on attendance and attitude.
MINIMUM AVERAGE: N/A
VALUE: $500.00
TERMS: One year only
NUMBER OF AWARDS: 3
DEADLINE FOR APPLICATIONS: August 19

CODE: SK/CO4H01/g
NAME: Co-operators 4-H Scholarship
SPONSOR: Saskatchewan 4-H Office, Rural Service Centre
ADDRESS: 3735 Thatcher Avenue, Saskatoon, Saskatchewan S7K 2H6
PROGRAM: Any
BASIS: Applicants must be at least 16 years old as of January 1, have completed at least 2 years in 4-H club work, and be currently registered as a member. The selection is based on 4-H activities and on a 500–1000-word essay on farm safety.
MINIMUM AVERAGE: N/A
VALUE: $1000.00
TERMS: One year only
NUMBER OF AWARDS: 1
DEADLINE FOR APPLICATIONS: July 15

CODE: SK/COG01/g
NAME: Cogema Canada Ltd
Scholarships Program for Northern
Residents
SPONSOR: Cogema Canada Ltd
(formerly AMOK Ltd)
ADDRESS: P.O. Box 9204, 817–825 45th
Street W., Saskatoon, Saskatchewan
S7K 3X5
PROGRAM: Various university
programs
BASIS: Offered to students enrolled in
a program of study that would be,
in the opinion of the Scholarship
Committee, of benefit to the North.
To be eligible, applicants must
qualify as northern residents.
MINIMUM AVERAGE: N/A
VALUE: $3500.00
TERMS: One year only
NUMBER OF AWARDS: 6
DEADLINE FOR APPLICATIONS: June 30

CODE: SK/COG02/g
NAME: Cogema Canada Ltd
Scholarships Program for Northern
Residents
SPONSOR: Delta Catalytic
ADDRESS: P.O. Box 9204, 817–825 45th
Street W., Saskatoon, Saskatchewan
S7K 3X5
PROGRAM: Various university
programs
BASIS: Offered to students enrolled in
a program of study that would be,
in the opinion of the Scholarship
Committee, of benefit to the North.
To be eligible, applicants must
qualify as northern residents.
MINIMUM AVERAGE: N/A
VALUE: $2000.00
TERMS: One year only
NUMBER OF AWARDS: 3
DEADLINE FOR APPLICATIONS: June 30

CODE: SK/CPA01/g
NAME: Lottie V.M. Teale Scholarship
SPONSOR: Canadian Paraplegic
Association, Saskatchewan Division
ADDRESS: 3 – 3012 Louise Street,
Saskatoon, Saskatchewan S7K 1M6

PROGRAM: Any. Must be at least half-
time.
BASIS: Awarded to a paid member of
the Canadian Paraplegic Association, Saskatchewan Division, who
has a spinal-cord injury or a similar disorder. Medical confirmation
of the condition is required. Applicants must be Canadian citizens or
landed immigrants.
MINIMUM AVERAGE: N/A
VALUE: Varies
TERMS: One year only
NUMBER OF AWARDS: 1
DEADLINE FOR APPLICATIONS: June 13

CODE: SK/CREG01/g
NAME: City of Regina Scholarships
SPONSOR: City of Regina, Public
Affairs Department
ADDRESS: P.O. Box 1790, Regina,
Saskatchewan S4P 3C8
PROGRAM: Various
BASIS: Applicants must be enrolled in
a bachelor's degree program with
specialization in an area related to
urban planning, economic develop-
ment, civic government, or popula-
tion.
MINIMUM AVERAGE: N/A
VALUE: $1000.00
TERMS: One year only. There are 3
other scholarships for students in
2nd, 3rd, and 4th years.
NUMBER OF AWARDS: 1
DEADLINE FOR APPLICATIONS:
September 1

CODE: SK/CUHS01/g
NAME: Credit Union High School
Graduate Award
SPONSOR: Credit Union High School
Graduate Award
ADDRESS: P.O. Box 3030, Regina,
Saskatchewan S4P 3G8
PROGRAM: Any post-secondary
institution in Saskatchewan
BASIS: Applicants must be Canadian
citizens residing in Saskatchewan.
The selection is based on commu-
nity service, extracurricular

activities, and leadership ability. Three letters of recommendation must accompany the application.
MINIMUM AVERAGE: 70.00
VALUE: $1000.00
TERMS: One year only
NUMBER OF AWARDS: 6
DEADLINE FOR APPLICATIONS: May 15

CODE: SK/CURR01/g
NAME: Gordon Currie Youth Development Bursary
SPONSOR: Gordon Currie Youth Development Fund
ADDRESS: Box 3763, Regina, Saskatchewan S4P 3N8
PROGRAM: Any
BASIS: Applicants must under the age of 25 and residents of Saskatchewan. Application forms are available from the Fund.
MINIMUM AVERAGE: N/A
VALUE: $1000.00
TERMS: One year only
NUMBER OF AWARDS: Varies
DEADLINE FOR APPLICATIONS: September 30

CODE: SK/DRS01/g
NAME: D.R. Simmons Memorial Scholarship
SPONSOR: Supervisor, Student Financial Services Branch
ADDRESS: Saskatchewan Education, 1855 Victoria Avenue, Regina, Saskatchewan S4P 3V5
PROGRAM: Any post-secondary program
BASIS: Awarded to graduating Grade 12 students of Indian or Métis ancestry. Applicants must be graduates of a Saskatchewan high school in the year the award is made.
MINIMUM AVERAGE: N/A
VALUE: $500.00
TERMS: One year only
NUMBER OF AWARDS: 2

CODE: SK/EMM01/g
NAME: Hannon Scholarship

SPONSOR: Registrar, College of Emmanuel and St Chad
ADDRESS: 1337 College Drive, Saskatoon, Saskatchewan S7N 0W0
PROGRAM: Pre-Theology
BASIS: Awarded to a student entering the Pre-Theology program at the college.
MINIMUM AVERAGE: N/A
VALUE: $2000.00
TERMS: One year only
NUMBER OF AWARDS: 2
DEADLINE FOR APPLICATIONS: July 1

CODE: SK/GAVIN1/g
NAME: Bill Gavin, Tom Gavin, and Colin Reichel Memorial Bursary
SPONSOR: Awards Office, Room 213.19, Administration/Humanities Building
ADDRESS: University of Regina, Regina, Saskatchewan S4S 0A2
PROGRAM: Any program. U of Regina preferred.
BASIS: Awarded to a student who has been heavily involved in soccer or hockey as a player or a coach or in the Boy Scouts. A letter of application and reference letters are required.
MINIMUM AVERAGE: N/A
VALUE: $500.00
TERMS: One year only
NUMBER OF AWARDS: 1
DEADLINE FOR APPLICATIONS: April 30

CODE: SK/GMM01/g
NAME: Grant Mitchell Memorial Bursary
SPONSOR: Bursary Committee, Sherwood Credit Union Administrative Office
ADDRESS: 1960 Albert Street, Regina, Saskatchewan S4P 2T4
PROGRAM: Full or part-time studies, including conferences
BASIS: Applicants must have been involved with co-operatives in Saskatchewan, demonstrate reasonable knowledge and understanding of co-operative principles and their

application, and indicate how the proposed study would contribute to the co-operative movement.
MINIMUM AVERAGE: N/A
VALUE: $500.00
TERMS: Renewable for a 2nd year upon application.
NUMBER OF AWARDS: Varies

CODE: SK/HOTA01/g
NAME: Heroes of Our Times Awards
SPONSOR: National Indian Brotherhood Trust Fund
ADDRESS: 3rd Floor, 47 Clarence Street, Ottawa, Ontario K1N 9K1
PROGRAM: Various
BASIS: Native applicants may apply for 5 separate awards: Walter Dieter Award, James Gosnell Award, Tom Longboat Award, and Tommy Prince Award.
MINIMUM AVERAGE: N/A
VALUE: $2000.00
TERMS: One year only
NUMBER OF AWARDS: 5
DEADLINE FOR APPLICATIONS: May 31

CODE: SK/IAAI01/g
NAME: Bun Allin Memorial Scholarship
SPONSOR: International Association of Arson Investigators
ADDRESS: 2260 11th Avenue, 18th Floor, Regina, Saskatchewan S4P 0J9
PROGRAM: Any
BASIS: Awarded on the basis of an essay (minimum of 2000 words) on a topic related to the fire sciences (e.g., arson, origin and cause of fire).
MINIMUM AVERAGE: N/A
VALUE: $1000.00
TERMS: One year only
NUMBER OF AWARDS: 1
DEADLINE FOR APPLICATIONS: September 1

CODE: SK/IODE01/g
NAME: IODE Bursary
SPONSOR: Mrs Win Morrey

ADDRESS: 114 Michener Drive, Regina, Saskatchewan S4V 0G8
PROGRAM: Full course load at the U of Regina
BASIS: Awarded to a Regina resident who is graduating from Grade 12. The selection is based on financial need and extracurricular activities. A transcript and character reference are required. Candidates may be interviewed.
MINIMUM AVERAGE: 75.00
VALUE: $800.00
TERMS: Awarded in 2 instalments.
NUMBER OF AWARDS: 1
DEADLINE FOR APPLICATIONS: June 1

CODE: SK/ISPC01/g
NAME: IPSCO Inc. Scholarships
SPONSOR: University of Regina, Awards Office
ADDRESS: 3737 Wascana Parkway, Regina, Saskatchewan S4S 0A2
PROGRAM: Engineering, Adminstration/Commerce, or Science
BASIS: Awarded to Saskatchewan students entering the U of Regina or the U of Saskatchewan. The selection is based on academic achievement, leadership skills, financial need, and an interest in working in the steel industry.
MINIMUM AVERAGE: 80.00
VALUE: $6000.00
TERMS: $1500 per year. Renewable provided the recipients maintain a high academic standing.
NUMBER OF AWARDS: 2
DEADLINE FOR APPLICATIONS: April 15

CODE: SK/JGRA01/g
NAME: Jennie E. Graham Bursaries
SPONSOR: University Women's Club
ADDRESS: Moosejaw, Saskatchewan
PROGRAM: Any
BASIS: Awarded to a male and a female graduate from the high schools of Moose Jaw. Financial need will be considered. Application forms are available in the high schools.

MINIMUM AVERAGE: N/A
VALUE: $500.00
TERMS: One year only. Tenable at the U of Regina or the U of Saskatchewan.
NUMBER OF AWARDS: 2
DEADLINE FOR APPLICATIONS: June 15

CODE: SK/LEAD01/g
NAME: Leader Post Carrier Foundation Education Grant
SPONSOR: Leader Post Education Grant
ADDRESS: 1964 Park Street, Box 2020, Regina, Saskatchewan S4P 3G4
PROGRAM: Any post-secondary program
BASIS: Awarded on the basis of financial need, extracurricular activities, and academic ability.
MINIMUM AVERAGE: N/A
VALUE: $1000.00
TERMS: One year only
NUMBER OF AWARDS: 2
DEADLINE FOR APPLICATIONS: May 31

CODE: SK/MAS0N1/g
NAME: Masonic Youth Scholarships
SPONSOR: Awards Selection Committee, Masonic Youth Trust Fund
ADDRESS: Box 870, Moosomin, Saskatchewan S0G 3N0
PROGRAM: Any Canadian post-secondary institution
BASIS: Offered to graduates of Saskatchewan high schools. The selection is based on academic achievement and extracurricular activities. An application is required.
MINIMUM AVERAGE: N/A
VALUE: $500.00
TERMS: One year only. Number of awards vary.
NUMBER OF AWARDS: 10 (approx.)
DEADLINE FOR APPLICATIONS: September 15

CODE: SK/MASON2/g
NAME: Ross Kirk Masonic Past Masters Association Inc. Bursary
SPONSOR: Chair, Bursary Committee,

c/o Past Masters Association Inc.
ADDRESS: 132 105th Street W., Saskatoon, Saskatchewan S7N 1N2
PROGRAM: Any
BASIS: Awarded to residents of Saskatchewan who have Masonic connections via the Masons, Eastern Star, Job's Daughter, or Demolay. Financial need, school and community leadership, and academic achievement are considered.
MINIMUM AVERAGE: N/A
VALUE: $300.00
TERMS: One year only
NUMBER OF AWARDS: 2
DEADLINE FOR APPLICATIONS: September 30

CODE: SK/MASON3/g
NAME: Wascana Masonic Lodge Bursaries
SPONSOR: Secretary Treasurer, Wascana Lodge No. 2
ADDRESS: 1930 Lorne Street, Regina, Saskatchewan S4P 2M1
PROGRAM: Any
BASIS: Awarded to members of Wascana Lodge No. 2 A.F. and A.M.G.R.S., their wives, widows, and children who are entering or continuing post-seconary studies. Financial need will be considered.
MINIMUM AVERAGE: N/A
VALUE: $500.00
TERMS: One year only
NUMBER OF AWARDS: 5
DEADLINE FOR APPLICATIONS: October 1

CODE: SK/MASON4/g
NAME: A.E. Smith Memorial Bursary
SPONSOR: P.J. Cameron, Chair, Bursary Committee
ADDRESS: 132 105th Street W., Saskatoon, Saskatchewan S7N 1N2
PROGRAM: Recreational Technology or Physical Education
BASIS: Applicants must be sponsored by a Mason. The selection is based on demonstrated leadership in athletics, participation in school

and community activities, and financial need.
MINIMUM AVERAGE: 75.00
VALUE: $300.00
TERMS: One year only
NUMBER OF AWARDS: 1
DEADLINE FOR APPLICATIONS: September 20

CODE: SK/MASON5/g
NAME: Saskatoon Chapter #4 Royal Arc Mason Past Masters Association Bursary
SPONSOR: Bursary Committee, Past Masters Association Inc.
ADDRESS: 132 105th Street W., Saskatoon, Saskatchewan S7N 1N2
PROGRAM: Any university program
BASIS: Applicants must have Masonic connections or be sponsored by a Mason. Financial need, academic standing, and character will be considered.
MINIMUM AVERAGE: N/A
VALUE: $300.00
TERMS: One year only
NUMBER OF AWARDS: 2
DEADLINE FOR APPLICATIONS: September 30

CODE: SK/MEDIA1/g
NAME: Media House Scholarship
SPONSOR: Selection Committee, c/o Media House Productions Inc.
ADDRESS: 1174 Winnipeg Street, Regina, Saskatchewan S4R 1J6
PROGRAM: Communications program: Radio, TV, Journalism, etc.
BASIS: Applicants must be Grade 12 graduates whose principal residence is in Saskatchewan. The letter of application must include education and career goals, details of community involvement, and a certified transcript of high school marks.
MINIMUM AVERAGE: 80.00
VALUE: $1500.00
TERMS: One year only
NUMBER OF AWARDS: 1
DEADLINE FOR APPLICATIONS: May 1

CODE: SK/MSSC01/g
NAME: Multiple Sclerosis Society of Canada Regina Chapter Bursary
SPONSOR: Multiple Sclerosis Society of Canada Regina Chapter
ADDRESS: 2329 Eleventh Avenue, Regina, Saskatchewan S4P 0K2
PROGRAM: Any of at least 2 years' duration
BASIS: Awarded to Saskatchewan residents who have MS or an immediate family member with MS. Recipients will be chosen on the basis of financial need, academic standing, volunteer work, and program of study.
MINIMUM AVERAGE: N/A
VALUE: $1000.00
TERMS: One year only
NUMBER OF AWARDS: 2
DEADLINE FOR APPLICATIONS: July 23

CODE: SK/NAP01/g
NAME: Napoleon Lafontaine Economic Development Scholarship Program
SPONSOR: Secretary, Selection Committee, Gabriel Dumont Institute of Native Studies and Applied Research
ADDRESS: 121 Broadway Avenue E., Regina, Saskatchewan S4N 0Z6
PROGRAM: Any diploma, certificate, or degree program
BASIS: Applicants must be Métis or Non-status Indians, have resided in Saskatchewan for at least 5 years, and be committed to working in an Aboriginal work environment upon the successful completion of studies. An application is required.
MINIMUM AVERAGE: 70.00
VALUE: $300.00
TERMS: One year only
NUMBER OF AWARDS: 1
DEADLINE FOR APPLICATIONS: October 1

CODE: SK/NLC02/g
NAME: Lord Strathcona Trust Fund
SPONSOR: Navy League of Canada,

Air Command HQ, Detachment Regina
ADDRESS: 2800 Broad Street, Queen Building, Regina, Saskatchewan S4P 4K6
PROGRAM: Physical education at any Saskatchewan institution
BASIS: Awarded to a member of a cadet corp/squadron who has been serving for at least 2 years. A transcript of marks is required with the application.
MINIMUM AVERAGE: N/A
VALUE: $750.00
TERMS: One year only
NUMBER OF AWARDS: 1
DEADLINE FOR APPLICATIONS: September 15

CODE: SK/NSSP01/g
NAME: Northern Spirit Scholarship Program
SPONSOR: Sask Power Northern Enterprise Fund
ADDRESS: P.O. Box 939, Saskatoon, Saskatchewan S7K 1A8
PROGRAM: Various
BASIS: Applicants must be permanent residents of northern Saskatchewan enrolled in full-time studies. The selection is based on academic achievement and commitment to entrepreneurial spirit in northern Saskatchewan.
MINIMUM AVERAGE: N/A
VALUE: $10,000.00
TERMS: $2500 per year, renewable for a total of 4 years. A "B" average must be kept. There are 4 awards for university programs and 4 for technology programs.
NUMBER OF AWARDS: 8
DEADLINE FOR APPLICATIONS: June 30

CODE: SK/OBEY01/g
NAME: Art Obey Memorial Award
SPONSOR: Tony Sparvier, TFHQ District Chiefs
ADDRESS: Box 1549, Fort Qu'Appelle, Saskatchewan S0G 1S0

PROGRAM: Any
BASIS: Awarded on the basis of leadership and commitment in the field of recreation or athletics for the Indian people of Saskatchewan. The recipient must be innovative, demonstrate respect for others, and act as a good role model.
MINIMUM AVERAGE: N/A
VALUE: This award has no monetary value at present.
NUMBER OF AWARDS: 1
DEADLINE FOR APPLICATIONS: September 22

CODE: SK/ODDR01/g
NAME: Oddfellows and Rebekah Lodges Scholarships
SPONSOR: Oddfellows and Rebekahs, Regina Branch
ADDRESS: 840 Rae Street, Regina, Saskatchewan S4T 2B2
PROGRAM: Any post-secondary program
BASIS: Awarded on the basis of financial need, academic standing in Grade 12, and potential toward chosen career.
MINIMUM AVERAGE: 75.00
VALUE: $500.00
TERMS: One year only
NUMBER OF AWARDS: 2
DEADLINE FOR APPLICATIONS: April 30

CODE: SK/PMA001/g
NAME: Past Masters Association, Inc., Bursary
SPONSOR: Chairman of the Bursary Committee
ADDRESS: c/o The Past Masters Association Inc., 132 105th Street W., Saskatoon, Saskatchewan S7N 1N2
PROGRAM: Any
BASIS: Applicants must be residents of Saskatchewan who have Masonic connections via the Masons, Eastern Star, Job's Daughter, or Demolay. Awarded on the basis of

financial need, school and community leadership, and scholarship.
MINIMUM AVERAGE: N/A
VALUE: $300.00
TERMS: One year only
NUMBER OF AWARDS: 2
DEADLINE FOR APPLICATIONS: August 10

CODE: SK/POT4-H/g
NAME: Potash Corporation of Saskatchewan Inc. 4-H Scholarship
SPONSOR: Saskatchewan 4-H Office, Rural Service Centre
ADDRESS: 3735 Thatcher Avenue, Saskatoon, Saskatchewan S7K 2H6
PROGRAM: Any university in Saskatchewan
BASIS: Awarded to any 4-H member entering his or her 1st year at a Saskatchewan university. Emphasis will be placed on a combination of scholastic ability, community involvement, and demonstrated 4-H leadership skills.
MINIMUM AVERAGE: N/A
VALUE: $500.00
TERMS: One year only
NUMBER OF AWARDS: 1
DEADLINE FOR APPLICATIONS: July 31

CODE: SK/PWP01/g
NAME: Parents Without Partners Award
SPONSOR: Parents Without Partners Inc.
ADDRESS: P.O. Box 1491, Regina, Saskatchewan S4T 3C2
PROGRAM: Any university program
BASIS: Applicant must be the child of a single parent who is a member of Parents Without Partners. An essay is required with the application.
MINIMUM AVERAGE: N/A
VALUE: $500.00
TERMS: One year only
NUMBER OF AWARDS: 1
DEADLINE FOR APPLICATIONS: February 1

CODE: SK/RCL001/g
NAME: Jack Moore Memorial Scholarships
SPONSOR: Regina Royal Canadian Legion, Saskatchewan Command
ADDRESS: 3079 5th Avenue, Regina, Saskatchewan S4T 0L6
PROGRAM: Any post-secondary program
BASIS: Awarded to the sons, daughters, or grandchildren of veterans. The selection is based on good academic standing and financial need.
MINIMUM AVERAGE: N/A
VALUE: $200.00
TERMS: One year only
NUMBER OF AWARDS: 8
DEADLINE FOR APPLICATIONS: August 15

CODE: SK/RCL002/g
NAME: Regina Branch Bursary
SPONSOR: Royal Canadian Legion, Regina Branch
ADDRESS: 1820 Cornwall Street, Regina, Saskatchewan S4P 2K2
PROGRAM: Any
BASIS: Applicant must be the child or grandchild of a veteran. A letter of recommendation is required. Financial need will be considered.
MINIMUM AVERAGE: N/A
VALUE: $500.00
TERMS: One year only
NUMBER OF AWARDS: Varies
DEADLINE FOR APPLICATIONS: January 8

CODE: SK/RCL003/g
NAME: Royal Canadian Legion Ladies Auxiliary Scholarships
SPONSOR: Royal Canadian Legion Ladies Auxiliary
ADDRESS: #D – 3081 5th Avenue, Regina, Saskatchewan S4T 0L6
PROGRAM: Any
BASIS: Applicants must be children of ex–service personnel, or of Legion or Ladies Auxilary members. A recent transcript and letters of recommendation from high school

and the Ladies Auxiliary Officer are required. Need, academic standing, and school activities are considered.
MINIMUM AVERAGE: N/A
VALUE: $300.00
TERMS: One year only
NUMBER OF AWARDS: Varies
DEADLINE FOR APPLICATIONS: July 31

CODE: SK/RCL004/g
NAME: Royal Canadian Legion, Saskatchewan Command, Ladies Auxiliary Bursary
SPONSOR: Royal Canadian Legion, Saskatchewan Command, Ladies Auxiliary
ADDRESS: Suite D, 3081 Fifth Avenue, Regina, Saskatchewan S4T 0L6
PROGRAM: Any post-secondary program
BASIS: Applicants considered are the children or grandchildren of ex–service personnel, Legion members (Ordinary, Life, or Associate), and Ladies Auxiliary members. Applications are also available from local Auxiliary units.
MINIMUM AVERAGE: N/A
VALUE: $300.00
TERMS: One year only
NUMBER OF AWARDS: N/A
DEADLINE FOR APPLICATIONS: May 31

CODE: SK/RCL005/g
NAME: Poppy Fund Bursary
SPONSOR: Canadian Legion
ADDRESS: 315 19th Street E., Saskatoon, Saskatchewan S7K 0A1
PROGRAM: Any
BASIS: Applicants must be Saskatoon residents and descendents of veterans. Financial need will be considered.
MINIMUM AVERAGE: N/A
VALUE: Varies
TERMS: One year only
NUMBER OF AWARDS: 8
DEADLINE FOR APPLICATIONS: August 1

CODE: SK/RCL006/g
NAME: Titus Bursary
SPONSOR: Canadian Legion
ADDRESS: 315 19th Street E., Saskatoon, Saskatchewan S7K 0A1
PROGRAM: Health-related
BASIS: Applicants must be Saskatoon residents and descendents of veterans. Financial need will be considered.
MINIMUM AVERAGE: N/A
VALUE: Varies
TERMS: One year only. Number of awards varies.
NUMBER OF AWARDS: 8 (approx.)
DEADLINE FOR APPLICATIONS: August 1

CODE: SK/RCSS01/g
NAME: Henry A. Kutama Christian Youth Leadership Scholarship
SPONSOR: Regina Roman Catholic Separate School Division #81
ADDRESS: 3328 Pike Avenue, Regina, Saskatchewan S4T 1S4
PROGRAM: Any
BASIS: Awarded to a student graduating from a Regina Separate School. The selection is based on commitment to others, Christian leadership, parish involvement, and academic standing.
MINIMUM AVERAGE: N/A
VALUE: $500.00
TERMS: One year only
NUMBER OF AWARDS: 1
DEADLINE FOR APPLICATIONS: May 24

CODE: SK/RNAMJ1/g
NAME: Saskatchewan Registered Nurses Association (Moose Jaw) Bursary
SPONSOR: SRNA Bursary Committee
ADDRESS: c/o Moose Jaw Union Hospital, 455 Fairford Street E., Moose Jaw, Saskatchewan S6H 1H3
PROGRAM: Nursing
BASIS: Applicants must be graduates of a Moose Jaw high school. Financial need will be considered.
MINIMUM AVERAGE: N/A

VALUE: $100.00
TERMS: One year only
NUMBER OF AWARDS: Varies
DEADLINE FOR APPLICATIONS:
September 30

CODE: SK/ROB01/g
NAME: Robertson Bursary
SPONSOR: Royal United Services
Institute of Regina
ADDRESS: 1660 Elphinstone Street,
Regina, Saskatchewan S4T 3N1
PROGRAM: Any university program
BASIS: Awarded to a student who is
entering the 1st year of university.
Preference is given to applicants
taking agriculture or related
studies, to the children or legal
wards of the Institute, members of
the Primary Reserves, or members
of a cadet corps in Saskatchewan.
MINIMUM AVERAGE: 75.00
VALUE: $200.00
TERMS: One year only
NUMBER OF AWARDS: 1
DEADLINE FOR APPLICATIONS: August
10

CODE: SK/RPC01/g
NAME: Ted Davis Memorial
Scholarship
SPONSOR: Regina Press Club,
Scholarship Committee Chairman
ADDRESS: 1437 Rose Street, Regina,
Saskatchewan S4R 2A1
PROGRAM: Any post-secondary
journalism program
BASIS: Applicants must be residents of
Saskatchewan who intend to study
journalism. Samples of work must
be sent along with an essay on
being a journalist.
MINIMUM AVERAGE: N/A
VALUE: $1000.00
TERMS: One year only
NUMBER OF AWARDS: 1
DEADLINE FOR APPLICATIONS: June 30

CODE: SK/SAAP01/g
NAME: Saskatchewan Awards
Program
SPONSOR: Saskatchewan Awards
Program
ADDRESS: Saskatchewan Education,
1855 Victoria Avenue, Regina,
Saskatchewan S4P 3V7
PROGRAM: Various post-secondary
programs
BASIS: Awarded to Saskatchewan
residents who are graduating from
Grade 12. The selection is based on
superiority in scholarship, leader-
ship, ability to cooperate, com-
munity involvement, and extra-
curricular activities.
MINIMUM AVERAGE: N/A
VALUE: $5000.00
TERMS: One year only
NUMBER OF AWARDS: 10
DEADLINE FOR APPLICATIONS:
September 6

CODE: SK/SACL01/g
NAME: Carol Ann Bursaries
SPONSOR: Saskatchewan Association
for Community Living
ADDRESS: 3031 Louise Street,
Saskatoon, Saskatchewan S7J 3L1
PROGRAM: Any approved program in
Saskatchewan
BASIS: Awarded to students pursuing
training leading to a career work-
ing with people who are mentally
handicapped.
MINIMUM AVERAGE: N/A
VALUE: $500.00
TERMS: One year only
NUMBER OF AWARDS: 10

CODE: SK/SACL02/g
NAME: G. Allan Roeher Institute
Bursaries
SPONSOR: Saskatchewan Association
for Community Living
ADDRESS: 3031 Louise Street,
Saskatoon, Saskatchewan S7J 3L1
PROGRAM: Any approved program in
Saskatchewan
BASIS: Awarded to students interested
in a field of study dealing with the
mental handicapped. Application
must include an outline of the field

of study and a recommendation from the provincial association.
MINIMUM AVERAGE: N/A
VALUE: $1000.00
TERMS: One year only. Value may vary.
NUMBER OF AWARDS: Varies

CODE: SK/SAHA01/g
NAME: Saskatchewan Amateur Hockey Association Scholarships
SPONSOR: SAHA Office
ADDRESS: Box 883, Regina, Saskatchewan S4P 3B1
PROGRAM: Any university or college in Saskatchewan
BASIS: Applicant must be a Grade 12 graduate who has been registered for at least 3 years with SAHA and is a registrant in good standing. The application must be made in the year of Grade 12 graduation.
MINIMUM AVERAGE: N/A
VALUE: $1000.00
TERMS: Awarded in 2 instalments.
NUMBER OF AWARDS: 11
DEADLINE FOR APPLICATIONS: August 15

CODE: SK/SASED1/g
NAME: Fuhrman Emergency Loan Program
SPONSOR: Saskatchewan Education – Student Assistance Program
ADDRESS: 1855 Victoria Avenue, Regina, Saskatchewan S4P 3V7
PROGRAM: Any at SIAST
BASIS: Applicants must be residents of Saskatchewan, with at least 60% of a full course load. Financial need must be verified by a SIAST counsellor.
MINIMUM AVERAGE: N/A
VALUE: $400.00
TERMS: Candidates may reapply.
NUMBER OF AWARDS: Varies

CODE: SK/SASED2/g
NAME: Federal-Provincial Fellowship Program
SPONSOR: Saskatchewan Education –

Official Minority Language Office
ADDRESS: 1855 Victoria Avenue, Regina, Saskatchewan S4P 3V7
PROGRAM: Any
BASIS: Applicants must be Canadian citizens and residents of Saskatchewan. Students must be full-time, with at least 60% of their course load in French.
MINIMUM AVERAGE: N/A
VALUE: $250.00
TERMS: This amount is given each semester.
NUMBER OF AWARDS: Varies
DEADLINE FOR APPLICATIONS: September 15

CODE: SK/SASED3/g
NAME: Federal-Provincial Fellowship Program
SPONSOR: Saskatchewan Education – Official Minority Language Office
ADDRESS: 1855 Victoria Avenue, Regina, Saskatchewan S4P 3V7
PROGRAM: Bachelor of Education, U of Regina
BASIS: Applicants must be Canadian citizens and residents of Saskatchewan. Students must be full-time, with at least 60% of their course load in French.
MINIMUM AVERAGE: N/A
VALUE: $250.00
TERMS: This amount is given each semester. A contract is required for all 4 years of the program.
NUMBER OF AWARDS: Varies
DEADLINE FOR APPLICATIONS: September 15

CODE: SK/SASED4/g
NAME: French Minority Language Travel Bursary
SPONSOR: Saskatchewan Education – Official Minority Language Office
ADDRESS: 1855 Victoria Avenue, Regina, Saskatchewan S4P 3V7
PROGRAM: Any outside Saskatchewan
BASIS: Applicants must have French as their 1st language and cannot

pursue studies in their own language in Saskatchewan. They must be full-time students with 80% of their course load in French.
MINIMUM AVERAGE: N/A
VALUE: Varies
TERMS: One year only. Bursary value is equivalent to one economy-class round-trip fare anywhere in Canada.
NUMBER OF AWARDS: Varies
DEADLINE FOR APPLICATIONS: September 15

CODE: SK/SASED5/g
NAME: French Summer Language Bursary Program
SPONSOR: Saskatchewan Education – Official Minority Language Office
ADDRESS: 1855 Victoria Avenue, Regina, Saskatchewan S4P 3V7
PROGRAM: U of Saskatchewan and others
BASIS: Applicants must be participants in the summer language program.
MINIMUM AVERAGE: N/A
VALUE: Bursary defrays the costs of tuition and other expenses.
NUMBER OF AWARDS: Varies
DEADLINE FOR APPLICATIONS: February 15

CODE: SK/SASED6/g
NAME: Official Languages Monitor Program
SPONSOR: Saskatchewan Education – Official Minority Language Office
ADDRESS: 1855 Victoria Avenue, Regina, Saskatchewan S4P 3V7
PROGRAM: Any
BASIS: This program involves work as an Official Language Monitor.
MINIMUM AVERAGE: N/A
VALUE: $11,200.00
TERMS: Amount includes salary and travel expenses. Part-time positions pay $3500.
NUMBER OF AWARDS: Varies
DEADLINE FOR APPLICATIONS: February 15

CODE: SK/SASED7/g
NAME: Achievement Awards
SPONSOR: Saskatchewan Education Awards Program Co-ordinator
ADDRESS: 1855 Victoria Avenue, Regina, Saskatchewan S4P 3V7
PROGRAM: Any
BASIS: Awarded to Sasakatchewan high school graduates on the basis of academic standing. Supporting documentation must be sent outlining the suitability of the candidate for a targetted career area.
MINIMUM AVERAGE: N/A
VALUE: $3000.00
TERMS: One year only
NUMBER OF AWARDS: Varies
DEADLINE FOR APPLICATIONS: September 1

CODE: SK/SASED8/g
NAME: General Proficiency Awards
SPONSOR: Saskatchewan Education Awards Program Co-ordinator
ADDRESS: 1855 Victoria Avenue, Regina, Saskatchewan S4P 3V7
PROGRAM: Any
BASIS: Awarded to Sasakatchewan high school graduates on the basis of academic standing.
MINIMUM AVERAGE: N/A
VALUE: $400.00
TERMS: One year only
NUMBER OF AWARDS: Varies

CODE: SK/SASED9/g
NAME: Scholars Awards
SPONSOR: Saskatchewan Education Awards Program Co-ordinator
ADDRESS: 1855 Victoria Avenue, Regina, Saskatchewan S4P 3V7
PROGRAM: Any
BASIS: Awarded to Saskatchewan high school graduates on the basis of academic standing and involvement in school and community affairs.
MINIMUM AVERAGE: N/A
VALUE: $5000.00
TERMS: One year only
NUMBER OF AWARDS: Varies

CODE: SK/SCKC01/g
NAME: Swift Current Kiwanis Club
Bursaries
SPONSOR: Chairman, Vocational
Guidance Committee
ADDRESS: Swift Current Kiwanis Club,
1118 Bothwell Street, Swift Current,
Saskatchewan S9H 1Z9
PROGRAM: Education, Engineering or
Technology
BASIS: Awarded to graduates of Swift
Current Comprehensive High
School: 2 bursaries for students
entering a teacher-training
program, 2 bursaries to students
entering Engineering or Tech-
nology programs, and one awarded
on the basis of financial need.
MINIMUM AVERAGE: N/A
VALUE: $300.00
TERMS: One year only. The bursary
based on financial need is worth
$400.
NUMBER OF AWARDS: 5

CODE: SK/SETE01/g
NAME: Saskatchewan Education
General Proficiency Awards
SPONSOR: Saskatchewan Education
Training and Employment
ADDRESS: Applicants should contact
their high school guidance office.
PROGRAM: Any
BASIS: Awarded to students registered
in publicly funded Saskatchewan
high schools who will be furthering
their education in a post-secondary
program. Eligible students will be
nominated by their high school
principal.
MINIMUM AVERAGE: N/A
VALUE: $400.00
TERMS: One year only
NUMBER OF AWARDS: 650

CODE: SK/SHB001/g
NAME: Saskatchewan Health Bursaries
SPONSOR: Bursary Administrator,
Saskatchewan Health
ADDRESS: 3475 Albert Street, Regina,
Saskatchewan S4X 6X6

PROGRAM: Respiratory Therapy
Program
BASIS: Awarded on the basis of
financial need. Selected candidates
must agree to do a period of 2
years' service in Saskatchewan.
MINIMUM AVERAGE: N/A
VALUE: Varies
NUMBER OF AWARDS: Varies
DEADLINE FOR APPLICATIONS: June 1

CODE: SK/SHB002/g
NAME: Saskatchewan Department of
Health Bursary Program
SPONSOR: Staff Development,
Department of Health
ADDRESS: 3475 Albert Street, Regina,
Saskatchewan S4S 6X6
PROGRAM: Health career-related
studies
BASIS: Applicants must provide the
following: outline of proposed
course of studies, letter of accept-
ance, résumé, and transcript of all
high school marks. Candidates
may be required to appear before
the bursary selection committee.
MINIMUM AVERAGE: N/A
VALUE: N/A
TERMS: Recipients will be expected to
provide a specified period of service in the province of Saskatchewan.
NUMBER OF AWARDS: N/A

CODE: SK/SKF01/g
NAME: Saskatoon Kiwanis Foundation
Talent Scholarship
SPONSOR: Saskatoon Kiwanis
Foundation, c/o Travelodge
ADDRESS: 106 Circle Drive W.,
Saskatoon, Saskatchewan S7l 4L6
PROGRAM: Performing arts-related
BASIS: Applicants must be partici-
pants in the School Variety Night
/ Lit Night in Saskatoon and wish
to continue training in music,
dance, etc.
MINIMUM AVERAGE: N/A
VALUE: Varies
TERMS: One year only

NUMBER OF AWARDS: Varies
DEADLINE FOR APPLICATIONS: May 15

CODE: SK/SMAS01/g
NAME: Society of Management
Accountants Scholarship
SPONSOR: Society of Management
Accountants of Saskatchewan
ADDRESS: 4601 Albert Street, Regina,
Saskatchewan S4S 6B8
PROGRAM: Accounting at any
approved educational institute
BASIS: Awarded to a Grade 12
graduate planning to pursue a
career in management accounting.
MINIMUM AVERAGE: 80.00
VALUE: $500.00
TERMS: One year only
NUMBER OF AWARDS: 1
DEADLINE FOR APPLICATIONS: August
10

CODE: SK/SMDC01/g
NAME: Saskatchewan Mining
Development Corporation
Scholarships
SPONSOR: Public Affairs Branch,
Saskatchewan Mining Development
Corporation
ADDRESS: 122 3rd Avenue N., Saska-
toon, Saskatchewan S7K 2H6
PROGRAM: Mineral-resource indus-
try–related programs
BASIS: Applicants must be entering
the 1st year of a program that will
prepare them for a career in the
mineral-resource industry in
Saskatchewan.
MINIMUM AVERAGE: N/A
VALUE: $1500.00
TERMS: One year only
NUMBER OF AWARDS: 5

CODE: SK/SOR01/g
NAME: Soroptimist Training Award
Program
SPONSOR: Cecilian Rotstein
ADDRESS: 25 Haultain Crescent,
Regina, Saskatchewan S4S 4B4
PROGRAM: Vocational or technical
training

BASIS: Awarded to women from
south Saskatchewan who are
preferably over 25 years old and
the head of a household. Community interest, career goals,
financial need, and personal
references will be considered.
MINIMUM AVERAGE: N/A
VALUE: $1500.00
TERMS: There will be finalist awards
of $300.
NUMBER OF AWARDS: Varies
DEADLINE FOR APPLICATIONS: January
15

CODE: SK/SPS01/g
NAME: Saskatoon Pharmacists' Society
Scholarship
SPONSOR: Dean of Pharmacy
ADDRESS: University of Saskatoon,
Saskatoon, Saskatchewan S7N 0W0
PROGRAM: Pharmacy, U of
Saskatchewan
BASIS: Awarded to a Saskatoon high
school graduate on the basis of
academic standing and financial
need.
MINIMUM AVERAGE: N/A
VALUE: $400.00
TERMS: One year only
NUMBER OF AWARDS: 1
DEADLINE FOR APPLICATIONS:
September 30

CODE: SK/SSCF01/g
NAME: South Saskatchewan
Community Foundation Award
SPONSOR: South Saskatchewan
Community Foundation
ADDRESS: 46 Wheaton Crescent,
Regina, Saskatchewan S4S 2Z2
PROGRAM: Any
BASIS: Awarded to students who are
blind within the meaning of the
White Cane Act.
MINIMUM AVERAGE: N/A
VALUE: Varies
NUMBER OF AWARDS: Varies
DEADLINE FOR APPLICATIONS: August
15

CODE: SK/SSTA01/g
NAME: Saskatchewan School Trustees Association Education Scholarship
SPONSOR: SSTTA
ADDRESS: 400 – 2222 13th Avenue, Regina, Saskatchewan S4P 3M6
PROGRAM: Any university program in Saskatchewan
BASIS: Awarded to a graduate of a Saskatchewan high school who is entering the 1st year of university. The selection is based on a short written essay, good character, community leadership, and financial need. Application forms are available from school board offices.
MINIMUM AVERAGE: N/A
VALUE: $1000.00
TERMS: One year only
NUMBER OF AWARDS: 1
DEADLINE FOR APPLICATIONS: September 1

CODE: SK/STAR01/g
NAME: Star-Phoenix Alumni Association Scholarship
SPONSOR: Star-Phoenix Carrier Alumni Association Inc.
ADDRESS: 204 5th Avenue N., Saskatoon, Saskatchewan S7K 2P1
PROGRAM: Any approved post-secondary institution
BASIS: Awarded to a Saskatchewan resident on the basis of financial need.
MINIMUM AVERAGE: N/A
VALUE: $1000.00
TERMS: One year only. The selection committee will consider any other sources of financial assistance each applicant is receiving.
NUMBER OF AWARDS: 1
DEADLINE FOR APPLICATIONS: May 31

CODE: SK/STEL01/g
NAME: Sasktel Scholarships
SPONSOR: Corporate Equity Officer
ADDRESS: 2121 Saskatchewan Drive, Regina, Saskatchewan S4P 3Y2
PROGRAM: Various, at any Saskatchewan university
BASIS: Awarded to Saskatchewan residents. Special consideration will be given to applicants who are members of the following groups: women, Aboriginal ancestry, disabled, or visible minorities.
MINIMUM AVERAGE: 70.00
VALUE: $1000.00
TERMS: One year only. Recipients may reapply for $1500 undergraduate awards in subsequent years.
NUMBER OF AWARDS: Varies
DEADLINE FOR APPLICATIONS: July 1

CODE: SK/STJA01/g
NAME: St John Ambulance Bursary
SPONSOR: Margaret MacLaren Memorial Fund, St John Council for Saskatchwan
ADDRESS: 2625 3rd Avenue, Regina, Saskatchewan S4T 0C8
PROGRAM: Any recognized university or technical institute
BASIS: The selection is based on proven leadership and ability. Preference will be given to qualified applicants with St John Ambulance affiliation. Financial need will be considered.
MINIMUM AVERAGE: N/A
VALUE: N/A
TERMS: One year only
NUMBER OF AWARDS: N/A
DEADLINE FOR APPLICATIONS: April 1

CODE: SK/STJA02/g
NAME: Margaret McLaren Memorial Bursary
SPONSOR: St John Ambulance Council for Saskatchewan
ADDRESS: 2625 3rd Avenue, Regina, Saskatchewan S4T 0C8
PROGRAM: Nursing – Diploma programs, B.Sc.
BASIS: Preference is given to students with St John Ambulance affiliation.
MINIMUM AVERAGE: N/A
VALUE: $1000.00
TERMS: Awards range in value from $700 to $1000.
NUMBER OF AWARDS: Varies

DEADLINE FOR APPLICATIONS: March
15

CODE: SK/STPR01/g
NAME: St Peter's Men's Club Award
SPONSOR: St Peter's Catholic Rectory
ADDRESS: 100 Argyle Street, Regina,
Saskatchewan S4R 4C3
PROGRAM: Any
BASIS: Applicant must be a member of
St Peter's Parish. The selection is
based on academic standing, and
on activities in the parish, school,
and community.
MINIMUM AVERAGE: N/A
VALUE: $475.00
TERMS: One year only
NUMBER OF AWARDS: 1
DEADLINE FOR APPLICATIONS: May 15

CODE: SK/WSCU01/g
NAME: Western Savings and Credit
Union Ltd Bursaries
SPONSOR: Administrative Assistant,
Western Savings & Credit Union
Ltd
ADDRESS: 177 1st Avenue N.E., Box
666, Swift Current, Saskatchewan
S9H 4X6
PROGRAM: Any
BASIS: Awarded to graduates of the
Swift Current Comprehensive High
School who plan to attend any uni-
versity, technical institute, or secre-
tarial college. An application is
required.
MINIMUM AVERAGE: N/A
VALUE: $1000.00
TERMS: One year only
NUMBER OF AWARDS: 4

YUKON TERRITORY

CODE: YT/CCC01/g
NAME: Robert Asbil Memorial
Scholarship
SPONSOR: The Rector, Christ Church
Cathedral
ADDRESS: Box 4489, Whitehorse,
Yukon Y1A 2R8
PROGRAM: Theological or religious
training
BASIS: The application must include
an official Grade 12 transcript.
MINIMUM AVERAGE: N/A
VALUE: $50.00
TERMS: One year only
NUMBER OF AWARDS: 1

CODE: YT/CLOW01/g
NAME: Julie Cruickshank Bursary
SPONSOR: CCLOW, c/o Yukon
College Counselling Centre
ADDRESS: Yukon College, Box 2799,
Whitehorse, Yukon Y1A 5K4
PROGRAM: Any
BASIS: Awarded to a Whitehorse

woman and a woman from a rural
community who are 25 years or
older and have lived in the Yukon
for at least 2 years. Financial need
will be considered.
MINIMUM AVERAGE: N/A
VALUE: $200.00
TERMS: One year only. A one-year
membership in the Canadian
Congress for Learning Opportunities for Women is included in
this bursary.
NUMBER OF AWARDS: 2
DEADLINE FOR APPLICATIONS:
September 30

CODE: YT/CLOW02/g
NAME: Mairi St. John Macdonald
Scholarship
SPONSOR: CCLOW, c/o Yukon
College Counselling Centre
ADDRESS: Yukon College, Box 2799,
Whitehorse, Yukon Y1A 5K4
PROGRAM: Any

BASIS: Awarded to a female Canadian citizen or landed immigrant who is at least 19 years of age and has not attended school for at least 3 years. Financial need will be considered.
MINIMUM AVERAGE: N/A
VALUE: $500.00
TERMS: One year only. A one-year membership in the Canadian Congress for Learning Opportunities for Women is included in this bursary.
NUMBER OF AWARDS: 1
DEADLINE FOR APPLICATIONS: August 31

CODE: YT/CVA01/g
NAME: Jinx Ross Memorial Scholarship
SPONSOR: Community Vocational Alternative
ADDRESS: 1148 1st Avenue, Whitehorse, Yukon Y1A 1A6
PROGRAM: Rehabilitation Medicine or related training
BASIS: Awarded to a Grade 12 Yukon student. An official Grade 12 transcript must accompany the application.
MINIMUM AVERAGE: N/A
VALUE: $300.00
TERMS: One year only
NUMBER OF AWARDS: 1
DEADLINE FOR APPLICATIONS: July 31

CODE: YT/DOE01/g
NAME: Lester B. Pearson College of the Pacific
SPONSOR: Yukon Education
ADDRESS: Box 2703, Whitehorse, Yukon Y1A 2C6
PROGRAM: International Baccalaureate
BASIS: Applicants should have completed Grade 11 and will take Grade 12 and 13 at the College, culminating in the International Baccalaureate examination. Applications are available from Yukon high schools or the Department of Education in January.
MINIMUM AVERAGE: N/A

VALUE: Varies
TERMS: Renewable
NUMBER OF AWARDS: 2
DEADLINE FOR APPLICATIONS: March 1

CODE: YT/ESTR01/g
NAME: Dawson City Chapter of O.E.S. Scholarship
SPONSOR: Chapter of the Order of the Eastern Star
ADDRESS: Secretary of Whitehorse Chapter, 505 Lambert Street, Whitehorse, Yukon Y1A 1Z8
PROGRAM: Any
BASIS: Awarded to a Grade 12 student who attended Robert Service Elementary Junior Secondary School in Dawson City. The selection is made by the principal of the school.
MINIMUM AVERAGE: N/A
VALUE: Varies
TERMS: One year only
NUMBER OF AWARDS: 1

CODE: YT/ESTR02/g
NAME: Eastern Star Religious Leadership Training Awards
SPONSOR: Chapter of the Order of the Eastern Star
ADDRESS: Grand Secretary, 505 Lambert Street, Whitehorse, Yukon Y1A 1Z8
PROGRAM: Any
BASIS: Open to a member of the Order, or the wife, husband, father, mother, sister, brother, child, stepchild, or grandchild of a member of a Chapter of the Order of the Eastern Star in British Columbia/Yukon.
MINIMUM AVERAGE: N/A
VALUE: Varies
TERMS: One year only
NUMBER OF AWARDS: Varies
DEADLINE FOR APPLICATIONS: March 31

CODE: YT/ESTR03/g
NAME: Elizabeth Bentley Order of the Eastern Star Scholarship Awards
SPONSOR: Chapter of the Order of the Eastern Star

ADDRESS: Grand Secretary, 505 Lambert Street, Whitehorse, Yukon Y1A 1Z8
PROGRAM: Any
BASIS: Open to a member of the Order, or the wife, husband, father, mother, sister, brother, child, stepchild, or grandchild of a member of a Chapter of the Order of the Eastern Star in British Columbia/Yukon. Financial need and the difficulty of the course taken are considered.
MINIMUM AVERAGE: N/A
VALUE: $450.00
TERMS: One year only
NUMBER OF AWARDS: 3
DEADLINE FOR APPLICATIONS: March 31

CODE: YT/IODE01/g
NAME: IODE Scholarship (Dawson)
SPONSOR: Regent, Dawson City Chapter IODE
ADDRESS: Box 242, Dawson City, Yukon Y0B 1G0
PROGRAM: Any
BASIS: Awarded to a Grade 12 student of Robert Service School in Dawson City. The selection is based on academic standing. An official Grade 12 transcript must accompany application.
MINIMUM AVERAGE: 65.00
VALUE: $350.00
TERMS: One year only
NUMBER OF AWARDS: 1

CODE: YT/ORP01/g
NAME: Order of the Royal Purple
SPONSOR: Principal, F.H. Collins Secondary School
ADDRESS: Box 2703, Whitehorse, Yukon Y1A 2C6
PROGRAM: Technical or vocational school
BASIS: Awarded to a student from F.H. Collins Secondary School who has been a resident of the Yukon Territory for 5 years. The application must include a statement of educational plans and an official

Grade 12 transcript. Financial need will be considered.
MINIMUM AVERAGE: N/A
VALUE: $500.00
TERMS: One year only
NUMBER OF AWARDS: 1
DEADLINE FOR APPLICATIONS: May 31

CODE: YT/PYUA01/g
NAME: Frances Nowasad Award
SPONSOR: Prosvita-Yukon Ukrainian Association
ADDRESS: Box 4826, Whitehorse, Yukon Y1A 2B0
PROGRAM: Any
BASIS: Awarded on the basis of academic standing, good citizenship, participation in school and/or community activities, and involvement in ethnic (or minority group) cultural activity.
MINIMUM AVERAGE: N/A
VALUE: $300.00
TERMS: One year only
NUMBER OF AWARDS: 1
DEADLINE FOR APPLICATIONS: June 15

CODE: YT/RCL01/g
NAME: Royal Canadian Legion Bursary, Whitehorse
SPONSOR: Royal Canadian Legion
ADDRESS: 306 Alexander Street, Whitehorse, Yukon Y1A 2L6
PROGRAM: Any
BASIS: Awarded to a son, daughter, or grandchild of a veteran. Applicant must be a graduate of a Yukon high school. The veteran's regimental number must be sent in with the application
MINIMUM AVERAGE: N/A
VALUE: Varies
TERMS: One year only
NUMBER OF AWARDS: 1
DEADLINE FOR APPLICATIONS: August 15

CODE: YT/SFAC01/g
NAME: Audrey McLaughlin Bursary
SPONSOR: Principal, F.H. Collins Secondary School

ADDRESS: Box 2703, Whitehorse, Yukon Y1A 2C6
PROGRAM: Any
BASIS: Applicants must be graduates of F.H. Collins Secondary School. The selection is based on interest and involvement in the community.
MINIMUM AVERAGE: N/A
VALUE: $200.00
TERMS: One year only
NUMBER OF AWARDS: 1

CODE: YT/SFAC02/g
NAME: Beta Sigma Phi Scholarship
SPONSOR: Students' Financial Assistance Committee, Department of Education
ADDRESS: Box 2703, Whitehorse, Yukon Y1A 2C6
PROGRAM: Arts
BASIS: Awarded to a female resident of the Yukon. An official Grade 12 transcript is required with the application.
MINIMUM AVERAGE: N/A
VALUE: $250.00
TERMS: One year only
NUMBER OF AWARDS: 1
DEADLINE FOR APPLICATIONS: August 31

CODE: YT/SFAC03/g
NAME: Canadian Army Yukon Scholarship
SPONSOR: Students' Financial Assistance Committee, Department of Education
ADDRESS: Box 2703, Whitehorse, Yukon Y1A 2C6
PROGRAM: Any eligible institution
BASIS: Awarded to a Grade 12 student from the Yukon Territory. An official Grade 12 transcript is required with the application.
MINIMUM AVERAGE: 60.00
VALUE: $100.00
TERMS: One year only
NUMBER OF AWARDS: 1
DEADLINE FOR APPLICATIONS: August 31

CODE: YT/SFAC04/g
NAME: Knights of Columbus Scholarship
SPONSOR: Students' Financial Assistance Committee, Department of Education
ADDRESS: Box 2703, Whitehorse, Yukon Y1A 2C6
PROGRAM: Any eligible institution
BASIS: Awarded to a Grade 12 student from the Yukon Territory. The selection is based on academic standing, financial need, and citizenship. A Grade 12 transcript, letters of recommendation, and a letter of admission from a post-secondary institute are required with the application.
MINIMUM AVERAGE: 60.00
VALUE: $500.00
TERMS: One year only
NUMBER OF AWARDS: 1
DEADLINE FOR APPLICATIONS: August 31

CODE: YT/SFAC05/g
NAME: Nicholas John Harach Scholarship
SPONSOR: Students' Financial Assistance Committee, Department of Education
ADDRESS: Box 2703, Whitehorse, Yukon Y1A 2C6
PROGRAM: Aviation technical training preferred
BASIS: Awarded to a student from the Yukon Territory. The selection is based on academic standing, extra-curricular activities, and contributions to student life. A Grade 12 transcript is required with the application.
MINIMUM AVERAGE: N/A
VALUE: $100.00
TERMS: One year only
NUMBER OF AWARDS: 1
DEADLINE FOR APPLICATIONS: August 31

CODE: YT/SFAC06/g
NAME: NorthwesTel Scholarship
Program
SPONSOR: Students' Financial
Assistance Committee, Department
of Education
ADDRESS: Box 2703, Whitehorse,
Yukon Y1A 2C6
PROGRAM: Various post-secondary
programs
BASIS: Awarded to a student from the
Yukon Territory entering Electrical
Engineering, Commerce, Business
Administration, Computer Science,
or Electronic Technician or Tech-
nology programs. A Grade 12 tran-
script is required with the appli-
cation.
MINIMUM AVERAGE: 70.00
VALUE: $2000.00
TERMS: $500 per year. Renewable for
up to 3 more years subsequent to a
review of academic progress.
Summer employment may also be
offered to recipients.
NUMBER OF AWARDS: 1
DEADLINE FOR APPLICATIONS: August
31

CODE: YT/SFAC07/g
NAME: Whitehorse Lion's Club
Bursary
SPONSOR: Students' Financial
Assistance Committee, Department
of Education
ADDRESS: Box 2703, Whitehorse,
Yukon Y1A 2C6
PROGRAM: Any
BASIS: Awarded to a Grade 12
graduate who has attended F.H.
Collins Secondary School for at
least one year. Extracurricular
activities and academic standing
will be considered. An official
Grade 12 transcript must accom-
pany the application.
MINIMUM AVERAGE: 65.00
VALUE: $500.00
TERMS: One year only
NUMBER OF AWARDS: 1

DEADLINE FOR APPLICATIONS: August
31

CODE: YT/SFAC08/g
NAME: Yukon Art Society
Scholarship
SPONSOR: Students' Financial
Assistance Committee, Department
of Education
ADDRESS: Box 2703, Whitehorse,
Yukon Y1A 2C6
PROGRAM: Visual Arts
BASIS: Awarded to a Yukon Sec-
ondary School Grade 12 graduate.
An official Grade 12 transcript
and a letter of recommenda-
tion from the art teacher or prin-
cipal must accompany the appli-
cation.
MINIMUM AVERAGE: N/A
VALUE: $250.00
TERMS: One year only
NUMBER OF AWARDS: 1
DEADLINE FOR APPLICATIONS:
September 30

CODE: YT/SFAC09/g
NAME: Yukon Huskys C.B. Radio
Club Scholarship
SPONSOR: Students' Financial
Assistance Committee, Department
of Education
ADDRESS: Box 2703, Whitehorse,
Yukon Y1A 2C6
PROGRAM: Technical program
BASIS: Awarded to a Yukon Grade 12
graduate, preferably enrolled in a
technical program. An official
Grade 12 transcript must accom-
pany the application.
MINIMUM AVERAGE: N/A
VALUE: $350.00
TERMS: One year only
NUMBER OF AWARDS: 1
DEADLINE FOR APPLICATIONS: August
31

CODE: YT/SFAC10/g
NAME: Yukon Northern Resources
Scholarships
SPONSOR: Students' Financial

Assistance Committee, Department of Education
ADDRESS: Box 2703, Whitehorse, Yukon Y1A 2C6
PROGRAM: Any
BASIS: Yukon students entering any year in an eligible institution, with the primary selection based on financial need and length of Yukon residency. An official Grade 12 transcript must accompany the application.
MINIMUM AVERAGE: N/A
VALUE: $1000.00
TERMS: One year only
NUMBER OF AWARDS: 1
DEADLINE FOR APPLICATIONS: August 31

CODE: YT/SYANA1/g
NAME: Society of Yukon Artists of Native Ancestry Scholarship Fund
SPONSOR: Society of Yukon Artists of Native Ancestry
ADDRESS: P.O. Box 6067, Whitehorse, Yukon Y1A 5L7
PROGRAM: Fine Arts (visual, literary, or performing)
BASIS: Awarded to a Yukon Grade 12 graduate or post-secondary student of Native ancestry who is enrolled in a fine-arts program. An application is required.
MINIMUM AVERAGE: N/A
VALUE: $1000.00
TERMS: One year only
NUMBER OF AWARDS: 1
DEADLINE FOR APPLICATIONS: July 31

CODE: YT/WRC01/g
NAME: Whitehorse Rotary Bursary
SPONSOR: Rotary Club of Whitehorse
ADDRESS: Box 4401, Whitehorse, Yukon Y1A 3T5
PROGRAM: Any
BASIS: Awarded to a Yukon high school graduate on the basis of community service who characterizes the values and objective of the Rotary International. A personal essay outlining community

service and 2 letters of recommendation are required.
MINIMUM AVERAGE: N/A
VALUE: $500.00
TERMS: One year only. Paid in 2 instalments.
NUMBER OF AWARDS: 1
DEADLINE FOR APPLICATIONS: August 31

CODE: YT/YCS01/g
NAME: Ted Parnell Memorial Scholarship
SPONSOR: President, Yukon Conservation Society
ADDRESS: Box 4163, Whitehorse, Yukon Y1A 3T3
PROGRAM: Environmental studies
BASIS: Applicants must be Yukon residents. The application must include a letter describing the applicant's interest in the environment, academic achievements, and future plans. An official Grade 12 transcript must also be included.
MINIMUM AVERAGE: N/A
VALUE: $500.00
TERMS: One year only
NUMBER OF AWARDS: 1
DEADLINE FOR APPLICATIONS: June 15

CODE: YT/YKFN01/g
NAME: Yukon Foundation Scholarships
SPONSOR: Yukon Foundation
ADDRESS: P.O. Box 4067, Whitehorse, Yukon Y1A 3S9
PROGRAM: Various
BASIS: The Foundation awards scholarships for Natives, women, and students studying history, drama, fine arts, music, science, mining, archaeology, health care, engineering, and biology. Yukon high school graduates and/or residents are given priority over other applicants.
MINIMUM AVERAGE: N/A
VALUE: Varies
TERMS: The Yukon Foundation awards a number of valuable

scholarships from a variety of funds.
NUMBER OF AWARDS: Varies
DEADLINE FOR APPLICATIONS: May 31

CODE: YT/YOP01/g
NAME: Yukon Order of Pioneers Scholarships
SPONSOR: Scholarship Committee, Yukon Order of Pioneers
ADDRESS: Box 5384, Whitehorse, Yukon Y1A 4Z2
PROGRAM: Any Canadian university
BASIS: Awarded to graduates of a Yukon high school. An official transcript and a personal résumé must accompany the application. Preference is given to post-graduate students.
MINIMUM AVERAGE: N/A
VALUE: $500.00
TERMS: One year only. Not tenable with any other major scholarships worth more than $500.
NUMBER OF AWARDS: 2
DEADLINE FOR APPLICATIONS: August 15

CODE: YT/YTA01/g
NAME: Doris Stenbraten Scholarship
SPONSOR: Scholarship Committee, Yukon Teachers' Association
ADDRESS: 2064 2nd Avenue, Whitehorse, Yukon Y1A 1A9
PROGRAM: Education preferred
BASIS: Preference will be given to a Grade 12 graduate who has completed the major portion of his/her training in the Yukon educational system.
MINIMUM AVERAGE: 75.00
VALUE: $700.00
TERMS: One year only. Not tenable with any other major scholarships.
NUMBER OF AWARDS: 1
DEADLINE FOR APPLICATIONS: August 30

Yukon students: See also BC/YT/SVI1/g and NT/YT/BX1/g.

14 Employment scholarships

Employment scholarships are a valuable component of your scholarship quest. Many large companies help the dependent children of their employees by paying for the tuition fees or contributing around $1000 to $2000 per year for the first degree taken by the student. As a rule, the employer requires a minimum average of 70 to 75 per cent. Some give more money to students going to university because the tuition fees are higher than for most colleges. Most employers will consider stepchildren, adopted children, and the dependents of retired or deceased employees.

I am always amazed by the number of parents who really aren't sure whether or not their union or employer offers some kind of scholarship. It's certainly worth asking the personnel manager or the head of human resources or the union representative about what there is to offer. This inquiry should be a formal one, in writing, and not just a casual question at the coffee machine. Quite often any scholarships are mentioned in company newsletters or posted on the bulletin board. It is easy to miss this kind of information, so don't expect someone to come and tell you all about it.

If it turns out that there are no employer-sponsored scholarships, parents can ask that the present company consider setting up a scholarship. Employer-sponsored scholarships are usually considered to be an employee benefit and so can be written off as a business expense. Such programs are registered with Revenue Canada.

Some organizations choose to have their employer scholarships run at arm's length to ensure fairness and to avoid the administrative hassles. The Association of Universities and Colleges of Canada manages the scholarships for more than 140 companies listed below. Any questions concerning employer scholarships in general or these in particular should be directed to

Association of Universities and Colleges of Canada
Awards Division
350 Albert St., Suite 600
Ottawa, Ontario
K1R 1B1

(AUCC-managed Company Scholarships are for the dependents of employees only.)

ABB Power Plants Segment
Abitibi-Price Inc.**
Air Canada**
Allied-Signal Aerospace Canada
Allied Signal Canada Inc.
Amoco Canada Petroleum
    Company Limited
Asten Canada Inc. (Dietrich v.
    Asten Scholarhip)
Ball Packaging Products Canada,
    Inc.
BASF Corporation
Beaver Lumber Company Limited
Bell Canada
Bendix Heavy Vehicle Systems
    Inc.**
Bristol-Myers Squibb Canada, Inc.
Browning-Ferris Industries, Inc.
Bull HN Information Systems
    Limited
Canadian Pacific Forest Products
    Limited
Canadian Reynolds Metals
    Company Ltd.
Canadian Tire Corporation Limited
    (Muriel G. Billes & A.J. Billes
    Scholarship)
Canron Inc. (Howard J. Lang
    Scholarship)**
Cargill Limited

CGC Inc.
Chevron Canada Resources
Clairol Canada**
Colgate-Palmolive Canada Inc.
La Compagnie Minière Québec
    Cartier
Consumers Distributing Company
    Limited
Consumers Packaging Inc.
    (undergraduate and graduate
    awards)
The Continental Insurance
    Companies Ltd.
Corby Distilleries Limited
Cyanamid Canada Inc.
Dominion Bridge
Domtar Inc. **
Equifax Canada
Falconbridge Limited (Kidd Creek
    Division)
Fedmet Inc.
Fisher Scientific Ltd.
Gaz Metropolitain Inc. (under-
    graduate and graduate awards)
Gencorp Automotive
General Chemical Canada Inc.**
General Signal Corporation
Gilbey Canada Inc.
Gulf Canada Resources Ltd.
HOJ Management Inc.

** No new awards are being offered at this time; however, renewals are being offered.

Holophane Canada Inc.
Frank W. Horner Inc.
IBM Canada Limited
ICI Canada Inc. (André Boily
Memorial Scholarship)
IOC (Compagnie Minière)
Ingersoll-Rand Canada Inc.
International Union of Bricklayers
and Allied Craftsmen (Harry C.
Bates Merit Scholarship)
Iron Ore Company of Canada
Johnson & Higgins Ltd.,
Kraft General Foods Canada Inc.
Lafarge Canada Inc.
Lennox Industries (Canada) Ltd.
(Bill Tracy Memorial Scholarship)
Libbey-St. Clair Limited**
Macmillan Bathurst Inc.
Maritime Telegraph & Telephone
Company (A. Gordon Archibald
Scholarship)
Merck Frosst Canada Inc.
Metropolitan Life Insurance
Company
Mobil Chemical Canada Ltd.
Mobil Oil Canada
Molson Breweries
The Molson Companies Limited
(John Molson Scholarship)
Monenco Agra Ltd.
Motorola Canada Limited
Navistar International Corporation
Canada
The New Brunswick Telephone
Company, Limited (Kenneth V.
Cox Scholarship)
Norfolk Southern Corporation
Phillips Cable Limited (Clifford F.
Jardim Scholarship)
PPG Canada Inc.
Proctor & Gamble Inc.

PWA Corporation**
Québec-Téléphone
RJR-Macdonald Inc.
James Richardson & Sons Limited
Rothmans, Benson & Hedges Inc.
St. Lawrence Seaway Authority
Sara Lee Foundation (Nathan
Cummings Scholarship)
Scott Paper Limited
Sears Canada Inc.
Shaklee Canada Inc.
State Farm Mutual Automobile
Insurance Company
Stone-Consolidated Inc.
Suncor Inc.
Surpass Chemicals Limited
Télébec Ltée
Teleglobe Canada
TransCanada Pipelines
Transport Canada
Twinpak Inc.
Ultramar Canada Inc.
Unilever Canada Limited
Unisys Canada Inc.
United Distilleries Inc. (Donald W.
McNaughton Scholarship)
VIA Rail Canada Inc.**
Versa Services Ltd.
Warner-Lambert Canada Inc.
Westfair Foods Limited**
Westinghouse Canada Inc.
Weston Bakeries Ltd.
Weyerhaeuser Canada Ltd.
Weyerhaeuser Canada Ltd. Grande
Prairie Operations
Witco Canada Inc.
Wood Gundy Inc. (C.E. Medland
Scholarship)
World Book, Educational Products
Wrigley Canada Inc.
Xerox Canada Inc.

Applications for these scholarships are available from the Association of Universities and Colleges of Canada. The standard deadline date for applications from the dependents of employees is June 1st of each year.

The following is a list of the organizations (in the West and Canada-wide) that offer scholarships and run them themselves.

Alberta Society of Engineering
    Technologists
Alberta Union of Public Employees
Amalgamated Clothing and Textile
    Workers Union, Local 459
Amoco Canada Petroleum Co.
Automotive Industries Association
    of Canada
Birks Family Foundation
Brewery, Winery and Distillery
    Workers, Local 300
Bridgestone/Firestone Canada Inc.
BC Government Employees' Union
BC Hospital Employee's Union
BC Maritime Employers'
    Association
BC Teachers Credit Union
BC Telephone
Campbell Soup Company
Canadian Army Welfare Fund
Canadian College of Teachers
Canadian National
Canadian Pacific Rail
Canadian Plumbing and Mechanical
    Contractors Association
Canadian Union of Public
    Employees, BC Division
Carling O'Keefe Breweries
Central Okanagan Teachers'
    Association
Champion Spark Plug Co. of
    Canada Ltd
City of Calgary Police Service and
    Fire Brigade
Civil Service Union No. 52
    (Edmonton)
Cominco Limited
Communications and Electrical
    Workers of Canada
Communications, Energy, and
    Paper Workers Union of Canada
Crestbrook Forest Industries Ltd
Crouse Hinds Ltd
Dairy Industry Credit Union
Department of Veteran Affairs
Dow Chemical Canada Inc.

Energy and Chemical Workers
    Union, Local 911
Ethyl Canada Inc.
Evans Products Company
Fletcher Challenge Canada
    (National Trust)
Ford Motor Company of Canada
    Ltd
Fraser Valley Real Estate Board
Grain Services Union (Regina)
Graphic Communications
    International Union (Washington,
    DC)
Graphic Communications
    International Union, Local 900M
Husky Oil
Imperial Oil Limited
Inco Limited
Independent Order of Foresters
Insurance Brokers Association,
    Alberta
Insurance Brokers Association of
    Saskatchewan
International Association of Fire
    Fighters
International Brotherhood of
    Teamsters (Washington, DC)
International Brotherhood of
    Teamsters, Local 395
International Logging Associatoin
International Union of Operating
    Engineers, Local 827-8278
International Woodworkers of
    America, Local 1-80
International Woodworkers of
    America, Local 1-423
Interprovincial Pipe Line Inc.
IWA Canada, Local 1-417
John Labatt Ltd
MacMillan Bloedel Ltd
Manitoba Government Employees
    Association
Manitoba Government Employees'
    Union
McDonald's Restaurants of Canada
    Limited

National Union of Provincial Government Employees
Okanagan Valley School Employees Union, Local 523
Pacific Coast Fishermen's Mutual Marine Insurance Co.
Petro Canada
Pipe Line Contractors' Association of Canada
Piping Industry Journeymen Training and General Industry Promotion
Placer CEGO Petroleum Limited
Polysar Rubber Corporation
Public Service Alliance of Canada
Rayonier Canada (BC) Limited
Real Estate Board of Greater Vancouver
Regina Professional Firefighters Association, Local 181
Retail, Wholesale Union, Local 517
Saskatchewan Government Employees Union, Regina
Saskatchewan Government Employees Union, Weyburn
Saskatchewan Government Employees Union, Yorkton
Saskatchewan Teachers Federation, Moose Jaw
Saskatoon Fire Fighters Union, Local 80
School Plant Officials Association of BC

Service Employees International Union
Stelco Inc.
Syncrude Canada Limited
Teamsters General Drivers Warehousemen Helpers, Local 979
Teamsters Joint Council No. 36
Teamsters Union, Local 979
Telecommunications Workers Union (BC)
Thompson Products Old Guard Association
Trans-Mountain Oil Pipeline Co.
Transport Canada
UBC Employees, CUPE Local 116
United Association of Plumbers and Steamfitters, Local 170
United Food and Commercial Workers' Union, Local 401
United Food and Commercial Workers' Union, Local 1518
University of Saskatchewan Employee's Union, CUPE Local 1975
Van-Tel Credit Union
Vancouver Municipal and Regional Employees' Union
Vancouver Police Dept.
Weston Bakeries Ltd
White Spot Limited
Woodward Stores Limited

15 Index of selected awards by special characteristics

The followings lists are an attempt to sort through the hundreds of scholarships in this book. Remember that each scholarship has its own code and that the code gives a lot of information. The first two letters give the province or territory. The last letter tells you what kind of scholarship it is. If the last letter is a "u," then it is a university award and can be found in the university scholarship list. The letter "c" stands for college, and so an item with this suffix can be found in the college scholarships list. The letter "g" means that the scholarship can be found in the general scholarship list. These are scholarships that, generally, can be used at either a college or university.

Please note that, in the interest of brevity, each scholarship is listed under its most prominent characteristic. It's also worth noting that many of the scholarships listed under "Extracurricular," "Community Service," and "Leadership" have the other two characteristics as part of their selection criteria.

Cross-reference by specific characteristic or requirement

4-H: AB/4-H001/g, AB/4-H002/g, AB/4-H003/g, AB/4-H004/g,
AB/4-H005/g, AB/4-H006/g, AB/4-H007/g, AB/4-H008/g, AB/4-H009/g,
AB/4-H010/g, AB4-H011/g, AB/4-H012/g, AB/4-H013/g, AB/4-H014/g,
AB/4-H015/g, AB/4-016/g, AB/4-H017/g, AB/4-H018/g, AB/4-H019/g,
AB/4-H020/g, AB/4-H021/g, AB/4-H022/g, AB/4-H023/g, AB/4-H024/g,
AB/4-H025/g, AB/4-H026/g, AB/4-H027/g, AB/4-H028/g, AB/4-H029/g,
AB/4-H030/g, AB/4-H031/g, AB/4-H032/g, AB/4-H033/g, AB/4-H034/g,
AB/4-H035/g, AB/LAKE08/c, BC/4-H001/g, BC/4-H002/g, BC/4-H003/g,
BC/4-H005/g, BC/4-H006/g, BC/4-H007/g, BC/4-H008/g, BC/4-H009/g,
BC/4-H010/g, BC/4-H011/g, BC/BRI108/u, BC/PC4-H1/g, SK/4-H001/g,

SK/4-H002/g, SK/CO4H01/g, SK/POT4-H/g, SK/SAS007/u,
SK/SAS010/u, SK/SAS011/u, SK/SAS024/u

Agriculture: AB/AWP01/g, AB/GPRC48/c, BC/4-H008/g, BC/BCCA01/g,
BC/BCCA02/g, BC/CVFI01/g, BC/UCFV01/c, BC/UCFV02/c,
MB/BRN019/u

Aircraft: BC/BCIT04/c

Alberta Correspondence School: AB/ALB033/u

Alumni: BC/BCIT01/c

American: BC/BRI124/u, BC/BRI121/u

Anti-drug/alcohol abuse: BC/VIC017/u

Arson: SK/IAAI01/g

Art: AB/AFA02/g, AB/LET031/u, BC/CACC01/g, BC/CACC02/g,
BC/CSB001/g, CA/CCAA01/g, CA/CPI001/g, CA/CSEA01/g,
CA/CSFS01/g, SK/REG012/u, SK/REG021/u

Athletics: AB/ALHER3/g, AB/ALHER6/g, AB/GPRC25/c,
AB/GPRC47/c, AB/LET019/u, AB/LETH03/c, AB/MRC010/c,
AB/MRC011/c, AB/SFB004/g, BC/BCAA01/g, BC/BRI107/u,
BC/CBO005/c, BC/HJS001/g, BC/NGR001/g, BC/PAA01/g,
BC/SFU006/u, BC/SFU033/u, BC/UCFV05/c, BC/UCFV06/c,
BC/VAN003/c, BC/VIC022/u, CA/AAP01/g, CA/CFSA01/g,
CA/PCO001/g, CA/TFOX01/g, MB/UAS01/g, NT/SNFS01/g,
SK/REG021/u, SK/SAS005/u, SK/SAS012/u, SK/SAS015/u, SK/SIA005/c

Basketball: AB/CAL054/u, AB/CAL055/u, AB/CAL058/u, BC/BRI064/u,
BC/HSBA01/g, BC/SSGBA1/g

BC Teachers: BC/BRI030/u

Bilingual: AB/CAL036/u, CA/PAGE01/g

Blue Cross: MB/MBC01/g, MB/MBC02/g, MB/WNG011/u

B'nai B'rith: BC/BRI084/u

Bowling: BC/YBS001g

Boys and Girls Clubs: AB/ALBO38/u, BC/B&G001/g

Cadets: AB/LSTS01/g, CA/NLC03/g, SK/NLC02/g

Canada Pension Plan: MB/CPP01/g

Canadian Daughters: BC/CDS01/g

Canadian Navy: CA/RCNBF1/g

Catholic Family Services: BC/CFS01/g

Catholic priesthood: SK/SASTM3/u

Catholic Women's League: SK/REGC11/u

Cattlemen: BC/BVCA01/g

Chinese: AB/CAL047/u, BC/BRI021/u

Christian work: BC/TWU005/u

Citizenship: AB/CAL044/u, AB/LET014/u, MB/BRN006/u

Co-ops: AB/CALC01/g, CA/LEM001/g, SK/GMM01/g

College transfer: AB/LET025/u, AB/LET026/u, AB/LET027/u, BC/SFU034/u, BC/SFU035/u

Communication: BC/SFU007/u

Community service: AB/ALB005/u, AB/ALB006/u, AB/ALB008/u, AB/ALB009/u, AB/GPRC02/c, AB/GPRC03/c, AB/GPRC05/c, AB/GPRC15/c, AB/GPRC18/c, AB/GPRC35/c, AB/GPRC37/c, AB/GPRC40/c, AB/GPRC46/c, AB/ICAA01/g, AB/KEY011/c, AB/KEY013/c, AB/LAKE09/c, AB/LAKE10/c, AB/MED004/c, BC/BCITO2/c, BC/BCITO3/c, BC/BCIT09/c, BC/BRI029/u, BC/BRI074/u, BC/CBO008/c, BC/DGS002/c, BC/DGS003/c, BC/DSS01/g, BC/KWA003/c, BC/KWA005/c, BC/KWA007/c, BC/KWA010/c, BC/SOR01/g, BC/SPARK1/g, CA/BBM001/g, CA/CAP001/g, CA/CMFS01/g, CA/TFOX01/g, MB/BRN013/u, SK/AECA01/g, SK/CUHS01/g, SK/CUMB01/c, SK/CUMB02/c, SK/CUMB03/c, SK/CUMB04/c, SK/CUMB05/c, SK/CUMB06/c, SK/CUMB07/c, SK/CUMB08/c, SK/CUMB09/c, SK/CUMB10/c, SK/CUMB11/c, SK/MEDIA1/g, SK/NWR001/c, SK/NWR003/c, SK/NWR004/c, SK/REG010/u, SK/REG014/u, SK/REG018/u, SK/SAS023/u, SK/SAS028/u, SK/SIA001/c, SK/SIA008/c, SK/SSTA01/g, YT/SFAC01/g, YT/WRC01/g

Conservation: CA/CWF001/g

Construction: AB/CCRB01/g

Correspondence courses: AB/CAL063/u

Creative writing: BC/BRI035/u, BC/BRI050/u, CA/UCOL01/g

Criminal justice: BC/VAN001/c

Criminology: BC/SFU013/u

Cross-country skiing: BC/BRI060/u

Cultural ability: BC/KWA004/c

Czechoslovakian: AB/LET012/u

Diabetes: SK/SAS027/u

Disabled: AB/CPA01/g, AB/GPMH01/g, AB/GPRC07/c, AB/LET030/u, AB/LET036/u, AB/MED022/g, AB/NACCF1/g, AB/SFB002/g, BC/APSD01/g, BV/BCIT12/c, BC/BCPF01/g, BC/BCPF02/g, BC/BCPF03/g, BC/BCPF04/g, BC/BCPF05/g, BC/BCPF06/g, BC/BCPF07/g, BC/BRI029/u, BC/BRI036/c, BC/BRI051/u, BC/BRI067/u, BC/BRI078/u, BC/BRI087/u, BC/BRI97/u, BC/OKA003/c, BC/SSD01/g, BC/TCDV01/g, BC/VIC005/u, CA/CCPA01/g, CA/CPA001/g,

NT/ARC003/c, SK/SAS019/u, SK/SOR01/g, SK/STEL01/g,
YT/CLOW01/g, YT/CLOW02/g, YT/SFAC02/c

Filipino: AB/SAIT03/g

Fine arts: AB/LET011/u, BC/CACCO4/g, BC/UCFV04/c, CA/EGF001/g,
SK/REG009/u

Flowers: CA/PHS001/g

Food technology: BC/BCIT08/c

Football: AB/ALB037/u, AB/ALHER7/g, AB/CAL009/u, BC/BRI070/u

Foreign students: AB/CAL056/u

Forest products: BC/VAN002/c

French: AB/ALB012/u, BC/LFAP01/g, BC/SFU016/u, CA/RCS001/g,
CA/SLBP01/g, MB/CUSB01/u, MB/CUSB02/u, SK/REGC13/u,
SK/SASED2/g, SK/SASED3/g, SK/SASED4/g, SK/SASED5/g,
SK/SASED6/g

French/English: BC/FPLP01/g

Gay and lesbian: BC/BRI066/u

Geophysics: CA/CSEG01/g

Girl Guides: BC/BRI069/u, CA/GGC01/g

Gliding: AB/SAIT01/c

Golf: CA/CGF001/g

Greek: BC/BRI023/u

Harvard: AB/ALHER4/g

Hearing impaired: AB/LET037/u, BC/KHISS1/g

Hiking: BC/BRI060/u

Hockey: AB/ALB021/u, AB/ALB019/u, AB/ALHER5/g, AB/CAL008/u,
AB/CAL011/u, BC/BCAHA1/g, BC/BRI131/u, SK/GAVIN1/g,
SK/SAHA01/g

Holstein Canada: CA/HOL01/g

Hong Kong resident: BC/BRI132/u

Horticulture: CA/VHRT01/g

IODE, veterans: BC/BRI073/u

Icelandic: BC/ICC01/g

Independent Order of Foresters: AB/IOF01/g, BC/IOF01/g

India: SK/SAS013/u

International baccalaureate: MB/WNG008/u, YT/DOE01/g

International students: BC/BRI016/u, BC/OKA005/c

AB/LETH08/c, AB/REDD02/c, AB/REDD03/c, AB/REDD04/c, AB/REDD06/c

Mennonite studies: MB/WNG005/u

Mensa: CA/MENS01/g

Mental handicap: AB/CACL01/g, AB/CAMH01/g, AB/PACL01/g, BC/ACL01/g, BC/KSCL01/g, BC/KSCL02/g, SK/SACL01/g, SK/SACL02/g

Military: AB/GPRC31/c, BC/BRI017/u, BC/BRI038/u, BC/BRI039/u, BC/BRI129/u, BC/BRI133/u, CA/AFP01/g, CA/LEO001/g, CA/RWRAS1/g, MB/DVA01/g, MB/WNG004/u, SK/ROB01/g

Mineral industry: SK/CAME01/g

Mining: BC/BCIT06/c, CA/WAMC01/g

Minorities: MB/HYDR01/g, SK/SAS029/u, SK/STELO1/g

Multiple Sclerosis: SK/MSSC01/g

Municipal government: AB/ENM01/g

Muscular Dystrophy: BC/MDA01/g, BC/MDA02/g

Native (First Nations Peoples): AB/AIIC01/g, AB/ALB029/u, AB/ALB036/u, AB/ALB041/u, AB/CAL023/u, AB/KEY009/c, AB/MED020/c, AB/MED021/c, AB/NCW01/g, AB/NOVA01/g, AB/SYNC02/g, BC/BCIT11/c, BC/BEMM01/g, BC/BRI033/u, BC/BRI035/u, BC/BRI063/u, BC/BRI078/u, BC/BRI081/u, BC/BRI114/u, BC/CBO003/c, BC/HAWC01/g, BC/IAS01/g, BC/MMMA01/g, BC/MNA01/g, BC/MOH001/g, BC/OKA014/c, BC/STF01/g, BC/VIC007/u, CA/CNA001/g, CA/CNA002/g, CA/CNN001/g, CA/DOE02/g, CA/EAN001/g, CA/ESP001/g, CA/ESSO1/g, CA/HUSK01/g, CA/INAC01/g, CA/ONW001/g, CA/PDG02/g, CA/PNWA01/g, CA/ROYAL1/g, MB/HYDR01/g, MB/POW01/g, NT/NWA01/g, NT/TTMF01/g, NT/YT/BX1/g, SK/AMOK01/g, SK/DRS01/g, SK/CHIEF1/g, SK/HOTA01/g, SK/NAP01/g, SK/OBEY01/g, SK/REGS01/u, SK/REGS02/u, SK/REGS03/u, SK/SAS003/u, SK/SAS025/u, SK/SIA003/c, SK/STEL01/g, YT/SYANA1/g, YT/YKFN01/g

Naval officers: AB/NOAC01/g, CA/RCNBF1/g

Navy League: CA/NLC01/g, CA/NLC02/g, CA/NLS001/g, CA/NLS002/g, SK/NLC01/g

Newfoundland: AB/NEWF01/g

Newspaper carriers: AB/MHN01/g, BC/VSUN01/g, BC/VSUN02/g

Northern Alberta: AB/PRPM01/g

Northern BC: BC/BRI105/u

Northern Canada: CA/ACUNS1/g

Spina Bifida: AB/SPA01/g

Stampede: AB/MED019/c

Sto:lo: BC/SSA01/g

Swedish: BC/BRI018/u

Talent: SK/SKF01/g

Teacher: AB/REDD07/c, CA/PDK001/g

Theatre: AB/REDD24/c

Track: BC/SSTF01/g

TransAlta Utilities: AB/ALB031/u, AB/CAL048/u, AB/MRC009/c

Tuberculosis: BC/BCLA01/g

Ukrainian: BC/SLIPY1/g, CA/UCPC01/g

Uncles and Aunts at Large: AB/CAL037/u

United Church: MB/WNG012/u

United Kingdom: BC/BRI076/u

Valedictorian: BC/CUC001/c

Veterans: AB/VET01/g, BC/BRI083/u, BC/BRI112/u

Visual arts: BC/AMAC01/g, BC/CACGV1/g, BC/SPACS1/g

Visually impaired: AB/SFB006/g, BC/BRI034/u, BC/BRI047/u,
BC/BRI051/u, BC/BRI052/u, BC/BRI091/u, BC/BRI105/u, BC/BRI107/u,
BC/CNIB01/g, BC/CNIB02/g, BC/CNIB03/g, BC/CNIB04/g,
BC/CNIB05/g, BC/CNIB06/g, BC/CNIB07/g, BC/CNIB08/g,
BC/CNIB09/g, BC/CNIB10/g, BC/CNIB11/g, CA/VIEW01/g,
CA/VIEW02/g, SK/SSCF01/g

War Amputations: BC/WAOC01/g

Wards of the Province, BC: BC/PTE01/g

Water: AB/AWW01/g

Wheelchair athletes: CA/CWSA01/g

Wildlife: NT/NWTW01/g

Women's Institute: BC/BCWI01/g, BC/BCWI03/g

Writing: BC/JGM01/g

YMCA: BC/YMCA01/g, BC/YMCA02/g, BC/YMCA03/g

Cross-reference by specific program of study

Accounting: BC/CGAA01/g, BC/ICA001/g, SK/ASBOS1/g,
SK/SMAS01/g

Administration: SK/ASBOS1/g, SK/REG017/u

Agricultural science: BC/BRI008/c, BC/BRI010/u, BC/BRI029/u

Agricultural technology: AB/LETH01/c, AB/LETH11/c, BC/UCFV01/c

Agriculture: AB/4-H001/g, AB/4-H003/g, AB/4-H008/g, AB/4-H009/g, AB/4-H020/g, AB/4-H026/g, AB/4-H029/g, AB/4-H032/g, AB/40MIL1/g, AB/APW002/g, AB/ALB038/u, AB/ALB039/u, AB/ALB045/u, AB/AWP01/g, AB/GPRC19/c, AB/GPRC48/c, AB/KGF01/g, AB/LAKE09/c, AB/REDD19/c, BC/4-H008/g, BC/BCCA02/g, BC/BRI009/u, BC/BRI117/u, BC/CVFI01/g, BC/UCFV02/c, MB/BRN019/u, SK/RUSI01/g, SK/SAS007/u, SK/SAS011/u, SK/SAS019/u, SK/SAS020/u, SK/SAS031/u

Aircraft maintenance: BC/BCIT04/c

Architecture: BC/BRI019/u

Art: BC/RBM01/g, CA/CSEA01/g, CA/CNA002/g, CA/EGF001/g, CA/PDG002/g, SK/REG026/u

Automotive: BC/OKA007/c, CA/AIAC01/g, CA/FELPR1/g

Aviation: BC/UCFV03/c, CA/CCPEP1/g, YT/SFAC05/g

Biology: AB/LET022/u, BC/SFU026/u

Biology technology: AB/REDD10/c

Broadcast communications: BC/BAC01/g, BC/BCIT11/c, BC/JGM01/g

Business: AB/ALB010/u, AB/ICAA01/g, AB/LET054/u, BC/KWA001/g, BC/KWA009/c, BC/OKA009/g, SK/CUMB13/c

Business administration: AB/GPRC41/c, AB/LAKE01/c, AB/LAKE10/g, AB/MED006/c, AB/MRC006/c, AB/MRC008/c, AB/REDD21/c, BC/CBO08/c, BC/SFU025/u

Business education: AB/KEY010/c, SK/BUJEA1/g

Catholic priesthood: SK/SASTM3/u

Chemical technology: AB/AELR01/g

Chemistry: BC/BRI029/u, BC/SFU027/u

College Preparatory: AB/REDD01/c, AB/REDD02/c, AB/REDD20/c

Commerce: AB/ARC01/g, AB/CAL043/u, AB/GPRC46/c, AB/MED006/c, AB/MED007/g, AB/P&G01/g, NT/ARC001/c, NT/ICA01/g, SK/SAS029/u

Communications: CA/RCS001/g, SK/MEDIA1/g

Computers: AB/CAL017/u, AB/GPRC27/c, AB/GPRC28/c, AB/KEY011/c, AB/MED005/c, AB/MED006/c, AB/REDD12/c, AB/REDD21/c, BC/SFU008/u, SK/REG017/u

Computer systems technology: AB/MED008/c, AB/MED020/c

Conservation: CA/CWF001/g, NT/NWTW01/g

Co-operative studies: CA/LEM001/g

Creative writing: BC/BRI033/u

Criminal justice: BC/VAN001/c

Dentistry: NT/DENT01/g

ESL (English as a Second Language): SK/SIA007/c

Early childhood development: AB/GPRC29/c, AB/KEY012/c, AB/REDD16/c, AB/MED009/c, AB/MED020/c

Economics: BC/BRI132/u

Education: AB/ALB023/u, AB/ATA01/g, AB/CAL006/u, AB/GPRC06/c, AB/GPRC19/c, AB/GPRC33/c, AB/LSTS01/g, AB/MED009/c, AB/MED010/c, AB/MED025/c, AB/PACLO1/g, AB/REDD07/c, AB/REDD13/c, AB/REDD14/c, AB/SFB003/g, BC/BRI027/u, BC/BRI030/u, BC/BRI031/u, BC/BRI041/u, BC/BRI053/u, BC/BRI056/u, BC/BRI119/u, BC/CBO009/c, BC/CBO10/c, CA/PDK001/g, MB/MTS001/g, SK/ASHE01/g, SK/REG012/g, SK/SAS001/u, SK/SAS002/u, SK/SAS009/u, SK/SAS021/u, SK/SAS022/u, SK/SAS023/u, SK/SASED3/g, SK/SASTM5/u, SK/SCKC01/g, YT/YTA01/g

Electronics technology: BC/BCIT13/c

Engineering: AB/ALB009/u, AB/APEGG1/g, AB/ARC01/g, AB/CAL007/u, AB/CAL017/u, AB/CAL018/u, AB/CAL030/u, AB/LET014/u, AB/MED011/c, AB/MRC007/c, AB/MRC009/c, AB/P&G01/g, AB/REDD08/c, AB/REDD25/c, BC/BCPF05/g, BC/BRI008/u, BC/BRI009/u, BC/BRI011/u, BC/BRI012/u, BC/BRI027/u BC/BRIO57/u, BC/BRI058/u, BC/BRI065/u, BC/CBO008/c, BC/SFU007/u, BC/SFU009/u, BC/VIC009/u, BC/VIC015/u, CA/CASH01/g, MB/HYDR01/g, MB/HYDR02/g, MB/HYDR03/g, NT/ARC01/g, NT/NAPEG1/g, SK/ISPC01/g, SK/SAS017/u, SK/SCKC01/g

Engineering transfer program: AB/LET021/u

English: AB/LET009/u, CA/SLBP01/g

Environmental sciences: AB/LAKE05/c, CA/BMM001/g, MB/MFA01/g, YT/YCS01/g

Environmental technology: NT/ARC002/c, NT/ARC003/c

Equine studies: AB/4-H023/g

Fine arts: AB/AUG005/u, AB/CAL059/u, AB/LET031/u, BC/CACC01/g, BC/CACC02/g, BC/CACC03/g, BC/CACC04/g, BC/CACGV1/g, BC/CACR01/g, BC/UCFV04/c, CA/CSFS01/g, YT/SYANA1/G

Flowers: CA/PHS001/g

Food science: AB/ALB024/u, BC/BCIT08/c, SK/ASHE01/g

Mathematics: BC/SFU028/u

Mennonite studies: MB/WNG005/u

Mentally handicapped: AB/CAMH01/g, AB/PACLO1/g, BC/KSCL01/g, BC/KSCL02/g

Metallurgical engineering: BC/BRI022/u

Mining: BC/BCIT06/c, BC/BCIT14/c, BC/CIMM01/g, CA/WAMC01/g, SK/SMDC01/g

Municipal government: AB/ENM01/g

Music: AB/ALB042/u, AB/ALB048/u, AB/CAL013/u, AB/CAL021/u, AB/CAL022/u, AB/CAL027/u, AB/CAL028/u, AB/CAL029/u, AB/CAL033/u, AB/CAL042/u, AB/CAL064/u, AB/GPRC24/c, AB/GPRC30/c, AB/LET023/u, AB/LET033/u, AB/LET034/u, BC/BCMEA1/g, BC/BRI014/u, BC/BRI015/u, BC/BRI025/u, BC/BRI026/u, BC/BRI068/u, BC/BRI99/u, BC/BRI100/u, BC/DGS004/c, BC/VANF01/g, BC/VIC004/u, BC/VIC008/u, BC/VIC010/u, BC/VIC012/u, BC/VIC013/u, BC/VIC014/u, BC/VIC018/u, BC/VIC023/u, BC/VIC024/u, BC/VIC025/u, BC/VIC027/u, BC/VIC032/u, MB/BRN001/u, MB/BRN012/u, MB/BRN015/u, MB/BRN018/u, SK/REGL04/u, SK/REGL09/u, SK/SAS004/u, SK/SAS006/u, SK/SAS018/u

Native studies: AB/SFB005/g

Nursing: AB/ALB047/u, AB/CAL010/u, AB/GPRC18/c, AB/GPRC31/c, AB/GPRC32/c, AB/KEY013/c, AB/KEY014/c, AB/LET028/u, AB/LETH07/c, AB/LETH08/c, AB/LETH10/c, AB/BRI113/u, BC/CBO008/c, BC/CBO10/c, BC/DAW01/g, BC/DCDH01/g, BC/PCN01/g, BC/PRRH01/g, BC/RNF01/g, BC/STJA01/g, BC/YMCA01/g, CA/STJA01/g, MB/MARN01/g, NT/YT/BX1/g, SK/RNAMJ1/g, SK/STJA02/g, SK/SIA004/c

Nutrition: BC/BRI032/u, BC/BRI118/u

Occupational health and safety: BC/BCIT07/c

Office administration: AB/GPRC14/c, BC/NEWC05/c

Outdoor education or environmental studies: CA/BMM001/g

Parks and recreation: AB/ARPA01/g

Performing arts: AB/CFGP02/g, AB/GPRC13/c, AB/GPRC39/c, AB/LET032/u, BC/VANF01/g, SK/SKF01/g

Petroleum industry: AB/SYNC01/g, AB/SYNC02/g, CA/ESS01/g, CA/HUSK01/g

Pharmacy: AB/REDD18/c, SK/ASHE01/g, SK/SPS01/g

Philosophy: BC/BRI132/u

Physical education: AB/LSTS01/g, AB/SFB004/g, BC/VIC026/u, SK/NLC02/g, SK/REG019/u, SK/REG022/u

Physics: BC/SFU029/u

Political science: BC/BRI1132/u, MB/BRN003/u

Pre-Dental: MB/BRN020/u

Pre-Employment trades: AB/GPRC17/c

Pre-Law: AB/GPRC46/c, AB/GPRC47/c

Pre-Management: AB/CAL005/u, AB/CAL046/u

Pre-Medicine: AB/LET010/u, SK/REG023/u

Pre-Theology: SK/EMM01/g

Real estate: BC/OKA013/c

Recreation: AB/ARC01/g, AB/LSTS01/g, AB/P&G01/g, AB/SAIT05/g, NT/ARC01/g, SK/SIA005/c, SK/MASON4/g

Rehabilitation medicine: AB/ALB025/u, AB/ALB028/u, AB/GPMH01/g, AB/GPRC42/c, AB/REDD15/c, YT/CV01/g

Remote sensing: CA/BAUS01/g

Respiratory therapy: SK/SHB001/g

Science: AB/MED007/c, BC/BRI008/u, BC/BRI009/u, BC/BRI111/u, BC/CAP003/c, BC/CAP004/c, BC/CAP005/c, BC/MAL001/c, BC/SFU030/u, BC/VIC021/u, CA/CASH01/g, SK/REG008/u, SK/REG017/u, SK/REGL05/u

Shipping and marine operations: BC/PMTI01/c, BC/PMTI02/c, BC/PMTI03/c, BC/PMTI04/c, BC/PMTI05/c

Social service: BC/DSS01/g, AB/NCW01/g, AB/NEWF01/g, BC/BRI045/u, BC/BEMM01/g

Sports: NT/SNFS01/g

Teacher assistant: AB/REDD17/c, YT/SFAC10/g

Technical: SK/CUMB05/c, SK/CUMB11/c, YT/ORP01/g, YT/SFAC09/g

Technology/Trades: BC/BCIT01/c, BC/BCITO2/c, BC/BCIT03/c, BC/BCIT05/c, BC/BCIT10/c, BC/BCIT12/c, BC/NEWC03/c, CA/CNW001/g, MB/HYDR01/g, SK/NWR003/c, SK/NWR004/c, SK/SCKC01/g

Theatre studies: AB/REDD24/c, BC/VAN01/g

Theological training: YT/CCC01/g

Tourism: BC/OKA009/C

Trades: AB/MED024/c

Transportation: CA/CNN001/g

Ukrainian studies: BC/SLIPY1/g

United World College: CA/DOE02/g

University transfer: AB/LAKE02/c, AB/KEY016/c, AB/MED011/c, AB/MED017/c, AB/MED018/c

Urban studies: SK/CREG01/g

Veterinary sciences: AB/4-H001/g, AB/4-H003/g, AB/4-H030/g, AB/GPRC38/c

Visual arts: AB/AFA01/g, AB/AFA02/g, BC/SPACS1/g, YT/SFAC08/g

Visual and performing arts: AB/GPRC21/c, BC/AMACO1/g, BC/CBO007/C, BC/SFU012/u, CA/CNA001/g, CA/ESP001/g

Vocational training: AB/SOR01/g, BC/CBO013/c, BC/YT/SVI1/g, CA/VHRT01/g, SK/SOR01/g

Water and wastewater technician: AB/AWW01/g

Women's studies: BC/KWA013/c

Cross-Reference by application deadline

DATE	CODE	NAME OF SCHOLARSHIP
September 1	AB/ALB048/u	Edmonton Musical Club Scholarship in Music
	AB/LETH01/c	Alberta Treasury Branches Bursary
	AB/LETH02/c	Andy Anderson Student Leadership Award
	AB/LETH03/c	Canada Winter Games Scholarship
	AB/LETH04/c	Dr. Frank Christie Award
	AB/LETH06/c	Frank M. and Lila Linn Thompson Scholarship (I)
	AB/LETH07/c	Frank M. and Lila Linn Thompson Scholarship (II)
	AB/LETH08/c	Frank M. and Lila Linn Thompson Scholarship (III)
	AB/LETH09/c	Lethbridge Community College Entrance Scholarship
	AB/LETH10/c	Siguard E. Hansen Scholarship
	AB/LETH11/c	Vencl Hrncirik Memorial Scholarship
	AB/LETH12/c	William Asbury Buchanan Bursary
	BC/BCLA01/g	British Columbia Lung Association Bursaries
	BC/LFAP01/g	La Foundation André Piolat Bourses
	BC/UCFV02/c	Chilliwack Horticultural Society Scholarships
	SK/CREG01/g	City of Regina Scholarships
	SK/IAAI01/g	Bun Allin Memorial Scholarship
	SK/REG006/u	Elmer Shaw Special Talent Entrance Scholarship

September 11	SK/CUMB10/c	Nipiwan Royal Canadian Legion Bursary
(cont.)		
September 12	SK/REGL01/u	Philip Assman Memorial Scholarships (Luther College)
	SK/REGL02/u	Harold A. Dietrich University Bursaries (Luther College)
	SK/REGL03/u	Entrance Scholarships for Excellence and Achievement (Luther College)
	SK/REGL04/u	Liefeld Music Scholarship (Luther College)
	SK/REGL05/u	Liefeld – Taube Science Scholarship (Luther College)
	SK/REGL06/u	Laurence M. Maxwell Memorial Scholarship (Luther College)
	SK/REGL07/u	Caroline Niebergall Scholarship (Luther College)
	SK/REGL08/u	St. Mark's Lutheran Church Anniversary Scholarship (Luther College)
	SK/REGL09/u	Robert and Gertrude Wagner Music Scholarship (Luther College)
September 15	AB/GPRC01/c	A.C.T. Auxiliary Bursary
	AB/GPRC02/c	Academic Staff Association Bursary
	AB/GPRC03/c	Alberta Power Limited Bursary
	AB/GPRC04/c	Alberta Union of Provincial Employees Bursary
	AB/GPRC05/c	Margaret Andersen Bursary
	AB/GPRC06/c	Henry N. Anderson Scholarship
	AB/GPRC07/c	Army, Navy and Air Force Veterans in Canada Award
	AB/GPRC08/c	BLHS Reunion '86 Bursary
	AB/GPRC09/c	Beta Sigma Phi Bursary
	AB/GPRC10/c	Bowes Family Mature Student Bursary
	AB/GPRC11/c	Elizabeth Jean Butler Scholarships
	AB/GPRC12/c	Canadian Forest Products Bursary
	AB/GPRC13/c	CFGP Performing Arts Scholarship
	AB/GPRC14/c	Chicken Village Office Administration Bursary
	AB/GPRC15/c	Daily Herald-Tribune Bursary
	AB/GPRC16/c	Edmonton Northlands Mature Student Bursary
	AB/GPRC17/c	Edmonton Northlands Pre-Employment Trades Bursaries
	AB/GPRC18/c	Fairview Health Complex District #59 Nursing Bursary
	AB/GPRC19/c	Elsworth Foy Memorial Bursary
	AB/GPRC20/c	Angel Fraser Memorial Scholarship
	AB/GPRC21/c	Grande Prairie Amateur Games Society Award

September 15 (cont.)	AB/REDD07/c	Central Alberta Teachers' Convention Association Educational Award
	AB/REDD08/c	Charles Henry Snell City of Red Deer Engineering Scholarship
	AB/REDD09/c	County of Red Deer #23 Tuition Award
	AB/REDD10/c	Edmonton Northlands Biology Technology Award
	AB/REDD11/c	Edmonton Northlands College Preparatory Award
	AB/REDD12/c	Edmonton Northlands Computer Systems Technology Award
	AB/REDD13/c	Edmonton Northlands Education – Elementary Award
	AB/REDD14/c	Edmonton Northlands Education – Secondary Award
	AB/REDD15/c	Edmonton Northlands Rehabilitation Services Award
	AB/REDD16/c	Georgia Belknap Endowment Early Childhood Education Entrance Award
	AB/REDD17/c	Georgia Belknap Endowment Teacher Assistant Entrance Award
	AB/REDD18/c	Helen Anderson Smith Pharmacy Technician Bursary
	AB/REDD19/c	Henry Wise Wood Memorial Award
	AB/REDD20/c	Ian Cannon Memorial Bursary
	AB/REDD21/c	Imperial Oil Limited Scholarship
	AB/REDD22/c	Red Deer College Students' Association Bachelor of Arts Entrance Award
	AB/REDD23/c	Red Deer College Students' Association General Studies Entrance Award
	AB/REDD24/c	Shauna O'Sullivan Memorial Award in Theatre
	AB/REDD25/c	TransAlta Utilities Engineering Award
	BC/CBO001/c	CUPE Local 3500 Bursary
	BC/CBO002/c	Drdul, Alex Memorial Bursaries
	BC/CBO004/c	UCC Entrance Scholarships
	BC/CBO006/c	UCC Student Financial Aid Fund
	BC/CBO007/c	Underwriters Insurance Agencies Award
	BC/LTKF01/g	Leon and Thea Koerner Foundation Grants
	BC/OKA008/c	Penticton Centre Award Fund
	BC/OKA009/c	Penticton Chamber of Commerce Business Scholarship
	BC/OKA012/c	Penticton University Women's Club Bursary
	BC/PVPA01/g	BC Principals' and Vice-Principals' Association Scholarships
	BC/RIHF01/g	Royal Inland Hospital Foundation Award(s)

September 30	BC/KWA013/c	Women's Equity Bursary
(cont.)	BC/NWC001/c	Northwest Community College Entrance Scholarships
	CA/RRS001/g	Rixon Rafter Scholarship
	NT/NAPEG1/g	NAPEGG Scholarship
	NT/SNFS01/g	Sport North Federation Scholarship
	SK/AECA01/g	Arcola East Community Association (AECA)
	SK/CURR01/g	Gordon Currie Youth Development Bursary
	SK/MASON2/g	Ross Kirk Masonic Past Masters Association Inc. Bursary
	SK/MASON5/g	Saskatoon Chapter #4 Royal Arc Mason Past Masters Association Bursary
	SK/NWR001/c	Canadian Tire Scholarship
	SK/NWR002/c	Adult Basic Education Scholarship
	SK/NWR003/c	RE/MAX Scholarship
	SK/NWR004/c	Technical Training Scholarship
	SK/RNAMJ1/g	Saskatchewan Registered Nurses Association (Moose Jaw) Bursary
	SK/SAS001/u	Sarah Jane Abrey Bursaries
	SK/SAS021/u	Evelyn Norgord Scholarship in Education
	SK/SAS022/u	Halvor and Betty Norgord Scholarship in Education
	SK/SAS023/u	Phi Delta Kappa Scholarship in Education
	SK/SASSP1/u	Frank and Elizabeth Weber Scholarship (St Peter's College)
	SK/SASSP2/u	Thomas and Marie Clandinin Scholarship (St Peter's College)
	SK/SASSP3/u	Co-operative Work Scholarship (St Peter's College)
	SK/SASSP4/u	St Peter's College Entrance Scholarships
	SK/SASTM1/u	St Thomas More College First-Year Scholarships
	SK/SASTM2/u	St Thomas More Knights of Columbus First-Year Scholarships
	SK/SASTM3/u	Rose Voytilla Scholarship
	SK/SASTM4/u	Knights of Columbus Bursaries
	SK/SASTM5/u	Maureen Haynes Memorial Scholarship
	SK/SIA002/c	E.A. Davies Scholarship Award (Kelsey)
	SK/SIA005/c	A.E. Smith Memorial Bursary (Kelsey)
	SK/SPS01/g	Saskatoon Pharmacists' Society Scholarship
	YT/CLOW01/g	Julie Cruickshank Bursary
	YT/SFAC08/g	Yukon Art Society Scholarship
October 1	AB/NACCF1/g	Dr. G.R.A. Rice Bursary
	BC/BRI024/u	Birks Family Foundation Bursary
	BC/BRI031/u	BC Telephone NITEP Bursary

October 15	BC/BRI130/u	Zonta Club of Vancouver Bursary
(cont.)	BC/KWA001/c	Phyllis Addinall Bauer Memorial Scholarship
	SK/CYP001/c	Cypress Hills Regional College Entrance Award
	SK/CYP002/c	South Saskatchewan Pipelines Scholarship
	SK/CYP003/c	Sask Oil Scholarship
	SK/CYP004/c	Swift Current Kiwanis Club Scholarship
	SK/SAS010/u	Howard Henderson Memorial Bursary (Agriculture)
	SK/SAS031/u	Bill Story Memorial Bursary in Agriculture
October 28	CA/CMSF01/g	Canadian Merit Scholarship Foundation Awards
October 30	AB/MRC010/c	Athletic Grants in Aid for MRC
	AB/MRC011/c	Jimmie Condon Athletic Scholarships
	AB/SFB006/g	Wayne Gretzky Scholarship
	BC/CNIB06/g	Martha Guest Memorial Bursary
	CA/AIAC01/g	Automotive Industries Association of Canada Scholarship
	CA/BBM001/g	Bobby Bauer Memorial Award
	SK/SIA006/c	Association of Canadian Community Colleges Bursary
October 31	AB/CAB01/g	Charlie Floyd Memorial Scholarship
	AB/MRC001/c	Board of Governors Entrance Scholarship
	AB/MRC002/c	City of Calgary Scholarships
	AB/MRC003/c	Dr. George W. Kerby Memorial Scholarship
	AB/MRC004/c	Mount Royal College Entrance Scholarships
	AB/MRC005/c	Native Calgarian Society Scholarship
	AB/MRC006/c	Nickle Family Foundation Scholarship – Business Administration
	AB/MRC007/c	Nickle Family Foundation Scholarship – Engineering
	AB/MRC008/c	Jim Sinclair Insurance Bursary
	AB/MRC009/c	TransAlta Utilities Engineering Scholarship
	BC/UCFV04/c	Michelene Catherine Allard Memorial Fine Arts Bursary
	BC/YMCA01/g	Adele Peet YMCA Memorial Bursary Award
	CA/CNN001/g	CN Native Educational Awards Program
	CA/IFJ001/g	International Fellowships in Jewish Studies
	CA/WAMC01/g	Sophia Wood Education Award
	SK/REGS03/u	SIFC Entrance Scholarship

January 15 (cont.)	CA/PAGE01/g	Page Program
	SK/SOR01/g	Soroptimist Training Award Program
January 31	CA/ACUNS1/g	Special Awards for Northern Residents
	CA/CSFS01/g	Canadian-Scandinavian Foundation Scholarship
	CA/PDK001/g	Phi Delta Kappa Scholarship Grants
	NT/ACNS01/g	Beverly and Oaminirjuao Caribou Management Scholarship Fund
February 1	CA/TFOX01/g	Terry Fox Humanitarian Award
	MB/MAN002/u	Isabel Auld Entrance Scholarship
	MB/MAN003/u	Queen Elizabeth II Entrance Scholarships
	SK/PWP01/g	Parents Without Partners Award
February 15	AB/CCRB01/g	Building and Construction Research Scholarship
	SK/SASED5/g	French Summer Language Bursary Program
	SK/SASED6/g	Official Languages Monitor Program
February 18	CA/SLBP01/g	Summer Language Bursary Program
February 28	BC/DCDH01/g	Dawson Creek and District Hospital Bursaries
	CA/MENS01/g	Mensa Canada Scholarship Program
	SK/REGS01/u	Eastview Rotary Indian/Native Entrance Scholarship (SIFC)
	SK/REGS02/u	Information Systems Management Scholarship, (SIFC)
	SK/SIA001/c	Constable Brian King Memorial Scholarship (Kelsey)
March 1	BC/CACGV1/g	Community Arts Council of Greater Victoria Bursaries
	BC/PAA01/g	Premier's Athletic Awards
	BC/TWU004/u	Trinity Western Academic Scholarship
	BC/YMCA03/g	Ellen Bell Memorial Scholarship
	CA/CDH001/g	C.D. Howe Memorial Foundation Scholarships
	CA/DOE02/g	Duke of Edinburgh United World College Scholarship
	SK/REG008/u	Faculty of Science 10th Anniversary Scholarship
	YT/DOE01/g	Lester B. Pearson College of the Pacific
March 2	MB/WNG002/u	Francis Winston Armstrong Entrance Scholarship
	MB/WNG003/u	Elinor F.E. Black Entrance Scholarship
	MB/WNG004/u	James H. Cameron Memorial Scholarship
	MB/WNG005/u	C.A. DeFehr Memorial Entrance Scholarship in Mennonite Studies
	MB/WNG006/u	Henry Edmison Duckworth Entrance Scholarships

March 15	BC/4-H006/g	4-H Scholarships
(cont.)	BC/CBO003/c	Macmillan, H.R. Indian Training Fund
	BC/STJA01/g	St John Ambulance Bursaries
	BC/VIC019/u	John Locke Malkin Entrance Scholarships
	BC/VIC020/u	T.S. McPherson Entrance Scholarships
	CA/LEO001/g	Leonard Foundation Financial Assistance Program
	CA/STJA01/g	St John Ambulance Bursary Award Program
	SK/STJA02/g	Margaret McLaren Memorial Bursary
March 21	AB/DROC01/g	Dr. Ed O'Connor Scholarships
March 26	MB/SOR01/g	Soroptimist Training Awards Program
March 31	AB/AFA02/g	Visual Arts Study Grant
	AB/GPRC30/c	Jazz North Scholarships
	AB/SAIT05/c	Don Moore Award
	AB/SAIT06/c	North Canadian Forest Industry
	BC/BRI076/u	A. Johnson Bursary
	BC/JGM01/g	Joseph Golland Memorial Scholarhip Award
	BC/KWA008/c	Kwantlen College Entrance Scholarships
	BC/LAC01/g	Langley Arts Council Fine Arts Scholarship
	BC/OKA006/c	Okanagan University College President's Entrance Scholarships
	CA/PHS001/g	Pat Humphreys Scholarship
	YT/ESTR02/g	Eastern Star Religious Leadership Training Awards
	YT/ESTR03/g	Elizabeth Bentley Order of the Eastern Star Scholarship Awards
April 1	AB/ALHER2/g	Michael Luchkovich Scholarships for Career Development
	AB/LET001/u	Chinook Scholarships
	AB/LET002/u	University of Lethbridge Achievement Scholarships
	AB/LET003/u	Early Entrance Scholarships
	BC/4-H001/g	Bill Alendal Scholarship
	BC/4-H002/g	Zoe Forstbauer 4-H Scholarship
	BC/4-H004/g	Interior Reforestation Scholarship
	BC/4-H005/g	Ralph Barichello Scholarship
	BC/4-H007/g	Norgan Foundation Scholarships
	BC/4-H008/g	BC Fairs Scholarships
	BC/4-H009/g	Farm Credit Corporation Scholarships
	BC/BRI040/u	CBC Prize in Playwriting
	BC/BRI092/u	Norman Mackenzie Alumni Entrance Scholarship
	BC/BRI093/u	Norman A. Mackenzie College Scholarships
	BC/BRI120/u	U.S.A. Alumni Scholarship
	BC/CLRK01/g	Dr. David Clarke Bursary

April 1 (cont.)	BC/SFU027/u	P.D. McTaggart-Cowan Scholarships in Chemistry
	BC/SFU028/u	P.D. McTaggart-Cowan Scholarships in Mathematics
	BC/SFU029/u	P.D. McTaggart-Cowan Scholarships in Physics
	BC/SFU030/u	Dean's Scholarship in Management and Systems Science
	BC/SFU031/u	Gordon M. Shrum National Scholarships
	BC/SFU032/u	Kenneth Strand National Scholarship
	BC/SFU033/u	Jack Diamond National Entrance Scholarships
	BC/SFU034/u	Honourable William M. Hamilton Scholarship
	BC/SFU035/u	Ken Caple Scholarships
	BC/TWU003/u	Trinity Western Entrance Scholarship
	BC/TWU005/u	Christian Ministries Bursary
	BC/TWU006/u	Trinity Western Bursary
	CA/CCPA01/g	Canadian Cerebral Palsy Association Scholarships
	CA/CFSA01/g	Canadian Figure Skating Association Athlete Trust Scholarship
	CA/MONA01/g	Eugene A. Forsey Essay Prize
	MB/BRN005/u	Brandon University Entrance Scholarship to the Music Program
	MB/BRN006/u	Elizabeth Ann Bremner Award
	MB/WNG001/u	Alumni Entrance Awards
	SK/STJA01/g	St John Ambulance Bursary
April 13	BC/CGAA01/g	Certified General Accountants' Association of BC Scholarship
April 14	BC/SFU005/u	Summit Scholarships
	BC/SFU025/u	Dean's Entrance Scholarships in the Faculty of Business Administration
April 15	AB/ALB008/u	Charlotte A. and J. Garner Caddel Memorial Leadership Scholarship
	AB/ICAA01/g	Institute of Chartered Accountants of Alberta High School Awards
	BC/BCCA01/g	BC Cattlemen's Association – Martin Riedmann Bursaries
	BC/BCIT02/c	President's Entrance Award Program
	BC/BRI001/u	National Scholarships
	BC/BRI002/u	Mount Pleasant Branch #177 – Royal Canadian Legion Scholarship
	BC/BRI003/u	Bert Henry Memorial Scholarships
	BC/BRI004/u	Chancellor's Entrance Scholarships (from Secondary School)
	BC/BRI006/u	President's Entrance Scholarships
	BC/BRI007/u	UBC Royal Institution Entrance Scholarships

April 15 (cont.)	BC/BRI008/u	Charles A. and Jane C.A. Banks Foundation Entrance Scholarships I
	BC/BRI009/u	Charles A. and Jane C.A. Banks Foundation Entrance Scholarships II
	BC/BRI010/u	University of BC Agricultural Sciences Alumni Entrance Scholarship
	BC/BRI011/u	Expo 86 Scholarship
	BC/BRI012/u	C.K. Choi Scholarship in Engineering
	BC/BRI013/u	University of BC Forestry Alumni Division Scholarship
	BC/BRI014/u	School of Music 25th Anniversary Entrance Scholarships
	BC/BRI015/u	Harry and Frances Adaskin Scholarship
	BC/BRI042/u	Margaret McDavid Fordyce Clark Memorial Scholarship
	BC/BRI074/u	Annie B. Jamieson Scholarship
	BC/BRI082/u	Labatt Breweries of British Columbia Scholarships
	BC/BRI088/u	W.H. MacInnes Entrance Scholarship in English
	BC/BRI089/u	W. H. MacInnes Entrance Scholarship in Latin
	BC/BRI090/u	W.H. MacInnes Entrance Scholarship in Mathematics
	BC/BRI094/u	Louise Elliot McLuckie Bursary
	BC/BRI100/u	School of Music, Twenty-fifth Anniversary Scholarship
	BC/BRI102/u	Percy W. Nelms Memorial Scholarship
	BC/BRI109/u	John Oliver Piercy Memorial Scholarship
	BC/BRI126/u	Amy Woodland Scholarship
	BC/BRI129/u	Katherine Ann Young Memorial Bursary
	BC/CAP002/c	Capilano College English Scholarship
	BC/CDS01/g	Canadian Daughters' Scholarship (Assembly No. 3, Kamloops)
	BC/CNIB01/g	William and Dorothy Ferrell Scholarship
	BC/CNIB11/g	Telesensory Scholarship
	BC/EKCC01/c	Crestbrook Forest Industries Ltd, Rotary Club of Cranbrook Scholarship
	BC/EKCC02/c	East Kootenay Community College Entrance Scholarships
	BC/EKCC03/c	Paul Sims Memorial Scholarship
	BC/RIHF01/g	Royal Inland Hospital Foundation Award(s)
	BC/TWU001/u	President's Scholarships
	BC/TWU002/u	President's Leadership Award
	BC/VIC001/u	President's Entrance Scholarships
	BC/VIC002/u	President's Regional Entrance Scholarships
	BC/VIC003/u	David Brousson Entrance Scholarship

April 15 (cont.)	BC/VIC004/u	Ralph Barbour Burry Memorial Scholarship in Music
	BC/VIC005/u	L. and G. Butler Scholarship for the Disabled
	BC/VIC007/u	C.H. Dowling Memorial Award
	BC/VIC008/u	Gertrude Huntly Durand Memorial Scholarship
	BC/VIC009/u	Faculty of Engineering: Dean's Entrance Scholarships
	BC/VIC010/u	Walter J. Fletcher Piano Scholarship
	BC/VIC011/u	Alyden Hamber IODE Entrance Scholarship
	BC/VIC012/u	Harbord Insurance Ltd Scholarship
	BC/VIC013/u	Willard E. Ireland Entrance Scholarship
	BC/VIC014/u	J.J. Johannesen Scholarship in Music Performance
	BC/VIC015/u	Betty and Gilbert Kennedy Entrance Scholarship in Engineering
	BC/VIC016/u	Labatt Breweries of British Columbia Limited Scholarship
	BC/VIC017/u	Alexander and Mary Mackenzie Entrance Scholarship
	BC/VIC018/u	Evelyn Marchant MacLaurin Memorial Scholarships in Music
	BC/VIC021/u	George Nelms Memorial Scholarship
	BC/VIC022/u	25th Olympiad Scholarship
	BC/VIC023/u	Performance Scholarship in Music
	BC/VIC024/u	Douglas Ross Memorial Scholarship
	BC/VIC025/u	Herbert and Eva Schaefer String Scholarship
	BC/VIC026/u	School of Physical Education Entrance Scholarship
	BC/VIC027/u	Daisie Thirlwall Scholarships in Violin
	BC/VIC028/u	University of Victoria Entrance Scholarships
	BC/VIC029/u	West Kootenay Power Scholarship
	BC/VIC030/u	Brian Williams Memorial Scholarship
	BC/VIC031/u	Victoria Musical Arts Society Scholarship
	CA/CNA001/g	Educational Scholarship Program
	CA/CNA002/g	Professional Development Grants
	CA/DOE01/g	Duke of Edinburgh's Award Program Award(s)
	CA/ESP001/g	Educational Scholarship Program
	CA/PDG002/g	Professional Development Grants
	SK/ISPC01/g	IPSCO Inc., Scholarships
	SK/REG009/u	Fine Arts Entrance Scholarships
	SK/SAS003/u	Chase Memorial Scholarships
	SK/SAS005/u	R.E. DuWors Scholarship
	SK/SAS008/u	Pearl Finley Scholarships

April 15 (cont.)	SK/SAS009/u	Maureen Hayes Memorial Scholarship
	SK/SAS012/u	Harry R. Hunking Scholarship
	SK/SAS013/u	India Canada Cultural Association Bursary
	SK/SAS015/u	Constable Brian King Memorial Bursaries
	SK/SAS017/u	Moore Memorial Award
	SK/SAS020/u	Frances Elizabeth Murray Scholarship
	SK/SAS025/u	Louis Riel Scholarship
	SK/SAS027/u	Salikin Diabetes Scholarships
	SK/SAS028/u	SASKEXPO '86 Bursary
	SK/SAS030/u	Clare and Margaret Sherrard Memorial Scholarship
	SK/SAS032/u	Toupin Family Memorial Bursary
	SK/SAS033/u	University Entrance Scholarships
	SK/SAS034/u	University of Saskatchewan Alumni Association Scholarships
April 19	SK/ASBOS1/g	Association of School Business Officials Saskatchewan Bursary
April 22	CA/COPP01/g	Paul Moreland/Copp Clark Longman Award
	AB/CFGP02/g	CFGP Scholarship
	AB/MAS0N1/g	Masonic Bursaries
	AB/SAIT01/c	Alberta "75" Scholarship (Gliding)
	BC/BCAHA1/g	BC Amateur Hockey Association Scholarship
	BC/BCYSA1/g	BC Youth Soccer Association Scholarship
	BC/CFS01/g	Barbara Hough Memorial Scholarship
	BC/CNIB02/g	June Gilmore English Memorial Fund
	BC/MAL001/c	Nicholas Plecas Endowment Entrance Scholarships in Science
	BC/OKA007/c	Penticton Auto Dealers Association Automotive Studies Bursary
	BC/PC4-H1/g	Petro-Canada 4-H Youth Leadership Award
	BC/YBS001g	Youth Bowling Congress Scholarship
	CA/SFAC07/g	Queen's University (Kingston, Ontario) National Bursary
	SK/GAVIN1/g	Bill Gavin, Tom Gavin, and Colin Reichel Memorial Bursary
	SK/ODDR01/g	Oddfellows and Rebekah Lodges Scholarships
	SK/REG001/u	Elmer Shaw Entrance Scholarship
	SK/REG002/u	Entrance Scholarships
	SK/REG003/u	Entrance Scholarships
	SK/REG004/u	Entrance Scholarships
	SK/REG005/u	Allan Blakeney Entrance Scholarship
	SK/REG020/u	Anne Rigney Entrance Scholarship

April 22 (cont.)	SK/REG021/u	University of Regina Special Entrance Scholarships
	SK/REG023/u	Frederick W. and Bertha A. Wenzel Entrance Bursary
May 1	BC/4-H003/g	Elizabeth Haddow Memorial Scholarship
	BC/BCMEA1/g	BC Music Educators' Association Scholarship
	BC/CBO011/c	Rose Hill Farmers' Institute Bursaries
	BC/CVFI01/g	Comox Valley Farmers' Institute Award
	BC/DGS004/c	Douglas College Music Scholarships
	BC/NGR001/g	Nancy Greene Scholarships
	BC/PCN01/g	Plateau Chapter of Nurses Award
	BC/RCL003/g	Royal Canadian Legion, Ladies Auxiliary, Branch 160, Bursary
	CA/FELPR1/g	Fel-Pro Automotive Technicians Scholarship Program Awards
	CA/GGC01/g	Girl Guides of Canada – Guides du Canada Scholarship
	CA/KofC01/g	Knights of Columbus Canadian Scholarship Program
	MB/BRN001/u	R.D. Bell String Scholarships
	MB/BRN002/u	Beta Sigma Phi Entrance Scholarship
	MB/BRN003/u	Procop and Dora Bilous Memorial Scholarship
	MB/BRN004/u	Brandon University Board of Governors Entrance Scholarship
	MB/BRN007/u	James Christie Memorial Scholarship
	MB/BRN008/u	Sarah Harriet Hall Memorial Academic Scholarships
	MB/BRN009/u	G.F. MacDowell Entrance Scholarships
	MB/BRN010/u	Professor G. MacNeill Memorial Scholarship
	MB/BRN011/u	Masonic Past Masters' Association of Manitoba Entrance Scholarship
	MB/BRN012/u	Orchard Memorial Entrance Scholarship
	MB/BRN013/u	Terry Penton Memorial Entrance Scholarship
	MB/BRN014/u	Robbins Entrance Scholarhips
	MB/BRN015/u	Carl and Lyle Sanders Scholarships in Music
	MB/BRN016/u	Simplot Canada Limited Entrance Scholarship
	MB/BRN018/u	Mary Smart Scholarships
	MB/BRN019/u	James Harvey Tolton Memorial Scholarship
	MB/BRN020/u	Westman Dental Group Scholarship
	MB/MTS001/g	Manitoba Teachers' Society Scholarships
	NT/DOH001/g	Health Bursary Program
	SK/MEDIA1/g	Media House Scholarship

May 4	AB/CFGP01/g	Roxanne Ashmead Memorial Scholarship
May 7	CA/AAH001/g	A.A. Heaps Scholarship
May 10	AB/ACA001/c	ACA Alumni Association Award
	AB/ACA002/c	Continuing Arts Association Foundation Scholarship
	AB/ACA003/c	Eaton Scholarship
	BC/CFUW01/g	Canadian Federation of University Women Sunshine Coast Bursary
May 15	AB/ALHER4/g	Charles S. Noble Scholarships for Study at Harvard
	AB/LSTS01/g	Lord Strathcona Trust Scholarship
	BC/ABCDE1/g	British Columbia Drama Scholarship
	BC/BRI005/u	Chancellor's Entrance Scholarships (from Regional Colleges)
	BC/BRI016/u	Adelphian Scholarship
	BC/BRI020/u	Association of Administrative and Professional Staff of UBC Scholarship
	BC/BRI027/u	Borden Packaging and Industrial Products – Canada Scholarship
	BC/BRI039/u	Canadian Army Remembrance Scholarship
	BC/BRI044/u	Columbia College A.J. Mouncey Memorial Scholarship
	BC/BRI047/u	Margaret Ruth Crawford Scholarship
	BC/BRI049/u	Lewis Cuming Scholarship
	BC/BRI059/u	Faculty Women's Club Magaret MacKenzie Scholarship
	BC/BRI061/u	Ferguson Scholarship
	BC/BRI069/u	Girl Guides of Canada Vancouver Area Council Elizabeth Rogers Trust Scholarship
	BC/BRI070/u	Frank Gnup Memorial Award
	BC/BRI075/u	Japanese-Canadian Citizens' Association BC Centennial Scholarship
	BC/BRI083/u	T.E. and M.E. Ladner Memorial Scholarship
	BC/BRI098/u	Margaret Morrow Scholarship, Nelson, BC
	BC/BRI101/u	Alan W. Neill Memorial Scholarship
	BC/BRI106/u	Percy W. Perris Salmon Arm Scholarship
	BC/BRI113/u	Nancy Ryckman Scholarship
	BC/BRI115/u	Sikh Students' Association Scholarship
	BC/BRI116/u	Terminal City Club Memorial Scholarship
	BC/BRI121/u	University of BC Alumni Southern California Scholarship
	BC/BRI122/u	Vancouver Estonian Society Scholarship
	BC/BRI124/u	Harold Anderson White Scholarship

May 15	BC/BRI128/u	Yates Memorial Scholarship Fund
(cont.)	BC/CACC01/g	Community Arts Council of Chilliwack Fine Arts Award
	BC/CACC02/g	Community Arts Council of Chilliwack Awards
	BC/CACC03/g	Jenny Child Memorial Award
	BC/CACC04/g	Mary Elizabeth Allan Memorial Award
	BC/CAFA01/g	Coquitlam Area Fine Arts Council Grants
	BC/CAP003/c	Science Faculty and Staff Scholarships
	BC/CAP004/c	Science Tuition Scholarships
	BC/CBO012/c	Rose Hill Farmers' Institute – Heritage Bursary
	BC/DIAC01/g	Diachem Industries Limited Soccer Scholarships
	BC/FCC02/g	Fletcher Challenge Canada Awards
	BC/HAWC01/g	Indian and Inuit Health Careers Program
	BC/HJS001/g	Harry Jerome Scholarship
	BC/RCL001/g	Royal Canadian Legion Branch #4 (Chilliwack) Bursaries
	BC/RCL002/g	Royal Canadian Legion Branch #4 (Chilliwack) Ladies Auxiliary Bursaries
	BC/UCFV07/c	UCFV Basic Education and Development Tuition Scholarships
	BC/UCFV09/c	University College of the Fraser Valley Student Society Bursary
	BC/UCFV10/c	UCFV Tuition Waiver Scholarships for High School Students
	CA/CIME01/g	Denis Cressey Marine Engineering Scholarship Trust
	CA/CSEA01/g	CSEA Berol Prismacolour National Art Scholarship
	CA/LDAC01/g	Carol Thompson Memorial Scholarship
	CA/UCOL01/g	Norma Epstein Award for Creative Writing
	SK/CUHS01/g	Credit Union High School Graduate Award
	SK/REG010/u	Dr George and Helen Ferguson Entrance Scholarship
	SK/SKF01/g	Saskatoon Kiwanis Foundation Talent Scholarship
	SK/STPR01/g	St Peter's Men's Club Award
May 24	SK/RCSS01/g	Henry A. Kutama Christian Youth Leadership Scholarship
May 30	AB/CALCO1/g	Calgary Co-op Scholarship
	BC/CBO008/c	John Thomas Gramiak Prize
	BC/CBO009/c	Sharon Anne Kask Memorial Bursary
	BC/CBO010/c	Charles Marshall Endowment

June 1	CA/IMA001/g	Imasco Scholarship
(cont.)	CA/MEF01/g	Mattinson Endowment Fund Scholarship for Disabled Students
	MB/MBC01/g	Manitoba Blue Cross Entrance Scholarship
	MB/MBC02/g	Manitoba Blue Cross Traveller's Award
	MB/MBC03/g	Bursary for Students with Special Needs
	NT/ARC003/c	Canada Scholars for Technology
	NT/GNWT02/g	Grade 12 Scholarships
	SK/IODE01/g	IODE Bursary
	SK/REG016/u	IODE James Henderson LL.D. Chapter Bursary
	SK/SAS014/u	Richard Glenn Johnston Bursaries
	SK/SAS037/u	C.F.M. Misselbrook Scholarship Fund
	SK/SHB001/g	Saskatchewan Health Bursaries
June 3	BC/BRI055/u	Alex Drdul Memorial Bursary
June 7	CA/CGF001/g	Canadian Golf Foundation Scholarship
June 12	CA/HOL01/g	Holstein Canada Scholarship
June 13	SK/CPA01/g	Lottie V.M. Teale Scholarship
June 15	AB/CAL033/u	Myrtle Cochran Paget Memorial Bursary
	AB/CAL065/u	University of Calgary Transfer Scholarships
	AB/NEWF01/g	Althea Shears Memorial Bursary
	AB/NOVA01/g	Nova Educational Awards for Natives
	BC/BRI125/u	Edmond T. Wong Bursaries
	BC/COL001/c	Columbia College Entrance Scholarships
	BC/RCL004/g	Frank Morris/Royal Canadian Legion Branch #13
	BC/SPARK1/g	S.P.A.R.K.S. Scholarship
	BC/STF01/g	Postsecondary Education Assistance to Status First Nations People
	CA/EAN001/g	Education Awards for Native Students
	CA/ESSO01/g	Native Educational Awards Program
	CA/HUSK01/g	Husky Oil Education Awards for Native People
	CA/PCO001/g	Petro-Canada Olympic Torch Fund
	NT/NWTW01/g	NT Wildlife Federation's Louis Lemieux Scholarship
	SK/JGRA01/g	Jennie E. Graham Bursaries
	YT/PYUA01/g	Frances Nowasad Award
	YT/YCS01/g	Ted Parnell Memorial Scholarship
June 20	CA/CASH01/g	Canada Scholarships
June 25	BC/RBM01/g	Robert Borsos Memorial Award
	MB/MAN001/u	Leader of Tomorrow Scholarships
	AB/AWNA01/g	C.A. Maclean Journalism Bursary
	AB/ENM01/g	Ernest Newman Memorial Bursary
June 30	AB/ALHER1/g	Alberta Heritage Scholarships (Alexander Rutherford)
	AB/AUG005/u	Fine Arts Performance Grants

June 30	MB/HYDR03/g	Engineering Entrance Scholarships
(cont.)	NT/NML01/g	Nanisivik Mines Ltd Scholarships
	SK/AMOK01/g	AMOK Scholarship
	SK/CAME01/g	CAMECO Entrance Scholarships
	SK/COG01/g	Cogema Canada Ltd Scholarships Program for Northern Residents
	SK/COG02/g	Cogema Canada Ltd Scholarships Program for Northern Residents
	SK/NSSP01/g	Northern Spirit Scholarship Program
	SK/REG018/u	Bert Fox/Ferguson University of Regina Alumni Entrance Scholarship
	SK/RPC01/g	Ted Davis Memorial Scholarship
July 1	AB/KGF01/g	Keith Gilmore Foundation Scholarship
	AB/PACL01/g	G. Allan Roeher Institute Bursaries
	AB/SFB003/g	Anna and John Kolesar Memorial Scholarship
	AB/SFB005/g	Pope John Paul II Commemorative Scholarships
	BC/ACL01/g	G. Allen Roeher Institute Bursaries for College Students
	BC/BRI131/u	Father David Bauer Scholarship
	BC/GLM01/g	Grand Lodge Masonic Bursaries
	BC/ICA001/g	Institute of Chartered Accountants of BC Scholarships
	BC/VAN002/c	British Columbia Forest Products Entrance Scholarship (Langara)
	NT/YACL01/g	Roeher Institute Bursaries
	NT/YT/BX1/g	Baxter Corporation Jean Goodwill Scholarships
	SK/EMM01/g	Hannon Scholarship
	SK/SAS004/u	C95 Bursary
	SK/SAS018/u	Evan and Elsie Morgan Scholarship
	SK/SAS029/u	SaskTel Scholarships
	SK/STEL01/g	Sasktel Scholarships
July 15	AB/4-H001/g	Her Majesty Queen Elizabeth "the Queen Mother" Scholarships
	AB/4-H002/g	4-H Foundation of Alberta Scholarship
	AB/4-H003/g	A & E Capelle LN Herfords Scholarship
	AB/4-H004/g	Alberta Farm and Ranch Writer's Award
	AB/4-H005/g	Alberta Treasury Branch Scholarships
	AB/4-H006/g	Alberta Wheat Pool Scholarships
	AB/4-H007/g	Alberta Ford and Mercury Dealer Scholarships
	AB/4-H008/g	Alberta Salers Association Scholarship
	AB/4-H009/g	Alpha Milk Company Scholarships
	AB/4-H010/g	Bale Bandits Scholarship
	AB/4-H011/g	Blue Klein Memorial Scholarship

July 15	AB/ALB024/u	Viscount Bennett Scholarships
(cont.)	AB/ALB025/u	Rosa H. Wolters Entrance Scholarship
	AB/ALB026/u	Harry W. Bass Memorial Bursaries
	AB/ALB027/u	Margaret Ann (Hardy) Simpson Award
	AB/ALB028/u	Canadian Foundation of Poliomyelitis and Rehabilation Bursaries (Alberta)
	AB/ALB030/u	Dr. K.A. Clark Memorial Bursary
	AB/ALB031/u	TransAlta Utilities Entrance Scholarships
	AB/ALB032/u	Percy Clubine Memorial Scholarship
	AB/ALB033/u	Mildred Rowe Weston Memorial Scholarships
	AB/ALB034/u	Alma Mater Entrance Scholarships
	AB/ALB035/u	Dymtro O. Pawluk Scholarships
	AB/ALB036/u	Harry A. and Frances Lepofsky Friedman Award
	AB/ALB038/u	David Butchart Pope Scholarships
	AB/ALB039/u	Alberta Egg Producers Scholarships
	AB/ALB040/u	Ralph and Isabel Steinhauer Scholarship
	AB/ALB041/u	City of Edmonton Entrance Scholarship
	AB/ALB043/u	Nickle Family Foundation Prize
	AB/ALB044/u	Trans Mountain Pipe Line Company Ltd Scholarships
	AB/ALB045/u	Melcor Developments Ltd Scholarship
	AB/ALB046/u	University of Alberta Entrance Scholarships
	AB/ALB047/u	PEO Memorial Scholarship
	AB/ALB049/u	Peace River Pioneer Memorial Bursaries
	AB/APEGG1/g	A.P.E.G.G.A. High School Awards for Engineering, Geology and Geophysics
	AB/ARC01/g	A Western Arctic Scholarship
	AB/CACL01/g	Bursaries in the Field of Mental Handicap
	AB/CAL006/u	Elizabeth and James McKenzie Andrews Bursaries
	AB/CAL007/u	Alex R. Cummings Bursary
	AB/CAL010/u	Thomas S. Dobson Scholarship
	AB/CAL011/u	Dr. A. Downey Memorial Award
	AB/CAL012/u	John and Sarra Fabbro Scholarships
	AB/CAL014/u	Fortune Industries Ltd Matriculation Bursary
	AB/CAL015/u	Bob Grainger Matriculation Bursary
	AB/CAL016/u	Bob Grainger Matriculation Bursary, Bow Valley Area
	AB/CAL017/u	Home Oil Company Ltd Centennial Matriculation Bursaries
	AB/CAL018/u	W.G. (Bill) Howard Memorial Foundation Matriculation Scholarships
	AB/CAL019/u	Kappa Alpha Theta Alumnae Club of Calgary Scholarship

July 15	AB/CAL061/u	Viscount Bennett Matriculation
(cont.)		Scholarships
	AB/CAL062/u	West Canadian Graphic Scholarship
	AB/CAL063/u	Mildred Rowe Weston Memorial
		Scholarships
	AB/IODE01/g	IODE Coronation Matriculation
		Bursaries
	AB/LET004/u	University of Lethbridge Entrance
		Scholarships
	AB/LET005/u	Oliver Collumbell Kelly Memorial
		Scholarship
	AB/LET006/u	Entrance and Continuing Scholarships
	AB/LET007/u	Frank M. and Lila Linn Thompson
		Scholarship
	AB/LET008/u	Lethbridge Science Fair Scholarship
	AB/LET009/u	Archdeacon Cecil Swanson Scholarship
	AB/LET010/u	Bigelow Fowler Clinic Scholarship
	AB/LET011/u	Entrance Scholarship in Fine Arts
	AB/LET012/u	Czechoslovak Canadian Cultural Society
		Scholarship
	AB/LET013/u	Ellison Enterprises Ltd Scholarship
	AB/LET014/u	Home Oil Company Ltd Scholarship
	AB/LET015/u	Palliser Distillers Scholarships
	AB/LET016/u	Robert H. Parsons Scholarship
	AB/LET017/u	Mary Agnes Crow Scholarships
	AB/LET018/u	Mildred Rowe Weston Scholarship
	AB/LET019/u	Canada Winter Games Scholarship
	AB/LET020/u	Royal Canadian Legion Alberta–N.W.T.
		Command Bursaries
	AB/LET021/u	TransAlta Utilities Scholarship
	AB/LET022/u	Neil D. Holmes Bursary
	AB/LET023/u	IODE Awards in Music
	AB/LET024/u	William Asbury Buchanan Bursary
	AB/LET025/u	College Transfer Scholarships
	AB/LET026/u	Transfer Student Scholarships
	AB/LET027/u	Lethbridge Community College Transfer
		Scholarships
	AB/LET028/u	School of Nursing Entrance Scholarship
	AB/LET029/u	William S. Kizema Memorial
		Scholarships
	AB/LET030/u	Gerald Trechka Memorial Scholarship
	AB/LET031/u	Fine Arts Entrance Scholarship (Art)
	AB/LET032/u	Fine Arts Entrance Scholarship.
		Dramatic Arts
	AB/LET033/u	Fine Arts Entrance Scholarship (Music)
	AB/LET034/u	Louise Needham Scholarship
	AB/LET035/u	Joseph Dorner Memorial Bursary
	AB/LET036/u	Scholarship for the Physically Disabled
	AB/LET037/u	Ryan Imbach Memorial Bursary for the
		Hearing Impaired

July 31	CA/LEM001/g	Lemaire Co-operative Studies Awards
(cont.)	MB/MFA01/g	Dr. Alan B. Beaven Scholarship
	MB/RRC001/c	Tom O'Brien Memorial Entrance Scholarship
	NT/NWA01/g	Native Women's Association of the NT Scholarship
	SK/POT4-H/g	Potash Corporation of Saskatchewan Inc. 4-H Scholarship
	SK/RCL003/g	Royal Canadian Legion Ladies Auxiliary Scholarships
	SK/SAS007/u	Farm Credit Corporation Canada Scholarships
	SK/SAS024/u	Potash Corporation of Saskatchewan Scholarship
	YT/CVA01/g	Jinx Ross Memorial Scholarship
	YT/SYANA1/g	Society of Yukon Artists of Native Ancestry Scholarship Fund
August 1	AB/LAKE01/c	Earle Associate Consulting Scholarship
	AB/LAKE02/c	Ed Jenson and Family Scholarship
	AB/LAKE03/c	Herman Huber Award
	AB/LAKE04/c	Husky Oil Entrance Scholarships
	AB/LAKE05/c	ISPAS Wildlife Refuge Scholarship
	AB/LAKE06/c	John Dahmer Community Involvement Scholarship
	AB/LAKE07/c	Lakeland College Scholarship for Excellence
	AB/LAKE08/c	Matt and Mary McDonald Memorial Award
	AB/LAKE09/c	Colchester and District Agricultural Society Scholarship
	AB/LAKE10/c	Peter J. Gulak Entrance Scholarship
	BC/BRI050/u	Roy Daniells Scholarship in Creative Writing
	BC/GDV01/g	Geraldo Donato Vertone Scholarship
	BC/MDA01/g	Derek Saltzberg Memorial Bursary
	BC/MDA02/g	Kit Davison Bursary
	BC/SSD01/g	Assistance Program for Students with Severe Disabilities
	NT/GNWT01/g	Igal Roth Memorial Scholarship
	SK/RCL005/g	Poppy Fund Bursary
	SK/RCL006/g	Titus Bursary
	SK/REG024/u	Groome Memorial Scholarship
August 2	BC/BCIT01/c	BCIT Alumni Association Entrance Award
	BC/BCIT03/c	Pacific Foundation of Applied Technology, Otto A. Kloss Awards
	BC/BCIT05/c	Simons Foundation Entrance Awards for Women
	BC/BCIT06/c	Teck Corporation Entrance Award
	BC/BCIT08/c	BC Dairy Foundation Entrance Awards
	BC/BCIT09/c	David Lloyd Entrance Awards

August 15 (cont.)	SK/REGC12/u	Jesuit Fathers Entrance Bursaries (Campion College)
	SK/REGC13/u	Knights of Columbus, Conseil Langevin Scholarship (Campion College)
	SK/REGC14/u	Saskatchewan Irish Club, Mary Reid Memorial Scholarship (Campion College)
	SK/SAHA01/g	Saskatchewan Amateur Hockey Association Scholarships
	SK/SSCF01/g	South Saskatchewan Community Foundation Award
	YT/RCL01/g	Royal Canadian Legion Bursary, Whitehorse
	YT/YOP01/g	Yukon Order Pioneers Scholarships
August 19	SK/CHIEF1/g	Touchwood – File Hills Qu'Appelle District Chiefs Scholarships
August 20	AB/RCL001/g	Royal Canadian Legion District #1 Bursaries
August 29	AB/RCL002/g	Royal Canadian Legion Ladies Auxiliary Alberta – N.W.T. Command Award
August 30	BC/CAP001/c	Capilano College Board Entrance Scholarships
	SK/ASHE01/g	Association of Saskatchewan Home Economists Regina Branch Scholarship
	YT/YTA01/g	Doris Stenbraten Scholarship
August 31	AB/SPA01/g	Spina Bifida Association of Northern Alberta Scholarship
	BC/BCWI01/g	Maple Women's Institute Scholarship
	BC/BCWI02/g	BC Women's Institute – Centennial Vocational Bursary
	BC/BCWI03/g	British Columbia Women's Institute Memorial Scholarship
	BC/IOF01/g	Independent Order of Foresters Bursaries
	BC/OKA017/c	Vernon Film Society Entrance Scholarship
	BC/VIC006/u	Canadian Union of Public Employees Scholarships
	CA/CCLOW1/g	Mairi St. John Macdonald Scholarship
	CA/CPA001/g	Morton Copnick Scholarship
	YT/CLOW02/g	Mairi St. John Macdonald Scholarship
	YT/SFAC02/g	Beta Sigma Phi Scholarship
	YT/SFAC03/g	Canadian Army Yukon Scholarship
	YT/SFAC04/g	Knights of Columbus Scholarship
	YT/SFAC05/g	Nicholas John Harach Scholarship
	YT/SFAC06/g	NorthwesTel Scholarship Program
	YT/SFAC07/g	Whitehorse Lion's Club Bursary
	YT/SFAC09/g	Yukon Huskys C.B. Radio Club Scholarship
	YT/SFAC10/g	Yukon Northern Resources Scholarships
	YT/WRC01/g	Whitehorse Rotary Bursary

16 Glossary of Terms

The various post-secondary institutions use a number of different words in their descriptions of scholarships and application forms. Here is a short list of definitions to help you.

Academic excellence: The quality of being an outstanding student achieving a high overall average in the senior grades.

Admission award: This is usually an amount of money given to a student by an institution as an incentive to attend a post-secondary course there.

Audition: An opportunity to perform or recite before a selection panel. These are usually offered to students entering a program of music or other performing arts.

Bursary: A sum of money given to a student primarily on the basis of financial need.

Community service: This is the general name given to any volunteer work that is done for the benefit of the community.

Co-op programs: These programs usually involve a term of school followed by a work term in a place of paid employment related to the school program.

Emergency loans: Small sums of money that are loaned without interest for a short term by institutions to students who are temporarily without funds.

Entrance award (or scholarship): This is much the same as an admission award.

Extracurricular activities: Any non credit activities that are sponsored by the high school for students. This includes such things as sports teams, students' council, and school band.

Fellowship: A sum of money awarded to a student pursuing post-secondary education usually beyond the baccalaureate level.

Full-time student: This definition may vary between post-secondary students, but usually refers to students taking four or more full-credit academic courses per academic year.

Grade Point Average (GPA): A system by which final course grades are given as a number with one decimal place as opposed to a percentage or letter grade. Some systems use a scale from 1.0 to 4.0, which is the highest grade. A specific Grade Point Average may be required to renew a scholarship.

Grant: A sum of money given to a student, usually on the basis of financial need.

In-course awards: These are scholarships and prizes given to students already enrolled in post-secondary programs. As a rule these are not awarded to first-year students.

Letter of recommendation: This is a letter written by a teacher, principal, or employer that emphasizes a candidate's suitability for a given scholarship or program.

Letter of reference: This is a letter that describes a person's education and/or employment experience. It is similar to a letter of recommendation, except that it is more passive and does not attempt to promote the candidate.

Loan: Financial assistance to be repaid. Student loan programs often defer the repayment of such loans until after the student has graduated.

Mentor: Experienced and trusted adviser.

Merit: Praiseworthy aspects or worthiness for an award.

Needs test: A process by which the financial need of an applicant can be determined. This may involve forms and/or an interview.

Portfolio: This is the name given to a portable case designed to protect drawings, paintings, and other artwork. Portfolio submissions are used by a selection committee to determine the most meritorious candidate.

Prize: Often a non-monetary award (book, medal, or trophy) given in recognition of achievement or success in a competition.

Renewable award: An award that can be maintained in subsequent years provided the renewal criteria are met. The number of periods of renewal are often limited.

Residence fees: The costs of a residence room and meal plan for an academic term.

Résumé: Also known as a curriculum vitae. This is a short document generated by an individual to give details of his or her education and work history.

Scholarship: A monetary award intended to recognize excellence in such things as academics or sports. Often used as an inducement for students to attend certain post-secondary institutions.

Scholarship coach: A person who helps prepare students to apply for scholarships.

Scholastic Aptitude Test (SAT): An American multiple-choice test made up of verbal and math questions. SAT scores are used in the United States as part of the post-secondary admission process. Occasionally, SAT scores are required for some scholarship applications, particularly those offered by American companies.

Transcript: An authorized copy of a student's academic record showing courses taken and grades received.

Tuition fees: The amount charged by colleges and universities for courses taken. These can vary depending on the institution and the program.

Responses

If you would like to offer comments or suggestions for future editions of *Winning Scholarships: A Student's Guide to Entrance Awards at Western Canadian Universities and Colleges*, please detach this page and send it to:

Michael J. Howell
Winning Scholarships: A Student's Guide
c/o University of Toronto Press
10 St Mary Street, Suite 700
Toronto, Canada M4Y 2W8

Comments _____

_____

_____

_____

_____

Suggestions _____

_____

_____

_____

We would especially like to hear from you if there is a scholarship you know about that is not listed in this book. Please send the name of the scholarship and an address or phone number of the sponsor.

(over)

Name of scholarship _____

_____

_____

Address of sponsor _____

_____

_____

_____

_____

We would also like to know if our readers have had any success with scholarships by using this book.

Your name _____

_____

Scholarship(s) won
Name   *Amount*

_____

_____

_____

_____

_____